Paragraphs and Essays

With Integrated Readings
Eleventh Edition

Lee Brandon
Mt. San Antonio College

Kelly Brandon
Santa Ana College

D1500931

WADSWORTH
CENGAGE Learning

Australia • Brazil • Japan • Korea • Mexico • Singapore • Spain • United Kingdom • United States

To Sharon

Paragraphs and Essays with Integrated Readings, **Eleventh Edition**
Lee Brandon, Kelly Brandon

Senior Publisher: Lyn Uhl

Director of Developmental English:
  Annie Todd

Development Editor: Karen Mauk

Associate Editor: Janine Tangney

Editorial Assistant: Melanie Opacki

Media Editor: Emily Ryan

Senior Marketing Manager: Kirsten Stoller

Marketing Coordinator: Ryan Ahern

Marketing Communications Manager:
  Martha Pfeiffer

Senior Content Project Manager:
  Margaret Park Bridges

Art Director: Jill Ort

Print Buyer: Sue Spencer

Senior Rights Acquisition Account Manager,
  Text: Katie Huha

Text Permissions Editor:
  Mary Dalton-Hoffman

Production Service: Books By Design, Inc.

Text Designer: Books By Design, Inc.

Photo Manager: John Hill

Cover Designer: Jill Ort

Cover Image: © Steve Chorney

Compositor: S4Carlisle Publishing Services

For product information and technology assistance, contact us at
Cengage Learning Customer & Sales Support,
1-800-354-9706

For permission to use material from this text or product, submit all requests online at **www.cengage.com/permissions.**
Further permissions questions can be e-mailed to
permissionrequest@cengage.com.

Library of Congress Control Number: 2009928730

Student Edition:
ISBN-13: 978-0-495-80180-1
ISBN-10: 0-495-80180-1

Wadsworth
20 Channel Center Street
Boston, MA 02210
USA

Cengage Learning is a leading provider of customized learning solutions with office locations around the globe, including Singapore, the United Kingdom, Australia, Mexico, Brazil, and Japan. Locate your local office at **international.cengage.com/region**

Cengage Learning products are represented in Canada by Nelson Education, Ltd.

For your course and learning solutions, visit **www.cengage.com.**

Purchase any of our products at your local college store or at our preferred online store **www.ichapters.com.**

Printed in the United States of America
2 3 4 5 6 7 13 12 11 10

Contents

Chapter 10   Process Analysis: Writing About Doing   193

Chapter 14   Definition: Clarifying Terms   309

Thematic Contents

Especially for Combining Writing Patterns and Integrating Reading Selections

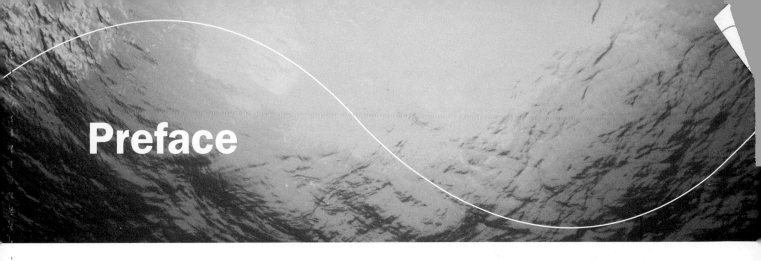

Preface

In this, the eleventh edition of *Paragraphs and Essays,* the surf writer, gallantly perched on a pencil, once more celebrates the "flow of writing." Like waves at a beach, writing is cyclical, moving forward and backward and forward again. The surf writer will always be searching for the "perfect wave," meaning the best possible expression. The recursive movement of writing and rewriting is the essence of good writing. Instruction in this book—comprehensive, flexible, relevant, and stimulating—is predicated on that systematic, relentless revision.

The Parts of a Flexible, Comprehensive Package of Instruction, Enhanced with Optional Reading-Based Writing

Written especially for English writing courses one level below freshman composition, *Paragraphs and Essays,* Eleventh Edition, contains highly accessible writing instruction that will enable students to learn especially by the contemplation of good examples and by practice, practice, practice of established techniques. Specifically, the Writing Process Worksheet, the Self-Evaluation Chart, annotated student demonstrations, and abundant topics and detailed prompts (reading-based, general, cross-curricular, and career-related) will support and guide the inexperienced writer from the foundation to the edifice of effective writing. Other specific features such as plentiful third-person exemplary reading selections and reading-based writing assignments will help students transition into advanced courses where objective writing and writing about reading material are customary.

Here is a layout of the particulars.

Part I   Linking Reading and Writing

* Reading techniques: underlining, annotating, outlining, taking notes
* Reading-based writing (the major form of text-based writing): summary, reaction, two-part response
* Giving credit for ideas and quotations: basic documentation
* Demonstrations, exercises, assignments

Part II   The Writing Process

* Stages of writing: exploring, organizing, writing
* Revising and editing

- Paragraphs and essays
- Demonstrations, exercises, assignments

Part III   Writing Paragraphs and Essays: Instruction, with Integrated Reading Selections

- Forms of discourse: descriptive narration, exemplification, analysis by division, process analysis, cause and effect, classification, comparison and contrast, definition, argument; with recognition that a single form often provides structure for paragraphs and essays but almost never occurs without the presence of other forms
- Forms of discourse adapted for career-related writing, with instruction and examples for the more career-minded students; for example, exemplification as incident report, comparison and contrast as product evaluation, and argument as workplace proposal
- Chapters 7 through 15 with identical formats: functional cartoons, writing instruction, an exercise in finding patterns in photos, two exercises in practicing patterns, model paragraphs and essays by student and professional writers, a student example of writing in stages, a student example of reading-based writing, writing prompts and topics (reading-based, general, cross-curricular, career-related), and a chapter summary

READING-BASED WRITING FOR DEVELOPMENTAL ENGLISH

Along with thorough instruction in basic writing skills and the writing process, Brandon books offer another dimension: reading-based writing. As a natural progression of linking reading and writing, reading-based writing moves students beyond the personal narratives to more analytical expression as they write about what they read. Reading-based writing provides substance for compositions and promotes critical thinking. Students engaged in reading-based writing will be able to transition more smoothly through developmental English and into freshman English composition, and to function better in courses across the curriculum.

READING-BASED WRITING DEFINED

The typical reading-based writing assignments in *Paragraphs and Essays* require students to read a source, write an analytical reply, and give credit to the originator(s) for borrowed words and ideas. Credit can be noted formally (MLA style with 2009 Update in the Brandon books) or informally, depending on the instructor's preference. Specific assignments in reading-based writing are the summary, the reaction (paragraph or essay), and the two-part response (with separated summary and reaction used to teach students the difference between the two). Although the reaction can, and often does, include personal experience and reflect individual perspectives, analytical and interpretive discussion should be at the center of the writing. The reaction can also incorporate summary to convey a broad aspect of the text, but summary is never the main concern of the reaction.

READING-BASED WRITING IN THE SYLLABUS

Depending on their objectives and student needs, instructors assigning reading-based writing will determine the extent of its use: (1) beginning with personal experience assignments and phasing in reading-based writing during the course; (2) interspersing reading-based writing assignments with other writing assignments; (3) working with the summary, the reaction (a critique), and the two-part response as one of several units of instruction; or (4) using reading-based writing throughout the semester. Many instructors have found that a summary works well as a diagnostic writing test at the beginning of the semester, and an in-class reading-based essay, with a brief outline annotated with a few quotes brought to class, works well for the final exam. Annotated student examples of the three different kinds of reading-based writing appear throughout Brandon books.

Part IV   Using Sources

- Finding and evaluating sources in the library and on the Internet
- Documenting sources
- Writing a short research paper in ten steps
- Demonstration, exercises

Part V   Handbook

- Sentence elements
- Sentence patterns
- Sentence combining
- Sentence rhetoric
- Diction
- Punctuation

Some Brandon Time-Tested Techniques

For the Student Companion Site, visit www.cengage .com/devenglish/brandon/ pe11e.

- The Writing Process Worksheet is available for students to print out from the Student Companion Site. Instructors can customize it on the Instructor Companion Site and print it out or post it online for students. This worksheet (page 6) guides students through the recursive stages of writing from exploring to organizing to writing, with emphasis on rewriting.
- Each of Chapters 7 through 15 includes a student paragraph and a student essay, one of which is presented with all stages of writing in the Writing Process Worksheet form, explicitly answering the familiar student question: "How does a student like me do this assignment?"
- The six major parts of revision are represented by the acronym CLUESS: **C**oherence, **L**anguage, **U**nity, **E**mphasis, **S**upport, and **S**entences. Inexperienced writers can easily latch onto that memory device and use it as a checklist for revision.
- Another acronym—COPS: **C**apitalization, **O**missions, **P**unctuation, and **S**pelling—provides a similar aid for editing.
- As students move through the course, they can track their progress and become more self-sufficient by using the Self-Evaluation Chart on the inside front cover.
- Another feature that directs students toward text in each of Chapters 7 through 15 is "Finding Patterns in Photos," which immediately follows the writing instruction. Written for either individual or group work, this exercise provides students with an opportunity to sharpen their critical-thinking skills as they match chapter patterns with photo content. It is especially good for spirited group discussions and follow-up writing assignments.

Other Features in *Paragraphs and Essays,* Eleventh Edition

- For the more career-minded or career-engaged students, instruction with examples of patterns of writing used at the workplace:

  Descriptive narration becomes an incident report
  Analysis by division becomes a career review
  Process analysis becomes a set of directions at a workplace
  Comparison and contrast becomes product, performance, or process evaluation
  Argument becomes a workplace proposal

- A focusing device for critical reading called "Mindset: Lock It In"
- Twenty-nine readings new to this edition
- Sixty-three readings with cultural and gender balance
- A restaurant review as a model form of analysis by division
- Nine cartoons that amuse while demonstrating patterns of thought
- An alternative Thematic Contents for readings
- A short story that highlights cause and effect in human behavior
- More writing topics than any other textbook on the market, including an abundance of reading-based writing topics phrased as prompts, and additional writing topics and prompts grouped as general, cross-curricular, and career-related topics
- An ESL unit in the text and extensive online practice exercises available to be assigned selectively by the instructor from comprehensive ESL instruction on *WriteSpace*
- Full-color design

INSTRUCTIONAL SUPPORT

The Annotated Instructor's Edition (AIE) contains immediate answers and teaching tips for exercises and activities.

The Instructor's Guide is now located on the Instructor Companion Site at www .cengage.com/devenglish/brandon/pe11e. You can either download the material for photocopying or obtain a hard-copy text booklet by contacting Cengage Learning, Higher Education, at 800-354-9706.

The Instructor's Guide on the Instructor Companion Site includes the following:

- Tips for new instructors on how to approach the text
- Sample syllabi (one annotated, the other direct), with suggestions for adaptations for different pedagogies and course lengths
- List of readings that are especially effective for reading-based writing
- Reproducible sentence-writing quizzes from the Handbook
- Reproducible quizzes on selected readings from Part III
- Instructions for ordering a printed quiz booklet from Cengage Learning, Higher Education, ideal for photocopying
- Suggestions for effective and time-saving approaches to instruction
- PowerPoint slides that can be downloaded and used to enhance classroom instruction
- Suggestions for ESL instruction
- Suggestions for teaching basic writers
- The Student's Answer Key

Answers to about half of the handbook exercises are now on the Instructor Companion Site. The instructor can make these answers available to students by printing them out or by posting them on the instructor's school web page. Instructors who do not post or distribute answers will now have almost twice as much uncorrected sentence writing exercise material for class discussion as was in the first through the tenth editions.

WEBSITE RESOURCES FOR STUDENTS

Paragraphs and Essays, Eleventh Edition, offers students additional opportunities to explore writing through the Student Companion Site. The features include the following:

- A printable copy of the Writing Process Worksheet
- Interactive quizzes in sentence writing
- Interactive quizzes in the writing process
- Interactive quizzes in writing with patterns
- Interactive quizzes in reading-based writing
- A brief guide to APA style
- Additional instruction in writing letters of recommendation and résumés
- Instructions in taking tests

WriteSpace is a flexible, interactive, and customizable program that assesses students of English at all skill levels. *WriteSpace* motivates and assists students with varying skill levels by providing tutorial support. *WriteSpace* includes (1) diagnostic skills assessments in writing and grammar skills with test results linked to individualized concept reviews and study paths for self-remediation, helping motivate and prepare students for coursework; (2) *Exercises and Writing Modules* (tutorials) that give students additional practice beyond the classroom; (3) *Associated Press Interactives & NewsNow* that allow you to incorporate current events, critical thinking, and visual literacy into your course; (4) *Plagiarism Prevention Zone* that helps you keep plagiarism problems to a minimum; (5) *Online Tutoring*; (6) an *Online Handbook*; and (7) a *Gradebook*.

Acknowledgments

We are profoundly indebted to the many instructors who have reviewed *Paragraphs and Essays* and helped it grow and remain fresh over the years. Here are a few of these thoughtful, imaginative reviewers: Thomas Beery, Lima Technical College; Dorothy Brown, Iowa Western Community College; Gricelle Gomez Cano, Houston Community College, Southeast; Linda Caywood-Farrell, Piedmont Community College; Diane Dowdey, Sam Houston State University; Tammy Frankland, Casper College; Craig Frischkorn, Jamestown Community College; William Gilbert, University of Houston, Downtown; Herbert Karl Green Jr., Camden County College; Sally C. Hall, Honolulu Community College; Carol S. Hamm, Seminole State College; William B. Harrison III, Georgia Perimeter College, Decatur; Jill A. Lahnstein, Cape Fear Community College; Daniel E. M. Landau, Santa Monica College; Elisabeth Leyson, Fullerton College; Christiane Moore, Houston Community College, Southeast; Christopher Nielson, Glendale Community College; Ida R. Page, Durham Technical Community College; Daniel W. Powell, Florida Community

College, Jacksonville; Elizabeth Remsburg-Shiroishi, Golden West College; Jude Roy, Madisonville Community College; Kathleen C. Swango, Bluegrass Community and Technical College; Joseph Szabo, Mercer County Community College; David Throne, Community College of Aurora; and Cheryl West, Brewton Parker College. Thanks also to the English departments at Mt. San Antonio College and Santa Ana College.

We also deeply appreciate the expert, dedicated work of freelance editors Karen Mauk, Mary Dalton-Hoffman, Robin Hogan, and Nancy Benjamin, and our colleagues at Cengage Learning: Annie Todd, Kirsten Stoller, Margaret Bridges, Rick Nicotera, Janine Tangney, Martha Pfeiffer, Katie Huha, and Melanie Opacki.

We are especially grateful to our family members for their cheerful, inspiring support: Sharon, Erin, Michael, Kathy, Shane, Lauren, Jarrett, Matthew, Jessica, and Deborah.

Lee Brandon and Kelly Brandon

Student Overview

"Every sentence, paragraph, and essay begins with a single word."

A VARIATION ON A FAMILIAR SAYING
(LEE BRANDON)

The Flow of Writing: Icon and Theme

You will see this icon frequently in *Paragraphs and Essays*:

Follow the line from top left over the waves, then down and around to the pencil with the little surf writer getting ready to hang ten.

Like the surf writer, you follow that pattern in writing, the pattern of the tide near the shore. In flowing cycles, the tide advances and withdraws, then regroups and proceeds again. The tide does not merely rush forward at one time and be done with it. Writing also moves in cycles with a rhythmic flow. You do not just write your message and walk away. Instead, you write—and, for revision and editing—back up, and rewrite, following that pattern until you are through. In writing, the back-and-forth movement is called *recursive.* It is the essence of the writing process.

In the coming pages, the icon will identify features that enable your own flow of writing and remind you of the importance of rewriting.

Paragraphs and Essays shows how to proceed from fragmented ideas to effective expression by blending instruction, examples, and practice. Like the surf writer going back again and again in looking for that perfect wave, you as a writer will go back again and again in quest of that perfect composition.

Practice with Principles

Some will tell you that to become a better writer you should practice. Others will say that to become a better writer you should learn the principles of writing.

Each view is a half-truth. If you practice without knowing what to do, you will get better only within your own limitations; any bad habits are likely to become more ingrained. If you are playing the piano with two fingers and you practice a lot, you may learn to play a great "Chopsticks," but Beethoven's "Moonlight Sonata" will remain beyond your reach.

In the same way, if you learn the principles of writing and do not practice them, they will never become a functioning part of your skills. The solution is in your hands. You are now gazing at a book with a well-rounded approach, one that combines sound techniques and sample writing practice. It is designed for use both in class and on your own.

Each chapter in this book begins with a list of chapter topics.

Chapter 1 links reading and writing.

Chapters 2 through 4 explain the three stages of the writing process.

Chapters 5 and 6 present forms of writing and support: Chapter 5, the paragraph; Chapter 6, the essay.

Chapters 7 through 15 focus on forms of discourse, commonly called *patterns of development*: descriptive narration, exemplification (explaining), analysis by division, process analysis, cause and effect, classification, comparison and contrast, definition, and argument.

Chapter 16 discusses how to write the research paper in ten steps.

Chapter 17, the Handbook, offers instruction in fundamentals and sentence writing. It also includes a brief guide for ESL students.

A Self-Evaluation Chart appears on the inside front cover of this book (see pages 3–4 for more information), and a Correction Chart appears on the inside back cover.

Strategies for Self-Improvement

Here are some strategies you can follow to make the best use of this book and to jump-start the improvement in your writing skills.

1. *Be active and systematic in learning.* Take advantage of your instructor's expertise by being an active class member—one who takes notes, asks questions, and contributes to discussion. Become dedicated to systematic learning. Determine your needs, decide what to do, and do it. Make learning a part of your everyday thinking and behavior.

2. *Read widely.* Samuel Johnson, a great English scholar, once said he did not want to read anything by people who had written more than they had read. William Faulkner, a Nobel Prize winner in literature, said, "Read, read, read.

Read everything—trash, classics, good and bad, and see how writers do it." Read to learn technique, to acquire ideas, and to be stimulated to write. Especially read to satisfy your curiosity and to receive pleasure. In this book reading is a companion to writing. You will often write about what you read. That approach is called *reading-based writing*.

3. *Keep a journal.* Keep a journal, even though it may not be required in your particular class. It is a good practice to jot down your observations in a notebook. Here are some activities for daily, or almost daily, journal writing:

- Summarize, evaluate, or react to reading assignments.
- Summarize, evaluate, or react to what you see on television and in movies, and to what you read in newspapers and in magazines.
- Describe and narrate situations or events you experience.
- Write about career-related matters you encounter in other courses or on the job.

Your journal entries may read like an intellectual diary, a record of what you are thinking about at certain times. Keeping a journal will help you to understand reading material better, to develop more language skills, and to think more clearly—as well as to become more confident and to write more easily so that writing becomes a comfortable, everyday activity. Your entries may also provide subject material for longer, more carefully crafted pieces. The most important thing is to get into the habit of writing something each day.

4. *Evaluate your writing skills.* Use the Self-Evaluation Chart on the inside front cover of this book to assess your writing skills by listing problem areas you need to work on. You may be adding to these lists throughout the entire term. Drawing on your instructor's comments, make notes on matters such as organization, development, content, spelling, vocabulary, diction, grammar, sentence structure, punctuation, and capitalization. Use this chart for self-motivated study assignments and as a checklist in all stages of writing. As you master each problem area, you can erase it or cross it out.

Most of the elements you record in your Self-Evaluation Chart are covered in *Paragraphs and Essays*. The table of contents, the index, and the Correction Chart on the inside back cover will direct you to the additional instruction you decide you need.

- *Organization/Development/Content*: List aspects of your writing, including the techniques of all stages of the writing process, such as freewriting, brainstorming, and clustering; the phrasing of a good topic sentence or thesis; and the design, growth, and refinement of your ideas.
- *Spelling/Vocabulary/Diction*: List common words marked as incorrectly spelled on your college assignments. Here, *common* means words that you use often. If you are misspelling these words now, you may have been doing so for years. Look at your list. Is there a pattern to your misspellings? Consult the Spelling section in the Handbook, Chapter 17, for a set of useful rules. Whatever it takes, master the words on your list. Continue to add troublesome words as you accumulate assignments. If your vocabulary is imprecise or your diction is inappropriate (if you use slang, trite expressions, or words that are too informal), note those problems as well.

- *Grammar/Sentence Structure*: List recurring problems in your grammar or sentence structure. Use the symbols and page references listed on the Correction Chart (inside back cover) or look up the problem in the index.
- *Punctuation/Capitalization*: Treat these problems the same way you treat grammar problems. Note that the Punctuation and Capitalization section in the Handbook numbers some rules; therefore, you can often give exact locations of the remedies for your problems.

Here is an example of how you might use your chart.

Self-Evaluation Chart

Organization/ Development/ Content	Spelling/ Vocabulary/ Diction	Grammar/ Sententce Structure	Punctuation/ Capitalization
needs more specific support such as examples, 137	avoid slang, 56	fragments, 439	difference between semicolons and commas, 443
refine outline, 46	avoid clichés such as "be there for me," 58	subject-verb agreement, 461	comma after long introductory modifier, 502
use clear topic sentence, 40	it's, its, 523	comma splice, 442	comma in compound sentence, 502
	you're, your, 524	vary sentence patterns, 437	
	rec<u>ei</u>ve, rule on, 520		

5. *Use the Writing Process Worksheet.* Record details about each of your assignments, such as the due date, topic, length, and form. The worksheet will also remind you of the stages of the writing process: explore, organize, and write. A blank Writing Process Worksheet for you to photocopy for assignments appears on page 6. Discussed in Chapter 2, it guides student work in almost every chapter. In reading-based writing you can include quotations and references with your outline. Your instructor may ask you to complete the form and submit it with your assignments.

STUDENT COMPANION SITE
For additional practice, visit www.cengage .com/devenglish/ brandon/pe11e.

6. *Take full advantage of the Student Companion Site and other technology.* Using a computer will enable you to write, revise, and edit more swiftly as you move, alter, check, and delete material with a few keystrokes. The Student Companion Site offers additional exercises and instructions. Many colleges have writing labs with instruction and facilities for networking and researching complicated topics. Used wisely, the Internet can provide resource material for compositions.

7. *Be positive.* To improve your English skills, write with freedom, but revise and edit with rigor. Work with your instructor to set attainable goals, and proceed at a reasonable pace. Soon, seeing what you have mastered and checked off your list will give you a sense of accomplishment.

While you progress in your English course, notice how you are getting better at content, organization, and mechanics as you read, think, and write.

Consequently, you can expect writing to become a highly satisfying pleasure. After all, once you learn to write well, writing can be just as enjoyable as talking.

Finally, do not compare yourself with others. Compare yourself before your learning experiences with yourself after your learning experiences and, as you improve, consider yourself what you are—a student on the path toward more effective writing, a student on the path toward success.

It is appropriate to end this overview with the same quotation that introduced it.

Every sentence, paragraph, and essay begins with a single word.

Let a word fall like thunder or a snowflake, to launch your thoughts.

Writing Process Worksheet

FLOW OF WRITING

Name _____ **Title** _____ **Due Date** _____

Use the back of this page or separate paper if you need more space.

Assignment

In the space below, write whatever you need to know about your assignment, including information about the topic, audience, pattern of writing, length, whether to include a rough draft or revised drafts, and whether your paper must be typed.

Stage One

Explore   Freewrite, brainstorm (list), cluster, or take notes as directed by your instructor.

Stage Two

Organize   Write a topic sentence or thesis; label the subject and focus parts.

Write an outline or an outline alternative. For reading-based writing, include references and short quotations with page numbers as support in the outline.

Stage Three

Write   On separate paper, write and then revise your paragraph or essay as many times as necessary for **c**oherence, **l**anguage (usage, tone, and diction), **u**nity, **e**mphasis, **s**upport, and **s**entences (**CLUESS**). Read your work aloud to hear and correct any grammatical errors or awkward-sounding sentences.

Edit any problems in fundamentals, such as **c**apitalization, **o**missions, **p**unctuation, and **s**pelling (**COPS**).

Part I

LINKING READING AND WRITING

Reading and writing are joined without seam. Reading activates your memory and provides you with substance for writing. Writing helps you examine your ideas and clarify what you have read. Reading and writing often blend as reading-based writing and together are the essence of critical thinking.

Chapter 1

Reading for Thinking, Discussion, and Writing

FLOW OF WRITING

Reading-Based Writing

THE WRITING COMPONENT

Reading-based writing was invented to help you fill those intimidating blank pages with thoughtful statements centered around what you have read, broadly called the *text*. *Text* is a term that includes items as diverse as photos, advertisements, online postings, and movies as sources for *text-based writing*, but in this book, we are concerned specifically with writing about reading, hence the term *reading-based writing*.

For instruction in this book, reading-based writing comes in three forms: summary, reaction, and two-part response. In writing a summary, you use your own words to restate the main ideas in what you have read. In writing a reaction, you comment critically on what you have read, while giving credit for the ideas and words you borrow. Then, in composing a two-part response, you write both a summary and a reaction, but you separate them to show your instructors that you know the difference between the two forms.

THE READING COMPONENT

Reading-based writing can also make you a better reader. When you are reading for a writing assignment, you concentrate more because you are thinking about how you will be using the content. When you are writing, your mind reflects back on what you have read, running ideas critically by your windows of experiences and knowledge. Reading-based writing represents the complete *you* as a thinking, feeling person in relation to what you have read. As we have said before, reading-based writing is the essence, or core, of critical thinking.

Reading-Based Writing and Other Approaches in Writing

Reading-based writing will serve you well in classrooms across your campus and also in your career. Of course, *Paragraphs and Essays* presents a range of writing approaches that may or may not make use of reading-based writing, including those called *personal experience, individual perspective, cross-curricular,* and *career-related*. All of those approaches are presented with instruction, examples, exercises, and suggested topics and prompts. Some approaches overlap, but each has a main thrust with variations imposed by particular writing objectives.

Reading-based writing is presented in this introductory chapter because most of the writing instruction in *Paragraphs and Essays* involves reading in some way. The abundant student and professional readings (more than sixty) were selected to stimulate thought and discussion, to provide content for writing, and to inform writing by strong examples of techniques and forms. Even reading-based writing has its own different forms, and reading itself has its own special techniques. Those techniques and forms are shown here in a concise outline of the instruction that covers the remainder of this chapter:

I. Reading techniques
   A. Underlining
   B. Annotating
   C. Outlining
   D. Taking notes

II. Reading-based writing forms
   A. Summary
   B. Reaction
   C. Two-part response

Reading Techniques

UNDERLINING

Imagine you are reading a chapter of several pages and you decide to underline and write in the margins. Immediately, the underlining takes you out of the passive, television-watching frame of mind. You are engaged. You are participating. It is now necessary for you to discriminate, to distinguish more important from less important ideas. Perhaps you have thought of underlining as a method designed only to help you with reviewing. That is, when you study the material the next time, you will not have to reread all of it; instead, you can review only the most important—those that are underlined—parts. However, even while you are underlining, you are benefiting from an imposed concentration, because this procedure forces you to think, to focus. Consider the following guidelines for underlining:

1. Underline the main ideas in paragraphs. The most important statement, the topic sentence, is likely to be at the beginning of the paragraph.

2. Underline the support for those main ideas.

3. Underline answers to questions that you bring to the reading assignment. These questions may have come from the end of the chapter, from subheadings that you turn into questions, from your independent concerns about the topic, or from questions posed by your instructor.

4. Underline only the key words. You would seldom underline all the words in a sentence and almost never a whole paragraph.

Does that fit your approach to underlining? Possibly not. Most students, in their enthusiasm to do a good job, overdo underlining.

The trick is to figure out what to underline. You would seldom underline more than about 30 percent of a passage, although the amount would depend on your purpose and the nature of the material. Following the preceding four suggestions will be useful. Learning more about the principles of sentence, paragraph, and essay organization in the following chapters will also be helpful.

ANNOTATING

Annotating, writing notes in the margins, is a practice related to underlining. You can do it independently, although it usually appears in conjunction with underlining to record your understanding and to extend your involvement in reading.

Writing in the margins represents intense involvement because it turns a reader into a writer. If you read material and write something in the margin as a reaction to it, then in a way you have had a conversation with the author. The author has made a statement and you have responded. In fact, you may have added something to the text; therefore, for your purposes, you have become a co-author or collaborator. The comments you make in the margin are of your own choosing according to your interests and the purpose you bring to the reading assignment. Your response in the margin may merely echo the author's ideas, it may question them critically, it may relate them to something else, or it may add to them.

The comments and marks on the following essay will help you understand the connection between writing and reading. Both techniques—underlining to indicate main and supporting ideas and annotating to indicate their importance and relevance to the task at hand—will enhance thinking, reading, and writing.

TOTAL INSTITUTIONS
Seymour Feshbach and Bernard Weiner

Total institution encompasses individual (thesis)

1   A <u>total institution</u> completely <u>encompasses</u> the <u>individual</u>, forming a barrier to the types of social intercourse that occur outside such a setting. Monasteries, jails, homes for the aged, boarding schools, and military academies are a few examples of total institutions.

1. Individual activities in same setting

2   <u>Total institutions</u> have certain <u>common characteristics</u>. <u>First</u>, the <u>individuals</u> in such environments must <u>sleep</u>, <u>play</u>, and <u>work</u> within the <u>same setting</u>. These are generally segmented spheres of activity in the lives of most individuals, but within a total institution one sphere of activity overlaps with others. <u>Second</u>,

2. All life within group

<u>each phase of life</u> takes place in the <u>company</u> of a <u>large group</u> of others. Frequently, sleeping is done in a barracks, food is served in a cafeteria, and so on. In such activities everyone is treated alike and must perform certain essential tasks. <u>Third, activities</u> in an institution are <u>tightly scheduled</u> according to a <u>master</u>

3. Activities tightly scheduled

<u>plan</u>, with set times to rise, to eat, to exercise, and to sleep. These institutional characteristics result in a <u>bureaucratic society</u>, which requires the hiring of other people for surveillance. What often results is a split in the groups within an institution into a large, managed group (inmates) and a small supervisory staff. There

Managed groups and staff at distance

tends to be <u>great social distance between</u> the <u>groups</u>, who <u>perceive each other</u> <u>according to stereotypes</u> and <u>have</u> severely <u>restricted communications</u>.

Two worlds—inside and outside

3   The <u>world of</u> the <u>inmate differs</u> greatly <u>from</u> the <u>outside world</u>. When one enters a total institution, all <u>previous roles</u>, such as father or husband, are <u>disrupted</u>. The <u>individual</u> is further <u>depersonalized</u> by the issuance of a uniform, confiscation of belongings, and gathering of personal information, as well as by more subtle touches like doorless toilets, record keeping, and bedchecks. The <u>effects</u> of an

Personality altered

institutional setting are so <u>all-encompassing</u> that one can meaningfully speak of an "<u>institutional personality</u>": a persistent manner of <u>behaving compliantly</u> and <u>without emotional involvement</u>.

Becomes psychotic, childlike, or depressive

4   Of course, there are <u>individual differences in adaptation</u> to the situation. They can be as extreme as <u>psychosis</u>, <u>childlike regression</u>, and <u>depression</u> or as mild as resigned compliance. <u>Most individuals do adjust</u> and build up a system of satisfactions, such as close friendships and cliques.

Individuals adjust but have trouble later on street

5   But because of these bonds and the fact that the habits needed to function in the outside world have been lost, <u>inmates face</u> great <u>problems</u> upon <u>leaving an</u> <u>institution</u>. A <u>shift from</u> the <u>top of</u> a <u>small society</u> to the <u>bottom of</u> a <u>larger one</u> may be <u>further demoralizing</u>.

OUTLINING

After reading, underlining, and annotating the piece, the next step could be outlining. If the piece is well organized, you should be able to reduce it to a simple outline so that you can, at a glance, see the relationship of ideas (sequence, relative importance, and interdependence).

The essay on total institutions can be outlined very easily:

Total Institutions
- I. Common characteristics
  - A. All activities in the same setting
  - B. All phases of life within a larger group
  - C. Activities scheduled according to a master plan
    - 1. Bureaucratic society
    - 2. Social distance between inmates and staff
- II. Adjusting to the world inside
  - A. Individual depersonalized
    - 1. Wears uniform
    - 2. No personal belongings
    - 3. No privacy
  - B. Adaptation
    - 1. Negative
      - a. Psychosis
      - b. Regression
      - c. Depression
    - 2. Positive
- III. Problems upon release outside
  - A. Adjusting to a different system
  - B. Encountering shock of going to the bottom of a new order

EXERCISE 1   Underlining, Annotating, and Outlining

Underline and annotate this passage. Then complete the outline that follows.

EFFECTIVE E-MAIL PRACTICES

1   Use short lines and short paragraphs. A short line length (perhaps 50 to 60 characters) is much easier to read than the 80-character line of most text editors. Similarly, short paragraphs (especially the first and last paragraph) are more inviting to read. Avoid formatting a long message as one solid paragraph.

2   Don't shout. Use all-capital letters only for emphasis or to substitute for italicized text (such as book titles). Do NOT type your entire message in all capitals: It is a text-based form of *shouting* at your reader and is considered rude (not to mention being more difficult to read).

3   Proofread your message before sending it. Do not let the speed and convenience of e-mail lull you into being careless. While an occasional typo or other surface error will probably be overlooked by the reader, excessive errors or sloppy language creates an unprofessional image of the sender.

4   Append previous messages appropriately. Most e-mail systems allow you to append the original message to your reply. Use this feature judiciously. Occasionally, it may be helpful for the reader to see his or her entire message replayed. More often, however, you can save the reader time by establishing the context of the original message in your reply. If necessary, quote pertinent parts of the original message. If the entire original message is needed, treat it as an appendix and insert it at the *end* of your reply—not at the beginning.

5   Use a direct style of writing and think twice; write once. Put your major idea in the first sentence or two. If the message is so sensitive or emotionally laden that a more indirect organization would be appropriate, you should reconsider whether e-mail is the most effective medium for the message. Because it is so easy to respond immediately to a message, you might be tempted to let your emotions take over. Such behavior is called "flaming" and should be avoided. Always assume the message you send will never be destroyed but will be saved permanently in somebody's computer file.

6   Do not neglect your greeting and closing. Downplay the seeming impersonality of computerized mail by starting your message with a friendly salutation, such as "Hi, Amos" or "Dear Mr. Fisher."

7   An effective closing is equally important. Some e-mail programs identify only the e-mail address (for example, "70511.753@compuserve.com") in the message header they transmit. Do not take a chance that your reader will not recognize you. Include your name, e-mail address, and any other appropriate identifying information at the end of your message.

(Adapted from Scot Ober, *Contemporary Business Communication*)

I. Short lines; short paragraphs

    A. _____

    B. _____

II. No shouting

    A. No entire message in capital letters

    B. Causes problems

        1. _____

        2. _____

III. Proofread message before sending

    A. Resist temptation to send without checking

    B. Errors create unprofessional image

IV. Append messages appropriately

    A. _____

    B. Often better to establish context in your message

    C. _____

V. Direct style with deliberation

  A. _____

  B. _____

VI. Greetings and closings

  A. _____

  B. Provide necessary information in closing

    1. _____

    2. _____

    3. _____

TAKING NOTES

Taking notes for reading-based writing in this book consists of underlining and annotating passages in reading selections and jotting down the relevant points for support in your outline as you organize your summary, reaction, or two-part response. While writing, you will use those notes for support as you refer directly to what you have read and use some quotations from it. You will also give credit to the source(s) you are reading, and—if your instructor requires you to do so—you will use documentation, including page numbers and identification of your source(s) for those ideas and words you borrow.

If you were doing a longer writing based on numerous sources outside this book, you would consult page 384 in Chapter 16, "Writing the Research Paper," which presents a well-organized system for using cards that group and coordinate borrowed ideas in relation to a basic outline of the ground you expect to cover. Of course, as you carefully and critically read sources in this book, you will naturally underline significant passages (often only a few words at a time) and annotate your reactions to what you read. Those annotations will vary according to your audience, their interests and background, and the nature of your topic. The sooner you settle on a topic and its natural divisions, the better, because only then you will be able to take those relevant notes.

If you already have at least a general topic before you read, you can easily formulate some basic questions to help you focus. Most reading-based writing prompts at the ends of Chapters 7 through 15 divide topics into parts that can serve as divisions for your outline. Reading some of the prompts and the entries called "Lock It In" before you read the selections will also be useful in helping you concentrate.

Here is an example of a reading-based writing prompt for the essay "Low Wages, High Skills" by Katherine S. Newman. "Transferable skills" are the operative words in organizing the response.

Low Wages, High Skills [title of Newman's essay]

Write a two-part response to the essay. Concentrate your critical thinking on Newman's idea that those who work at Burger Barn have transferable skills. Relate those specific skills to what you have experienced in a low-pay service job. Use direct references to and quotations from the essay. Agree or disagree with Newman.

Putting together a simple outline in advance and allowing some writing space between lines will provide you with room to pencil in references and quotes, with page numbers. Then when you write your outline or reaction, you can just incorporate your notes without having to refer back to the reading(s).

Here is an example of how you can place notes inside outlines. It is an excerpt from student Alex Mylonas's reading-based reaction to the short story "The Use of Force" by William Carlos Williams. During his first reading, he underlined and annotated freely; then later he selected phrases as support in his outline, which he submitted with a long paragraph assignment. His reaction appeared in a previous edition of this book.

I. The surface conflict
   A. Doctor-patient relationship
   B. Physical struggle
     1. Girl won't cooperate
     2. Doctor uses force to examine her throat
II. The inner conflict
   A. Doctor versus himself
     1. Wants to be professional
     2. Loses self-control
       "attractive little thing," p. 333
       "damned little brat," p. 333
     3. Loses sight of objective
       "got beyond reason," p. 334
   B. Emotional (brutal) side wins
       "It was a pleasure to attack her," p. 335
       "blind fury," p. 335

Reading-Based Writing Forms

WRITING A SUMMARY

The **summary**, the purest form of reading-based writing, is a rewritten, shortened version of a source in which you use your own wording to express the main ideas. Learning to summarize effectively will help you in many ways. Summary writing reinforces comprehension skills in reading, because it requires you to discriminate among the ideas in the target reading passage. Summaries are usually written in the form of a well-designed paragraph or set of paragraphs. Frequently, they are used in collecting material for research papers and in writing conclusions to essays.

The following rules will guide you in writing effective summaries.

1. Cite the author and title of the text.

2. Reduce the length of the original by about two-thirds, although the exact reduction will vary, depending on the content of the original.

3. Concentrate on the main ideas and include details only infrequently.

4. Change the original wording without changing the idea.

5. Do not evaluate the content or give an opinion in any way (even if you see an error in logic or fact).

6. Do not add ideas (even if you have an abundance of related information).

7. Do not include any personal comments (that is, do not use *I*, referring to self).

8. Use quotations only infrequently. (If you do use quotations, however, enclose them in quotation marks.)

9. Use some author tags ("says York," "according to York," or "the author explains") to remind the reader(s) that you are summarizing the material of another writer.

EXERCISE 2   Evaluating a Summary

Apply the rules of summary writing to the following summary of "Total Institutions," page 12. Mark the instances of poor summary writing by using rule numbers from the preceding list.

TOTAL INSTITUTIONS

A total institution completely encompasses the individual. Total institutions have certain common characteristics. Institutions provide the setting for all rest, recreation, and labor. Residents function only within the group. And residents are directed by a highly organized schedule, which, I think, is what they need or they wouldn't be there. There residents are depersonalized by being required to wear a uniform, abandon personal items, and give up privacy. Some adapt in a negative way by developing psychological problems, but most adapt in a positive way by forming relationships with other residents. Several popular movies, such as *The Shawshank Redemption*, show how prison society works. Once outside the total institution, individuals must deal with the problem of relearning old coping habits. They must also withstand the shock of going from the top of a small society to the bottom of a larger one. Society needs these total institutions, especially the jails.

The following is an example of an effective summary.

A SUMMARY OF "TOTAL INSTITUTIONS"
Michael Balleau

In "Total Institutions," Seymour Feshbach and Bernard Weiner explain that a total institution encompasses the lives of its residents, who share three common traits: The residents must do everything in the same place, must do things together, and must do things according to the institution's schedule. The institution takes away the residents' roles they had in society, takes away their appearance by issuing uniforms, takes away their personal property by confiscation, and takes away their privacy by making life communal. The authors say that some residents adapt negatively by developing psychological problems, but most form relationships and new roles within the institution. Upon release, these residents must learn to function in the free world all over again, as they start at the bottom of society. This shift "may be further demoralizing."

WRITING A REACTION

The reaction statement is another kind of reading-based writing, one in which you incorporate your views. Some reactions require evaluation with a critical-thinking emphasis. Some focus on simple discussion of the content presented in the reading and include summary material. Others concentrate on the writer's experience as related directly to the content of the passage.

The following paragraph is student Tanya Morris's reaction statement to "Total Institutions." She could have expanded her ideas to write an essay. Her instructor did not require her to provide page-number locations of her references and quotations.

INSTITUTIONS ALWAYS WIN
Tanya Morris

The short essay "Total Institutions," by Seymour Feshbach and Bernard Weiner, is a study of conflicts in controlled environments. The common characteristics of such places are in personal combat with the individual, in which the resident is stripped of his or her choices and made to "sleep, play, and work within the same setting." The resident who tries to assert his or her uniqueness is controlled by a master plan. That plan is enforced by personnel who become the masters of surveillance, set up social barriers, and maintain control over their underlings. The result is "a bureaucratic society." Cut off from the free world, the resident is in conflict with significant matters of newness—clothes, facilities, regulations, and roles. The authors explain that almost always the institution wins, sometimes converting the resident into a disturbed person or an amiable robot among other inmates. But at some point after that conversion, the institutionalized person may be returned to the free world. There a new conflict arises for the inmate, who goes from "the top of a small society to the bottom of a larger one." The authors of this essay are very clear in showing just how comprehensive these institutions are in waging their war, regardless of the motives, against individuality. After all, they are "total." As such, they should be, whenever possible, avoided.

WRITING A TWO-PART RESPONSE

As you have seen, the reaction response includes a partial summary or is written with the assumption that readers have read the original piece. However, your instructor may prefer that you separate the forms—for example, by presenting a clear, concise summary followed by a reaction. This format is especially useful for critical examination of a text or for problem-solving assignments because it requires you to understand and repeat another's views or experiences before responding. The most comprehensive reading-based writing form, the two-part response also helps you avoid the common problem of writing only a summary of the text when your instructor wants you to both summarize and react.

TOTAL INSTITUTIONS: A SUMMARY AND A REACTION
Michael Balleau

Part I: Summary

In "Total Institutions," Seymour Feshbach and Bernard Weiner explain that a total institution encompasses the lives of its residents, who share three common traits: The residents must do everything in the same place, must do things together, and must do things according to the institution's schedule. The institution takes away the residents' roles they had in society, takes away their appearance by issuing uniforms, takes away their personal property by confiscation, and takes away their privacy by making life communal. The authors say that some residents adapt negatively by developing psychological problems, but most form relationships and new roles within the institution. Upon release, these residents must learn to function in the free world all over again as they start at the bottom of society. This shift "may be further demoralizing."

Part 2: Reaction [Page-number documentation was not required.]

The basic ideas in "Total Institutions" gave me an insight into the behavior of my older cousin. Let's call him George. He spent almost five years in prison for a white collar crime he committed at the bank where he worked. Before George was incarcerated, he was an individual, almost to the extreme of being a rebel. When he got out, he was clearly an institutionalized person. Following the pattern of institutionalized behavior laid out in "Total Institutions," George had become a group person without knowing it. Many of "the habits needed to function in the outside world [had] been lost." Even at home after he returned, he had to be around people. He wanted some of us to be with him all the time, and he liked the noise of a radio or television. When we went out, he found it difficult to make decisions, even in buying a simple item, such as a shirt, or ordering food in a restaurant. Once when he was driving, we were stopped by a police officer because his car's taillight was out, and George became transformed into someone who was on automatic pilot in answering questions. It was his "institutional personality." Minutes later, he seemed hostile and had bad, unwarranted things to say about the officer. Altogether, George did five years in prison, and it took him about three more to adjust before he seemed like sort of what he was before. He was certainly never the same. As the authors say, every person reacts differently to "total institutions," and some institutions are more extreme than others, but each one has a profound effect on the resident's individuality.

Kinds of Support for Reading-Based Writing

In your reading-based writing assignments, you are likely to use three methods in developing your ideas: explanations, direct references to the reading selection, and quotations from the reading selection.

- Your explanations will often be expressed in patterns, such as causes and effects, comparison and contrast, definition, and exemplification. These forms are presented with others in depth in Chapters 7 through 15.

- Your references will point your reader(s) directly toward original ideas in sources. The more specific the references, the more helpful they will be to your readers.
- Your quotations will be words borrowed from sources and credited to those sources. You will use quotation marks around those words, which will appear as sentences or as partial sentences blended with your own words.

These concepts are important in all reading-related writing, but they are especially important in the reading-based writing you will be doing in Chapters 7 through 15 of this textbook.

Basic Formal Documentation in Reading-Based Writing

Borrowing words or ideas without giving credit to the originator is called **plagiarism** and is not acceptable scholarship, regardless of whether it is intentional. As you use sources from your textbook, your instructor will ask you to document the ideas of others formally or informally. Informally, you will credit a source by title or author's name. Formally, you will indicate the precise location of all the original ideas you have borrowed according to a system. (See "Plagiarism" in Chapter 16, pages 386–387, for more details.)

CITATIONS

Documenting sources for papers based on written material is systematic. Most English instructors use MLA (Modern Language Association) style, the system used in this chapter and explained further in Chapter 16, "Writing the Research Paper." Mainly, you need to remember that when using material from a source, you must give enough information so that the reader will recognize it or be able to find it in its original context. Here are the most common principles of documentation that can be used for textbook or other restricted sources, whether it is quoted, paraphrased (restated), or summarized.

If you use the author's name in introducing a quotation, then usually give only the page number.

> **Example:** Suzanne Britt says that "neat people are bums and clods at heart" (255).

If you use the author's name in introducing a borrowed idea, then usually give only the page number.

> **Example:** Suzanne Britt believes that neat people are weak in character (255).

If you do not use the author's name to introduce a quotation or an idea, then usually give both the author's name and the page number:

> **Example:** Music often helps Alzheimer's patients think more clearly (Weiss 112).

WORKS CITED

Work(s) Cited lists the sources used, meaning those that appear in citations, as shown in the previous section. Each kind of publication has its own order of parts and punctuation. You need not memorize them. They are given in detail in

Chapter 16, on pages 377–382, and some can be found on the Internet by keying in "MLA Form."

Here is an example of a Work Cited entry for the previous edition of this book, pertaining to the student paragraph on page 228. Other examples can be found at the end of the next two student works and on page 378 of Chapter 16, under "An Anthology or Textbook." Note the punctuation between parts and the order of those parts: author's name (last, first), title of composition (quotation marks for a short work, italics for a long work), edition; name of the anthology, editor(s) of the anthology, place of publication, publisher, date of publication, pages on which the selection appears, and medium of publication.

Work Cited

Blaylock, Richard. "More Than the Classroom." *Paragraphs and Essays with Integrated Readings*. Ed. Lee Brandon and Kelly Brandon. 10th ed. Boston: Houghton, 2008. 228. Print.

Examples of Student Reading-Based Writing

Your reading-based paragraph or essay may include ideas from newspapers, magazines, online sources, or books. To make classwork simpler for you here, most of the reading-based assignments relate to selections included in this book. When you are writing about something you have read, just write as you usually would, but bring in ideas and quotations from that source. You may also want to refer to more than one source. You may even use ideas from other sources to contrast with your own. For example, you may say, "Unlike Fred M. Hechlinger in 'The First Step in Improving Sex Education: Remove the Hellfire' (351), I believe that public schools should not offer sex education." Do not feel that all points you make must agree with the views in the reading selections.

STUDENT PARAGRAPH WITH DOCUMENTATION

Here is a student paragraph illustrating how to incorporate ideas and document them.

SEXIST MEN AS VICTIMS
Jackie Malone

Sexist men are victims of their own bias against females. Because they cannot accept women as full human beings, they themselves are smaller in dimension. In Irwin Shaw's "The Girls in Their Summer Dresses," Michael looks at his wife, but he doesn't see a full human being. In fact for a moment he does not even recognize her as his wife; he just sees a sexual object: "what a pretty girl, what nice legs" (314). Because he sees her and other women that way, he cannot ever have the relationship with her that she deserves and that he would find fulfilling. Of course, thinking of women as just soft and cuddly has its effects on men in other ways. The man as father who thinks that way may very well regard his own daughter as one limited in her ranges of activities and limited in her potential. He may be one of those fathers who immediately stereotype their daughters as headed for a "life of the affections," not like a son's, "earning a living" (Lurie 249). Unfortunately, these men cannot accept females as their equals in any important respect, and, in doing so, they deprive themselves, as well as others.

Works Cited

Lurie, Alison. "Pink Kittens and Blue Spaceships." *Paragraphs and Essays: A Worktext with Readings*. Ed. Lee Brandon. 8th ed. Boston: Houghton, 2001. 249–50. Print.

Shaw, Irwin. "The Girls in Their Summer Dresses." *Paragraphs and Essays with Integrated Readings*. Ed. Lee Brandon and Kelly Brandon. 11th ed. Boston: Cengage, 2011. 233–36. Print.

STUDENT ESSAY WITH DOCUMENTATION

"Listening to the Air" Guitar

JOSEPH PONCA

The essay was written for this assignment: "Write a brief reading-based essay on a reading selection. Use MLA style in providing credit for your citations and Work Cited [instructor choice in this case]." In prewriting this assignment, Joseph Ponca composed an outline of his main points and filled in the supporting points and details with comments about his experience and insights and with short quotations from and references to (with page numbers) "Listening to the Air."

Relating reading
selection
to personal
experience

Thesis

1   When I read "Listening to the Air," by John (Fire) Lame Deer, I thought of something I saw last summer. While on vacation in Oklahoma, I went to a powwow. One dance involved a group of Native American boys in full native dress of paint, beads, and buckskin. They were dancing to honor the spirits, but between dances one of the boys looked upward to an airplane making contrails across the sky. Then his mind seemed to wander, and he began a strumming motion on his feathered staff as if it were a stringed instrument. He was playing air guitar, and it made me think of how, in a couple of minutes, he lived in two worlds—the dance taking him back with tribal chants and the air guitar returning him to music of his generation, as he looked at the airplane. That is sort of what the essay made me do.

General reference

Blended quotations

2   John (Fire) Lame Deer has the message and Richard Erdoes does the writing about what "civilization" has done to people. Lame Deer thinks we have separated ourselves from nature too much. He says we "have changed men into . . . office workers, into time-clock punchers . . . and women into housewives, truly fearful creatures" who overfurnish the home and overregulate home life. He "sometimes" prefers "tar-paper shacks" to our "luxury homes" and outhouses to bathrooms. He believes we are so afraid of the world that we "don't want to see, feel, smell, or hear it" (382).

Transition

Topic sentence

3   Reading that, my reactions are immediate. I do not care to live in a shack permanently or use an outhouse on a regular basis. I prefer the fresh smell of soap to the stale smell of day-old sweat, and breath freshener to halitosis. I prefer not to work or eat in a smoke-filled room. I prefer my food well-cooked with sauces, and I want my milk pasteurized and fortified. I do not want to chew on a raw kidney—or even a cooked one. After work, I like a reclining chair and a cool drink and a big-screen TV.

Transition and
topic sentence

Blended quotation

4   But Lame Deer shocks me into thought about my artificial life with his colorful examples of "old-fashioned full-bloods" chewing on uncooked buffalo intestines and organ meat (383). I am reminded that we do not know what a good tomato or green bean tastes like, unless we grow one in the garden. My great-grandmother did, and she had dozens of warm and scary frontier stories that were as good as the ones in *Little House on the Prairie*. She was almost a century closer to real life than I ever will be. She was my bridge, much as Lame Deer is.

Topic sentence	5	Sometimes I am able to create the feeling that I am "listening to the air." Nothing relaxes me more than backpacking, my favorite hobby. That is when I get closer to nature, walking the trails, sleeping under the stars with the earth an inch under my body, and preparing my food. But even then I am walking on hundred-dollar boots, snoozing in a sleeping bag filled with goose down provided by creatures I will never see, and eating a freeze-dried meal cooked on my portable gas stove, as I sip water I have purified chemically. And so on.
Meaning	6	Lame Deer makes me think. He puts me in touch with what once *was* for his tribe. He makes me feel guilty. He makes me feel I should take more responsibility and have more conscience for what we do to our environment, to fellow creatures, and to people. I do not want to go back to where my grandparents were, but I do not want to forget them and what was their everyday life. So, my feet are set in this artificial world. I console myself
Reflecting back to the introduction		with thoughts of greater longevity, comfort, and technological pleasures. Like the Indian boy in his tribal dress playing the air guitar on his feathered staff, I am urged to stand in both worlds.

Work Cited

Lame Deer, John, and Richard Erdoes. "Listening to the Air." *Sentences, Paragraphs, and Beyond: A Worktext with Readings*. Ed. Lee Brandon and Kelly Brandon. 4th ed. Boston: Houghton, 2001. 281–83. Print. [Lame Deer's essay can be found on the Internet by keying in the title and the author's last name on Google.]

Professional Essay with Applications

The following essay demonstrates many of the elements of good writing that we have been exploring. To help you evaluate and write in response to the selection, the essay is underlined, annotated, and accompanied by a set of discussion and critical-thinking questions and then by several reading-based writing suggestions. Taking a look at the questions and writing suggestions before you read the essay may help you focus your reading.

The Struggle to Be an All-American Girl

ELIZABETH WONG

The title of the reading may suggest that Elizabeth Wong would experience success if she became an "all-American girl." But then the question is, Would she enjoy as an adult what she had wanted as a child?

MINDSET

Lock It In

Must one relinquish one's own cultural identity to assume another cultural identity?

Setting—childhood	1	It's still there, the <u>Chinese school</u> on Yale Street <u>where</u> my brother and <u>I used to go</u>. Despite the new coat of paint and the high wire fence, the school I knew ten years ago <u>remains</u> remarkably, stoically the <u>same</u>.

Goes reluctantly to Chinese school	2	Every day at 5 p.m., instead of playing with our fourth- and fifth-grade friends or sneaking out to the empty lot to hunt ghosts and animal bones, my brother and <u>I had to go</u> to Chinese school. No amount of kicking, screaming, or pleading could dissuade <u>my mother</u>, who was <u>solidly determined to have us learn</u> the <u>language of our heritage</u>.

3   Forcibly, she walked us the seven long, hilly blocks from our home to school, depositing our defiant tearful faces before the stern principal. My only memory of him is that he swayed on his heels like a palm tree, and he always clasped his impatient twitching hands behind his back. I recognized him as a repressed maniacal child killer, and knew that if we ever saw his hands we'd be in big trouble.

Smell—Chinese vs. American	4	We all sat in little chairs in an empty auditorium. The room smelled like Chinese medicine and imported faraway mustiness. Like ancient mothballs or dirty closets. <u>I hated that smell.</u> <u>I favored crisp new scents.</u> <u>Like</u> the <u>soft French perfume</u> that <u>my American teacher</u> wore in <u>public school</u>.

5   Although the <u>emphasis at</u> the <u>school</u> was <u>mainly language</u>—speaking, <u>reading</u>, <u>writing</u>—the lessons always began with an exercise in politeness. With the entrance of the teacher, the best student would tap a bell and everyone would get up, kowtow, and chant, "*sing san ho,*" the phonetic for "How are you, teacher?"

Subject material— Chinese vs. American	6	<u>Being ten years old, I had better things to learn than ideographs</u> copied painstakingly in lines that ran right to left from the tip of a *moc but*, a real ink pen that had to be held in an awkward way if blotches were to be avoided. After all, <u>I could do</u> the <u>multiplication tables</u>, <u>name</u> the <u>satellites of Mars</u>, and <u>write reports</u> on *Little Women* and *Black Beauty*. <u>Nancy Drew</u>, my favorite book heroine, <u>never spoke Chinese</u>.

Language—Chinese vs. American	7	The <u>language</u> was a <u>source</u> of <u>embarrassment</u>. More times than not, I had tried to disassociate myself from the nagging loud voice that followed me wherever I wandered in the nearby American supermarket outside Chinatown. The <u>voice</u> belonged to <u>my grandmother</u>, a fragile woman in her seventies who could outshout the best of the street vendors. Her humor was raunchy, her Chinese rhythmless, patternless. It was quick, it was <u>loud</u>, it was <u>unbeautiful</u>. It was <u>not like</u> the <u>quiet</u>, <u>lilting romance of French</u> or the <u>gentle refinement</u> of the <u>American South</u>. <u>Chinese</u> sounded <u>pedestrian</u>. <u>Public</u>.

Rewards for learning English well	8	In <u>Chinatown</u>, the <u>comings and goings</u> of hundreds of <u>Chinese</u> on their daily tasks <u>sounded chaotic and frenzied</u>. I did not want to be thought of as mad, as talking gibberish. <u>When I spoke English, people nodded at me, smiled sweetly, said encouraging words</u>. Even the people in my culture would cluck and say that I'd do well in life. "My, doesn't she move her lips fast," they would say, meaning that I'd be able to keep up with the world outside Chinatown.

Brother reinforces cultural bias	9	<u>My brother</u> was <u>even more fanatical than I about speaking English</u>. He was especially <u>hard on</u> my <u>mother</u>, criticizing her, often cruelly, for her pidgin speech—smatterings of Chinese scattered like chop suey in her conversation. "It's not 'What it is,' Mom," he'd say in exasperation. "It's 'What *is* it; what *is* it, what *is* it!'" Sometimes Mom might leave out an occasional "the" or "a," or perhaps a verb of being. He would stop her in mid-sentence: "Say it again, Mom. Say it right." When he tripped over his own tongue, he'd blame it on her: "See, Mom, it's all your fault. You set a bad example."

Cultural divorce	10	<u>After two years of writing</u> with a *moc but* and <u>reciting words</u> with multiples of meanings, I finally <u>was granted</u> a <u>cultural divorce</u>. I was <u>permitted</u> to <u>stop Chinese school</u>.

Embraces other cultures	11	I <u>thought of myself as multicultural</u>. I <u>preferred tacos to egg rolls; I enjoyed Cinco de Mayo more than Chinese New Year</u>.
No reconciliation	12	<u>At last</u>, I was <u>one of you</u>; I <u>wasn't one of them</u>.
Sad	13	<u>Sadly</u>, I <u>still am</u>.

EXERCISE 3   Discussion and Critical Thinking

1. By what steps is Wong transformed into an "all-American girl"?

2. Who or what influenced her the most?

3. How does she feel about her transformation?

4. Why can't Wong do anything about her transformation?

5. What advice would you give to her?

6. What advice do you think the author would give to her daughter?

EXERCISE 4   Suggestions for Reading-Based Writing

On separate paper, complete one of the following reading-based responses.

1. Write a summary of Wong's essay.

2. Write a two-part response composed of labeled summary and reaction parts.

3. In a reaction, analyze the essay as a transformation that Wong experienced. Concentrate on stages of her change, using time as the principle for order, or emphasize how different parts of society—school, neighborhood, and family—influenced her to set aside her culture and adopt another. Resist the temptation to write only a summary.

4. Write a reaction in which you discuss Wong's struggle to be an all-American girl. Explain exactly what happened and, in your estimation, why it happened. Discuss what you have learned by direct experience and by observation. Have you or has someone you know gone through a similar experience of wanting to be part of some other group, such as cultural, ethnic, or social class (from working class to upper middle or upper)? When you were a young teenager, did you sometimes want to divorce your parents? If you discuss your personal experience, do so by relating it to Wong's experience, as you use quotations from and references to her essay.

EXERCISE 5   Incorporating Quotations

Introduce the sentence as it is, select a key part of each sentence and blend it with your words in a new sentence, or paraphrase (reword) the sentence. Include citations if your instructor prefers.

Examples:

Wong: "At last, I was one of you; I wasn't one of them."
Introducing: Wong concludes with a confession: "At last, I was one of you; I wasn't one of them." (paragraph 12)

Wong: "I thought of myself as multicultural."
Blending: She considered herself "multicultural." (paragraph 11)

Wong: "The language was a source of embarrassment."
Paraphrasing: She was ashamed of her own language. (paragraph 7)

1. Wong: "Sadly, I still am." (paragraph 13)

2. Wong: "Even the people in my culture would cluck and say that I'd do well in life." (paragraph 8)

3. Wong: "When I spoke English, people nodded at me, smiled sweetly, said encouraging words." (paragraph 8)

EXERCISE 6   Form for Works Cited

Write a Works Cited entry for "The Struggle to Be an All-American Girl" by Elizabeth Wong. Refer to pages 20–21 for instruction and example.

Journal Writing

Your journal entries are likely to be concerned primarily with the relationship between the reading material and you—your life experiences, your views, your imagination. The reading material will give you something of substance to write about, but you will be writing especially for yourself, developing confidence and ease in writing so that writing becomes a comfortable part of your everyday activities, as speaking already is.

These journal entries will be part of your intellectual diary, recording what you are thinking about a certain issue. They will help you understand the reading material; help you develop your writing skills, in uncovering ideas that can be used on other assignments; and help you think more clearly and imaginatively. Because these entries are of a more spontaneous nature than the more structured writing assignments, organization and editing are likely to be of less concern.

Each journal entry should be clearly dated and, if reading related, should specify the title and author of the original piece.

Even if your instructor wants you to concentrate on what you read for your journal writing, he or she might not want you to be restricted to the material in this text. Fortunately, you are surrounded by reading material in newspapers, magazines, and, of course, textbooks from other courses. These topics can serve you well, especially if you want to begin your journal writing now.

Cross-Curricular and Career-Related Writing

This textbook includes cross-curricular and career-related writing topics at the end of Chapters 7 through 15. These suggestions offer a wide range of subject material to those of you who would like to write about subjects you have encountered across campus, at work, and in your search for a career. Some of that writing may include ideas coming directly from your reading. Those ideas can be documented with a listing of the source, which usually includes the name of the author, title of the work, place of publication, publisher, date, page numbers, and medium of publication. The citations for quotations or specific references can be made in the same fashion as the ones for textbook sources.

WRITER'S GUIDELINES: Reading for Thinking, Discussion, and Writing

1. **Underlining** helps you to read with discrimination.

   * Underline the main ideas in paragraphs.
   * Underline the support for those ideas.
   * Underline answers to questions that you bring to the reading assignment.
   * Underline only the key words.

2. **Annotating** enables you to actively engage the reading material.

   * Number parts if appropriate.
   * Make comments according to your interests and needs.

3. **Outlining** the passages you read sheds light on the relationship of ideas, including the major divisions of the passage and their relative importance.

4. **Summarizing** helps you concentrate on main ideas. A summary

   * cites the author and title of the text.
   * is usually shorter than the original by about two-thirds, although the exact reduction will vary depending on the content of the original.
   * concentrates on the main ideas and includes details only infrequently.
   * changes the original wording without changing the idea.
   * does not evaluate the content or give an opinion in any way (even if the original contains an error in logic or fact).
   * does not add ideas (even if the writer of the summary has an abundance of related information).
   * does not include any personal comments by the writer of the summary (therefore, no use of *I*, referring to self).

- seldom contains quotations (although, if it does, only with quotation marks).
- includes some author tags ("says York," "according to York," or "the author explains") to remind the reader(s) that it is a summary of the material of another writer.

5. Two other types of reading-based writing are

- the reaction, which shows how the reading relates to you, your experiences, and your attitudes; also, it is often a critique of the worth and logic of the piece.
- the two-part response, which includes a summary and a reaction that are separate.

6. Most ideas in reading-based papers are developed in one or more of these three ways:

- explanation
- direct references
- quotations

7. Documenting is giving credit to borrowed ideas and words.

- Informal documentation gives credit to sources as directed by your instructor.
- Formal documentation gives credit to sources according to published guidelines, such as those provided by the MLA (Modern Language Association).

Part II THE WRITING PROCESS

Think of writing as swimming. If you were a nonswimmer and you jumped into the water without instructions, at best you would swim awkwardly. At worst you would sink. You may face similar dilemmas in writing. If you choose the sink-or-swim method, hope for hidden talent or good luck. A better choice is the writing process, an approach that all writers use, to some degree, with modifications for different writing situations. Whether you call it the flow of writing or the writing process, it is all here in the next five chapters.

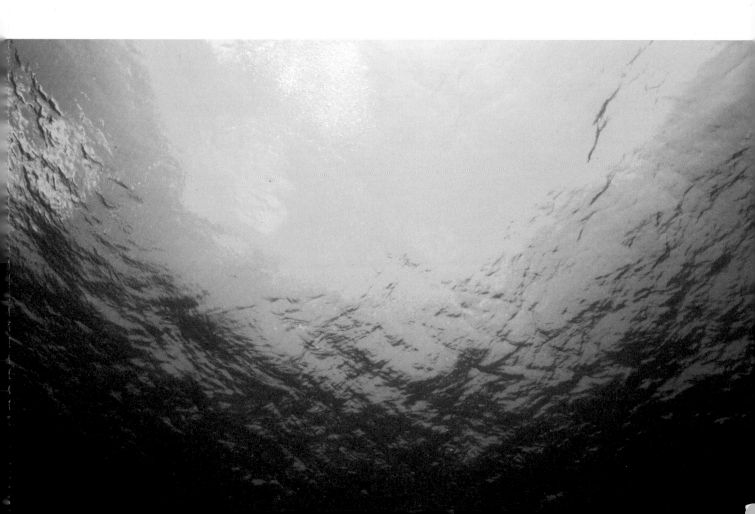

Chapter 2

The Writing Process: Stage One
Exploring / Experimenting / Gathering Information

The Writing Process Defined

The writing process consists of a set of strategies that will help you proceed from idea or purpose to the final statement of a paragraph or an essay. As presented here, the different strategies move from

Stage One: Exploring / Experimenting / Gathering Information
to
Stage Two: Writing the Controlling Idea / Organizing and Developing Support
to
Stage Three: Writing / Revising / Editing.

These stages are described in Chapters 2, 3, and 4, respectively. Altogether they represent what is called the **writing process**.

The process of writing is **recursive**, which means "going back and forth." In this respect, writing is like reading. If you do not understand what you have read, you back up and read it again. After you reread the entire passage, you may still go back and reread selectively. The same can be said of your writing. If, for example, you have reached Stage Two and you are working with an outline only to discover that your subject is too broad, you may want to back up and narrow your topic sentence or thesis and then adjust your outline. You may even return to an early cluster of ideas to see how you can use a smaller grouping of them. Revision, in Stage Three, is usually the most recursive part of all. You will go over your material again and again until you are satisfied that you have expressed yourself the best you can.

The Writing Process Worksheet

The blank Writing Process Worksheet on page 6, with brief directions for the three stages of the writing process, is designed to be duplicated and completed with each major writing assignment. It gives you clear, consistent guidance and provides your instructor with an easy format for finding and checking information. Customarily this worksheet is stapled to the front of your rough and final drafts.

The Assignment

Particulars of the assignment, frequently the most neglected parts of a writing project, are often the most important. If you do not know, or later cannot recall, specifically what you are supposed to do, you cannot do satisfactory work. An otherwise excellent composition on a misunderstood assignment may get you a failing grade, a sad situation for both you and your instructor.

As an aid to recalling just what you should write about, the Writing Process Worksheet provides space and guidance for you to note these details: information about the topic, audience, pattern of writing, length of the paper, whether to include a rough draft or revised drafts, whether your paper must be typed, and the date the assignment is due.

At the time your instructor gives that information, it will probably be clear; a few days later, it may not be. By putting your notes on the assignment portion of the worksheet, you remind yourself of what you should do and also indicate to your instructor what you have done.

Your Audience

More so than most points on the assignment portion of the worksheet, the matter of audience requires special consideration. At the outset of your writing project, you should consider your readers. Their needs, interests, and abilities should determine the focus of your subject, the extent of your explanation, your overall style, and your word choice. We usually make those adjustments automatically when we are speaking; it is easy to forget to do so when we are writing.

Stage One Strategies

Certain strategies commonly grouped under the heading *prewriting* can help you get started and develop your ideas. These strategies—freewriting, brainstorming, clustering, and gathering information—are very much a part of writing. The understandable desire to skip to the finished statement is what causes the most common student-writer grief: that of not filling the blank sheet or of filling it but not significantly improving on the blankness. The prewriting strategies described in this section will help you attack the blank sheet constructively with imaginative thought, analysis, and experimentation. They can lead to clear, effective communication.

FREEWRITING

Freewriting is an exercise that its originator, Peter Elbow, has called "babbling in print." When you freewrite, you write without stopping, letting your ideas tumble forth. You do not concern yourself unduly with the fundamentals of writing, such as punctuation and spelling. Freewriting is an adventure into your memory and imagination. It is concerned with discovery, invention, and exploration. If you are at a loss for words on your subject, write in a comment such as "I do not know what is coming next" or "blah, blah, blah," and continue when relevant words come. It is important to keep writing. Freewriting immediately eliminates the blank page and thereby helps you break through an emotional barrier, but that is not the only benefit. The words that you sort through in that idea kit will include some you can use. You can then underline or circle those words and even add notes on the side so that the freewriting continues to grow even after its initial spontaneous expression.

The way you proceed depends on the type of assignment: working with a topic of your choice, working from a restricted list of topics, or working with a prescribed topic.

The *topic of your choice* affords you the greatest freedom of exploration. You would probably select a subject that interests you and freewrite about it, allowing your mind to wander among the many parts of that subject, perhaps mixing fact and fantasy, direct experience, and hearsay. A freewriting about music might uncover areas of special interest and knowledge, such as jazz or folk rock, that you would want to pursue further in freewriting or other prewriting strategies.

Working from a *restricted list* requires a more focused freewriting. With the list, you can, of course, experiment with several topics to discover what is most suitable for you. If, for example, "career choice," "career preparation," "career guidance," and "career prospects" are on the restricted list, you would probably select one and freewrite about it. If it works well for you, you would probably proceed with the next step of your prewriting. If you are not satisfied with what you uncover in freewriting, you would explore another item from the restricted list.

When working with a *prescribed topic*, you focus on a particular topic and try to restrict your freewriting to its boundaries. If your topic specifies a division of a subject area such as "political involvement of your generation," then you would tie those key words to your own information, critical thinking, and imaginative responses. If the topic asks for, let's say, your reactions to a specific poem, then that poem would give you the framework for your free associations with your own experiences, creations, and opinions.

You should learn to use freewriting because it will often serve you well, but you need not use it every time you write. Some very short writing assignments do not call for freewriting. An in-class assignment may not allow time for freewriting.

Nevertheless, freewriting is often a useful strategy in your toolbox of techniques. It can help you get words on paper, break emotional barriers, generate topics, develop new insights, and explore ideas.

Freewriting can lead to other stages of prewriting and writing, and it can also provide content as you develop your topic.

The following example of freewriting, and the writing, revising, and editing examples in Chapters 3 and 4, are from student Betsy Jackson's work titled "If I Were a Traffic Cop." She selected her topic, bad drivers, from a restricted list. If she had been working with a prescribed topic, she might have been told to concentrate on only one aspect of bad drivers, such as the need for driver education, the need for better laws, or the cost of bad driving. Then she would have done some research. However, she had no such limitation and, therefore, thought about bad drivers broadly. After her freewriting, she went back over her work looking for an idea that might be limited enough to use as the basis for a paper. Here is what she wrote:

All kinds

Drunk drivers

If I were a cop

Tailgaters

Lane changers
Left turners on red
Too fast, too slow
Don't yield

Causes
Effect

Just driving around on streets and freeways can be a scary experience because of all the bad drivers. Whenever I see them, sometimes I just laugh. Sometimes I get mad. Sometimes I get irritated. Sometimes I get scared. It's not just the young drivers or the old drivers it's <u>all kinds</u>. And all types of people no matter what the nationality or the types of vehicles they drive. Pickup drivers are worse as a group but bad drivers come in all kinds of vehicles. I think someone should do something about them. The worst are the <u>drunk drivers</u>. I don't see them in the morning. But I see them late at night when I'm driving home from work. They should be put away. But a lot of others should be getting serious tickets. Especially the bad ones. <u>Make me a cop</u>—a supercop—a Rambo cop and I'll go after the bad ones. Some of them cause a lot of accidents and get people all mad. Blah. Blah. Blah. Take <u>tailgaters</u> for example. And what about the drivers that go into the emergency lanes on the freeways to pass when there's a jam. And then you've got the <u>lane changers</u> that don't even give signals. And those that just <u>keep going</u> and <u>turn left when</u> the <u>light turns red</u>. Then you've got the ones that drive <u>too fast</u> and <u>too slow</u>. And you've got the ones that <u>don't stop</u> for <u>pedestrians</u>. Blah. Blah. Blah. I guess we all have our pet peeves about bad drivers and everyone would like to be a cop sometimes. I guess if you talked to them some would have reasons. Maybe they're <u>late</u> for work or they are <u>mad</u> about something. Or maybe there's an <u>emergency</u>. Whatever it is, I get concerned when they <u>take my life in their hands</u>.

After her freewriting session, Jackson examined what she had written for possible ideas to develop for a writing assignment. As she recognized those ideas, she underlined important words and phrases and made a few notes in the margins. By reading only the underlined words in her freewriting, you can understand what is important to Jackson; it was not necessary for her to underline whole sentences.

In addition to putting some words on that dreaded blank sheet of paper, Jackson discovered that she had quite a lot to say about drivers and that she had selected a favorable topic to develop. The entire process took no more than five minutes. Had she found only a few ideas or no promising ideas at all, she might have freewritten on another topic. Although in going back over her work she saw some errors, especially in wording and sentence structure, she did not correct them because the purpose of freewriting is discovery, not revising or editing. She was confident that she could continue with the process of writing a paper as she followed her flow of thought.

EXERCISE 1   Freewriting

Try freewriting on a broad topic such as one of the following:

an event that was important to you in your youth
a concert, a movie, or a television program
the ways you use your computer
drug use—causes, effects, a friend with a problem
gang membership—causes, effects, an experience
the benefits of using a word processor
ways of disciplining children
why a person is a hero or role model to you
a great or terrible party
a bad or good day at school
why a college education is important

Following the example in Jackson's freewriting, underline and annotate the phrases that may lead to ideas you could explore further.

BRAINSTORMING

Brainstorming features important words and phrases that relate in various ways to the subject area or to the specific topic you are concerned with. Brainstorming includes two basic forms: (1) asking and answering questions and (2) listing.

Big Six Questions

One effective way to get started is to ask the big six questions about your subject: *Who? What? Where? When? Why? How?* Then let your mind run free as you jot down answers in single entries or lists. Some of the big six questions may not fit, and some may be more important than others, depending on the purposes of your writing. For example, if you were writing about the causes of a situation, the *Why?* question could be more important than the others; if you were concerned with how to do something, the *How?* question would predominate. If you were writing in response to a reading selection, you would confine your thinking to questions appropriately related to the content of that reading selection.

Whatever your focus for the questions is, the result is likely to be numerous ideas that will provide information for continued exploration and development of your topic. Thus your pool of information for writing widens and deepens.

Jackson continued with the topic of bad drivers, and her topic tightened to focus on particular areas.

Who?   bad drivers; me as a cop
What?   driving badly, recklessly, unsafely; a cop's job
Where?   on every roadway
When?   all the time
Why?   hurried, disrespectful, self-centered, sick, addiction, hostile, irresponsible
How?   lane-changing, driving illegally in emergency lane, not signaling, passing on the shoulder, tailgating, turning left on red, rolling stop, speeding, driving while intoxicated

Notice that each question is answered in this example, but with some topics some questions may not fit. As Jackson addressed the *Why?* and *How?* questions, her brainstorming produced long lists, suggesting that those areas were strong possibilities for the focus of her paper.

Listing

Simply making a list of words and phrases related to your topic is another effective way to brainstorm, especially if you have a defined topic and a storehouse of information. This strategy is favored by many writers.

Knowing from the outset that she was concerned mainly with the behavior of drivers, Jackson might have gone directly to making a list indicating what drivers do or how they drive. She then might have selected perhaps four ideas from this list for her framework and circled them for future reference.

(unsafe lane changers)
driving illegally in the emergency lane
not signaling
passing on the shoulder
(tailgating)
(turning left on red)
turning right on red without stop
rolling stop
speeding
driving too slow in fast lane
(driving while intoxicated)
driving while on cell phone
driving while reading road map
truck in car lanes
drivers dumping trash

Even if you do not have a focused topic, you may find a somewhat random listing useful, merely writing phrases as they occur to you. This exploratory activity is similar to freewriting. After you have established such a list, you can sort out and group the phrases as you generate your topic and find its natural divisions. Feel free to accept, reject, or insert phrases.

EXERCISE 2   Brainstorming

Further explore the topic you worked with in Exercise 1 by first answering the big six questions and then making a list.

Big Six Questions

Who? _____

What? _____

Where? _____

When? _____

Why? _____

How? _____

List

_____

_____

_____

_____

_____

_____

_____

_____

_____

_____

CLUSTERING

In **clustering**, double-bubble your topic—that is, write it down in the middle of the page and draw a double circle around it—and then respond to the question "What comes to mind?" Draw a single bubble around other ideas on spokes radiating from the hub that contains the topic. Any bubble can lead to another bubble or to numerous bubbles in the same way. This strategy is sometimes used instead of, or before, making an outline to organize and develop ideas.

The more restricted the topic inside the double bubble, the fewer the number of spokes that will radiate with single bubbles. For example, a topic such as "high school dropouts" would have more spokes than "reasons for dropping out of high school."

Here is Jackson's cluster on the subject of bad drivers. She has drawn dotted lines around subclusters that seem to relate to a workable, unified topic.

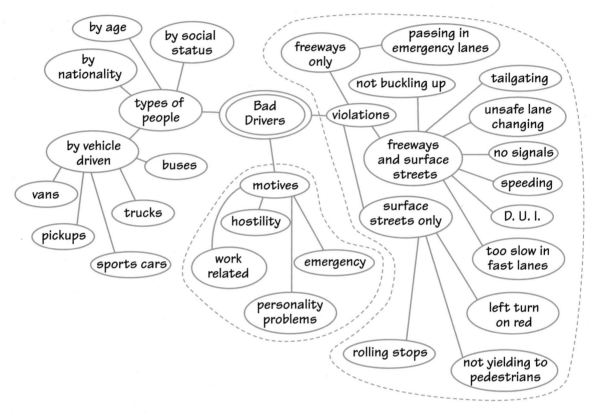

EXERCISE 3   Clustering

Continuing with your topic, develop a cluster of related ideas. Draw dotted lines around subclusters that have potential for focus and more development.

GATHERING INFORMATION

For reading-related writing—especially the kind that requires a close examination of the selection—you will gather information by reading print or electronic sources, such as the Internet; make notes; and perhaps outline or summarize (see Chapter 1) the text. Of course, you may also want to make notes for other topics to write about as they occur to you. This kind of note taking can be combined with other strategies such as brainstorming and clustering. It can even take the place of them. It can also be used in conjunction with strategies such as outlining.

Student Betsy Jackson at this point is writing about personal experience. If she wanted to include statistics or an authoritative statement, she might do some library research or interview a police officer. In either case, she would take notes.

WRITER'S GUIDELINES: The Writing Process: Stage One

The writing process consists of strategies that will help you proceed from idea or purpose to the final statement of a paragraph or an essay. Throughout all stages of the writing process, you should consider your audience. Stage One offers four approaches:

STUDENT COMPANION SITE
For additional practice, visit www.cengage.com/devenglish/brandon/pe11e.

1. **Freewriting** consists of writing without stopping, letting ideas tumble forth.

   - Freewriting involves breaking down emotional barriers, generating topics, discovering ideas, and exploring ideas.
   - Your approach to freewriting will depend on whether you work on a topic of your choice (great freedom), a topic from a restricted list (more focused), or an assigned topic (concentration on one idea).
   - You need not use freewriting for all writing experiences. You would probably not use it for very short assignments, in-class assignments with limited time, outline and summary assignments, or assignments on topics you know well.

2. **Brainstorming** is used for quickly developing key words and phrases that relate to your topic. It includes two basic forms: the big six questions and listing.

   - You may ask *Who? What? Where? When? Why?* and *How?* questions about your topic, ignoring questions that do not fit.
   - Or, you may simply list points on likely divisions of your topic.

3. **Clustering** is a visual way of showing connections and relationships. It is sometimes used with an outline and sometimes in place of one.

   - Start by double-bubbling your topic.
   - Then, in response to the question *What comes to mind?* single-bubble other ideas on spokes radiating from the hub.

4. **Gathering information** can take the form of reading with underlining, annotating, and note taking.

Chapter 3

The Writing Process: Stage Two
Writing the Controlling Idea / Organizing and Developing Support

The most important advice this book can offer you is *state your controlling idea and support it.* If you have no controlling idea—no topic sentence for a paragraph or thesis for an essay—your writing will be unfocused, and your readers may be confused or bored. But if you organize your material well, so that it supports and develops your controlling idea, you can present your views to your readers with interest, clarity, and persuasion.

Stating the controlling idea and organizing support can be accomplished effectively and systematically. How? This chapter presents several uncomplicated techniques you can use in Stage Two of the writing process.

Defining the Controlling Idea

If you tell a friend you are about to write a paragraph or an essay, be prepared to hear the question "What are you writing about?" If you answer, "Public schools," your friend will probably be satisfied with the answer but not very interested. The problem is that the phrase *public schools* offers no sense of limitation or direction. It just indicates your subject, not what you are going to do with it. *An effective controlling statement, called the **topic sentence** for a paragraph and the **thesis** for an essay, has both a subject **and** a focus.* The **subject** is what you intend to write about. The **focus** is what you intend to do with your subject.

Example: <u>Long homework assignments for children</u> <u>can interrupt family life</u>.
                                    subject   focus

In some instances the subject will follow the focus:

<u>The time has come</u> for a national law legalizing
        focus

<u>physician-assisted suicide for the terminally ill</u>.
                        subject

In other instances the subject will divide the focus:

<u>Four factors establish</u> <u>Elvis Presley</u> <u>as the greatest entertainer of</u>
        focus   subject   focus

<u>the twentieth century</u>: appearance, singing ability, style, and
influence.

Writing the Controlling Idea as a Topic Sentence or Thesis

The effective controlling idea presents a focus that can be developed with supporting information. The ineffective one is vague, too broad, or too narrow.

Vague: <u>Public schools</u> <u>are great</u>.
                    subject   focus

Better: <u>Public schools</u> <u>do as well academically as private schools,</u>
                    subject   focus
                <u>according to statistics</u>. [made more specific]

Too Broad: <u>Public schools</u> <u>are too crowded</u>.
                    subject   focus

Better: <u>Bidwell Elementary School</u> <u>is too crowded</u>. [limiting the
                        subject   focus
                <u>subject to a particular school</u>]

Too Narrow: <u>American public schools</u> <u>were first established in Philadelphia</u>
                        subject   focus
                <u>in 1779</u>. [only a fact]

Better: <u>The first public schools in America</u> <u>were founded to meet certain</u>
                            subject   focus
                <u>practical needs</u>. [made more specific by indicating aspects]

In writing a sound controlling idea, be sure that you have included both the subject and the focus and that the whole statement is not vague, too broad, or too narrow. Instead, it should be phrased so that it invites development. Such phrasing can usually be achieved by limiting time, place, or aspect. The limitation may apply to the subject (instead of schools in general, a specific school), or it may apply to the focus (you might compare the subject to something else, as in "do as well academically"). You might limit both the subject and the focus.

EXERCISE 1   Evaluating Topic Sentences

In the following controlling ideas, underline and label the subjects (S) and focus (F). Also judge each one as effective (E) or ineffective (I).

Example:

__I__   <u>Basketball</u> <u>is an interesting sport</u>.
                    S   F

____ 1. Students who cheat in school may be trying to relieve certain emotional pressures.

____ 2. Shakespeare was an Elizabethan writer.

____ 3. The quarterback in football and the general of an army are alike in significant ways.

____ 4. Animals use color chiefly for protection.

____ 5. Portland is a city in Oregon.

____ 6. Life in the ocean has distinct realms.

____ 7. Rome has had a glorious and tragic history.

____ 8. Boston is the capital of Massachusetts.

____ 9. The word *macho* has a special meaning to the Hispanic community.

____ 10. The history of plastics is exciting.

EXERCISE 2   Evaluating Topic Sentences

In the following controlling ideas, underline and label the subjects (S) and focus (F). Also judge each one as effective (E) or ineffective (I).

____ 1. An experience in the first grade taught me a valuable lesson about honesty.

____ 2. The Internet has changed the way many people shop.

____ 3. President Lincoln was assassinated at the Ford Theater.

____ 4. The dictionary has an interesting history.

____ 5. The world is a place of many contrasts.

____ 6. Rap music can be classified on the basis of the intent of its writers/ composers.

____ 7. Mumbai is one of the most densely populated cities in the world.

_____ 8. What I have seen while working in a fast-food place has made me lose my appetite.

_____ 9. My physical education teacher is called "Coach."

_____ 10. Count Dracula's reputation is based on his exploits as a nocturnal creature.

EXERCISE 3   Writing Topic Sentences

Complete the following entries to make each one a solid topic sentence. Only a subject and part of the focus are provided. The missing part may be more than a single word.

Example: Car salespeople behave differently, depending on _the car they are selling and the kind of customer they are serving._

1. A part-time job can offer _____

2. My school's athletic program should be _____

3. It is almost universally accepted that smoking is _____

4. Students caught cheating should be _____

5. Health care should be _____

6. One of the effects of the rising cost of a college education is _____

   _____

7. Offering constructive criticism to a friend who did not ask can _____

   _____

8. People who appear on television talk shows are frequently _____

9. The slang of a particular group reveals _____

10. Gestures and facial expressions usually communicate _____

EXERCISE 4   Writing Topic Sentences

Convert each of the following subjects into a topic sentence.

1. Bumper stickers _____

2. Rudeness _____

3. The true character of my neighbor _____

4. Many homeless people _____

5. Being able to use a computer _____ _____

6. Dieting _____

7. The basic forms of jazz and classical music _____

8. Educated citizens _____

9. The required labeling of rock music CDs _____

10. Smoking _____

Your topic sentence or thesis can come from any of several places. You may be able to generate it at Stage One, in your initial freewriting, brainstorming, clustering, or gathering information, or you may be given an assigned topic. In any case, your procedure is the same at this point. You need to work on the statement—just that one sentence—until you have developed an interesting subject and a well-defined focus. The statement may be a bit more mechanical than the one you actually use in your paragraph or essay, but it can easily be reworded once you reach Stage Three of the writing process: writing, revising, and editing.

The controlling idea will probably not pop into your head fully developed. It is more likely to be the result of repeated revisions. Even when you are revising a paper you have written, you may go back and rephrase your topic sentence or thesis. That is part of the back-and-forth (recursive) nature of the writing process.

In the following example, note how Jackson reworks her controlling idea several times before she settles on a statement that is well focused and able to be developed.

Subject	Focus
Bad drivers	can be found everywhere. (too broad)
Someone	should do something about bad drivers. (vague)
Bad driving	has existed in the United States for more than a century. (too broad)
If I were a traffic cop	I'd crack down on certain types of bad drivers. (workable)

Jackson has limited the subject by reducing it to the hypothetical situation of being a traffic cop. She has limited the focus by dealing with only "certain types of bad drivers," not all bad drivers.

EXERCISE 5 Writing Your Topic Sentence

Using a topic you worked with in Chapter 1 or one from the list on page 35, write a topic sentence or thesis. Mark the subject and focus parts.

Organizing Support

You have now studied the first part of the seven-word sentence "State your controlling idea and support it." In the first stage of the writing process (described in Chapter 2), you explored many ideas, experimented with them, and even developed some approaches to writing about them. You may also have gathered information through reading and note taking. The techniques of that first stage have already given you some initial support. The next step is to organize your ideas and information into a paragraph or an essay that is interesting, understandable, and compelling.

Three tools can help you organize your supporting material: listing (a form of brainstorming), clustering, and outlining. You will probably use only one of these organizing tools, depending on course requirements, the assignment, or individual preference. In the continuing demonstration of Betsy Jackson's work, each tool is shown.

LISTING

Lists are the simplest and most flexible of the organizing tools. Listing need be nothing more than a column of items presenting support material in a useful sequence (time, space, or importance). As you work with your support material, you can cross out words or move them around on the list. By leaving vertical space between items, you can easily insert new examples and details. Jackson took phrases from the list she had made in Stage One and wrote them below her topic sentence.

<u>If I were a traffic cop,</u> <u>I would crack down on certain types of bad drivers</u>.
         subject   focus

drunk drivers—most dangerous, top priority, off the road
tailgaters—hostile, hurried, cause accidents, irritating
unsafe lane changers—rude, cause accidents
left-turners on red—reckless, accident prone

CLUSTERING

Chains of circles radiating from a central double-bubbled circle form a cluster that shows the relationship of ideas. In the following example, Jackson has developed part of her Stage One cluster (a section noted by a dotted line on page 38).

<u>If I were a traffic cop,</u> <u>I'd crack down on certain types of bad drivers</u>.
         subject   focus

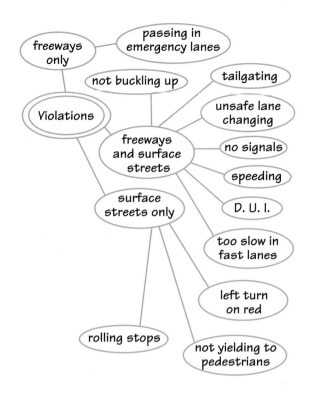

OUTLINING

Outlining is the tool that most people think of in connection with organizing. Because it is flexible and widely used, it will receive the most emphasis in this stage of the writing process. Outlining does basically the same thing that listing and clustering do. Outlining divides the controlling idea into sections of support material, divides those sections further, and establishes sequence.

An outline is a framework that can be used in two ways: (1) It can indicate the plan for a paragraph or an essay you intend to write, and (2) it can show the organization of a passage you are reading. The outline of a reading passage and the outline as a plan for writing are identical in form. If you intend to write a summary of a reading selection, then a single outline might be used for both purposes.

The two main outline forms are the **sentence outline** (each entry is a complete sentence) and the **topic outline** (each entry is a key word or phrase). The topic outline is more common in writing paragraphs and essays.

In the following topic outline, notice first how the parts are arranged on the page: the indentations, the number and letter sequences, the punctuation, and the placement of words. Then read Jackson's outline and see how the ideas in it relate to one another.

Main Idea (will usually be the topic sentence for a paragraph or the thesis for an essay)

  I. Major support

    A. Minor support

      1. Explanation, detail, example

      2. Explanation, detail, example

    B. Minor support

      1. Explanation, detail, example

      2. Explanation, detail, example

II. Major support
  A. Minor support
     1. Explanation, detail, example
     2. Explanation, detail, example
  B. Minor support
     1. Explanation, detail, example
     2. Explanation, detail, example

Here is Betsy Jackson's outline:

<u>If I were a traffic cop,</u> <u>I would crack down on certain types of bad drivers.</u>
              subject   focus

I. Drunks
II. Unsafe lane changers
   A. Attitude
      1. Rude
      2. Bullying
   B. Results
      1. Accidents
      2. People irritated
III. Left-turners on red
   A. Attitude
      1. Self-centered
      2. Putting self above law
   B. Results
      1. Bad collisions
      2. Mass anger
IV. Tailgaters
   A. Motives
      1. Hostility
      2. Rushed
      3. Impatient
   B. Effects
      1. Accidents
      2. Road fights

The foundation of an effective outline, and, hence, of an effective paragraph or essay, is a strong controlling idea. Always begin by writing a sound topic sentence or thesis, one with a specific subject and a well-defined treatment. Then divide the focus into parts. The nature of the parts will depend on what you are trying to do in the focus. Just consider the thought process involved. What kinds of material would best support or explain that topic sentence or thesis? How should you organize that material? Should you present a series of examples? a description of a process? a story of human struggle? a combination of methods?

Among the most common forms of dividing and organizing ideas are the following:

• **Narration**: division of time or incident to tell a story

I.   Situation

II. Conflict

III. Struggle

IV. Outcome

V.   Meaning

- **Exemplification**: division into several examples

  I.   First example

  II. Second example

  III. Third example

- **Analysis by division**: division into steps telling how something is done

  I.   Preparation

  II. Steps
       A. Step 1
       B. Step 2
       C. Step 3

- **Process analysis**: division of a unit into parts (for example, a pencil has an eraser, a wooden barrel, and a lead)

  I.   First part

  II. Second part

  III. Third part

- **Causes and effects**: division into causes or effects

  I.   Cause (or effect) one

  II. Cause (or effect) two

  III. Cause (or effect) three

These patterns and others are the subjects of individual chapters in this book.

EXERCISE 6   Completing Outlines

Fill in the missing parts of the following outlines. It may be helpful to consider, in each case, whether you are dealing with time, examples, causes, effects, parts, or steps. The answers will vary, depending on your individual experiences and views.

1. <u>Borrowing</u> <u>is the mother of trouble</u>.
       subject   focus

    I.   Received five credit cards in mail

    II. Saw numerous commercials on television

         A. One about _____

         B. Another about _____

    III. Made purchases with the credit card

    IV. Two months later _____

2. <u>A successful job interview</u> <u>depends on several factors</u>.
           subject   focus

   I. Good appearance

      A. _____

      B. _____

  II. Behaving properly

 III. Being qualified

      A. Education

      B. _____

 IV. Knowing something about the employer

3. <u>Joe's drug addiction</u> <u>had significant effects on his life</u>.
           subject   focus

   I. Developed mental health problems

      A. _____

      B. _____

  II. Developed _____

 III. Lost his job

 IV. Lost _____

4. <u>A college education</u> <u>is important for several reasons</u>.
           subject   focus

   I. Offers personal enrichment

  II. Fulfills curiosity

 III. Provides contacts that may be satisfying later

 IV. _____

5. <u>An ordinary person</u> <u>can be an environmentalist every day</u>.
           subject   focus

   I. Limit use of internal combustion engines

  II. Avoid using and dumping poisonous chemicals

 III. _____

 IV. _____

      A. Save newspapers

      B. Save _____

      C. _____

6. <u>Cooking spaghetti</u> <u>is not difficult</u>.
  subject   focus

   I. Get pan, water, and pasta

  II. Boil water in pan

 III. _____

 IV. Cook pasta until _____

  V. Remove pasta from pan and rinse the pasta in cold water

7. <u>An excellent doctor</u> <u>must have three qualities</u>.
  subject   focus

  I. _____

 II. _____

 III. _____

8. <u>Some drivers</u> <u>break traffic laws selectively</u>.
  subject   focus

  I. Make rolling stops

 II. _____

 III. _____

EXERCISE 7   Writing Your Outline

Using the subject you converted into a topic sentence or thesis (Exercise 5), compose a topic outline.

WRITER'S GUIDELINES: The Writing Process: Stage Two

1. The most important advice this book can offer you is *state your controlling idea and support it*. If you have no controlling idea—no topic sentence for a paragraph or thesis for an essay—your writing will be unfocused and your readers may be confused or bored. But if you organize your material well, so that it supports and develops your controlling idea, you can present your views to your readers with interest, clarity, and persuasion.

2. An effective controlling statement, called the **topic sentence** for a paragraph and the **thesis** for an essay, has both a subject and a focus. The **subject** is what you intend to write about. The **focus** is what you intend to do with your subject.

> **Example:** <u>Long homework assignments for children</u> <u>can interrupt family life</u>.
>   subject   focus

3. Three tools can help you organize your supporting material: listing, clustering, and outlining.

- Listing presents support material as a column of items in a useful sequence (time, space, or importance).
- Clustering uses chains of circles radiating from a central double-bubbled circle to show the relationship of ideas.
- Outlining can be used in two ways: to plan the structure and content of something you intend to write and to reveal the structure and content of something you read.

A typical outline looks like this:

Main Idea (will usually be the topic sentence for the paragraph or the thesis for the essay)
  I. Major support
    A. Minor support
      1. Explanation, detail, example
      2. Explanation, detail, example
    B. Minor support
      1. Explanation, detail, example
      2. Explanation, detail, example
  II. Major support
    A. Minor support
      1. Explanation, detail, example
      2. Explanation, detail, example
    B. Minor support
      1. Explanation, detail, example
      2. Explanation, detail, example

Chapter 4

The Writing Process: Stage Three
Writing / Revising / Editing

Writing the First Draft

In Stage Three of the writing process, your work begins to assume its final form. Use your outline, or alternative form of organization, as a guide in composing your paragraph or essay. For college work, your controlling idea should almost always be clearly stated early in the paper. The Roman-numeral parts of the outline will provide the framework for the main ideas of a paragraph assignment or for the topic sentence ideas in an essay. Supporting information—details, examples, quotations—is likely to be used in approximately the same order as it appears in the outline. Keep in mind that you should not be bound absolutely by the outline. Outlines often need to be redone just as your initial writing needs to be redone.

Most writers do best when they go straight through their first draft without stopping to polish sentences or fix small problems. Try that approach. Using the information in your outline and ideas as they occur to you, go ahead and simply write a paragraph or an essay. Do not be slowed down by possible misspelled words, flawed punctuation, or ungraceful sentences. You can repair those problems later.

Whether you write in longhand or on a computer depends on what works better for you. Some writers prefer to do a first draft by hand, mark it up, and then go to the computer. Computers save you time in all aspects of your writing, especially revision.

The following paragraph is Betsy Jackson's first draft, which includes some errors in spelling, grammar, and punctuation. Notice how it follows the order of topics in her outline; it also includes some new ideas.

RAMBO TRAFFIC COP

I. Drunks

II Unsafe lane changers
  A. Character
    1. Rude
    2. Bullying
  B. Results
    1. Accidents
    2. People upset

III. Left-turners on red
  A. Attitude
    1. Self-centered
    2. Putting self
      above law
  B. Kinds
    1. Age
    2. Sex
  C. Results
    1. Collisions
    2. Mass irritation

IV. Tailgaters
  A. Motives
    1. Hostility
    2. Rushed
  B. Effects
    1. Accidents
    2. People upset

Make me a traffic cop, and I'll crack down on certain types of drivers. First off are the drunks. I'd zap them off the highways right off, and any cop would. But what I'm really talking about is the jerks of the highway. Near the top are the uptight lane changers, for example, this morning when I was driving to school, I saw several. I could of carved at least a couple notches in a vilation pad, and I wasn't even cranky. They cut off people and force their way in, and leave behind upset and hurt people. Then there's the left-turn bullies the ones that keep moving out when the yellow turn to red. They come in all ages and sexes, they can be young or old, male or female. Yesterday, I saw this female in a pick-up barrel right out into the teeth of a red light. She had a baby on board. She had lead in her foot. She had evil in her eye. She was hostile and self-centered. Taking advantage of others. She knew that the facing traffic would probably not pull out and risk a head-on crash. The key word there is probably but many times these people with a green light do move out and colide with the left turn bullies. Third, I'd sap the tailgaters. No one goes fast enough for these guys. I'm not alone in this peeve. One bumper sticker reads, "Stay back. I chew tobacky." And James Bond sprayed cars that chased him. Since the first is dirty and the second is against the law, if I had the clout of a Rambo cop I'd just rack up a lot of tailgater tickets. But there's a lot of road demons out there. Maybe it's good I'm not a traffic cop, Rambo or otherwise, cause traffic cops are suppose to inforce hundreds of laws. I don't know if I'd have time cause I have my own pet peeves in mind.

If part of the development of your topic seems out of balance or needs more support, subtract or add material as necessary. Don't be afraid to change the outline. Often going back and forth between the initial draft and the outline will prevent your final work from seeming mechanical. Occasionally, as you discover that you need to expand or diminish a part, it may be useful to review your Stage One for details and opportunities.

EXERCISE 1   Writing Your Rough Draft

On a separate sheet of paper, use the topic you developed in Chapters 2 and 3, and write a rough draft of a paragraph or an essay as directed by your instructor.

Revising

The term **first draft** suggests quite accurately that there will be other drafts, or versions, of your writing. Only in the most dire situations, such as an in-class examination when you have time for only one draft, should you be satisfied with a single effort.

What you do beyond the first draft is revision and editing. **Revision** includes checking for organization, content, and language effectiveness. **Editing** (discussed later in this chapter) involves a final correcting of simple mistakes and fundamentals such as spelling, punctuation, and capitalization. In practice, editing and revising are not always separate activities, although writers usually wait until the next-to-the-last draft to edit some minor details and attend to other small points that can be easily overlooked.

Successful revision almost always involves intense, systematic rewriting. You should learn to look for certain aspects of skillful writing as you enrich and repair your first draft. To help you recall these aspects so that you can keep them in mind and examine your material in a comprehensive fashion, this textbook offers a memory device—an acronym in which each letter suggests an important feature of good writing and revision. This device enables you to memorize the features of good writing quickly. Soon you will be able to recall and refer to them automatically. These features need not be attended to individually when you revise your writing, although they may be, and they need not be attended to in the order presented here. The acronym is CLUESS (pronounced "clues"), which provides this guide: **C**oherence, **L**anguage, **U**nity, **E**mphasis, **S**upport, and **S**entences.

Each of these features of good writing can be approached with a set of techniques you can apply easily to your first draft. They are presented here with some details, examples, and supporting exercises. See the Writer's Guidelines at the end of this chapter for a concise list of these features and a set of questions you can apply to your own writing and to peer editing.

COHERENCE

Coherence is the orderly relationship of ideas, each leading smoothly and logically to the next. You must weave your ideas together so skillfully that the reader can easily see how one idea connects to another and to the central thought. This central thought, of course, is expressed in the topic sentence for a paragraph and in the thesis for an essay. You can achieve coherence efficiently by using the following:

Overall pattern
Transitional terms
Repetition of key words and important ideas
Pronouns
Consistent point of view

Overall Pattern

Several chapters in this book discuss strategies for an overall pattern of organization or order. Three basic patterns prevail: **time** (chronology), **space** (spatial arrangement), and **emphasis** (stress on ideas). Sometimes you will combine patterns. The coherence of each can be strengthened by using transitional words such as the following:

> **For a time pattern:** *first, then, soon, later, following, after, at that point*
> **For a space pattern:** *up, down, right, left, beyond, behind, above, below*
> **For an emphasis pattern:** *first, second, third, most, more*

Transitional Terms

By using transitional terms, you can help your readers move easily from one idea to another. The transitional term in each of the following sentences is italicized.

> *First*, I realized I had to get a job to stay in school.
> *At the same time*, my track coach wanted the team to spend more hours working out.
> We were, *after all*, the defending champions.
> *Finally*, I dropped one of my courses.

Repetition of Key Words and Important Ideas

Repeat key words and phrases to keep the main subject in the reader's mind and to maintain the continuity necessary for a smooth flow of logical thought. (See the section on Emphasis later in this chapter.)

Pronouns

Pronouns, such as *he, her, them,* and *it*, provide natural connecting links in your writing. Why? Every pronoun refers to an earlier noun (called the **antecedent** of the pronoun) and thus carries the reader back to that earlier thought. Here are some examples.

> I tried to buy *tickets* for the concert, but *they* were all sold.
> Assertive *people* tend to make decisions quickly. However, *they* may not make the wisest decisions.
> *Roger* painted a picture of *his* father's pickup truck. *It* was so good that *his* professor asked *him* to enter *it* in an art show.

Consistent Point of View

Point of view shows the writer's relationship to the material, the subject, and it usually does not change within a passage.

If you are conveying personal experience, the point of view will be *first person*, or *I*, which can be either involved (a participant) or detached (an observer).

The *second person*, *you* and *your*, is usually reserved for how-to writing in college assignments.

If you are presenting something from a distance, geographical or historical (for example, telling a story about George Washington), the point of view will be *third person*, and the participants will be referred to as *he, she,* and *they*.

Along with the consistency of perspective, you should avoid shifts in number (*she* to *they*) and verb tense (*is* to *was*).

Being consistent in these matters will promote coherence.

LANGUAGE

In the revision process, the word **language** takes on a special meaning, referring to usage, tone, and diction. If you are writing with a computer, consider using the thesaurus feature, but keep in mind that no two words share precisely the same meaning.

Usage

Usage is the kind or general style of language we use. All, or almost all, of us operate on the principle of appropriateness. If I used *ain't* as part of my explanations in this textbook, you would be surprised and probably disappointed; you would think about my word choice rather than about what I have to say. Why would you be surprised? Because *ain't* is not appropriate for my audience in this situation. If you write an essay containing slang, you will probably be understood, but if the slang is not appropriate, you will draw unfavorable attention to your message. That does not mean that slang does not have its place—it does. It can be imaginative and colorful. Often, though, it is only a weak substitute for a more precise vocabulary.

Usage is an important part of writing and revising. Judge what is appropriate for your audience and your purpose. What kind of language is expected? What kind of language is best suited for accomplishing your purpose?

Most of the material in the Handbook (Chapter 17) consists of explanations of standard, mainly formal, English grammar. Using standard verb tenses and pronoun cases will help you to write effectively. The Handbook offers clear explanations and examples. As you practice the principles of standard English in your writing and revising, you will master them.

Tone

Have you ever heard someone say, "Don't talk to me in that tone of voice" or "I accepted what she was saying, but I didn't like the tone she used when she told me"? **Tone** in these contexts means that the sound of the speaker's voice and maybe the language choices conveyed disrespect to the listener. The tone could have represented any number of feelings about the subject matter and the audience. Tone can have as many variations as you can have feelings: it can, for example, be sarcastic, humorous, serious, cautionary, objective, groveling, angry, bitter, sentimental, enthusiastic, somber, outraged, or loving.

Let's say you are getting a haircut. Looking in those panoramic mirrors bordered with pictures of people with different styles of haircuts, you see that the hair stylist is cutting off too much hair. You could use different tones in giving him or her some timely how-to instructions.

Objective: "If you don't mind, what I meant to say was that I would like a haircut proportioned similar to that one there in the picture of Tom Cruise from *Jerry Maguire*."
Humorous: "I hesitate to make suggestions to someone who is standing at my back and holding a sharp instrument near my throat, but I'm letting my hair grow out a bit. I don't want you to take off a lot in the back and on the sides."

Angry and sarcastic: "Look man, when I sat down, I said I wanted my hair cut in the design of Tom Cruise in *Jerry Maguire*. The way you're hacking at it, you must've thought I said *Top Gun*."

Servile: "I really like the way you cut my hair, and I can see that you are proportioning it with great care, but I would like my hair to be a bit longer than the style that I think you're working on. Do you remember how I used to get my hair cut about a year ago, a little longer on the sides and more bushy on top? You came up with a great style that everyone liked. Could you give me one similar to that?"

Overbearing: "Damn it, buddy. Will you watch what you're doing! I asked for a haircut, not a shave. If God had wanted me to have bare skin above my shoulders, he would've put the hair on my feet."

In speech, feelings and attitudes are represented by inflection, loudness, word choice, and language patterns. In writing, tone is conveyed mainly by word choice and order; it is closely related to style—the variations in the way you write, depending on your purpose. Your purpose is simply to present a particular idea in a particular context. The context implies the audience; it is important to use the tone appropriate to your audience.

Usually your tone will be consistent throughout your presentation, although for the informal essay often assigned in college, you may choose to begin in a light-hearted, amusing tone before switching to a more serious, objective mode.

Diction

Diction is word choice. If you use good diction, you are finding the best words for a particular purpose in addressing a certain audience. There is some overlap, therefore, between usage and diction. I may look at an area in the subway and present my reaction in the following way:

Poor Diction:

This part of the subway is really a mess. Everywhere I look I can see things people have thrown away, which have fallen through the grates above. Along with the solid items are liquids. On the walls are a hodge-podge of posters and writing. The whole area is very dirty and very unpleasant.

Note how the scene comes to life with better word choice:

Good Diction:

[Before me I saw] an unspeakable mass of congealed oil, puddles of dubious liquid, and a mishmash of old cigarette packets, mutilated and filthy newspapers, and the debris that filtered down from the street above. [The walls were a display of posters]—here a text from the Bible, there a half-naked girl, here a pair of girl's legs walking up the keys of a cash register—all scribbled over with unknown names and well-known obscenities. . . .

The difference between these two passages is obvious. The first is general. Terms such as "very dirty" and "very unpleasant" carry little meaning. The author has not made us see. The word *very* is an empty modifier. The second passage is specific. You can visualize what the writer is saying through the specific diction, the detail. The first is general and, for content, hardly goes beyond a single phrase—mess in the subway.

The following list shows the difference between general and specific words.

General	Specific	More Specific
food	fruit	juicy, ripe peach
mess	litter	candy wrappers, empty cans
drink	soda	Diet Pepsi
odor	kitchen smell	aroma of coffee brewing

Another aspect of diction is freshness and originality of expression. To achieve those distinctions, you should avoid clichés, which are trite, familiar phrases. Consider this sentence:

> When the prince married Cinderella, her sisters went green with envy because she was now on easy street, leaving them out in the cold.

Those words were written by a person who does not care about communicating in a clear and interesting manner. It would be far better to say:

> When the prince married Cinderella, her sisters were envious because they had no suitors.

This list shows some clichés to avoid:

young at heart	quick as a flash
rotten to the core	slow but sure
uphill battle	other side of the coin
more than meets the eye	breathless silence
bitter end	acid test
as luck would have it	better late than never
last but not least	six of one, half dozen of the other

Clichés are ready-made expressions. A cliché master manipulates language as if it were a prefabricated building going up, not bothering to use any imagination and leaving little opportunity for his or her audience to use theirs. Good diction, however, reflects the writer as an individual and is fresh, original, and clear.

UNITY

A controlling idea, stated or implied, establishes **unity** in every piece of good writing. It is the central point around which the supporting material revolves. For a paragraph, the elements are the topic sentence and the supporting sentences. For an essay, the elements are the thesis and the supporting developmental paragraphs. All the supporting material should be related to the topic sentence or thesis, and it should all be subordinate to the topic sentence or thesis. Unity can be strengthened and made more apparent if you restate the topic sentence or thesis at the end of the unit and if you repeat key words and phrases from time to time. A good check on unity is to ask yourself if everything in your paragraph or essay is subordinate to and derived from the controlling idea.

Do not confuse unity and coherence. Whereas coherence involves the clear movement of thought from sentence to sentence or paragraph to paragraph, unity means staying on the topic. A unified and coherent outline would become incoherent if the parts were scrambled, but the outline technically would still be unified. These qualities of writing go together. You should stay on the topic and make clear connections.

EMPHASIS

Emphasis, a feature of most good writing, helps the reader focus on the main ideas by stressing what is important. It can be achieved in several ways but mainly through placement of key ideas and through repetition.

Placement of Ideas

The most emphatic part of any passage, whether a sentence or a book, is the last part, because we usually remember most easily what we read last. The second most emphatic part of a passage is the beginning, because our mind is relatively uncluttered when we read it. For these reasons, among others, the topic sentence or thesis is usually at the beginning of a piece, and it is often restated at the end in an echoing statement.

Repetition of Key Words and Important Ideas

Repetition is one of the simplest devices in your writer's toolbox. The words repeated may be single words, phrases, slightly altered sentences, or synonyms. Repetition keeps the dominant subject in the reader's mind and maintains the continuity necessary for a smooth flow of logical thought.

You can use this valuable technique easily. If, as is done in the following example, you are discussing the effects of the school dropout problem, then the word *effect(s)*, along with synonyms such as *result(s)* or *consequence(s)*, and *school dropout(s)*, is likely to be repeated several times. Moreover, phrases giving insight into the issue may be repeated, perhaps with slight variation. Phrases and their repetitions are underlined in this passage:

The causes of the school <u>dropout</u> problem have received much attention recently, but the <u>effects</u> are just as important. One obvious <u>result</u> is that of unemployment or low-paying employment. The student who <u>drops out</u> of school is likely to be <u>dropping</u> into poverty, perhaps even into a lifelong condition. Another <u>effect</u> is juvenile crime. The young person who has no prospects for a good job and no hope all too frequently turns to illegal activities. A third <u>result</u> concerns the psychological well-being of the <u>dropout</u>. Although <u>withdrawing</u> from school seems to offer a quick, viable solution to perceived problems, it almost immediately has <u>consequences</u> for the <u>dropout</u>'s self-esteem. Of course, these <u>effects</u> may also be tied to causes, such as drugs, poverty, crime, or psychological problems, but devastating <u>repercussions</u> are there at the far end of the causes-and-effects continuum, and youngsters who are contemplating <u>dropping out</u> should consider them with care.

A word of warning: The effective use of word and phrase repetition should not be confused with an irritating misuse of word repetition. We all at times get stuck on certain words, and the result is a negative response from our audience. Consider this awkward use of repetition:

> She looked at him and frowned. He returned the look and then looked away at a stranger looking for his lost keys.

That's too many *look*'s. Consider this version:

> She looked at him [*or, even better,* She frowned at him]. He glared back and then glanced away at a stranger searching for his lost keys.

The second version preserves the idea of people "looking" by using synonyms. It is more precise and does not grate on the reader's mind as the first does.

SUPPORT

How much **support** as evidence or explanation does a piece of writing need? A good developmental paragraph fulfills its function by developing the topic sentence. An essay is complete when it fulfills its function of developing a thesis. Obviously, you will have to judge what is complete. With some subjects, you will need little supporting and explanatory material. With others, you will need much more. Incompleteness, not overdevelopment, is more common among beginning writers. Besides having enough support, be sure the points of support are presented in the best possible sequence.

Consider the following paragraph. Is it complete? Does the writer make the main idea clear and provide adequate support for it? Are the ideas in the right order?

> A cat's tail is a good barometer of its intentions. By various movements of its tail a cat will signal many of its wants. Other movements indicate its attitudes. An excited or aggressively aroused cat will whip its entire tail back and forth.

At first glance, this paragraph seems complete. It begins with a concise topic sentence telling us that a cat's tail is a good barometer of its intentions. It adds information of a general nature in the following two sentences. Then it presents a supporting example about the aggressively aroused cat. But the paragraph is not explicit; there is insufficient supporting material for the opening generalization. The paragraph leaves the reader with too much information to fill in. What are some other ways that cats communicate their intentions with their tails? How do they communicate specific wishes or desires? Is their communication effective? If the passage is to answer these or other questions that may come into the reader's mind, it must present more material to support the beginning generalization. The original paragraph that follows begins with a concise topic sentence that is then supported with particulars.

> A cat's tail is a good barometer of its intentions. An excited or aggressively aroused cat will whip its entire tail back and forth. When I talk to Sam, he holds up his end of the conversation by occasionally flicking the tip of his tail. Mother cats move their tails back and forth to invite their kittens to play. A kitten raises its tail perpendicularly to beg for attention;

older cats may do so to beg for food. When your cat holds its tail aloft while crisscrossing in front of you, it is trying to say, "Follow me"—usually to the kitchen, or more precisely, to the refrigerator. Unfortunately, many cats have lost their tails in refrigerator doors as a consequence.

(Michael W. Fox, "What Is Your Pet Trying to Tell You?")

We can strengthen our understanding of good support by analyzing the structure of the model paragraph, putting to use the information we have assimilated to this point in the discussion. The paragraph begins with the highest generalization (the main idea in the topic sentence): "A cat's tail is a good barometer of its intentions." It is followed immediately with six supporting statements and ends with a final sentence to add humor to the writing. If we place this material in outline form, we can easily see the recurrent pattern in the flow of thought from general to particular.

Topic sentence (highest generalization)

A cat's tail is a good barometer of its intentions.

Major support

1. An excited or aggressively aroused cat will whip its entire tail back and forth.

Major support

2. When I talk to Sam, he holds up his end of the conversation by occasionally flicking the tip of his tail.

Major support

3. Mother cats move their tails back and forth to invite their kittens to play.

Major support

4. A kitten raises its tail perpendicularly to beg for attention;

Major support

5. older cats may do so to beg for food.

Major support

6. When your cat holds its tail aloft while crisscrossing in front of you, it is trying to say, "Follow me"—usually to the kitchen, or more precisely, to the refrigerator.

Added for humor

Unfortunately, many cats have lost their tails in refrigerator doors as a consequence.

SENTENCES

In the revision process, the word **sentences** refers to the variety of sentence patterns and the correctness of sentence structure.

Variety of Sentences

A passage that offers a variety of simple and complicated sentences satisfies the reader, just as various simple and complicated foods go together in a good meal. The writer can introduce variety by including both short and long sentences, by using different sentence patterns, and by beginning sentences in different ways (see pp. 437–438).

Length

In revising, examine your writing to make sure that sentences vary in length. A series of short sentences is likely to make the flow seem choppy and the thoughts disconnected. However, single short sentences often work very well. Because they are uncluttered with supporting points and qualifications, they are often direct and forceful. Consider using short sentences to emphasize points and to introduce ideas. Use longer sentences to provide details or show how ideas are related.

Variety of Sentence Patterns

Good writing includes a variety of sentence patterns. Although there is no limit to the number of sentences you can write, you may be pleased to discover that the conventional English sentence appears in only four basic patterns (see pp. 417–426).

Simple: She did the work well.
Compound: She did the work well, and she was well paid.
Complex: Because she did the work well, she was well paid.
Compound-Complex: Because she did the work well, she was well paid, and she was satisfied.

An analysis of these patterns with suggestions and exercises for combining sentences is given in the Handbook.

Each of the four sentence patterns listed has its own purposes and strengths. The simple sentence conveys a single idea. The compound sentence shows, by its structure, that two somewhat equal ideas are connected. The complex sentence shows that one idea is less important than another; that is, it is dependent on, or subordinate to, the idea in the main clause. The compound-complex sentence has the scope of both the compound sentence and the complex sentence.

Variety of Sentence Beginnings

Another way to provide sentence variety is to use different kinds of beginnings. A new beginning may or may not be accompanied by a changed sentence pattern. Among the most common beginnings, other than starting with the subject of the main clause, are those using a prepositional phrase, a dependent clause, or a conjunctive adverb such as *therefore*, *however*, or *in fact* (see p. 438).

- Prepositional phrase (in italics)

    In your fantasy, you are the star.
    Like casino owners, game show hosts want you to be cheery.

- Dependent clause (in italics)

    When the nighttime Wheel of Fortune *debuted*, the slot was occupied by magazine shows.
    As Pat Sajak noted, viewers often solve the puzzle before the contestants do.

- Conjunctive adverb (in italics)

    Now you know.
    Therefore, you feel happy, excited, and a bit superior.

Problems with Sentences

A complete sentence must generally include an independent clause, which is a group of words that contains a subject and a verb and can stand alone. Some groups of words may sound interesting, but they are not really sentences. Three common problem groupings are the fragment, the comma splice, and the run-on (see pp. 437–449).

- A sentence **fragment** is a word grouping that is structurally incomplete.

  Because he left. [This is a dependent clause, not a complete sentence.]
  Went to the library. [This has no subject.]
  She being the only person there. [This has no verb.]
  Waiting there for help. [This has neither subject nor verb.]
  In the back seat under a book. [Here we have two phrases but no subject or verb.]

- A **comma splice** consists of two independent clauses with only a comma between them.

  The weather was bad, we canceled the picnic. [A comma by itself cannot join two independent clauses.]

- A **run-on** differs from the comma splice in only one way: It has no comma between the independent clauses.

  The weather was bad we canceled the picnic.

Fragments, comma splices, and run-ons can easily be fixed (see the Handbook) during the revising and editing stages of your writing. A computerized grammar checker may help you find these problems.

If you frequently have problems with sentence structure and awkwardness of phrasing, be especially suspicious of long sentences. Test each sentence of fifteen or more words for flaws. Try writing shorter, more direct sentences until you gain confidence and competency. Then work with sophisticated patterns.

See the Writer's Guidelines at the end of this chapter for a concise summary of the strategies for effective revision.

Editing

Editing, the final stage of the writing process, involves a careful examination of your work. Look for problems with **c**apitalization, **o**missions, **p**unctuation, and **s**pelling (COPS). (See capitalization, p. 515; omissions, p. 435; punctuation, p. 501; and spelling, p. 519.)

Because you can find spelling errors in writing by others more easily than you can in your own, a computerized spell checker is quite useful. However, it will not detect wrong words that are correctly spelled, so you should always proofread. It is often helpful to leave the piece for a few hours or a day and then reread it as if it were someone else's work.

Before you submit your writing to your instructor, do what almost all professional writers do before sending their material along: Read it aloud, to yourself or to a willing audience. Reading material aloud will help you catch any awkwardness of expression, omission and misplacement of words, and other problems that are easily overlooked by an author.

As you can see, writing is a process and is not a matter of just sitting down and producing a statement. The parts of the process from prewriting to revising to editing are connected, and your movement is ultimately forward, but this process allows you to go back and forth in the recursive manner discussed in Chapters 2 and 3. If your outline is not working, perhaps the flaw is in your topic sentence. You may need to go back and fix it. If one section of your paragraph is skimpy, perhaps you will have to go back and reconsider the pertinent material in your outline or clustering. There you might find more details or alter a statement so that you can move into more fertile areas of thought.

Student Demonstration of All Stages of the Writing Process

Here we see how Betsy Jackson worked through the entire writing process. In Stage One, she freewrote, brainstormed, and developed a cluster of ideas. In Stage Two, she composed a good topic sentence, developed further a part of her cluster from Stage One, and drew up an outline based on the cluster. Then, in Stage Three, we see one of her early drafts, her revision and editing of that draft, and finally the finished version.

Note that Jackson has used a Writing Process Worksheet, which has been lengthened for you to be able to see all parts of her work. You will find a full-size blank worksheet on page 6, which can be photocopied, filled in, and submitted with each assignment if your instructor directs you to do so.

Writing Process Worksheet

Name *Betsy Jackson*   **Title** *If I Were a Traffic Cop*   **Due Date** *Monday, June 5, 8 a.m.*

Use the back of this page or separate paper if you need more space.

Assignment

In the space below, write whatever you need to know about your assignment, including information about the topic, audience, pattern of writing, length, whether to include a rough draft or revised drafts, and whether your paper must be typed.

Write a paragraph of about 200 to 300 words on a topic from the list—bad drivers. Discuss types for the pattern. Use some examples. Write for readers who have probably shared your experiences. Include this completed worksheet, one or more rough drafts marked for revision, and a typed final paper.

Stage One

Explore   Freewrite, brainstorm (list), cluster, or take notes as directed by your instructor.

Freewriting (abbreviated here)

drunks

Every day when I drive to school I see bad drivers. Sometimes I'm mad. Sometimes I'm irritated. Sometimes I'm scared. I think someone should do something about them. The <u>drunk drivers</u> are the worst. They should be put away. But a lot of the other should be getting tickets too. Some of the drivers are worse than others. Make me a cop, a supercop, a rambo cop, and I'll go after the worst. Maybe I'd just go after the ones that bother me. Some bad drivers cause a lot of accidents and get people all angry. Take the <u>tailgaters</u> for example. And what about the <u>drivers that go into the emergency lanes</u> on the freeways to pass when there's a jam. And then you've got the <u>lane changers</u> and the <u>people that don't signal</u> and <u>those that keep going and turning left when</u> the <u>light turns red</u>. Then you've got the people that <u>drive too fast</u> and <u>too slow</u>. And you've got the ones that <u>don't stop</u> for <u>pedestrians</u>. <u>All kinds</u> of bad drivers are out there—young, old, male, female, insane, drunk, angry, and rushed.

tailgaters
lane changers
no signals
run lights
too fast/slow
all kinds

Clustering

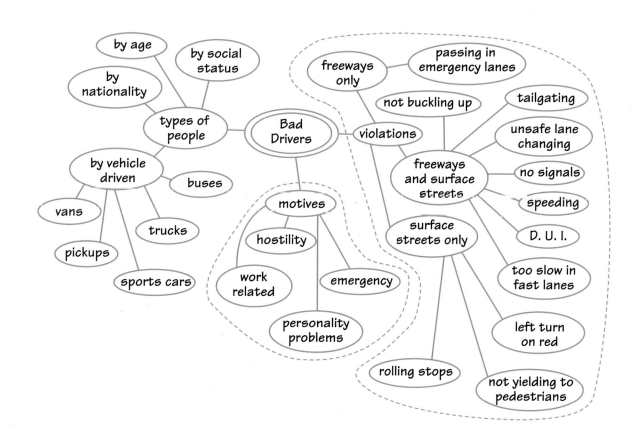

Brainstorming (Big Six Questions)

Who?   bad drivers; me as a cop
What?   driving badly, recklessly, unsafely; a cop's job
Where?   on every roadway
When?   all the time

Why?   hurried, disrespectful, self centered, sick, addiction, hostile,
        irresponsible

How?   lane-changing, driving illegally in emergency lane, not signaling,
        passing on the shoulder, tailgating, turning left on red, rolling stop,
        speeding, driving while intoxicated

Stage Two

Organize Write a topic sentence or thesis; label the subject and the focus parts.

If I were a traffic cop, I would crack down on certain types of drivers.
          subject   focus

Write an outline or an outline alternative. For reading-based writing, include references and short quotations with page numbers as support in the outline.

   I. Drunks
  II. Unsafe lane changers
     A. Character
       1. Rude
       2. Bullying
     B. Results
       1. Accidents
       2. People upset
 III. Left-turners on red
     A. Attitude
       1. Self-centered
       2. Putting self above law
     B. Kinds
       1. Age
       2. Sex
     C. Results
       1. Collisions
       2. Mass irritation
 IV. Tailgaters
     A. Motives
       1. Hostility
       2. Rushed
     B. Effects
       1. Accidents
       2. People upset

Stage Three

Write On separate paper, write and then revise your paragraph or essay as many times as necessary for **c**oherence, **l**anguage (usage, tone, and diction), **u**nity, **e**mphasis, **s**upport, and **s**entences (**CLUESS**). Read your work aloud to hear and correct any grammatical errors or awkward-sounding sentences.

Edit any problems in fundamentals, such as **c**apitalization, **o**missions, **p**unctuation, and **s**pelling (**COPS**).

Rough Draft: Writing, Revising, Editing

Rambo Traffic Cop

Make me a traffic cop, and I'll crack down on certain types of drivers. First off are the drunks. I would zap them off the highways right off, and any cop would. But what I'm really talking about is the jerks of the highway. Near the top are the up-tight lane changers, for example, this morning when I was driving to school, I saw several. I could of carved at least a couple notches in a vilation pad, and I wasn't even cranky. They cut off people and force their way in, and leave behind upset and hurt people. Then there's the left-turn bullies the ones who keep moving out when the yellow turn to red. They come in all ages and sexes, they can be young or old, male or female. Yesterday, I saw this female in a pick-up barrel right out into the teeth of a red light. She had a baby on board. She had lead in her foot. She had evil in her eye. She was hostile and self-centered. Taking advantage of others. She knew that the facing traffic would probably not pull out and risk a head-on crash. The key word there is probably but many times people with a green light do move out and colide with the left turn bullies. Third, I'd sap the tailgaters. No one goes fast enough for these guys. I'm not alone in this peeve. One bumper sticker reads, "Stay back. I chew tobacky." And James Bond sprayed cars that chased him. Since the first is dirty and the second is against the law, if I had the clout of a Rambo cop I'd just rack up a lot of tailgater tickets. But there's a lot of road demons out there. Maybe it's good I'm not a traffic cop, Rambo or otherwise, cause traffic cops are suppose to inforce hundreds of laws. I don't know if I'd have time cause I have my own pet peeves in mind.

Final Draft

IF I WERE A TRAFFIC COP
Betsy Jackson

Topic sentence

Support

Support

Support (example)

Support

Restated topic sentence

<u>If I were a traffic cop, I would crack down on certain types of drivers</u>. My primary target would be <u>drunk drivers</u>. I would arrest them immediately, and any cop would. But the jerks on the highway are what I am really concerned about here. Near the top of my hit list are the <u>unsafe lane changers</u>. They cut off other drivers and force their way in, leaving behind upset and injured people. This morning when I was driving to school, I could have carved at least a couple of notches in a citation pad, and I was not even cranky. Then there are the <u>left-turn bullies</u>, the ones who keep moving out when the yellow turns to red. They come in all ages and sexes. Yesterday, I saw this female in a pickup barrel right out into the teeth of a red light. She had a baby on board, lead in her foot, and evil in her eye. She was hostile and self-centered, taking advantage of others. She knew that the facing traffic would probably not pull out and risk a head-on crash. The key word there is "probably," but many times people with a green light do move out and collide with the left-turn bullies. Fourth, I would zap the <u>tailgaters</u>. No one goes fast enough for them. Many of my fellow drivers agree. One bumper sticker reads, "Stay back. I chew tobacky." And James Bond sprayed oil on cars that chased him. Since the first is unsanitary and the second illegal, if I had the authority of a Rambo-cop, I would just issue a lot of tailgater tickets. <u>These four types of road demons would feel my wrath</u>. But maybe it is good I am not a traffic cop, Rambo or otherwise, because traffic cops are supposed to enforce hundreds of laws. I do not know if I would have time because I would be concentrating on this private list of obnoxious drivers.

EXERCISE 2   Revising and Editing a First Draft

Revise the following student first draft. Then check for capitalization, omissions (oversights or grammar problems), punctuation, and spelling (COPS). Space is provided for you to add, delete, move, and correct material.

PAIN UNFORGETTABLE
James Hutchison

One evening in 1968 while I was working the swing shift at the General Tire Recapping Plant. I came up with the greatest pain of my life because of a terible accident. Raw rubber was heated up in a large tank. Pryor to its being fed into an extruder. I was recapping large off-road tires. The lowering platform was in the up position the chain snapped. It sent the heavy platform crashing down into the tank. This caused a huge wave of steaming water to surge out of the tank. Unfortunately, I was in its path the wave hit my back just above my waist. The sudden pain shook me up. I could not move. My clothes were steaming I freaked out.

Sentences

- Are the sentences varied in length and beginnings?
- Are the sentences varied in pattern (simple, compound, complex, and compound-complex)?
- Are all problems with sentence structure (fragments, comma splices, and run-ons) corrected?

3. Editing

- Are all problems in such areas as **c**apitalization, **o**missions, **p**unctuation, and **s**pelling (**COPS**) corrected?

Chapter 5

Writing the Paragraph

The Paragraph Defined

Defining the word *paragraph* is no easy task because there are four different kinds of paragraphs, each one having a different purpose:

Introductory: Usually the first paragraph in an essay, it gives the necessary background and indicates the main idea, called the **thesis**.

Developmental: A unit of several sentences, it expands on an idea. This book features the writing of developmental paragraphs.

Transitional: A very brief paragraph, it merely directs the reader from one point in the essay to another.

Concluding: Usually the last paragraph in an essay, it makes the final comment on the topic.

The following paragraph is both a definition and an example of the developmental paragraph.

Topic sentence

Support

Support

The developmental paragraph contains three parts: the subject, the topic sentence, and the support. The **subject** is what you will write about. It is likely to be broad and must be focused or qualified for specific focus. The **topic sentence** contains both the subject and the focus—what you will do with the subject. It carries the central idea to which everything else in the paragraph is subordinated. For example, the first sentence of this paragraph is a topic sentence. Even when not stated, the topic sentence as an underlying idea unifies the paragraph. The **support** is the evidence or reasoning by which a topic sentence is developed. It

Support

Concluding sentence

comes in several basic patterns and serves any of the four forms of expression: narration, description, exposition, and argumentation. These forms, which are usually combined in writing, will be presented with both student and professional examples in the following chapters. <u>The **developmental paragraph**, therefore, is a group of sentences, each with the function of supporting a controlling idea called the topic sentence.</u>

Basic Paragraph Patterns

The most important point about a developmental paragraph is that it should state an idea and support it. The support, or development, can take several forms, all of which you already use. It can do the following:

* Give an account (tell a story).
* Describe people, things, or events.
* Explain by analyzing, giving examples, comparing, defining, showing how to do something, or showing causes.
* Argue that something should be done or resisted, that something is true or untrue, or that something is good or bad.

(All of these forms of expression are discussed with examples in Chapters 7 through 15.) You will not find it difficult to write solid paragraphs once you understand that good writing requires that main ideas have enough support so that your reader can understand how you have arrived at your main conclusions.

Usually the developmental paragraph will be indented only one time. However, you will note in your reading that some writers, especially journalists, break a paragraph into parts and indent more than once in developing a single idea. That arrangement, called a **paragraph unit**, is fairly common in magazine and newspaper articles (frequently with each sentence indented) but less so in college writing.

Two effective patterns of conventional paragraph structure are shown in Figure 5.1. Pattern A merely states the controlling idea, the topic sentence, and develops it; Pattern B adds a concluding sentence following the development.

Example of Pattern A:

PITY, ANGER, AND ACHIEVEMENT PERFORMANCE

Topic sentence

Support

Support

It is generally thought that pity and sympathy are "good" emotions and that anger is a "bad" emotion. <u>However, attribution theorists have pointed out that the consequences of these emotional expressions are complex.</u> In one investigation, Graham (1984) gave subjects (twelve-year-old children) false failure feedback during an achievement task. For some children, this was accompanied by the remark: "I feel sorry for you" as well as body postures and facial gestures that accompany sympathy (head down, hands folded, etc.). To other students, the experimenter said: "I am angry with you." Students receiving the pity feedback tended to blame the failure on themselves (low ability) and their performance declined. On the other hand, students receiving anger feedback attributed their failure to lack of effort and their performance subsequently increased. <u>This is not to advocate that sympathy is always detrimental and anger always facilitative.</u> Rather, the consequences of feedback depend on how

Figure 5.1
Paragraph Patterns

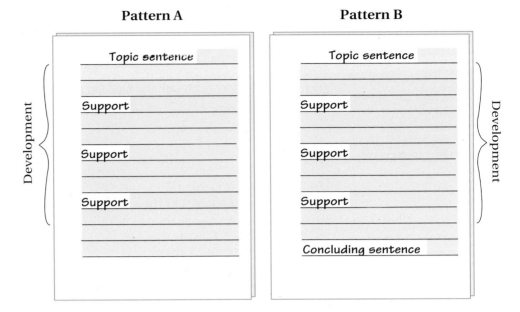

that feedback is construed and what it means to the recipient of the communication. Other kinds of feedback, such as praise for success at an easy task and excessive and unsolicited helping, also tend to convey that the student is "unable" and therefore have some negative consequences.

(Seymour Feshbach and Bernard Weiner, from *Personality*)

Example of Pattern B:

PRIMITIVE METHODS OF LIE DETECTION

Topic sentence

Support

Throughout history there have been efforts to distinguish the guilty from the innocent and to tell the liars from the truthful. For example, a method of lie detection practiced in Asia involved giving those suspected of a crime a handful of raw rice to chew. After chewing for some time, the persons were instructed to spit out the rice. The innocent person was anticipated to do this easily, whereas the guilty party was expected to have grains of rice sticking to the roof of the mouth and tongue. This technique relied on the increased sympathetic nervous system activity in the presumably fearful and guilty person. This activity would result in the drying up of saliva that, in turn, would cause grains of rice to stick in the mouth. A similar but more frightening technique involved placing a heated knife blade briefly against the tongue, another method used for criminal detection. An innocent person would not be burned while the guilty party would immediately feel pain, again because of the relative dryness of the mouth. Many of these methods relied (unknowingly) on the basic physiological principles that also guided the creation of the polygraph.

Support

Concluding sentence

(Seymour Feshbach and Bernard Weiner, from *Personality*)

EXERCISE 1 Analyzing a Paragraph

Read the following paragraph carefully.

1. Is the paragraph developed in Pattern A (topic sentence/development) or Pattern B (topic sentence/development/restated topic sentence)?

2. Identify the parts of the paragraph pattern by underlining and annotating them. Use the two example paragraphs as models.

TYPES OF NIGHTCLUBBERS
Jerry Lopez

Dancers are not the only men who go to nightclubs. Having worked in and attended various clubs, I have come to realize they attract about four different types of guys, who can be grouped by the way they act. First there are the dancers. They are out on the floor most of the night. They are not concerned with their appearance. They usually wear jeans or shorts and a tee shirt. They are there to dance and sweat. Then there are the posers. They go to model and show off their clothes and hair. They won't dance for fear of messing up their appearance or, even worse, sweating! The third group is the scammers. Scammers go to pick up women. They usually stand around and check out the body parts of other people as they pass by. A person close to them can see the lust in their eyes. There are also the boozers or druggies. They can be seen stumbling around, falling down, or lying in some corner where they have passed out. At times I am a member of a fifth group: the observers.

EXERCISE 2 Analyzing a Paragraph

Read the following paragraph carefully.

1. Is the paragraph developed in Pattern A (topic sentence/development) or Pattern B (topic sentence/development/restated topic sentence)?

2. Identify the parts of the paragraph pattern by underlining and annotating them. Use the two example paragraphs as models.

THE FIGHTING, FOUNDING MOTHERS
Maxine Johnson

People argue a lot about the prospects of women in the military fighting in combat, but in the War of Independence, several women distinguished themselves in combat situations. In 1775, Paul Revere got the main credit for riding to warn the Patriots that the British were coming on a military move on Concord and Lexington, Massachusetts. The fact is that, although he did warn some

Patriots, he was stopped by the British. Who did get through? Several people, including Sybil Ludington, a teenage woman who fearlessly rode her horse like the wind. Another famous woman was known as Molly Pitcher. Her real name was Mary Hayes. She went with her husband to the battlefield, where she brought the men pitchers of water (hence her nickname) and helped load the cannon her husband fired. When her husband was shot at the Battle of Monmouth in 1778, she took over the cannon and fought bravely. At the end of the battle, won by the Patriots, she carried a wounded man for two miles. More than two hundred years ago, these women proved that their gender can be soldiers in every sense.

The Writing Process and the Paragraph

Learning to write a well-designed developmental paragraph will help you write longer assignments, because the developmental paragraph is often an essay in miniature.

Therefore, you can approach both the developmental paragraph and the essay in the same manner—namely, by working through the three stages of the writing process described in Chapters 2 through 4. In this chapter, we will go through the basic stages and strategies once again. Here is a summary of them:

- Stage One: Exploring / Experimenting / Gathering Information

  Freewrite, brainstorm (answer questions or make lists), cluster, take notes (if doing research or analyzing a reading selection).

- Stage Two: Writing the Controlling Idea / Organizing and Developing Support

  Compose your topic sentence with a subject and a focus.
  Complete an outline or an outline alternative.

- Stage Three: Writing / Revising / Editing

  Write a first draft; then revise and edit as many drafts as necessary to reach the final draft.

Student Demonstration of All Stages of the Writing Process

Here is how one student, Vera Harris, moved from an idea to a topic sentence to an outline to a paragraph. Vera Harris returned to college while she still had a full-time job as a hairdresser. When her instructor asked her to write a paragraph about types of people she had encountered, she naturally considered her customers for the subject of her paragraph—what she would write about. But she also had a special interest in dogs, and cleverly she was able to include that interest. Although she knew her topic rather well, she worked with some prewriting techniques that allowed her to get her ideas flowing onto paper.

She used the Writing Process Worksheet for guidance, thus also providing her instructor with a record of the development of her work. Her worksheet has been lengthened for you to be able to see her work in its entirety. You will find a full-size blank worksheet on page 6, which can be photocopied, filled in, and submitted with each assignment if your instructor directs you to do so.

Writing Process Worksheet

Name Vera Harris   **Title** Customers Are Like Canines   **Due Date** Monday, Nov. 13, 8 a.m.

Use the back of this page or separate paper if you need more space.

Assignment

In the space below, write whatever you need to know about your assignment, including information about the topic, audience, pattern of writing, length, whether to include a rough draft or revised drafts, and whether your paper must be typed.

Write a paragraph of classification in which you group people according to their behavior. Keep your audience in mind as you select words and as you develop your ideas in an appropriate way. Submit this completed Writing Process Worksheet, a rough draft marked for revision, and a typed final draft of about 250 words.

Stage One

Explore   Freewrite, brainstorm (list), cluster, or take notes as directed by your instructor.

Freewriting (partial)

Types of customers

I have worked in beauty shops for a long time, and I've naturally made a lot of observations about my customers. I could write about what they look like and how they behave and how they tip and lots of things. When I first started to work, I guess at first I thought of them as pretty much the same but then I started to see them as types mainly as to how they acted and I remember way back then I sometimes thought of how they reminded me of dogs. I don't mean that in any bad way but just that human beings have their personalities and their appearances and all and so do dogs.

Both dogs and customers can be grouped

Brainstorming (Big Six Questions)

Who?   my customers
What?   the way they act
Where?   in the beauty salon
When?   for the years I have worked
Why?   their basic nature
How?   behavior sometimes like dogs—hounds, Dobermans, terriers, bulldogs, cockers, poodles, mixed, retrievers, boxers

Brainstorming (Listing)

Kinds of dogs
   hounds
   Dobermans
   terriers
   bulldogs
   cockers
   poodles
   mixed
   retrievers
   pit bulls
   boxers

Clustering

Stage Two	**Organize** Write a topic sentence or thesis; label the subject and the focus parts.

The customers in the beauty shop where I work remind me of types of dogs
subject
(of which I am fond).
focus

Write an outline or an outline alternative. For reading-based writing, include references and short quotations with page numbers as support in the outline.

   I. Poodles (major support)
     A. High-strung (minor support)
     B. Need attention (minor support)
  II. Doberman pinschers (major support)
     A. Demanding (minor support)
     B. Need watching (minor support)
 III. Bulldogs (major support)
     A. Act mean (minor support)
     B. Will back down (minor support)
 IV. Cocker spaniels (major support)
     A. Lovable (minor support)
     B. Faithful (minor support)
     C. Easy to please (minor support)

Stage Three	**Write** On separate paper, write and then revise your paragraph or essay as many times as necessary for **c**oherence, **l**anguage (usage, tone, and diction), **u**nity, **e**mphasis, **s**upport, and **s**entences (**CLUESS**). Read your work aloud to hear and correct any grammatical errors or awkward-sounding sentences. Edit any problems in fundamentals, such as **c**apitalization, **o**missions, **p**unctuation, and **s**pelling (**COPS**).

Rough Draft: Writing, Revising, Editing

CUSTOMERS ARE LIKE CANINES
Vera Harris

Language
Punctuation
Sentences
Punctuation

~~I have worked~~ ^{Over the years while working} in a beauty salon ~~for a long time. There,~~ I have come across almost every kind of salon customer, each with her own unique looks and personality. ^{Because} I am also a dog lover and have observed numerous dogs

Language

with care it is easier to classify these people if I ~~compare them with~~ ^{relate them to} canine types—but in a playful rather than a mean way. The first group is made up

Language

of poodles. Poodles are very prissy, ^{and high-strung} with a constant need for attention. Their

Emphasis
Spelling
Omission

hair is usually over-styled. They think puffballs in soft colors look great. The ~~next group~~ ^{last—} and largest group—is made up of cocker spani^els. The ¢ockers

Language

are very lovable ^{and} the most faithful. They enjoy being ^{groomed and stroked, but they are easy to please.} ~~pampered.~~ Cockers like

Sentences

to see me every week and ^{to} visit with others. Sometimes I can almost see their

Sentences
Language

tails wagging. Then come the Doberman pinchers. This type scares me the most. Dobies are hard to please. If one hair goes the wrong way, I will see

their upper lip rise up to ~~show~~ ^{expose} eyeteeth, as if they are snarling. I rarely turn

Punctuation

my back while working on this type—a Dobie might bite. The ~~last~~ ^{third} group ^{members,} the

Language

bulldogs, are not as mean as Dobies. Bulldogs act mean and tough, but if ~~you~~ ^{one does not}

Punctuation

~~don't~~ show fear when they get bossy they will back down. This type needs

Language

to feel in charge, even if ~~it's me~~ ^{I am} leading them around on a leash. No matter what, canines and customers are my best friends.

Final Draft

CUSTOMERS ARE LIKE CANINES
Vera Harris

Topic sentence

Over the years while working in a beauty salon, I have come across almost every kind of salon customer, each with her own unique looks and personality. Because I am also a dog lover and have observed numerous dogs with care, it is easier to classify these people if I relate them to canine types—but in a playful rather than a mean way. The first group is made up of poodles.

Support

Poodles are very prissy and high-strung, with a constant need for attention. Their hair is usually over-styled. They think puffballs in soft colors look great.

Support

Then come the Doberman pinschers. This type scares me the most. Dobies are hard to please. If one hair goes the wrong way, I will see their upper lip rise up to expose eyeteeth. I rarely turn my back while working on this type—a Dobie might bite. The third group members, the bulldogs, are not as mean as

Support

Dobies. Bulldogs act mean and tough, but if one does not show fear when they

Support

get bossy, they will back down. This type needs to feel in charge, even if I am leading them around on a leash. The last—and largest—group is made up of cocker spaniels. The cockers are very lovable and the most faithful. They enjoy being groomed and stroked, but they are easy to please. Cockers like to see

Concluding sentence

me every week and to visit with others. Sometimes I can almost see their tails wagging. No matter what, canines and customers are my best friends.

EXERCISE 3 Writing a Paragraph

Select one of the following topic sentences and, on separate paper, write a paragraph based on it.

1. I made that argument at the time, but if I had a second chance, I wouldn't repeat it.

2. It was the worst piece of news I ever had to deliver.

3. I confronted authority and learned from the experience.

4. It was an act of generosity I will never forget.

5. Sometimes there are good reasons for lying.

6. Alcohol addiction has physical, social, and vocational effects.

7. There are several ways to show affection.

8. The job didn't pay well, but it provided me with a good education in balancing my budget, managing my time, and dealing with the public.

9. Teenagers like music for obvious reasons.

10. Homeless people are in their situation for different reasons.

WRITER'S GUIDELINES: Writing the Paragraph

STUDENT COMPANION SITE
For additional practice, visit www.cengage .com/devenglish/ brandon/pe11e.

1. The **developmental paragraph** is a group of sentences, each with the function of stating or supporting a controlling idea called the **topic sentence**.

2. The developmental paragraph contains three parts: the subject, the topic sentence, and the support.

3. The two main patterns of the developmental paragraph are (A) topic sentence and support, and (B) topic sentence, support, and concluding sentence.

Pattern A	Pattern B

Pattern A

Topic sentence
_____
Support _____
_____
Support _____
_____
Support _____
_____
_____

Development {

Pattern B

Topic sentence
_____
Support _____
_____
Support _____
_____
Support _____
_____
Concluding sentence

} Development

4. The topic sentence includes what you are writing about—the **subject**—and what you intend to do with that subject—the **focus**.

<u>Being a good parent</u> <u>is more than providing financial support</u>.
     subject   focus

5. The **outline** is a pattern for showing the relationship of ideas. It can be used to reveal the structure and content of something you read or to plan the structure and content of something you intend to write. The following topic outline shows how the parts are arranged on the page as well as how the ideas in it relate to one another.

Main Idea (will usually be the topic sentence for the paragraph or the thesis for the essay)
  I. Major support
     A. Minor support
       1. Details (specific information of various kinds)
       2. Details
     B. Minor support
       1. Details
       2. Details
 II. Major support
     A. Minor support
     B. Minor support
       1. Details
       2. Details
       3. Details

Chapter 6

Writing the Essay

The Essay Defined in Relation to the Developmental Paragraph

The essay is as difficult to define as the paragraph, but the paragraph definition gives us a framework. Consider the definition from Chapter 5: The **developmental paragraph** "is a group of sentences, each with the function of supporting a controlling idea called the topic sentence."

The main parts of the developmental paragraph are the topic sentence (subject and focus), support (evidence and reasoning), and, often, a concluding sentence. Now let's use that framework to define the essay: The **essay** is a group of paragraphs, each with the function of supporting a controlling idea called the thesis.

These are the main parts of the essay:

Introduction: presents the thesis, which states the controlling idea—much like the topic sentence for a paragraph but on a larger scale.
Development: introduces evidence and reasoning—the support.
Transition: points out divisions of the essay (seldom used in the short essay).
Conclusion: provides an appropriate ending—often a restatement of or reflection on the thesis.

Thus, considered structurally, the essay can be an expanded developmental paragraph. That does not mean that all paragraphs can grow to be essays or that all essays can shrink to become paragraphs. For college writing, however, a

Figure 6.1
Paragraph and Essay
Compared

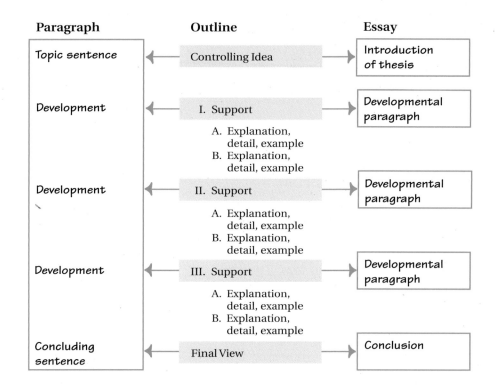

Paragraph	Outline	Essay
Topic sentence	Controlling Idea	Introduction of thesis
Development	I. Support	Developmental paragraph
	A. Explanation, detail, example B. Explanation, detail, example	
Development	II. Support	Developmental paragraph
	A. Explanation, detail, example B. Explanation, detail, example	
Development	III. Support	Developmental paragraph
	A. Explanation, detail, example B. Explanation, detail, example	
Concluding sentence	Final View	Conclusion

good understanding of the parallel between well-organized paragraphs and well-organized essays is useful.

As you learn how to write effective paragraphs—with strong topic sentences and strong support—you also learn how to organize an essay. You just expand the process, as shown in Figure 6.1.

Like the paragraph, the essay may also assume different patterns. It may be primarily one form of discourse: narration, description, exposition, or argumentation. It may also be a combination, varying from paragraph to paragraph and even within paragraphs. Regardless of its pattern, the essay will be unified around a central idea, or thesis. The **thesis** is the assertion or controlling purpose. All the other parts of the essay will be subordinate to the thesis and will support it. As with the paragraph, the main point—here, the thesis—will almost certainly be stated, usually in the first paragraph, and again—more often than not—at the end of the essay. The essay on Elvis on page 84 illustrates this pattern.

The only difference in concept between the topic sentence and the thesis is one of scope: The topic sentence unifies and controls the content of the paragraph, and the thesis does the same for the essay. Because the essay is longer and more complex than the typical paragraph, the thesis may suggest a broader scope and may more explicitly indicate the parts.

Paragraph:

Short Essay:

GOOD KING ELVIS

A messiah, a jester, a reckless jerk—or a soulful singer from the Deep South—Elvis at different times to different people was all these things. <u>His fans mirror every facet of their idol.</u>   *Introduction*

Thesis

<u>For some fans the attraction is appearance.</u> "I liked him because of his looks," says Sue Scarborough, forty-nine, of Lexington, Kentucky, as she waits with her husband to tour Grace-land. She grins good-naturedly at her husband and gives him an affectionate nudge in the ribs when he says, "My wife really likes Elvis, but I'm not jealous because he is dead—I think." Her response tells all: "My husband's a good man at drivin' a truck and fishin' for bass, but no one'll ever paint his picture on velvet."   *Topic sentence*

Support

<u>For others, Elvis was a king with a common touch and humanitarian instincts.</u> "He didn't put on airs," says Jeff Graff, twenty, of Cleveland, Ohio. "He went out of his way to help people." His friend nods his head in agreement. "Elvis must've given away a hundred Cadillacs in his day." Others in line break in to tell stories about the generosity of this good man who once walked among them.   *Topic sentence*

Support

<u>The speakers at Graceland who get the most attention are those who actually met Elvis and have information about his basic good-ness.</u> "I met him in 1960 when I was twelve years old," says Billie Le Jeune of Memphis, who visits Graceland once or twice a month: "He asked me what my favorite subject was." A few others have stories equally compelling. The crowd listens in awe and envy.   *Topic sentence*

Support

<u>Along with these talkers at Graceland are the writers, who sum up the range of Elvis's qualities.</u> On the pink fieldstone wall outside Graceland, which for years has functioned as an unauthorized bulletin board, the graffiti runs like this: ELVIS IS LOVE; I DID DRUGS WITH ELVIS; and most cryptic of all—ELVIS DIDN'T DESERVE TO BE WHITE.   *Conclusion*

GOOD KING ELVIS

Topic sentence

Support

Support
Support

Concluding sentence

A messiah, a jester, a reckless jerk—or a soulful singer from the Deep South—Elvis at different times to different people was all these things. <u>His fans mirror every facet of their idol.</u> "I liked him because of his looks," says Sue Scarborough, forty-nine, of Lexington, Kentucky, as she waits with her husband to tour Grace-land. "He didn't put on airs," says Jeff Graff, twenty, of Cleveland, Ohio. "He went out of his way to help people." "I met him in 1960 when I was twelve years old," says Billie Le Jeune of Memphis, who visits Graceland once or twice a month: "He asked me what my favorite subject was." On the pink fieldstone wall outside Graceland, which for years has functioned as an unauthorized bulletin board, the graffiti runs like this: ELVIS IS LOVE; I DID DRUGS WITH ELVIS; and most cryptic of all—ELVIS DIDN'T DESERVE TO BE WHITE.

I. Appearance

II. Helped people

III. Basic goodness

(Jim Miller, "Forever Elvis")

Special Paragraphs Within the Essay

Developmental paragraphs were discussed in Chapter 5, and because paragraphs of transition (usually short and having a simple structure) are almost never needed in short essays, we will focus our attention on paragraphs of introduction and conclusion.

INTRODUCTIONS

A good introductory paragraph does many things. It attracts the reader's interest, states or points toward the thesis, and moves the reader smoothly into the body paragraphs, the developmental paragraphs. Here are some introductory methods:

- a direct statement of the thesis
- background
- definition of term(s)
- quotation(s)
- a shocking statement
- question(s)
- a combination of two or more methods on this list

You should not decide that some of the methods are good and some are bad. Indeed, all are valid, and the most common one is the last, the combination. Use the approach that best fits each essay. Resist the temptation to use the same kind of introduction in every essay you write.

Each of the following statements is an introductory paragraph. The thesis is the same in all of them, yet each uses a different introductory method. Notice the great variety here.

Subject
Treatment

Direct Statement of Thesis: Anyone on the road in any city near midnight on Friday and Saturday is among dangerous people. They are not the product of the witching hour; they are the product of the "happy hour." They are called drunk drivers. <u>These threats to our lives and limbs</u> need to be covered by federal laws with strong punitive provisions.

Subject
Treatment

Background: In one four-year period in California (2005–2009), 17,942 people were injured and 6,632 were killed by drunk drivers. Each year, the same kinds of figures come in from all our states. The federal government does virtually nothing. Drunk driving has reached the point of being a national problem of huge proportions. <u>This slaughter of innocent citizens should be stopped by following the lead of many other nations and passing federal legislation with strong punitive provisions.</u>

Subject
Treatment

Definition: Here is a recipe. Take two thousand pounds of plastic, rubber, and steel, pour in ten gallons of gas, and start the engine. Then take one human being of two hundred pounds of flesh, blood, and bones, pour in two glasses of beer in one hour, and put him or her behind the wheel. Mix the two together, and the result may be a drunken driver ready to cause death and destruction. <u>This problem of drunk driving</u> can and should be covered by federal legislation with strong punitive provisions.

Quotation: The National Highway Traffic Safety Administration has stated that 50 percent of all fatal accidents involve intoxicated drivers and that

Subject

Treatment

"75 percent of those drivers have a Blood Alcohol Content of .10 percent or greater." That kind of information is widely known, yet the carnage on the highways continues. This problem of drunk driving should be addressed by a federal law with strong punitive provisions.

Subject

Treatment

Shocking Statement and Questions: Almost 60,000 Americans were killed in the Vietnam War. What other war kills more than that number every four years? Give up? It is the war with drunk drivers. The war in Vietnam ended more than three decades ago, but our DUI war goes on, and the drunks are winning. This deadly conflict should be covered by a federal law with strong punitive provisions.

Subject

Treatment

Questions and a Definition: What is a drunk driver? In California it is a person with a blood alcohol content of .08 percent or more who is operating a motor vehicle. What do those drivers do? Every year some of them kill more than 16,000 people nationwide. Those are easy questions. The difficult one is, What can be done? One answer is clear: Drunk drivers should be covered by federal laws with strong punitive provisions.

All these introductory methods are effective. Some others, however, are ineffective because they are too vague to carry the thesis or because they carry the thesis in a mechanical way. The mechanical approach may be direct and explicit, but it usually numbs the reader's imagination and interest.

Avoid: The purpose of this essay is to write about the need for strong punitive national laws against drunk driving.

Avoid: I will now write a paper about the need for strong punitive national laws against drunk driving.

The length of an introduction can vary, but the typical length for the introductory paragraph of a student essay is three to five sentences. If your introduction is shorter than three, be certain that it conveys all you want to say. If it is longer than five, be certain that it only introduces and does not try to expand on ideas. That function is reserved for the developmental paragraphs; a long and complicated introduction may make your essay top-heavy.

EXERCISE 1 Writing an Introduction

Select one of the following theses (altering it a bit to suit your own ideas, if you like) and, on separate paper, write at least three introductions for it, using a different method for each one. Underline the thesis in each paragraph, and label the subject and focus parts.

1. Marriages come in different shapes and sizes.

2. Career choices are greatly influenced by a person's background.

3. *Friendship* is just one word, but friends are of different kinds.

4. The spirit of sports has been corrupted by money.

5. Sexual harassment at work often goes unreported for practical reasons.

CONCLUSIONS

Your concluding paragraph should give the reader the feeling that you have said all you want to say about your subject. Like introductory paragraphs, concluding paragraphs are of various types. Here are some effective ways of concluding a paper:

• Conclude with a final paragraph or sentence that is a logical part of the body of the paper; that is, one that functions as part of the support. In the following example, there is no formal conclusion. This form is more common in the published essay than in the student essay.

> One day he hit me. He said he was sorry and even cried, but I could not forgive him. We got a divorce. It took me a while before I could look back and see what the causes really were, but by then it was too late to make any changes.
>
> (Maria Campos, "A Divorce with Reasons")

• Conclude with a restatement of the thesis in slightly different words, perhaps pointing out its significance or making applications.

> Do not blame it on the referee. Do not even blame it on the fight managers. Put the blame where it belongs—on the prevailing mores that regard prize fighting as a perfectly proper enterprise and vehicle of entertainment. No one doubts that many people enjoy prize fighting and will miss it if it should be thrown out. And that is precisely the point.
>
> (Norman Cousins, "Who Killed Benny Paret?")

• Conclude with a review of the main points of the discussion—a kind of summary. This is appropriate only if the complexity of the essay makes a summary necessary.

> As we have been made all too aware lately in this country, the more energy we conserve now, the more we'll have for the future. The same holds true for skiing. So take the Soft Path of energy conservation as you ski. You will not only be able to make longer nonstop runs, but you will have more energy to burn on the dance floor.
>
> (Carl Wingus, "Conserving Energy as You Ski")

• Conclude with an anecdote related to the thesis.

> Over the harsh traffic sounds of motors and horns and blaring radios came the faint whang-whang of a would-be musician with a beat-up guitar and a money-drop hat turned up at his feet. It all reminded me of when I had first experienced the conglomeration of things that now assailed my senses. This jumbled mixture of things both human and nonhuman was, in fact, the reason I had come to live here. Then it was different and exciting. Now it is the reason I am leaving.
>
> (Brian Maxwell, "Leaving Los Angeles")

• Conclude with a quotation related to the thesis.

> He [Johnny Cash] had, of course, long since attained a legendary stature few performers ever achieved. Terri Clark, a country songstress two generations removed, captured a sense of it in a statement released Friday. "What

really made him stand out, more than the back-beats, the TV shows, the hit records, was how he stood up for the little people, the way he believed in the right things. . . . He was a beacon for both musical and personal integrity, and he set a bar most of us can only gaze at."

(Dave Tianen, "A Music Legend Fades to Black")

There are also many ineffective ways of concluding an essay. Do not conclude with the following:

- a summary when a summary is unnecessary
- a complaint about the assignment or an apology about the quality of the work
- an afterthought—that is, something you forgot to discuss in the body of the essay
- a tagged conclusion—that is, a sentence beginning with such phrases as *In conclusion, To conclude, I would like to conclude this discussion,* or *Last but not least*
- a conclusion that raises additional problems that should have been settled during the discussion

The conclusion is an integral part of the essay and is often a reflection of the introduction. If you have trouble with the conclusion, reread your introduction. Then work for a roundness or completeness in the whole paper.

Student Demonstration of All Stages of the Writing Process

Let's see now how one student wrote an essay by working her way through all the stages of the writing process.

Our student writer, Leah, is an inmate at a California prison where, for several years, she was enrolled in a small, low-cost college program. In her English class, her assignment was to write a personal essay of 500 to 800 words. Her instructor suggested she concentrate on a recent development or event at the prison that had changed her life, for better or worse.

Several topics interested her. There was the problem of overcrowding: She lived in an institution built for 900 inmates, and the population was now 2,200. She also considered education. After spending some time in routine prison work and aimless activities, she discovered school and found it highly satisfying. Then there were the accomplishments of her Native American friends at the prison. After years of arguing their case, they had finally obtained permission from the institution to build a sweat lodge for religious purposes, and it was now in operation. That was a subject she knew well, and it was one for which she held the most enthusiasm. She was ready to proceed, knowing that the writing process would provide her with strategies and give her direction.

Leah used the Writing Process Worksheet for guidance, thus also providing her instructor with a record of the development of her work. Her worksheet has been lengthened for you to be able to see parts of her work in their entirety. You will find a full-size blank worksheet on page 6, which can be photocopied, filled in, and submitted with each assignment if your instructor directs you to do so.

Writing Process Worksheet

Name Leah   **Title** Prison Sweat Lodge   **Due Date** Tuseday, April 11, at 1 p.m.

Use the back of this page or separate paper if you need more space.

Assignment

In the space below, write whatever you need to know about your assignment, including information about the topic, audience, pattern of writing, length, whether to include a rough draft or revised drafts, and whether your paper must be typed.

Write a personal essay of 500 to 800 words about some aspect of your prison life that has changed recently. This will be mainly about how something is done; therefore, you will probably organize your discussion by time. Write for a general cross section of the population, one that will probably not have shared the experience you write about. Submit this completed worksheet, a rough draft marked for revision, and a typed final draft.

Stage One

Explore   Freewrite, brainstorm (list), cluster, or take notes as directed by your instructor.

Freewriting

- First Leah started freewriting, which enabled her to probe her memory and see which aspects of the subject most interested her. She wrote without stopping, letting her ideas tumble forth in a rich free association on the subject of "sweat lodge." •

Have sweat lodge now

For several years I have wanted to worship in the way that I did when I was on the reservation. These people here at prison were discriminating against me, I thought. I knew that the other people here could go to the chaplain and to the chapel and they could do so without people complaining or going to any bother. I didn't know why they did not allow me to follow my own religious preference. Then I talked to the other Indian sisters here at prison and they told me that they had been working for many years to get a sweat lodge. I started working with them. It took years of work, but it is worth it for now <u>we have a sweat lodge</u> where we can go for our ceremonies. It makes me feel good. I look forward to it. I <u>have used it once a week for most</u> of the <u>last year</u>. When I am nervous and when things are tense on the prison grounds, I think about the sweat lodge and just thinking about it gives me some peace. Then <u>when I go there and sweat</u> for a period of time I seem to feel that I am leaving the prison grounds and I am <u>at peace</u> with the universe. It is <u>a ceremony</u> that is <u>important</u> to me and also to the prison. We even have women who are not Indians who are interested and we teach them about Indian ways and we all learn from what we do. What else is there to say. I could go on and on. That is what I have to say. I love the sweat lodge which we call the sweats. I think it is the most important thing in my life now. I used to be bitter toward the prison for denying me my rights, but now I am even <u>at peace</u> with them—most of the time. I remember when we were trying to get approval and . . . [partial]

Ceremony important

At peace

Brainstorming (Big Six Questions)

- Leah continued with the subject of the prison sweat lodge, and her topic tightencd to focus on particular areas. Although she could have listed the annotations and the words she underlined in her freewriting, she began with the big six questions for her framework.

Who?   American Indian inmates and others
What?   sweat lodge—how it was started—the politics—the ceremonies
Where?   California Institution for Women—off the yard
When?   1989, before, after, long time in planning and building
Why?   spiritual, physical, self-esteem, educational
How?   preparation, steps

Brainstorming (Listing)

- Leah then proceeded to write three useful lists based on her answers to the questions.

Sweat lodge	*Ceremony*	*Result*
Problems in building it	Preparation	Relaxed
Reasons	Blankets	Spiritually clean
Fairness	Rocks	Peaceful
Who helped	Fire	
Time to build	Water	
	Tobacco and sweet grass	
	Sweating	
	Passing pipe	
	Tearing down	

Clustering

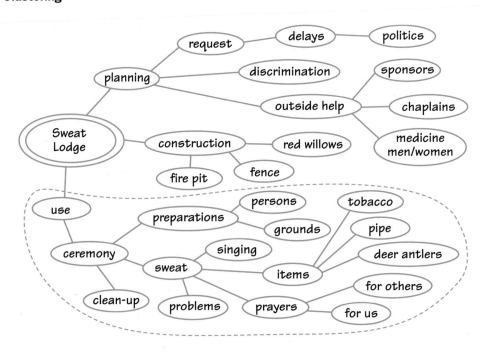

- Notice that after completing her basic cluster, Leah went back and drew a broken boundary around subclusters that offered encouraging areas for focus.

Some subclusters, usually with further clustering to provide details, can work as well as an outline for providing structure and content for the development of an essay.   •

Stage Two   **Organize**   Write a topic sentence or thesis; label the subject and the focus parts.

• After freewriting, brainstorming, and clustering, Leah was ready to focus. She was ready to concentrate on one aspect of her larger topic that could reasonably be developed in an essay of 500 to 800 words. She also wanted to establish a direction for the essay that would target her audience, who knew little about her topic. It would be necessary to explain her topic in detail so that uninformed readers could easily understand. Moreover, she would avoid any Native American words that her audience might not know. Although the sweat lodge was developed in an atmosphere of controversy in which she and others often had to be persuasive, she anticipated that readers of this essay would be open-minded and interested. She would simply inform them about her experience with the sweat lodge, giving a personal perspective. She would also have to avoid using prison slang, because this essay was for an assignment in a college writing class.

Leah made three attempts to write a sentence with both a subject (what she would write about) and a treatment (what she would do with her subject). She wanted the treatment to be just right, not vague or too broad or too narrow.   •

I want to explain how we use sweats and why.
Using the prison sweat lodge involves specific practices that contribute to my well-being.

I want to discuss the <u>prison sweat lodge</u>, <u>what we do in the preparation period,</u>
                                    subject
<u>what we do when we were inside for the ceremony, and what we do afterward</u>.
                                    focus

• Her third attempt satisfied her, and the statement became her thesis. Later she would reword it.   •

Write an outline or an outline alternative. For reading-based writing, include references and short quotations with page numbers as support in the outline.

• Leah's next task was to organize her material. Although she might have used the part of her cluster marked by the dotted lines, she chose the outline form. The outline shows the relationship of ideas, suggests ways to divide the essay according to Leah's thesis, and indicates support. The divisions are Preparation, Ceremony, and Ceremony completion and site restoration. Those items are Leah's Roman-numeral headings.   •

I. Preparation
  A. Fasting
    1. Duration
    2. Only water
  B. Heat rocks
    1. Thirty to fifty
    2. Build fire

C. Set up lodge

    1. Permission from sponsor

    2. Cover framework

II. Ceremony

  A. Movement

    1. Going and coming

    2. Passing sacred objects

  B. Establishing attitude

  C. Sweating

  D. Praying and singing

  E. Purification rites

    1. Tobacco ties

    2. Sage

    3. Sweet grass

III. Ceremony completion and site restoration

  A. Personal

    1. Water down

    2. Eat and drink

    3. Change

  B. Site

    1. Remove and store blankets

    2. Move rocks

Stage Three

Write   On separate paper, write and then revise your paragraph or essay as many times as necessary for **c**oherence, **l**anguage (usage, tone, and diction), **u**nity, **e**mphasis, **s**upport, and **s**entences (**CLUESS**). Read your work aloud to hear and correct any grammatical errors or awkward-sounding sentences.

Edit any problems in fundamentals, such as **c**apitalization, **o**missions, **p**unctuation, and **s**pelling (**COPS**).

• The following is an early draft that shows Leah's revision process. The draft also includes some editing (COPS). •

RAZOR WIRE SWEAT LODGE

My tribe is
~~I am a~~ Pomo ~~Indian~~, one ~~tribe~~ of ~~many here~~ on the prison grounds. I have had

Rewrite
tremendous interest in my ~~Ancestry~~ and their customs, and the cultures of

all Indian tribes. The sacred sweat ceremonies, ~~I've~~ found to be one of the

Rewrite
most interesting. Many women of ~~all~~ races here in the facility have also taken

interest and found ~~peace~~ within themselves from participating in the sweats. I

want to discuss the prison sweat lodge, what we do in the preparation period,

what we do when ~~we're~~ inside for the ceremony, and what we do afterward.

Rewrite for stronger topic sentence

The first step to sweating [in our prison facility] is the preparation period. Before anyone can sweat there are many requirements [concerning] ~~in~~ what we wear, / ~~how we are instructed (depending on how many times we've gone),~~ and how we act. [For] ~~T~~wenty-four hours before the sweat, we fast. [Participants should drink only] ~~We can only drink~~ water or juices, but if

Coherence

someone has health problems we will excuse them. The lava rocks have to [heat] ~~in~~ the fire approximately three hours before we start sweating. The fire has to be built just right in a little house shape. [We put] ~~Putting~~ all the rocks in the middle with the wood standing like a teepee around them; then the paper [is] stuffed

Organize
Be more concise

between and around the wood. Once ~~there's~~ [there is] a good fire going then we ~~start~~ tend to the sweat lodge itself. Because we have no tarp to put on the sweat lodge, the state has provided us with plenty of blankets. The blankets have to cover the [s]weat lodge fully. We put at least three layers of blankets on the sweat lodge. We make sure we leave about eight inches of blanket around the bottom of the sweat lodge. [By] ~~Around~~ this time, some women have started

Coherence

making their tobacco ties. These ties are used for [sending] ~~putting your~~ prayer on. We've ~~got to~~ [must] make sure the sponsor is somewhere by the sweat lodge at all times. ~~Also about~~ [As for] the rock[s], we use thirty to fifty of them, it depends on their size and how many women are sweating that day. Then the women are told to change into only muu muu[s]; the state provides them also. Then ~~we're~~ [we are] read[y] to go inside. The preparation period is very important ~~and~~ [but] everyone looks forward to it being over.

Once everyone is inside the sweat lodge, there are certain things ~~you~~ [we] must do. ~~The way we enter is~~ first we enter counterclockwise [once] and inside we [conduct all parts of the ceremony] ~~maintain everything we do~~ counterclockwise. There are four rounds in the sweat, [each of] which last[s] about twenty to thirty minutes ~~each~~. We stress that no one [should] break our circle inside the sweat lodge, but it ~~is possible.~~ [sometimes happens.] Some women ~~can't~~ [cannot]

Coherence

handle the heat inside [so] we never make them stay. The praying and singing is in the Sioux language because our outside sponsor is Sioux. Not everyone

Rephrase

has to sing or pray. ~~It's~~ [It is] up to ~~them.~~ [the individual.] As someone finishes a prayer ~~they say~~

Agreement

Be more concise

Verb tense

she mentions all her relatives;
~~for all their relations,~~ then the next person prays. Before ~~anyone even~~ *we* enter~~s~~ the sweat ~~they~~ *we* have to make sure they have peace and good feelings with all other members. The tobacco ties hang over our heads in the sweat or around our necks. ~~Also~~ we take in sage with us and smudge ourselves with it *for purification*. After each round, new hot rocks are brought in. As these rocks are place*d* in the fire sweet grass is put on them. ~~All~~ *What* we do inside the sweat lodge is not only for ourselves, but ~~for~~ *through* our prayers for others. We maintain ourselves with humility during the whole sweat.

When the sweat is over we enter the final phase. We come out and throw our tobacco ties in *to* the fire pit. The *n* ~~first thing~~ we ~~do is~~ hose ourselves down with plenty of cold water. The refreshments are opened and someone goes after food. Once ~~we've~~ *we have* eaten and changed our clothes we start taking down the sweat. The blankets have to be taken off the same way they were put on and folded up ~~good~~ *carefully.* The leftover wood has to be put away and ~~on both~~ the blankets and the wood ~~we put their covers~~ *must be covered.* Any garbage ~~that's~~ *that has* been left around is thrown in *to* the Dumpster. Then we lock the gate and bid our farewells until the next weekend. After ~~it's~~ *f it is* all over ~~you really~~ *we* feel ~~a sense of~~ *physically,* refresh~~ness~~*ed* clean and peaceful.

Rewrite

Move to end

Using The sweat lodge is a custom of most~~ly all~~ Indian tribes. Certain Indian tribes go about it differently ~~than~~ *from* others but once ~~they're~~ *they are* all inside everyone feels of one whole being. All three steps ~~I've~~ *I have* gone through are helpful for a successful sweat ceremony. ~~Many of us members~~ *Each week we* look forward to these ceremonies ~~every week~~. They help us cope better with the prison system.

Final Draft

RAZOR WIRE SWEAT LODGE
Leah

My Indian tribe is Pomo, one of twenty-one represented at this prison. I have always had tremendous interest in my ancestors and their customs, and in the cultures of all Indian tribes. The sacred sweat ceremony itself is at the center of my life. Here at prison it has taken on a special meaning. In fact, many women of other races here have also found peace within themselves as a result of participating with me and other Native Americans in the sweats. <u>Each Saturday we have a routine: We make preparations, we sweat, and we conclude with a post-sweat activity.</u>

Thesis

Topic sentence

<u>Before we sweat, we must prepare ourselves and the facility</u>. For twenty-four hours before the sweat, we fast. We do not eat anything and drink only water or juices, but if someone has a health problem, we will excuse her. As for clothing, we wear simple, loose dresses such as the prison-issued muu muus. We bring tobacco ties, sage leaves, sweet grass, and sometimes a pipe. Preparing the facility is more complicated than preparing ourselves. About thirty-five lava rocks must be heated in a fire approximately three hours before we start sweating. The wood for the fire has to be placed in a tepee shape around the pile of rocks and ignited. Once the fire is hot, we tend to the sweat lodge itself. Because we have no tarp to put on the sweat lodge frame, the state provides us with blankets. We use these to cover the lodge fully, draping it with about three layers and leaving an opening to the east. Finally we are ready to go inside. The preparation period is very important, but everyone looks forward to its being over.

Topic sentence

<u>From this point on through the ceremony, everything must be done according to rules</u>. First we enter counterclockwise, and once inside we conduct all parts of the ceremony counterclockwise. There are four rounds in the sweat, each of which lasts about twenty to thirty minutes. We stress that no one should break our circle inside the sweat lodge, but it sometimes happens. Some women cannot handle the steam and the heat, so we never make them stay. Those who do stay are free to participate in the singing and praying or not. The four rounds are similar. For each, six hot rocks are brought in, and six dippers of water are poured onto the rocks. The number six indicates the four directions and the sky and the ground. As someone finishes a prayer (usually in Sioux because our sponsor is a Sioux), she mentions her relatives, for this ceremony is also for others. Then another person follows. As sweet grass burns outside on the fire, we sit in the hot steam and rub sage leaves on our bodies for purification. We maintain ourselves with humility during the whole event.

Topic sentence

<u>When the sweat is over, we enter the final phase</u>. We come out and throw our tobacco ties into the fire pit, and the smoke takes our prayers to the sky. Then we hose ourselves down with plenty of cold water and open the refreshments we brought. Once we have eaten and changed our clothes, we start dismantling the sweat. The blankets have to be taken off the same way they were put up and then folded carefully. The leftover wood has to be put away, and the blankets and wood must be covered. Any garbage that has been left around is thrown into the Dumpster. Then we lock the gate to our facility and bid farewell.

Using a sweat lodge is a custom of most Indian tribes. Certain Indian tribes go about it differently from others, but in here when we are together in the lodge, we feel like one whole being. Each week we look forward to this ceremony. It helps us cope better with the prison system. After it is over, we feel physically refreshed, clean, and peaceful.

EXERCISE 2 Completing a Writing Process Worksheet

Select one of the following theses (altering it if you like, even by taking the opposite position) and complete a Writing Process Worksheet at least through Stage Two. (Photocopy the blank form on page 6.)

1. The date [marriage, class, game, job] was a disaster [success].

2. I will never forget my first encounter with racial prejudice [cruelty to animals, inhumanity].

3. The kind of music I listen to reflects the kind of person I would like to be.

4. A preoccupation with a single activity or concern throws life out of balance.

5. The importance of student government is often overlooked.

6. A death in the family can teach a person a great deal about life.

7. The way a person drives reveals his or her personality.

8. The way I drive depends on my mood.

9. The way I keep my room [car, house, yard, desk] is a reflection of the way I think [regard life].

10. One of my most embarrassing moments has become, in retrospect, only a humorous recollection.

WRITER'S GUIDELINES: Writing the Essay

1. The **essay** is a group of paragraphs, each with the function of stating or supporting a controlling idea called the **thesis**.

   • The main parts of an essay are the introduction, development, and conclusion.
   • The essay can be considered an amplification of a developmental paragraph.

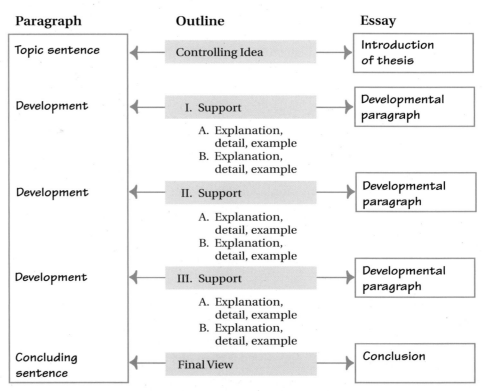

2. The **introduction** contains the thesis within a context of comments that give an adequate perspective on the topic. There are many good introductory methods, which include presenting a direct statement of the thesis, background, definition of term(s), quotation(s), a shocking statement, question(s), and a combination of two or more of these methods.

3. The **conclusion** makes a final comment on the development of your thesis. If you do not know how to conclude, reread your introduction for ideas.

4. You can depend on the three stages of the writing process to help you write paragraphs and essays. In the first stage, you are encouraged to explore relevant ideas and perhaps generate a topic sentence or thesis. In the second stage, you move naturally to a precise statement of your topic sentence or thesis and to an organized plan for your support material. Finally, you do the actual writing, revising, and editing of your paragraph or essay. This process also allows for recursive movement: You can go back and forth as you rework your material.

Part III   WRITING PARAGRAPHS AND ESSAYS: INSTRUCTION, WITH INTEGRATED READING SELECTIONS

Part III discusses—and also demonstrates through reading selections—how our thoughts often occur in flexible, useful patterns. As you write in classes across the campus, notice how many regular writing assignments—especially papers and essay tests—expect you to describe, narrate, analyze (in many forms such as causes and effects, comparison and contrast, and definition), or argue a point. Following the same principles, you may be asked to use similar forms at the workplace as you write incident reports, proposals, evaluations, and recommendations. Although one form may indicate purpose and generally guide organization, it is important to note that written passages are almost always a combination of forms.

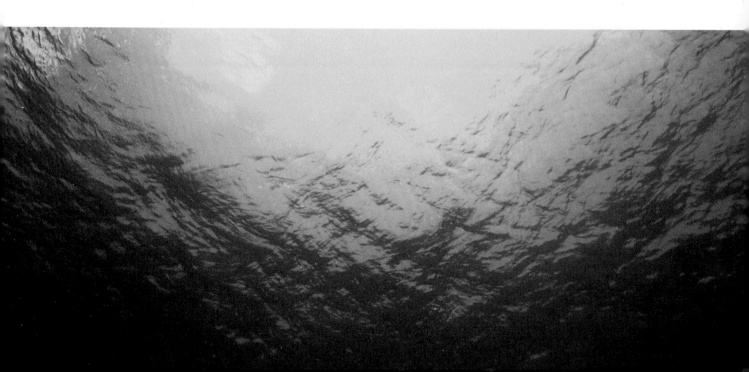

Chapter 7

Descriptive Narration
Moving Through Space and Time

WHEN TO USE DESCRIPTIVE NARRATION

FOR COLLEGE WRITING ASSIGNMENTS

Descriptive narratives are commonly written in many different college subject areas:

- In English composition classes you will probably write some paragraphs and essays about your experiences, showing what happened and giving impressions of how things appeared.
- In police science and fire science classes, you may report on scenes and incidents you observed during ride-alongs and visits to stations.
- In classes as varied as sociology, education, ecology, psychology, and music and art appreciation, your reports of what you experienced during field trips and personal visits are likely to be among course requirements.

IN CAREERS AND AT THE WORKPLACE

- At the workplace, you may be called upon to write descriptive narratives in incident reports, case studies, employee evaluations, proposals, comparative evaluations of products or services, quality control reports, or testimonials promoting products or services.

DESCRIPTIVE NARRATION IN A CARTOON

At home with the police

Writing Descriptive Narration

As patterns of writing, description and narration are almost always associated. You would almost never describe something without relating it to something else, especially to a story or a narrative. And you would seldom narrate something (tell the story) without including some description. A narrative moves through time; a description usually moves through space. In this chapter the two patterns are linked as descriptive narration. Either one may be emphasized, but the two blend seamlessly. First we will examine their individual principles.

THE NARRATIVE DEFINED

In our everyday lives, we tell stories and invite other people to do so by asking questions such as "What happened at work today?" and "What did you do last weekend?" We are disappointed when the answer is "Nothing much." We may be equally disappointed when a person does not give us enough details—or maybe gives us too many and spoils the effect. After all, we are interested in people's stories and in the people who tell them. We like the narrative.

What is the narrative? *The narrative is an account of an incident or a series of incidents that make up a complete and significant action.* Each narrative has five parts: situation, conflict, struggle, outcome, and meaning.

NARRATIVE PATTERNS

The five narrative patterns are described here as they relate directly to the action. In a broader sense, you might use other terms such as setting, concern, sequence of events, completion, and significance (or recommended response).

Situation

Situation is the background for the action. The situation may be described only briefly, or it may even be implied. ("To celebrate my seventeenth birthday, I went to the Department of Motor Vehicles to take my practical test for my driver's license.")

Conflict

Conflict is friction, such as a problem in the surroundings, with another person, or within the individual. The conflict, which is at the heart of each narrative, produces struggle. ("It was raining and my appointment was the last one of the day. The examiner was a serious, weary-looking man who reminded me of a bad boss I once had, and I was nervous.")

Struggle

Struggle, which need not be physical, is the manner of dealing with conflict. The struggle adds action or engagement and generates the plot. ("After grinding on the ignition because the engine was already on, I had trouble finding the windshield wiper control. Next I forgot to signal until after I had pulled away from the curb. As we crept slowly down the rain-glazed street, the examiner told me to take the emergency brake off. All the while, I listened to his pen scratching on his clipboard. 'Pull over and park,' he said solemnly.")

Outcome

Outcome is the result of the struggle. ("After I parked the car, the examiner told me to relax, and then he talked to me about school. When we continued, somehow I did not make any errors, and I got my license.")

Meaning

Meaning is the significance of the story, which may be deeply philosophical or simple, stated or implied. ("Calmness promotes calmness.")

VERB TENSE

Because most narratives relate experience in time order, the verb tense is likely to be the past ("She *walked* into the room") rather than the present ("She *walks* into the room"), although you may use either. An unnecessary change in tense tends to distract or confuse readers.

Two generalizations may be useful as you work with verb tense.

- Most narratives (often summaries) based on literature are written in the present tense.

    Tom Sawyer *pretends* that painting the fence *is* a special pleasure. His friends *watch* him eagerly. He *talks* and *displays* his joy. They *pay* him to do his work.

- Most historical events and personal experiences are written in the past tense.

    The Battle of Gettysburg *was* the decisive encounter in the Civil War. Although General Lee, the Confederate general in charge of the overall strategy, *was* a wise and experienced man, he *made* some tactical blunders that *led* to a devastating victory by the Union forces.

> We *walked* down the path to the well-house, attracted by the fragrance of the honeysuckle with which it *was covered*. Someone *was* drawing water and my teacher *placed* my hand under the spout. As the cool stream *gushed* over one hand she *spelled* into the other the word *water*, first slowly, then rapidly.
>
> (Helen Keller, *The Story of My Life*)

Although Helen Keller chose the conventional past tense for verbs in the last passage, she might have chosen the present tense for a sense of immediacy.

The two main points about tense are the following:

- The generalizations about verb-tense selection (using past for the historical and the personal and using present for fiction) are useful.
- The verb tense in a passage should change only when the shift is needed for clarity and emphasis.

POINT OF VIEW

Point of view shows the writer's relationship to the material and the subject, and it usually does not change within a passage.

If you are conveying personal experience, the point of view will be **first person**, which can be either involved (as a participant) or detached (as an observer). The involved perspective uses *I* more prominently than the detached perspective does.

If you are presenting something from a distance—geographical or historical (for example, telling a story about George Washington)—the point of view will usually be **third person**, and the participants will be referred to as "he," "she," and "they."

DIALOGUE

Dialogue is used purposefully in narration to characterize, particularize, and support ideas. It shows us how people talk and think, as individuals or as representatives of society. Not every narrative requires dialogue.

Note in the following paragraph that the snatches of dialogue are brief. The language will ring true to Asian immigrants and those who have been around Asian immigrants. It is starkly realistic yet sympathetically engaging in context so that we are convinced of its authenticity and drawn into the story. As narrator, the author was present when the utterances in this paragraph were made.

> My brother was even more fanatical than I about speaking English. He was especially hard on my mother, criticizing her, often cruelly, for her pidgin speech—smatterings of Chinese scattered like chop suey in her conversation. "It's not 'What it is,' Mom," he'd say in exasperation. "It's 'What *is* it; what *is* it, what *is* it!'" Sometimes Mom might leave out an occasional "the" or "a," or perhaps a verb of being. He would stop her in mid-sentence: "Say it again, Mom. Say it right." When he tripped over his own tongue, he'd blame it on her: "See, Mom, it's all your fault. You set a bad example."
>
> (Elizabeth Wong, "The Struggle to Be an All-American Girl")

ORDER

The **order** will be essentially time, moving from conflict to meaning. Flashbacks within the sequence are used infrequently in college assignments. (See page 109 for a list of transitional words that promote coherence in the progression of time.)

DESCRIPTIVE PATTERNS

Description is the use of words to represent the appearance or nature of something. It is not merely the work of an indifferent camera: Instead, often going beyond sight, it includes details that will convey a good representation. Just what details the writer selects will depend on several factors, especially the type of description and the dominant impression the writer is trying to convey.

Types of Description

Depending on how you wish to treat your subject material, your description is likely to be either objective or subjective.

Effective **objective description** presents the subject clearly and directly as it exists outside the realm of emotions. If you are explaining the function of the heart, the characteristics of a computer chip, or the renovation of a manufacturing facility, your description will probably feature specific, impersonal details. Most technical and scientific writing is objective in this sense. It is likely to be practical and utilitarian, making little use of speculation or poetic technique and featuring mainly what can be seen.

Effective **subjective description** is also concerned with clarity and it may be direct, but it conveys a feeling about the subject and sets a mood while making a point. Because most expression involves personal views, even when it explains by analysis, subjective description (often called **emotional description**) has a broader range of uses than objective description.

Descriptive passages can be a combination of objective and subjective description; only the larger context of the passage will reveal the main intent. The following description of a baseball begins with objective treatment and then moves to subjective.

Objective treatment moving to subjective treatment

> It weighs just over five ounces and measures between 2.86 and 2.94 inches in diameter. It is made of a composition-cork nucleus encased in two thin layers of rubber, one black and one red, surrounded by 121 yards of tightly wrapped blue-gray wool yarn, 45 yards of white wool yarn, 53 more yards of blue-gray wool yarn, 150 yards of fine cotton yarn, a coat of rubber cement, and a cowhide (formerly horsehide) exterior, which is held together with 216 slightly raised red cotton stitches. Printed certifications, endorsements, and outdoor advertising spherically attest to its authenticity. . . . Feel the ball, turn it over in your hand; hold it across the seam or the other way, with the seam just to the side of your middle finger. Speculation stirs. You want to get outdoors and throw this spare and sensual object to somebody or, at the very least, watch somebody else throw it. The game has begun.

(Roger Angell, "On the Ball")

The following subjective description, also on the subject of baseball, is designed to move the emotions while informing.

The following details relate to the paradoxes.

Note the emotional appeals, the subjective approach.

The Babe was a bundle of paradoxes. Somehow one of the most appealing things about him was that he was neither built, nor did he look like, an athlete. He did not even look like a ballplayer. Although he stood six feet two inches and weighed 220 pounds, his body was pear-shaped and even when in tip-top condition he had a bit of a belly. His barrel always seemed too much for his legs, which tapered into a pair of ankles as slender almost as those of a girl. The great head perched upon a pair of round and unathletic shoulders, presented a moon of a face, the feature of which was the flaring nostrils of a nose that was rather like a snout. His voice was deep and hoarse, his speech crude and earthy, his ever-ready laughter a great, rumbling gurgle that arose from the caverns of his middle. He had an eye that was abnormally quick, nerves and muscular reactions to match, a supple wrist, a murderous swing, and a gorgeously truculent, competitive spirit.

(Paul Gallico, "Babe Ruth")

Techniques of Descriptive Writing

As a writer of description, you will need to focus your work to accomplish four specific tasks:

- Emphasize a single point (dominant impression).
- Choose your words with care.
- Establish a perspective from which to describe your subject (point of view).
- Position the details for coherence (order).

Dominant Impression

See if you can find the dominant impression in this description:

Please help me find my dog. He is a mongrel with the head of a poodle and the body of a wolfhound, and his fur is patchy and dingy-gray. He has only three legs, but despite his arthritis, he uses them pretty well to hobble around and scratch his fleas and mange. His one seeing eye is cloudy, so he runs with his head sideways. His ragged, twisted ears enable him to hear loud sounds, which startle his troubled nervous system and cause him to howl pitifully. If you give him a scrap of food, he will gum it up rapidly and try to wag his broken tail. He answers to the name of Lucky.

Of course, the dominant impression, what is being emphasized, is "misery," or "unlucky," not "lucky." The dominant impression emerges from a pattern of details, often involving repetition of one idea with different particulars. Word choice, which is of paramount importance, depends on your purpose in writing and on your audience.

If you are in a restaurant, and you say to your companion, "This food is good," your companion may understand all he or she needs to understand on the subject. After all, your companion can see you sitting there chewing the food, smacking your lips, and wiping the donut glaze off your chin. But if you write that sentence and send it to someone, your reader may be puzzled. Although the reader may know you fairly well, he or she may not know the meaning of "good" (to eat? to purchase for others? to sell?) or of "this food" (What kind? Where is it? How is it special? How is it prepared? What qualities does it have?).

To convey your main concern effectively to readers, you will want to give some sensory impressions. These sensory impressions, collectively called *imagery*, refer to that which can be experienced by the senses—what we can see, smell, taste, hear, and touch. You may use *figures of speech* to convey these sensory impressions; figures of speech involve comparisons of unlike things that, nevertheless, have something in common.

The imagery in this passage is italicized.

Topic sentence	Sitting here in Harold's Hefty Burgers at midnight, I am convinced that I am eating the ultimate form of food. The *buns* are *feathery soft* to the touch but *heavy* in the hand and *soggy* inside. As I take a full-mouth, no-nonsense bite, the *melted cheese* and *juices cascade* over my fingers and make little *oil slicks* on the *vinyl table* below. I *chew noisily* and happily like a puppy at a food bowl, stopping occasionally to flush down the *rich, thick taste of spicy animal fat* with a *swig* from a *chilled mug of fizzing root beer* that *prickles my nose*. Over at the grill, *the smell of frying onions creeps away* stealthily on *invisible feet* to conquer the neighborhood, turning hundreds of ordinary *citizens* like me into drooling, stomach growling, fast-food addicts, who *trudge* in from the night like the walking dead and *call out* the same order, time after time. "Hefty Burger." "Hefty Burger." "Hefty Burger."
Dominant impression	
Image (touch)	
Images (sight) Image (sound)	
Image (taste)	
Image (smell)	
Figure of speech	
Note movement	
through time Image (sight)	
and space Image (sound)	

(Dale Scott, "Hefty Burger")

In reading Scott's enthusiastic endorsement of the Hefty Burger, the reader will have no trouble understanding the idea that he liked the food. Through imagery, Scott has involved the reader in what he has seen, smelled, heard, tasted, and touched. He has also used figures of speech, including these examples:

Simile: a comparison using *like* or *as*   "chew noisily and happily like a puppy"

Metaphor: a comparison using   "feathery [instead of 'delicately'] soft"
    word replacement

Personification: an expression   "smell of frying onions creeps away
    giving human characteristics   stealthily on invisible feet to conquer"
    to something not human   [instead of "spreads to entice"]

Subjective description is likely to make more use of imagery, figurative language, and words rich in associations than is objective description. But just as a fine line cannot always be drawn between the objective and the subjective, a fine line cannot always be drawn between word choice in one and in the other. However, we can say with certainty that whatever the type of description, careful word choice will always be important. Consider the following points about word choice (diction), point of view, and order.

Word Choice: General and Specific, Abstract and Concrete

To move from the general to the specific is to move from the whole class or group of items to individual ones; for example,

General	Specific	More Specific
food	hamburger	Hefty Burger
mess	grease	oil slicks on the table
drink	soda	mug of root beer
odor	smell from grill	smell of frying onions

Words are classified as abstract or concrete, depending on what they refer to. *Abstract words* refer to qualities or ideas: *good, ordinary, ultimate, truth, beauty, maturity, love.* Concrete words refer to things or a substance; they have reality: *onions, grease, buns, table, food.* Specific concrete words, sometimes called *concrete particulars*, often support generalizations effectively and convince the reader of the accuracy of the description.

Never try to give all the details in a description. Instead, be selective. Pick only those details that you need to project a dominant impression, always taking into account the knowledge and attitudes of your readers. To reintroduce an idea from the beginning of this section, description is not photographic. If you wish to describe a person, select the traits that will project your intended dominant impression. If you wish to describe a landscape, do not give all the details that you might find in a picture; on the contrary, pick the details that support your intended dominant impression. That extremely important dominant impression is directly linked to your purpose. It is created by the judicious choice and arrangement of images, figurative language, and revealing details.

Point of View

Point of view shows the writer's relationship to the subject, thereby establishing the perspective from which the subject is described. It rarely changes within a passage. Two terms usually associated with fiction writing, *first person* and *third person*, also pertain to descriptive writing.

If you want to convey personal experience, your point of view will be *first person*, which can be either involved (point of view of a participant) or uninvolved (point of view of an observer). The involved perspective uses *I* more prominently than the uninvolved. Student Dale Scott's paragraph "Hefty Burger" uses first person, involved.

If you want to present something from a detached position, especially from a geographical or historical distance (see "Babe Ruth" and "On the Ball"), your point of view will be *third person*, and you will refer to your subjects by name or by third-person pronouns such as *he, she, him, her, it, they,* and *them,* without imposing yourself as an *I* person.

Order

The point of view you select may indicate or even dictate the order in which you present descriptive details. If you are describing your immediate surroundings while taking a walk (first person, involved), the descriptive account would naturally develop spatially as well as chronologically—in other words, in both space and time.

Some descriptive pieces—for example, the one on Babe Ruth—may follow an idea progression for emphasis and not move primarily through space or time. Whatever appropriate techniques you use will guide your reader and thereby aid coherence.

All three elements—dominant impression, point of view, and order—work together in a well-written description.

The dominant impression of the paragraph "On the Ball" is of an object remarkably well designed for its purpose. The point of view is third person, and the order of the description moves from the core of the baseball outward.

The paragraph "Babe Ruth" emphasizes the idea of paradox (something that appears to be a contradiction). The details are presented from a detached point of view (third person) and appear in order from physique to overall appearance to behavior. The details show a person who was not built like an athlete and did not look like an athlete yet was one of the most famous athletes of all time. Collectively those details convey the dominant impression of "Ruth, the paradox."

Scott's "Hefty Burger" can also be evaluated for all four elements:

* *Dominant impression*: good food (images, figurative language, other diction). The reader experiences the incident as the writer did because of the diction.
* *Word choice*: general or specific; abstract or concrete. The general and abstract have been made clear by use of the specific and the concrete. Of course, not all abstract words need to be tied to the concrete, nor do all general words need to be transformed to the specific. As you describe, use your judgment to decide which words fit your purposes—those needed to enable your audience to understand your ideas and to be persuaded or informed.
* *Point of view*: first person, involved.
* *Order*: chronological (time) for the eating; spatial (space) for the grill and neighborhood.

Transitional Words

Consider using the following transitional words to improve coherence by connecting ideas with ideas, sentences with sentences, and paragraphs with paragraphs.

FOR DESCRIPTION (place): above, over, under, below, nearby, near, across, beyond, among, to the right, to the left, in the background, in the foreground, further, beside, opposite, within sight, out of sight

FOR NARRATION (time): after, before, later, earlier, initially, soon, recently, next, today, tomorrow, yesterday, now, then, until, currently, when, finally, not long after, immediately, (at) first, (at) last, third, previously, in the meantime, meanwhile

FOR ALL PATTERNS OF WRITING: The HOTSHOT CAT words: however, otherwise, therefore, similarly, hence, on the other hand, then, consequently, also, thus (See pages 427–428 for additional transitional words.)

CAREER-RELATED WRITING: WORKPLACE REPORTS

At the workplace, numerous reports fit the pattern of narrative writing: trip reports, status reports (from investigation or development of something such as a program or product), or incident reports (one of the most universal from industry to industry).

In most instances the incident report denotes problems. Something unforeseen has occurred, and it must be documented: an accident, a theft, a disturbance, a dangerous condition, a lost child, an act of vandalism, an equipment failure, or a health emergency other than one caused by an accident. A report on one of these incidents is likely to be written as an important record. It may be the essential information on which law enforcement acts, equipment is replaced, clients are served, safety is assured, security is established, or the physical plant is protected.

These reports are sometimes dictated, but they are more often written by the person most directly related to an incident. Your ability to write an effective report will aid your company and reflect well on you as an intelligent, educated employee. Although the procedure and the form of these incident reports will vary, there are some principles that can be applied to all; these principles follow the basic narrative form.

Situation: Identify the kind of problem.

Conflict: Indicate when and where it occurred.

Struggle and outcome: Provide an account of what happened.

Meaning: If appropriate, write a recommendation for what could be done to avoid a repetition of such an incident if it is appropriate to do so.

Follow these guidelines in writing an incident report:

* Write in the first person (*I*), for you are the one who is writing the report.
* Start with the date, time, and your reason for involvement.
* If you use the words of anyone reporting on the incident, enclose them in quotation marks and acknowledge the source of those words.
* Use facts, not opinions.
* Do not step outside your work expertise and become a psychologist, philosopher, physician, or moralist. If you do, should this report make its way to a court case, what you say will be discredited.
* Use past tense; you are writing about something that has already happened.
* Use mostly active voice. For example, write, "Mills made the report," not "The report was made by Mills."
* Identify those involved. Drop the titles, such as Mr., Mrs., Dr., and so on. After the first reference to the person in the report, use only the surname or the first initial and the surname.

See pages 129–130 for an example of an incident report.

FINDING PATTERNS IN PHOTOS

EXERCISE 1   A Text-Based Activity for Groups or Individuals

Cheating student

Imagine that you are working on a final examination. Letter grades will be calculated on a curve. You are trying to convey your understanding of the course content to your instructor. Then you look to your left and see a fellow student (the one in the photo) with a cheat card in the palm of his hand. He is part of your competition. His use of the card may mean the difference between your making a lower or higher grade. You are on a bubble for your grade point average. The final grade may determine whether you can transfer to the university of your choice or not. You look to the front of the room where your instructor sits at his desk, his gaze locked on a stack of bluebook finals he is marking from another class. For a moment you are torn. You have never snitched. You have said publicly you do not believe in snitching. But much is riding on the results of this test. You continue with your work. You finish early. The cheating student is still on task—and still consulting his illegal notes. You use your cell phone camera to take a picture (as shown), in case you need evidence. You are about to submit your test. It is time to do the right thing. But what is the right thing?

Complete the following outline.

Topic Sentence or Thesis: There are occasions when a single event can make people reevaluate a principle they have always upheld, in this case *never snitching*.

    I. Extended example

        A. _____

        B. _____

    II. Example in relation to personal code of conduct

        A. _____

        B. _____

    III. Decision (to snitch or not to snitch)

        A. _____

        B. _____

If your instructor directs you to do so, write a paragraph or short essay based on this imaginary experience.

© Chuck Savage/Corbis

Practicing Narrative Patterns

Some narratives are more structured than others, but all have the same basic patterns. The parts, especially conflict and struggle, will vary in extent, depending on the circumstances.

EXERCISE 2   Writing Patterns

Fill in the blanks to complete the pattern for the topic "A Random, Unexpected, and Welcome Act of Kindness" or for another topic of your choice. Add descriptive details as needed.

(Situation)   I. _____

(Conflict)   II. _____

(Struggle)   III. _____

                A. _____

                B. _____

                C. _____

                    (Or more) _____

(Outcome) IV. _____

(Meaning) V. _____

EXERCISE 3   Writing Patterns

Fill in the blanks to complete the pattern for the topic "Dealing with an Unpleasant Person at Work" or for another topic of your choice. Add descriptive details as needed.

(Situation)   I. _____

(Conflict)   II. _____

(Struggle)   III. _____

                A. _____

                B. _____

                C. _____

                    (Or more) _____

(Outcome) IV. _____

(Meaning) V. _____

Practicing Descriptive Patterns

Description, which is almost always used with other patterns, is very important and often neglected. The following exercises feature descriptive writing that supports a dominant impression of colorful action.

EXERCISE 4 Working with Word Choice

Improve the following sentences by supplying specific and concrete words. Use images when they serve your purposes.

Example: The animal was restless and hungry.
The gaunt lion paced about the cage and chewed hungrily on an old shoe.

1. The fans were happy.

2. She was in love.

3. Confusion surrounded him.

4. The traffic was congested.

5. The dessert impressed the diner.

6. The woman liked her date.

7. The salesman was obnoxious.

8. The room was cluttered.

9. His hair was unkempt.

10. The room smelled bad.

EXERCISE 5 Completing Descriptive Patterns

Fill in the blanks. This is a useful procedure for prewriting a descriptive paragraph or essay. Consider using it for your writing assignment in this chapter. Suggested topic: a location on campus, such as a classroom, the cafeteria, the student aid office, the stadium, a playing field, a lab, or the parking lot at night.

What is your subject? _____

What is the dominant impression? _____

What is the situation? (Include some movement or action to provide a narrative framework, even if it is only you walking through an area.) _____

What is the order of details? _____

What details support the dominant impression? (Use listing or clustering.)

Listing

1. _____

2. _____

3. _____

4. _____

5. _____

Clustering

Insert your topic in the double bubble and fill in details in the blank single bubbles.

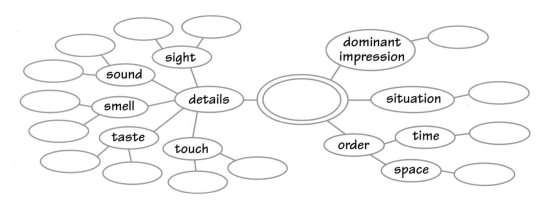

Explain your narrative framework. It need not be complicated.

- Situation _____

- Conflict _____

- Struggle _____

- Outcome _____

- Meaning _____

Readings for Critical Thinking, Discussion, and Writing

READING STRATEGIES AND OBJECTIVES

Underlining and annotating these reading selections will help you answer the questions that follow the selections, discuss the material in class, and prepare for reading-based writing assignments. As you underline and annotate, pay special attention to the author's writing skills, logic, and message, and consider the relevance of the material to your own experiences and values.

Most selections begin with a Mindset suggestion that can help you create a readiness for connecting with what you are about to read.

PARAGRAPH

One More Time

GARY SOTO

A highly acclaimed author and educator, Gary Soto, born April 12, 1952, grew up in a barrio in Fresno, California. He is the author of eleven poetry collections for adults, essays, nonfiction books, biographies, and numerous books for young readers, including Living Up the Street, *from which this passage is taken. Transitional words are underlined.*

Narration

Situation

Conflict

Struggle

Outcome

Meaning (implied)

Along with my brother and sister I picked grapes <u>until</u> I was fifteen, before giving up and saying that I'd rather wear old clothes than stoop like a Mexican. Mother thought I was being stuck-up, even stupid, because there would be no clothes for me in the fall. I told her I didn't care, but when Rick and Debra rose at five in the morning, I lay awake in bed feeling that perhaps I had made a mistake but unwilling to change my mind. <u>That fall</u> Mother bought me two pairs of socks, a packet of colored T-shirts, and underwear. The T-shirts would help, I thought, but who would see that I had new underwear and socks? I wore a new T-shirt <u>on the first</u> day of school, <u>then</u> an old shirt on Tuesday, <u>then</u> another T-shirt on Wednesday, and <u>on Thursday</u> an old Nehru shirt that was embarrassingly out of style. <u>On Friday</u> I changed into the corduroy pants my brother had handed down to me and slipped into my last new T-shirt. I worked like a magician, blinding my classmates, who were all clothes-conscious and small-time social climbers, by arranging my wardrobe to make it seem larger than it really was. But <u>by spring</u> I had to do something—my blue jeans were almost silver and my shoes had lost their form, puddling like black ice around my feet. <u>That spring</u> of my sixteenth year, Rick and I decided to take a labor bus to chop cotton. In his old Volkswagen, which was more noise than power, we drove <u>on a Saturday morning</u> to West Fresno—or Chinatown as some call it—parked, walked slowly toward a bus, and stood gawking at the winos, toothy blacks, Okies, *Tejanos* with gold teeth, whores, Mexican families, and labor contractors shouting "Cotton" or "Beets," the work of spring.

EXERCISE 6   Discussion and Critical Thinking

1. Write a phrase or a concise sentence to indicate each part of the narration as annotated.

  a. Situation:

  b. Conflict:

  c. Struggle:

  d. Outcome:

  e. Meaning (implied, not stated):

2. Of the five senses (sight, sound, touch, smell, taste), which one is used as images for descriptive writing?

3. List two phrases that convey images of sight. Use quotation marks around the words you quote.

The Story of a Well-Made Shield

N. SCOTT MOMADAY

This discussion of the Plains Indian shield reveals a great deal about Native American culture. The two short passages here are from In the Presence of the Sun: Stories and Poems. *They include description, a narrative, and a drawing, telling and showing how the designs on the shields signify far more than mere decoration or artistic imagination*

MINDSET

Lock It In

Imagine you are a Native American warrior on the plains and you are about to paint an image, really your personal icon, on your shield. It will represent what you are and will protect you. This is a final draft. Unlike your writing, you can never revise it. What will you draw?

Now in the dawn before it dies, the eagle swings low and wide in a great arc, curving downward to the place of origin. There is no wind, but there is a long roaring on the air. It is like the wind—nor is it quite like the wind—but more powerful.

A Word on the Plains Shield

Oyate awicahipi kin hehan lyou waslahy el wasicu wan Ble eciyape ci Jack Carrigan kici mazopiye yuhapi ca he Sitting Bull's shield kiu he opeton. Mr. One Bull says he can draw the shield. Please send him paper and colors. Green grass color, dark blue, brown scarlet. Yes Sitting Bull's father Jumping Bull gave him this shield and named him Sitting Bull. Jumping Bull made this shield from a vision. When Sitting Bull wears his shield he paints his horse in a certain way. Yes his father gave him this painting. When they have a shield they are not supposed to tell a lie or think wrong. If they do they are wounded or killed. When Sitting Bull's band was brought to the Standing Rock Agency, a white man, in a store with Jack Carrigan, by the name of Billie (William McNider) bought Sitting Bull's shield.

"With Regard to Sitting Bull,"
Given by His Nephew, One Bull,
and Transcribed by His Grandniece,
Mrs. Cecelia One Bull Brown

1   In its basic form the Plains shield is round and made of durable materials. It is relatively small and light in weight. A diameter of twenty-four inches is close to the average. The manufacture consists of hide and adornments. The hide is thick and dried to a remarkable hardness; it is most often the hide of a bison. Only in a limited sense can the shield rightly be considered armor, although it is strong enough to repel missiles, stones and clubs certainly, but also arrows and even balls and bullets shot from firearms, especially if the blow is glancing. But first and above all the shield is medicine.

2   The Plains shield reflects the character of the Plains culture, also known as the Horse culture or Centaur culture. It evidences a nomadic society and a warrior ideal. Those who carried shields were hunters and fighters whose purpose it was to raid, to capture, and to demonstrate extraordinary bravery.

3   The aesthetic aspects of the Plains shield [are] pronounced; the shield is a unique work of art. Without exception great care is given to the decoration of a proper shield. The artwork on many Plains shields is highly evolved in terms of proportion, design, symmetry, color, and imagination. Plains shield art is the equal of the great ledgerbook drawings of the nineteenth century, which in turn have been compared to Archaic Greek vase painting. It is an art of high order and singular accomplishment.

4   The shield bears a remarkable relationship to the individual to whom it belongs. Indeed the relationship is so immediate, so intimate as to be virtually impossible to define. In a real sense the Plains warrior *is* his shield. It is his personal flag, the realization of his vision and his name, the object of his holiest quest, the tangible expression of his deepest being. In bearing his shield he says, "My shield stands for me, and I stand for my shield. I am, and I am my shield!"

5   The shield is a mask. The mask is an appearance that discloses reality beyond appearance. Like other masks, it bespeaks sacred mystery. The shield is what you see, believes the Plains warrior. It reflects your own reality, as it does mine, he says. It reveals to you the essence of your self. It charms you, frightens you, disarms you, renders you helpless. You behold my shield, and you are transfixed or transformed, perhaps inspired beyond your imagining. Nothing will ever be the same again, for you have entered into the presence of my power. Oh, my enemy! Behold my shield!

6   The shield is involved in story. The shield is its own story. When the shield is made visible it means: Here is the story. Enter into it and be created. The story tells of your real being.

7   The shields in this gathering exist quintessentially in the element of language, and they are directly related to the stories, songs, spells, charms, and prayers of the Native American oral tradition.

8   And the shields are meditations that make a round of life. The shield stories are meant to be told aloud, either to oneself or to another or to others, one each day for sixteen consecutive days, in which on the fourth, eighth, twelfth, and sixteenth days the storyteller and his listener or listeners might fast in order to be hale and worthy and pure in spirit. The stories ought to be told in the early morning or late afternoon, when the sun is close to the horizon, and always in the presence of the sun.

The Floating Feathers Shield

9   When Gai-talee was still a boy, learning how to hunt, he had a wonderful dream. In it he saw a great bear on the side of a mountain. The bear stood still for a long time, waiting in the shadow of a high stone ridge near timberline. Then a shape hurtled on the ridge, and the bear reared suddenly and took in his claws an eagle from the air. For a moment there was an awful frenzy; then again the stillness, and dark feathers floating and fluttering down on a little wind.

10   Gai-talee told Many Magpies of the shield he wanted, and it was made according to his dream. Gai-talee raided many times in Mexico, and he carried his shield with him. They say that Gai-talee's shield is well known below the Llano Estacado.

EXERCISE 7   Discussion and Critical Thinking

1. In paragraph 1, is the description mainly objective or subjective?

2. In what way is each shield an individual work of art?

3. Why is the idea of a dominant impression relevant to shield painting?

4. What kind of imagery is naturally dominant on the shield?

5. In "The Floating Feathers Shield," how is movement suggested?

6. In what way does the shield reflect the Plains culture?

No Tears for Frankie

GINA GREENLEE

Freelance writer Gina Greenlee recalls a bully from her childhood, his death, and his funeral, which she attended. This article was first published in the "Lives" section of the New York Times Magazine.

MINDSET

Lock It In

If you had the opportunity to attend the funeral of the person who had done you the most harm in your whole life and that harm were horrific, would you go? And if you did, as you looked on the corpse, do you think you would be trying to find it in your heart to forgive that person, or might you be mainly interested in verifying the coroner's report? Ponder that question as you read an account of someone who experienced that situation.

1   I was in the fifth grade when Frankie died. It was 1971. My whole class planned to attend the funeral, since we knew him. My father thought going might give me nightmares, but I insisted. I had never seen a dead person before. Most of all, I wanted to be sure that the little creep would never touch me again.

2   Frankie lived in Lower Manhattan where run-down tenements along Avenues A, B and C were on the verge of becoming the crack houses of the '80s. At the time, I lived nearby. Then in 1970 my family moved into an apartment in Coop Village on Grand Street and F.D.R. Drive. It was only three blocks—and a world—away from the projects to a predominantly white middle-class community on the East River. Overnight at school, I became "that black girl who lives in the rich Jew buildings." Or at least that's what Frankie and my other African-American classmates thought I was. It became a familiar chant of theirs as I made my way through my old neighborhood to get to school.

3   Frankie and I were in the same grade, but I was 10 and he was 12 because he had been left back twice. He tormented all of the girls in our class. But Frankie relished singling me out—the only black girl in a sea of Jewish girls dotted with Latinas—and he had done so since I first arrived from another school in third grade.

4   He never did any schoolwork. Instead, for the first three periods Frankie's curriculum was mayhem; by fourth period he was usually in the principal's office; and by the fifth, he was back in class unremorseful and pumped to do it again. He only got worse in that working-class, urban-blight panacea, the after-school program. It was a nice idea: children whose parents were unavailable

at 3 o'clock because they were working stayed after school to study, improve skills and tackle extra-credit projects. I spent those afternoons trying to stay alive.

5   Frankie and his crew would grab my breasts, genitals and buttocks when the teachers weren't looking. Their hands, quick as filthy street rats, darted across my private parts in assembly line, during dance rehearsals and yard processions. They would leave scrawled notes in my book bag that read, "I'm gonna beat you up after school," or "I'll get you in the stairwell."

6   One spring afternoon, I had made it through another harrowing two hours after school, only to be cornered on the stairs by the whole nasty lot. They taunted me to walk down ahead of them. I managed each step as if it were my first, balancing myself on the chalk-blue shellacked handrail as I peered through the landing divider reminiscent of a wire cage, hoping to see another student, teacher, anyone. Frankie shoved me, and I tumbled one full flight, landing on my knees, my favorite brown plaid dress above my ears, easy pickings for the tiny vultures who cackled obscenities while snatching at my body, punching and kicking me. That day, I understood the depth of Frankie's perversity.

7   When I told a friend that our classroom emptied out at 3 p.m., leaving me alone with Frankie's boys, without having to share another detail, she said, "Come to my house after school." I had enjoyed two afternoons of baking cookies and doll playing when I let slip that my parents thought I was in class. My friend's mother welcomed me to play at her home anytime as long as my parents knew. "Why were you at Amy's and not in the after-school program?" my father asked me later that night. I didn't tell him because I didn't think he could help me. His interventions would only inspire retaliations and spiral me deeper into the mess.

8   I did try to tell my teachers, but nobody believed me. They chuckled and said, "Frankie just has a crush on you." That's what I told my father 15 years after the attacks, when he asked me if I had told my teachers. I guess in their world, 12-year-old boys don't sexually attack 10-year-old girls. What world did they come from, anyway? What world was I in, and how could I fix it so Frankie would disappear?

9   One morning when my teachers had stepped away from the classroom, Frankie and his boys shoved me into the coat closet and held the door shut while I was alone with Frankie. It was dark. As he kept touching me, I tried to push him away and screamed to be let out. But Frankie's friends held steadfast until the teachers arrived; then they scrambled to their seats. None of the other kids said a word. But in front of them all, I told Frankie that I hated his guts and hoped he would die.

10   Quite accommodating, he lay in a casket later that year. I didn't shed a tear. My heart was hardened, though. As usual, Frankie was up to no good—tampering with public property with the boys—when he got himself electrocuted. I was 10, and I was glad.

EXERCISE 8   Discussion and Critical Thinking

1. Use phrases or sentences to indicate these parts of this narrative:

   Situation:

   Conflict:

   Struggle:

   Outcome:

   Meaning:

2. Why didn't Gina Greenlee shed a tear?

3. Having read this essay, do you think that this event made Greenlee generally a more compassionate or a less compassionate human being? Explain.

4. Is this an essay that only a person who has been bullied dreadfully can understand, or can it be appreciated by anyone? Explain.

5. What would you say to people who would have forgiven Frankie in his casket?

More

JUDITH ORTIZ COFER

Born in Puerto Rico in 1952, Judith Ortiz Cofer moved with her parents to New Jersey, where she learned a new language and a new culture while in elementary school. Now an author and a university professor, she writes poignantly about her experiences trying to embrace two cultures with different customs and different languages. This essay comes from Silent Dancing: A Partial Remembrance of a Puerto Rican Childhood *(1990).*

MINDSET

Lock It In

Have you ever known a person or a couple who lived in one house most of their lives so that the house seemed to take on the character of its tenants and tell their story by its growth and furnishings? Judith Ortiz Cofer has had that experience with her grandparents, and, to her, their house seems to have its own life.

1   My grandmother's house is like a chambered nautilus; it has many rooms, yet it is not a mansion. Its proportions are small and its design simple. It is a house that has grown organically, according to the needs of its inhabitants. To all of us in the family it is known as *la casa de Mamá*. It is the place of our origin; the stage for our memories and dreams of island life.

2   I remember how in my childhood it sat on stilts; this was before it had a downstairs. It rested on its perch like a great blue bird, not a flying sort of bird, more like a nesting hen, but with spread wings. Grandfather had built it soon after their marriage. He was a painter and housebuilder by trade, a poet and meditative man by nature. As each of their eight children were born, new rooms were added. After a few years, the paint did not exactly match, nor the materials, so that there was a chronology to it, like the rings of a tree, and Mamá could tell you the history of each room in her casa, and thus the genealogy of the family along with it.

3   Her room is the heart of the house. Though I have seen it recently, and both woman and room have diminished in size, changed by the new perspective of my eyes, now capable of looking over countertops and tall beds, it is not this picture I carry in my memory of Mamá's casa. Instead, I see her room as a queen's chamber where a small woman loomed large, a throne-room with a massive four-poster bed in its center which stood taller than a child's head. It was on this bed where her own children had been born that the smallest grandchildren were allowed to take naps in the afternoon; here too was where Mamá secluded herself to dispense private advice to her daughters, sitting on the edge of the bed, looking down at whoever sat on the rocker where generations of babies had been sung to sleep. To me she looked like a wise empress right out of the fairy tales I was addicted to reading.

4   Though the room was dominated by the mahogany four-poster, it also contained all of Mamá's symbols of power. On her dresser instead of cosmetics there were jars filled with herbs: *yerba buena*, *yerba mala*, the making of purgatives and teas to which we were all subjected during childhood crises. She had a steaming cup for anyone who could not, or would not, get up to face life on any given day. If the acrid aftertaste of her cures for malingering did not get you out of bed, then it was time to call *el doctor*.

5   And there was the monstrous chifforobe she kept locked with a little golden key she did not hide. This was a test of her dominion over us; though my cousins and I wanted a look inside that massive wardrobe more than anything, we never reached for that little key lying on top of her Bible on the dresser. This was also where she placed her earrings and rosary at night. God's word was her security system. This chifforobe was the place where I imagined she kept jewels, satin slippers, and elegant sequined, silk gowns of heart-breaking fineness. I lusted after those imaginary costumes. I had heard that Mamá had been a great beauty in her youth, and the belle of many balls. My cousins had other ideas as to what she kept in that wooden vault: its secret could be money (Mamá did not hand cash to strangers, banks were out of the question, so there were stories that her mattress was stuffed with dollar bills, and that she buried coins in jars in her garden under rosebushes, or kept them in her inviolate chifforobe); there might be that legendary gun salvaged from the Spanish-American conflict over the Island. We went wild over suspected treasures that we made up simply because children have to fill locked trunks with something wonderful.

6   On the wall above the bed hung a heavy silver crucifix. Christ's agonized head hung directly over Mamá's pillow. I avoided looking at this weapon suspended over where her head would lay; and on the rare occasions when I was allowed to sleep on that bed, I scooted down to the safe middle of the mattress, where her body's impression took me in like a mother's lap. Having taken care of the obligatory religious decoration with a crucifix, Mamá covered the other walls with objects sent to her over the years by her children in the States. *Los Nueva Yores* were represented by, among other things, a postcard of Niagara Falls from her son Hernán, postmarked, Buffalo, N.Y. In a conspicuous

gold frame hung a large color photograph of her daughter Nena, her husband and their five children at the entrance to Disneyland in California. From us she had gotten a black lace fan. Father had brought it to her from a tour of duty with the Navy in Europe (on Sundays she would remove it from its hook on the wall to fan herself at Sunday mass). Each year more items were added as the family grew and dispersed, and every object in the room had a story attached to it, a *cuento* which Mamá would bestow on anyone who received the privilege of a day alone with her. It was almost worth pretending to be sick, though the bitter herb purgatives of the body were a big price to pay for the spirit revivals of her story-telling.

EXERCISE 9   Vocabulary Highlights

Write a short definition of each word as it is used in the essay. (Paragraph numbers are given in parentheses.) Be prepared to use the words in sentences.

perspective (3)	inviolate (5)
massive (3)	suspended (6)
dispense (3)	obligatory (6)
acrid (4)	conspicuous (6)
chifforobe (5)	bestow (6)

EXERCISE 10   Discussion and Critical Thinking

1. Ortiz Cofer says her grandmother's house "is like a chambered nautilus" (paragraph 1), which is a mollusk with a spiral, pearly lined shell with a series of air-filled chambers. In what ways is that figure of speech (simile) a good representation of the house?

2. Name at least two other comparisons she uses in describing the house.

3. Ortiz Cofer helps you imagine what she saw by using details. List five specific, concrete visual images she uses in paragraph 6.

4. What is the benefit of using the Spanish phrases?

5. Reading this essay, do you have the feeling that you are learning more about a particular culture or universal conditions and behavior?

Yearning for Love

CHANTRA SHASTRI

Having lived in America for five years, Chantra Shastri asks for freedom—freedom to make a choice in marriage, a choice based on love. In the annotation, the first column indicates images for description, and the second indicates parts of the narrative pattern. The topic sentence and concluding sentences are single-underlined; the descriptive phrases are double-underlined.

MINDSET

Lock It In

If your parents know your head and you know your heart, does the heart trump the head? It is your call.

Descriptive	Narration
	Situation
	Conflict
	Struggle
Sight	
Touch	
Sound	
Sound	
	Outcome
Metaphor	Meaning

I need not go beyond myself to find examples of love, at least the yearning for love. My home is now America, but I have not left India far behind. There, in ways still cherished by my traditional family, freedom is based on gender, and I am a female. My parents expect women to cook, clean, and nurture. My parents expect me to marry the man of their choice, although my brother will have the freedom to choose his own mate. If I disobey, I will no longer be recognized by my parents. It is easy to give in to such a custom; it is difficult to disobey. My parents have always believed as they do. I cannot change them, nor do I want to, but I wish they would accept my difference in this different country. I think my mother understands. Last week, I saw her crying while she ironed our clothes. When I asked her why she was crying, she wiped the warm tears off her thin, soft cheeks and pretended not to hear me as she sang. Her singing made me sad because I knew why she had cried, and she knew I knew. I seized the opportunity to say, "I don't want an arranged marriage," but she sang on even louder, singing a song of a distant home. In times such as these, like my father, she too covers her ears with the thick dried mud of tradition. She doesn't want to hear me. It is easier that way.

EXERCISE 11   Discussion and Critical Thinking

1. Why did Shastri's mother cry?

2. What chance does Shastri have to make her own choice?

3. What would you advise her to do?

4. How does the specific example of Shastri's mother crying imply more than it actually says?

When student Mike Kavanagh looked at the assignment to write a paragraph of descriptive narration about something he knew well, he had no trouble in selecting a subject. As a drag racer for sport and prize money, he had built up his car, a 1968 Camaro, to thunder down the track at more than two hundred miles per hour, with all his senses raw to the wind.

His Writing Process Worksheet shows you how his writing evolved from idea to final draft. To conserve space here, the freewriting and the rough draft marked for revision have been omitted. The balance of his worksheet has been lengthened for you to be able to see parts of his work in their entirety.

You will find a full-size blank worksheet on page 6. It can be photocopied, filled in, and submitted with each assignment if your instructor directs you to do so.

FLOW OF WRITING

Writing Process Worksheet

Name Mike Kavanagh   **Title** The Drag   **Due Date** Monday, March 27, 9 a.m.

Use the back of this page or separate paper if you need more space.

Assignment   In the space below, write whatever you need to know about your assignment, including information about the topic, audience, pattern of writing, length, whether to include a rough draft or revised drafts, and whether your paper must be typed.

Write a paragraph of descriptive narration about something you have experienced, an event that occurred in a short period of time, maybe a minute or less. Write so that an uninformed audience can understand what you did, how you did it, and how you felt. About 250 to 300 words. Submit this completed worksheet, a rough draft marked for revision, and a typed final draft.

Stage One   **Explore**   Freewrite, brainstorm (list), cluster, or take notes as directed by your instructor.

Clustering

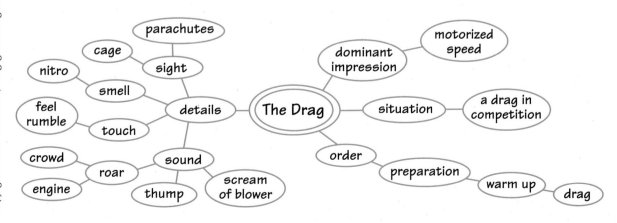

Stage Two

Organize Write a topic sentence or thesis; label the subject and the focus parts.

I climb into the cockpit for my drag.
subject   focus

Write an outline or an outline alternative. For reading-based writing, include references and short quotations with page numbers as support in the outline.

I. Preparation
   A. Take position
   B. Strap in
      1. Straps merge
      2. Buckle
II. Warm up
   A. Fire motor
      1. Feel rumble
      2. Hear blower
      3. Smell nitro
   B. Dry hop tires
III. Drag
   A. Green light
   B. Thrust
   C. Braking
      1. Regular brakes
      2. Parachutes
   D. Success
      1. Scoreboard
      2. Feeling

Stage Three

Write On separate paper, write and then revise your paragraph or essay as many times as necessary for **c**oherence, **l**anguage (usage, tone, and diction), **u**nity, **e**mphasis, **s**upport, and **s**entences (**CLUESS**). Read your work aloud to hear and correct any grammatical errors or awkward-sounding sentences.

Edit any problems in fundamentals, such as **c**apitalization, **o**missions, **p**unctuation, and **s**pelling (**COPS**).

Final Draft
[The topic sentence and concluding sentence are single-underlined.]

THE DRAG
Mike Kavanagh

Descriptive   Narration
                  Situation

                  Conflict

                  Struggle

                  Outcome
                  Meaning

As I climb into the cockpit for my drag, I hear the roar of the crowd and the thundering blasts in the background. Engulfed in an iron cage, I strap myself down. First over the shoulders, then from the waist, and finally from between my legs the straps merge and then buckle at my belly button. This is to ensure my stability in the ironclad, two-hundred-and-thirty-miles-per-hour street rocket. My crew then signals me to fire up the three thousand horsepower motor mounted at my back. With the push of a button, I feel the rumble of the motor, hear the scream of the blower, and smell the distinctive odor of nitro in the air. I then move up to the starting line to dry hop my rear tires for better traction. I quickly thrust the accelerator pedal to the floor. I am shot forward about two hundred feet. Letting off the accelerator pedal and pulling the brake handle allows me to come to a slow stop. A low continuous thump from the motor echoes through my head as I reverse back to the starting line. As I creep forward, I stage the beast and wait for the lights to change to green. This feels like an eternity. The lights flicker yellow, yellow, yellow, GREEN! I stab the pedal to the floor. I am flung thirteen hundred and twenty feet faster than I can say my name. When I pull the brake and parachute handles simultaneously, I lunge back from the force of the billowing chutes. I climb out of the jungle gym and look up at the scoreboard, which reads 5.26 seconds at 230.57. There is nothing else like rocketing down the track at 230 m.p.h.

EXERCISE 12   Discussion and Critical Thinking

1. Is this paragraph mainly descriptive, mainly narrative, or equally balanced?

2. Annotate in the margin and underline at least one image of sound, sight, touch, and smell.

3. Although you probably have not drag raced competitively, you can get a good sense of what it is like to do so by reading this paragraph. What details and what phrasing convince you that the author is writing from experience?

4. What is the dominant impression?

5. List four words of transition used in the first five sentences.

READING-BASED WRITING

Rituals as Comfort Food for the Soul

ADAM RENSKY

Student Adam Rensky selected this assignment from a list: "Write a brief reading-based reaction to a reading selection from your textbook. Demonstrate your understanding of the text by analyzing it and relating it to your experience. Include quotations from and references to the text to convey the author's techniques of description and narration, and use MLA style in providing credit for your citations and in listing the work cited [see Chapter 1]."

1   When I was a child, my father and I used to take walks. Our path never varied: South from our house to make a right turn at the second corner, on past my elementary school, then across from the Youth Center where I had Boy Scout meetings, by a middle school I would later attend, and down an oak-lined street before turning back on my home street. We did that more than a hundred times. Recently on a nostalgic day, I drove the route to measure what usually seemed a short distance at the time, but was exactly one and a quarter miles.

Topic sentence

Transition

2   Looking back, I now know the walks were as valuable as comfort food, though there was no apparent calculation by my father to make them so. Those were the times when I could say what I wanted to say and ask what I wanted to ask. My father talked about the hardships and fulfillments of growing up in the Hill Country of Texas. I talked about the joys and agonies of a kid growing up right there in the city of Covina, California. Geographical differences, a lot of time, and a lot of cares seemed to blend in stories and questions and answers and peaceful silences, as we walked.

Topic sentence
Transition
Blended quotation

Summary and interpretation follow

Quotation

Quotation

Blended quotation

Blended quotation

3   "Closets and Keepsakes" by Willi Coleman carries the same theme, as her memories are brought back by the sight of "a straightening comb" and other relics of the past (101). Her essay is an account of a comforting ritual with her mother. Each week as a child, she sat on the floor, with her head between her mother's knees, and her mother combed her hair and talked with her. That was Coleman's special time. It was as satisfying as comfort food, the childhood treat that somehow still evokes soothing memories when life cries out for relief, as it did long ago. She says, "Our sessions together could halt time, still waters, and predict the future" (101). Both mother and child unburdened their feelings, and the occasion occurred each week at the same time, at the same place, and in the same way. Looking back, she knows that hair care was always secondary to talking—to talking freely. She says, "It never crossed my mind to hold back the hurt, fear, or anger" (102). Her mother, who worked weekdays as a housekeeper for those who were often disrespectful, had plenty of her own problems, but she "talked with ease and listened with undivided attention" (101). Those were special, comforting moments between just mother and child. Coleman "moved away from those Saturday hair sessions, as if from a safe harbor" (102).

Relating text to experience

4   Much has been said about comfort foods, but the fact is that parent-child rituals—just little repeated activities, such as playing board games, changing oil in the car, gardening, playing catch, or shooting baskets—have provided and, at least in recollection, still can provide special comfort too. For Willi Coleman, comfort was sitting on the floor, getting her hair combed and swapping worries, complaints, and stories. For me, it was that mile and a quarter walk, doing the same kind of thing that Willi Coleman did, for the same reasons. It is later that one puts ever-upgrading labels of meaning on experiences such as those.

Work Cited

Coleman, Willi. "Closets and Keepsakes." *Paragraphs and Essays: A Worktext with Readings.* Ed. Lee Brandon. 8th ed. Boston: Houghton, 2001. 101–3. Print.

CAREER-RELATED WRITING

The content of your writing will, of course, depend on your academic and vocational experiences. If you have a job or have worked for pay, you can write narratives about your experiences. Perhaps you are already in the career field of your choice; if so, you could write about a specific event that has given you insight into that field or a reason for your commitment to it. Or perhaps you have already taken college chasses relating to your career choices; then you could write a report—incident, progress, or investigative—about something you have witnessed or read about, using a standard form (such as the one that follows) as you practice a kind of writing you will likely use at the workplace.

Incident Report of the Falling Shoppers

DOUGLAS ROSS

As an optional assignment, student Douglas Ross had the choice of writing a narrative about an event that occurred at work, especially one that was written up as a report or could have been. One event stood out in Ross's mind. He had written an incident report about an accident that occurred in his presence when he worked for a regional market chain. The report had been favorably reviewed by a district manager, and Ross was promoted soon after that time to a full-time senior checker. Here, he recreates what he reported on that day, composing a form similar to the store template for incident reports.

Employee Report

Form 117-Incident

- ☒ Accident
- ☐ Reported theft
- ☐ Disturbance
- ☐ Dangerous condition
- ☐ Lost child
- ☐ Vandalism
- ☐ Health emergency
- ☐ Other

Business and Location: [Name and address of business omitted by student request]

Time: July 27, 2009, at 09:33 a.m.

Employee Name: Douglas Ross

Situation

Incident Report: At 09:33 a.m. I was working the cash register at Station 3 when I saw an elderly couple approach my empty customer slot from the nearby newspaper, book, and magazine rack. The woman was

Conflict

Struggle

walking ahead of the man, who carried a small bag of fruit in one hand and a loaf of fresh bakery bread in the other. A younger woman with a shopping cart full of items had also spotted the open slot and headed that way. The wife started walking faster, turned to her husband, said something I couldn't hear, and motioned for him to follow her. He increased his pace and followed. Then he staggered and lost his balance and lunged forward, hitting his wife, who had turned away from him. Thrown off balance, she also lunged forward and struck a display of pastries, knocking it down as she fell to her knees. By this time, her husband had fallen, striking his head on the tile floor.

I came to their aid quickly, helping the woman to her feet. The man rolled over and sat there. I said I would call paramedics. The woman asked the man if he were hurt. He said he would be all right. I got on the phone and called Supervisor Kennedy, who was out at the loading dock. He said I should call paramedics anyway, because the man was still sitting on the floor.

While we were waiting for the paramedics, the man took an oblong loop of stiff plastic binding material from his foot and showed it to me. He explained that it had apparently been left by the magazine rack where it had been used to tie a bundle of newspapers. He said he had stepped on one side of it and, when he did, the other side of it popped up like a small hula hoop and caught his other foot as he was about to take another step. Then he fell and hit his wife, who also fell.

Outcome

The paramedics came and examined the husband and wife, Carl and Ruth Sutton [names changed]. The paramedics asked them about abrasions and pains. They said they needed no further medical care or examination. The paramedics completed a report on the particulars, now attached to this one. Mr. and Mrs. Sutton said they would go to their family doctor.

Supervisor Kennedy took down additional information and gave them his business card. Mrs. Sutton asked me if I had witnessed what happened. I said I saw them fall. She looked at my badge and wrote my name and employee number down in her address book. I gave the loop of plastic binding to Supervisor Kennedy.

Meaning

Recommendation: When stocking the shelves with any items that are bound, the binding should be carefully disposed of. As a further precaution, it would be a good idea to clip the loops of plastic bindings so that no one could trip over them even if they were left on the floor.

Suggested Topics and Prompts for Writing Descriptive Narration

STUDENT COMPANION SITE
For additional practice, visit www.cengage .com/devenglish/ brandon/PE11e.

You will find a blank Writing Process Worksheet on page 6 of this book and on the Student Companion Site. It can be photocopied or printed out, filled in, and submitted with your assignment, if your instructor directs you to do so.

READING-BASED WRITING

Reading-based writing requires you to read critically, write a reply that shows you understand what you have read, and give credit for ideas you borrow and words you quote. The form can be a summary, a reaction, or a two-part response (with separated summary and reaction). Documentation, in which you give credit for borrowed ideas and words, can be either formal (MLA) or informal, as directed by your instructor. Both the forms of reading-based writing and documentation are discussed with examples in Chapter 1. Definitions of the three forms follow. Any form can be used for any reading selection in this book.

Summary

- The summary is a statement presenting only the main points of what you have read by using different wording without altering the meaning, adding information, or showing bias.
- It is the purest form of reading-based writing.

Reaction

- In the reaction, the meaning of what you have read will be central to your topic sentence of your paragraph or to the thesis of your essay.
- Although the reaction is not a personal narrative by itself, it may include personal experience to explain elements of the text. For example, if your source is about driving styles, your own experiences as a driver or an observer of drivers could be relevant in your analysis of the text.
- The reaction may incorporate a summary to convey a broad view of what you have read, but your summary should never be the main part of your reaction.

The Two-Part Response

- The two-part response separates the summary from the reaction.
- This form will give you practice in separating your objective summary in the first part from your more personal evaluation, interpretation, or application in the second part, the reaction.

READING-BASED WRITING TOPICS

"The Story of a Well-Made Shield"

1. Using what you have learned from Momaday, sketch a shield design for yourself or someone you have known, or know of (family member, friend, someone in the news, or a fictional character from a television program or movie), basing the design on a defining moment in the subject's life. Then write a descriptive narration in which you explain what Momaday means when he writes, "My shield stands for me." Refer to the essay and use quotations. Submit your writing with your drawing of the proposed shield. If time permits, transfer your design to an improvised shield made of poster board or cardboard cut from a box.

"No Tears for Frankie"

2. Write a reactive paragraph or essay that includes an integrated summary of the text and comments on the author's behavior and feelings. Use quotations and

references. Under the circumstances, would you have expected Greenlee to consider any degree of forgiveness for her deceased tormentor? What if there had been grieving family members in the audience? Although Frankie seemed to be the worst kind of bully, is there anything that might be learned about him— call on your knowledge of bullies—that might make him seem less malicious?

"More"

3. Write a summary of "More."

4. Write a two-part response to "More." Following the summary, write a reaction in which you discuss how Ortiz Cofer makes the house seem alive by personalizing it and by comparing it to a sea creature. Use references and quotations. Consider extending that discussion by relating Ortriz Cofer's observations to a house you know or remember well. Concentrating on an individual room and the overall layout, you would probably explain how over a period of time that house took on the character of those who lived there.

"Yearning for Love"

5. Assume that you are a psychologist or the personal-advice columnist for a large newspaper, and Chantra Shastri has written her paragraph to you. Realizing that she has a life ahead of her and her family is asking her to choose between independence and family, what would you suggest that she should do? Another possible extension of the issue: What advice would you give Shastri's parents if they wrote to you and said that most American marriages end in divorce and that they, the parents, could make a better decision for a sound marriage, one that is more mature and nonemotional, one that is based on what they knew about both Shastri and the young man they had already selected?

"Rituals as Comfort Food for the Soul"

6. Write a reaction in which you discuss your own repeated comforting experience similar to those discussed by Rensky. Include direct references to and quotations from his essay. Use techniques of descriptive narration as you write about your own comfort sessions—a repeated activity that brought you closer to a parent by providing you with occasions for talking. Consider activities such as cooking, shooting baskets, playing catch, hiking, shopping, playing board games, gardening, washing the car, driving to and from school, and so on.

GENERAL TOPICS

7. Write about an occasion when you finally decided to do some work you had sworn not to, such as cooking fast foods, mowing lawns, working in the fields, babysitting, or working at the car wash. Explain why you changed your mind and what you learned from the experience. For a helpful model on a similar topic, review "One More Time" by Gary Soto on page 115.

8. Describe and narrate an exciting moment you have experienced or witnessed. It need not be a sporting event, but it can be. For a helpful model on a similar topic, review "The Drag" on page 127.

9. Write a descriptive narration based on a topic sentence such as this: "One experience showed me what _____ [pain, fear, anger, love, sacrifice, dedication, joy, sorrow, shame, pride] was really like."

10. Write a descriptive narration about a fire, a riot, an automobile accident, a rescue, shoplifting, or some other unusual happening you witnessed.

11. Write a descriptive narration that supports (or opposes) the idea of a familiar saying such as one of the following:

    a. You never know who a friend is until you need one.

    b. A person who is absent is soon forgotten.

    c. Better to be alone than to be in bad company.

    d. Borrowing is the mother of trouble.

    e. A person who marries for money earns it.

    f. The person who lies down with dogs gets up with fleas.

    g. Never give advice to a friend.

    h. If it isn't broken, don't fix it.

    i. Nice people finish last.

    j. Every person has a price.

    k. You get what you pay for.

    l. Haste makes waste.

    m. The greatest remedy for anger is delay.

Objective Description

Give your topic some kind of narrative framework or purpose beyond simply writing a description. As you develop your purpose, consider the knowledge and attitudes of your readers. You might be describing a lung for a biology instructor, a geode for a geology instructor, a painting for an art instructor, or a comet for an astronomy instructor. Or maybe you could pose as the seller of an object, such as a desk, a table, or a bicycle. Describe one of the following topics:

12. A simple object, such as a pencil, cup, sock, dollar bill, coin, ring, or notebook

13. A human organ, such as a heart, liver, lung, or kidney

14. A visible part of your body, such as a toe, a finger, an ear, a nose, or an eye

15. A construction, such as a room, desk, chair, commode, or table

16. A mechanism, such as a bicycle, tricycle, wagon, car, motorcycle, can opener, or stapler

Subjective Description

The narrative framework (something happening) is especially useful in providing order and vitality to descriptive writing. Here are three possibilities for you to consider:

17. Personalize a trip to a supermarket, a stadium, an airport, an unusual house, a mall, the beach, a court, a church, a club, a business, the library, or the police station. Describe a simple conflict in one of those places while emphasizing descriptive details.

18. Pick a high point in any event and describe the most important few seconds. Think how a scene can be captured by a video camera and then give focus by applying the dominant impression principle, using relevant images of sight, sound, taste, touch, and smell. The event might be a ball game, graduation ceremony, wedding ceremony, funeral, dance, concert, family gathering, class meeting, rally, riot, robbery, fight, proposal, or meal. Focus on subject material that you can cover effectively in the passage you write.

19. Pick a moment when you were angry, sad, happy, confused, lost, rattled, afraid, courageous, meek, depressed, or elated. Describe how the total context of the situation contributed to your feeling.

CROSS-CURRICULAR TOPICS

20. Write a paragraph or an essay of descriptive narration about a visit, an observation, or a field trip to a museum, a concert, an institution, or a workplace.

21. Write about a unit of time in which feverish action occurs. You could select a pivotal moment in history (the assassination of a president, a turning point in a battle, the first encounter between two groups of people), in science (the discovery of a process or product), in music (a composer conducting his or her own musical composition), or in art appreciation (a painter finishing a famous painting). Content from other courses will provide most of the framework; your imagination can provide the details. Be inventive, but base your invention on what you know of individuals and the time period. Consult textbooks. Talk to instructors.

CAREER-RELATED TOPICS

22. Adapt the form on page 110 for one of the following topics. For a helpful model on a similar topic, review "Incident Report of the Falling Shoppers" on pages 129–130.

    • Write a descriptive narrative account of an encounter between a customer and a salesperson. Explain what went right and what went wrong.
    • Write a descriptive narrative of an employee handling a customer's complaint. Evaluate the procedure.
    • Using a workplace form you are familiar with, write an incident report about an event such as an accident, a theft, or a disturbance.

23. Write a descriptive narrative account of a work-related encounter between a manager and a worker and briefly explain the significance of the event.

24. Describe a well-furnished, well-functioning office or other work area. Be specific.

25. Describe a computer-related product; give special attention to the dominant trait that gives the product its reputation.

26. Describe a person groomed and attired for a particular job or interview. Be specific in giving details pertaining to the person and in naming the place or situation. Describe yourself from a detached point of view if you like.

WRITER'S GUIDELINES: Descriptive Narration

Narration

1. Include these parts so that you will be sure you have a complete narrative:

   - situation
   - conflict
   - struggle
   - outcome
   - meaning

2. Use these techniques or devices as appropriate:

   - images that appeal to the senses (sight, smell, taste, hearing, touch) and other details to advance action
   - dialogue
   - transitional devices (such as *next, soon, after, later, then, finally, when, following*) to indicate chronological order

3. Give details concerning action.

4. Be consistent with point of view and verb tense.

5. Keep in mind that most narratives written as college assignments will have an expository purpose; that is, they explain a specific idea.

6. Consider working with a short time frame for short writing assignments. The scope would usually be no more than one incident of brief duration for one paragraph. For example, writing about an entire graduation ceremony might be too complicated, but concentrating on the moment when you walked forward to receive the diploma or the moment when the relatives and friends come down on the field could work very well.

Description

In objective description, use direct, practical language appealing mainly to the sense of sight. In subjective description, appeal to the reader's feelings, especially through the use of figurative language and the use of images of sight, sound, smell, taste, and touch. Use concrete, specific words if appropriate.

Apply these questions to your writing:

- What is the subject?
- What is the dominant impression I am trying to convey?
- What details support the dominant impression?
- What is the situation?
- What is the order of the details?
- What is the point of view? (Is it first or third person? involved or objective?)

Consider giving the description a narrative framework. Include some action. Use the writing process.

- Write and then revise your paragraph or essay as many times as necessary for **c**oherence, **l**anguage (usage, tone, and diction), **u**nity, **e**mphasis, **s**upport, and **s**entences (**CLUESS**).

- Read your work aloud to hear and correct any grammatical errors or awkward-sounding sentences.
- Edit any problems in fundamentals, such as **c**apitalization, **o**missions, **p**unctuation, and **s**pelling (**COPS**).

Incident Report

1. Identify the kind of problem and the location. This may be part of a form provided by your employer.

2. Indicate when the problem occurred.

3. Provide an account of what happened.

4. Write in the first person (*I*); you are the one who is writing the report.

5. Start with the date, time, and your reason for involvement.

6. Include quotation marks if you use the words of anyone reporting on the incident and give the name of the person whose words you use.

7. Use facts, not opinions.

8. Remain objective. Do not step outside your work expertise and become a psychologist, philosopher, physician, or moralist.

9. Use past tense. You are writing about something that has already happened.

10. Use mostly active-voice verbs. For example, write, "Mills wrote the report," not "The report was written by Mills."

11. Identify those involved. Drop the titles, such as Mr., Mrs., Dr., and so on. After the first reference to the person in the report, use only the surname or the first initial and the surname.

12. If appropriate, write a recommendation for what could be done to avoid a repeat of such an incident.

Exemplification:
Writing with Examples

WHEN TO USE EXEMPLIFICATION

FOR COLLEGE WRITING ASSIGNMENTS

- In all classes, probably the most common constructive comment on a paper is "Be specific." That problem can often be remedied by giving examples. If you write only, "Women were active participants in the War of Independence," you will generalize. But if you add, "Two female heroes were teenager Sybil Ludington, who outraced Paul Revere to warn the colonists in Lexington, and a soldier's wife, Mary Hayes (AKA Molly Pitcher), who not only served soldiers water but also fought beside them," you will provide specific supportive information.

- Across the curriculum, exemplification strengthens sentences, paragraphs, essays, reports, research papers, case studies, and field-trip reports.

IN CAREERS AND AT THE WORKPLACE

- As you look for that initial job in your career field or a better job later on, examples will help you connect commonplace generalizations, as found in most applications, with revealing and vivid accounts of your abilities and accomplishments.

- At the workplace, examples can provide crucial information in incident reports, accident reports, case studies, recommendations, evaluations, support for proposals, and testimonials for products and services.

EXEMPLIFICATION IN A CARTOON

THE QUIGMANS   by Buddy Hickerson

B. Hickerson, copyright Los Angeles Times Syndicate. Reprinted by permission.

"So what do you have that's fresh?"

Writing Exemplification

Exemplification means using examples to explain, convince, or amuse. Lending interest and information to writing, exemplification is one of the most common and effective ways of developing ideas. Examples may be developed in a sentence or more, or they may be only phrases or even single words, as in the following sentence: "Children like packaged breakfast foods, such as Wheaties, Cheerios, and Rice Krispies."

CHARACTERISTICS OF GOOD EXAMPLES

As supporting information, the best examples are specific, vivid, and representative. These three qualities are closely linked; collectively, they must support the topic sentence of a paragraph and the thesis of an essay.

You use examples to inform or convince your reader. Of course, an example by itself does not necessarily prove anything. We know that examples can be found on either side of an argument, even at the extreme edges. Therefore, in addition to providing specific examples so that your reader can follow you precisely and vivid ones so that your reader will be interested, you should choose examples that are representative. Representative examples are examples that your reader can consider, accept as appropriate, and, in some instances, even match with examples of his or her own. If you are writing about cheating and you give one specific, vivid, and representative example, your reader should be able to say, "That's exactly what happens. I can imagine just how the incident occurred." The reader might even have in mind examples that are similar.

TECHNIQUES FOR FINDING EXAMPLES: LISTING AND CLUSTERING

Writing a good paragraph or essay of exemplification begins, as always, with prewriting. The techniques you use will depend on what you are writing about. If you were writing about cheating at school, you might work effectively with a list, perhaps including a few insights into your topic if you have not already formulated your controlling statement. The following is one such list compiled by student Lara Olivas as she developed her essay in the demonstration on pages 156–158; she has circled items she thinks she can use.

Student Cheating
When I copied homework
Looking at a friend's test answers
A student with hand signals
Jake and his electronic system
Time for planned cheating
Those who got caught
(A person who bought a research paper)
Jess, who copied from me
The Internet "Cheaters" source
The two students who exchanged identities
(More work than it's worth)
(More stress than it's worth)
The teacher's assistant and his friends
(The girl from the biology class)

If you are pretty well settled on your subject and you expect to use several different kinds of examples, clustering may work very well for you. Student Garabed Yegavian, whose paragraph appears on pages 154–155, first used clustering to explore and then transferred much of his information to an outline. Yegavian's cluster is shown here.

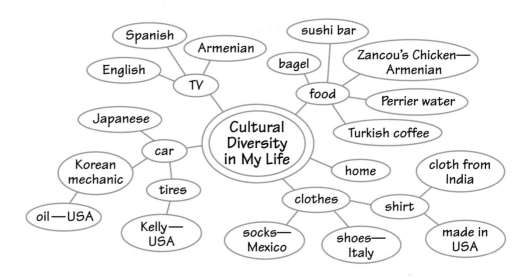

NUMBER AND ORDER OF EXAMPLES

After you have explored your topic and collected information, you must decide whether to use only one example with a detailed explanation, a few examples with a bit less information, or a cluster of examples. A well-stated topic sentence or thesis will guide you in making this decision. When you are writing about a personal topic, you will probably have far more examples than you can use.

If your example is an incident or a series of incidents, you will probably use time order, reinforcing that arrangement with terms such as *next, then, soon, later, last,* and *finally*. If your examples exist in space (maybe in different parts of a room), then you would use space references (*up, down, left, right, east, west, north,* and *south*). Arranging examples by emphasis means going from the most important example to the least important or from the least to the most important.

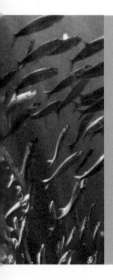

Transitional Words

Consider using the following transitional words to improve coherence by connecting ideas with ideas, sentences with sentences, and paragraphs with paragraphs.

FOR EXEMPLIFICATION: for example, as an example, another example, for instance, such as, including, specifically, especially, in particular, to illustrate, as an illustration, that is, i.e. (meaning *that is*), e.g. (meaning *for example*)

FOR ALL PATTERNS OF WRITING: The <u>H</u>OTSHOT <u>CAT</u> words: <u>H</u>owever, <u>O</u>ther-wise, <u>T</u>herefore, <u>S</u>imilarly, <u>H</u>ence, <u>O</u>n the other hand, <u>T</u>hen, <u>C</u>onsequently, <u>A</u>lso, <u>T</u>hus (See pages 427–428 for additional transitional words.)

FINDING PATTERNS IN PHOTOS

EXERCISE 1   A Text-Based Activity for Groups or Individuals

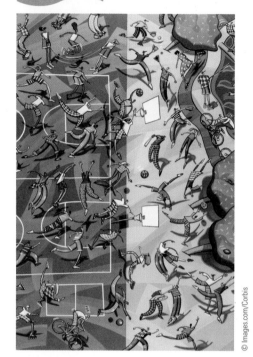

Crowded park

This photo of a painting shows a crowded park. Imagine that you are there in the painting. You have decided to get some exercise by just walking around. You need to clear your mind so that you can write a composition for your English class. You are searching for a topic in which you can use some specific examples to illustrate a point about something within your neighborhood. As you stroll, you begin looking at all the different ways others are getting their exercise. In fact, you take out a notepad and begin jotting down the different ways people get exercise. You find fifteen different forms. List these forms of exercise here:

1. _____   9. _____

2. _____   10. _____

3. _____   11. _____

4. _____   12. _____

5. _____   13. _____

6. _____   14. _____

7. _____   15. _____

8. _____

You now have an idea for writing a paragraph or an essay about your little crowded park. You could use specific examples from your observations to write on this topic: "My little neighborhood park is usually quite crowded, but people find many enjoyable ways to get their exercise."

If your instructor directs, write a paragraph or an essay in which you use numerous examples from your imaginary stroll within the photo. If you like, make some of the examples more specific by giving names (made-up names, celebrity names, or names of people you know) to those who are exercising. To be really imaginative, you could briefly interview a few of these imaginary people.

Practicing Patterns of Exemplification

The simple patterns in the following exercise will help you see the relationship between purpose and example(s).

EXERCISE 2   Listing to Brainstorm Examples

Make a list of examples that could support the following topic sentence or thesis. Then circle four you might use in writing a paragraph or an essay on that topic. The first item is provided.

Controlling idea: Some people let television watching interfere with their real lives.

Specific occasions where you have observed people watching television instead of doing what they intended or expected to be doing:

Family gathering on a holiday _____

_____

_____

_____

_____

_____

_____

Readings for Critical Thinking, Discussion, and Writing

READING STRATEGIES AND OBJECTIVES

Underlining and annotating these reading selections will help you answer the questions that follow the selections, discuss the material in class, and prepare for reading-based writing assignments. As you underline and annotate, pay special attention to the author's writing skills, logic, and message, and consider the relevance of the material to your own experiences and values.

Many selections begin with a Mindset suggestion that can help you create a readiness for connecting with what you are about to read.

PARAGRAPH

Dropping Way Out*

DAVID LEVINE

Every day, three thousand students give up on high school—for good. They push open the doors and walk out. They turn their backs on school. Drop out, way out. Here we have one of numerous examples of dropout experiences discussed by freelance author David Levine in his essay "I'm Outta Here."

MINDSET

Lock It In

Imagine you are seventeen and you have just dropped out of high school and into a minimum-pay job. How long do you hold that breath of freedom before the stress begins?

Situation

Think about it. In some ways it seems perfect. Quit school. Just say No—no more pressure, no more stupid rules, no more deadlines, no more uncaring teachers, no more snobby, clique-conscious peers. Nearly every high school student has imagined what it would be like. Beth Kierny did more than imagine. A few months into her senior year at Columbia High School, in East Greenbush, New York, she dropped out of school. Beth is a shy eighteen-year-old with dark, curly hair who hated getting up early for classes. She thought it would be great. She'd just get a job, sleep in later, work at some cool place instead of sitting in boring classes, and lead an easier, more interesting life.

Conflict

But without a diploma, Beth found it difficult to get a job. She had to finally settle for one at the Hessmart gas station a few miles down Route 20. Being the youngest and newest employee, she got stuck working the worst shifts. Often she had to get up even earlier than she had to for school—

Struggle

sometimes she had to be *at work* by 7:00 a.m. Or she'd have to work the midnight shift, which was scary because one never knew if the place might get held up. Or she'd have to work weekends, when her friends were all out partying. The money was terrible—at minimum wage she cleared maybe

Outcome
Meaning
(implied: Don't drop out)

$90 a week—and she couldn't afford a car, so she had to take cabs to and from work, which cost almost ten bucks a day. That didn't leave much for her share of the $425 a month in rent on their small apartment behind the Burger King.

EXERCISE 3 Discussion and Critical Thinking

1. What topic is illustrated?

2. Does Levine use one example or many examples? Why?

3. What other pattern of writing is used to develop the example?

* Title by authors of this textbook.

ESSAYS

Little Brother Is Watching

ERIC GALL

On his YouTube listing, Eric Gall calls himself a "Toronto ad guy (writer/creative director), music guy (composer), video guy (shooter), and book guy," who attended Queen's University. As a freelancer, he has written for the National Post *and the* Queen's Journal.

1   In late 2006, Michael Richards, Seinfeld's shock-haired neighbor Kramer, found out the hard way that messing up in public is now a whole lot messier. Thanks to the cell phone video camera and the Internet's latest killer app—YouTube.com—Richards' racist meltdown at a heckler during a standup routine in L.A. was viewed by millions. As Richards discovered, Little Brother is watching, again and again, and he is e-mailing the link to all his friends.

2   Back in 2005, when Chad Hurley, Steve Chen, and Jawed Karim founded YouTube, they thought they were building a place where ordinary people could share their favorite camcorder movies, TV moments, and, yes, cell phone clips. And share they did. One would have to have been living on one of the more desolate craters on Pluto not to have seen the Backstreet Boys' "I Want It That Way" as lip-synched by two Chinese pranksters. Arguably the site's tipping point, their dorm-made video spawned a million imitations and clicked YouTube to the top of every browser bookmark list.

3   What Chad, Steve, and Jawed couldn't have predicted was that they were bringing George Orwell's dystopic *1984* to life in a way no one saw coming. While Orwell's protagonist, Winston Smith, lived a miserable existence, at least he knew he was being watched as he carried out life's mundane tasks. It was not the same case with University of Missouri quarterback Chase Daniel, whose moment of fame came during a game on November 4, 2006. He didn't anticipate being filmed as he sat on the bench performing his own digital download—from nose to mouth—and having his little picnic uploaded onto the World Wide Web. Students worldwide have also happily uploaded cell phone videos of teachers "losing it" in class—some actually hitting their students. Many of these educators, it is alleged, were pushed to the brink by their pupils for the very purpose of being surreptitiously filmed.

4   Beyond the facility to humiliate, there is a positive side to the power of YouTube. Two Los Angeles cops were caught on a cell phone camera "subduing" an alleged perp (another of the site's recent top hits). While their YouTube moment now has them slapping their own foreheads, it demonstrates that "the whole world is in fact watching." So what better way is there to blow the whistle than to use the powers of online video blogs, especially if you've tried and failed by every other means? That's what Michael DeKort, former Lockheed Martin engineer on the US Coast Guard's "Deepwater" project, did when nobody would listen to his concerns about serious security flaws the company and the coast guard were determined to ignore. His ten-minute "kitchen confidential" shot on grainy home video finally caught the eye of the navy, congress and, crucially, other Lockheed and coast guard personnel eager to corroborate his story—not to mention the media and two dozen lawyers eager to help him advance and defend his case.

5   Other "good" causes are also getting their fifteen minutes of infamy via the site. Take the Canadian-made Dove commercial that shows an ordinary woman being transformed through the magic of technology into an impossibly beautiful billboard model in just ninety seconds. Within hours of its arrival on the site, the ad was on its way to becoming a global phenomenon—selling

soap and reinforcing the idea that images, especially digitally produced ones, can't be trusted.

6   Orwell's Big Brother and YouTube's Little Brother both have potent methods of exerting thought control over those who mess up in public. For his crimes against the Party, *1984*'s protagonist Winston Smith faced compulsory re-education (also known as torture and brainwashing) courtesy of the Thought Police. For Michael Richards, the L.A. police, and anyone else caught in an embarrassing scenario, there is "voluntary" cultural sensitivity training, along with anger management classes and public apologies, which ironically are also available on—you guessed it—YouTube.

7   But if we're smart, we won't wait until our "Kramer moment" is being end-lessly replayed by sniggering surfers from Moose Jaw to Mogadishu. We'll just make sure we never do anything embarrassing, illegal, or stupid ever again. Right?

8   Yeah, sure. See you on YouTube.

EXERCISE 4   Vocabulary Highlights

Write a short definition of each word as it is used in the essay. (Paragraph numbers are given in parentheses.) Be prepared to use these words in sentences.

spawned (2)   corroborate (4)

dystopic (3)   infamy (5)

mundane (3)   phenomenon (5)

surreptitiously (3)   scenario (6)

subduing (4)   ironically (6)

EXERCISE 5   Discussion and Critical Thinking

1. Overall, according to Gall, is YouTube more harmful or more helpful to society? for what reason(s)?

2. Does the example of Michael Richards (Kramer) show a positive or negative effect of "Little Brother"?

3. There is much discussion of Big Brother in the novel *1984* about a science fiction (or an eerily current) time when society is under almost constant surveillance. What is wrong with having cameras almost everywhere?

4. Should there be laws against "staging"—provoking people into committing irrational or embarrassing acts with the purpose of setting up those people to be filmed for YouTube or other sites? Why or why not?

5. Does the author take up the issue of existing laws or the need for laws to protect citizens against unwelcome filming?

6. In what way does Gall suggest that the current filming is even worse than that practiced against Winston Smith in *1984*?

7. Why does Gall begin and end with references to Michael Richards?

Who's Cheap?

ADAIR LARA

Adair Lara is an award-winning newspaper columnist for the San Francisco Chronicle *and the author of five books and dozens of magazine articles. Her best-selling memoir about raising a teenage daughter,* Hold Me Close, Let Me Go, *was published by Random House (2001). Her specialty is writing about her experiences in first-person point of view.*

MINDSET

Lock It In

Imagine you are the female of a heterosexual couple on a first date, and the food server leaves the check on the table evenly between you and the guy. Would you say, "Let me pay," "I'll pay," "Let me pay half," "I'll pay half," or nothing?

1   It was our second date, and we had driven one hundred miles up the coast in my car to go abalone-diving. When I stopped to fill the tank at the only gas station in sight, Craig scowled and said, "You shouldn't get gas here. It's a rip-off."

2   But he didn't offer to help pay. And that night, after dinner in a restaurant, he leaned over and whispered intimately, "You get the next one." Though he was sensitive and smart, and looked unnervingly good, Craig was as cheap as a two-dollar watch.

3   This is not an ethical dilemma, you're all shouting. Lose the guy, and fast.

4   Lose the guy? Is this fair? My friend Jill is always heading for the john when the check comes, but I don't hear anybody telling me to lose her. And she's far from the only cheap woman I know. A lot of us make decent money these days, yet I haven't seen women knocking over tables in fights for the lunch tab. In fact, many women with 20/20 vision seem to have trouble distinguishing the check from the salt, pepper, and other tabletop items. But if a guy forgets to chip in for gas or gloats too long over the deal he got on his Nikes, he's had it.

5   Why is this double standard so enduring? One reason is that, while neither sex has a monopoly on imperfection, there *are* such things as flaws that are much more distasteful in one sex than in the other. Women seem especially unpleasant when they get drunk, swear or even insist on pursuing an argument they'll never win. And men seem beneath contempt when they're cheap.

6   These judgments are a holdover from the days when women stayed home and men earned the money. Though that old order has passed, we still associate men with paying for things. And besides, there's just something appealing about generosity. Buying something for someone is, in a sense, taking care of her. The gesture says, "I like you, I want to give you something." If it comes from a man to whom we are about to entrust our hearts, this is a comforting message. We miss it when it's not forthcoming.

7   Then why *not* dump on cheap men?

8   Some men are just skinflints and that's it. My friend Skye broke up with her boyfriend because when they went to the movies he doled out M&Ms to her one at a time. Craig, my date back at the gas station, liked to talk about how he'd bought his car—which in California, where I live, is like buying shoes—as a special present to himself.

9   This kind of cheapness is ingrained; you'll never change it. That guy who parks two miles away to avoid the parking lot fee was once a little boy who saved his birthday money without being told to. Now he's a man who studies the menu and sputters, "Ten dollars for *pasta*?" His stinginess will always grate on you, since he is likely to dole out his feelings as parsimoniously as his dollars.

10   On the other hand, I know a wonderful man, crippled with debts from a former marriage, who had to break up with a woman because she never paid her share, and he was simply running out of money. Though she earned a lot more than he did, she couldn't expand her definition of masculinity to include "sometimes needs to go Dutch treat."

11   To men, such women seem grasping. One friend of mine, who spends a lot of money on concerts and theater and sailing but not on restaurants he considers overpriced, has evolved a strategy for women who are annoyed at the bohemian places he favors. If his date complains, he offers to donate to the charity of her choice the cost of an evening at her favorite spot. "Some women have bad values," he says, "And if the idea of spending money on a good cause, but not on her, makes her livid, I know she's one of them."

12   I had a bracing encounter with my own values when I told my friend Danny the humorous (I thought) story of a recent date who asked if I wanted a drink after a concert, then led me to the nearest water fountain.

13   Danny gave one of his wry looks. "Let's get this straight," he said, laughing. "As a woman, you are so genetically precious that you deserve attention just because you grace the planet. So, of course, he should buy you drinks. He should also drive the car, open the door, ask you to dance, coax you to bed. And then when you feel properly pampered, you can let out that little whine about how he doesn't treat you as an equal."

14   On second thought, I guess I'd rather buy my own drink.

15   So here's the deal. Before dumping a guy for ordering the sundowner dinner or the house white, better first make sure that you aren't burdening the relationship with outdated ideas of how the sexes should behave. Speaking for myself, I know that if a man looks up from the check and says, "Your share is eleven dollars," part of me remembers that, according to my mother, *my* share was to look charming in my flowered blouse.

16   Wanting the man to pay dies hard. What many of us do now is *offer* to split the check, then let our purses continue to dangle from the chair as we give him time to realize that the only proper response is to whip out his own wallet.

17   Is this a game worth playing? It's up to you, but consider that offering to help pay implies that the check is his responsibility. And this attitude can work both ways. My sister gets angry when her husband offers to help clean the house. "Like it's *my* house!" she snorts.

18   Like it's *his* check.

EXERCISE 6   Vocabulary Highlights

Write a short definition of each word as it is used in the essay. (Paragraph numbers are given in parentheses.) Be prepared to use these words in sentences.

intimately (2)	grate (9)
unnervingly (2)	dole (9)
ethical (3)	parsimoniously (9)
dilemma (3)	bohemian (11)
gloats (4)	genetically (13)

EXERCISE 7   Discussion and Critical Thinking

1. Lara uses examples to explain how she came to a conclusion on who—male, female, or both—should pay on dates. What does she think about the occasion of her second date with Craig when he does not pay for the gas or meal?

2. What examples does she use to show that some men are just "skinflints"?

3. In your estimation, who is worse on the 1–10 cheapness scale, the one-at-a-time M&Ms guy or the water-fountain guy?

4. In paragraph 9, Lara says that some men have ingrained cheapness and that men who are stingy with money are likely to be stingy with feelings. She offers no other support. Do you agree with her generalization? Why or why not?

5. The author seems impressed by the man (in paragraph 11) who says he takes dates to cheap restaurants and if they complain, he offers to give the money he saved to a worthy cause of his date's choice. Then if she does not accept, he assumes she is just interested in having the fine meal for herself. Do you think that is likely a good way to discover his date's value system (as

he believes), or is it likely that he has just devised a good way to avoid paying more?

6. What paragraph carries Lara's conclusion on her main question?

Tortillas

JOSÉ ANTONIO BURCIAGA

A distinguished publisher and writer, José Antontio Burciaga died in 1996, leaving a rich legacy of poems, short stories, and essays. His essay here defines one of the most basic Hispanic foods, tortillas. *Much more than a mere recipe, this definition is colorfully layered with historical, regional, and personal context.*

1   My earliest memory of *tortillas* is my *Mamá* telling me not to play with them. I had bitten eyeholes in one and was wearing it as a mask at the dinner table.

2   As a child, I also used *tortillas* as hand warmers on cold days, and my family claims that I owe my career as an artist to my early experiments with *tortillas*. According to them, my clowning around helped me develop a strong artistic foundation. I'm not so sure, though. Sometimes I wore a *tortilla* on my head, like a *yarmulke*, and yet I never had any great urge to convert from Catholicism to Judaism. But who knows? They may be right.

3   For Mexicans over the centuries, the *tortilla* has served as the spoon and the fork, the plate and the napkin. *Tortillas* originated before the Mayan civilizations, perhaps predating Europe's wheat bread. According to Mayan mythology, the great god Quetzalcoatl, realizing that the red ants knew the secret of using maize as food, transformed himself into a black ant, infiltrated the colony of red ants, and absconded with a grain of corn. (Is it any wonder that to this day, black ants and red ants do not get along?) Quetzalcoatl then put maize on the lips of the first man and woman, Oxomoco and Cipactonal, so that they would become strong. Maize festivals are still celebrated by many Indian cultures of the Americas.

4   When I was growing up in El Paso, *tortillas* were part of my daily life. I used to visit a tortilla factory in an ancient adobe building near the open *mercado* in Ciudad Juárez. As I approached, I could hear the rhythmic slapping of the *masa* as the skilled vendors outside the factory formed it into balls and patted them into perfectly round corn cakes between the palms of their hands. The wonderful aroma and the speed with which the women counted so many dozens of *tortillas* out of warm wicker baskets still linger in my mind. Watching them at work convinced me that the most handsome and *deliciosas tortillas* are handmade. Although machines are faster, they can never adequately replace generation-to-generation experience. There's no place in the factory assembly line for the tender slaps that give each *tortilla* character. The best thing that can be said about mass-producing *tortillas* is that it makes it possible for many people to enjoy them.

5   In the *mercado* where my mother shopped, we frequently bought *taquitos de nopalitos*, small tacos filled with diced cactus, onions, tomatoes, and *jalapeños*. Our friend Don Toribio showed us how to make delicious, crunchy

taquitos with dried, salted pumpkin seeds. When you had no money for the filling, a poor man's *taco* could be made by placing a warm *tortilla* on the left palm, applying a sprinkle of salt, then rolling the *tortilla* up quickly with the fingertips of the right hand. My own kids put peanut butter and jelly on *tortillas*, which I think is truly bicultural. And speaking of fast food for kids, nothing beats a *quesadilla*, a *tortilla* grilled-cheese sandwich.

6   Depending on what you intend to use them for, *tortillas* may be made in various ways. Even a run-of-the-mill *tortilla* is more than a flat corn cake. A skillfully cooked homemade *tortilla* has a bottom and a top; the top skin forms a pocket in which you put the filling that folds your *tortilla* into a taco. Paper-thin *tortillas* are used specifically for *flautas*, a type of taco that is filled, rolled, and then fried until crisp. The name *flauta* means *flute*, which probably refers to the Mayan bamboo flute; however, the only sound that comes from an edible *flauta* is a delicious crunch that is music to the palate. In México *flautas* are sometimes made as long as two feet and then cut into manageable segments. The opposite of *flautas* is *gorditas*, meaning *little fat ones*. These are very thick small *tortillas*.

7   The versatility of *tortillas* and corn does not end here. Besides being tasty and nourishing, they have spiritual and artistic qualities as well. The Tarahumara Indians of Chihuahua, for example, concocted a corn-based beer called *tesgüino*, which their descendants still make today. And everyone has read about the woman in New Mexico who was cooking her husband a *tortilla* one morning when the image of Jesus Christ miraculously appeared on it. Before they knew what was happening, the man's breakfast had become a local shrine.

8   Then there is *tortilla* art. Various Chicano artists throughout the Southwest have, when short of materials or just in a whimsical mood, used a dry *tortilla* as a small, round canvas. And a few years back, at the height of the Chicano movement, a priest in Arizona got into trouble with the Church after he was discovered celebrating mass using a *tortilla* as the host. All of which only goes to show that while the *tortilla* may be a lowly corn cake, when the necessity arises, it can reach unexpected distinction.

EXERCISE 8   Discussion and Critical Thinking

1. Does the author assume his audience already knows what a *tortilla* is?

2. Where is the simplest, most direct definition of a *tortilla*?

3. In addition to exemplification, which of these patterns of development— description, narration, process analysis, and classification—does Burciaga use?

4. Which paragraphs carry the most vivid examples?

5. What different aspects of life does Burciaga bring into his discussion through examples?

Liked for Myself

MAYA ANGELOU

As a child, Maya Angelou (Marguerite), author of the autobiographical book I Know Why the Caged Bird Sings, *was raped by a friend of her mother. In this excerpt she has only recently come to live in her grandmother's home in rural Arkansas. There, psychologically wounded by her experience, she does not speak. She is desperate for self-confidence. She needs to be liked for the person she is.*

MINDSET

Lock It In

If you had to pick one person who came along at your time of need and pointed you or booted you in the right direction, who would that person be?

1   For nearly a year, I sopped around the house, the Store, the school, and the church, like an old biscuit, dirty and inedible. Then I met, or rather got to know, the lady who threw me my first life line.

2   Mrs. Bertha Flowers was the aristocrat of Black Stamps. She had the grace of control to appear warm in the coldest weather, and on the Arkansas summer days it seemed she had a private breeze which swirled around, cooling her. She was thin without the taut look of wiry people, and her printed voile dresses and flowered hats were as right for her as denim overalls for a farmer. She was our side's answer to the richest white woman in town.

3   Her skin was a rich black that would have peeled like a plum if snagged, but then no one would have thought of getting close enough to Mrs. Flowers to ruffle her dress, let alone snag her skin. She didn't encourage familiarity. She wore gloves too.

4   I don't think I ever saw Mrs. Flowers laugh, but she smiled often. A slow widening of her thin black lips to show even, small white teeth, then the slow effortless closing. When she chose to smile on me, I always wanted to thank her. The action was so graceful and inclusively benign.

5   She was one of the few gentlewomen I have ever known, and has remained throughout my life the measure of what a human being can be. . . .

6   One summer afternoon, sweet-milk fresh in my memory, she stopped at the Store to buy provisions. Another Negro woman of her health and age would have been expected to carry the paper sacks home in one hand, but Momma said, "Sister Flowers, I'll send Bailey up to your house with these things."

7   She smiled that slow dragging smile, "Thank you, Mrs. Henderson. I'd prefer Marguerite, though." My name was beautiful when she said it. "I've been meaning to talk to her, anyway." They gave each other age-group looks. . . .

8   There was a little path beside the rocky road, and Mrs. Flowers walked in front swinging her arms and picking her way over the stones.

9   She said, without turning her head, to me, "I hear you're doing very good school work, Marguerite, but that it's all written. The teachers report that they have trouble getting you to talk in class." We passed the triangular farm on our left and the path widened to allow us to walk together. I hung back in the separate unasked and unanswerable questions.

10   "Come and walk along with me, Marguerite." I couldn't have refused even if I wanted to. She pronounced my name so nicely. Or more correctly, she spoke each word with such clarity that I was certain a foreigner who didn't understand English could have understood her.

11   "Now no one is going to make you talk—possibly no one can. But bear in mind, language is man's way of communicating with his fellow man and it is language alone which separates him from the lower animals." That was a totally new idea to me, and I would need time to think about it.

12   "Your grandmother says you read a lot. Every chance you get. That's good, but not good enough. Words mean more than what is set down on paper. It takes the human voice to infuse them with the shades of deeper meaning."

13   I memorized the part about the human voice infusing words. It seemed so valid and poetic.

14   She said she was going to give me some books and that I not only must read them, I must read them aloud. She suggested that I try to make a sentence sound in as many different ways as possible.

15   "I'll accept no excuse if you return a book to me that has been badly handled." My imagination boggled at the punishment I would deserve if in fact I did abuse a book of Mrs. Flowers'. Death would be too kind and brief.

16   The odors in the house surprised me. Somehow I had never connected Mrs. Flowers with food or eating or any other common experience of common people. There must have been an outhouse, too, but my mind never recorded it.

17   The sweet scent of vanilla had met us as she opened the door.

18   "I made tea cookies this morning. You see, I had planned to invite you for cookies and lemonade so we could have this little chat. The lemonade is in the icebox."

19   It followed that Mrs. Flowers would have ice on an ordinary day, when most families in our town bought ice late on Saturdays only a few times during the summer to be used in the wooden ice-cream freezers.

20   She took the bags from me and disappeared through the kitchen door. I looked around the room that I had never in my wildest fantasies imagined I would see. Browned photographs leered or threatened from the walls and the white, freshly done curtains pushed against themselves and against the wind. I wanted to gobble up the room entire and take it to Bailey, who would help me analyze and enjoy it.

21   "Have a seat, Marguerite. Over there by the table." She carried a platter covered with a tea towel. Although she warned that she hadn't tried her hand at baking sweets for some time, I was certain that like everything else about her the cookies would be perfect.

22   They were flat round wafers, slightly browned on the edges and butter-yellow in the center. With the cold lemonade they were sufficient for childhood's lifelong diet. Remembering my manners, I took nice little lady-like bites off the edges. She said she had made them expressly for me and that she had a few in the kitchen that I could take home to my brother. So I jammed one whole cake in my mouth and the rough crumbs scratched the insides of my jaws, and if I hadn't had to swallow, it would have been a dream come true.

23   As I ate she began the first of what we later called "my lessons in living." She said that I must always be intolerant of ignorance but understanding of illiteracy. That some people, unable to go to school, were more educated and even more intelligent than college professors. She encouraged me to listen carefully to what country people called mother wit. That in those homely sayings was couched the collective wisdom of generations.

24   When I finished the cookies she brushed off the table and brought a thick, small book from the bookcase. I had read *A Tale of Two Cities* and found it up to my standards as a romantic novel. She opened the first page and I heard poetry for the first time in my life.

25 "It was the best of times and the worst of times. . . ." Her voice slid in and curved down through and over the words. She was nearly singing. I wanted to look at the pages. Were they the same that I had read? Or were there notes, music, lined on the pages, as in a hymn book? Her sounds began cascading gently. I knew from listening to a thousand preachers that she was nearing the end of her reading, and I hadn't really heard, heard to understand, a single word.

26 "How do you like that?"

27 It occurred to me that she expected a response. The sweet vanilla flavor was still on my tongue and her reading was a wonder in my ears. I had to speak.

28 I said, "Yes, ma'am." It was the least I could do, but it was the most also.

29 "There's one more thing. Take this book of poems and memorize one for me. Next time you pay me a visit, I want you to recite."

30 I have tried often to search behind the sophistication of years for the enchantment I so easily found in those gifts. The essence escapes, but its aura remains. To be allowed, no, invited, into the private lives of strangers, and to share their joys and fears, was a chance to exchange the Southern bitter wormwood for a cup of mead with Beowulf or a hot cup of tea and milk with Oliver Twist. When I said aloud, "It is a far, far better thing that I do, than I have ever done . . ." tears of love filled my eyes at my selfishness.

31 On that first day, I ran down the hill and into the road (few cars ever came along it) and had the good sense to stop running before I reached the Store.

32 I was liked, and what a difference it made. I was respected not as Mrs. Henderson's grandchild or Bailey's sister but for just being Marguerite Johnson.

33 Childhood's logic never asks to be proved (all conclusions are absolute). I didn't question why Mrs. Flowers had singled me out for attention, nor did it occur to me that Momma might have asked her to give me a little talking to. All I cared about was that she had made tea cookies for *me* and read to *me* from her favorite book. It was enough to prove that she liked me.

EXERCISE 9   Vocabulary Highlights

Write a short definition of each word as it is used in the essay. (Paragraph numbers are given in parentheses.) Be prepared to use these words in sentences.

taut (2)	leered (20)
voile (2)	cascading (25)
benign (4)	sophistication (30)
infuse (12)	essence (30)
valid (13)	aura (30)

EXERCISE 10   Discussion and Critical Thinking

1. In what way can Mrs. Bertha Flowers be seen as an extended example in this essay?

2. What are her most outstanding character traits?

3. What techniques (part of the struggle) does Mrs. Flowers use to encourage Marguerite to speak?

4. What does Mrs. Flowers mean by the word *educated*?

5. What does the narrator mean by "childhood's logic" (paragraph 33)?

6. What are "lessons in living" (paragraph 23)? In what way can this episode be called such a lesson?

7. Which one of the five parts of the narrative pattern—situation, conflict, struggle, outcome, meaning—is the lesson of this episode?

STUDENT PARAGRAPH AND ESSAYS

Traveling the World at Home

GARABED YEGAVIAN

An Armenian-American student, Garabed Yegavian has traveled to many countries and encountered many cultures. Living in Southern California, he is constantly reminded that he lives in a global community, but this assignment focused his attention on specific, persuasive examples.

Living in California can be like traveling the world. It is morning! Responding to my alarm clock made in China, I get out of my bed, which was constructed in the United States, and step onto a Persian rug. I'm ready to start my Saturday. I walk to my closet to find my clothes: pants from Indonesia, shirt of fabric from India but made in North Carolina, socks from Mexico, shoes from Italy. For late breakfast I have a bagel and cream cheese. I sit in front of my television to see what is happening in the world today. I flip through the channels—English, Spanish, Chinese—until I get to the local Armenian station for an update. After an hour I'm ready to go. I drive to my Korean friend's garage, where he fills my car with oil refined in a plant down by Long Beach. I pay him with my American dollars, and I'm off for tires. On the way to the tire shop, I stop for some lunch. Zancou's Chicken is the place for me today. I order Armenian-style chicken and a bottle of Perrier water and enjoy my feast. Done with lunch, I motor to the tire shop where an immigrant worker from El Salvador fits American Kelly tires on my car. I drink a small cup of Turkish coffee with the manager and talk about business here in America. After a while, my car is ready, and I leave for a mid-afternoon snack. Where to go? There are just too many choices. I decide to go to a Japanese restaurant near my home. There I eat sushi made with fish caught from the waters off Peru, drink Japanese saki, and reflect on my day's experiences. In miles I had not gone far, but who needs to travel the world when one lives in Southern California?

EXERCISE 11   Discussion and Critical Thinking

1. Underline the topic sentence of the paragraph.

2. Circle each specific example.

3. As Yegavian's community becomes more global, does it become less American, more American, or just a different kind of American? Explain.

4. Do you welcome this kind of change and find it rather exciting, as Yegavian apparently does? Why or why not?

5. To what extent is your environment similar to the one presented in this paragraph?

Lara Olivas was asked to write an essay on unproductive student behavior, developing her ideas mainly with examples. Of numerous topics that came to mind, one stood out: cheating. It was a practice she had observed for years and had very briefly experimented with and rejected. Wanting to do something a bit different, she considered all the reasons that cheating is not a good idea and came up with a practical one: Cheating is hard work, and cheaters sometimes work harder at cheating than others do at their work.

Olivas's Writing Process Worksheet shows how her writing evolved from idea to final draft. To conserve space here, the freewriting and the rough drafts marked for revision have been omitted. The balance of her worksheet has been lengthened for you to be able to see her other work in its entirety.

You will find a full-size blank worksheet on page 6, which can be photocopied, filled in, and submitted with each assignment if your instructor directs you to do so.

Writing Process Worksheet

Name Lara Olivas   **Title** Cheating Is Not Worth the Bother   **Due Date** Wednesday, May 17, 9.00 a.m.

Use the back of this page or separate paper if you need more space.

Assignment

In the space below, write whatever you need to know about your assignment, including information about the topic, audience, pattern of writing, length, whether to include a rough draft or revised drafts, and whether your paper must be typed.

Write a 500- to 750-word essay of exemplification on the topic of unproductive student behavior. Fellow students and the instructor will probably be familiar with your subject but not your examples and your view. Submit this completed worksheet, one or more rough drafts marked for revision, and a typed final draft.

Stage One

Explore   Freewrite, brainstorm (list), cluster, or take notes as directed by your instructor.

Listing

STUDENT CHEATING

When I copied homework
Looking at a friend's test answers
A student with hand signals
Jake and his electronic system
Time for planned cheating
Those who got caught
(A person who bought a research paper)
Jess, who copied from me
The Internet "Cheaters" source
The two students who exchanged identities
(More work than it's worth)
(More stress than it's worth)
The teacher's assistant and his friends
(The girl from the biology class)

Stage Two

Organize   Write a topic sentence or thesis; label the subject and the focus parts.

<u>Cheating students</u> <u>often put themselves under more stress than honest students.</u>
　　　subject　　　　　　　　　　　　　　　　　　focus

Write an outline or an outline alternative. For reading-based writing, include references and short quotations with page numbers as support in the outline.

　I. Student who bought paper
　　　A. Had trouble with form
　　　　　1. Prewriting
　　　　　2. Drafts

B. Had trouble with quality

C. Drops class

II. Student with cheat cards

A. Had a system

B. Sometimes under suspicion

C. Experienced stress

Stage Three

Write   On separate paper, write and then revise your paragraph or essay as many times as necessary for **c**oherence, **l**anguage (usage, tone, and diction), **u**nity, **e**mphasis, **s**upport, and **s**entences (**CLUESS**). Read your work aloud to hear and correct any grammatical errors or awkward-sounding sentences.

Edit any problems in fundamentals, such as **c**apitalization, **o**missions, **p**unctuation, and **s**pelling (**COPS**).

Final Draft

CHEATING IS NOT WORTH THE BOTHER
Lara Olivas

I knew many students who took college prep classes all the way through high school and never read a book in an English class. They read Cliffs Notes or Monarch Notes, or they copied work from other people who did. But they weren't cheating just in English classes. They had systems of cheating in every class. Cheating became a way of life. They were always conniving and scheming. I am not that pure. I have tried cheating, but I soon rejected it. I did not learn that way, and I lost my self-esteem. I also feared getting caught; and I discovered that most of the time cheating was hard, stressful work. So I never became, like some of my friends, a master cheater, but I did become a master observer of cheaters because students almost always see more than teachers do. <u>What I learned was that cheaters often put themselves under more stress than honest students</u>.

<u>Even the student who pays for school work can become a victim of stress</u>. I remember a student in my junior composition class who needed a research paper, so he found a source and bought one for seventy-five dollars. The first trouble was that he had to submit the work in stages: the topic, the working bibliography, the note cards, the outline, the rough draft, and the final. Therefore, he went to the library and started working backwards. Of course, he couldn't turn in only the bib cards actually used in the paper, and next he had to make out note cards for the material he "would be" documenting, and even make out more. After having all kinds of trouble, he realized that the bought paper was of "A" quality, whereas he had been a "C" student. He went back to his source and was told he should change the sentence structure and so on to make the paper weaker. Finally he dropped the class after spending more time on his paper than I did on mine.

<u>Then during my senior year, a female student in Biology 2 became another subject for my study in cheating</u>. She was sitting next to me, so I could see everything she did. She kept her cheat cards in her bra. This is the way she did it. On the day of the test, she would wear a loose-fitting blouse or dress. Then when the instructor was not watching, she would hunch her shoulders like a buzzard sleeping and slump so that she could look down the front of her own dress. Sometimes she'd have to fiddle around down there to get the cheat card to pop into place. Her writing was tiny. I know about the writing because one day the teacher left the room, and she just took a card out and

Thesis

Topic sentence

Specific example

Order by time

Topic sentence

Specific example

Order by time

used it openly. If the instructor stared at her when she was looking down, she would blow inside her dress as if she were trying to cool off her bosom or something. Then she would smile at the instructor and shake her head and pucker her lips to show how hot it was. Her strategy worked because she did perspire due to the stress. The tests were mainly on muscles and bones and weren't that difficult. She probably worked harder in rigging the cheat cards on her underwear than I did in memorizing information.

Cluster of examples

There were dozens of other examples—the writing on seats, hands, arms, legs, and cuffs; the hand signs, blinks, and coughs; and the plagiarism of all kinds. There were even the classes where cheating would never be caught because some teachers did not watch carefully during the tests, and others didn't read carefully later. But for the most part, the cheaters were the ones who had the most anxiety and often the ones who did the most work—work that was never directed toward learning.

EXERCISE 12　Discussion and Critical Thinking

1. Why did Olivas give up cheating?

2. What evidence is there that the two students she discusses experienced stress?

3. Does Olivas use a large number of specific examples to support her points or does she develop her examples in detail?

4. As Olivas develops her examples in paragraphs, what other pattern of writing emerges?

READING-BASED WRITING

Grading a Professor's Writing

MASON ARNOLD

Student Mason Arnold had an unusual topic. He was asked to write an evaluation of an essay about students who wanted their grade changed. His text was "Making the Grade" by Kurt Wiesenfeld, a professor who reported that for one grading period, about 10 percent of his physics students at Georgia Tech had contacted him after his classes ended, with seemingly trivial, nonacademic arguments for a higher grade. Specifically, Arnold's task was to assign Professor Wiesenfeld a letter grade based mainly on the effectiveness of his examples.

1　　In writing "Making the Grade," Professor Kurt Wiesenfeld uses three kinds of examples: students with bad values and poor performance, real-world problems, and a culture that allows the unqualified to cause those problems. He is concerned.

2　　Ten percent of his students are the offenders. He gives examples of visits, phone calls, and e-mails from students who want their grades raised for nonacademic reasons. Although these are the ones who do not work

Summary with quotation		hard or perform well, they try to make the professor feel guilty about their low grades, as they beg and make excuses. He says it is the "disgruntled consumer approach. . . . If they don't like their grade, they go to the 'return' counter to trade it in for something better" (184).

Summary with quotation

3   In the same way the students have not been serious and careful about their studies, some people have not been serious and careful at work. In short, they may not be qualified. Wiesenfeld says most of his students are engineering majors, and he is fearful that if they do not get "the answer right" when they are on the job, problems may occur (184). He gives examples of a light tower collapsing, a building beam breaking, and a dorm floor being unlevel (184). He uses these examples to say that those problems could be caused by engineers who were careless students. That may not be the case. He does not know anything about those who were responsible.

Interpretation and summary

Quotation
Reference
Question of logic

4   Wiesenfeld traces the blame for loss of respect for education to both individuals and society. He says society is "saturated with surface values" connected with the idea that a degree is something to be traded for a "job, which means money" and that a degree is often treated as more important than an education (185). The students are mainly to blame, but they reflect the view of society. He even says teachers are inconsistent in their grading standards, which is true. But he does not give specific examples, certainly not the kind he finds for the sniveling students and the engineering errors. The fact is that some students try to con their professors because they know from experience and observation that sometimes the con works. There are lots of examples on any campus and in any department.

Blended quotations and paraphrasing

Evaluation
Critical comment on use of examples

5   For that one shortcoming, I have lowered Professor Kurt Wiesenfeld's grade to a B+. If he e-mails, telephones, or visits to say he would have done better had his classes been smaller and his committee meetings shorter, I will just tell him that for the good of society I will not accept his excuses.

Evaluation as conclusion

Work Cited

Wiesenfeld, Kurt. "Making the Grade." *From Self to Sources: Essays and Beyond.* Ed. Lee Brandon. Boston: Houghton, 2003. 183–86. Print.

Suggested Topics and Prompts for Writing Exemplification

STUDENT COMPANION SITE
For additional practice, visit www.cengage .com/devenglish/ brandon/Pe11e.

You will find a blank Writing Process Worksheet on page 6 of this book and on your Student Companion Site. It can be photocopied or printed out, filled in, and submitted with your assignment, if your instructor directs you to do so.

READING-BASED WRITING

Reading-based writing requires you to read critically, write a reply that shows you understand what you have read, and give credit for ideas you borrow and words you quote. The form can be a summary, a reaction, or a two-part response (with separated summary and reaction).

Documentation, in which you give credit for borrowed ideas and words, can be either formal (MLA) or informal, as directed by your instructor. Both the forms of reading-based writing and documentation are discussed with examples in Chapter 1. Definitions of the three forms follow. Any form can be used for any reading selection in this book.

Summary

- The summary is a statement presenting only the main points of what you have read by using different wording without altering the meaning, adding information, or showing bias.
- It is the purest form of reading-based writing.

Reaction

- In the reaction, the meaning of what you have read will be central to your topic sentence of your paragraph or to the thesis of your essay.
- Although the reaction is not a personal narrative by itself, it may include personal experience to explain elements of the text. For example, if your source is about driving styles, your own experiences as a driver or an observer of drivers could be relevant in your analysis of the text.
- The reaction may incorporate a summary to convey a broad view of what you have read, but your summary should never be the main part of your reaction.

The Two-Part Response

- The two-part response separates the summary from the reaction.
- This form will give you practice in separating your objective summary in the first part from your more personal evaluation, interpretation, or application in the second part, the reaction.

READING-BASED WRITING TOPICS

"Dropping Way Out"

1. Write a reaction to this paragraph in which you discuss how typical Beth Kierny is of students who drop out of high school. Compare her with a person or persons you have known who have also gone from the world of school to the world of work.

2. Write a reaction in which you make the same argument as Levine. Give Levine credit for the ideas you borrow and provide your own examples, pointing out their similarity to the account of Beth Kierny.

"Little Brother Is Watching"

3. Write a two-part response—a summary of and a reaction to this essay. In your summary restate Gall's main ideas. In your reaction evaluate his views on the positive and negative effects of the use of candid or staged films on YouTube and similar websites. Are Gall's views well-supported by examples? Has his range of examples essentially covered the content of YouTube films you have seen? Does he—by implication or statement—give enough attention to instances of filmed bullying, harassment, and vandalism? Or, is YouTube site management taking care of most of those problems?

4. Write a reaction to Gall's essay in which you address a youthful friend or relative as you suggest a set of sensible principles about the rights and responsibilities of someone filming and then publishing candid scenes featuring oneself, others, or a situation. Relate your comments to the content of Gall's

essay by using references and quotations. Consider using some of your own examples in your discussion.

5. Gall writes about surveillance in two societies. In the novel *1984*, everyone is being watched by the Thought Police of a totalitarian state. In our contemporary society, we are being watched by our fellow citizens, and some of them have cameras ready to film us without our permission. Explain to what extent the two societies are different. Refer to and use quotations from the essay.

"Who's Cheap?"

6. Write a reading-based paragraph or essay in which you address some of the questions in Exercise 7. Agree or disagree with Adair Lara, as you examine her use of numerous examples leading to a conclusion that from now on she will pay her part of the check. Keep in mind that at the end of her essay, Lara knows what she'll say after the meal. She'll say, "I'll pay half," not "Let me pay half." Discuss the difference and whether it matters from your male or female perspective. Consider using some examples from your own experience.

"Traveling the World at Home"

7. Write a reaction to this paragraph in which you explain why the author's examples are reason for celebration or grief—or something in between. In your view, has the expansion of free trade been mainly good or bad for the American economy? Provide some of your own examples.

"Cheating Is Not Worth the Bother"

8. Write a reaction in which you agree or disagree with Lara Olivas's view that "cheating is not worth the bother." Consider discussing how to compete with cheaters. Evaluate her examples and incorporate your own examples from personal experience.

"Grading a Professor's Writing"

9. Write a paragraph or an essay of reaction in which you agree or disagree with the views of the professor and then with the criticism of the professor by student Mason Arnold.

GENERAL TOPICS

10. Write a paragraph or essay in which you use examples to discuss one of the most common foods in your culture or in your family. Used in different ways and on different occasions, the food might be dumplings, corn bread, biscuits, rice, potatoes, beans, fry bread, greens, bagels, muffins, or spaghetti. Include colorful examples that you recall, especially during childhood. For a helpful model on a similar topic, review "Tortillas" on pages 149–150.

11. Write a paragraph or essay in which you use an extended example with several instances to discuss a critical period in your life when a special person helped you survive and grow. Be specific in referring to events and your predicament. For a helpful model on a similar topic, review "Liked for Myself" on pages 151–153.

12. Choose or modify one of the following statements as a topic sentence for a paragraph or a thesis for an essay. Support the statement with specific examples.

    a. Television commercials are often amusing [misleading, irritating, sexist, racist, useless, fascinating].
    b. Rap music often carries important messages [makes me sick, brings out the best in people, brings out the worst in people, degrades women, promotes violence, presents reality, appeals to our better instincts, tells funny stories].
    c. Rock groups do not have to be sensational in presentation and appearance to be popular.
    d. A person can be an environmentalist in everyday life.
    e. Many people who consider themselves law-abiding citizens break laws on a selective basis.
    f. People who do not have a satisfying family life will find a family substitute.
    g. Country music appeals to some of our most basic concerns.

CROSS-CURRICULAR TOPIC

13. Use examples to write a paragraph or an essay in the following kinds of assignments.

    a. In preparation for an anticipated essay test question in another class, write a paragraph or an essay with an extended example or several specific examples.
    b. Reports: Focus on one or more examples as representative of a much larger group, for example, a focused discussion of one work of art in a museum grouping of pieces by style or a study of a particular typical student in a class visit for an education class.

CAREER-RELATED TOPICS

14. Use specific examples to support one of the following statements as applied to business or work.

    a. It's not what you know, it's who you know.
    b. Don't burn your bridges.
    c. Like Legos, business is a matter of connections.
    d. The customer is always right.
    e. A kind word turns away wrath.

15. Discuss how a specific service or product can benefit its users. Use an example or examples.

WRITER'S GUIDELINES: Exemplification

1. Use examples to explain, convince, or amuse.

2. Use examples that are vivid, specific, and representative.

   - Vivid examples attract attention.
   - Specific examples are identifiable.
   - Representative examples are typical and therefore the basis for generalization.

3. Tie your examples clearly to your thesis.

4. Draw your examples from what you have read, heard, and experienced.

5. Brainstorm a list or cluster of possible examples before you write.

6. The order and number of your examples will depend on the purpose stated in your topic sentence or thesis.

7. Use the writing process.

   - Write and then revise your paragraph or essay as many times as necessary for **c**oherence, **l**anguage (usage, tone, and diction), **u**nity, **e**mphasis, **s**upport, and **s**entences (**CLUESS**).
   - Read your work aloud to hear and correct any grammatical errors or awkward-sounding sentences.
   - Edit any problems in fundamentals, such as **c**apitalization, **o**missions, **p**unctuation, and **s**pelling (**COPS**).

Chapter 9

Analysis by Division
Examining the Parts

FLOW OF WRITING

WHEN TO USE ANALYSIS BY DIVISION

FOR COLLEGE WRITING ASSIGNMENTS

- If a writing assignment in any class requires that you divide your subject into parts and discuss how the parts relate to make up a unit, then you will turn to analysis by division. The principle is essentially the same regardless of the unit: a short story, a person, an organism, a rock, a painting, or a piece of music.

IN CAREERS AND AT THE WORKPLACE

- Whether you are preparing for a career or are engaged in a career, analysis by division will serve you well as you deal with any unit: requirements to complete your degree (how each one is part of the unit and relates to the other parts), the chain of command at work (each part, or level, with responsibilities and rewards), the job description at the workplace (each aspect separate and all related to a work assignment), the performance review (made up of categories of how you will be [are] evaluated and, perhaps, how you [will] evaluate others).

ANALYSIS BY DIVISION IN A CARTOON

THE QUIGMANS   **by Buddy Hickerson**

Date with a movie critic.

Writing Analysis by Division

PROCEDURE

If you need to explain how something works or exists as a unit, you will write an analysis by division. You will break down a unit (your subject) into its parts and explain how each part functions in relation to the operation or existence of the whole. The most important word here is *unit*. You begin with something that can stand alone or can be regarded separately: a poem, a heart, a painting, a car, a bike, a person, a school, a committee. The following procedure will guide you in writing an analysis by division: Move from subject to principle, to division, to relationship.

Step 1. Begin with something that is a unit (subject).

Step 2. State one principle by which the unit can function.

Step 3. Divide the unit into parts according to that principle.

Step 4. Discuss each of the parts in relation to the unit.

You might apply that procedure to writing about a good boss in the following way:

1. Unit	Manager
2. Principle of function	Effective as a leader
3. Parts based on the principle	Fair, intelligent, stable, competent in the field
4. Relationship to the unit	Consider each part in relation to the person's effectiveness as a manager.

ORGANIZATION

In an essay of analysis by division, the main parts are likely to be the main points of your outline or main extensions of your cluster. If they are anything else, reconsider your organization. A basic outline of an analysis by division might look like this:

Thesis: To be effective as a leader, a manager needs specific qualities.
I. Fairness
II. Intelligence
III. Stability
IV. Competence in the field

SEQUENCE OF PARTS

The order in which you discuss the parts will vary according to the nature of the unit and the way you view it. Here are some possible sequences for organizing the parts of a unit:

- **Time**: The sequence of the parts in your paragraph or essay can be mainly chronological, or time-based (if you are dealing with something that functions on its own, such as a heart, with the parts presented in relation to stages of the function).
- **Space**: If your unit is a visual object, especially if, like a pencil, it does nothing by itself, you may discuss the parts in relation to space. In the example of the pencil, the parts of the pencil begin at the top with the eraser and end at the bottom with the pencil point.
- **Emphasis**: Because the most emphatic location of any piece of writing is the end (the second most emphatic point is the beginning), consider placing the most significant part of the unit at the end.

Transitional Words

Consider using the following transitional words to improve coherence by connecting ideas with ideas, sentences with sentences, and paragraphs with paragraphs.

FOR ANALYSIS BY DIVISION:
Time or numbering: first, second, third, another, last, finally, soon, later, currently, before, along with, another part (section, component)

Space: above, below, to the left, to the right, near, beyond, under, next to, in the background, split, divide

Emphasis: most important, equally important, central to the, to this end, as a result, taken collectively, with this purpose in mind, working with the, in fact, of course, above all, most of all, especially, primarily, without question

FOR ALL PATTERNS OF WRITING: the <u>H</u>OTS<u>H</u>OT <u>C</u>AT words: <u>H</u>owever, <u>O</u>therwise, <u>T</u>herefore, <u>S</u>imilarly, <u>H</u>ence, <u>O</u>n the other hand, <u>T</u>hen, <u>C</u>onsequently, <u>A</u>lso, <u>T</u>hus (See pages 427–428 for additional transitional words.)

TWO USES OF ANALYSIS BY DIVISION: THE RESTAURANT REVIEW AND THE CAREER REVIEW

From the wide range of uses of analysis by division mentioned in the introduction, two are featured in this chapter.

Restaurant Review

Definition

The **restaurant review** is an article of one or more paragraphs that describes three elements: ambiance, service, and food.

- **Ambiance** is the atmosphere, mood, or feeling of a place. For restaurants, it may begin with landscaping and architecture (building style). Ambiance is certainly produced by what is inside, such as the furnishings, seating, style, upkeep, sounds, sights, smells, behavior of other customers, and management style—whatever produces that mood or the feeling, even if it is franchise plastic and elevator music.
- **Service** is mainly concerned with food delivery and those who do it: their attitude, manners, helpfulness, promptness, accuracy, and availability. Self-service or pickup establishments would be judged by similar standards.
- **Food** is the emphasis—its variety, quality, quantity, price, and presentation.

Writing the Review

- Use first person (*I*) as you relate your experience in a particular restaurant or chain.
- If possible, base your evaluation on more than one food item. Here is a low-cost way to do that: Dine with others and ask your companions to order different foods. Then ask them if you can taste (two small bites will suffice) what they are served, thus increasing your experience. Offering to pay a portion of their check may make others more receptive to sharing their food.
- While you are dining, use a simple outline or listing to make sure you have information on ambiance, service, and food. Copy names of foods and prices from the menu. Use quotation marks around any descriptive phrases for items you copy.
- You need not separate comments on ambiance, service, and food or present them in a particular order, but be specific in your details and examples. Use quotation marks for any descriptive phrases you borrow from the menu.

An example of a professional restaurant review, "Food, Service Hit and Miss at Gianno's," appears on pages 179–180.

Career Review

The career review is a summary of a career, which you will personalize by relating it to your background, interests, aptitude, and other relevant vocational matters.

The organization and development of your career review follow the basic procedure for writing an analysis by division as you move from unit to division to development. It is logical, systematic, and highly manageable.

- The unit for an essay is the career field and your quest of that career field.
- The parts of that unit arc the parts of the career field and your quest. Those parts can be further subdivided.
- The extent of the dividing may vary, depending on your particular purpose (assignment), the expected audience, and, if applicable, your current involvement in the career field.
- Your college library has an abundance of material that will inform you with career information you can summarize in your review. Your best overall source is probably the *Occupational Outlook Handbook* by the U.S. Department of Labor. It is available in print and online, and is ideal for you to summarize selectively for your career review. Updated and published every two years, the handbook covers hundreds of career fields, providing information about earnings, prerequisites of training and education, expected job prospects, job duties, and working conditions. Of course, you should give credit to your source(s) in your Work(s) Cited at the end of your review. This is the online address, which can be used for locating the source online or in the library or for giving credit in your Work(s) Cited.

   United States. Dept. of Labor. *Occupational Outlook Handbook*, 2008–09 Edition. Web. 19 Dec. 2009.

- The following main-part outline shows some useful divisions for an essay as a career review. For a shorter essay, just select the main parts that fit the assignment you have in mind. For an even shorter assignment of a paragraph, subdivide one of these Roman-numeral parts for basic organization of your career review, or analysis by division.

Unit: (the career itself)
Divisions: (parts of the unit, the career itself)
  I. My background, interests, and aptitude
  II. My desired field—an overview
  III. Working conditions, pay, benefits
  IV. Requirements for employment
  V. My step-by-step plan to enter this field

See pages 186–187 for an example of a student career review in the form of an analysis by division.

FINDING PATTERNS IN PHOTOS

EXERCISE 1   A Text-Based Activity for Groups or Individuals

Working mother

The artwork is titled "Working Mother." The working mother obviously has several roles in which she deals with needs, each one insistently demanding. Simultaneously she confronts a crying infant, bills, work, another child (?), and a tight time schedule. Those needs are enough, but to some mothers they are not all.

Focus on a working mother you know who is juggling different roles. Then select six roles from the left column, rank them according to what you know about the working mother you have in mind, and list those roles on the lines in the right column.

1. Mother   I.   _____

2. Financial manager of household   II.   _____

3. Worker outside the home   III. _____

4. Wife   IV. _____

5. Stepmother   V.   _____

6. Daughter   VI. _____

7. Daughter-in-law

8. Student

9. Family recreational director (scouts, little league, dance)

10. Spiritual leader

If your instructor directs you to do so, write a paragraph or an essay based on the six roles shown in your outline. Discuss the importance of prioritizing and creating balance.

Consider personalizing this subject if it touches your life or that of someone you know well.

Practicing Patterns of Analysis by Division

In analysis by division, Roman-numeral headings are almost always parts of the unit you are discussing as your subject. Learning to divide the unit into parts will help you move through your assignment quickly and efficiently.

EXERCISE 2   Writing Patterns

Fill in the blanks as if you were organizing material for a paragraph or an essay. Have a specific unit in mind.

1. Unit: friend, relative, hero, or role model

   Principle: that which defines the person

   The name of the person (may be fictitious): _____

   I. _____

   II. _____

   III. _____

   IV. _____

2. Unit: physical object such as a pencil, shoe, baseball, or pair of glasses

   Principle: that which makes the object functional

   Specific name of the unit: _____

   I. _____

   II. _____

   III. _____

   IV. _____

EXERCISE 3   Writing Patterns

Fill in the blanks as if you were organizing material for a paragraph or an essay. Have a specific unit in mind.

1. Unit: movie, television program, or novel

   Principle: that which makes the unit excellent

   Specific name of the unit: _____

   I. _____

   II. _____

   III. _____

   IV. _____

2. Unit: family, relationship, club, or class

   Principle: that which makes the unit excellent

   Specific name of the unit: _____

       I. _____

      II. _____

     III. _____

     IV. _____

Readings for Critical Thinking, Discussion, and Writing

READING STRATEGIES AND OBJECTIVES

Underlining and annotating these reading selections will help you answer the questions that follow the selections, discuss the material in class, and prepare for reading-based writing assignments. As you underline and annotate, pay special attention to the author's writing skills, logic, and message, and consider the relevance of the material to your own experiences and values.

Some selections begin with a Mindset suggestion that can help you create a readiness for connecting with what you are about to read.

PARAGRAPHS

Golden Oldies

JERRY BRATCHER

Freelance writer Jerry Bratcher reflects on one of our treasured shared experiences. He reminds us that all the songs we call "golden oldies" have common characteristics, and we note that his discussion of those characteristics is an analysis by division.

MINDSET
Lock It In

Do you have a song that is golden to you—that special song, maybe an "our song"? If so, how was it chosen?

Unit

Principle

Part 1

Part 2

Radio stations have made golden oldies their entire program. Television infomercials have beckoned those from a particular oldie period to listen to and buy CD collections. "Golden oldies" has become a term with components familiar to all of us. Anyone can love the songs, but only listeners who were around to hear them first can truly cherish all their dimensions. Golden oldies are the songs that resonate in our memories. Merely hearing one triggers a series of related emotions and recollections, which is what makes them golden. Not all songs can be both golden and oldie. *Oldie* means it must have originated in a clearly defined historical past, probably more than ten years ago. The person who hears an oldie on the radio is reminded of the historical time of its origin; thus, the oldie will be suggestive of what was going on culturally. Though that message need not be profound, somehow, in music, style, and lyrics the golden oldie will reveal its context. More important for the individual listener,

Part 3
Part 4

the golden oldie must have emerged at a key time in his or her life, usually in the adolescent to early adulthood range, a time of acute emotions and restless hormones. Additionally, for an oldie to be truly golden, a poignant response to the song must be shared with others of its host generation. Thus, a song treasured by only two people might be a sentimental favorite, but if it is not sanctioned by the media industry and millions of people, that's all it is. If you are not old enough to cherish a golden oldie, just wait around. Hum, chant, whistle, tap your toe, or shake your booty patiently. You probably have dozens of golden oldies in the making. A few words of warning: Your descendants not yet born may someday scorn the tunes you treasure.

EXERCISE 4   Discussion and Critical Thinking

Complete the following pattern.

Subject: golden oldie

Principle of division: components for a definition according to the common use of the term

Parts (components):

   I. Historical origin: ten or more years old

   II. Revealing of _____

   III. Personal: _____

   IV. Must be shared _____

The Zones of the Sea

LEONARD ENGEL

In this paragraph reprinted from The Sea, *published by Time-Life Books, the author shows that the sea can be divided into four zones.*

The life of the ocean is divided into distinct realms, each with its own group of creatures that feed upon each other and depend on each other in different ways. There is, first of all, the tidal zone, where land and sea meet. Then comes the realm of the shallow seas around the continents, which goes down to about 500 feet. It is in these two zones that the vast majority of marine life occurs. The deep ocean adds two regions, the zone of light and the zone of perpetual darkness. In the clear waters of the western Pacific, light could still be seen at a depth of 1,000 feet through the portholes of the *Trieste* on its seven-mile dive. But for practical purposes the zone of light ends at about 600 feet. Below that level there is too little light to support the growth of the "grass" of the sea—the tiny, single-celled green plants whose ability to form sugar and starch with the aid of sunlight makes them the base of the great food pyramid of the ocean.

EXERCISE 5   Discussion and Critical Thinking

1. What are the four zones of the sea?

2. Is the paragraph organized by space or by time?

3. What characterizes each zone?

4. Draw a cross section of the sea to show the four zones. Make it as elaborate as you like.

ESSAYS AND RESTAURANT REVIEW

Men Are from Mars, Women Are from Venus

JOHN GRAY

As a writer, marriage counselor, and seminar leader, John Gray specializes in understanding and dealing with gender difference. This excerpt comes from his best-selling book Men Are from Mars, Women Are from Venus *(1992), in which he says men and women are so different they might as well have come from different planets. Like all generalizations, his do not perfectly fit all individuals within groups (genders), but he provides much for you to consider.*

1   The most frequently expressed complaint women have about men is that men don't listen. Either a man completely ignores [a woman] when she speaks to him, or he listens for a few beats, assesses what is bothering her, and then proudly puts on his Mr. Fix-It cap and offers her a solution to make her feel better. He is confused when she doesn't appreciate this gesture of love. No matter how many times she tells him that he's not listening, he doesn't get it and keeps doing the same thing. She wants empathy, but he thinks she wants solutions.

2   The most frequently expressed complaint men have about women is that women are always trying to change them. When a woman loves a man she feels responsible to assist him in growing and tries to help him improve the way he does things. She forms a home-improvement committee, and he becomes her primary focus. No matter how much he resists her help, she persists—waiting

for any opportunity to help him or tell him what to do. She thinks she's nurturing him, while he feels he's being controlled. Instead, he wants her acceptance.

3   These two problems can finally be solved by first understanding why men offer solutions and why women seek to improve. Let's pretend to go back in time, where by observing life on Mars and Venus—before the planets discovered one another or came to Earth—we can gain some insights into men and women.

4   Martians value power, competency, efficiency, and achievement. They are always doing things to prove themselves and develop their power and skills. Their sense of self is defined through their ability to achieve results. They experience fulfillment primarily through success and accomplishment.

5   Everything on Mars is a reflection of these values. Even their dress is designed to reflect their skills and competence. Police officers, soldiers, businessmen, scientists, cab drivers, technicians, and chefs all wear uniforms or at least hats to reflect their competence and power.

6   They don't read magazines like *Psychology Today, Self,* or *People.* They are more concerned with outdoor activities, like hunting, fishing, and racing cars. They are interested in the news, weather, and sports and couldn't care less about romance novels and self-help books.

7   They are more interested in "objects" and "things" rather than people and feelings. Even today on Earth, while women fantasize about romance, men fantasize about powerful cars, faster computers, gadgets, gizmos, and new more powerful technology. Men are preoccupied with the "things" that can help them express power by creating results and achieving their goals.

8   Achieving goals is very important to a Martian because it is a way for him to prove his competence and thus feel good about himself. And for him to feel good about himself he must achieve these goals by himself. Someone else can't achieve them for him. Martians pride themselves on doing things all by themselves. Autonomy is a symbol of efficiency, power, and competence.

9   Understanding this Martian characteristic can help women understand why men resist so much being corrected or being told what to do. To offer a man unsolicited advice is to presume that he doesn't know what to do or that he can't do it on his own. Men are very touchy about this, because the issue of competence is so very important to them.

10   Because he is handling his problems on his own, a Martian rarely talks about his problems unless he needs expert advice. He reasons: "Why involve someone else when I can do it by myself?" He keeps his problems to himself unless he requires help from another to find a solution. Asking for help when you can do it yourself is perceived as a sign of weakness.

11   However, if he truly does need help, then it is a sign of wisdom to get it. In this case, he will find someone he respects and then talk about his problem. Talking about a problem on Mars is an invitation for advice. Another Martian feels honored by the opportunity. Automatically he puts on his Mr. Fix-It hat, listens for a while, and then offers some jewels of advice.

12   This Martian custom is one of the reasons men instinctively offer solutions when women talk about problems. When a woman innocently shares upset feelings or explores out loud the problems of her day, a man mistakenly assumes she is looking for some expert advice. He puts on his Mr. Fix-It hat and begins giving advice; this is his way of showing love and of trying to help.

13   He wants to help her feel better by solving her problems. He wants to be useful to her. He feels he can be valued and thus worthy of her love when his abilities are used to solve her problems.

14   Once he has offered a solution, however, and she continues to be upset it becomes increasingly difficult for him to listen because his solution is being rejected and he feels increasingly useless.

15   He has no idea that by just listening with empathy and interest he can be supportive. He does not know that on Venus talking about problems is not an invitation to offer a solution.

16   Venusians have different values. They value love, communication, beauty, and relationships. They spend a lot of time supporting, helping, and nurturing one another. Their sense of self is defined through their feelings and the quality of their relationships. They experience fulfillment through sharing and relating.

17   Everything on Venus reflects these values. Rather than building highways and tall buildings, the Venusians are more concerned with living together in harmony, community, and loving cooperation. Relationships are more important than work and technology. In most ways their world is the opposite of Mars.

18   They do not wear uniforms like the Martians (to reveal their competence). On the contrary, they enjoy wearing a different outfit every day, according to how they are feeling. Personal expression, especially of their feelings, is very important. They may even change outfits several times a day as their mood changes.

19   Communication is of primary importance. To share their personal feelings is much more important than achieving goals and success. Talking and relating to one another is a source of tremendous fulfillment.

20   This is hard for a man to comprehend. He can come close to understanding a woman's experience of sharing and relating by comparing it to the satisfaction he feels when he wins a race, achieves a goal, or solves a problem.

21   Instead of being goal oriented, women are relationship oriented; they are more concerned with expressing their goodness, love, and caring. Two Martians go to lunch to discuss a project or business goal; they have a problem to solve. In addition, Martians view going to a restaurant as an efficient way to approach food: no shopping, no cooking, and no washing dishes. For Venusians, going to lunch is an opportunity to nurture a relationship, for both giving support to and receiving support from a friend. Women's restaurant talk can be very open and intimate, almost like the dialogue that occurs between therapist and patient.

22   On Venus, everyone studies psychology and has at least a master's degree in counseling. They are very involved in personal growth, spirituality, and everything that can nurture life, healing, and growth. Venus is covered with parks, organic gardens, shopping centers, and restaurants.

23   Venusians are very intuitive. They have developed this ability through centuries of anticipating the needs of others. They pride themselves on being considerate of the needs and feelings of others. A sign of great love is to offer help and assistance to another Venusian without being asked.

24   Because proving one's competence is not as important to a Venusian, offering help is not offensive, and needing help is not a sign of weakness. A man, however, may feel offended because when a woman offers advice he doesn't feel she trusts his ability to do it himself.

25   A woman has no conception of this male sensitivity because for her it is another feather in her hat if someone offers to help her. It makes her feel loved and cherished. But offering help to a man can make him feel incompetent, weak, and even unloved.

26   On Venus it is a sign of caring to give advice and suggestions. Venusians firmly believe that when something is working it can always work better. Their nature is to want to improve things. When they care about someone, they freely point out what can be improved and suggest how to do it. Offering advice and constructive criticism is an act of love.

27   Mars is very different. Martians are more solution oriented. If something is working, their motto is don't change it. Their instinct is to leave it alone if it is working. "Don't fix it unless it is broken" is a common expression.

28   When a woman tries to improve a man, he feels she is trying to fix him. He receives the message that he is broken. She doesn't realize her caring attempts to help him may humiliate him. She mistakenly thinks she is just helping him to grow.

EXERCISE 6   Discussion and Critical Thinking

Although this essay is structured as comparison and contrast, it is organized on a subject-by-subject pattern, and each subject (men and women) is covered separately as an analysis by division. Paragraphs 4 through 15 make up an analysis by division about men, and paragraphs 16 through 28 do the same for women.

1. What are the divisions that make up the nature of men in paragraphs 4 through 15?

2. What are the divisions that make up the nature of women in paragraphs 16 through 28?

3. Is Gray serious about his insights? What in this excerpt indicates his intention?

4. Does Gray oversimplify gender differences? Explain.

5. Do his views apply equally to different income and social classes?

6. How do styles in communication affect multiple areas of relationships—values, careers, friendships, activities, family, and so on?

7. Do the people you know fit into these behavioral patterns detailed by Gray? Discuss.

8. Is he suggesting that men and women should break out of their patterns of thinking and behaving? Explain.

9. How do you account for the enormous success of the book from which this excerpt came?

Americanization Is Tough on "Macho"

ROSE DEL CASTILLO GUILBAULT

What does macho *mean to you? If someone calls you or a person you respect "macho," are you pleased or offended? Or, are you perhaps unsure and listen on, reserving judgment and trying to determine what the speaker means. The fact is that* macho *has two distinctly different meanings.*

MINDSET

Lock It In

If you are a male and a person calls you *macho*, do you say "thank you," punch that person in the nose, or just consider the speaker?

1   What is *macho*? That depends on which side of the border you come from.

2   Although it's not unusual for words and expressions to lose their subtlety in translation, the negative connotations of *macho* in this country are troublesome to Hispanics.

3   Take the newspaper descriptions of alleged mass murderer Ramon Salcido. That an insensitive, insanely jealous, hard-drinking, violent Latin male is referred to as *macho* makes Hispanics cringe.

4   "*Es muy macho*," the women in my family nod approvingly, describing a man they respect. But in the United States, when women say, "He's so macho," it's with disdain.

5   The Hispanic *macho* is manly, responsible, hardworking, a man in charge, a patriarch. A man who expresses strength through silence. What the Yiddish language would call a *mensch*.

6   The American *macho* is a chauvinist, a brute, uncouth, selfish, loud, abrasive, capable of inflicting pain, and sexually promiscuous.

7   Quintessential *macho* models in this country are Sylvester Stallone, Arnold Schwarzenegger, and Charles Bronson. In their movies, they exude toughness, independence, masculinity. But a closer look reveals their machismo is really violence masquerading as courage, sullenness disguised as silence and irresponsibility camouflaged as independence.

8   If the Hispanic ideal of *macho* were translated to American screen roles, they might be Jimmy Stewart, Sean Connery, and Laurence Olivier.

9   In Spanish, *macho* ennobles Latin males. In English it devalues them. This pattern seems consistent with the conflicts ethnic minority males experience in this country. Typically the cultural traits other societies value don't translate as desirable characteristics in America.

10   I watched my own father struggle with these cultural ambiguities. He worked on a farm for twenty years. He laid down miles of irrigation pipe, carefully plowed long, neat rows in fields, hacked away at recalcitrant weeds and drove tractors through whirlpools of dust. He stoically worked twenty-hour days during harvest season, accepting the long hours as part of agricultural work. When the boss complained or upbraided him for minor mistakes, he kept quiet, even when it was obvious the boss had erred.

11   He handled the most menial tasks with pride. At home he was a good provider, helped out my mother's family in Mexico without complaint, and was indulgent with me. Arguments between my mother and him generally had to do with money, or with his stubborn reluctance to share his troubles. He tried to work them out in his own silence. He didn't want to trouble my mother—a course that backfired, because the imagined is always worse than the reality.

12   Americans regarded my father as decidedly un-*macho*. His character was interpreted as nonassertive, his loyalty non-ambition, and his quietness, ignorance. I once overheard the boss's son blame him for plowing crooked

rows in a field. My father merely smiled at the lie, knowing the boy had done it, but didn't refute it, confident his good work was well known. But the boss instead ridiculed him for being "stupid" and letting a kid get away with a lie. Seeing my embarrassment, my father dismissed the incident, saying "They're the dumb ones. Imagine, me fighting with a kid."

13   I tried not to look at him with American eyes because sometimes the reflection hurt.

14   Listening to my aunts' clucks of approval, my vision focused on the qualities America overlooked. "He's such a hard worker. So serious, so responsible." My aunts would secretly compliment my mother. The unspoken comparison was that he was not like some of their husbands, who drank and womanized. My uncles represented the darker side of *macho*.

15   In a patriarchal society, few challenge their roles. If men drink, it's because it's the manly thing to do. If they gamble, it's because it's how men relax. And if they fool around, well, it's because a man simply can't hold back so much man! My aunts didn't exactly meekly sit back, but they put up with these transgressions because Mexican society dictated this was their lot in life.

16   In the United States, I believe it was the feminist movement of the early 1970s that changed *macho*'s meaning. Perhaps my generation of Latin women was in part responsible. I recall Chicanas complaining about the chauvinistic nature of Latin men and the notion they wanted their women barefoot, pregnant, and in the kitchen. The generalization that Latin men embodied chauvinistic traits led to this interesting twist of semantics. Suddenly a word that represented something positive in one culture became a negative prototype in another.

17   The problem with the use of *macho* today is that it's become an accepted stereotype of the Latin male. And like all stereotypes, it distorts the truth.

18   The impact of language in our society is undeniable. And the misuse of *macho* hints at a deeper cultural misunderstanding that extends beyond mere word definitions.

EXERCISE 7   Vocabulary Highlights

Write a short definition of each word as it is used in the essay. (Paragraph numbers are given in pa†rentheses.) Be prepared to use these words in sentences.

subtlety (2)	recalcitrant (10)
connotations (2)	stoically (10)
alleged (3)	upbraided (10)
quintessential (7)	transgressions (15)
ambiguities (10)	embodied (16)

EXERCISE 8   Discussion and Critical Thinking

1. What is Hispanic *macho*?

2. What is American *macho*?

3. What other examples of the different definitions of *macho* can you provide?

4. The author's father worked "stoically." What does the word *stoical* imply about how a person looks at life with its many problems?

5. How does the author relate the word *macho* to the feminist movement?

6. Would the word *patriarch* be regarded differently by people with different cultural or political views?

7. What makes the author's view valuable?

8. To what kind of audience is this piece directed?

RESTAURANT REVIEW

Food, Service Hit and Miss at Gianno's

JOHN BATCHELOR, SPECIAL TO THE *GREENSBORO NEWS & RECORD*

(Thursday, January 12, 2006 1:00 am)

John Batchelor is a freelance contributor who has been reviewing restaurants for more than 20 years. You can reach him at P.O. Box 20848, Greensboro, NC 27420, or send e-mail to jebatchelor@netscape.net. To find his recent columns on the Internet, go to www.gotriad.com and click on dining. For older columns, click on News Archives.

MINDSET

Lock It In

Think of one restaurant that has—for its good or bad ambiance, food, and service—made a strong impression on you, and now you are ready to become a restaurant critic.

1   Renovations at Gianno's a couple of years ago have created a sort of Tuscan look, with wood beams overhead, beige stippled walls and tile floors. Seating is a bit crowded, and hard surfaces reflect sound, generating a noisy ambiance. This is a family-friendly restaurant, and the many children add to the volume.

2   A chalkboard at the entry describes the evening's specials but does not include prices. When we inquired, our server was not able to provide that information. Service in general proved problematic, ranging from slow but accurate to very slow with errors and omissions.

3   I could not help noticing a sign in the bar area: "This is not Burger King. You don't get it your way. You get it my way, or you don't get a damn thing." In an

establishment that is supposed to be in the hospitality business, this is a bad joke, and I don't think management should have allowed such a posting.

4   Gianno's began as a pizza specialty restaurant. My wife and I liked the firm, flavorful crust on Gianno's Pizza ($11.95). A mild tomato sauce hosted fresh mushrooms, onions, green peppers and black olives, plus sausage and pepperoni that tasted pretty much standard for area pizza.

5   Calamari ($6.95) provided a solid start to one evening's experience. The ample serving of thin-sliced rings and baby squid arrived crisp, hot and tender, with a tasty marinara sauce. The chopped spinach in Oysters Rockefeller ($6.95/six) didn't taste fresh. Most of the flavor came from the bacon and Parmesan cheese; there was no sauce, and the overall effect tilted toward dry.

6   Entree prices include a house salad of iceberg lettuce, cucumber, red onion and Roma tomato slices—rather lean in comparison to other area restaurants, but at least a salad is included. Or you can upgrade ($1.95) to spinach salad with chopped tomato, red onion, a bacon product and toasted croutons.

7   Lasagna ($8.95) produced a good meaty flavor from ground beef, ricotta cheese and tomato sauce. This is an easy recommendation.

8   Veal Saltinbocca ($14.25) had been sauteed with bits of prosciutto, spinach and portabello mushrooms, then layered with melted mozzarella. The veal was a little firm, but acceptable at the price, and it tasted good. Spinach and ricotta cheese ravioli completed the presentation.

9   A chalkboard-posted Beef Tenderloin ($18.95) was ordered medium; it arrived well done, gray throughout, albeit still tender. No one checked back for satisfaction. We entered a complaint when the check arrived, and the manager came over and volunteered to delete the charge.

10   Two seafoods made positive impressions. Grilled Salmon ($15.95) was nice and moist, served in combination with eight medium-large deveined, tender shrimp over linguine. Capers, artichokes and diced tomatoes had been scattered on top, along with a dollop of lemon butter. Pecan Crusted Trout ($14.25) had been pan-fried, creating a delightfully crisp exterior; a light baking rendered the interior fully cooked yet moist. This was placed over rice with a dab of lemon butter.

11   We never received salads on one visit. The manager gave us a card for a free Italian Nachos appetizer on a return visit. Though compensating somewhat for the omission, this procedure makes you come back in order to receive the free item as opposed to a procedure that makes you want to come back. Our waiter provided a free tiramisu—a custardy, chocolate-coffee flavored rendition that we really enjoyed.

12   On balance, some of the food at Gianno's would merit a return visit, some would not. I'm sure that if the service we received were typical, the restaurant would not have established the popular following that it has. But my experience cannot be ignored, hence a lower rating than I would have wished.

Gianno's Stone Oven
1124 Eastchester Drive
High Point
885-0762

Hours: 1 a.m.–11 p.m. Monday–Saturday

Sanitation grade: A (99.5)

Credit cards: Visa, MC, Discover

ABC permits: All

Appetizers: $4.95–$8.95

Soups: $2.25

Sandwiches: $5.95–$6.95

Handicapped accessibility: All seating on entry level

Kid friendly: Children's menu available

Healthy choices: Not identified on menu

Most recent visit: Dec. 22, 2005

Pizza: $9.85–$12.95
Salads: $2.95–$7.85
Entrees: $7.75–$21.65, including salad
Desserts: Approximately $2.95–$3.95
  (selections vary daily)
Theme: Casual Italian

Food: ** Flavors abundant and enjoyable, usually
Ambiance: Acceptable. Noisy, crowded.
Service: Acceptable. Slow, inattentive, error-filled.
Value: **½ Quantities are generous, prices very competitive
Overall rating: *

EXERCISE 9   Discussion and Critical Thinking

1. Which paragraph covers the ambiance (meaning the special atmosphere or mood created by the environment—the design, furnishings, sound, light, smell)?

2. Which paragraphs cover the quality and price of food?

3. Which paragraphs cover the quality of the service?

4. Does John Batchelor say how many times he visited Gianno's?

5. At a minimum, how many times should a reviewer visit a restaurant before evaluating it?

6. On what can readers base the credibility (accepting the person as an authority) of the reviewer; that is, why believe him or her?

7. Is one part of a review—ambiance, food, service—most important to you? If so, why?

STUDENT PARAGRAPH AND ESSAYS

Student Nancy Samuels was faced with writing on the topic of "a personal, popular, or historical hero." She didn't have to go to the library. Right in her household she found her subject—her mother. She writes of an ordinary person who faced a difficult challenge and succeeded, in a situation in which others gave up too easily. You can follow her writing process by studying her Writing Process Worksheet. To conserve space here, the freewriting and the first draft with revisions and editing have been deleted from her submission.

You will find a full-size blank worksheet on page 6, which can be photocopied, filled in, and submitted with each assignment if your instructor directs you to do so.

Writing Process Worksheet

Name <u>Nancy Samuels</u>   **Title** <u>More Than Ordinary</u>   **Due Date** <u>Tuesday, May 4, 9:30 a.m.</u>

Use the back of this page or separate paper if you need more space.

Assignment   In the space below, write whatever you need to know about your assignment, including information about the topic, audience, pattern of writing, length, whether to include a rough draft or revised drafts, and whether your paper must be typed.

Write a paragraph of analysis by division about a personal, popular, or historical hero. Name the hero and stress the traits that make that person a hero. Assume that your readers do not know your subject well. Submit this completed worksheet, one or more rough drafts, and a typed final draft.

Stage One   **Explore** Freewrite, brainstorm (list), cluster, or take notes as directed by your instructor.

Listing

Unit: Mother
Principle of function: person as hero
Parts based on the principle:
   optimistic
   persevering
   considerate
   courageous
   tolerant
   self-sacrificing

Stage Two   **Organize** Write a topic sentence or thesis; label the subject and the focus parts.

<u>My mother</u> is the best example of a hero I can think of.
    subject   focus

Write an outline or an outline alternative. For reading-based writing, include references and short quotations with page numbers as support in the outline.

  I. Optimistic
    A. Would not believe bad news
    B. Consulted several doctors
    C. Had a positive goal
 II. Persevering
    A. Becomes my brother's therapist
    B. Worked with him for three years
III. Courageous
    A. Does not listen to others
    B. Would not accept failure

IV. Self-sacrificing

    A. Concentrating on helping son

    B. Neglected self

Stage Three

Write On separate paper, write and then revise your paragraph or essay as many times as necessary for **c**oherence, **l**anguage (usage, tone, and diction), **u**nity, **e**mphasis, **s**upport, and **s**entences (**CLUESS**). Read your work aloud to hear and correct any grammatical errors or awkward-sounding sentences.

Edit any problems in fundamentals, such as **c**apitalization, **o**missions, **p**unctuation, and **s**pelling (**COPS**).

Final Draft

MORE THAN ORDINARY
Nancy Samuels

Topic sentence
(Unit and principle)

    <u>My mother is the best example of a hero I can think of</u>. No one will read about her in a book about heroes, but within her small circle of friends, her traits of heroism are well-known. My younger brother is the special beneficiary of her heroism. He was in an accident when he was five years old, and the doctor told us that he would never walk. My mother listened respectfully, but

(Part) Trait

she didn't believe him. She had <u>optimism</u>. She went to another doctor and then another. Finally she found one who prescribed exercises. She worked with

(Part) Trait

my brother for three years. Day after dismal day, she <u>persevered</u>. It wasn't just her working with him that helped my brother. It was her raw courage in

(Part) Trait

the face of failure. My brother worked with her. They both were <u>courageous</u>. We other family members weren't. To us my brother and mother were acting like a couple of people blinded by hope. We thought my mother especially, the leader, was in prolonged denial. But in three years my brother was walking. He won't be an athlete; nevertheless, he gets around. We're proud of him, but we

Trait

know—and he knows—that without Mother he would never have walked. She <u>sacrificed</u> years of her life for him. Of course, she's not a miracle worker. Most of the time, doctors are right, and some injured people can never walk. But the ones, like my brother, who somewhere have that hidden ability need that special someone like my mother. She's more than ordinary. She's a hero.

EXERCISE 10   Discussion and Critical Thinking

1. What are the main traits of Samuels's heroic mother?

2. Is she a miracle worker?

3. Will her kind of strength always succeed? Explain.

4. Would she have been heroic if she had not succeeded in helping her son?

READING-BASED WRITING

. . . .

Elvis Presley: King of the Twentieth Century

EMMETT DAVIS

Emmett Davis faced an assignment in analysis by division in which he would discuss the qualities that made a person successful. He was expected to refer to at least two sources. Davis turned to the early days of rock and roll, his special interest. Almost every source he skimmed, both on the Internet and in his college library's database, contained discussion of Elvis Presley, who became his subject.

MINDSET

Lock It In

If you believe someone else is the "King," then annotate and underline this essay and be prepared to argue.

1   After having moved a decade into the twenty-first century, we still look back and revise lists of top people of the previous one hundred years. One much-discussed category is the Greatest Performers in Popular Music. Although I have trouble choosing the top person in some categories, in this one I have no problem. Of course, it's Elvis Presley. Four factors stand out and make my choice easy: he was good looking, he could sing, he had style, and he influenced the main world of popular music, which we call "rock 'n' roll."

2   As for his looks, he was darkly handsome, some would say even beautiful, with thick, unruly hair and a sneering smile that appealed to the rebellious side of young people. Dick Clark, producer and host of *American Bandstand* for four decades, said that youth "copied his style. People imitated his gestures, dressed like him, wanted to be him (or his woman)" (148). Much has been made of the young Elvis and the old Elvis. The young was the person of slender body in a leather jacket. From that image he soon morphed into his spangled outfit phase, a reflection of his ties with country music entertainers but also becoming the model for the glitter look of numerous rock stars. Unfortunately, toward the end of his life, he put on too much weight and favored white bejeweled jump suits.

3   As for singing, he had a powerful, deep voice with a wide range similar to the big voices in rhythm and blues and black gospel music he had listened to and loved as he grew up in Mississippi and Tennessee. Early in his career he was sometimes criticized for not sounding more like traditional crooners. Although it was true that he did howl, wail, and shout in certain arrangements, he could sing religious songs and simple love ballads such as "Teddy Bear" and "Love Me Tender" with great clarity and warmth.

4   When he was on stage, his style was personal, as he shook his hips and belted out songs like "Heartbreak Hotel" and "You Ain't Nothin' But a Hound Dog." While making the guitar respectable, he popularized the driving rhythm of rock. He made music more personal and more aggressive. His body language may look tame today, but in the 1950s, it was revolutionary.

5   Because he was so different and so good, he influenced and inspired others who would become famous artists of rock 'n' roll. Groups like the Beatles and the Rolling Stones gave him credit for his innovations. His

influence even extends to academia. In 1995 the University of Mississippi convened an international conference entitled "In Search of Elvis." Professor Vernon Chadwick, who helped organize the conference, said that Elvis "is better known and in many cases more influential than William Faulkner" (Geier 14). Though Chadwick's statement may have upset some of his colleagues, it is well in line with what many of his fans believe.

6   Some fanatical fans believe Elvis is off hiding in the witness protection program and shopping at the K-Marts and Wal-Marts of the world, but, to me, he's alive in a more important way: he's a legend—he's the Greatest Performer in Popular Music for the Twentieth Century.

Works Cited

Clark, Dick. "Remembering 'Presleymania.'" *Newsweek* 8 June 1998: 148. Print.

Geier, Thom. "Eggheads for Elvis." *U.S. News & World Report* 7 Aug. 1995: 14. Print.

EXERCISE 11   Discussion and Critical Thinking

1. Circle the thesis.

2. What is the unit being considered?

3. What is the principle for dividing the unit?

4. Underline the topic sentences that indicate the parts of the unit and, in the margin to the left, use single words to annotate those parts.

5. Emmett Davis has no reservation in picking his "King." Of course, this is all a matter of opinion, but would you argue for another person? If so, who and why?

Air Traffic Control as a Career

ROGER MYERS

One of the suggested assignments was to write an essay about a career choice. The entire process would be analyzed. That satisfied the interests of student Roger Myers, who had recently chosen a career field, following several years of vacillation.

1   Since my senior year in high school, I have changed my career goals several times. I was set on being a pilot, an anthropologist, and a teacher. At one time I even made plans to move to Alaska and work in construction and outdoor recreation. After exploring those careers by reading, talking to people in those fields, and taking some courses, I expanded my search and decided on my career for good. Now my short-range and long-range career goals are in place. I intend to be an air traffic controller.

2   I discovered the field when I was taking college aeronautics courses. One was in navigation and communication. On a field trip, we visited a local airport and went up into the control tower to watch landings and take-offs. I was fascinated by the way tower operators directed traffic. I signed up for an introductory course in air traffic control, which included more firsthand observations in the same tower.

Nature of the Work

3   The nature of the work can be reduced to two words: safety and expedition. Safety means simply to keep the aircraft from running into each other. Expedition means to maintain schedules. As every air traveler knows, the two important things are to reach the destination on time and without getting hurt.

4   There are basically three kinds of air traffic controllers. First there are the control tower operators. They work in a glassed-in cage above the airport. Their main job is to direct aircraft landings and departures. For departures, they direct pilots to taxi from terminals to the runway and finally give permission for take-offs. For arrivals, they receive information from other controllers about incoming flights and give information to pilots, including weather conditions, other traffic in the area, points for reporting in the landing patterns, and permission to land. The landings and the take-offs are coordinated. All of this is done routinely by the operators if the weather is good.

5   If the weather is bad, usually meaning limited visibility, another group of air traffic controllers are engaged: the approach controllers. They are often located in a radar room under the control tower. They use instruments to maintain separation between landing aircraft, guiding pilots on flight paths through low clouds and fog. During good weather they are likely to contact aircraft as they approach the airport and guide them in their descents, finally turning them over to the control tower for movement through the traffic pattern and to a safe landing.

6   A third group of controllers are responsible for enroute flight, monitoring and regulating the upper airspace between airports. There are twenty-one such control centers staffed by about seven hundred controllers. Enroute controllers work in teams using sophisticated radar equipment to maintain

vertical and horizontal separation between aircraft. They also warn pilots about bad weather conditions and other potential hazards.

Working Conditions, Benefits, Pay, and Retirement

7   All three kinds of air traffic controllers work a basic 40-hour week and sometimes work overtime. Because the operation of air traffic occurs at all times, controllers work in shifts. Pay varies, depending on the job, but in 2000, the middle 50 percent of controllers made between $62,000 and $101,000. Senior controllers can make almost $150,000. Benefits include 13 to 26 days of vacation and health and life insurance. Because of the mental stress involved in making life-or-death decisions daily, controllers are allowed to retire after working for 25 years, are permitted to retire at the age of 50 with 20 years on the job, and must retire at the age of 56.

Training, Employment, and Job Outlook

8   Air traffic controllers are employed by the Federal Civil Service system. Most controllers go through this procedure: pass a rigorous series of tests, complete the Federal Aeronautics Association Academy for air traffic control, pass another series of examinations, begin work as an apprentice, and gradually become a certified controller. Continued employment requires yearly physical and performance examinations, as well as periodic drug tests.

9   Individuals with military experience in air traffic control can bypass some of the requirements. They have a major advantage over other applicants because of their occupational knowledge (covered by a large part of the initial examinations) and because they have been certified as air traffic controllers according to basically the same standards used in the civilian field.

10   The job outlook is good, although the competition is keen. Despite recent airline downsizing, the airflight industry continues to thrive and will continue to grow. Even in the worst of times, air traffic controllers are not laid off.

My Final Approach

11   Although I could take the examination for the FAA Academy and probably do well because I have a good basic knowledge of the career field and have passed similar tests for my private pilot's license, I intend to complete two years at my community college and enlist in the United States Air Force. I have talked to recruiters who have assured that I can be guaranteed entrance to the military school for air traffic controllers. In the service, I can learn on the job and, upon being discharged in four years, be in an almost certain position to move into the FAA program. It is possible that I will enjoy military life and remain in the service as an air traffic controller.

Work Cited

United States. Dept. of Labor. *Occupational Outlook Handbook.* 2008–09 Edition. Web. 19 Dec. 2009.

EXERCISE 12   Discussion and Critical Thinking

1. What is the unit for analysis by division?

2. What are the divisions?

3. What is the principle on which the division is based?

4. What paragraph discusses that principle?

5. What double meaning does the last section, My Final Approach, carry?

Suggested Topics and Prompts for Writing Analysis by Division

STUDENT COMPANION SITE
For additional practice, visit www.cengage .com/devenglish/ brandon/PE11e.

You will find a blank Writing Process Worksheet on page 6 of this book and on your Student Companion Site. It can be photocopied or printed out, filled in, and submitted with your assignment, if your instructor directs you to do so.

READING-BASED WRITING

Reading-based writing requires you to read critically, write a reply that shows you understand what you have read, and give credit for ideas you borrow and words you quote. The form can be a summary, a reaction, or a two-part response (with separated summary and reaction). Documentation, in which you give credit for borrowed ideas and words, can be either formal (MLA) or informal, as directed by your instructor. Both the forms of reading-based writing and documentation are discussed with examples in Chapter 1. Definitions of the three forms follow. Any form can be used for any reading selection in this book.

Summary

- The summary is a statement presenting only the main points of what you have read by using different wording without altering the meaning, adding information, or showing bias.
- It is the purest form of reading-based writing.

Reaction

- In the reaction, the meaning of what you have read will be central to your topic sentence of your paragraph or to the thesis of your essay.
- Although the reaction is not a personal narrative by itself, it may include personal experience to explain elements of the text. For example, if your source is about driving styles, your own experiences as a driver or an observer of drivers could be relevant in your analysis of the text.

- The reaction may incorporate a summary to convey a broad view of what you have read, but your summary should never be the main part of your reaction.

The Two-Part Response

- The two-part response separates the summary from the reaction.
- This form will give you practice in separating your objective summary in the first part from your more personal evaluation, interpretation, or application in the second part, the reaction.

READING-BASED WRITING TOPICS

"Golden Oldies"

1. Write a paragraph or an essay of reaction in which you analyze your favorite golden oldie by discussing its divisions, such as when it originated, what it reveals about the culture of that time, and how the oldie touches your life and the lives of others. Refer to and quote from the paragraph.

2. If a song you have in mind is not at least ten years old, put it forward as a candidate for "golden oldie" status by discussing the same divisions indicated in the previous topic. Refer to and quote from the paragraph.

"Men Are from Mars Women Are from Venus"

Although this essay is structured as comparison and contrast, it is organized in a subject-by-subject pattern, and each subject (men and women) is covered separately as an analysis by division. Paragraphs 4 through 15 make up an analysis by division about men, and paragraphs 16 through 28 do the same for women.

3. Select either the first unit (4–15) or the second (16–28), and evaluate it for accuracy. Does Gray oversimplify or stereotype or are his generalizations mostly sound? Do his views correspond with what you know about gender? Do they apply to people at all social levels? Use examples from what you have learned in school and from your experience. Refer to and quote from the essay.

"Americanization Is Tough on 'Macho'"

4. Write a summary of this essay, and underline the main idea and double-underline the parts of the definition, which takes the form of analysis by division.

5. Author Rose del Castillo Guilbault makes the point that there are two definitions of "macho"—the positive and the negative, essentially the Hispanic and the American. The qualities, or traits, of each are given in paragraphs 5 and 6. Relying on your familiarity with the term, write a reaction that focuses on either the positive or the negative as you would apply the term to someone you know, a character from the media, or a well-known public figure. Discuss at least three of the traits. Refer to and quote from the essay.

"Food, Service Hit and Miss at Gianno's"

6. Write a two-part response in which you first summarize and then react to Batchelor's restaurant review. Be specific. Discuss the parts—ambiance,

service, and food—by pointing out the usefulness and/or the shortcomings of his discussion of each part. Refer to the review and use quotations.

"Elvis Presley: King of the Twentieth Century"

7. Write a reaction in which you generally agree or disagree with Emmett Davis's view. Discuss Elvis's qualities: Are these divisions the right ones? Is Elvis the greatest in these ways collectively? Refer directly to the essay and use quotations. Should he have discussed Elvis's record sales and movie career?

8. If you believe some other performer is greater than Elvis and deserves to be called "King," then write a reaction to argue your point by referring to Davis's essay, by using quotations, and by introducing other factors that should be considered.

GENERAL TOPICS

9. Write a restaurant review in which you divide your evaluation into three parts: ambiance, service, and food. You can even use subtitles for those three parts. You need not pick an expensive or elegant establishment. A fast-food place may do or even your school cafeteria, though you may find much more originality and charm in a small, single-owner café. If there is no table service, then evaluate the counter service—the speed of service, the cheerfulness and overall appearance of the attendant, and the accuracy of the order. Pay attention to the cleanliness and whether the décor, music in the background, and seating enhance or detract from your dining experience. If the place has a reputation, is that reputation justified? Be specific in your descriptions of all parts, give prices, and use a five-star rating system for each part. For a helpful model on a similar topic, review "Food, Service Hit and Miss at Gianno's" on pages 179–181.

10. Write a paragraph or essay about a person you know who has struggled mightily to help himself or herself, or to help others and, therefore, deserves the title "hero." Structure your writing around the person's achievements and, especially, traits. For a helpful model on a similar topic, review "More Than Ordinary" on page 183.

11. Choose one of the following subjects, narrow it to a focused topic, divide it into parts, and analyze it. For example, the general "a wedding ceremony" could be narrowed to the particulars "Jason and Lisa's wedding ceremony."
    a. A machine such as an automobile, a computer, a camera
    b. A city administration, a governmental agency, a school board, a student council
    c. A ceremony—wedding, graduation
    d. A holiday celebration, a pep rally, a sales convention, a religious revival
    e. An offensive team in football (any team in any game)
    f. A family, a relationship, a gang, a club, a sorority, a fraternity
    g. An album, a performance, a song, a singer, an actor, a musical group, a musical instrument
    h. A movie, a television program, a video game
    i. Any well-known person—athlete, politician, criminal, writer

CROSS-CURRICULAR TOPIC

12. Consider the units of material in a class you are taking or have taken. Each unit has its parts: a musical composition in a music appreciation class, a short story in an English class, an organ such as a heart in a biology class, a government in a political science class, a management team in a business class, a family in a sociology class, a painting in an art history class, a teacher or student in an education class, and so on. Select one unit, consult your textbook(s), talk to your instructor(s), and follow the procedure for writing an analysis by division. Credit your sources, and use quotation marks around material you borrow.

CAREER-RELATED TOPICS

13. Write an analysis by division of your own career field or a career field that interests you. For a paragraph unit, write about one aspect, such as your background and aptitude, an overview of the field, working conditions and benefits, requirements for employment, or your plan for entering the field. For a longer analysis, write about several or all of the parts. For a helpful model on a similar topic, review "Air Traffic Control as a Career" on pages 186–187; for directions and a reference to good source material, see "Career Review" on pages 167–168.

14. Explain how the parts of a product function as a unit.

15. Explain how each of several qualities of a specific person—such as his or her intelligence, sincerity, knowledgeability, ability to communicate, manner, attitude, and appearance—makes that individual an effective salesperson, manager, or employee.

16. Explain how the demands or requirements for a particular job represent a comprehensive picture of that job.

17. Explain how the aspects of a particular service (such as friendly, competent, punctual, confidential) work together in a satisfactory manner.

WRITER'S GUIDELINES: Analysis by Division

Almost anything can be analyzed by division—for example, how the parts of the ear work in hearing, how the parts of the eye work in seeing, or how the parts of the heart work in pumping blood throughout the body. Subjects such as these are all approached with the same systematic procedure.

1. This is the procedure.

- **Step 1.** Begin with something that is a unit.
- **Step 2.** State the principle by which that unit functions.
- **Step 3.** Divide the unit into parts according to the principle.
- **Step 4.** Discuss each of the parts in relation to the unit.

2. This is the way you might apply that procedure to a good boss.

• Unit	Manager
• Principle of function	Effective as a leader
• Parts based on the principle	Fair, intelligent, stable, competent in the field
• Relationship to the unit	Consider each part in relation to the person's effectiveness as a manager.

3. This is how a basic outline of analysis by division might look.

Thesis: To be effective as a leader, a manager needs specific qualities.
  I. Fairness
  II. Intelligence
  III. Stability
  IV. Competence in the field

4. The restaurant review will almost certainly use the analysis-by-division pattern.

   • The main parts of a typical review are ambiance, service, and food.
   • The review should contain specific descriptive details, examples, and information from the menu.

5. The career review is another form of analysis by division.

   • The unit is the career quest itself.
   • The parts are the relevant matters that make up the entire quest for a career.
   • The following main-part outline shows some useful divisions for an essay as a career review. For a shorter essay, just select the main parts that fit the assignment you have in mind. For an even shorter assignment of a paragraph, subdivide one of these Roman-numeral parts for basic organization of your career review, or analysis by division.

   Unit: (the career itself)
   Divisions: (parts of the unit, the career itself)
     I. My background, interests, and aptitude
     II. My desired field—an overview
     III. Working conditions, pay, benefits
     IV. Requirements for employment
     V. My step-by-step plan to enter this field

6. Use the writing process.

   • Write and then revise your paragraph or essay as many times as necessary for **c**oherence, **l**anguage (usage, tone, and diction), **u**nity, **e**mphasis, **s**upport, and **s**entences (**CLUESS**).
   • Read your work aloud to hear and correct any grammatical errors or awkward-sounding sentences.
   • Edit any problems in fundamentals, such as **c**apitalization, **o**missions, **p**unctuation, and **s**pelling (**COPS**).

Chapter 10

Process Analysis
Writing About Doing

FLOW OF WRITING

WHEN TO USE PROCESS ANALYSIS

FOR COLLEGE WRITING ASSIGNMENTS

Much of your college work appears as process analysis. Instructors and instructional materials, such as this textbook, are explaining how things are done or how things occurred.

- In labs you experiment with processes and learn to perform tasks. To demonstrate your knowledge of what you have learned and your ability to perform tasks, you write paragraphs, essays, and reports, and you take tests.
- Having a systematic pattern for organization for writing these process analyses will enable you to write with efficiency.

IN CAREERS AND AT THE WORKPLACE

Process analysis is central to both career preparation and workplace activities. You learn what to do and how to perform.

- As you work with others, as a member of a team or as a supervisor of new employees, you will need to write memos and directives as process analysis to explain what to do and how something is or was done.
- Whether you do the technical writing or advertising copy, you will need to explain, often in writing, how your products and services are used and how they are beneficial.

THE QUIGMANS by Buddy Hickerson

"Hold still, it's my first day!"

Writing Process Analysis

If you have any doubt about how frequently we use process analysis, just think about how many times you have heard people say, "How do you do it?" or "How is [was] it done?" Even when you are not hearing those questions, you are posing them yourself when you need to make something, cook a meal, assemble an item, take some medicine, repair something, or figure out what happened. In your college classes, you may have to discover how osmosis occurs, how a rock changes form, how a mountain was formed, how a battle was won, or how a bill goes through the legislature.

If you need to explain how to do something or how something was (is) done, you will engage in **process analysis**. You will break down your topic into stages, explaining each so that your reader can duplicate or understand the process.

TWO TYPES OF PROCESS ANALYSIS: DIRECTIVE AND INFORMATIVE

The questions How do I do it? and How is (was) it done? will lead you into two different types of process analysis—directive and informative.

Directive process analysis explains how to do something. As the name suggests, it gives directions for the reader to follow. It says, for example, "Read me, and you can bake a pie [tune up your car, read a book critically, write an essay, take some medicine]." Because it is presented directly to the reader, it usually addresses the reader as "you," or it implies the "you" by saying something such as "First [you] purchase a large pumpkin, and then [you]. . . ." In the same way, this textbook addresses you or implies "you" because it is a long how-to-do-it (directive process analysis) statement.

Informative process analysis explains how something was (is) done by giving data (information). Whereas the directive process analysis tells you what to do in the future, the informative process analysis tells you what has occurred or what is occurring. If it is something in nature, such as the formation of a mountain, you can read and understand the process by which it emerged. In this type of process analysis, you do not tell the reader what to do; therefore, you will seldom use the words *you* or *your*.

WORKING WITH STAGES

Preparation or Background

In the first stage of directive process analysis, list the materials or equipment needed for the process and discuss the necessary setup arrangements. For some topics, this stage will also provide technical terms and definitions. The degree to which this stage is detailed will depend on both the subject itself and the expected knowledge and experience of the projected audience.

Informative process analysis may begin with background or context rather than with preparation. For example, a statement explaining how mountains form might begin with a description of a flat portion of the earth made up of plates that are arranged like a jigsaw puzzle.

Steps or Sequence

The actual process will be presented here. Each step or sequence must be explained clearly and directly, and phrased to accommodate the audience. The language, especially in directive process analysis, is likely to be simple and concise; however, avoid dropping words such as *and*, *a*, *an*, *the*, and *of*, and thereby lapsing into "recipe language." The steps may be accompanied by explanations about why certain procedures are necessary and how not following directions carefully can lead to trouble.

Order

The order will usually be chronological (time based) in some sense. Certain transitional words are commonly used to promote coherence: *first*, *second*, *third*, *then*, *soon*, *now*, *next*, *finally*, *at last*, *therefore*, *consequently*, and—especially for informative process analysis—words used to show the passage of time such as hours, days of the week, and so on.

BASIC FORMS

Consider using this form for the directive process (with topics such as how to cook something or how to fix something).

How to Prepare Spring Rolls
 I. Preparation
    A. Suitable cooking area
    B. Utensils, equipment
    C. Spring roll wrappers
    D. Vegetables, sauce

II. Steps

    A. Season vegetables

    B. Wrap vegetables

    C. Fold wrappers

    D. Deep-fry rolls

    E. Serve rolls with sauce

Consider using this form for the informative process (with topics such as how a volcano functions or how a battle was won).

How Coal Is Formed

 I. Background or context

    A. Accumulation of land plants

    B. Bacterial action

    C. Muck formation

II. Sequence

    A. Lignite from pressure

    B. Bituminous from deep burial and heat

    C. Anthracite from metamorphic conditions

COMBINED FORMS

Combination process analysis occurs when directive process analysis and informative process analysis are blended, usually when the writer personalizes the account. For example, if I tell you from a detached point of view how to write a research paper, my writing is directive process analysis, but if I tell you how I once wrote a research paper and give you the details in an informative account, then you may very well learn enough so that you can duplicate what I did. Thus, you would be both informed and instructed. Often the personalized account is more interesting to the general reader, but if, for example, you need to assemble a toy the night before your child's birthday you just want information.

Many assignments are done as a personalized account. A paper about planting radish seeds may be informative—but uninspiring. However, a paper about the time you helped your grandpa plant his spring garden (giving all the details) may be informative, directive, and entertaining. It is often the cultural framework provided by personal experience that transforms a pedestrian directive account into something memorable. That is why some instructors ask their students to explain how to do something within the context of experience.

CAREER-RELATED WRITING AS PROCESS ANALYSIS

When you are new on the job, you will be expected first to learn how to execute your job description according to employer expectations, doing work the "company way." Knowing the techniques for process analysis presented here will help you master the workplace subject material more easily. Then at some point, you will probably be expected to train others. The training you do may require you both to talk and to write. Whatever the method, knowing how to deliver a clear, logical, and correct process analysis will be an asset. Fortunately for you, the two basic organizational patterns of process analysis— directive and informative—are as logical as they are simple.

Process analysis will serve you particularly well in writing memos and guidance sheets, and in giving PowerPoint presentations. In PowerPoint presentations you can treat your outline as an overview as part of your introduction and then proceed to discuss the specific steps or stages for development. Keep in mind that these techniques for writing process analysis in your current class differ little from what you will be doing at work. The essay on pages 215–216, "Doing a Flame Hair Tattoo," offers both an outline and a written example of what can be done with a single unit of workplace process.

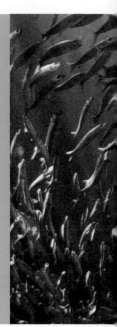

Transitional Words

Consider using the following transitional words to improve coherence by connecting ideas with ideas, sentences with sentences, and paragraphs with paragraphs.

FOR PROCESS ANALYSIS:
Preparation and Background: at the outset, before stages develop, before steps occur, before work begins, as preparation for, in anticipation of, in laying the groundwork

Steps and Stages: first, second, third, another step, next, now, then, at this point, at this stage, at this step, after, at last, finally, subsequently, to begin with, initially, after that, afterward, at the same time, concurrently, meanwhile, soon, during the process, during . . . , in order to, for a minute, for a . . .

FOR ALL PATTERNS OF WRITING: The <u>HOTSHOT CAT</u> words: <u>H</u>owever, <u>O</u>therwise, <u>T</u>herefore, <u>S</u>imilarly, <u>H</u>ence, <u>O</u>n the other hand, <u>T</u>hen, <u>C</u>onsequently, <u>A</u>lso, <u>T</u>hus (See pages 427–428 for additional transitional words.)

USEFUL PREWRITING PROCEDURE

All the strategies of freewriting, brainstorming, and clustering can be useful in writing a process analysis. However, if you already know your subject well, you can simply make two lists, one headed *Preparation* or *Background* and the other *Steps* or *Sequence*. Then jot down ideas for each. After you have finished with your listing, you can delete parts, combine parts, and rearrange parts for better order. That editing of your lists will lead directly to a formal outline you can use in Stage Two of the writing process. Following is an example of listing for the topic of how to prepare spring rolls.

Preparation	*Steps*
stainless steel bowl	slice and mix vegetables
deep-fry pan	add sauce to vegetables
spoon	beat eggs
damp cloth	place wrappers on damp cloth
spring roll wrappers	add 2 to 3 tablespoons of vegetables per wrapper
eggs	fold and seal wrapper with egg
sauce	freeze for later or deep-fry immediately
cabbage	serve with sweet-and-sour sauce
celery	
carrots	
bean sprouts	

FINDING PATTERNS IN PHOTOS

EXERCISE 1   A Text-Based Activity for Groups or Individuals

Valerie changes the oil in her car

Imagine you are Valerie in the photo, and you are not a mechanic. Nevertheless, you have calculated you can save a lot of money by switching to self-service in oil changing. You e-mailed a friend with a weird sense of humor and asked him to fax you the steps for changing oil. He called and volunteered to do the work. Being an independent person, you said you only want the steps. Later when you heard a noise on your front porch, you investigated and discovered he had quickly come and gone, leaving behind tools, an oil filter, cans of oil, and a list of steps. One problem: He jumbled the order of the steps. You are not amused. Determined to do the work yourself, you look at the items, scratch your head, and begin rearranging the list.

In the following blanks, place the steps from the right-hand column in the correct order. Add steps if you like.

If your instructor requires, use the outline as a framework to write a brief process-analysis paper on changing the oil in your car.

1. _____   A. Dispose of used oil at a recycling center.

2. _____   B. Use wrench to unscrew and remove oil filter.

3. _____   C. Pour oil into crankcase.

4. _____   D. Place catch pan under oil drain plug.

5. _____   E. Drain oil.

6. _____   F. Use wrench to remove oil drain plug.

7. _____   G. Replace oil drain plug.

8. _____   H. Run engine for two minutes.

9. _____   I. Coat oil filter gasket with oil and install oil filter.

10. _____   J. Turn off engine.

11. _____   K. Wait a few minutes to check and adjust oil level.

Practicing Patterns of Process Analysis

A definite pattern underlies a process analysis. In some presentations, such as with merchandise to be assembled, the content reads as mechanically as an outline, and no reader objects. In other presentations, such as your typical college assignments, the writing should be well developed and interesting. Regardless of the form you use or the audience you anticipate, keep in mind that in process analysis the pattern will provide a foundation for the content.

EXERCISE 2   Completing Patterns of Directive Process Analysis

Using directive process analysis, fill in the blanks to complete this pattern for "writing an essay."

I. Preparation (Prewriting)

    A. Understand assignment

    B. _____

    C. Write the controlling idea

    D. _____

II. Steps (Writing)

    A. Draft

    B. _____

    C. _____

EXERCISE 3   Completing Patterns of Directive Process Analysis

Using directive process analysis, fill in the blanks to complete this pattern for "planting a lawn."

I. Preparation

    A. Obtain tools

    B. Obtain _____

    C. Obtain _____

    D. Obtain _____

II. Steps

    A. _____

    B. _____

    C. Cultivate soil

    D. _____

    E. Cover seed with mulch and fertilizer

    F. _____

EXERCISE 4   Completing Patterns of Informative Process Analysis

Using informative process analysis, fill in the blanks to complete this pattern. Use a topic from a subject you are studying or have studied and explain some phenomenon such as how a volcano, a hurricane, a tidal wave, cell division, tree growth, a common cold, a sunburn, a blister, a headache, chapped lips, land erosion, quicksand, computer crash, asthma, fossil, fog, or the like occurs.

I. Background

A. _____

B. _____

C. _____

II. Sequence

A. _____

B. _____

C. _____

D. _____

EXERCISE 5   Completing Patterns of Informative Process Analysis

Using informative process analysis, fill in the blanks to complete this pattern. Use a topic from a subject you are studying or have studied and explain some phenomenon such as how a tornado, dust storm, rip tide, osmosis, human growth, flu, termite damage, skin cancer, tooth cavity, baldness, wrinkling, airplane flight, rise and fall of tides, rainbow, radar, rust on metal, egg hatching, egg fertilization, HIV, frog croaking, cricket chirping, or the like occurs.

I. Background

A. _____

B. _____

C. _____

II. Sequence

A. _____

B. _____

C. _____

D. _____

Readings for Critical Thinking, Discussion, and Writing

READING STRATEGIES AND OBJECTIVES

Underlining and annotating these reading selections will help you answer the questions that follow the selections, discuss the material in class, and prepare for reading-based writing assignments. As you underline and annotate, pay special attention to the author's writing skills, logic, and message, and consider the relevance of the material to your own experiences and values.

One selection begins with a Mindset suggestion that can help you create a readiness for connecting with what you are about to read.

PARAGRAPHS

How to Sharpen a Knife

FLORENCE H. PETTIT

The simplest tasks are often the most poorly done because we assume that we know how to do them and do not seek instruction. Florence H. Pettit explains here how to sharpen a knife properly, and what we learn reminds us that we could probably take lessons on performing any number of everyday chores.

Setup

Steps

1

2

3

4

5

6

If you have never done any whittling or wood carving before, the first skill to learn is how to sharpen your knife. You may be surprised to learn that even a brand-new knife needs sharpening. Knives are never sold honed (finely sharpened), although some gouges and chisels are. It is essential to learn the firm stroke on the stone that will keep your blades sharp. The sharpening stone must be fixed in place on the table, so that it will not move around. You can do this by placing a rubber inner tube or a thin piece of foam rubber under it. Or you can tack four strips of wood, if you have a rough worktable, to frame the stone and hold it in place. Put a generous puddle of oil on the stone—this will soon disappear into the surface of a new stone, and you will need to keep adding more oil. Press the knife blade flat against the stone in the puddle of oil, using your index finger. Whichever way the cutting edge of the knife faces is the side of the blade that should get a little more pressure. Move the blade around three or four times in a narrow oval about the size of your fingernail, going *counterclockwise* when the sharp edge is facing right. Now turn the blade over in the same spot on the stone, press hard, and move it around the small oval *clockwise*, with more pressure on the cutting edge that faces left. Repeat the ovals, flipping the knife blade over six or seven times, and applying lighter pressure to the blade the last two times. Wipe the blade clean with a piece of rag or tissue and rub it flat on the piece of leather strop at least twice on each side. Stroke *away*, from the cutting edge to remove the little burr of metal that may be left on the blade.

EXERCISE 6   Discussion and Critical Thinking

1. What type of process analysis (informative or directive) is used?

2. To what type of audience (well informed, moderately informed, or poorly informed on the topic) does the writer direct this selection?

3. What is the prevailing tone (objective, humorous, reverent, argumentative, cautionary, playful, ironic, ridiculing) of this selection?

In text:

- A horizontal line shows the point at which the preparation (materials, setup, explaining words, and so on) ends and the steps begin. The steps are numbered in the margin.

How to Eat an Ice Cream Cone

L. RUST HILLS

Our simple behavior may seem absurd when examined with solemn deliberation. Here, L. Rust Hills explains how to eat an ice cream cone, even when things go wrong. Perhaps this piece is so successful because the author describes techniques and behavior (with a bit of exaggeration) that we are all familiar with but have not really considered.

Grasp the cone with the right hand firmly but gently between thumb and at least one but not more than three fingers, two-thirds of the way up the cone. Then dart swiftly away to an open area, away from the jostling crowd at the stand. Now take up the classic ice-cream-cone-eating stance: feet from one to two feet apart, body bent forward from the waist at a twenty-five-degree angle, right elbow well up, right forearm horizontal, at a level with your collarbone and about twelve inches from it. But don't start eating yet! Check first to see what emergency repairs may be necessary. Sometimes a sugar cone will be so crushed or broken or cracked that all one can do is gulp at the thing like a savage, getting what he can of it and letting the rest drop to the ground, and then evacuating the area of catastrophe as quickly as possible. Checking the cone for possible trouble can be done in a second or two, if one knows where to look and does it systematically. A trouble spot some people overlook is the bottom tip of the cone. This may have been broken off. Or the flap of the cone material at the bottom, usually wrapped over itself in that funny spiral construction, may be folded in a way that is imperfect and leaves an opening. No need to say that through this opening—in a matter of perhaps thirty or, at most, ninety seconds—will begin to pour hundreds of thousands of sticky molecules of melted ice cream. You know in this case that you must instantly get the paper napkin in your left hand under and around the bottom of the cone to stem the forthcoming flow, or else be doomed to eat the cone far too rapidly. It is a grim moment. No one wants to eat a cone under that kind of pressure, but neither does anyone want to end up with the bottom of the cone stuck to a messy napkin. There's one other alternative—one that takes both skill and courage: Forgoing any cradling action, grasp the cone more firmly between thumb and forefinger and extend the other fingers so that they are out of the way of the dripping from the bottom, then increase the waist-bend angle from twenty-five to thirty-five degrees, and then eat the cone, *allowing* it to drip out of the bottom onto the ground in front of you! Experienced and thoughtful cone-eaters enjoy facing up to this kind of sudden challenge.

EXERCISE 7   Discussion and Critical Thinking

1. What type of process analysis (informative or directive) is used?

2. To what type of audience (well informed, moderately informed, or poorly informed on the topic) does the writer direct this selection?

3. What is the prevailing tone (objective, humorous, reverent, argumentative, cautionary, playful, ironic, ridiculing) of this material?

ESSAYS

Attitude

GARRISON KEILLOR

Author, humorist, and storyteller, Garrison Keillor is best known as host of A Prairie Home Companion *straight from Lake Wobegon, long featured on National Public Radio. In this essay, first published in* The New Yorker, *he tells us how to play slow-pitch softball with "attitude."*

1   Long ago I passed the point in life when major-league ballplayers begin to be younger than yourself. Now all of them are, except for a few aging trigenarians and a couple of quadros who don't get around on the fastball as well as they used to and who sit out the second games of doubleheaders. However, despite my age (thirty-nine), I am still active and have a lot of interests. One of them is slow-pitch softball, a game that lets me go through the motions of baseball without getting beaned or having to run too hard. I play on a pretty casual team, one that drinks beer on the bench and substitutes freely. If a player's wife or girlfriend wants to play, we give her a glove and send her out to right field, no questions asked, and if she lets a pop fly drop six feet in front of her, nobody agonizes over it.

2   Except me. This year. For the first time in my life, just as I am entering the dark twilight of my slow-pitch career, I find myself taking the game seriously. It isn't the bonehead play that bothers me especially—the pop fly that drops untouched, the slow roller juggled and the ball then heaved ten feet over the first baseman's head and into the next diamond, the routine singles that go

through outfielders' legs for doubles and triples with gloves flung after them. No, it isn't our stone-glove fielding or pussyfoot baserunning or limp-wristed hitting that gives me fits, though these have put us on the short end of some mighty ridiculous scores this summer. It's our attitude.

3   Bottom of the ninth, down 18–3, two outs, a man on first and a woman on third, and our third baseman strikes out. *Strikes out!* In slow-pitch, not even your grandmother strikes out, but this guy does, and after his third strike—a wild swing at a ball that bounces on the plate—he topples over in the dirt and lies flat on his back, laughing. *Laughing!*

4   Same game, earlier. They have the bases loaded. A weak grounder is hit toward our second baseperson. The runners are running. She picks up the ball, and she looks at them. She looks at first, at second, at home. We yell, "Throw it! Throw it!" and she throws it, underhand, at the pitcher, who has turned and run to back up the catcher. The ball rolls across the third-base line and under the bench. Three runs score. The batter, a fatso, chugs into second. The other team hoots and hollers, and what does she do? She shrugs and smiles ("Oh, silly me"); after all, it's only a game. Like the afore-mentioned strikeout artist, she treats her error as a joke. They have forgiven themselves instantly, which is unforgivable. It is *we* who should forgive them, who can say, "It's all right, it's only a game." They are supposed to throw up their hands and kick the dirt and hang their heads, as if this boner, even if it is their sixteenth of the afternoon—*this* is the one that really and truly breaks their hearts.

5   That attitude sweetens the game for everyone. The sinner feels sweet remorse. The fatso feels some sense of accomplishment; this is no bunch of rumdums he forced into an error but a team with some class. We, the sinner's teammates, feel momentary anger at her—dumb! dumb play!—but then, seeing her grief, we sympathize with her in our hearts (any one of us might have made that mistake or one worse), and we yell encouragement, including the shortstop, who, moments before, dropped an easy throw for a force at second. "That's all right! Come on! We got 'em!" we yell. "Shake it off! These turkeys can't hit!" This makes us all feel good, even though the turkeys now lead us by ten runs. We're getting clobbered, but we have a winning attitude.

6   Let me say this about attitude: Each player is responsible for his or her own attitude, and to a considerable degree you can *create* a good attitude by doing certain little things on the field. These are certain little things that ballplayers do in the Bigs, and we ought to be doing them in the Slows.

7   **1.** When going up to bat, don't step right into the batter's box as if it were an elevator. The box is your turf, your stage. Take possession of it slowly and deliberately, starting with a lot of back-bending, knee-stretching, and torso-revolving in the on-deck circle. Then, approaching the box, stop outside it and tap the dirt off your spikes with your bat. You don't have spikes, you have sneakers, of course, but the signifi-cance of the tapping is the same. Then, upon entering the box, spit on the ground. It's a way of saying, "This here is mine. This is where I get my hits."

8   **2.** Spit frequently. Spit at all crucial moments. Spit correctly. Spit should be *blown*, not ptuied weakly with the lips, which often results in dribble. Spitting should convey forcefulness of purpose, concentration, pride. Spit down, not in the direction of others. Spit in the glove and on the fingers, especially after making a real knucklehead play; it's a way of saying, "I dropped the ball because my glove was dry."

9   **3.** At bat and in the field, pick up dirt. Rub dirt in the fingers (especially after spitting on them). Toss dirt, as if testing the wind for velocity and direction. Smooth the dirt. Be involved with dirt. If no dirt is available (e.g., in the outfield), pluck tufts of grass. Fielders should be grooming their areas constantly between plays, flicking away tiny sticks and bits of gravel.

10   **4.** Take your time. Tie your laces. Confer with your teammates about possible situations that may arise and conceivable options in dealing with them. Extend the game. Three errors on three consecutive plays can be humiliating if the plays occur within the space of a couple of minutes, but if each error is separated from the next by extensive conferences on the mound, lace-tying, glove adjustments, and arguing close calls (if any), the effect on morale is minimized.

11   **5.** Talk. Not just an occasional "Let's get a hit now" but continuous rhythmic chatter, a flow of syllables: "Hey babe hey babe c'mon babe good stick now hey babe long tater take him downtown babe . . . hey good eye good eye."

12   Infield chatter is harder to maintain. Since the slow-pitch pitch is required to be a soft underhand lob, infielders hesitate to say, "Smoke him babe hey low heat hey throw it on the black babe chuck it in there back him up babe no hit no hit." Say it anyway.

13   **6.** One final rule, perhaps the most important of all: When your team is up and has made the third out, the batter and the players who were left on base do not come back to the bench for their gloves. *They remain on the field, and their teammates bring their gloves out to them.* This requires some organization and discipline, but it pays off big in morale. It says, "Although we're getting our pants knocked off, still we must conserve our energy."

14   Imagine that you have bobbled two fly balls in this rout and now you have just tried to stretch a single into a double and have been easily thrown out sliding into second base, where the base runner ahead of you had stopped. It was the third out and a dumb play, and your opponents smirk at you as they run off the field. You are the goat, a lonely and tragic figure sitting in the dirt. You curse yourself, jerking your head sharply forward. You stand up and kick the base. How miserable! How degrading! Your utter shame, though brief, bears silent testimony to the worthiness of your teammates, whom you have let down, and they appreciate it. They call out to you now as they take the field, and as the second baseman runs to his position he says, "Let's get 'em now," and tosses you your glove. Lowering your head, you trot slowly out to right. There you do some deep knee bends. You pick grass. You find a pebble and fling it into foul territory. As the first batter comes to the plate, you check the sun. You get set in your stance, poised to fly. Feet spread, hands on hips, you bend slightly at the waist and spit the expert spit of a veteran ballplayer—a player who has known the agony of defeat but who always bounces back, a player who has lost a stride on the base paths but can still make the big play.

15   This is *ball*, ladies and gentlemen. This is what it's all about.

EXERCISE 8   Discussion and Critical Thinking

1. Is the process analysis part of this essay informative or directive?

2. What is the source of "attitude," as Keillor would like to see it demonstrated on his slow-pitch team?

3. Why does he skip over the preparation stage?

4. Keillor provides us with six steps. Are the steps to be performed in a particular order?

5. In what other sports is attitude important? Give some examples of attitude-building rituals in other sports.

6. What attitude-building behavior is used by people outside sports: at school, at work, at worship, on the road?

7. What is the tone of this essay and what does Keillor expect readers to do?

Flirting Fundamentals

GERALDINE BAUM

Flirting, like all human behavior, can be studied and analyzed. Although we flirt without conscious effort, to the psychologist the techniques and procedures are as predictable as those associated with fear and hunger. Los Angeles Times staff writer Geraldine Baum, no psychologist herself, reports the findings of the foremost specialist in this area, Monica Moore.

MINDSET
Lock It In

Imagine you are a single guy and there she is across the room giving off more signals than a cop directing traffic in Times Square. But you are not sure whether you or the person behind you is the target, so you just watch the body language. You are cool.

1   You probably shouldn't know about Monica Moore's research. You *think* you want to know, but really you don't. If you did, you'd be too self-conscious to do what comes naturally. For while the rest of us fumble through life clutching our hearts and throats, this woman observes us and simply knows.

2   For almost twenty years, Moore, an experimental psychologist, has been studying flirting. In fact, she has spent a career turning an immensely subtle art into science. Which is a little like reducing Mona Lisa's smile into a neurological tic.

3   Moore, a professor at St. Louis' Webster University, and her teams of graduate students spent hundreds of hours in bars and student centers covertly watching women and men court, and painstakingly recording every smile and laugh. After feeding all the data into a computer, Moore came up with a catalogue of fifty-two gestures women use to signal their interest in men. Think of it as L.L. Bean's Love Collection. This is one of those studies congressmen like to rail against when it involves a federal grant. But Moore, the Jane Goodall of human courtship, is quite serious about her work.

4   "People see flirting as so frivolous," she says. "But I'd argue that to know about all this is very important because it helps explain human relations." Like Charles Darwin, Moore began with the premise that women make the initial choice of a mate. And from there the courtship process begins. Western cultures wrongly assume men control the process, she says, because they focus on the far more obvious second stage of courtship: The approach. But Moore contends it all begins when girl eyes boy—and smiles or smoothes her skirt or licks her lips. And study after study showed that how attractive a woman is, is less important than her flirting skills.

5   "So she gets the first turn, then he gets a turn. Each time one signals the other they are reaffirming their choice. Either one can opt out at any time along the way." In fact, Moore's studies decode the obvious. The only surprise is that such excruciatingly erotic behavior can sound so boring. Listen to her description of "neck presentation": "The woman tilted her head sideways to an angle of approximately 45 degrees. This resulted in the ear almost touching the ipsilateral shoulder, thereby exposing the opposite side of the neck. Occasionally the woman stroked the exposed neck area with her fingers. . . ."

6   But Moore isn't writing for *True Romance*. Rather, she publishes in such scintillating academic journals as *Semiotica* and *Ethology and Sociobiology*.

7   The best part of her study on gestures, which included observing 200 women over two years, is the list. To attract a man, women most often smile, glance, primp, laugh, giggle, toss their heads, flip their hair, and whisper. Sometimes they hike their skirts, pat a buttock, hug, request a dance, touch a knee, and caress. Moore's description of one of the most frequent signals—"solitary dancing"—would make anyone who has ever been in a singles bar squirm. "While seated or standing, the woman moved her body in time to the music. A typical male response was to request a dance."

8   In fact, there is something risky about Moore's work and she knows it. And so after one of her students came back from spring break boasting that it took twelve minutes of signaling to get a man to her side at an airport bar—and then she ignored him—Moore instituted an ethics policy for her graduate students. "I didn't want them to misuse their knowledge," Moore says.

9   Moore began her research in flirting in the late 1970s when she herself was a graduate student in search of a dissertation topic. Her adviser suggested she pick something fun, and all she could think was: "Food, sex, food, sex, food, sex." Later Moore heard an anthropologist lecture about biological theories of human female choice, which started Moore wondering how women made decisions about who they choose.

10   Moore interviewed 100 women asking what it was about the men they were seeing that made them sexy. But interviewing techniques presented too many problems, so she decided she had to make objective observations

11   Moore doesn't have a similar list of men's gestures. All she knows is that men send out undirected signals of power and attractiveness by puffing up their chests or checking their watch or smoothing their ties. "But they don't do what women do," she says. "Once a woman looks around the room, she settles on one or two men and starts sending out the signals."

12   It's amazing how intricate her research is. Once in a bar her teams of graduate students—always one man and one woman because couples are rarely noticed when there are singles around—would randomly select a female subject. Then one member of the team would talk into a small tape recorder and keep track of her every movement. The other member of the team would keep track of all the responses made by men.

13   In the next few years Moore hopes to use her catalogue to find out more about women's choices and she wants to explore whether flirting drops off after marriage. "I don't think so, but it will be fascinating to find out," says Moore, who is 41 and married with a child.

The 52 Ways Women Flirt

Psychologist Monica Moore provides this list of behaviors (listed in descending order of occurrence).

Facial/Head Patterns	Posture Patterns	
Smile	Solitary dance	Thigh touch
Room-encompassing glance	Lean	Placement
Laugh	Point	Approach
Short, darting glance	Dance (acceptance)	Foot to foot
Fixed gaze	Parade	Request dance
Hair flip	Aid solicitation	Hug
Head toss	Play	Frontal body contact
Head nod	Brush	Breast touch
Giggle	Knee touch	Hang
Whisper	Shoulder hug	Lateral body contact
Neck presentation		
Lip lick	**Gestures**	
Pout	Gesticulation	Caress (back)
Coy smile	Caress (object)	Arm flexion
Face to face	Primp	Caress (torso)
Kiss	Caress (leg)	Buttock pat
Eyebrow flash	Caress (arm)	Tap
Lipstick application	Hand hold	Caress (face/hair)
	Palm	Hike skirt

14   She says there are only six other academics that she knows of in the world who have done human courtship studies. Most are sexologists. "Whenever I presented my work at meetings of psychologists, I was always in a room packed with voyeurs," she says. "I had no one to talk to until I found the Society for the Scientific Study of Sex."

EXERCISE 9   Vocabulary Highlights

Write a short definition of each word as it is used in the essay. (Paragraph numbers are given in parentheses.) Be prepared to use these words in sentences.

subtle (2)	scintillating (6)
neurological (2)	intricate (12)
frivolous (4)	voyeurs (14)
reaffirming (5)	lateral (list)
excruciatingly (5)	gesticulation (list)

EXERCISE 10   Discussion and Critical Thinking

1. Is the study of the science of flirting important or not important? Why?

2. What does Moore say about the female's role in mate selection?

3. How far does her research go?

4. What is typical behavior when a woman who is interested in attracting a man enters a room?

5. How do Moore's research teams operate?

6. Do you think Moore's research is most valid when applied to settings for singles or does it have wide application? Explain.

7. Moore is curious about whether flirting (with the spouse) drops off after marriage. What do you think?

8. Do you regard Moore's study as a serious one within the field of sociology or anthropology? Explain.

CAREER-RELATED WRITING

A Successful Interview

C. EDWARD GOOD AND WILLIAM FITZPATRICK

Freelance authors C. Edward Good and William Fitzpatrick describe the interview as systematic. To be successful in an interview, a person being interviewed must understand the system. In this way, the interviewee will not only follow what is going on and anticipate questions but also in some instances, be able to control the flow of the interview.

1   Facing the interview might make you apprehensive, but there is no reason to fear it. It is your real opportunity to get face to face with your product's potential buyer and bring to bear all of your personal selling skills. If you go into the situation with confidence based on preparation and not on ego, you are more likely to come out a winner. Take the time to prepare properly. The interview has been your goal thus far in the job search, so it is your stepping stone to future success. Be positive, be enthusiastic, and rely on your experience in communicating with people.

The Interview

2   The interviewer will probably take the following steps with you:

Establish Rapport. The interviewer's responsibility is to put you at ease, both physically and emotionally. The more relaxed you are, the more you will trust the interviewer and open up to him or her. Skilled interviewers will not put you in front of a desk. They will put the chair beside the desk so there are no barriers between you or will not use a desk at all. Initial conversation will be about trivial matters such as the weather, parking, or any subject to get you talking.

3   *Determine Your Qualifications.* The interviewer has to find out as early as possible if you are technically qualified (on the surface) for the job. Time is valuable, and an interviewer can't waste it on unqualified candidates. The determination is made by a review of the application and your résumé. This can turn into a simple yes and no session as the interviewer matches your qualifications against the requirements for the position. During this phase, information is gathered to develop questions later on in the conversation. This technique is called blueprinting.

4   *Explain the Company and the Job.* At this point in the interview, the interviewer will try to get you excited about wanting to work for the company. He or she generally will cover job responsibilities and company benefits to interest you even further.

5   *Determine Your Suitability.* The interviewer now has to determine if you are the best candidate. In many cases this is a subjective judgment based upon impressions of your conduct and your ability to handle the questions posed to you. In this part of the interview you will be asked situational questions, which may or may not be directly related to your future duties. The interviewer may even ask some startling questions to get your response. The technique used is to ask open-ended questions (those that require more than a one-word answer) during this phase, rather than close-ended questions (those that only require a simple yes or no).

6   *Conclusion.* Now it is the interviewer's responsibility to review the major points you covered during the interview and get you out of the office in a

timely manner. The interviewer should ensure all of your questions have been answered and will generally let you know what the next step is and when a decision will be made.

7   As you can see, an interview is a planned and controlled process. As stated, a trained and skilled interviewer will guide you through the steps and will know exactly how to keep you on track. The managers in the second and subsequent interviews may not follow a planned agenda and may even have trouble staying on track themselves. If you understand what is happening, you can take control. The rules for the interview are based on one theory only. If you were called, you probably are qualified for the job. Your task is to show the company you are the best qualified of the candidates who are competing. Here are some suggestions for doing that.

8   *Always Be Positive.* Losers dwell on past losses, winners dwell on future successes. Don't worry about where you have been, worry about where you're going. Make sure your accomplishments are related to your capabilities.

9   *Listen, Listen, Listen.* Throughout the interview, concentrate to be sure you're really listening to what the interviewer has to say. It looks very bad when you ask a question the interviewer just answered.

10   *State Your Qualifications, Not Your Drawbacks.* Tell them what you can do; let them wonder about what you can't do.

11   *Ask Questions.* Be sure to ask intelligent, well-thought-out questions that indicate you are trying to find out what you can do for the company. Base any statements on proven experience, not dreams and hopes.

12   *Watch Out for Close-Ended Questions.* Be wary of interviewers who ask close-ended questions. They probably don't know what they are doing. If you begin to hear a series of questions that require only a yes or no, the other candidates are probably hearing the same questions. If the interviewer asks three candidates the same question and all he gets are three no answers, he won't be able to distinguish among the three. If all the answers are the same, he can't make an intelligent choice. Your strategy, then, is to turn these close-ended questions into open-ended ones so you can put a few intelligent sentences together. In this way, you will distinguish yourself from the other yes and no candidates.

13   *Stay Focused.* Concentrate on the conversation at hand. Don't get off on extraneous matters that have nothing to do with the job or your qualifications.

14   *Don't Get Personal.* Keep personal issues out of the interview. Never confide in an interviewer no matter how relaxed and comfortable you feel. If you feel the urge to bare your soul, your feelings should tell you the interviewer is very skilled and followed the first step of the interview extremely well.

15   *Rehearse.* Plan some answers to obvious questions. Why did you leave your previous position? Why did you choose your academic major? What are your training and experience going to do for the company?

16   *Maintain Eye Contact.* If you can't look interviewers in the eye, they won't believe your answer. Further, there are no answers written on the ceiling, so if you get in a bind, don't look up for divine guidance. The answer is not on the ceiling. It's in your head.

17   *Pause a Moment.* Take a moment before each answer to consider what you will say. Don't answer the question in a rush, but reflect a moment to get it straight.

18   *Take Notes.* If you plan on taking notes, ask first. Some people are uncomfortable when their words are written down. Do not attempt to record the conversation.

19   *Multiple Interviewers.* If you are interviewed by more than one person, answer all of them equally. Begin with the questioner, let your eyes go to each of the others as you continue your answer, and finally come back to the original questioner. Each of them will then feel you are speaking to him or her alone.

20   *Don't Drink, Don't Smoke.* In fact, don't ingest anything at all. Although it is polite to accept a proffered cup of coffee or a soft drink, it is not polite to spill it in your lap. You will be nervous, so don't take the chance. Remember, they are merely trying to establish rapport. Besides, you can't maintain eye contact while drinking or eating.

21   *Likely Open-Ended Questions.* What follows are some properly formulated open-ended questions you may hear later. Get used to the format and prepare answers. Keep them down to a couple of sentences, not paragraphs.

   1. In your relationship with your previous supervisor, would you mind giving an example of how you were alike or not alike?
   2. How would you define success?
   3. Would you demonstrate some methods you would use to cause a marginal employee to rise to his or her full potential?
   4. How can a team atmosphere improve your personal effectiveness?
   5. If you were a problem, how would you solve yourself?

After the Interview

22   When the interview concludes, don't linger, but don't run out the door, either. If the interviewers haven't indicated when a decision will be reached, ask them. This will give them the impression that you might have other offers you are considering. When you get back to your car, take out a professional-looking note card (purchased in advance for just this purpose) and write (in longhand with roller pen or a fountain pen) a brief thank-you note to all the people in the company who interviewed you.

23   Take the note to the post office and mail it the same day. It is important that the note reach the interviewers the next day. You hope it will hit their desk at the same time they are comparing your résumé with those of other candidates. You now have the advantage of having at least two documents on their desk. It might not help, but it certainly won't hurt.

EXERCISE 11   Discussion and Critical Thinking

   1. Is this essay informative or directive?

   2. What are the major steps that an interviewer is likely to follow?

   3. Are the suggestions presented in any sequence that need be followed?

4. Is the interview process discussed here formal or informal or a combination?

5. How does this "planned and controlled process" (paragraph 7) compare with interviews you have participated in?

STUDENT PARAGRAPH AND ESSAY

A Summary of "How Low-Balling Works on Your Mind"

LARRY GARDNER

The assignment for student Larry Gardner was to write a summary of a selection, "How Low-Balling Works on Your Mind." He was directed to annotate the preparation and steps and to italicize the transitional words.

Preparation
Steps

1

2

3
4

In "How Low-Balling Works on Your Mind," Sharon S. Brehm discusses what she says may be "the most unscrupulous of all compliance techniques" (199). Low-balling can be used in many undertakings, but it is used mostly in selling. In selling automobiles, the salesperson *first* wins the customer over by agreeing to a good price for a vehicle. The ball thrown is a high pitch, a good one to hit. The customer is pleased and begins thinking of ownership. *Then* the salesperson comes back and throws the low ball: the sales manager says that the price is not enough because of the vehicle's special feature(s) and that the sale can be made only if the price is increased. *Next* the salesperson expresses regret and claims to be on the customer's side. *Finally* the customer, already emotionally committed to the deal and maybe identifying with the seemingly supportive salesperson, accepts whatever the sales manager said or a negotiated higher price. The customer has been low-balled.

Work Cited

Brehm, Sharon S. "How Low-Balling Works on Your Mind." *Paragraphs and Essays: A Worktext with Readings.* Ed. Lee Brandon. 9th ed. Boston: Houghton, 2005. 322–24. Print.

CAREER-RELATED WRITING

Student Tina Sergio was mainly interested in the law program, but in her English class she had an opportunity to write on a topic from another discipline at her school, cosmetology. With that, a school field of study and her work experience came together, and she wrote about the preparation for and the steps of an exotic, creative process she occasionally performs at her workplace to the considerable satisfaction of herself and her clients.

You will find a full-size blank worksheet on page 6, which can be photocopied, filled in, and submitted with each assignment if your instructor directs you to do so.

Writing Process Worksheet

Name Tina Sergio   **Title** Doing a Flame Hair Tattoo   **Due Date** Thursday, March 9, 11 a.m.

Use the back of this page or separate paper if you need more space.

Assignment

In the space below, write whatever you need to know about your assignment, including information about the topic, audience, pattern of writing, length, whether to include a rough draft or revised drafts, and whether your paper must be typed.

Write a process-analysis essay about a procedure you have done at a workplace. Your audience will be those who may be familiar with your topic but have not performed the procedure. It may be helpful to imagine that you have just been promoted and your replacement needs to be instructed, in writing, about the performance of a specific task. Include the preparation stage and the steps. Use one or more illustrations. Submit a completed Writing Process Worksheet and a typed final draft with a marked first draft. Because you are already familiar with your topic, you may skip the Stage One part of the worksheet.

Stage One

Explore Freewrite, brainstorm (list), cluster, or take notes as directed by your instructor.

[Omitted because of the student's familiarity with her topic.]

Stage Two

Organize Write a topic sentence or thesis; label the subject and the focus parts.

<u>Doing the Flame Hair Tattoo well</u> <u>requires careful preparation and specific steps</u>.
       subject   focus

Write an outline or an outline alternative. For reading-based writing, include references and short questions with page numbers as support in the outline.

  I. Preparation
     A. Consult with the customer about the Flame Hair Tattoo
     B. Gather materials
     C. Gather tools
 II. Steps
     A. Make stencil designs, still consulting with the customer
     B. Pre-cut the customer's hair
     C. Perform the bleach procedure
        1. Mix the bleach
        2. Apply the bleach with a brush
        3. Monitor the chemical processing of the bleach
     D. Dye the customer's bleached hair
        1. Mix the colors
        2. Brush in the colors
        3. Monitor the chemical processing of the colors
     E. Admire the unique creation: the Flame Hair Tattoo

Stage Three

Write On separate paper, write and then revise your paragraph or essay as many times as necessary for **c**oherence, **l**anguage (usage, tone, and diction), **u**nity, **e**mphasis, **s**upport, and **s**entences (**CLUESS**). Read your work aloud to hear and correct any grammatical errors or awkward-sounding sentences.

Edit any problems in fundamentals, such as **c**apitalization, **o**missions, **p**unctuation, and **s**pelling (**COPS**).

This essay is annotated, with underlines for transitional words.

Final Draft

DOING A FLAME HAIR TATTOO
Tina Sergio

1   As a hair stylist for several years, I have seen many styles emerge, become popular, and then disappear. Sometimes they resurface again with variations, sort of like men's neckties. Their popularity may be national, regional, or local. They may be trends or just fads. One of my creations is the Flame Hair Tattoo. It is like a tattoo because it is permanently set in the hair, at least until the hair grows or is rebleached and redyed. Doing this design well requires careful preparation and specific steps. Keep in mind that this is a procedure I use, as a cosmetologist, in a hair styling salon. Because it deals with some strong chemicals, I do not recommend that inexperienced persons attempt it in their home.

I. Preparation
A. Willing customer

2   Preparation is extremely important because once I start, I cannot afford to delay the sequence of steps. <u>First</u>, of course, I need a customer. Often now, it is a person who has been referred after having seen one of my creations on the street. Let us say this person (with dark hair) asks me for a hair tattoo. I start by showing some photographs of satisfied clients, then explain what I can do, and give the price. <u>After</u> we agree on a style and particular colors, I need to make sure I have a large, flexible piece of thin cardboard, an X-acto knife, a drawing pencil, a paper plate, shampoo, towels, cream bleach, cream developer, a 1-inch-wide and a small paintbrush, tints in shades of the intended flames, scissors, and clippers with a number 2 attachment. All of these items are at my disposal in my fully equipped beauty salon. The customer is sitting in an adjustable chair.

B. Obtain materials
C. Obtain tools

II. Steps
A. Make stencils

3   The sequence <u>begins</u>. My <u>first step</u> is to prepare stencils that will become a wall of flames extending around the client's head and licking at the top. As the client watches and I explain what I am doing, I draw outlines of flames for stencils on my piece of cardboard. <u>At that point</u> the client can still make minor changes in the shading and design. <u>Then</u> I cut out the stencils with the X-acto knife, tracing the lines I have drawn on the cardboard, as shown in Figure 10.1. The annotations indicate the approximate locations of colors that will be added.

B. Pre-cut hair
C. Perform bleach procedure

1. Mix bleach

4   <u>Next, before starting</u> the bleaching process, I clip and buzz the hair to no more than 1/8 inch with the scissors and number 2 clippers. <u>After</u> making sure the cut hair is whisked or blown off the client's head, I am ready for the bleach. I mix a cream bleach first with equal parts of 20 volume cream developer and then with equal scoops of a powdered bleach. I stir this mixture until no lumps are left and it has a consistency of mayonnaise. The consistency is important, for if it is too runny, it might leave its own blurry design.

Figure 10.1
One Flame

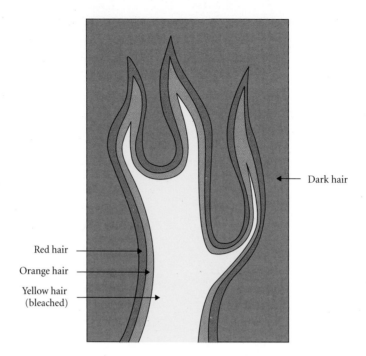

Dark hair

Red hair

Orange hair

Yellow hair
(bleached)

2. Apply bleach

5   Now is the time to apply the bleach, but before applying it, I ask an assistant to hold each stencil firmly in place as I work. Using the larger brush, I apply bleach generously to the open areas of each stencil, making sure all the edges are covered to produce a flame image before it is removed. After completing the last stencil, I reapply the bleach carefully with the larger brush, making sure that each part of the band of flames appears in flowing, even lines. With the application of bleach completed, I cover the treated hair with a plastic bag and let the chemicals process for an hour or until the bleached portions reach a pale yellow color. Once the hair has processed, I rinse out the bleach and gently shampoo the hair one time. After towel drying the hair, I am ready to start the coloring process.

3. Process bleach

D. Dye hair

6   The first step of the coloring process is to select and display the colors. I use semi-permanent dyes of the brand Fudge. After deciding which colors to use, I squeeze each onto a paper plate in separate piles, sometimes mixing them, just as an artist might in painting with oils. Next, using the small paintbrush, I first outline and then fill in the flames, always going from light colors to dark. I make much use of a hand mirror so the client knows what I am doing as I work. By stages, I add the yellows, oranges, and reds—whatever the design calls for as I figuratively set his or her hair on fire.

1. Mix colors
2. Brush in colors

3. Process colors

7   With the colors in place, processing takes at least thirty minutes. After that time is up, I wash the hair with shampoo one more time. The Flame Hair Tattoo is finished. The client's head is "permanently" ablaze with flames from temple to temple, moving upward from the hairline and across the top of the head.

E. Admire the creation

8   This style is not for everyone, but those who like the Flame Hair Tattoo wear it with pride and pleasure. They are having fun. I regard my hair tattoos in much the same way. No two designs are exactly the same. Each hair color and head conformation is a different medium and a new challenge for my craft and art.

EXERCISE 11   Discussion and Critical Thinking

1. In what way is this an essay of directive process analysis?

2. Why might Sergio's essay also be considered an informative process analysis?

3. Underline the thesis.

4. Draw a line between the preparation and the steps.

Suggested Topics and Prompts for Writing Process Analysis

STUDENT COMPANION SITE

For additional practice, visit www.cengage .com/devenglish/ brandon/PE11e.

You will find a blank Writing Process Worksheet on page 6 of this book and on your Student Companion Site. It can be photocopied or printed out, filled in, and submitted with your assignment, if your instructor directs you to do so.

READING-BASED WRITING

Reading-based writing requires you to read critically, write a reply that shows you understand what you have read, and give credit for ideas you borrow and words you quote. The form can be a summary, a reaction, or a two-part response (with separated summary and reaction). Documentation, in which you give credit for borrowed ideas and words, can be either formal (MLA) or informal, as directed by your instructor. Both the forms of reading-based writing and documentation are discussed with examples in Chapter 1. Definitions of the three forms follow. Any form can be used for any reading selection in this book.

Summary

- The summary is a statement presenting only the main points of what you have read by using different wording without altering the meaning, adding information, or showing bias.
- It is the purest form of reading-based writing.

Reaction

- In the reaction, the meaning of what you have read will be central to your topic sentence of your paragraph or to the thesis of your essay.
- Although the reaction is not a personal narrative by itself, it may include personal experience to explain elements of the text. For example, if your source is about driving styles, your own experiences as a driver or an observer of drivers could be relevant in your analysis of the text.
- The reaction may incorporate a summary to convey a broad view of what you have read, but your summary should never be the main part of your reaction.

The Two-Part Response

- The two-part response separates the summary from the reaction.
- This form will give you practice in separating your objective summary in the first part from your more personal evaluation, interpretation, or application in the second part, the reaction.

READING-BASED WRITING TOPICS

"Attitude"

1. Write a summary of this essay.

2. Write a reaction in which you focus on Keillor's intent in writing this essay. Explain whether he is just trying to be funny or whether he is serious about the game and the behavior of his fellow players. Discuss his choice of words and his use of examples, as well as the overall content. Refer directly to the essay and use quotations.

3. Write a reaction in which you apply his idea about taking his game "seriously" to another sport, thereby discussing how to perform certain tasks, customs, or rituals in your sport in the "proper" way. Use some references to and quotations from the essay in explaining how your approach is similar to that of Keillor.

"Flirting Fundamentals"

4. In this article, newspaper writer Geraldine Baum discusses Monica Moore as an experimental psychologist. The subject is flirting techniques. Write a combined summary and evaluation of Moore's study of flirting, which is itself largely a process analysis. It is sexy as a subject—is it scientific? (Does it have a hypothesis? Is it tested? Are there positive results? Has it been retested, with the same results?) Do your observations confirm Moore's insights? Her team observations are based on certain locations, certain age groups, and certain lifestyles. Are the locations, age groups, and lifestyles too restrictive or at least restrictive enough to bias her conclusions? Specifically, do you know some young women who would insist they use few, if any, of the "52 Ways Women Flirt"? Would some regard Moore's study as sexist? What does your experience tell you about those questions?

"A Successful Interview"

5. Using the interview process discussed in this essay, describe an interview you experienced as either an interviewer or an interviewee. Refer to and quote from this essay.

6. As a group, prepare for a practice interview, conduct it, and write about the results of this activity. Refer to and quote from this essay.
   a. Create and define an imaginary company or decide on a company you are all familiar with, such as Wal*Mart, JCPenney, or Sears.

b. Divide the class into three groups: those who are interviewing; those who are being interviewed (looking for a job); and those who are watching, taking notes, and advising other groups.

c. All groups prepare for mock interviews: deciding on job specifications (duties, pay, benefits, etc.), phrasing questions, and anticipating questions.

d. Rehearse.

e. Conduct interviews.

f. Take notes.

g. Write an informative process analysis based on a particular interview and related to the procedure described in the essay. You will discuss the background and sequence parts and evaluate the performance of the interviewers and the person being interviewed. For a more focused piece of writing, you could concentrate only on the person being interviewed.

"A Summary of 'How Low-Balling Works on Your Mind'"

7. In a reaction, apply the parts of this summary to a situation you have experienced. Automobile and real estate sales are often occasions for the low-balling scam experience.

GENERAL TOPICS

8. In a paragraph or essay, explain how to perform a simple task at home (cleaning an oven), at school (dissecting a frog in a biology lab), or at work (building a display for a product). For a helpful model on a similar topic, review "How to Sharpen a Knife" on page 201.

9. For an amusing, light-hearted how-to-do-it paragraph or essay, write about how to gracefully eat Chinese food (using chopsticks), fried chicken (using hands), watermelon (using mouth and hands), or Arabic food (using fingers). For a helpful model on a similar topic with humor, review "How to Eat an Ice Cream Cone" on pages 202–203.

10. Write a paragraph or an essay on one of the following topics. Although they are phrased as directive topics, each can be transformed into a how it-was-done informative topic by personalizing it and explaining stage by stage how you, someone else, or a group did something. For example, you could write either a directive process analysis about how to deal with an obnoxious person or an informative process analysis about how you or someone else dealt with an obnoxious person. Keep in mind that the two types of process analysis are often blended, especially in the personal approach. Many of these topics will be more interesting to you and your readers if they are personalized.

Most of the topics require some narrowing to be treated in a paragraph. For example, writing about playing baseball is too broad; writing about how to throw a curve ball may be manageable.

a. How to end a relationship without hurting someone's feelings

b. How to pass a test for a driver's license

c. How to get a job at _____

d. How to perform a magic trick

e. How to repair _____

f. How to assemble _____

g. How to learn about another culture

h. How to approach someone you would like to know better

CROSS-CURRICULAR TOPICS

11. Write a paragraph or an essay about a procedure you follow in your college work in a science (chemistry, biology, geology) lab. You may explain how to analyze a rock, how to dissect something, how to operate something, how to perform an experiment.

12. Write a paragraph or an essay about how to do something in an activity or performance class, such as drama, physical education, art, or music.

CAREER-RELATED TOPIC

13. Pretend you are going on vacation, and your boss says there will be a replacement for you, and you should write a paragraph or an essay about a particular task (not a very complicated one) so that the temporary employee can do that part of your work. Imagine that the temp will not have seen your workstation so you must explain in detail and perhaps even do a drawing to go with your writing. Now write that process analysis. Refer back to the instruction at the beginning of this chapter. For a helpful model on a similar topic, review "How to Sharpen a Knife" on page 201 or "Doing a Flame Hair Tattoo" on pages 215–216.

WRITER'S GUIDELINES: Process Analysis

1. Decide whether your process analysis is mainly directive or informative, and be appropriately consistent in using pronouns and other designations.

   • For directive process analysis, use the second person, addressing the reader as *you*. The *you* may be understood, even if it is not written.

   • For informative process analysis, use the first person, speaking as *I* or *we*, or the third person, speaking about the subject as *he*, *she*, *it*, or *they*, or by name.

2. Consider using these basic forms.

Directive	**Informative**
I. Preparation	I. Background
A.	A.
B.	B.
II. Steps	II. Sequence
A.	A.
B.	B.
C.	C.

3. Listing is a useful prewriting activity for process analysis. Begin with the Roman-numeral headings indicated in number 2.

4. The order of a process analysis will usually be chronological (time based) in some sense. Certain transitional words are commonly used to promote coherence: *first*, *second*, *third*, *then*, *soon*, *now*, *next*, *finally*, *at last*, *therefore*, and *consequently*.

5. Career-related process analysis takes the same conventional form.

6. Use the writing process.
   - Write and then revise your paragraph or essay as many times as necessary for **c**oherence, **l**anguage (usage, tone, and diction), **u**nity, **e**mphasis, **s**upport, and **s**entences (**CLUESS**).
   - Read your work aloud to hear and correct any grammatical errors or awkward-sounding sentences.
   - Edit any problems in fundamentals, such as **c**apitalization, **o**missions, **p**unctuation, and **s**pelling (**COPS**).

Chapter 11

Cause and Effect
Determining Reasons and Outcomes

WHEN TO USE CAUSE AND EFFECT

FOR COLLEGE WRITING ASSIGNMENTS

• Cause-and-effect questions are at the center of scientific investigation. They are also common-place in reading assignments, class discussion, reports, research papers, and tests. If you want to study for an examination or just to be prepared for class discussion, highlight any situation, event, or trend and list relevant causes and effects. Try that approach with these general topics: gang activity, high blood pressure, obesity, divorce rate, drug addiction, inflation, economic depression, drought, flood, political change, racism, foreign policy, earthquake, volcanic eruption, or tax increase.

IN CAREERS AND AT THE WORKPLACE

• Businesses and other institutions deal constantly with reasons and results. For the individual, the rise and fall of careers are usually tied to causes and effects. Businesses need to make money. Institutions need to function well. Helping them do so requires the use of cause-and-effect analysis in almost every measurable respect. Cause-and-effect issues are subjects of progress reports, performance reviews, memos, and proposals. Accountability, a key word in measuring effectiveness, is based on causes and effects. Being able to understand and explain cause and effect will make you indispensable in any vocational field.

CAUSE AND EFFECT IN A CARTOON

THE QUIGMANS   by Buddy Hickerson

The desert wedding is a greatly feared event, mostly because of the tossing of the bridal cactus.

Writing Cause and Effect

Causes and effects deal with reasons and results; they are sometimes discussed together and sometimes separately. Like other forms of writing to explain, writing about causes and effects is based on natural thought processes. The shortest, and arguably the most provocative, poem in the English language—"I/Why?"—is posed by an anonymous author about cause. Children are preoccupied with delightful and often exasperating "why" questions. Daily we encounter all kinds of causes and effects. The same subject may raise questions of both kinds.

> The car won't start. Why? [*cause*]
> The car won't start. What now? [*effect*]

At school, from the biology lab to the political science classroom, and at work, from maintaining relationships to changing procedures, causes and effects are pervasive.

EXPLORING AND ORGANIZING

One useful approach to developing a cause-and-effect analysis is *listing*. Write down the event, situation, or trend you are concerned about. Then on the left side, list the causes; on the right side, list the effects. From them you will select the main causes or effects for your paragraph or essay. Here is an example.

Causes	Event, Situation, or Trend	Effects
Low self-esteem	Joining a gang	Life of crime
Drugs		Drug addiction
Tradition		Surrogate family relationship
Fear		Protection
Surrogate family		Ostracism
Protection		Restricted vocational opportunities
Neighborhood status		

As you use prewriting techniques to explore your ideas, you need to decide whether your topic should mainly inform or mainly persuade. If you intend to inform, your tone should be coolly objective. If you intend to persuade, your tone should be subjective. In either case, you should take into account the views of your audience as you phrase your ideas. You should also take into account how much your audience understands about your topic and develop your ideas accordingly.

COMPOSING A TOPIC SENTENCE OR A THESIS

Now that you have listed your ideas under causes and effects, you are ready to focus on the causes, on the effects, or, occasionally, on both.

Your controlling idea, the topic sentence or the thesis, might be one of the causes: "It is not just chance; people have reasons for joining gangs." Later, as you use the idea, you would rephrase it to make it less mechanical, allowing it to become part of the flow of your discussion. If you wanted to personalize the work—thereby probably making it more interesting—you could write about someone you know who joined a gang. You could use the same basic framework, the main causes, to indicate why this particular person joined a gang.

WRITING AN OUTLINE

Your selection of a controlling idea takes you to the next writing phase: completing an outline or outline alternative. There you need to

- consider kinds of causes and effects.
- evaluate the importance of sequence.
- introduce ideas and work with patterns.

In its most basic form, your outline, derived mainly from points in your listing, might look like one of the following:

Paragraph of causes
Topic sentence: It is not just chance; people have reasons for joining gangs.

I. Low self-esteem (cause 1)
II. Surrogate family (cause 2)
III. Protection (cause 3)

Essay of effects

Thesis: One is not a gang member without consequences.

I. Restricted vocational opportunities (effect 1)
II. Life of crime (effect 2)
III. Drug addiction (effect 3)
IV. Ostracism from mainstream society (effect 4)

CONSIDERING KINDS OF CAUSES AND EFFECTS

Causes and effects can be primary or secondary, immediate or remote.

Primary or Secondary

Primary means "major," and **secondary** means "minor." A primary cause may be sufficient to bring about the situation (subject). For example, infidelity may be a primary (and possibly sufficient by itself) cause of divorce for some people but not for others, who regard it as secondary. Or, if country X is attacked by country Y, the attack itself, as a primary cause, may be sufficient to bring on a declaration of war. But a diplomatic blunder regarding visas for workers may be of secondary importance, and, though significant, it is certainly not enough to start a war over.

Immediate or Remote

Causes and effects often occur at a distance in time or place from the situation. The immediate effect of sulfur in the atmosphere may be atmospheric pollution, but the long-range, or remote, effect may be acid rain and the loss of species. The immediate cause of the greenhouse effect may be the depletion of the ozone layer, whereas the long-range, or remote, cause is the use of CFCs (chlorofluorocarbons, commonly called Freon, which are found in such items as Styrofoam cups). Even more remote, the ultimate cause may be the people who use the products containing Freon. Your purpose will determine the causes and effects appropriate for your essay.

EVALUATING THE IMPORTANCE OF SEQUENCE

The sequence in which events occur(red) may or may not be significant. When you are dealing with several sequential events, determine whether the sequence of events has causal connections; that is, does one event bring about another?

Consider this sequence of events: Joe's parents get divorced, and Joe joins a gang. We know that one reason for joining a gang is to gain family companionship. Therefore, we may conclude that Joe joined the gang to satisfy his need for family companionship, which he lost when his parents divorced. But if we do so, we may have reached a wrong conclusion, because Joe's joining the gang after the family breakup does not necessarily mean that the two events are related. Maybe Joe joined the gang because of drug dependency, low self-esteem, or a need for protection.

In each case, examine the connections. To assume that one event is *caused* by another just because it *follows* the other is a logical error called a **post hoc** ("**after this**") **fallacy**. An economic depression may occur after a president takes office, but that does not necessarily mean the depression was caused by the new administration. It might have occurred anyway, perhaps in an even more severe form.

Order

The order of the causes and effects you discuss in your paper may be based on time, space, emphasis, or a combination.

- *Time*: If one stage leads to another, as in a discussion of the causes and effects of upper atmospheric pollution, your paper would be organized best by time.
- *Space*: In some instances, causes and effects are best organized by their relation in space. For example, the causes of an economic recession could be discussed in terms of local factors, regional factors, national factors, and international factors.
- *Emphasis*: Some causes and effects may be more important than others. For instance, if some causes of divorce are primary (perhaps infidelity and physical abuse) and others are secondary (such as annoying habits and laziness), a paper about divorce could present the secondary causes first, and then move on to primary causes to emphasize the latter as more important.

In some situations, two or more factors (such as time and emphasis) may be linked; in that case, select the order that best fits what you are trying to say, or combine orders.

Transitional Words

Consider using the following transitional words to improve coherence by connecting ideas with ideas, sentences with sentences, and paragraphs with paragraphs.

FOR CAUSE AND EFFECT:
Cause: as, because, because of, due to, for, for the reason that, since, bring about, another cause, for this reason, one cause, a second cause, another cause, a final cause

Effect: accordingly, finally, consequently, hence, so, therefore, thus, as a consequence, as a result, resulting

FOR ALL PATTERNS OF WRITING: The <u>HOTSHOT CAT</u> words: <u>H</u>owever, <u>O</u>therwise, <u>T</u>herefore, <u>S</u>imilarly, <u>H</u>ence, <u>O</u>n the other hand, <u>T</u>hen, <u>C</u>onsequently, <u>A</u>lso, <u>T</u>hus (See pages 427–428 for additional transitional words.)

INTRODUCING IDEAS AND WORKING WITH PATTERNS

In presenting your controlling idea—probably near the beginning for a paragraph or in an introductory paragraph for an essay—you will almost certainly want to perform two functions:

1. *Discuss your subject.* For example, if you are writing about the causes or effects of divorce, begin with a statement about divorce as a subject.

2. *Indicate whether you will concentrate on causes or effects or combine them.* That indication should be made clear early in the paper. Concentrating on one—causes or effects—does not mean you will not mention the other; it only means you will emphasize one of them. You can bring attention to your main concern(s)—causes, effects, or a combination—by repeating key words such as *cause, reason, effect, result, consequence,* and *outcome.*

The most likely pattern for your work is one of those shown in Figure 11.1. These patterns may look familiar to you. We discussed similar patterns in Chapters 5 and 6.

Figure 11.1
Patterns for Paragraph and Essay

For Paragraph

Subject and Topic Sentence

Cause or Effect 1

Cause or Effect 2

Cause or Effect 3

Reflection on Topic Sentence

For Essay

Subject and Thesis

Topic Sentence

Cause or Effect 1

Topic Sentence

Cause or Effect 2

Topic Sentence

Cause or Effect 3

Conclusion

FINDING PATTERNS IN PHOTOS

EXERCISE 1   A Text-Based Activity for Groups or Individuals

As we gaze at the photo on page 228 of a glove and a baseball sharing space with syringes and vials, we may be disappointed at what "our national pastime" has become, but we are probably not shocked. After all, numerous well-known athletes have tested positive for illegal performance-enhancing drugs, while others have been charged with using those drugs at some time in their past career. Learning from the media about the drug-related charges, suspensions, lawsuits, testimonies, and confessions has prompted many of us to become more cynical about the purity of sports, to question sports ethics, and even to reexamine our own values.

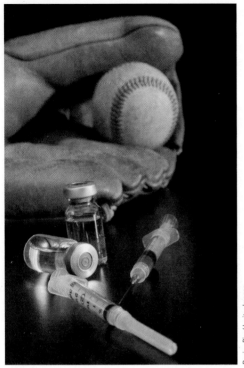

Baseball glove with syringes and vials

Either as individuals or in groups, as directed by your instructor, make two lists—one for causes and the other for effects. First list the causes with the possible motives of players (the users), of the suppliers (personal trainers, pushers, manufacturers), of the teams (management and sponsors), and even of the fans. Then change your focus from causes to effects on the same entities: players, suppliers, teams, and fans.

Causes (why)	Trend	Effects (results)
_____		_____
_____		_____
_____		_____
_____		_____
_____		_____
_____		_____
_____		_____

Possible Assignments (as directed by instructor):

1. Class discussion of individual work

2. Class reports from group discussions

3. Writing assignment of a paragraph or essay emphasizing either causes or effects on sports generally, a specific sport, or a specific player, with reference(s) to the photo

A SPECIFIC USE OF CAUSE AND EFFECT: THE SHORT STORY REVIEW

Short Story Review

A **short story** is a brief, imaginative narrative, with numerous functional elements (all of which can be analyzed): setting, conflict, characters, plot, theme, and point of view.

The overarching element of the short story is usually the plot. In the simplest terms, the plot begins when a character in a setting experiences (with or without being aware) a conflict. The plot develops as the character deals with the conflict in a single scene or sequence of scenes. All of this narrative is related from a first-person (*I*) or a third-person (*he, she, they*) point of view. The entire presentation has a theme, the underlying generalization or fictional point.

Short stories are fiction, meaning they are not a report of what has actually happened, though they may be based squarely on an author's experience.

Writing the Short Story Review

One theory about why we enjoy fiction—in print and film—is that we can analyze it. The events of our lives may often appear too complicated and close for us to figure out, but with fiction we can see connections more clearly. We can dissect fiction, examine the parts and their relationships, and speculate about what it all means. We can even relate fiction to our own experiences.

Like most writing, the short story review (analysis) is a combination of writing forms, but one form—analysis by division, comparison and contrast, cause and effect, or narration—may provide much of the pattern. For a short review, you will likely emphasize one aspect of the short story—setting, conflict, plot, character(s), theme, point of view—though you may touch on several.

- Develop your ideas by referring directly to the story; by explaining; and by using summaries, paraphrases, and quotations. Avoid the temptation to oversummarize.
- Use present tense in relating events in the story. For example, "Jude is trying to survive," not "Jude was trying to survive." Use quotation marks around the words you borrow and provide documentation if directed to do so by your instructor.
- Although a short story review is mainly analytical, it may include your speculation and call forth references to your personal experience.

A short story for analysis, "The Girls in Their Summer Dresses," begins on page 233. A student review on a short story, "The Use of Self-Analysis," appears on pages 248–249.

Practicing Patterns of Cause and Effect

A detailed outline and your subsequent writing may include a combination of causes and effects, but almost always either causes *or* effects will be emphasized and will provide the main structure of your paper. Whether you are writing a basic outline for an assignment outside of class without a significant time constraint or you are writing in class under the pressure of time, you will always have a chance to jot down prewriting lists and a simple outline.

EXERCISE 2   Completing Patterns of Cause and Effect

Complete the following cluster on teenage parenthood. Then select three primary causes or three primary effects that could be used in writing a paragraph or an essay on this topic.

Causes   Effects

Teenage
Parenthood

Primary causes

1. _____

2. _____

3. _____

Primary effects

1. _____

2. _____

3. _____

EXERCISE 3   Completing Patterns of Cause and Effect

Complete the following cluster on a bad diet. Then select three primary causes or three primary effects that could be used in writing a paragraph or an essay on this topic.

Causes   Effects

Bad
Diet

Primary causes   Primary effects

1. _____   1. _____

2. _____   2. _____

3. _____   3. _____

EXERCISE 4   Completing a Pattern of Cause

Fill in the blanks to complete this outline of cause.

Causes for dropping out of high school

I. Family tradition

II. _____

III. _____

IV. _____

EXERCISE 5   Completing a Pattern of Effect

Fill in the blanks to complete this outline of effect.

Effects of becoming a parent

I. Pride

II. _____

III. _____

IV. _____

Readings for Critical Thinking, Discussion, and Writing

READING STRATEGIES AND OBJECTIVES

Underlining and annotating these reading selections will help you answer the questions that follow the selections, discuss the material in class, and prepare for reading-based writing assignments. As you underline and annotate, pay special attention to the author's writing skills, logic, and message, and consider the relevance of the material to your own experiences and values.

Some selections begin with a Mindset suggestion that can help you create a readiness for connecting with what you are about to read.

PARAGRAPHS

Why Marriages Fail

ANNE ROIPHE

As novelist and journalist, Anne Roiphe has been especially concerned with the topic of contemporary relationships. In this essay, first published in Family Weekly, *she concentrates on two phenomena all too frequently linked: marriage and divorce.*

Topic sentence

Cause

Cause

When we look at how we choose our partners and what expectations exist at the tender beginnings of romance, some of the reasons for disaster become quite clear. We all select with unconscious accuracy a mate who will re-create with us the emotional patterns of our first homes. Dr. Carl A. Whitaker, a marital therapist and emeritus professor of psychiatry at the University of Wisconsin, explains, "From early childhood on, each of us carried models for marriage, femininity, masculinity, motherhood, fatherhood, and all the other family roles." Each of us falls in love with a mate who has qualities of our parents, who will help us rediscover both the psychological happiness and miseries of our past lives. We may think we have found a man unlike Dad, but then he turns to drink or drugs, or loses his job over and over again or sits silently in front of the TV just the way Dad did. A man may choose a woman who doesn't like kids just like his mother or who gambles away the family savings just like his mother. Or he may choose a slender wife who seems unlike his obese mother but then turns out to have other addictions that destroy their mutual happiness.

EXERCISE 6   Discussion and Critical Thinking

1. The author says that in our romances we experience unconscious attempts to re-create our childhood emotional patterns and, therefore, select mates similar to our parents. Does she argue that this practice is the only cause of failed marriages?

2. Roiphe's examples of how one may duplicate the conditions found in one's childhood home tend toward family problems. Does she allow for more positive influences from the family of one's childhood?

3. Elsewhere in the essay from which this paragraph is taken, Roiphe says we can overcome the stress produced by the bad family patterns we have re-created, but we also have to deal with real-life problems such as "failure at work, disappointments, exhaustion, bad smells, bad colds, and hard times." Which do you think are more significant causes of marriage failure—the unconscious psychological patterns we have chosen or the real-life problems? Why?

Family Heroes and Role Models

MARIAN WRIGHT EDELMAN

We are not born with values. We do not survive and prosper by ourselves. Any person who has succeeded should be able to look back and recognize those who provided a heritage through example and instruction. Marian Wright Edelman pays homage to her family and community for what her generation of black children received. This paragraph comes from her book The Measure of Our Success: A Letter to My Children and Yours *(1992).*

The legacies that parents and church and teachers left to my generation of Black children were priceless but not material: a living faith reflected in daily service, the discipline of hard work and stick-to-it-ness, and a capacity to struggle in the face of adversity. Giving up and "burnout" were not part of the language of my elders—you got up every morning and you did what you had to do and you got up every time you fell down and tried as many times as you had to to get it done right. They had grit. They valued family life, family rituals, and tried to be and to expose us to good role models. Role models were of two kinds: those who achieved in the outside world (like Marian Anderson, my namesake) and those who didn't have a whole lot of education or fancy clothes but who taught us by the special grace of their lives the message of Christ and Tolstoy and Gandhi and Heschel and Dorothy Day and Romero and King that the Kingdom of God was within—in what you are, not what you have. I still hope I can be half as good as Black church and community elders like Miz Lucy McQueen, Miz Tee Kelly, and Miz Kate Winston, extraordinary women who were kind and patient and loving with children and others and who, when I went to Spelman College, sent me shoeboxes with chicken and biscuits and greasy dollar bills.

EXERCISE 7   Discussion and Critical Thinking

1. What is the subject at the center of this discussion?

2. Which sentence most clearly indicates why black children of Edelman's generation developed a good set of values?

3. What were the three main legacies, or causes, of the value system of Edelman's generation?

4. What kinds of role models were causal factors?

5. Give two examples of role models (one of each kind) offered by Edelman.

SHORT STORY

The Girls in Their Summer Dresses

IRWIN SHAW

Is Irwin Shaw writing only about two individuals in this short story, or do the characters represent a general, and long-standing, division between the sexes?

MINDSET

Lock It In

Imagine you are a woman. And imagine you can read minds. Your husband is staring at you across the room. You read his mind: "She looks great. She's absolutely stunning. Oops! She's my wife." Overall, would you be happy?

1   Fifth Avenue was shining in the sun when they left the Brevoort. The sun was warm, even though it was February, and everything looked like Sunday morning—the buses and the well-dressed people walking slowly in couples and the quiet buildings with the windows closed.

2   Michael held Frances' arm tightly as they walked toward Washington Square in the sunlight. They walked lightly, almost smiling, because they had slept late and had a good breakfast and it was Sunday. Michael unbuttoned his coat and let it flap around him in the mild wind.

3   "Look out," Frances said as they crossed Eighth Street. "You'll break your neck."

4   Michael laughed and Frances laughed with him.

5   "She's not so pretty," Frances said. "Anyway, not pretty enough to take a chance of breaking your neck."

6   Michael laughed again. "How did you know I was looking at her?"

7   Frances cocked her head to one side and smiled at her husband under the brim of her hat. "Mike, darling," she said.

8   "O.K.," he said. "Excuse me."

9   Frances patted his arm lightly and pulled him along a little faster toward Washington Square. "Let's not see anybody all day," she said. "Let's just hang around with each other. You and me. We're always up to our neck in people, drinking their Scotch or drinking our Scotch; we only see each other in bed. I want to go out with my husband all day long. I want him to talk only to me and listen only to me."

10   "What's to stop us?" Michael asked.

11   "The Stevensons. They want us to drop by around one o'clock and they'll drive us into the country."

12   "The cunning Stevensons," Mike said. "Transparent. They can whistle. They can go driving in the country by themselves."

13   "Is it a date?"

14   "It's a date."

15   Frances leaned over and kissed him on the tip of the ear.

16   "Darling," Michael said, "this is Fifth Avenue."

17   "Let me arrange a program," Frances said. "A planned Sunday in New York for a young couple with money to throw away."

18   "Go easy."

19   "First let's go to the Metropolitan Museum of Art," Frances suggested, because Michael had said during the week he wanted to go. "I haven't been there in three years and there're at least ten pictures I want to see again. Then we can take the bus down to Radio City and watch them skate. And later we'll go down to Cavanaugh's and get a steak as big as a blacksmith's apron, with a bottle of wine, and after that there's a French picture at the Filmarte that every-body says—say, are you listening to me?"

20   "Sure," he said. He took his eyes off the hatless girl with the dark hair, cut dancer-style like a helmet, who was walking past him.

21   "That's the program for the day," Frances said flatly. "Or maybe you'd just rather walk up and down Fifth Avenue."

22   "No," Michael said. "Not at all."

23   "You always look at other women," Frances said. "Everywhere. Every damned place we go."

24   "No, darling," Michael said, "I look at everything. God gave me eyes and I look at women and men and subway excavations and moving pictures and the little flowers of the field. I casually inspect the universe."

25   "You ought to see the look in your eye," Frances said, "as you casually inspect the universe on Fifth Avenue."

26   "I'm a happily married man." Michael pressed her elbow tenderly. "Example for the whole twentieth century—Mr. and Mrs. Mike Loomis. Hey, let's have a drink," he said, stopping.

27   "We just had breakfast."

28   "Now listen, darling," Mike said, choosing his words with care, "it's a nice day and we both felt good and there's no reason why we have to break it up. Let's have a nice Sunday."

29   "All right. I don't know why I started this. Let's drop it. Let's have a good time."

30   They joined hands consciously and walked without talking among the baby carriages and the old Italian men in their Sunday clothes and the young women with Scotties in Washington Square Park.

31   "At least once a year everyone should go to the Metropolitan Museum of Art," Frances said after a while, her tone a good imitation of the tone she had used at breakfast and at the beginning of their walk. "And it's nice on Sunday. There're a lot of people looking at the pictures and you get the feeling maybe Art isn't on the decline in New York City, after all—"

32   "I want to tell you something," Michael said very seriously. "I have not touched another woman. Not once. In all the five years."

33   "All right," Frances said.

34   "You believe that, don't you?"

35   "All right."

36   They walked between the crowded benches, under the scrubby city-park trees.

37   "I try not to notice it," Frances said, "but I feel rotten inside, in my stomach, when we pass a woman and you look at her and I see that look in your eye and that's the way you looked at me the first time. In Alice Maxwell's house. Stand-ing there in the living room, next to the radio, with a green hat on and all those people."

38   "I remember the hat," Michael said.

39   "The same look," Frances said. "And it makes me feel bad. It makes me feel terrible."

40   "Sh-h-h, please, darling, sh-h-h."

41   "I think I would like a drink now," Frances said.

42   They walked over to a bar on Eighth Street, not saying anything, Michael automatically helping her over curbstones and guiding her past automobiles. They sat near a window in the bar and the sun streamed in and there was a

small, cheerful fire in the fireplace. A little Japanese waiter came over and put down some pretzels and smiled happily at them.

43   "What do you order after breakfast?" Michael asked.

44   "Brandy, I suppose," Frances said.

45   "Courvoisier," Michael told the waiter. "Two Courvoisiers."

46   The waiter came with the glasses and they sat drinking the brandy in the sunlight. Michael finished half his and drank a little water.

47   "I look at women," he said. "Correct. I don't say it's wrong or right. I look at them. If I pass them on the street and I don't look at them, I'm fooling you, I'm fooling myself."

48   "You look at them as though you want them," Frances said, playing with her brandy glass. "Every one of them."

49   "In a way," Michael said, speaking softly and not to his wife, "in a way that's true. I don't do anything about it, but it's true."

50   "I know it. That's why I feel bad."

51   "Another brandy," Michael called. "Waiter, two more brandies."

52   He sighed and closed his eyes and rubbed them gently with his fingertips. "I love the way women look. One of the things I like best about New York is the battalions of women. When I first came to New York from Ohio that was the first thing I noticed, the million wonderful women, all over the city. I walked around with my heart in my throat."

53   "A kid," Frances said. "That's a kid's feeling."

54   "Guess again," Michael said. "Guess again. I'm older now. I'm a man getting near middle age, putting on a little fat and I still love to walk along Fifth Avenue at three o'clock on the east side of the street between Fiftieth and Fifty-seventh Streets. They're all out then, shopping, in their furs and their crazy hats, everything all concentrated from all over the world into seven blocks—the best furs, the best clothes, the handsomest women, out to spend money and feeling good about it."

55   The Japanese waiter put the two drinks down, smiling with great happiness.

56   "Everything is all right?" he asked.

57   "Everything is wonderful," Michael said.

58   "If it's just a couple of fur coats," Frances said, "and forty-five-dollar hats—"

59   "It's not the fur coats. Or the hats. That's just the scenery for that particular kind of woman. Understand," he said, "you don't have to listen to this."

60   "I want to listen."

61   "I like the girls in the offices. Neat, with their eyeglasses, smart, chipper, knowing what everything is about. I like the girls on Forty-fourth Street at lunchtime, the actresses, all dressed up on nothing a week. I like the salesgirls in the stores, paying attention to you first because you're a man, leaving lady customers waiting. I got all this stuff accumulated in me because I've been thinking about it for ten years and now you've asked for it and here it is."

62   "Go ahead," Frances said.

63   "When I think of New York City, I think of all the girls on parade in the city. I don't know whether it's something special with me or whether every man in the city walks around with the same feeling inside him, but I feel as though I'm at a picnic in this city. I like to sit near the women in the theatres, the famous beauties who've taken six hours to get ready and look it. And the young girls at the football games, with the red cheeks, and when the warm weather comes, the girls in their summer dresses." He finished his drink. "That's the story."

64   Frances finished her drink and swallowed two or three times extra. "You say you love me?"

65   "I love you."

66   "I'm pretty, too," Frances said. "As pretty as any of them."

67   "You're beautiful," Michael said.

68　"I'm good for you," Frances said, pleading. "I've made a good wife, a good housekeeper, a good friend. I'd do any damn thing for you."

69　"I know," Michael said. He put his hand out and grasped hers.

70　"You'd like to be free to—" Frances said.

71　"Sh-h-h."

72　"Tell the truth." She took her hand away from under his.

73　Michael flicked the edge of his glass with his finger. "O.K," he said gently. "Sometimes I feel I would like to be free."

74　"Well," Frances said, "any time you say."

75　"Don't be foolish." Michael swung his chair around to her side of the table and patted her thigh.

76　She began to cry silently into her handkerchief, bent over just enough so nobody else in the bar would notice. "Someday," she said, crying, "you're going to make a move."

77　Michael didn't say anything. He sat watching the bartender slowly peel a lemon.

78　"Aren't you?" Frances asked harshly. "Come on, tell me. Talk. Aren't you?"

79　"Maybe," Michael said. He moved his chair back again. "How the hell do I know?"

80　"You know," Frances persisted. "Don't you know?"

81　"Yes," Michael said after a while, "I know."

82　Frances stopped crying then. Two or three snuffles into the handkerchief and she put it away and her face didn't tell anything to anybody. "At least do me a favor," she said.

83　"Sure."

84　"Stop talking about how pretty this woman is or that one. Nice eyes, nice breasts, a pretty figure, good voice." She mimicked his voice. "Keep it to yourself. I'm not interested."

85　Michael waved to the waiter. "I'll keep it to myself," he said.

86　Frances flicked the corners of her eyes. "Another brandy," she told the waiter.

87　"Two," Michael said.

88　"Yes, Ma'am; yes, Sir," said the waiter, backing away.

89　Frances regarded Michael coolly across the table. "Do you want me to call the Stevensons?" she asked. "It'll be nice in the country."

90　"Sure," Michael said. "Call them."

91　She got up from the table and walked across the room toward the telephone. Michael watched her walk, thinking what a pretty girl, what nice legs.

EXERCISE 8　Discussion and Critical Thinking

1. Point out the significance of the setting, either stated or implied.

2. Indicate the main conflict (and any secondary conflict).

3. Name the central character(s) and his or her (their) traits.

4. State the point of view (first or third person).

5. How does the behavior of both characters change after Michael starts looking at other women?

6. Would you say one is more at fault in this argument? Explain.

7. What is the significance of Michael's last observation of Frances?

8. What do you think will happen to their marriage? Why?

9. What would be your advice to the couple?

10. Briefly discuss the theme (what the story means, what it says about an individual specifically or human nature generally).

VIEWS ON VIOLENCE

Depending on the perspective of an individual, violence may be regarded in quite different ways. Here, in three essays, we have three different views.

- "The Ghetto Made Me Do It" makes a case for significantly taking into account the traumatic, violent childhood of those who go on to commit violent crimes.
- "Enough Is Enough" stresses the need for a perpetrator of violent crimes to accept personal responsibility without casting primary blame on society generally or family specifically. She says that most youngsters growing up in a difficult environment struggle to do what is right and do not play the "victim game."
- "From 'Kick Me' to 'Kiss Me'" is written by an inmate who was raised in an environment of violence, learned to be violent, and is now learning about herself.

The Ghetto Made Me Do It

FRANCIS FLAHERTY

This essay by freelance author Francis Flaherty was first published in In These Times, *a magazine from Chicago.*

MINDSET

Lock It In

The title states Felicia Morgan's plea to a murder charge. Can you imagine you would let her go free? Or, would you lock her up?

1   When Felicia "Lisa" Morgan was growing up, her parents would sit down to meals with guns next to their plates. They were defending themselves—against each other.

2   "This was Lisa's dinner," explains attorney Robin Shellow. "She was seven at the time."

3   If nothing else, Lisa Morgan's childhood in a poor, inner-city Milwaukee neighborhood starkly illustrates the tragic effects of omnipresent urban violence. "Mom shot dad," Shellow says. "And Mom shot boyfriend. . . . [Lisa's] uncle, who was actually her age, was murdered. Two days later, her other uncle was murdered. Her sister's boyfriend was paralyzed from the neck down by gunfire. Her brother was shot at and injured. Her mother once had set her father on fire."

4   If this weren't enough tragedy in one young life, Lisa Morgan's mother was a drug addict and Lisa was raped at age 12.

The "Ghetto Defense"

5   So perhaps it's not too surprising that Morgan, as a teenager, committed six armed robberies and one intentional homicide in the space of 17 minutes in October 1991. The victims were girls; the stolen objects were jewelry, shoes, and a coat. The dead girl was shot at point-blank range.

6   What *is* surprising—to the legal establishment, at least—is the approach Robin Shellow used in defending Morgan. In the girl's neighborhood and in her family, Shellow argued, violence is a *norm*, an occurrence so routine that Morgan's 17 years of exposure to it have rendered her not responsible for her actions.

7   This "ghetto defense" proved fruitless in Morgan's case. In court, the young woman was found both sane and guilty. Unless Shellow wins on appeal, Morgan will be behind bars well into [this] century.

8   But despite its failure for Morgan, Shellow's "cultural psychosis" or "psychosocial history" strategy has taken hold. "I've gotten hundreds of calls from interested attorneys," Shellow says. Already, the defense is being floated in courtrooms around the nation. It's eliciting both enthusiasm and outrage.

The Defense Is a Medical One

9   Technically, Shellow's defense is a medical one. She believes that Morgan suffers from post-traumatic stress disorder (PTSD) and other psychological ailments stemming from her lifelong exposure to violence.

10   Like other good lawyers, Shellow knows that the law abhors broadly applicable excuses, so she emphasizes the narrowness of her claim. Morgan belongs to a very small group of inner-city residents with "tremendous intra-familial violence," only some of whom might experience PTSD. She also stresses the unrevolutionary nature of the defense, medically and legally. PTSD has been recognized as a malady in standard diagnostic texts since 1980, she says, and it has been employed as a criminal defense for Vietnam veterans, battered wives, and many other trauma victims.

11   Despite Shellow's attempts to show that her defense is neither new nor broad, the case is ringing loud alarms. For, however viewed, her strategy sets up an inflammatory equation between inner-city conditions and criminal exculpation. The implication is that if you grew up in a poor, violent neighborhood and you commit a crime, you may go scot-free.

12   Yet why not a ghetto defense? After all, if a Vietnam veteran can claim PTSD from the shock of war, why shouldn't a similar defense be available for a young black reared in the embattled precincts of Bed-Stuy [Bedford-Stuyvesant neighborhood of New York City]? Sounds sensible, no? Isn't a ghetto like a battlefield?

Compare These Neighborhoods to War Zones

13   Alex Kotlowitz, who chronicled the lives of two Chicago black boys in *There Are No Children Here*, goes even further. He says the inner city can be worse than war. "You hear constant comparisons of these neighborhoods to war zones, but I think there are some pretty significant differences," he says. "In war, there's at least a sense that someday there will be a resolution, some vision that things could be different. That is not the case in the inner cities. There is no vision. And there's no sense of who's friend and who's foe."

14   There are other analogies that make the ghetto defense seem very legitimate. For instance, despite traditional self-defense principles, a battered wife in some jurisdictions can kill her sleeping husband and be legally excused for the homicide. The reason is the psychological harm she has sustained from her life of fear and violence.

15   Why not Lisa Morgan? Hasn't her life been debilitatingly violent and fearful?

16   These arguments make some lawyers hopeful about the future of Shellow's pioneering strategy. But most observers are pessimistic. "We'll get nowhere with it," says famous defense lawyer William Kunstler.

The Poor Instead of the Powerful

17   Why? One reason is that the American justice system often favors the powerful over the poor. For generations, for instance, the bloodiest crime in the nation—drunk driving—was punished with a relative wrist slap. By contrast, a recent federal law mandates that those convicted of the new crime of carjacking get socked with a minimum and mandatory 15-year sentence.

18   What explains these disparate approaches? Simple: protection of the affluent classes. Light penalties for drunk driving protect the affluent because they often drive drunk. Harsh carjacking penalties protect the affluent because they are the usual carjacking victims. "The middle class sees carjacking [laws] as protecting them from people coming out of some poor neighborhood and just showing up in *their* neighborhood and committing a crime in which they are at risk of dying," says Professor James Liebman of Columbia University School of Law.

19   Because the ghetto defense protects the poor instead of the powerful, Kunstler and others doubt it has a bright future. Other factors further dim the strategy's chances. Fear is a main one, says Professor Liebman. The ghetto defense brings a gulp from jurors because "their first thought is, 'If he's not responsible, then none of those people are,'" he reasons. And we all know what that means: riots, mayhem, Los Angeles.

20   Social guilt raises even higher the hurdles for the ghetto defense. To allow such a defense is a tacit admission that we—society—tolerate a situation so hobbling that its victims have become unaccountable for their actions. "If it ain't them who's guilty, it's us," says Michael Dowd, director of the Pace University Battered Women's Justice Center in New York. And "it's just too horrific for us to accept responsibility, too horrific to say, 'I'm responsible for what happened in L.A.' We will be able to accept the [ghetto] defense at the same moment that we are seriously moved to eradicate the realities behind that defense."

21   What are the biggest criticisms of the ghetto defense? One focuses on the victim's identity. Battered spouses and battered children are accused of killing precisely those who hurt them. This endows the crime with a certain rough justice. But in a ghetto defense case, the victim is usually an innocent stranger.

22   Others, like Kotlowitz, worry that the ghetto defense might dislodge the cornerstone of our justice system: personal responsibility. "We have to be careful not to view people growing up in neighborhoods completely as victims; they are both victims and actors," he warns. "We can't absolve them from responsibility."

23   Lisa Morgan "went up to someone she didn't know, stole a jacket from her, and then just blew her away," he says. "There's no way as a society that we can excuse that. We can understand it, but we can't excuse it."

24   He raises a fundamental question. Everyone can point to scars from the past—alcoholic parents, tragic love, etc.—and claim exculpation. And if all are excused, who is responsible?

25   Another worry is diminished standards. "[The ghetto defense] lowers expectations," Kotlowitz continues. "It says, 'OK, I understand what you've been through, so it's OK to go out and hurt somebody.' And once you lower your expectations, particularly with kids, they will meet only those lower expectations."

A Disease Is a Disease

26   It's only fair to note that other criminal defenses also have these weaknesses. For instance, the victim of a PTSD-afflicted veteran is often an innocent passerby, and the battered-spouse doctrine certainly raises questions about personal responsibility and lowered expectations.

27   And if, as seems likely, some ghetto residents do have PTSD largely as a result of their living conditions, it's hard to see why this ailment should be exculpatory for veterans, say, but not for ghetto residents. After all, a disease is a disease, and how you got it is irrelevant.

28   How deep go the wounds from the ghetto? Here are two incidents in Morgan's life: "When Felicia was about 11, her mother put a knife to her throat and threatened to kill her," according to a psychologist's report in the case. "Felicia escaped by running into the basement, where she 'busted the lights out with my hand' so that her mother could not see her." Then, when she was 12, the landlord attacked her. "Felicia fought him off by throwing hot grease onto him, but he finally subdued her, tied her hands to the bed, stuffed her mouth with a sock and raped her."

29   How does one live like this? Morgan gives a hint. "My ears be open," she told the psychologist, "even when I'm asleep."

30   This was a *child*. Society did nothing to stop these daily depredations upon her. While the legal propriety of the ghetto defense is an important question, the biggest question of all in this story has nothing to do with personal responsibility. It has to do with society's responsibility to poor children like Morgan. What does it say about our society that such a defense was conceived? How can things have come to this pass?

EXERCISE 9   Vocabulary Highlights

Write a short definition of each word as it is used in the essay. (Paragraph numbers are given in parentheses.) Be prepared to use these words in sentences.

omnipresent (3)	exculpation (11)
rendered (6)	sustained (14)
eliciting (8)	debilitatingly (15)
abhors (10)	tacit (20)
malady (10)	eradicate (20)

EXERCISE 10   Discussion and Critical Thinking

1. What writing pattern does Flaherty use in the first four paragraphs that serve as an introduction to her essay?

2. Which sentence in which paragraph contains the definition of "ghetto defense"?

3. What is post-traumatic stress disorder?

4. Does Attorney Shellow argue that all poor people living in the ghetto be granted excuses for any crimes they commit? If not, what is she arguing?

5. How is Morgan's case arguably similar to and different from those of battered spouses?

6. How is Morgan's case arguably similar to those of certain Vietnam veterans with PTSD who committed homicide?

7. According to Alex Kotlowitz, how can the inner-city environment be worse than that of a war zone?

8. According to the ghetto defense, where does responsibility lie, with the person or with society?

9. What is your opinion of the ghetto defense?

10. If the ghetto defense has validity, should the concept be extended to anyone who has had extremely violent experiences—"Everyone can point to scars from the past—alcoholic parents, tragic love, etc." (paragraph 24)?

11. Imagine you were a juror judging Morgan's case. How would you have voted and why?

Enough Is Enough

JUDY SCHEINDLIN AND JOSH GETLIN

Judy Scheindlin is best known as the star of Judge Judy, *a top-rated American reality-based television court show. For twenty-five years prior to her media stardom, she served as a family court judge in New York. This commentary comes from a book written with Josh Getlin, titled* Don't Pee on My Leg and Tell Me It's Raining.

MINDSET

Lock It In

In a purely practical sense, would it be better to have Madonna or Judge Judy as a mother?

1   As a family court judge, I looked down daily on a pageant of dysfunction that would curl your hair. After twenty-four years on the bench, I came to realize that these are not legal problems. They mirror what is wrong with our society, reflecting just how far we have strayed from personal responsibility and old-fashioned discipline.

2   Most of the kids I prosecuted during my early years in court were involved in petty thefts, but as the 70s passed into the 80s, both the incidence and the ferocity of juvenile crime accelerated. A new breed of delinquents was born, and the system did not have a clue how to treat them. We still don't.

3   To show you the price we pay, let me share some of my experiences in family court. The first case is heard at 9:30 a.m. A boy I'll call Elmo, 15, has been charged for a second time with selling crack cocaine. His lawyer argues that Elmo's troubles started when his grandmother died. In his grief, he had no choice but to deal the hard stuff. "Get a better story," I fire back, startling the boy, who is looking smug. "Nobody goes out and sells drugs because Grandma died."

4   Next is a youth I'll call Tito, a delinquent who confesses to mugging an 80-year-old man in broad daylight. Tito's older brother has just been sent to prison for murder. Tito was very close to his brother, the boy's lawyer insists, and his crime was a result of post-traumatic stress. "You'll have to do better than that," I snap.

5   Then comes a woman who is addicted to crack. She's already given birth to two crack-addicted babies, and she didn't report to her drug-rehab program as promised. Her excuse: She lost the address. "What do you want, a road map?" I exclaim.

6   Welcome to my world.

7   I believe that you deal with these problems the way you would deal with any crisis in a family: by setting strict limits and by showing compassion. As the mother of five children, I know that you have to get tough at the same time that you show love. Family court should be no different. I think we should send a tough message to first-time offenders every chance we get, in the hopes that perhaps there will not be a second offense.

8   The primary obligation of any civilized society is to preserve the peace and protect its citizens. Only after that should you worry about the lawbreakers and their rehabilitation. This might be our last chance to do something about the future of these delinquents—and our own safety. Here are my suggestions for improving our juvenile system.

Spend Public Money on Good Kids

9   The vast majority of the children who suffer from poverty, neglect, and even abuse do not commit crimes. They struggle in their chaotic environments, with little or no support. But for years our concerns have been with those who break the law.

10   A recent set of photographs in my local newspaper illustrated this inversion of priorities. In one picture was a state-of-the-art gymnasium, with Nautilus equipment and gleaming free weights—part of the recreational complex at a state detention facility. The other photo was of an overcrowded, deteriorating inner-city junior high school with peeling paint and broken windows. What kind of insanity is this? We should offer offenders food, clothing, and a bed, plus vocational and academic training. Period. The money we save by not dressing up our detention facilities should be spent on the good kids who struggle just to get by.

No Rules of Confidentiality for Juvenile Offenders

11   It is impossible for judges to sentence intelligently if they do not know the offender's criminal history. If a youngster turns his or her life around, those records can be sealed or expunged at age 25. If he does not, that record should follow him to the grave.

Make Them Earn Early Release

12   Convicted juveniles, like adult offenders, often gain early and undeserved release from jail. In my opinion, early release should be earned. Juveniles should qualify only if they complete an academic or vocational course of study. The rest should stay behind bars their full term.

Enact a National Curfew

13   Most lawbreaking by youngsters takes place at a time when these kids should be at home. I recommend a national curfew for kids under 18. If parents cannot or will not set limits, then society must do it for them, for their protection and its own.

Make the Parents Pay

14   Too many people treat the juvenile system as a joke. That would change overnight if we required parents to pay for their children's defense attorneys according to their means, even if it is a percentage of their welfare benefits.
15   Furthermore, in too many states, welfare keeps flowing while the kids are in jail, or middle-class parents continue to claim children as tax deductions even as the state pays for their upkeep in detention facilities. We must demand that parents reimburse the state for housing their failures.

No Public Assistance for Parents of Dropouts

16   Kids need an education to have hope for the future. It makes sense to insist that children stay in school or go off welfare. Our message should be clear to everyone: If you want to eat, you have to work. If you stay in school, we'll support you. Otherwise, support yourself. No exceptions. Does it sound like I'm cracking down on the poor? Far from it. If a middle-class kid drops out of school, the $2,750 tax break that his parents claim for him should be eliminated. Without proof that a child is attending school, parents should lose the exemption.
17   If I had to boil my message down to one sentence, it would be that people create their own opportunities. As a woman, a mother, and a judge who has seen our criminal system deteriorate for nearly a quarter of a century, I have had it with the victim game. A delinquent is responsible for his crime. Parents are responsible for their children.

18   The prescription so far has been to give them more social programs, and that remedy has failed. Self-discipline, individual accountability, and responsible conduct are the answer. They have always been the answer, but America got lost. It is time to get back on course.

EXERCISE 11   Discussion and Critical Thinking

1. According to Judge Judy, what is wrong with our society?

2. How does she use the case of Elmo in her argument?

3. What is her reaction to the lawyer's plea that Tito's crime was caused by his post-traumatic stress?

4. How does she feel about showing compassion to first-time offenders?

5. What is Judge Judy's economic message to parents of delinquents?

6. Do you agree with her judicial tough-love approach? Why or why not?

7. Do you agree with her view that "self-discipline, individual accountability, and responsible conduct are the answer" (paragraph 18)? Explain.

STUDENT ESSAY

From "Kick Me" to "Kiss Me"

SHANDRA BRYSON (PSEUDONYM)

Victims of abuse do not always feel sorry for themselves. They also do not always protect others who are being abused. These are shocking conclusions reached by Shandra Bryson, a victim who now looks at herself thoughtfully.

1   I can identify with people who were physically abused as children. I am one of them, and I've got all kinds of scars. In prison, I am surrounded by people with a background similar to mine. Like me, they are trying to leave a whole pattern of thinking and behavior behind. Here in prison, a woman I know filed a grievance against a guard who, she said, had struck her numerous times. When the Watch Commander read the statement, he said, "You didn't fill in this part that says, 'Action Requested'?" Her answer was immediate. "I want people to stop beating me unless I deserve it." A former victim of child abuse, she was taking an important step. The final

Thesis

one would occur when she stopped believing that she should be beaten for any reason. Some people might think that understanding is simple, but it isn't. <u>First, one has to understand what happens to a person who gets beat on every day.</u>

2   When I was a little kid, my father used to abuse me—in ways I don't want to describe just yet. Abuse was a normal part of my life. He especially liked to throw things such as ashtrays, books, the TV remote control, and beer cans (usually with beer in them). Then if he missed, he'd get even madder and chase me down and pound me with his fists.

Effect

<u>Naturally I figured out it would be better to be hit with a flying object than to be pounded, so I learned to move toward whatever he threw.</u> He never seemed to catch on. I'd lunge toward something like an ashtray, and it'd hit me—fleshy parts like my seat were the best targets—and then I'd cry, and he'd stop. Sometimes he'd say how sorry he was and how I got him all upset. It always was my fault.

Effect

3   Of course, I believed it was my fault. <u>Whenever he hit me, however he did it, I knew I deserved it, if not for the immediate mischief, for something else—I was wicked.</u> I always felt more guilt than anger. My life was full of guilt-producing incidents. I received bad grades in school. I embarrassed him in front of his friends. I got in his way around the house. The food I cooked was never as good as that cooked by my mother, who'd disappeared four years after I was born—which was another source of guilt because she probably didn't like me. There were plenty of reasons for me to feel guilty, and I didn't neglect any of them.

4   But I wasn't the only one around the house who felt guilty. <u>My little brother had his share of guilt feelings.</u> For him, it was not my father he had to watch out for. My father thought Joey could do no wrong. <u>I was the one who beat Joey.</u> When my father was out, I slapped Joey around and threw things—ashtrays, books, hair brushes, whatever I had. Pretty soon I had me a little whiner to pick on, so I could feel better. I even had him apologizing, acting mousier than I ever did, and even cutting on himself.

Effect

5   Finally, when I went to school with bruises for the hundredth time, a teacher took me to the principal, and I told all. <u>The result was juvenile hall, followed by a half-dozen foster homes and a pattern of beating by adults in all kinds of situations—even by men I lived with.</u>

Effect

Effects

6   Being abused is bad. <u>It made me feel guilty. It made me want to be abused. And it made me want to be an abuser.</u> Now I'm working on undoing the pattern of thinking that I've had all these years. I want to take the "Kick me" sign off my back and replace it with one that reads "Kiss me." But right now I'm all so mixed up in changing that if someone did kiss me, I don't know whether I'd kiss back or kick.

EXERCISE 12   Discussion and Critical Thinking

1. Does the author seem to understand her situation well in terms of causes and effects? Explain.

2. How would you relate the content of this essay to the two previous essays on the causes of violence?

3. If you were a judge in a case in which Shandra Bryson were the defendant, and you knew the story of her childhood, would you consider her family history in determining her incarceration or treatment? How do you think you might rule and what would you say to her?

STUDENT PARAGRAPH AND ESSAY

Responding to an assignment on a topic organized mainly around causes and effects, Richard Blaylock chose to write about the consequences of his becoming a college student. With much trepidation, at thirty-three he had enrolled in the evening program at a local community college. The reasons for his being there were multiple, and so, surprising to him, were the results.

Blaylock's Writing Process Worksheet shows how his writing evolved from idea to final draft. To conserve space here, the freewriting and the rough drafts marked for revision have been omitted. The balance of his worksheet has been lengthened for you to be able to see his other work in its entirety.

You will find a full-size blank worksheet on page 6, which can be photocopied, filled in, and submitted with each assignment if your instructor directs you to do so.

Writing Process Worksheet

Name <u>Richard Blaylock</u>   **Title** <u>The Classroom and Beyond</u>   **Due Date** <u>Tuesday, May 9, noon</u>

Use the back of this page or separate paper if you need more space.

Assignment

In the space below, write whatever you need to know about your assignment, including information about the topic, audience, pattern of writing, length, whether to include a rough draft or revised drafts, and whether your paper must be typed.

In a paragraph of 200 to 300 words, discuss the causes or effects of any new element in your life at any point. The element could be a relationship, death, health problem, marriage, college program, new job, or winning ticket in the lottery. Submit this completed worksheet, a rough draft marked for revision, and a typed final draft.

Stage One

Explore Freewrite, brainstorm (list), cluster, or take notes as directed by your instructor.

Listing

Causes	Event, Situation, or Trend	Effects
Boss's suggestion	My going to college	Family pride
Company pays		Wife inspired

My desire	Personal growth
Family support	More competitive at work
	Better pay
	Work scholarship
	Tired
	School friendships

Stage Two   **Organize** Write a topic sentence or thesis; label the subject and the focus parts.

<u>My decision to enroll in college night school</u> <u>would offer more benefits than I</u>
                              subject   focus
<u>could have imagined</u>.

Write an outline or an outline alternative. For reading-based writing, include references and short quotations with page numbers as support in the outline.

I. Effects on family
  A. Wife inspired
  B. Family proud
II. Effects on me
  A. Learn usable skills
  B. More confident
  C. More curious
III. Effects at work
  A. In line for better pay
  B. Soon given new responsibilities
  C. Given new respect

Stage Three   **Write** On separate paper, write and then revise your paragraph or essay as many times as necessary for **c**oherence, **l**anguage (usage, tone, and diction), **u**nity, **e**mphasis, **s**upport, and **s**entences (**CLUESS**). Read your work aloud to hear and correct any grammatical errors or awkward-sounding sentences.

Edit any problems in fundamentals, such as **c**apitalization, **o**missions, **p**unctuation, and **s**pelling (**COPS**).

Final Draft

THE CLASSROOM AND BEYOND
Richard Blaylock

"We think you would benefit from our work-study program," he said to me. He was not my high school counselor, and I wasn't 18. He was the division manager, and he had just offered to pay my expenses for attending a local community college. At 33, I was working for a large company in a dead-end job, dead-end because I was not qualified for any management positions. Naturally, I enrolled in college. More benefits than I expected were to follow. I had hardly started when the first response greeted me: my family was clearly proud. I heard my two kids in elementary school bragging about me to kids in the neighborhood. They even brought me some of their tough homework questions. My wife had lots of questions about college. We talked about taking a class together. Unlike me, she had been a good student in high school. Then I had had no interest in going on to college. Now I did, and one thing led to another. A geography class connected me with a geology class. A political science class moved me to subscribe to the Los Angeles *Times*. I became more curious about a variety of subjects, and I felt more confident in dealing with ideas. At work my supervisors started asking me to become more involved in ongoing projects and planning. By the time I had taken my second English class, I was writing reports with much more confidence and skill. Now, after receiving a good job review and being interviewed by my plant manager, I am in line for a promotion that I once thought was beyond my reach. At most, I had expected a classroom. I found much more.

EXERCISE 12   Discussion and Critical Thinking

1. Is this an essay mainly of causes or effects?

2. Circle the topic sentence.

3. Underline each effect.

READING-BASED WRITING: SHORT STORY REVIEW

The Use of Self-Analysis

GLORIA MENDEZ

This essay explains that the first-person point of view places the central character in "The Use of Force" in close focus, with all his strengths and weaknesses there on the surface for our analysis—and for his own. The underlinings and margin notes have been added to show how Mendez organized her final draft.

Thesis	1	One of the main thrusts in "The Use of Force" is point of view. <u>The narrator, a doctor, tells his own story, a story about his encounter with an uncooperative patient but also—and mostly—a story about the narrator's transformation from a mature, rational person to someone of a lower order who has lost considerable self-respect.</u> This transformation happens
Parts of support		in stages of changes in attitude that occur during his arrival, his early attempt at obtaining cooperation, his loss of self-control, and his reflection on his behavior.
Topic sentence	2	<u>When the doctor arrives at the small farmhouse, he feels like an outsider.</u>
Causes		The family is self-conscious and not sure about how to act around a doctor. They are poor, and out of concern for the daughter, are spending some of their meager funds to get a diagnosis and possible treatment. The doctor sees
Quotation and references		that they are "all very nervous, eyeing me up and down distrustfully . . ." (330). They tell him very little, wanting to get their money's worth.
Topic sentence	3	<u>The doctor initially follows standard procedure.</u> He sees that the daughter
Cause		is feverish and panting. With concern about a local diphtheria epidemic, he asks the mother if she had looked at the girl's throat. In a foreshadowing
Quotations and references		that the doctor does not catch, the mother says, "I tried to . . . but I couldn't see." Moving to the hands-on stage, he asks the girl to open her mouth. "Nothing doing." He tries a gentle approach, shows her he has no concealed

Cause		weapons by opening his hands. But her mother mentions the word "hurt," and the doctor grinds his "teeth in disgust"(330). He maintains his composure as he approaches her. She loses hers, as she tries to scratch his eyes out and succeeds in knocking his glasses to the floor.
Topic sentence	4	<u>Both his tact and his attitude change</u>. The parents are embarrassed;
Effect		they apologize, threaten the daughter, and awkwardly try to help the
Causes		doctor. He's disgusted with them, however; they've done all the wrong things. But he admires the girl, even saying he had "already fallen in love
Quotations and references		with the savage brat" (330). He knows that her anger is caused by her fear of him. He decides to use force—for her own good. The possibility that she has diphtheria is there. The girl's resistance builds: she screams and struggles. He uses a "wooden tongue depressor," and she chews it "into splinters" (331).
Topic sentence	5	<u>It is during this phase of the incident that the doctor joins the struggle</u>
Quotations and references		<u>at her level</u>. As he admits, "But now I also had grown furious—at a child. I
Effect		tried to hold myself down but I couldn't." He goes for heavier equipment—a metal spoon. He convinces himself that he must get the "diagnosis now or never." Whether his rationality or truth prevailed in that decision, he does know that he "had got beyond reason" (331). "I could have torn the child
Causes		apart in my fury. It was a pleasure to attack her. My face was burning
Effect		with it." He has truth and reason on his side, but his emotions as "a blind fury" are in control. He mounts the "final unreasoning assault" and wins. She has an infected throat, and he has exposed it, but she still tries to
Quotations and references		attack "while tears of defeat blinded her eyes" (331).
Topic sentence	6	<u>The final stage, the recognition, is there throughout the last part of the</u>
		<u>story</u>. If the doctor had dismissed the incident, we would have thought him insensitive. If the doctor had savored the experience, we would have called
Effect		him sadistic. But the doctor, with obvious regret, has admitted that he had "grown furious," lost restraint, "got beyond reason," felt a "longing for
Quotations and references		muscular release," and gone on "to the end" (332).
Conclusion	7	The "use of force" has two effects in this story. The girl resents the force and becomes alternately defensive and offensive. The doctor uses force
Effects		and becomes so caught up in the physical and emotional conflicts that he is responding to the wrong motive for acting. It is the point of view that highlights the doctor's feelings of guilt in retrospect. This feeling comes across much more poignantly because this story is, after all, a confessional.

Work Cited

Williams, William Carlos. "The Use of Force." *Paragraphs and Essays: A Worktext with Readings*. Ed. Lee Brandon. 8th ed. Houghton, 2001. 330–33. Print.

Suggested Topics and Prompts for Writing Cause and Effect

STUDENT COMPANION SITE
For additional practice, visit www.cengage .com/devenglish/ brandon/pe11e.

You will find a blank Writing Process Worksheet on page 6 of this book and on your Student Companion Site. It can be photocopied or printed out, filled in, and submitted with your assignment, if your instructor directs you to do so.

READING-BASED WRITING

Reading-based writing requires you to read critically, write a reply that shows you understand what you have read, and give credit for ideas you borrow and words you quote. The form can be a summary, a reaction, or a two-part response (with separated summary and reaction). Documentation, in which you give credit for borrowed ideas and words, can be either formal (MLA) or informal, as directed by your instructor. Both the forms of reading-based writing and documentation are discussed with examples in Chapter 1. Definitions of the three forms follow. Any form can be used for any reading selection in this book.

Summary

- The summary is a statement presenting only the main points of what you have read by using different wording without altering the meaning, adding information, or showing bias.
- It is the purest form of reading-based writing.

Reaction

- In the reaction, the meaning of what you have read will be central to your topic sentence of your paragraph or to the thesis of your essay.
- Although the reaction is not a personal narrative by itself, it may include personal experience to explain elements of the text. For example, if your source is about driving styles, your own experiences as a driver or an observer of drivers could be relevant in your analysis of the text.
- The reaction may incorporate a summary to convey a broad view of what you have read, but your summary should never be the main part of your reaction.

The Two-Part Response

- The two-part response separates the summary from the reaction.
- This form will give you practice in separating your objective summary in the first part from your more personal evaluation, interpretation, or application in the second part, the reaction.

READING-BASED WRITING TOPICS

"Why Marriages Fail"

1. Roiphe says that "we all select with unconscious accuracy a mate who will re-create with us the emotional patterns of our first homes." In a reaction either agree or disagree with that statement and its support, and explain your own views by discussing the causal factors in a marriage you are familiar with.

"The Girls in Their Summer Dresses"

2. Write a reading-based paragraph or essay of agreement or disagreement with one or more of the following statements. Paraphrase the statements if you like. Use references, quotations, and reasoning to support your views. Or write your own controlling statement(s).

a. "That is the way men are, and Frances should learn to love them or leave them."

b. "Michael is a self-centered male chauvinist, and he is at fault."

c. "The day started well, turned bad, and got worse because of (his or her) behavior."

d. "They have different definitions of love, and (he or she) deserves someone better."

e. "Their marriage can be saved if (he or she) will change."

3. Pretend you are "Dear Abby" or a marriage counselor by correspondence, and write advice on what Michael and Frances should do. Imagine that you have already read this short story as a very revealing document of their differences and that they know you have read it. Refer to their behavior and quote what they say as you discuss this eventful day.

"The Ghetto Made Me Do It"

4. In a reaction write about one or more of the questions posed by the author:

• If under certain conditions a Vietnam veteran or a battered spouse can use post-traumatic stress disorder as a defense, then why cannot a brutalized product of the ghetto such as Felicia Morgan use the same or a similar defense?

• What is the role of personal responsibility in the commission of a crime, regardless of what the perpetrator has experienced?

• To what extent is society responsible when a person such as Felicia Morgan grows up under such horrific conditions?

Refer directly to the essay and use quotations from it. Evaluate Flaherty's use of evidence such as examples and comparisons.

"Enough Is Enough"

5. Write either a summary of or a two-part response to Judge Judy's essay. In your reaction, agree or disagree with her views. You may use your own examples as support of your views.

"From 'Kick Me' to 'Kiss Me'"

6. Write a reaction in which you use Bryson's words to help you understand the depth of her problems and to speculate about the chances for her recovery.

Views on Violence

7. Write a reaction in which you apply Judge Judy's philosophy (see pages 237, 242) expressed in "Enough Is Enough" to the two inmates in "The Ghetto Made Me Do It" and "From 'Kick Me' to 'Kiss Me.'" Explain what you think she would do and say in sentencing each inmate, assuming that they were both convicted of assaulting a stranger in separate cases. Use at least one quotation from or reference to each essay.

GENERAL TOPICS

8. Write a paragraph or an essay about people who have influenced you in important ways. How have they caused you to be who you are and are becoming?

Consider giving credit to historical figures, family members, close friends, and other individuals from your community, neighborhood, or school. For a helpful model on a similar topic, review "Family Heroes and Role Models" on page 232.

9. Write a paragraph or an essay of cause and effect in which you discuss how your life has changed, is changing, or will change as a result of your ongoing education. For a helpful model on a similar topic, review "The Classroom and Beyond" on pages 247–248.

10. Select one of the following topics as a subject (situation, circumstance, or trend) for your paragraph or essay and then determine whether you will concentrate on causes, effects, or a combination. You can probably write a more interesting, well-developed, and therefore successful paragraph or essay on a topic you can personalize. For example, a discussion about a specific young person who contemplated, attempted, or committed suicide is probably a better topic idea than a general discussion of suicide. If you do not personalize the topic, you will probably have to do some basic research to supply details for development.

   a. Having or getting a job
   b. Alcoholism
   c. Gambling
   d. Moving to another country, state, or home

CROSS-CURRICULAR TOPIC

11. From a class that you are taking or have taken, select a subject that is especially concerned with causes and effects and develop a topic. Begin by selecting an event, a situation, or a trend in the class content and make a list of the causes and effects; that procedure will almost immediately show you whether you have a topic you can discuss effectively. Class notes and textbooks can provide you with more specific information. If you use textbooks or other materials, give credit or make copies of the sources. Instructors across the campus may have suggestions for studies of cause and effect. Some areas for your search include history, political science, geology, astronomy, psychology, philosophy, sociology, business, real estate, child development, education, fashion merchandising and design, psychiatric technician program, nursing, police science, fire science, nutrition and food, physical education, and restaurant and food-service management.

CAREER-RELATED TOPICS

12. Discuss the effects (benefits) of a particular product or service on the business community, family life, society generally, a specific group (age, income, interest), or an individual.

13. Discuss the needs (thus the cause of development) by individuals, families, or institutions for a particular product or type of product.

14. Discuss the effects of using a certain approach or philosophy in sales, human resources management, or customer service.

WRITER'S GUIDELINES: Cause and Effect

1. Determine whether your topic should mainly inform or mainly persuade, and consider your purpose and audience.

2. Use listing to brainstorm cause-and-effect ideas. This is a useful form:

Causes	Event, Situation, or Trend	Effects
1.		1.
2.		2.
3.		3.
4.		4.

3. Decide whether to concentrate on causes, effects, or a combination of causes and effects. Most paragraphs will focus only on causes or only on effects. Many short essays will discuss causes and effects but will use one as the framework for the piece. A typical basic outline might look like this:

Topic sentence of paragraph or thesis of essay
I. Cause or Effect 1
II. Cause or Effect 2
III. Cause or Effect 3

4. Do not conclude that something is an effect merely because it follows something else.

5. Emphasize your main concern(s)—causes, effects, or a combination—by repeating key words such as *cause*, *reason*, *effect*, *result*, *consequence*, and *outcome*.

6. Causes and effects can be primary or secondary, immediate or remote.

7. The order of causes and effects in your paper may be based on time, space, emphasis, or a combination.

8. The short story review is likely to include the following:

- In a short paper, you would probably use one or more of the short story's elements: setting, conflict, characters, plot, point of view, theme.
- Develop your ideas by referring directly to the story; by explaining; and by using summaries, paraphrases, and quotations.
- Use the present tense in relating events in the story.

9. Use the writing process.

- Write and then revise your paragraph or essay as many times as necessary for **c**oherence, **l**anguage (usage, tone, and diction), **u**nity, **e**mphasis, **s**upport, and **s**entences (**CLUESS**).
- Read your work aloud to hear and correct any grammatical errors or awkward-sounding sentences.
- Edit any problems in fundamentals, such as **c**apitalization, **o**missions, **p**unctuation, and **s**pelling (**COPS**).

Chapter 12

Classification
Establishing Groups

FLOW OF WRITING

WHEN TO USE CLASSIFICATION

FOR COLLEGE WRITING ASSIGNMENTS

If you are writing a statement of any length—sentence, paragraph, essay, or report—that is based on the phrase "different kinds—or classes—of [*your subject*]," you will use classification.

- In an English composition course, as you work on the techniques for classifying as a pattern of thought, you might write about classes of students or heroes.
- In a history course you might write about different classes of democracy, leaders, citizens, or government.
- In a geology course you might write about different classes of rocks or minerals.

Each of those classes will be formed according to a single principle that indicates your focus.

IN CAREERS AND AT THE WORKPLACE

Whether in preparation for a vocation or at the workplace, one deals critically with the formation of groups.

- Careers can be grouped according to common denominators of job descriptions, conditions, benefits, and requirements.
- Clients, products, and services are commonly grouped, or classified, in reports and by focus groups for analysis.

CLASSIFICATION IN A CARTOON

THE QUIGMANS   by Buddy Hickerson

THE MOST UNPLEASANT THING ABOUT BEING THE ONLY STUDENT IN THIS CLASS WILL BE WHEN I ASK YOU TO BREAK UP INTO GROUPS.

Writing Classification

To explain by classification, you put persons, places, things, or ideas into groups or classes based on their characteristics. Whereas analysis by division deals with the characteristics of just one unit, classification deals with more than one unit, so the subject is plural.

To classify efficiently, try following this procedure:

1. Select a plural subject.

2. Decide on a principle for grouping the units of your subject.

3. Establish the groups, or classes.

4. Write about the classes.

SELECTING A SUBJECT

When you say you have different kinds of neighbors, friends, teachers, bosses, or interests, you are classifying; that is, you are forming groups.

In naming the different kinds of people in your neighborhood, you might think of different groupings of your neighbors, the units. For example, some neighbors are friendly, some are meddlesome, and some are private. Some neighbors have yards like Japanese gardens, some have yards like neat-but-cozy parks, and some have yards like abandoned lots. Some neighbors are affluent, some are comfortable, and some are struggling. Each of these sets is a classification system and could be the focus of one paragraph in your essay.

USING A PRINCIPLE TO AVOID OVERLAPPING

All the sets in the preceding section are sound because each group is based on a single concern: neighborly involvement, appearance of the yard, or wealth. This one concern, or controlling idea, is called the **principle**. For example, the principle of neighborly involvement controls the grouping of neighbors into three classes: friendly, meddlesome, and private.

All the classes in any one group must adhere to the controlling principle for that group. You would not say, for example, that your neighbors can be classified as friendly, meddlesome, private, and affluent, because the first three classes relate to neighborly involvement, but the fourth, relating to wealth, refers to another principle. Any one of the first three—the friendly, meddlesome, and private—might also be affluent. The classes should not overlap in this way. Also, every member should fit into one of the available classes.

ESTABLISHING CLASSES

As you name your classes, rule out easy, unimaginative types such as *fast/medium/slow*, *good/average/bad*, and *beautiful/ordinary/ugly*. Look for creative, original phrases and unusual perspectives as shown in these simple forms.

Subject: neighbors
Principle: neighborhood involvement
Classes: friendly, meddlesome, private

Subject: neighbors
Principle: yard upkeep
Classes: immaculate, neat, messy

Subject: neighbors
Principle: wealth
Classes: affluent, comfortable, struggling

Complex classifications are based on one principle and then subgrouped by another related principle. The following example classifies neighbors by their neighborly involvement. It then subgroups the classes on the basis of motive.

I. Friendly
  A. Civic-minded
  B. Want to be accepted
  C. Gregarious
II. Meddlesome
  A. Controlling
  B. Emotionally needy
  C. Suspicious of others
III. Private
  A. Shy
  B. Snobbish
  C. Secretive

Transitional Words

Consider using the following transitional words to improve coherence by connecting ideas with ideas, sentences with sentences, and paragraphs with paragraphs.

FOR CLASSIFICATION: classify, (to) group, categorize, the first class, the second class, the third class, another class, a subclass, another subclass

FOR ALL PATTERNS OF WRITING: The <u>HOTSHOT CAT</u> words: <u>H</u>owever, <u>O</u>therwise, <u>T</u>herefore, <u>S</u>imilarly, <u>H</u>ence, <u>O</u>n the other hand, <u>T</u>hen, <u>C</u>onsequently, <u>A</u>lso, <u>T</u>hus (See pages 427–428 for additional transitional words.)

DEVELOPING THE CLASSIFICATION

Here is an example of a student paragraph that demonstrates the steps for writing classification:

Subject: shoppers in a department store
Principle: reasons for shopping
Classes: looking, sales, special-item shoppers

I. Looking shoppers
II. Sales shoppers
III. Special-item shoppers

SORTING THEM OUT
José Morales

Transitional words
Class 1

Transitional words
Class 2

Transitional words
Class 3

I've had several kinds of customers at my job at Target. Specifically, I can <u>group</u> most of them into three classes: the looking shopper, the sales shoppers, and the special-item shoppers. The <u>first</u> and largest <u>class</u> is the *looking shoppers*. One can see them wandering around all over the store as if they were lost or maybe out for exercise. They stop for discoveries here and there, but they don't want to be bothered by salespersons. They're pretty harmless, except sometimes they bump into each other. And quite infrequently they buy something. The <u>next class</u>, the *sales shoppers*, are the ones who have read the advertisements. They may even be carrying an advertisement with them, matching pictures and numbers with items. If a salesperson can help them get to the merchandise before someone else does, they're grateful; otherwise, get out of their way. They are single-minded and ruthless. Beware of verbal assaults and vicious bodily contact at the sales tables. The <u>last group</u> is my favorite. It is the *special-item shoppers*. They know what they want, but they would like good quality and a good price. They are usually friendly, and they are appreciative of good service. On a given day, one person may move from one group to another, and when the person does, his or her behavior changes. After serving more than three thousand customers, I can identify and classify them almost immediately.

EXERCISE 1 Avoiding Overlapped Classes

Mark each set of classes as OK or OL (overlapping); circle the classes that overlap.

	Subject	Principle	Classes
	Example:		
OL	community college students	intentions	vocational
			academic transfer
			specialty needs
			(hardworking)
1.	airline flights	passenger seating	first class
			business
			coach
2.	country singers	clothing trademark	hat
			overalls
			decorative costume
			expensive
3.	schools	ownership	private
			religious
			public
4.	faces	shape	round
			square
			oval
			beautiful
			broad
			long
5.	dates	behavior resembling aquatic animals	sharks
			clams
			jellyfish
			cute
			octopuses

FINDING PATTERNS IN PHOTOS

EXERCISE 2   A Text-Based Activity for Groups or Individuals

Yard sale

Imagine you are surrounded by clutter. Your loved ones and your inner parents are telling you it is time for a yard sale. It is an early Saturday morning. Traffic has not started to move much outside. You go through your house, your garage, and your toolshed, picking up items you need to lose. You put them on the lawn. You can bring more out later. You hastily make a sign, "Yard Sale," and are about to hang it on the back of your car parked curbside when it occurs to you that your items are jumbled. It is still early. Why not organize? You can classify the items according to their uses and place them in common areas marked with colored signs. You can have your own department store. Then when someone asks a question such as, "You got any old vinyl records?" you can point to a portion of the lawn that is marked "Entertainment."

Now it is time to classify. Come up with six or more phrases for groups of items that are commonly found at yard sales, and list some of the items you often see.

If your instructor directs, use your outline to write a paragraph or short essay of classification about this imagined preselling experience.

I. _____   IV. _____

   A. _____   A. _____

   B. _____   B. _____

   C. _____   C. _____

II. _____   V. _____

   A. _____   A. _____

   B. _____   B. _____

   C. _____   C. _____

III. _____   VI. _____

   A. _____   A. _____

   B. _____   B. _____

   C. _____   C. _____

© Felicia Martinez/Photo Edit

VII. _____   VIII. _____

    A. _____   A. _____

    B. _____   B. _____

    C. _____   C. _____

Practicing Patterns of Classification

Because the basic pattern of classification consists of classes, the initial outline is predictable: It uses Roman-numeral headings for the classes, although some classes may be longer and more complex than others.

EXERCISE 3   Completing Patterns of Classification

Fill in the blanks to identify classes that could be discussed for each subject.

1. *Subject:* Professional athletes

   Principle: Why they participate in sports

   Classes:

   I. Glory

   II. _____

   III. _____

2. *Subject:* Pet owners

   Principle: Why they own (need) pets

   Classes:

   I. Companionship

   II. _____

   III. _____

3. *Subject:* Dates or prospective spouses

   Principle: The way they can be compared to vehicles

   Classes:

   I. Economy (Taurus, Corolla, Civic)

       A. Low cost

       B. Low maintenance

       C. _____

   II. Minivans (Caravan, Quest, Odyssey)

       A. Practical

       B. _____

       C. _____

III. Luxury (Porsche, BMW, Mercedes, Lexus)

   A. High cost

      1.   Initial

      2.   _____

   B. _____

   C. Impressive features

      1.   _____

      2.   Unnecessary

Readings for Critical Thinking, Discussion, and Writing

READING STRATEGIES AND OBJECTIVES

Underlining and annotating these reading selections will help you answer the questions that follow the selections, discuss the material in class, and prepare for reading-based writing assignments. As you underline and annotate, pay special attention to the author's writing skills, logic, and message, and consider the relevance of the material to your own experiences and values.

Some selections begin with a Mindset suggestion that can help you create a readiness for connecting with what you are about to read.

PARAGRAPH

Styles of Leadership

WILLIAM M. PRIDE, ROBERT J. HUGHES, AND JACK R. KAPOOR

Written by three business professors, this paragraph is excerpted from a college textbook. It refers mainly to business institutions and the workplace, but it also covers all social units that depend on leadership, from the family to nations.

MINDSET
Lock It In

Was your favorite teacher of all time authoritarian, laissez-faire, democratic, or a combination of those?

For many years, leadership was viewed as a combination of personality traits, such as self-confidence, concern for people, intelligence, and dependability. Achieving a consensus on which traits were most important was difficult, however, and attention turned to styles of leadership behavior. In the last few decades, several styles of leadership have been identified: authoritarian, laissez-faire, and democratic. The **authoritarian leader** holds all authority and responsibility, with communication usually moving from top to bottom. This leader assigns workers to specific tasks and expects orderly, precise results. The leaders at United Parcel Service employ authoritarian leadership. At the other extreme is the **laissez-faire leader**, who gives authority to employees.

With the laissez-faire style, subordinates are allowed to work as they choose with a minimum of interference. Communication flows horizontally among group members. Leaders at Apple Computer are known to employ a laissez-faire leadership style in order to give employees as much freedom as possible to develop new products. The **democratic leader** holds final responsibility but also delegates authority to others, who participate in determining work assignments. In this leadership style, communication is active both upward and downward. Employee commitment is high because of participation in the decision-making process. Managers for both Wal-Mart and Saturn have used the democratic leadership style to encourage employees to become more than just rank-and-file workers.

EXERCISE 4   Discussion and Critical Thinking

1. Underline the topic sentence.

2. What is the subject of this paragraph?

3. What is the principle that divides the subject into classes?

4. This paragraph is obviously concerned with explaining the different styles of leadership, without showing favor. Do you have a preference? If so, what is your preference and why?

5. In the textbook *Business*, seventh edition, this paragraph is followed by another with this first sentence: "Today most management experts agree that no one 'best' managerial leadership style exists." How do you think the authors explain such a statement?

ESSAYS

How Do I Love Thee?

ROBERT J. TROTTER

How one loves depends on many things, including who is loving and who is being loved, but each love has certain components. Robert Trotter, using the system developed by R. J. Sternberg, details the different types of love by giving explanations and by providing examples.

MINDSET

Lock It In

Imagine you are in love with a critical thinker. On one poignant occasion, you whisper fervently, "I love you!" "How do you define 'love'?" your critical-thinking companion says. For a moment you are at a loss for words. Would you provide a definition? If so, what? Or would you just give your critical thinker a copy of the following essay?

1   Intimacy, passion, and commitment are the warm, hot, and cold vertices of Sternberg's love triangle. Alone and in combination they give rise to eight possible kinds of love relationships. The first is nonlove—the absence of all three components. This describes the large majority of our personal relationships, which are simply casual interactions.

2   The second kind of love is liking. "If you just have intimacy," Sternberg explains, "that's liking. You can talk to the person, tell about your life. And if that's all there is to it, that's what we mean by liking." It is more than nonlove. It refers to the feelings experienced in true friendships. Liking includes such things as closeness and warmth but not the intense feelings of passion or commitment.

3   If you just have passion, it's called infatuated love—the "love at first sight" that can arise almost instantaneously and dissipate just as quickly. It involves a high degree of physiological arousal but no intimacy or commitment. It's the 10th-grader who falls madly in love with the beautiful girl in his biology class but never gets up the courage to talk to her or get to know her, Sternberg says, describing his past.

4   Empty love is commitment without intimacy or passion, the kind of love sometimes seen in a 30-year-old marriage that has become stagnant. The couple used to be intimate, but they don't talk to each other any more. They used to be passionate, but that's died out. All that remains is the commitment to stay with the other person. In societies in which marriages are arranged, Sternberg points out, empty love may precede the other kinds of love.

5   Romantic love, the Romeo and Juliet type of love, is a combination of intimacy and passion. More than infatuation, it's liking with the added excitement of physical attraction and arousal but without commitment. A summer affair can be very romantic, Sternberg explains, but you know it will end when she goes back to Hawaii and you go back to Florida, or wherever.

6   Passion plus commitment is what Sternberg calls fatuous love. It's Hollywood love: Boy meets girl, a week later they're engaged, a month later they're married. They are committed on the basis of their passion, but because intimacy takes time to develop, they don't have the emotional core necessary to sustain the commitment. This kind of love, Sternberg warns, usually doesn't work out.

7   Companionate love is intimacy with commitment but no passion. It's a long-term friendship, the kind of committed love and intimacy frequently seen in marriages in which the physical attraction has died down.

8   When all three elements of Sternberg's love triangle come together in a relationship, you get what he calls consummate love, or complete love. It's the kind of love toward which many people strive, especially in romantic relationships. Achieving consummate love, says Sternberg, is like trying to lose weight, difficult but not impossible. The really hard thing is keeping the weight off after you have lost it, or keeping the consummate love alive after you have achieved it. Consummate love is possible only in very special relationships.

(a) Nonlove	(b) Friendship	(c) Infatuation	(d) Empty love

(e) Romantic love	(f) Fatuous love	(g) Companionate love	(h) Consummate love

.... indicates absence   _____ indicates presence

EXERCISE 5   Discussion and Critical Thinking

1. What are the eight different types of love described by Trotter?

2. What examples does Trotter use? Which ones are general and which are specific? What additional examples can you think of, taken from what you have read and what you have seen in movies and on television?

3. Trotter says that "consummate love is possible only in very special circumstances." What do you think he means in saying that? Do you agree with him?

Living Environments

AVI FRIEDMAN

Avi Friedman, winner of the United Nations World Habitat Award and internationally acclaimed architect, is especially concerned with how the perimeter and interior of a house need to be expanded and changed to fit the space needs and budget of its owners. A professor at the McGill School of Architecture, Friedman wrote this essay for the Montreal Gazette.

MINDSET
Lock It In

What do the design and condition of your residence say about what you are?

1   When invited to design a home, I first like to know what kind of dwellers my clients are. In our first meeting, I ask them to take me on a guided tour of their current residence and describe how each room is used—when and by whom. Walking through hallways, scanning the interior of rooms, peeping into closets, looking at kitchen cupboards, and pausing at family photos have helped me devise several common categories of occupants.

2   The "neat" household regards the house as a gallery. The home is spotless. The placement of every item, be it hanging artwork, a memento on a shelf, or furniture, is highly choreographed. The color scheme is coordinated and the lighting superb. It feels as if one has walked into an *Architectural Digest* magazine spread. Recent trends, professional touches, and carefully selected pieces are the marks of the place.

3   The "utilitarian" family is very pragmatic. They are minimalists, believing that they get only what they need. Environmental concerns play an important role in buying goods. The place, often painted in light tones, is sparsely decorated with very few well-selected items. Souvenirs from a recent trip are displayed and some photos or paintings are on the wall. They will resist excess consumption and will squeeze as much use as they can from each piece.

4   The home of the "collector" family is stuffed to the brim. It is hard to find additional space for furniture or a wall area to hang a painting. Books, magazines, and weekend papers are everywhere. Newspaper cutouts and personal notes are crammed under magnets on the fridge door. The collector family seems to pay less attention to how things appear and more to comfort. Stress reduction is a motto. Being an excessively clean "show house" is not a concern. Placing dirty breakfast dishes in the sink and the morning paper in the rack before leaving home is not a priority as long as things are moving along.

5   Of course, these are only a few household types, but at the end of a house tour, I have a pretty good idea about my clients. More than the notes that I take during a meeting, these real-life images tell me all about my client's home life and desired domestic environment. When I began practicing, I quickly realized house design is about people more than architecture. As hard as I might try, I will never be able to tailor a new personality to someone by placing them in a trendy style, one that does not reflect who they really are. I can attempt to illustrate options other than their current life habits and decorating choices. But in the end, when they move into their new place, they will bring along their old habits.

6   My experience has taught me some homeowners have been trying hard to emulate lifestyles and décors that are really not theirs. The endless decorating shows on television and the many magazines that crowd supermarket racks provide a tempting opportunity to become someone else. Some homeowners are under constant pressure, it feels, to undergo extreme makeovers and borrow rather than mature into their natural selves. They search for a readymade packaged interior style rather than discovering their own.

7   I am often at a loss when clients ask me what style I subscribe to, or solicit advice on the style they are to adopt. I reply that styles are trendy and comfort is permanent, and that they should see beyond the first day of occupancy into everyday living. Sipping a freshly brewed coffee on the back porch on a summer Sunday and letting the morning paper litter the floor while watching a squirrel on the tree across the yard is a treasured moment. It will never be able to fit into a well-defined architectural style. Home design needs to create the backdrop for such opportunities. It is these types of moments that make us enjoy life.

8   If someone wants to read, why not have a wall of books? Does someone love listening to music? Then a music room or corner should be created, even if it is not trendy. Does someone want to interact with the children? He or she might add a hobby space, even if it is outdated and cannot be found in most magazines.

9   Referring to technological advances, the renowned French architect Le Corbusier once described the home as a "machine for living." It is partially true. Home is the site where mundane and utilitarian activities take place. It is also where special moments, uniquely ours, are created and treasured.

EXERCISE 6   Vocabulary Highlights

Write a short definition of each word as it is used in the essay. (Paragraph numbers are given in parentheses.) Be prepared to use these words in sentences.

choreographed (2)	solicit (7)
pragmatic (3)	technological (9)
minimalists (3)	mundane (9)
sparsely (3)	utilitarian (9)
emulate (6)	uniquely (9)

EXERCISE 7   Discussion and Critical Thinking

1. Underline the thesis.

2. Does Friedman's classification cover all lifestyles, or categories of occupants? Explain.

3. Friedman specifies three categories of occupants—neat, utilitarian, collector. Does he seem to favor one or is he nonjudgmental? Explain.

4. How might one household type regard another? For example, how might the neat household type regard the collector household type, and vice versa?

5. What subdivisions do you see for some of Friedman's three household types? For example, are there degrees of a household being neat and a household being stuffed?

6. What is your personal evaluation of the three household types?

7. Evaluate this essay for the extent of the author's classification and the effectiveness of his development.

Why We Carp and Harp

MARY ANN HOGAN

Nag. Nag. Nag. Stop! Stop! Stop! We know nagging, don't we? After all, we've heard so much of it that we're experts, right? Maybe not. Listen to what this expert says about types of naggers. She points out that in this sophisticated world, some people specialize in certain kinds of nagging. This article was first published in the Los Angeles Times.

MINDSET

Lock It In

Should Hallmark or Shoe Box market a line of constructive nagging cards in different categories?

1   Bring those dishes down from your room! Put those scissors away. . . . I told you not to smoke in the kitchen and you shouldn't be smoking anyway! Take your feet off the table! Why do I have to tell you again and again! . . . ? The hills are alive with the sound of nagging—the gnawing, crescendoing timbre of people getting in each other's face. Parents nag children, wives nag husbands, husbands nag wives, friends nag friends . . . "*Use* your fork . . . *Stop* spending money like water . . . *Can't* you be ready on time? . . . *Act* like an adult . . ." Nagging, of course, has been around since the first cave husband refused to take out the cave garbage. But linguists, psychologists, and other scholars are just now piecing together what nagging really is, why we do it, and how to stop it before we nag each other to death.

2   Common perception holds that a nag is an unreasonably demanding wife who carps at a long-suffering husband. But in truth, nagging is universal. It happens in romances, in families, in businesses, in society—wherever people gather and one person wants another to do something he or she doesn't want to do. "It's a virus. You pick it up through kissing, shaking hands and standing in crowded rooms with people who have perfect children, wonderful husbands and sterilized homes," says humor columnist Erma Bombeck, whose family members nag her as artfully as she nags them. "It makes you feel good—like you're getting something done. Most of us want perfection in this world," she adds.

3   Thus, doctors can nag patients to lose their potbellies; accountants can nag timid clients to buy low; bosses can nag workers to get things done on time; special interest groups can nag the public to save the planet and send money; and the government can nag everyone to pay their taxes on time, to abstain from drink if they're pregnant, and, while they're at it, to Buy American. And when the going gets desperate, the desperate get nagging: Our recession-plagued nation, experts say, could be headed for a giant nag jag.

4   "When people are generally dissatisfied, they tend to harp at other people more," says Bernard Zilbergeld, a Bay Area psychologist. Naggers tend to fall into four categories—friendly, professional, social, and domestic—that range from the socially acceptable to the toxic.

5   The Friendly Ones are proud of their art. "My sisters call me a nag, but that's not necessarily a bad thing," says Bari Brenner, a 44-year-old Castro Valley resident who describes herself as "a third-generation nag" with a low tolerance for

procrastinators. "I get things done. The truth is I'm organized, they're not. I can see the big *picture*. They can't. We're going on a trip to England. 'Did you call the travel agent?' 'No.' 'Well, *call* the travel agent . . . book the hotel . . . call *now*!' It's the same thing at work. Nagging can be a means to an end."

6   Professional Nags—people who do it for a living—have to disguise what they do to get what they want. "I have to nag all the time—but you have to be careful about using the word *nag*," says Ruth Holton, a lobbyist for Common Cause, the good-government advocacy group. "I have to ask [legislators] for the same thing over and over again, year in, year out. But if they perceive what you're doing as nagging, they'll say, 'I've heard this 100 times before,' and they'll shut down. There's a fine line between artful persistence and being perceived as a nag."

7   Social nags don't see themselves as naggers. The U.S. Surgeon General's office peppers us with health warnings and calls it education. Environmentalists harp on people to recycle and save the rain forest, all in the name of the Greater Good. "One person's nagger is another person trying to save the world," says Arthur Asa Berger, a popular culture critic at San Francisco State University.

8   Then, somewhere beyond the limits of social convention, lies the dangerous world of the good old-fashioned Domestic Nag. Observers of the human condition, from the Roman poets to the purveyors of prime-time TV, have mined domestic nagging's quirkiness for laughs. But behavioral experts say that's where nagging can run amok. At best, domestic nagging is irritating. In Neil Simon's *The Odd Couple*, Felix wanted Oscar to clean up his act. Oscar liked being a slob, Felix nagged, nothing changed, and Felix finally moved out. At its worst, domestic nagging is murderous. In England last May, a 44-year-old businessman strangled his wife after 15 years of her nagging finally made him snap. In January, a judge ruled that the wife's verbal abuse justifiably provoked him and gave the husband an 18-month suspended sentence.

9   What causes this dynamic of domestic demolition? At the root of nagging, behavioralists say, lies a battle for control. It begins with a legitimate request: "I need you to hear me . . . to be with me . . . to be around, to do things like take out the garbage." But the person being asked doesn't want to change and sees the request as a threat to his or her control of the status quo. So the request is ignored.

10   "From the nagger's point of view, the naggee isn't listening," says Andrew Christensen, a UCLA psychology professor who has studied nagging for four years. "From there, it escalates. The further you withdraw, the more I nag. The naggee's point of view is, 'If I don't respond, maybe you'll shut up.'" The original request gets lost in the power struggle. The nagging takes on a life of its own. The desperate refrain of "Take out the garbage" can stand for a whole universe of complaints, from "You never do anything around here" to "I hate your stupid brown shoes!" "Sometimes I go through the house saying, 'Dammit, close the cupboards! Don't leave the towels on the floor! What's so hard about moving a vacuum cleaner across the hall. . . .' Bang! Bang! Bang! The list goes on," says a 40-year-old Mill Valley mother of two schoolchildren. "It's like the tape is stuck on replay and nobody's listening."

11   UCLA's Christensen calls it the "demand-withdraw pattern." In 60 percent of the couples he's studied, women were in the demanding, or nagging, role. In 30 percent of the cases, men were the demanders. In 10 percent, the roles were equal. "It may be that, traditionally, women have been more interested in closeness and sharing feelings, and men have been more interested in privacy," he says.

12   The scenario of the man coming home from work and the woman spending the day with the kids feeds the gender stereotype of the female nag. "He wants to sit in front of the TV, she's primed to have an empathetic listener,"

Christensen says. "The reverse is true with sex. There, men tend to be in the nagging role. Either way, one feels abandoned, neglected, and deprived, the other feels intruded upon. It's a stalemate."

13   Communications experts say there is a way to end the nagging. Both people have the power to stop. What it takes is earnest willingness to step out of the ritual. The naggee could say: "You keep bringing up the issue of the garbage. I'd like to sit down and talk about it." But the gesture would have to be heartfelt, not an exercise in lip service. The nagger could write a note instead of carping. "People tend to react differently to written communication," says Zilbergeld. In either case, the effect is paradoxical: When the nagger stops, it leaves room for the naggee to act. When the naggee listens, there's nothing to nag about.

14   And if it doesn't stop? "It gets more and more robotic," says Gahan Wilson, the *New Yorker* magazine artist who explored the fate of the Nag Eternal in a recent cartoon. "We spend much of our lives on automatic pilot."

EXERCISE 8   Vocabulary Highlights

Write a short definition for each word as it is used in the essay. (Paragraph numbers are given in parentheses.) Be prepared to use these words in sentences.

crescendoing (1)	status quo (9)
timbre (1)	escalates (10)
advocacy (adj.) (6)	scenario (12)
purveyors (8)	stalemate (12)
demolition (9)	paradoxical (13)

EXERCISE 9   Discussion and Critical Thinking

1. What is being classified?

2. What is the classification based on?

3. Where is the thesis stated?

4. Translate the basic parts of the classification in paragraph 4 into a simple topic outline.

I. Friendly _____   II. Professional _____

   A. _____   A. _____

   B. _____   B. _____

III. Social _____   IV. Domestic _____

    A. _____   A. _____

    B. _____ .   B. _____

5. What do the behavioralists say is at the root of nagging?

STUDENT PARAGRAPH AND ESSAY

For all the years he could remember, Boris Belinsky has observed doctors from up close and at a distance. It was only natural, therefore, that, when asked to classify a group of people according to their behavior, he chose doctors.

His Writing Process Worksheet shows you how this writing evolved from idea to final draft. To conserve space here, the freewriting and two rough drafts have been omitted. The balance of his worksheet has been lengthened for you to be able to see his other work in its entirety.

You will find a full-size blank worksheet on page 6, which can be photocopied, filled in, and submitted with each assignment if your instructor directs you to do so.

Writing Process Worksheet

Name _Boris Belinsky_   **Title** _Doctors Have Their Symptoms, Too_   **Due Date** _Friday, March 20, 8 a.m._

Use the back of this page or separate paper if you need more space.

Assignment

In the space below, write whatever you need to know about your assignment, including information about the topic, audience, pattern of writing, length, whether to include a rough draft or revised drafts, and whether your paper must be typed.

Write a paragraph of classification in which you group people according to their behavior in a particular vocation area. Your audience—your instructor and your peers—will be somewhat aware of the career field you select but will lack your insights. Submit a completed worksheet, a rough draft marked for revision, and a typed final draft of about 250 words.

Stage One

Explore Freewrite, brainstorm (list), cluster, or take notes as directed by your instructor.

Clustering

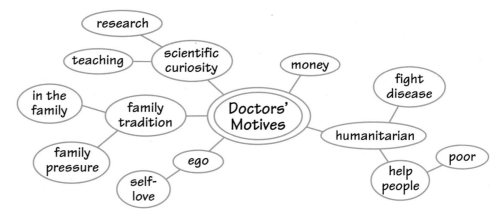

Stage Two

Organize Write a topic sentence or thesis; label the subject and the focus parts.

Doctors can be classified according to their motives for choosing their field of work.

Write an outline or an outline alternative. For reading-based writing, include references and short quotations with page numbers as support in the outline.

I. Motive: to make money
   A. Slow with patients
   B. Fast with bills
II. Motive: to pursue scientific interests
   A. Work in labs
   B. Teach in medical schools
III. Motive: to help people
   A. Spend much time with patients
   B. Have good standards
      1. May locate in poor areas
      2. Advocate preventative methods
      3. Do volunteer work

Stage Three

Write On separate paper, write and then revise your paragraph or essay as many times as necessary for **c**oherence, **l**anguage (usage, tone, and diction), **u**nity, **e**mphasis, **s**upport, and **s**entences (**CLUESS**). Read your work aloud to hear and correct any grammatical errors or awkward-sounding sentences.

Edit any problems in fundamentals, such as **c**apitalization, **o**missions, **p**unctuation, and **s**pelling (**COPS**).

Final Draft

DOCTORS HAVE THEIR SYMPTOMS, TOO
Boris Belinsky

Because I come from a large family that unfortunately has had a lot of illnesses, I have learned to classify doctors according to why they became doctors. As doctors can diagnose illnesses by the symptoms they identify, I can figure out doctors' motives by their symptoms, by which I mean

Topic sentence

Support (class)

Support (class)

Support (class)

Concluding sentence

behavior. Some doctors have chosen the field of medicine because they want to make <u>money</u>. They hurry to visit their patients (customers) waiting in multiple office spaces, answer few questions and never sit down. Although slow to respond to desperate phone calls, they are fast with the bills. The second class is the group with <u>scientific</u> interests. Not as much concerned about money, they are often found in university hospitals, where they teach and work on special medical problems. They may be a bit remote and explain symptoms in technical terms. The third group is my favorite: those who became doctors to <u>help people</u>. They spend much time with patients, often practice in areas that are not affluent, advocate preventative methods, and do volunteer work. <u>Not all doctors easily fall into these three groups, but virtually every one has a tendency to do so.</u>

READING-BASED WRITING

Community College Pressures

JOEL FOLLETTE

For an essay assignment in freshman composition, Joel Follette was asked to read the essay "College Pressures" and to apply its basic ideas to his experience at the community college he attends. Initially, he thought he was writing about two opposing worlds, Yale and Mt. San Antonio College, but then he found some similarities.

1   All college students have pressures. In his essay "College Pressures," William Zinsser describes the "modern undergraduate primarily as a driven creature," who is "fearful of risk" and "goal-obsessed." He says various harmful pressures exist "throughout American education" (78). Although he has some good insights, his focus is on Yale University, not a community college, such as the one I attend. The pressures he writes about—economic, parental, peer, and self-induced—do exist at Mt. San Antonio College in Southern California to some extent, but they take very different forms.

2   Zinsser says the Yale students feel economic pressure because they are looking for a "passport to security," and only good grades will get that for them (74). They are competing for slots in famous programs in law and medicine, such as the ones at Yale and Harvard. Other economic pressures come from the cost of education. He says some Yale students work part time during the school year and full time during the summer and still get loans. Students I know in the evening program at my school also have economic problems. I have a full-time job the year round in a company that makes cardboard boxes. I work overtime whenever I can get it without missing classes. I have a wife, who works part time, and two children in elementary school. I, too, have loans, but they are for a little house we bought last year and for a car that I first leased and then bought in a foolish transaction. Unlike Yale, my school only costs a few hundred dollars a year for the three classes I take in evening school each semester, but I passed on a job offer with a good salary because the new hours would have interfered with my class schedule.

3   Zinsser links economic pressure with parental pressure (75). The parents of most Yale students are paying for their education, and those parents expect results. They expect their offspring to do well in class and to major in a field that will pay well. He says the students want "to fulfill their parents' expectations." They often feel guilty if they do not do well and

neglect their own preferences in what to study. Although that may exist to a lesser degree at my community college, usually the parents themselves do not have a college degree and now they are not paying all the college costs for their children, although a large percentage of students in day school still live at home. Most evening students work full time, and the family pressure comes from a spouse and maybe children. When I get home on class nights at ten-thirty and see my kids sleeping and my tired wife, I know why I am going to college, and I feel guilty if I do not do well. And, to some extent like the students at Yale, I am thinking about security, not so much about being a doctor but about having a better job.

4   The other two pressures discussed by Zinsser, the peer and self-induced (76), are also linked. Again, there are big differences between the students at Yale and Mt. San Antonio College. Zinsser says that Yale students are very competitive, and they often "do more than they are expected to do" in order to excel (77). He uses the term "grade fever" (77). I have a *B* average and I know I have to make some As to offset some Cs, but I don't feel I am competing with my peers. We talk about grades, and usually ask each other about grades when we get tests or papers back. But I haven't seen a lot of competition. Of course, we have our pride, and we're embarrassed if we don't do well. Then we feel as if we have let ourselves and others down. According to my friend at UCLA, the students there are so grade conscious they hardly talk about their grades. Last semester one of his peers jumped to his death from a high-rise dorm room after finals. We do not jump here. I did see a guy kick a trash can one day after getting low marks on a research paper.

5   At all schools, pressures do exist. They may come from different sources and arrive in different degrees, but they are out there. Sometimes we do it to ourselves, and sometimes people do it to us. Pressures are the forces that may get in the way of our getting a good education, because we become too practical. But pressures are also what keep us going when we are dog-tired, sleepy, and cranky. I think Zinsser would say that if we did not have so many of these pressures that we might just sit down and read a good book—and that just might be the best education of it all.

Work Cited

Zinsser, William. "College Pressures." *Blair & Ketchum's Country Journal* 4 (April 1979): 72–78. Print.

EXERCISE 10   Discussion and Critical Thinking

1. Circle the thesis and underline all topic sentences.

2. What is the main pressure?

3. Which pressure differs to the greatest extent between Yale students and evening division community college students? Explain.

4. Is Follette a typical community college student? Discuss.

5. Are your pressures different from the ones mentioned here?

Suggested Topics and Prompts for Writing Classification

You will find a blank Writing Process Worksheet on page 6 of this book and on your Student Companion Site. It can be photocopied or printed out, filled in, and submitted with your assignment, if your instructor directs you to do so.

READING-BASED WRITING

Reading-based writing requires you to read critically, write a reply that shows you understand what you have read, and give credit for ideas you borrow and words you quote. The form can be a summary, a reaction, or a two-part response (with separated summary and reaction). Documentation, in which you give credit for borrowed ideas and words, can be either formal (MLA) or informal, as directed by your instructor. Both the forms of reading-based writing and documentation are discussed with examples in Chapter 1. Definitions of the three forms follow. Any form can be used for any reading selection in this book.

Summary

- The summary is a statement presenting only the main points of what you have read by using different wording without altering the meaning, adding information, or showing bias.
- It is the purest form of reading-based writing.

Reaction

- In the reaction, the meaning of what you have read will be central to your topic sentence of your paragraph or to the thesis of your essay.
- Although the reaction is not a personal narrative by itself, it may include personal experience to explain elements of the text. For example, if your source is about driving styles, your own experiences as a driver or an observer of drivers could be relevant in your analysis of the text.
- The reaction may incorporate a summary to convey a broad view of what you have read, but your summary should never be the main part of your reaction.

The Two-Part Response

- The two-part response separates the summary from the reaction.
- This form will give you practice in separating your objective summary in the first part from your more personal evaluation, interpretation, or application in the second part, the reaction.

READING-BASED WRITING TOPICS

"Styles of Leadership"

1. Write a reaction or two-part response. In the reaction part, explain why you think that one style is best or that each one has its advantages or disadvantages, depending on the situation.

"How Do I Love Thee?"

2. Write a two-part response to this essay. First, summarize this essay. Then apply the main ideas to an expression (or expressions) of love presented in a reading elsewhere in this book. Consider "The Girls in Their Summer Dresses," pages 233–236 (What kind of love does Frances seek and what kind of love does Michael seek?), and "Yearning for Love," page 124 (What kind of love does Chantra Shastri seek and what does her culture dictate?). Or, summarize the essay; then discuss at least three loves you are familiar with.

3. Discuss this classification as it relates to different cultures and value systems.

"Living Environments"

4. Using the three categories of occupants—neat, utilitarian, and collector—discussed by Avi Friedman, write about three families you are familiar with. Use references and quotations.

5. Write a two-part response with separate summary and reaction sections.

"Why We Carp and Harp"

6. Pick one of the classes of naggers—friendly, professional, social, or domestic—and show in a paragraph or an essay how the category can be divided into subclasses. Refer to and quote from Hogan's essay.

7. Write a reaction in which you classify people who are frequently nagged (the naggees), such as those in a family, at work, and at school. Refer to and quote from Hogan's essay.

8. Hogan says women are more likely to nag than men by 60 percent to 30 percent. Discuss how John Gray in "Men Are from Mars, Women Are from Venus" on pages 173–176 explains that strong tendency. Refer to and quote from both essays.

9. In a paragraph or an essay of reaction, discuss how control as in "Control Freak" can relate to all four classes of naggers. Use references and quotations.

GENERAL TOPICS

10. Write a paragraph or an essay in which you classify a vocational group—lawyers, teachers, police officers, clergy, shop owners–according to their reasons for choosing their field: curiosity about or interest in the field, wanting to make money, or wanting to help others. For a helpful model on a similar topic, review "Doctors Have Their Symptoms, Too" on pages 271–272.

11. Clarify your own pressures as a college student. For a helpful model on a similar topic, review "Community College Pressures" on pages 272–273.

12. Write a paragraph or an essay using one of the topics listed here. Divide your topic into groups according to a single principle.

a. Drinkers
b. Waitresses
c. Dates
d. Smiles
e. TV watchers
f. Sports fans
g. Churchgoers
h. Laughs
i. Riders on buses or airplanes
k. Rock music
l. Beards
m. Pet owners

CROSS-CURRICULAR TOPIC

13. Write a paragraph or an essay on one of the following terms.

- Business: Types of real estate sales, banking, management styles, interviews, evaluations.
- Geology: Types of rocks, earthquakes, mountains, rivers, erosion, faults
- Biology: Types of cells, viruses, proteins, plants
- Psychology: Types of stressors, aggression, adjustments, love
- Sociology: Types of families, parents, deviants
- Music: Types of instruments, singers, symphonies, operas, folk songs, rock, rap

CAREER-RELATED TOPICS

14. Discuss the different types of employees you have observed.

15. Discuss the different qualities of products or services in a particular field.

16. Discuss different types of customers with whom you have dealt (perhaps according to their purpose for seeking your services or products).

WRITER'S GUIDELINES: Classification

1. Follow this procedure for writing paragraphs and essays of classification:
   - Select a plural subject.
   - Decide on a principle for grouping the units of your subject.
   - Establish the groups, or classes.
   - Write about the classes.

2. Avoid uninteresting phrases for your classes, such as *good/average/bad*, *fast/medium/slow*, and *beautiful/ordinary/ugly*.

3. Avoid overlapping classes.

4. The Roman-numeral parts of your outline will probably indicate your classes.

   I. Class one
   II. Class two
   III. Class three

5. If you use subclasses, clearly indicate the different levels.

6. Following your outline, give somewhat equal (however much is appropriate) space to each class.

7. Use the writing process.

- Write and then revise your paragraph or essay as many times as necessary for **c**oherence, **l**anguage (usage, tone, and diction), **u**nity, **e**mphasis, **s**upport, and **s**entences (**CLUESS**).
- Read your work aloud to hear and correct any grammatical errors or awkward-sounding sentences.
- Edit any problems in fundamentals, such as **c**apitalization, **o**missions, **p**unctuation, and **s**pelling (**COPS**).

Chapter 13

Comparison and Contrast
Showing Similarities and Differences

FLOW OF WRITING

WHEN TO USE COMPARISON AND CONTRAST

FOR COLLEGE WRITING ASSIGNMENTS

- For good reasons, comparison and contrast topics for tests and special assignments are common-place across the curriculum. They require the student to acquire, organize, and evaluate ideas. The sources on either side of a comparison and con-trast may be abundant in the library and especially on the Internet, but usually the precise relationship of ideas must be established by the student writer.

- A comparison and contrast statement for a test or a special assignment will almost always be a paragraph or an essay.

IN CAREERS AND AT THE WORKPLACE

- At the workplace, employees prepare comparison and contrast studies in anticipation of modifying, acquiring, inventing, or discontinuing products, services, or procedures. The forms for such studies are likely to be standardized and computer-generated, but they employ many of the same principles used in this chapter.

- In determining career choice while still in college, you may use comparison and contrast to assess job descriptions, employment opportunities, and personal satisfaction in different fields.

COMPARISON AND CONTRAST IN A CARTOON

THE QUIGMANS   by Buddy Hickerson

B. Hickerson, copyright Los Angeles Times Syndicate. Reprinted with permission.

Evening with a flight attendant.

Writing Comparison and Contrast

DEFINING COMPARISON AND CONTRAST

Comparison and contrast is a method of showing similarities and differences between subjects. Comparison is concerned with organizing and developing points of similarity; contrast serves the same function for differences. In some instances, a writing assignment may require that you cover only similarities or only differences. Occasionally, an instructor may ask you to separate one from the other. Usually, you will combine them within the larger design of your paragraph or essay.

WORKING WITH THE 4 *P*s

Regardless of the nature of your topic for writing, you will develop your ideas by using a procedure called the 4 *P*s: purpose, points, patterns, and presentation.

PURPOSE

In most of your writing, the main purpose will be either to inform or to persuade.

Informative Writing

If you want to explain something about a topic by showing each subject in relationship with others, then your purpose is informative. For example, you might be comparing two composers, Beethoven and Mozart. Both were musical geniuses, so you might decide that it would be senseless to argue that one is superior to the other. Instead, you choose to reveal interesting information about both by showing them in relation to each other. The emphasis of your writing would be on insights into their characteristics, the insights heightened because the characteristics are placed alongside each other.

Persuasive Writing

If you want to show that one actor, one movie, one writer, one president, one product, or one idea is better than another, your purpose is persuasive. Your argument will take shape as you write, beginning with emphasis in the topic sentence or thesis and reinforcement by repetition throughout your paper, in each case indicating that one side is superior.

> **Example:** The extended example that follows is by student Judy Urbina. She chose to write a comparison and contrast dual paragraph-and-essay assignment arguing that Batman is more credible than Superman.

POINTS

Points are the phrases that will be applied somewhat equally to both sides of your comparison and contrast topic. They usually begin to emerge in freewriting, become more precise in brainstorming, and assume the major part of the framework in the outline. When writing an assigned topic based on lectures and reading, you will probably be able to select these points quickly. The subject material itself may dictate the points. For example, if you were comparing the governments of the United States and Canada, you would probably use these three points: executive, legislative, and judicial.

Listing is one of the most useful techniques for discovering points.

1. Make a list of points that can be applied to both sides of your topic.

> **Example:** Judy Urbina listed points relating to Superman and Batman.

physical abilities	weapons they use	enemies
motives for fighting crime	company they keep	compassion
helpers	upbringing	romantic interests

2. Then, select several of the strongest points as they relate to your controlling statement.

> **Example:** Urbina selected the three most relevant points.

upbringing	motives	enemies

3. Finally, incorporate these points into your controlling idea: the topic sentence or thesis. (You may rewrite this controlling statement for your final composition(s).

> **Example:** Urbina composed this controlling statement.

"Taking into account their upbringing, motives, and enemies, one can argue that Batman is more credible than Superman."

PATTERNS

Now you will choose between two basic patterns of organization: (1) subject by subject (opposing) or (2) point by point (alternating). In long papers you may mix the two patterns, but in most college assignments, you will probably select just one and make it your basic organizational plan.

In comparison and contrast, the outline works especially well in indicating relationships and sequence. As with most other writing forms we have worked with, the sequence of a comparison-and-contrast paragraph or essay can be based on time, space, or emphasis. Emphasis is the most likely order.

Example: Figures 13.1 and 13.2 show the two patterns as Urbina applied them to both the paragraph (on the left) and the essay (on the right).

In the subject-by-subject approach, organize your material around the subjects—the sides of the comparative study, as shown in Figure 13.1. In the point-by-point approach, organize your paper mainly around the points that you apply to the two subjects, as shown in Figure 13.2.

Figure 13.1
Subject-by-Subject
Organization

For Paragraph

Topic sentence
  I. Superman
    A. Upbringing
    B. Motives
    C. Enemies
  II. Batman
    A. Upbringing
    B. Motives
    C. Enemies

For Essay

Introduction with thesis
  I. Superman
    A. Upbringing
    B. Motives
    C. Enemies
  II. Batman
    A. Upbringing
    B. Motives
    C. Enemies
Conclusion

Figure 13.2
Point-by-Point Organization

For Paragraph

Topic sentence
  I. Upbringing
    A. Superman
    B. Batman
  II. Motives
    A. Superman
    B. Batman
  III. Enemies
    A. Superman
    B. Batman

For Essay

Introduction with thesis
  I. Upbringing
    A. Superman
    B. Batman
  II. Motives
    A. Superman
    B. Batman
  III. Enemies
    A. Superman
    B. Batman
Conclusion

PRESENTATION

The two patterns of organization—subject by subject and point by point—are equally valid, and each has its strengths for presentation of ideas.

As shown in Figure 13.1, the subject-by-subject pattern presents materials in large blocks, which means the reader can see two large, separate bodies of material. However, if the material is also complex, the reader has the burden of remembering ideas from one part to the next. Parallel development of ideas and cross-references in the second portion of the paragraph or essay can often offset that problem. Transitional words and phrases also help to establish coherence.

The point-by-point pattern shown in Figure 13.2 provides an immediate and direct relationship of points to subject. Therefore, it is especially useful in arguing that one side is superior to the other, in dealing with complex topics, and in working with longer compositions. But because of its systematic nature, if development is not sufficient, it can appear mechanical and monotonous. You can avoid that ping-pong effect by developing each idea thoroughly.

Some writers believe that the subject-by-subject form works best for short (paragraph-length) assignments, and the point-by-point form works best for longer pieces (essays).

> **Examples:** In the following examples, the topic of Superman and Batman is presented in the final draft stage of the paragraph form and then in the essay form. Note that the paragraph (often, as here, an essay in miniature) is expanded into an essay by developing the topic sentence, the supporting points, and the restated topic sentence into separate paragraphs: introduction, middle paragraph, middle paragraph, middle paragraph, and conclusion. Although both the paragraph and the essay make good observations and illustrate the use of pattern, for this topic the full essay would probably be more suitable in fulfilling the writer's purpose. In both the paragraph and the essay, Urbina uses a point-by-point arrangement.

Here is the paragraph, followed by the essay on page 283.

SUPERMAN AND BATMAN (PARAGRAPH)

Topic sentence

I. Upbringing
   A. Superman

   B. Batman

II. Motives
   A. Superman
   B. Batman

III. Enemies
   A. Superman

   B. Batman

<u>Both Superman and Batman are heroes, but only one is truly a superhero, and taking into account their upbringing, motives, and criminal targets, that is Batman.</u> Upbringing was not gentle for either. Superman came from Krypton, a planet that was about to self-destruct. His parents sent him as a baby on a spaceship to Earth. There he would be adopted by an ordinary farm family. His adoptive parents named him Clark Kent and reared him well. In the same generation, far away in Gotham, Bruce Wayne, the future Batman, was born to a contented, wealthy family. Tragically, his parents were killed in his presence during a mugging. He inherited the family wealth and was raised by his kindly butler. Those very different backgrounds provided Superman and Batman with powerful but different motives for fighting crime. Superman was programmed in his space capsule to know about the forces of good and evil on Earth and to fight the bad people. Unlike Superman, Batman learned from experience. Both have gone on to fight many bad people, but each one has a special enemy. For Superman, it is Lex Luthor, who has studied Superman and knows all about him, even his outstanding weakness—the mineral Kryptonite. For Batman, it is the Joker, who, as a wicked teenager, was the mugger-murderer of his parents. Many spectacular battles have ensued for

both crime fighters, and one has reached the top in his profession. Superman offers overwhelming physical strength against crime, but Batman displays cunning and base passion. As he strikes fear in the hearts of the wicked, he's not just winning; he is getting even. Most people would cheer Superman on. However, they would identify more with Batman, and he is the superhero.

Concluding statement

SUPERMAN AND BATMAN (ESSAY)

1   During the Depression in the 1930s, Superman and Batman were created as the first big comic-book heroes. More than two thousand similar but lesser characters were to follow. Both Superman and Batman have been enormously successful, but one seems to have more personality and is probably closer to most of us emotionally. Which hero wins out in this struggle for our hearts and minds? <u>Taking into account their upbringing, motives, and criminal targets,</u> <u>one can argue that it is Batman who is more credible.</u>

Thesis

2   <u>Neither came originally from a home environment we are likely to identify</u> <u>with completely.</u> Superman was conceived on the planet Krypton by a highly intelligent couple. His life was threatened because Krypton was going to destruct. Superman's parents bundled him up in a kiddie spacecraft and launched him on a long journey to Earth to save his life. He was raised on a farm by Jonathan and Martha Kent, who adopted him and grew to love him as their own. Batman, however, had an upbringing to which we can more easily imagine as a complete pattern. Really Bruce Wayne in disguise, Batman was left an orphan by his parents, who were killed in a mugging right in front of him. Fortunately for Bruce Wayne, his parents were rich, and he inherited millions when they died. He was raised by his butler, unlike Superman, who was nurtured by a conventional adoptive mom and dad. Obviously the upbringing of these two heroes had a lot to do with the kind of heroes they grew up to be.

I. Upbringing
A. Superman

B. Batman

3   <u>Both comic book heroes had different motives for confronting killers</u> <u>and spoilers.</u> Superman instinctively knew he was sent to Earth to fight crime. When his birth parents shipped him off to Earth as an infant, they programmed the spacecraft to educate him on the ways of the Earthlings. Superman's adoptive parents reinforced those lessons by teaching him that he had to hide his powers and use them for the well-being of the human race. To the contrary, Batman soon became a revenge-driven vigilante after his parents were killed in the mugging, so he decided to devote his life to fighting crime, with his butler as a domestic accomplice. To Batman no criminal is a good criminal. Although all of us citizens know we should not take the law into our own hands, nevertheless, we celebrate Superman and Batman as heroes, all the time identifying more with the guy in the fancy bat car.

II. Motives
A. Superman

B. Batman

4   <u>Like all superheroes, each of these two has an arch enemy.</u> Superman's arch enemy is Lex Luthor, who has a brilliant criminal mind. Lex Luthor is always trying to destroy Superman. He knows everything about Superman, right down to his weakness—the mineral Kryptonite. Batman's main enemy is the Joker. As a teen the Joker killed Batman's parents. Then Batman "accidentally" dropped the Joker into acid and permanently disfigured his face, so they are constantly getting into battles. More people are able to relate to Batman because most of us at least think about vengeance if someone has done us wrong. Superman just wants to fight for "truth, justice, and the American way," all worthwhile values, but they're abstract.

III. Enemies
A. Superman

B. Batman

Superman does not offer love or self-knowledge as keys to a perfect world. He offers only physical strength. Displaying more cunning and base passion,

Batman preys on fears and insecurities of criminals as keys to a perfect world. He wants to keep the bad men and women intimidated and on the run. His presence in Gotham strikes fear in the hearts of the wicked. Neither crime fighter is much concerned about rehabilitation. Mainly they knock heads. But Batman seems to enjoy his work more than Superman because Batman's getting even. The fact that we are in touch with that source of satisfaction says as much about us as it does about Batman.

CAREER-RELATED WRITING AS COMPARISON AND CONTRAST

Imagine you are on a career quest and you have narrowed the vocational fields to two. At that point you will naturally be thinking about comparing and contrasting to make the better choice. Or what if you are already at your workplace and you have to decide between two products, two services, two management styles, or two employees being considered for hiring, firing, or advancing? What pattern of thought does your mind shift to? Of course, again it is comparison and contrast.

If your mind just drifts around—going back and forth, up and down, sideways and other ways—then the ideas that come out of your mouth or computer will be jumbled. If, on the other hand, you have a system—say, the 4 *P*s: p̲urpose, p̲oints, p̲attern, and p̲resentation—you can move clearly and logically regardless of whether your comments will be written or spoken. If you need to make an oral presentation, maybe in PowerPoint, you can communicate with sense and continuity. You will just consider your audience, organize your thoughts, and proceed, following a simple outline.

In the example shown on pages 302–303, student Daphne Lee compares and contrasts two businesses. The subject could just as easily have been two ways of determining customer confidence, two locations for break rooms, two ride-sharing plans, or two software products used at the workplace. In her case, Lee sets out to argue for a reassessment of two fast-food restaurants by applying the points of ambiance, menu, and taste test before reaching a conclusion in her essay written for a college composition class. In a written statement for work, she might have provided a less personal context, but she would have used the same flexible, adaptable system. After all, the 4 *P*s function well in college assignments and in workplace tasks.

Transitional Words

Consider using the following transitional words to improve coherence by connecting ideas with ideas, sentences with sentences, and paragraphs with paragraphs.

FOR COMPARISON AND CONTRAST:
Comparison: in the same way, similarly, likewise, also, by comparison, in a like manner, as, with, as though, both, like, just as
Contrast: but, by contrast, in contrast, despite, however, instead, nevertheless, on (to) the contrary, in spite of, still, yet, unlike, even so, rather than, otherwise

FOR ALL PATTERNS OF WRITING: The <u>HOTSHOT CAT</u> words: <u>H</u>owever, <u>O</u>therwise, <u>T</u>herefore, <u>S</u>imilarly, <u>H</u>ence, <u>O</u>n the other hand, <u>T</u>hen, <u>C</u>onsequently, <u>A</u>lso, <u>T</u>hus (See pages 427–428 for additional transitional words.)

FINDING PATTERNS IN PHOTOS

EXERCISE 1   A Text-Based Activity for Groups or Individuals

Executive and man with skateboard

Your subject is lifestyles. Your specific subjects are two men. If you were to study these two individuals in a sociology class, with the intention of writing a paragraph or short essay of comparison and contrast, how might you use the 4 *P*s? First give the men names and then let the photo and your imagination do the talking.

Purpose: Do you want to argue that one person is better than the other person to explain their differences or, perhaps, to speculate about the workplace conditions each would prefer? Assume that both are successful at work.

Answer: _____

Points: Make a list of points—the phrases that could relate to the two subjects and could be main divisions of your outline for your writing. Some possibilities to consider, along with your own, are appearance, body language, equipment, passion (as in interests), success, goals, concerns, and influence.

List: _____   _____   _____

_____   _____   _____

_____   _____   _____

Pattern: Now select three or four points you could use for a paragraph or an essay and place them in a subject-by-subject or a point-by-point pattern.

Subject by subject

I. _____

    A. _____

    B. _____

    C. _____

II. _____

    A. _____

Point by point

I. _____

    A. _____

    B. _____

II. _____

    A. _____

    B. _____

Bill Varie/Corbis

B. _____   III. _____

C. _____   A. _____

B. _____

Presentation: If your instructor directs you to do so, write a paragraph or an essay using one of the patterns.

Practicing Patterns of Comparison and Contrast

Shorter compositions such as paragraphs are likely to be arranged subject by subject, and longer compositions such as essays are likely to be arranged point by point, although either pattern can work in either length. In longer works, especially in published writing, the two patterns may be mixed. Being able to organize your material quickly and effectively according to the pattern that is best for your material is important to your success as a writer. Even in a timed assignment, make a simple scratch outline that will guide you in writing a piece that is unified and coherent.

EXERCISE 2   Completing Patterns of Comparison and Contrast

Fill in the blanks to complete the following outlines.

A. Point-by-Point Outline

John: Before and after marriage

I. Way of talking (content and manner)

A. _____

B. John: After

II. _____

A. John: Before

B. John: After

III. _____

A. John: Before

B. _____

B. Subject-by-Subject Outline

Topic: Two jobs you have had (or another approved topic)

I. _____ (job)

A. _____ (point)

B. _____ (point)

C. _____ (point)

II. _____ (job)

A. _____ (point)

B. _____ (point)

C. _____ (point)

Readings for Critical Thinking, Discussion, and Writing

Underlining and annotating these reading selections will help you answer the questions that follow the selections, discuss the material in class, and prepare for reading-based writing assignments. As you underline and annotate, pay special attention to the author's writing skills, logic, and message, and consider the relevance of the material to your own experiences and values.

Some selections begin with a Mindset suggestion that can help you create a readiness for connecting with what you are about to read.

PARAGRAPHS

Blue as in Boy, Pink as in Girl

SHARON S. BREHM

This paragraph comes from "Stereotypes, Prejudices, and Discrimination," a chapter in Social Psychology, *a college textbook by Sharon S. Brehm. Comparing males and females, she maintains that discrimination based on gender begins at birth and never stops.*

MINDSET

Lock It In

Looking back, can you say you were conditioned and indirectly encouraged to move toward your current major or career choice, or did you, for the most part, naturally follow your inclinations? If you had different-gender siblings, are you aware of any discrimination (to your advantage or disadvantage) directed toward you (knowingly or unknowingly) by your parents or guardians?

When a baby is born, the first words uttered ring loud and clear: "It's a boy!" or "It's a girl!" In many hospitals, the newborn boy immediately is given a blue hat and the newborn girl a pink hat. The infant receives a gender-appropriate name and is showered with gender-appropriate gifts. Over the next few years, the typical boy is supplied with toy trucks, baseballs, pretend tools, toy guns, and chemistry sets; the typical girl is furnished with dolls, stuffed animals, pretend make-up kits, kitchen sets, and tea sets. As they enter school, many expect the boy to earn money by delivering newspapers and to enjoy math and computers, while they expect the girl to babysit and to enjoy crafts, music, and social activities. These distinctions persist in college, as more male students major in economics and the sciences and more female students in the arts, languages, and humanities. In the workforce, more men become doctors, construction workers, auto mechanics, airplane pilots, investment bankers and engineers. In contrast, more women become secretaries, schoolteachers, nurses, flight attendants, bank tellers, and housewives. Back on the home front, the life cycle begins again when a man and woman have their first baby and discover that "It's a girl!" or "It's a boy!" The traditional pinks and blues are not as distinct as they used to be. Many gender barriers of the past have been broken down, and the colors have somewhat blended together. Nevertheless, **sexism**—prejudice and discrimination based on a person's gender—still exists. Indeed, it begins with the fact that sex is the most conspicuous social category we use to identify ourselves and others.

EXERCISE 3   Discussion and Critical Thinking

1. Is Brehm trying mainly to inform or to persuade?

2. Is this paragraph more comparison or contrast?

3. What points does Brehm use?

4. Does Brehm use the alternating or opposing pattern?

5. Given a choice, would girls naturally choose dolls and boys trucks? In other words, are boys and girls just different by inclination genetically? Discuss.

6. Does your experience tell you that Brehm is right or wrong? If she is right, would you use the terms "prejudice" and "discrimination" to characterize the situation? Explain.

Public and Private

RICHARD RODRIGUEZ

Every person has a public life and a private life, and the character of each is colored by a variety of cultural forces. If the family in the United States includes parents born in Mexico, then the public life may be conducted mainly in English and the private life mainly in Spanish. In this passage from "Private Language, Public Language," Rodriguez says cultural contrast is natural and even complementary.

For me there were none of the gradations between public and private society so normal to a maturing child. Outside the house was public society; inside the house was private. Just opening or closing the screen door behind me was an important experience. I'd rarely leave home all alone or without reluctance. Walking down the sidewalk, under the canopy of tall trees, I'd warily notice the—suddenly—silent neighborhood kids who stood warily watching me. Nervously, I'd arrive at the grocery store to hear there the sounds of the *gringo*— foreign to me—reminding me that in this world so big, I was a foreigner. But then I'd return. Walking back toward our house, climbing the steps from the sidewalk, when the front door was open in summer, I'd hear voices beyond the screen door talking in Spanish. For a second or two, I'd stay, linger there, listening. Smiling, I'd hear my mother call out, saying in Spanish (words), "Is that you, Richard?" all the while her sounds would assure me: *You are home now; come closer; inside. With us.*

EXERCISE 4   Discussion and Critical Thinking

1. What is the topic sentence of this paragraph?

2. What sounds especially remind Rodriguez of the separation between private or public society?

3. What part of the house separates public and private society?

4. Is the pattern used in this paragraph point by point or subject by subject?

ANALOGY

Analogy is a method of organizing and developing ideas by comparison. In an analogy, a writer explains or clarifies an unfamiliar subject by likening it to a familiar but strikingly different subject. Writers use analogy to make the new, the different, the complex, or the difficult more understandable for the reader. Analogy, therefore, explains, clarifies, illustrates, and simplifies; it does not prove anything.

In the following model analogy, Emerson compares society to a wave. Most analogies, like this model, are part of a larger piece of writing.

> Society is a wave. The wave moves onward, but the water of which it is composed does not. The same particle does not rise from the valley to the ridge. Its unity is only phenomenal. The persons who make up a nation today, next year die, and their experience dies with them.
>
> (Ralph Waldo Emerson, "Self-Reliance")

Writers usually announce the analogy and then develop it. In addition, analogies, as a rule, rise spontaneously from the material as the writer's thoughts flow. Study the following model. Notice that the writer announces the comparison in the first sentence. To make the meaning clear, he compares the atmosphere of the earth to a window.

> The atmosphere of Earth acts like any window in serving two very important functions. It lets light in and it permits us to look out. It also serves as a shield to keep out dangerous or uncomfortable things. A normal glazed window lets us keep our house warm by keeping out cold air, and it prevents rain, dirt, and unwelcome insects and animals from coming in. As we have already seen, Earth's atmospheric window also helps to keep our planet to a comfortable temperature by holding back radiated heat and protecting us from dangerous levels of ultraviolet light.
>
> Lately, we have discovered that space is full of a great many very dangerous things against which our atmosphere guards us. It is not a perfect shield, and sometimes one of these dangerous objects does get through. There is even some evidence that a few of these messengers from space contain life, though this has by no means been proven yet.
>
> (Lester Del Ray, The Mysterious Sky)

The steps for writing the analogy are identical to those of writing comparison and contrast.

Heavenly Father, Divine Goalie

CHARLES PREBISH

Not many thinkers would connect sports with religion. Beginning with a basic idea from fellow writer Richard Lipsky about the religious overtones of games, Charles Prebish extended the comparison and produced an intriguing analogy.

In *How We Play the Game*, Richard Lipsky tells us (of baseball), "The game takes place in an atmosphere of piety. In many ways the ballplayers themselves can be seen as priests who represent us in a liturgy (game) that is part of a sacred tradition." Lipsky's comment reveals that far too little has been said about the role of the player in sport religion. In other words, we need to reflect on the actors in sport religion. It would be incorrect, though, to suggest that it is only the actual players who fulfill the role of religious participants in sport. We must include the coaches and officials as well, in their role as functionaries in the religious process. They are not untrained, either. Sport, no doubt, has its own seminaries and divinity schools in the various minor leagues and training camps that school the participants in all aspects of the tradition, from theology to ritual. The spectators, as video viewers, radio listeners, or game-going die-hards, form the congregation of sport religion. Their attendance is not required for all religious observances, but they do attend at specified times to share in religious rites. And they bear the religious symbols of their faith: the pennants, emblems, hats, coats, gloves, and whatever other objects the media geniuses can promote to signify the glory of sport in general and the home team in particular. The sport symbol may not be the cross, rosary, mezuzah, but it is no less valuable to the owner, and is likely considered to be just as powerful as its traditional counterpart, or more so.

EXERCISE 5   Discussion and Critical Thinking

1. What is the basis of the analogy?

2. What are the points of comparison?

ESSAYS

Chick Flicks vs. Macho Movies: Can You Tell the Difference?

KATHY SHASKAN

At Kathy Shaskan's Women's Forum.com, also known as "Mother Bee/Blossom Fuller" homepage, you'll get "laughs and inspiration . . . for women only" from an Internet writer and cartoonist. Here she has her go at movies for certain kinds of men and women, without poking fun all in one direction. Read her paired differences as a kind of outline or a set of points for discussion. You can do the composition writing later.

MINDSET

Lock It In

When you hear a phrase such as "chick flick" or "macho movie," do you suddenly experience a heartfelt desire or a gut-wrenching compulsion to head for a cinema house? Maybe you just get infuriated that anyone would use phrases like those in referring to the real women and real men you know. Or perhaps you have some other reaction you would like to share with your fellow students.

	The Chick Flick	The Macho Movie
1	The main relationship is between a man and a woman.	The main relationship is between a man and his sworn enemy (or sometimes his submachine gun or sports car).
2	There are lots of close-ups so you can see every emotion on the character's face.	There are lots of long shots so you can see every bit of blood, bone, and grey matter that explodes from the character's face.
3	The villains are people you see every day, like cheating husbands and nasty bosses.	The villains are people you'll probably never see in a lifetime, like heads of cocaine cartels and man-eating aliens.
4	The villain's worst act is something awful like sleeping with her best friend's spouse.	The villain's worst act is something awful like stealing a nuclear weapon.
5	A chick flick always includes child actors so they can add humanity and warmth to the story.	A macho movie includes child actors so they can be kidnapped and add suspense to the story.
6	The characters learn to respect one another through long talks and thoughtful actions.	The characters learn to respect one another by beating each other up.
7	If someone gets a disease, it's inevitably cancer or heart failure.	If someone gets a disease, it's inevitably a rare form of radiation poisoning or an exotic parasitic infection picked up in space.
8	There will be at least one emotional death.	There will be at least twenty unemotional deaths.
9	There will be at least one grunting, gooey depiction of childbirth.	There will be at least one grunting, gooey scene of hand-to-hand combat.
10	The chick flick will feature at least one scene where the lead character interacts with her mother.	The macho movie will feature at least one scene where the lead character interacts with a digital readout counting down to zero.
11	The climactic scene involves an explosion of passion.	The climactic scene involves an explosion of a car, bridge, or other man-made structure.
12	A happy ending is when the lead character finds love.	A happy ending is when the lead character finds the villain and blows him to smithereens.

EXERCISE 6   Discussion and Critical Thinking

1. Are the terms "chick flicks" and "macho movies" valid labels of popular films, or are they demeaning terms that stereotype? Explain.

2. Which are the four best comparative points?

3. Name one film that fits most of the characteristics for being a chick flick or a macho movie.

4. Though both genders are ridiculed (perhaps playfully), one side is treated a bit more severely. Referring to numbered pairs, indicate which side gets the worst treatment in clear-cut cases.

5. What audience would you expect for this reading selection?

6. Is it possible for a "chick flick" or a "macho movie" to be a high-quality film? You define the term "high-quality." If the answer is yes, give an example.

7. Is it possible that terms such as "chick" and "macho" can be applied to other media (especially television shows and songs), and many sporting events and activities?

Two Ways to Belong in America

BHARATI MUKHERJEE

A distinguished author of numerous books of both fiction and nonfiction, Bharati Mukherjee was born in India and became a citizen of the United States, where she has lived for more than forty-five years. This essay was written for the New York Times *in response to a debate in Congress about the rights of legal immigrants.*

1   This is a tale of two sisters from Calcutta, Mira and Bharati, who have lived in the United States for some 35 years, but who find themselves on different sides in the current debate over the status of immigrants. I am an American citizen and she is not. I am moved that thousands of long-term residents are finally taking the oath of citizenship. She is not.

2   Mira arrived in Detroit in 1960 to study child psychology and pre-school education. I followed her a year later to study creative writing at the University of Iowa. When we left India, we were almost identical in appearance and attitude. We dressed alike, in saris; we expressed identical views on politics, social issues, love, and marriage in the same Calcutta convent-school accent. We would endure our two years in America, secure our degrees, then return to India to marry the grooms of our father's choosing.

3   Instead, Mira married an Indian student in 1962 who was getting his business administration degree at Wayne State University. They soon acquired the labor certifications necessary for the green card of hassle-free residence and employment.

4   Mira still lives in Detroit, works in the Southfield, Michigan, school system, and has become nationally recognized for her contributions in the fields of preschool education and parent-teacher relationships. After 36 years as a legal immigrant in this country, she clings passionately to her Indian citizenship and hopes to go home to India when she retires.

5   In Iowa City in 1963, I married a fellow student, an American of Canadian parentage. Because of the accident of his North Dakota birth, I bypassed labor-certification requirements and the race-related "quota" system that favored the applicant's country of origin over his or her merit. I was prepared for (and even welcomed) the emotional strain that came with marrying outside my ethnic community. In 33 years of marriage, we have lived in every part of North America. By choosing a husband who was not my father's selection, I was opting for fluidity, self-invention, blue jeans and T-shirts, and renouncing 3,000 years (at least) of case-observant, "pure culture" marriage in the Mukherjee family. My books have often been read as unapologetic (and in some quarters overenthusiastic) texts for cultural and psychological "mongrelization." It's a word I celebrate.

6   Mira and I have stayed sisterly close by phone. In our regular Sunday morning conversations, we are unguardedly affectionate. I am her only blood relative on this continent. We expect to see each other through the looming crises of aging and ill health without being asked. Long before Vice President Gore's "Citizenship U.S.A." drive, we'd had our polite arguments over the ethics of retaining an overseas citizenship while expecting the permanent protection and economic benefits that come with living and working in America.

7   Like well-raised sisters, we never said what was really on our minds, but we probably pitied one another. She, for the lack of structure in my life, the erasure of Indianness, the absence of an unvarying daily core. I, for the narrowness of her perspective, her uninvolvement with the mythic depths or the superficial pop culture of this society. But, now, with the scapegoatings of "aliens" (documented or illegal) on the increase, and the targeting of long-term legal immigrants like Mira for new scrutiny and new self-consciousness, she and I find ourselves unable to maintain the same polite discretion. We were always unacknowledged adversaries, and we are now, more than ever, sisters.

8   "I feel used," Mira raged on the phone the other night. "I feel manipulated and discarded. This is such an unfair way to treat a person who was invited to stay and work here because of her talent. My employer went to the I.N.S. and petitioned for the labor certification. For over 30 years, I've invested my creativity and professional skills into the improvement of *this* country's pre-school system. I've obeyed all the rules, I've paid my taxes, I love my work, I love my students, I love the friends I've made. How dare America now change its rules in midstream? If America wants to make new rules curtailing benefits of legal immigrants, they should apply only to immigrants who arrive after those rules are already in place."

9   To my ears, it sounded like the description of a long-enduring, comfortable yet loveless marriage, without risk or recklessness. Have we the right to demand, and to expect, that we be loved? (That, to me, is the subtext of the arguments by immigration advocates.) My sister is an expatriate, professionally generous and creative, socially courteous and gracious, and that's as far as her Americanization can go. She is here to maintain an identity, not to transform it.

10   I asked her if she would follow the example of others who have decided to become citizens because of the anti-immigration bills in Congress. And here, she surprised me. "If America wants to play the manipulative game, I'll play it, too," she snapped. "I'll become a U.S. citizen for now, then change back to India when I'm ready to go home. I feel some kind of irrational attachment to India that I don't to America. Until all this hysteria against legal immigrants, I was totally happy. Having my green card meant I could visit any place in the world I wanted to and then come back to a job that's satisfying and that I do very well."

11   In one family, from two sisters alike as peas in a pod, there could not be a wider divergence of immigrant experience. America spoke to me—I married it—I embraced the demotion from expatriate aristocrat to immigrant nobody, surrendering those thousands of years of "pure culture," the saris, the delightfully accented English. She retained them all. Which of us is the freak?

12   Mira's voice, I realize, is the voice not just of the immigrant South Asian community but of an immigrant community of the millions who have stayed rooted in one job, one city, one house, one ancestral culture, one cuisine, for the entirety of their productive years. She speaks for greater numbers than I possibly can. Only the fluency of her English and the anger, rather than fear, born of confidence in her education, differentiate her from the seamstresses, the domestics, the technicians, the shop owners, the millions of hard-working but effectively silenced documented immigrants as well as their less fortunate "illegal" brothers and sisters.

13   Nearly 20 years ago, when I was living in my husband's ancestral homeland of Canada, I was always well-employed but never allowed to feel part of the local Quebec or larger Canadian society. Then, through a Green Paper that invited a national referendum on the unwanted side effects of "nontraditional" immigration, the government officially turned against its immigrant communities, particularly those from South Asia.

14   I felt then the same sense of betrayal that Mira feels now. I will never forget the pain of that sudden turning, and the casual racist outbursts the Green Paper elicited. That sense of betrayal had its desired effect and drove me, and thousands like me, from the country.

15   Mira and I differ, however, in the ways in which we hope to interact with the country that we have chosen to live in. She is happier to live in America as expatriate Indian than as an immigrant American. I need to feel like a part of the community I have adopted (as I tried to feel in Canada as well). I need to put roots down, to vote and make the difference that I can. The price that the immigrant willingly pays, and that the exile avoids, is the trauma of self-transformation.

EXERCISE 7   Vocabulary Highlights

Write a short definition of each word as it is used in the essay. (Paragraph numbers are given in parentheses.) Be prepared to use these words in sentences.

sari (2)	expatriate (9)
perspective (7)	divergence (11)
scapegoating (7)	cuisine (12)
adversaries (7)	referendum (13)
subtext (9)	trauma (15)

EXERCISE 8   Discussion and Critical Thinking

1. Considering their motives for emigrating to the United States and their behavior here, are the author and her sister more similar or more dissimilar?

2. What does the author think is positive about the behavior of both her and her sister?

3. The author's sister feels she has been used and rejected because she has not become a citizen and changed her cultural identity. What is your opinion of that view?

4. If you emigrated to a country with a distinctly different culture, do you think you would try to assimilate into the culture of your adoptive country or mostly try to maintain the culture of your birth country? If you had children, how might they behave?

5. The author and her sister are first-generation visitors—one to stay, adopt the new culture, become a citizen; the other to work and retain the major parts of her Indian culture. One would expect any children of the author almost certainly to adopt the values of America. What would you speculate about the cultural values of her sister's children, if any, who might be born in the United States? What type of clothing are the children of each sister likely to wear?

Neat People vs. Sloppy People

SUZANNE BRITT

In this comparison-and-contrast essay from her book Show and Tell, *freelance author Suzanne Britt discusses two kinds of people. You are likely to agree or disagree strongly with her conclusion.*

MINDSET

Lock It In

Before you read this essay, think of the sloppiest person and the neatest person you know, and answer this question: Which one would you prefer to share an apartment with?

1   I've finally figured out the difference between neat people and sloppy people. The distinction is, as always, moral. Neat people are lazier and meaner than sloppy people.

2   Sloppy people, you see, are not really sloppy. Their sloppiness is merely the unfortunate consequence of their extreme moral rectitude. Sloppy people carry in their mind's eye a heavenly vision, a precise plan, that is so stupendous, so perfect, it can't be achieved in this world or the next.

3   Sloppy people live in Never-Never Land. Someday is their métier. Someday they are planning to alphabetize all their books and set up home catalogs. Someday they will go through their wardrobes and mark certain items for tentative mending and certain items for passing on to relatives of similar shape and size. Someday sloppy people will make family scrapbooks into which they will put newspaper clippings, postcards, locks of hair, and the dried corsage from their senior prom. Someday they will file everything on the surface of their desk, including the cash receipts from coffee purchases at the snack shop. Someday they will sit down and read all the back issues of the *New Yorker*.

4   For all these noble reasons and more, sloppy people never get neat. They aim too high and wide. They save everything, planning someday to file, order, and straighten out the world. But while these ambitious plans take clearer and clearer shape in their heads, the books spill from the shelves onto the floor, the clothes pile up in the hamper and closet, the family mementos accumulate in every drawer, the surface of the desk is buried under mounds of paper and the unread magazines threaten to reach the ceiling.

5   Sloppy people can't bear to part with anything. They give loving attention to every detail. When sloppy people say they're going to tackle the surface of the desk, they really mean it. Not a paper will go unturned; not a rubber band will go unboxed. Four hours or two weeks into their excavation, the desk looks exactly the same, primarily because the sloppy person is meticulously creating new piles of papers with new headings and scrupulously stopping to read all the old book catalogs before he throws them away. A neat person would just bulldoze the desk.

6   Neat people are bums and clods at heart. They have cavalier attitudes toward possessions, including family heirlooms. Everything is just another dust-catcher to them. If anything collects dust, it's got to go and that's that. Neat people will toy with the idea of throwing the children out of the house just to cut down on the clutter.

7   Neat people don't care about process. They like results. What they want to do is get the whole thing over with so they can sit down and watch the rasslin' on TV. Neat people operate on two unvarying principles: Never handle any item twice, and throw everything away.

8   The only thing messy in a neat person's house is the trash can. The minute something comes to a neat person's hand, he will look at it, try to decide if it has immediate use and, finding none, throw it in the trash.

9   Neat people are especially vicious with mail. They never go through their mail unless they are standing directly over a trash can. If the trash can is beside the mailbox, even better. All ads, catalogs, pleas for charitable contributions, church bulletins and money-saving coupons go straight into the trash can without being opened. All letters from home, postcards from Europe, bills and paychecks are opened, immediately responded to, then dropped in the trash can. Neat people keep their receipts only for tax purposes. That's it. No sentimental salvaging of birthday cards or the last letter a dying relative ever wrote. Into the trash it goes.

10   Neat people place neatness above everything, even economics. They are incredibly wasteful. Neat people throw away several toys every time they walk through the den. I knew a neat person once who threw away a perfectly good dish drainer because it had mold on it. The drainer was too much trouble to wash. And neat people sell their furniture when they move. They will sell a La-Z-Boy recliner while you are reclining in it.

11   Neat people are no good to borrow from. Neat people buy everything in expensive little single portions. They get their flour and sugar in two-pound bags. They wouldn't consider clipping a coupon, saving a leftover, reusing plastic nondairy whipped cream containers or rinsing off tin foil and draping it over the unmoldy dish drainer. You can never borrow a neat person's newspaper to see what's playing at the movies. Neat people have the paper all wadded up and in the trash by 7:05 a.m.

12   Neat people cut a clean swath through the organic as well as the inorganic world. People, animals, and things are all one to them. They are so insensitive. After they've finished with the pantry, the medicine cabinet, and the attic, they will throw out the red geranium (too many leaves), sell the dog (too many fleas), and send the children off to boarding school (too many scuff marks on the hardwood floors).

EXERCISE 9   Vocabulary Highlights

Write a short definition of each word as it is used in the essay. (Paragraph numbers are given in parentheses.) Be prepared to use these words in sentences.

rectitude (2)   meticulously (5)

stupendous (2)   scrupulously (5)

métier (3)   cavalier (6)

tentative (3)   heirlooms (6)

excavation (5)   swath (12)

EXERCISE 10   Discussion and Critical Thinking

1. Is this essay mainly comparison or contrast?

2. Is Britt trying mainly to inform or to persuade?

3. What are the main points for this study?

4. Is the pattern mainly point by point or subject by subject?

5. What is the moral distinction between the neat and the sloppy?

6. Britt says that sloppy people are morally superior to neat people. How does that idea differ from common assumptions?

7. To what extent is Britt serious, and to what extent is she just being humorous?

8. It can be argued that Britt presents the two extremes of neatness and sloppiness. Do you agree, or do you think she favors one side? Explain.

9. Of the two extremes of neatness and sloppiness, what qualities would a person in the middle have? Or, do most people tend decidedly toward an extreme?

Student Thung Tran takes us on an international journey to explore the different experiences of women in Vietnam and America. Born in Vietnam, Thung Tran emigrated to America as a young girl. After observing her mother make the unsteady transition from Vietnamese woman to American woman, Tran was well qualified to write this comparison-and-contrast paragraph. Her paragraph "Wives and Mothers in Vietnam and in America" immediately follows with a completed Writing Process Worksheet and her final draft. To conserve space here, the freewriting and rough drafts have been omitted.

You will find a full-size blank worksheet on page 6, which can be photocopied, filled in, and submitted with each assignment if your instructor directs you to do so.

Writing Process Worksheet

Name Thung Tran   **Title** Wives and Mothers in Vietnam and in America   **Due Date** Wednesday, February 16, 10 a.m.

Use the back of this page or separate paper if you need more space.

Assignment

In the space below, write whatever you need to know about your assignment, including information about the topic, audience, pattern of writing, length, whether to include a rough draft or revised drafts, and whether your paper must be typed.

Write a paragraph of comparison and contrast about two people or two types of people who are culturally different. Use the subject-by-subject pattern. Assume that your readers do not know your subjects well. Turn in this completed worksheet, one or more rough drafts, and a typed final draft.

Stage One

Explore Freewrite, brainstorm (list), cluster, or take notes as directed by your instructor.

Listing

cultural background

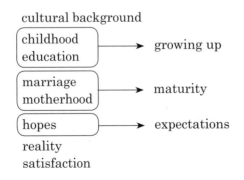

reality
satisfaction

Stage Two   **Organize** Write a topic sentence or thesis; label the subject and the focus parts.

Vietnamese immigrants discover just how American culture is different
subject
from Vietnamese culture, especially for the women who become wives and
focus
mothers.

Write an outline or an outline alternative. For reading-based writing, include references and short quotations with page numbers as support in the outline.

   I. Vietnam
      A. Growing up
      B. Maturity
      C. Expectations
  II. America
      A. Growing up
      B. Maturity
      C. Expectations

Stage Three   **Write** On separate paper, write and then revise your paragraph or essay as many times as necessary for **c**oherence, **l**anguage (usage, tone, and diction), **u**nity, **e**mphasis, **s**upport, and **s**entences (**CLUESS**). Read your work aloud to hear and correct any grammatical errors or awkward-sounding sentences.

Edit any problems in fundamentals, such as **c**apitalization, **o**missions, **p**unctuation, and **s**pelling (**COPS**).

Final Draft

WIVES AND MOTHERS IN VIETNAM AND IN AMERICA
Thung Tran

Topic sentence

I. Vietnam
  A. Growing up
  B. Maturity
  C. Expectations

II. America
  A. Growing up
  B. Maturity
  C. Expectations

Concluding sentences

Fleeing from communism, many Vietnamese left their country to resettle with their families in the United States. Here they discovered just how American culture is different from Vietnamese culture, especially for the women who become wives and mothers. In Vietnam, a young girl is educated in Confucian theories: "Obey your father as a child, and your husband when you get married." Living with her in-laws after her marriage, her role is that of child bearer and housekeeper. She has to be a good wife, a good mother, and a good daughter-in-law if she wants to be happy. She is the first to rise and the last to go to bed in a household that includes her husband and his parents. She will seldom make decisions and will always be obedient. She expects her husband to support the family financially, protect her, and help his relatives direct the family. In American society the female has a different pattern of experiences. As a girl she learns to think for herself and develop her talents. After she marries, unlike her Vietnamese counterpart, she is likely to work outside the home. Because she provides a part of the financial support, she expects her husband to share some of the work of raising the children, keeping the house, and maintaining a relationship with the in-laws on both sides, who probably live in a separate house. In America, ideally, the wife and mother will probably have more independence in the home and more responsibilities outside the home. In Vietnam the wife may be left with a secure position but few options.

EXERCISE 11   Discussion and Critical Thinking

1. Underline key words and phrases in the paragraph.

2. List any references to the other side that Tran uses to emphasize her comparison.

3. Does Tran shade the evidence to favor one side? Explain.

4. In ideal circumstances, what advantages does each woman experience?

READING-BASED WRITING

Struggling Against Silence

LYDIA HSIAO

For her comparison-and-contrast assignment, Lydia Hsiao was asked to read an essay of personal experience from her textbook and to relate it point by point to her life in a reading-based essay. In her textbook, Rereading America, *Hsiao found an excerpt from* The Woman Warrior *by Maxine Hong Kingston. The result was essentially a comparative study, one that helped Hsiao understand her own struggle and triumph. Hsiao's instructor asked her to document her essay formally. (However, essays written from single textbook sources are often presented with only informal references to indicate quoted and otherwise borrowed material.)*

1   In "Silence," a selection from Maxine Hong Kingston's autobiographical *The Woman Warrior*, the author portrays herself as an individual with timid charac-

Thesis
teristics. I have much in common with this author. Since both of us are Chinese and learned English as a second language, our experiences in school are very similar. As I read of her struggle to communicate, her thoughts blend with my thoughts and her words become my words.

Point and topic sentence   2   We both come from a strict Chinese background and were taught that "a ready
Blended quotation
tongue is an evil" (Kingston 252). We were also taught to keep to ourselves. We
First citation, with
author's last name
were never taught to communicate with those outside our culture. This back-ground may have caused my self-consciousness and my paralyzing fear of being embarrassed. During my first year in the United States, I attended middle school in Riverside, California. I was constantly teased about my Chinese accent, even though initially I felt certain I did not have one, for I had attended an American school in Taiwan. Perhaps my fellow students reacted as they did because I was the only Chinese girl in school. Nevertheless, as a result of this treatment, I

Quotation
became silent whenever possible, and if I mispronounced a word during class,
Second citation for
author, without author's
last name
I could not help but be disgusted by my own mistake, causing me even greater embarrassment. Kingston says, "[They] scared the voice away" (254). The result was that, like Kingston, my potential was for years undiscovered.

Transition   3   In the same way Kingston allowed silence to "[paint] layers of black over [her
Point and topic sentence
life]" (254), silence continued to create a thicker darkness in *my* life. It first
Blended quotation
embarrassed me; then it soon robbed me of my self-esteem. As Kingston says,
Blended quotation
"[Talking] takes up that day's courage" (252). It was almost as if silence was more than a curtain. It seemed to grow its own body and walk beside me. That silence became my sinister friend, taking advantage of my willingness to accept this cruel school life, tricking me into believing that home was the only place I could find my voice. The monster silence kept me quiet.

Transition Point and topic sentence Blended quotation Blended quotation Blended quotation	4	As my keeper, <u>that silence</u> also sent a message to others. It was often a signal for people not to intrude, and, of course, it was used to prevent rejection. Like Kingston, "I enjoyed the silence" (253). It concealed words that would lead to my embarrassment, sounds that might make my already cracked confidence shatter into millions of pieces like safety glass in a car crash. Thus, in Kingston's words, soon "it did not occur to me [that] I was supposed to talk" (253). But Kingston also said that "if [she couldn't] talk, [she] couldn't have a personality" (254). Thus, silence, my wicked companion that protected me from getting hurt, now led me into retreat from life.
Point and topic sentence	5	But both Kingston and I would achieve a breakthrough against silence. Kingston defeated her silence when she became a writer and published her writings, making her voice known. I made my voice known through my high school experience. When I moved to an area where more Asians lived, I made a supreme attempt to connect and associate with people who were willing to accept my differences in speaking. I was determined not to give in to silence. Through those interactions with new friends, silence slowly lost its hold on me. However, I still often ask people whether or not I have an accent. Interestingly enough, my Chinese friends say I do, and my Caucasian friends say I do not. I can never understand why that would be the case. Maybe a Chinese accent can be detected only by someone who knows the accent, or maybe a Chinese accent is something to be expected and, therefore, some people imagine they hear it. No matter what, I am still curious and, sometimes, feeling a bit insecure. I listen to myself. Again I am not far from Kingston, who said that even
Blended quotation		when she recited her Chinese lessons, she was two persons, "one chanting, one listening."
Transition Blended quotation Blended quotation	6	<u>Now</u>, when I begin to lose confidence and the dark curtain begins to fall or the monster begins to stir (Is it one, or both?), I remind myself that the best way to fight, as Kingston says, "is not to pause or stop to end the embarrassment, [but to keep] going until . . . the last word" (255). Like Kingston, I intend "to let people know [I] have a personality and a brain" (253).

Work Cited

Kingston, Maxine Hong. "Silence." *The Woman Warrior.* In *Rereading America.* Ed. Gary Colombo, Robert Cullen, and Bonnie Lisle. New York: Bedford/St. Martin's, 1998. 252–55. Print.

EXERCISE 12   Discussion and Critical Thinking

1. Is Hsiao's purpose to inform or to persuade?

2. Circle the thesis.

3. Is Hsiao's pattern of organization point by point or subject by subject?

4. Which image, the curtain or the monster, best fits her experience with silence? Why?

5. Can silence be caused by factors other than cultural? If so, what are they?

A Fast-Food Face-Off

DAPHNE LEE

Daphne Lee's assignment was to write a comparison-and-contrast essay in which she would show that one business was superior to the other. Reflecting her career interest in food service management, she chose two fast-food establishments.

1   "Burger joints are all alike. Their food is all the same—salty and greasy—so who cares which one you select!" Those were the lines I rehearsed silently while pulling my car into a Wendy's parking lot somewhere in the city of Orange, California. We were on our way to the semi-annual medical checkup for my daughter Angelina when she dramatically stated that she was so hungry she could die any second now. Pathetically, I am one of those hopelessly-in-love-with-my-child kinds of mothers, so I drove around in an unfamiliar city trying to find her a McDonald's, the only fast food restaurant she would tolerate since she was two years old. Oddly, there were no McDonald's restaurants within a five-mile radius, so I hesitantly pulled up to the nearest fast food place, which turned out to be a Wendy's. Obviously, Angelina was really hungry, for she entered with me without a protest. This was our first time at a Wendy's, and I truly expected it to probably be my last. But it was during my visit to Wendy's that I changed my opinion about fast food chains. Although McDonald's and Wendy's serve about the same clientele, the restaurants are more different than similar.

2   When I entered Wendy's, I immediately noticed the distinct difference between Wendy's and McDonald's in their ambiance. The interior design of Wendy's is simple and plain: a few booths, and many tables and chairs. Mainly earthy tones such as natural wood and leafy green surrounded me. The design offered homely comfort. No bold decorations on walls, tables, or seats demanded my attention. Another difference was the smell. When I walked into Wendy's, no familiar scent of fried foods and hamburgers greeted me. As I looked around while standing in line, I noticed how quiet the place was. There were only subdued chatterings from diners, plus some noises from the kitchen and the cashier area, but for a fast food restaurant environment Wendy's was almost silent.

3   On the other hand, the McDonald's interior design, including but not limited to the booth seats, tables, chairs, décor on the walls, is all done with their color scheme of bright red and yellow. It seems to grab and captivate customers' visual sensation in an instant. In the olfactory department, McDonald's is filled with the scent of French fries and burgers and is accompanied by a hint of sweetness. These odors attack customers' olfactory receptors like a typhoon and jostle their digestive systems into overdrive. Yet the most prominent difference from Wendy's is probably the noise level. At McDonald's there are always children running up and down the aisles, jumping and going wild in the Jungle Gyms, tugging and giggling under the tables—all of this punctuated by disciplinary warnings loudly "whispered" by the parents. No doubt, McDonald's is an optimal place for sensory overload.

4   Studying Wendy's menu, I found that, although many of the items are similar to those of McDonald's, Wendy's provides a wider selection, including some foods that wouldn't be considered fast. Among the 99-cent mainstays are baked potatoes with sour cream and chives, chili, and stuffed pitas. There is even a well-stocked salad bar. On the minus side, for dessert

Wendy's has only a few selections of milk shakes and chocolate chip cookies. Predictably, McDonald's is long on the sandwich list and short on nontraditional foods. Instead of everyday specialties, their promotional items are usually restricted to certain days. But Mac wins in the dessert lineup, with several kinds of cookies, milk shakes, apple turnovers, and soft-serve ice cream decorated by an assortment of sprinkles.

5   Angelina and I pondered the menu for a while before placing our order. I never hesitate in McDonald's. I get a large diet Coke, we share an extra large order of French fries, and she gets a Chicken McNuggets Happy Meal. Faced with more choices at Wendy's, we decided on a Spicy Chicken Sandwich Combo that came with a large order of French fries and a large diet Coke, an orange drink, an order of Chicken Nuggets, and a baked potato loaded with sour cream and chives. Angelina did not want a Wendy's Kid's Meal because the toy was not as "cool" as the one offered at McDonald's.

6   After picking up the food, we took a seat near a large window for our taste test. Examining and carefully blowing on a piece of hot chicken. Angelina dipped it into the sweet and sour sauce and then took a small bite. To my surprise, she continued to eat and even started on the French fries without complaint. I was skeptical as well; I took a breath and bit into the Spicy Chicken Sandwich. I was delighted. It has a soft bun, a crispy piece of lettuce and tomato, a hint of spices, and crunchy chicken meat, not excessively greasy tasting. In contrast, the McDonald's Spicy Chicken Sandwich, which I once considered the only palatable sandwich, usually has soggier chicken meat and greasier taste, although their buns are probably better tasting than those at Wendy's. McDonald's also supplies more lettuce than Wendy's. Next, I tried the Wendy's Chicken Nuggets, and I knew why Angelina liked them. They are meatier with thinner breading than McDonald's, so they are juicier and lighter tasting than Chicken McNuggets. When it comes to the taste of the French fries, we both agreed that McDonald's is the champion, but Wendy's is the first runner-up.

7   This visit to Wendy's has changed my preconception about fast food restaurants. The fast food restaurants are not all the same for me, anymore. In fact, we have been exploring other fast food establishments since that visit to Wendy's. At this point, our choice or, rather, my daughter's choice has been Wendy's more frequently than McDonald's. While we think that Wendy's surpasses McDonald's in many areas, it is difficult for us not to visit McDonald's occasionally. For Angelina, there is always a "cool" toy that McDonald's is advertising, which she must have. As for me, McDonald's brings back the memories of my little baby girl's face gleaming with smiles as she excitely played at the Jungle Gym, or the way her eyes lit up when she tasted the French fries with ketchup for the first time. The foods served in fast food places generally are considered to be unhealthful, but for many busy families fast foods are the only option to home-cooked meals. Now my range of choices has widened.

EXERCISE 13   Discussion and Critical Thinking

1. Circle the thesis.

2. Is the pattern point by point or subject by subject?

3. Is Lee's purpose to inform or to persuade?

4. Based on your experiences, are Lee's assessments of Wendy's and McDonald's sound?

5. How do the first two sentences of the essay reconcile with the next-to-the-last sentence?

Suggested Topics and Prompts for Writing Comparison and Contrast

STUDENT COMPANION SITE

For additional practice, visit www.cengage .com/devenglish/ brandon/pe11e.

You will find a blank Writing Process Worksheet on page 6 of this book and on your Student Companion Site. It can be photocopied or printed out, filled in, and submitted with your assignment, if your instructor directs you to do so.

READING-BASED WRITING

Reading-based writing requires you to read critically, write a reply that shows you understand what you have read, and give credit for ideas you borrow and words you quote. The form can be a summary, a reaction, or a two-part response (with separated summary and reaction). Documentation, in which you give credit for borrowed ideas and words, can be either formal (MLA) or informal, as directed by your instructor. Both the forms of reading-based writing and documentation are discussed with examples in Chapter 1. Definitions of the three forms follow. Any form can be used for any reading selection in this book.

Summary

- The summary is a statement presenting only the main points of what you have read by using different wording without altering the meaning, adding information, or showing bias.
- It is the purest form of reading-based writing.

Reaction

- In the reaction, the meaning of what you have read will be central to your topic sentence of your paragraph or to the thesis of your essay.
- Although the reaction is not a personal narrative by itself, it may include personal experience to explain elements of the text. For example, if your source is about driving styles, your own experiences as a driver or an observer of drivers could be relevant in your analysis of the text.
- The reaction may incorporate a summary to convey a broad view of what you have read, but your summary should never be the main part of your reaction.

The Two-Part Response

- The two-part response separates the summary from the reaction.

- This form will give you practice in separating your objective summary in the first part from your more personal evaluation, interpretation, or application in the second part, the reaction.

READING-BASED WRITING TOPICS

"Blue as in *Boy*, Pink as in *Girl*"

1. Write a paragraph or an essay patterned on three or more of the main points of this reading selection—colors, names, toys, activities, college majors, careers—in which you discuss your own family or another family you know well, with attention to at least one male child and one female child. Be sure to use references to and quotations from this source.

"Public and Private"

2. The author writes about living in a bicultural world divided into the public place and the private place. The idea of a bicultural world is familiar to all of us in various times in our lives. Discuss the significance of that idea and apply it to two different worlds you have lived in: different ethnic groups, different social and economic groups, different generations, different families, or different countries or regions. In your discussion, or reaction, refer to Rodriguez's paragraph and use quotations.

"Two Ways to Belong in America"

3. As a reaction to this essay, discuss two immigrants you know who are similar to the two sisters in significant ways. Use your own examples of their "two ways to become an American." Include your own evaluations of the two ways. Do you favor one way over the other as being better for the well-being of American society or do you see the two ways as merely different without one being better than the other? Use some references and quotations from the essay.

4. Write a reaction in which you explain Bharati Mukherjee's views and either agree or disagree with them. Use references and quotations from the essay.

"Chick Flicks vs. Macho Movies: Can You Tell the Difference?"

5. If you see validity in Shaskan's study, pick several of the points and discuss them in more detail as a reaction by using at least one specific example of a film for each gender. Use references to and quotations from Shaskan's points.

6. In a reaction, evaluate this set of points for effectiveness in showing just how different some films can be. Discuss which gender (in the sense that "chicks" and "machos" are gender) Shaskan favors, if either. Explain the degree to which she is accurate in grouping certain films. Discuss what she may be saying about the nature of many men and many women on the basis of the characteristics of the entertainment they enjoy. Comment on the idea that most entertainment media appeal to basic instincts in a superficial way. Consider using examples. Use references to and quotations from Shaskan's points.

"Neat People vs. Sloppy People"

7. The sloppy people side: Using ideas and points from this essay (vision, action, dealing with clutter, attitudes toward saving items), discuss two people you have known to argue that Britt's view is correct. Refer to and quote from her essay.

8. The neat people side: Using ideas and points from this essay (vision, action, dealing with clutter, attitudes toward saving items), discuss two people you have known to argue that Britt's view is wrong. Refer to and quote from her essay.

9. Write a reading-based paragraph or essay to show how Britt uses exaggerations, imaginative examples, and colorful expressions to support her points of comparison and contrast. Use references and quotations.

10. Write a paragraph or an essay in which you sympathize with Britt because you, too, have had to put up with neat freaks—or, take the opposing view. Use references to and quotations from Britt's essay and specific references to your experiences.

11. Write a summary of or a two-part response to Britt's essay.

GENERAL TOPICS

12. Write about two men or two women in two different societies, or cultures. Begin with whatever they have in common and then discuss how their experiences and behavior are different. You want instead to consider different aspects of one society: city and suburb, male and female, straight and gay, young and old, and so on. As you compare and contrast, keep in mind that you are generalizing and that individuals differ within groups—avoid stereotyping. For a helpful model on a similar topic, review "Wives and Mothers in Vietnam and in America" on page 299.

13. Compare and contrast one or more of the following topics. If you have had experience with the subject, consider personalizing your paragraph or essay by using examples from what you have done or observed.

    a. Two generations of college students

    b. Two types of (or specific) police officers, doctors, teachers, preachers, students, or athletes

    c. Living at college and living at home

    d. A small college and a large university or a four-year college and a community college

    e. Dating and going steady, living together and being married, or a person before and after marriage

    f. Shopping malls and neighborhood stores

14. Select one of the following subjects to develop an analogy in a paragraph or an essay. For a helpful model of the analogy, review "Heavenly Father, Divine Goalie" on page 290.

   a. Riding the merry-go-round and dating

   b. Juggling and paying bills

   c. Driving on the freeway and pursuing a career

   d. Going fishing and looking for a job

   e. Shopping in a supermarket and getting an education

   f. Caring for a child and caring for a dog

   g. Driving in traffic and fighting on a battlefield

   h. Sleeping and watching television

   i. Learning a new culture from an immigrant's viewpoint and learning an environment from an infant's viewpoint

   j. Looking for Elvis and looking for truth (or the Holy Grail, an honest person, a unicorn, the Loch Ness monster, Big Foot, or the Abominable Snowman)

CROSS-CURRICULAR TOPICS

15. In the fields of nutritional science and health, compare and contrast two diets, two exercise programs, or two pieces of exercise equipment.

16. Compare and contrast your field of study (or one aspect of it) as it existed some time ago (specify the years) and as it is now. Refer to new developments and discoveries, such as scientific breakthroughs and technological advances, cultural diversity, and changing cultural values.

CAREER-RELATED TOPICS

17. Select two competing businesses and write a paragraph or essay to show that one is better. Support should come from your experience, independent judgment, and, perhaps, from the Internet or library sources. Use points that apply somewhat equally to both businesses. You will see that those are the same kinds of points that would be used as key headings in a PowerPoint presentation at the workplace. For a helpful model on a similar topic, review "A Fast-Food Face-Off" on pages 302–303.

18. Compare and contrast two pieces of office equipment or two services with the purpose of showing that one is better.

19. Compare and contrast two management styles or two working styles.

20. Compare and contrast two career fields to argue that one is better for you.

21. Compare and contrast a public school with a business.

WRITER'S GUIDELINES: Comparison and Contrast

1. *Purpose*: During the exploration of your topic, define your purpose clearly.

   • Decide whether you are writing a work that is primarily comparison, primarily contrast, or balanced.
   • Determine whether your main purpose is to inform or to persuade.

2. *Points*

   • Indicate your points of comparison or contrast, perhaps by listing.
   • Eliminate irrelevant points.

3. *Patterns*

   • Select the subject-by-subject or the point-by-point pattern after considering your topic and planned treatment. The point-by-point pattern is usually preferred in essays. Only in long papers is there likely to be a mixture of patterns.
   • Compose an outline reflecting the pattern you select.
   • Use this basic outline for the subject-by-subject pattern:

      I. Subject X
         A. Point 1
         B. Point 2
      II. Subject Y
         A. Point 1
         B. Point 2

   • Use this basic outline for the point-by-point pattern:

      I. Point 1
         A. Subject X
         B. Subject Y
      II. Point 2
         A. Subject X
         B. Subject Y

4. *Presentation*

   • Give each point more or less equal treatment. Attention to each part of the outline will usually ensure balanced development.
   • Use transitional words and phrases to indicate comparison and contrast and to establish coherence.
   • Use a carefully stated topic sentence for a paragraph and a clear thesis for an essay. Each developmental paragraph should have a topic sentence broad enough to embrace its content.

5. Use the writing process.

   • Write and then revise your paragraph or essay as many times as necessary for **c**oherence, **l**anguage (usage, tone, and diction), **u**nity, **e**mphasis, **s**upport, and **s**entences (**CLUESS**).
   • Read your work aloud to hear and correct any grammatical errors or awkward-sounding sentences.
   • Edit any problems in fundamentals, such as **c**apitalization, **o**missions, **p**unctuation, and **s**pelling (**COPS**).

Definition
Clarifying Terms

WHEN TO USE DEFINITION

FOR COLLEGE WRITING ASSIGNMENTS

In all classes you will need to define both abstract and concrete terms in discussion and writing. Mastering techniques in defining can save you time and help you get credit for what you know. An identification item on a test requires only a sentence- or paragraph-long definition. An extended discussion of a term can require the bulk of an essay or a research paper.

IN CAREERS AND AT THE WORKPLACE

Whether preparing for a vocation or performing at the workplace, you will encounter terms that are at the center of discussion and, often, debate.

- In career preparation, you will be expected to define your career and relate that definition to your value system. Just what is an accountant, a teacher, a nurse, an oceanographer, a coach, a physical therapist, or a pilot in the context of your anticipated life?
- At the workplace, you may ponder and have to explain terms as difficult as *business ethics* or *integrity* and as simple as a product or service.

DEFINITION IN A CARTOON

THE QUIGMANS   by Buddy Hickerson

B. Hickerson, copyright Los Angeles Times Syndicate. Reprinted by permission.

Writing Definition

Most definitions are short; they consist of a **synonym** (a word or phrase that has about the same meaning as the term to be defined), a phrase, or a sentence. For example, we might say that a hypocrite is a person "professing beliefs or virtues he or she does not possess." Terms can also be defined by **etymology**, or word history. *Hypocrite* once meant "actor" (*hypocrites*) in Greek because an actor was pretending to be someone else. We may find this information interesting and revealing, but the history of a word may be of limited use because the meaning has changed drastically over the years. Sometimes definitions occupy a paragraph or an entire essay. The short definition is called a **simple definition**; the longer one is known as an **extended definition**.

TECHNIQUES FOR WRITING SIMPLE DEFINITIONS

If you want to define a term without being abrupt and mechanical, you have several alternatives. All of the following techniques allow you to blend the definition into your developing thought.

- *Basic dictionary meaning.* You can quote the dictionary's definition, but if you do, you are obliged to indicate your source, which you should do directly and explicitly. Always give the complete title of the dictionary, such as "*American Heritage Dictionary of the English Language* says." Do not write, "*Webster's* says." Dozens of dictionaries use the "*Webster's*" designation as part of their title.

- *Synonyms.* Although no two words have exactly the same meaning, synonyms often follow as if in parentheses.

  He was guilty of the ancient sin of *hubris*, of excessive pride.

- *Direct explanation.* You can state the definition.

  This spontaneous and loyal support of our preconception—this process of finding "good" reasons to justify our routine beliefs—is known to modern psychologists as *rationalizing*—clearly a new name for a very ancient thing.
  (James Harvey Robinson, "On Various Kinds of Thinking")

- *Indirect explanation.* You can imply the definition.

  Trance is a similar abnormality in our society. Even a mild mystic is *aberrant* in Western civilization.
  (Ruth Benedict, *Patterns of Culture*)

- *Analytical or formal definition.* In using this method, you define by placing the term (the subject) in a class (genus) and then identifying it with characteristics that show how it differs from other members of the same class, as the following examples show:

Subject	Class	Characteristics
A democracy	is a form of government	in which voters elect representatives to manage society.
A wolf	is a dog-like mammal	that is large and carnivorous, with coarse fur; erect, pointed ears; and a bushy tail.
Jazz	is a style of music	that features improvisation and performance.

EXERCISE 1   Writing Simple Definitions

Complete the following formal definitions.

Subject	Class	Characteristics
1. A workaholic	is a person	
2. Dreadlocks	is a natural hairstyle	
3. A hawk		that has a short, hooked bill and strong claws.
4. Hay fever		affecting the mucous membranes of the upper respiratory tract and the eyes, causing sneezing, running nose, and itchy, watery eyes.
5. A muumuu	is a dress	

6. Bongos   are two connected drums

7. A patriot

8. A desert   is a large land area

9. Jealousy   is a state of mind

10. Sociology

Dictionary Entries—Which One to Use

Suppose that you do not know the meaning of the term in italics in the following sentence:

That kind of cactus is *indigenous* to the Mojave Desert.

As you consider the term in context, you look at the dictionary definitions.

in•dig•e•nous \ ĭn-dĭj´ə-nəs \ *adj.* **1.** Originating and living or occurring naturally in an area or environment. See synonyms at **native**. **2.** Intrinsic; innate. [From Latin *indigena*, a native. See INDIGEN.]
(*American Heritage Dictionary of the English Language*, 4th ed.)

The first definition seems to fit the context of *indigenous*. It is followed by a reference: "See synonyms at **native**." Then you look at the second set of definitions: "Intrinsic; innate." The words are synonyms. You can see that only *native* fits. To provide more information for the reader, the dictionary also presents *native* with a special treatment of synonyms as indicated by the reference.

Looking under the word *native*, you find this definition:

Synonyms   native, indigenous, endemic, autochthonous, aboriginal
These adjectives mean of, belonging to, or connected with a specific place or country by virtue of birth or origin. *Native* implies birth or origin in the specified place: *a native New Yorker; the native North American sugar maple*. *Indigenous* specifies that something or someone is native rather than coming or being brought in from elsewhere: *an indigenous crop; the Ainu, a people indigenous to the northernmost islands of Japan*. Something *endemic* is prevalent in or peculiar to a particular locality or people: *endemic disease*. *Autochthonous* applies to what is native and unchanged by outside sources: *autochthonous folk melodies*. *Aboriginal* describes what has existed from the beginning; it is often applied to the earliest known inhabitants of a place: *the aboriginal population; aboriginal nature*. See also synonyms at **crude.**
Usage Note   When used in reference to a member of an indigenous people, the noun *native*, like its synonym *aborigine*, can evoke unwelcome stereotypes of primitiveness or cultural backwardness that many people now seek to avoid. As is often the case with words that categorize people,

the use of the noun is more problematic than the use of the corresponding adjective. Thus a phrase such as *the peoples native to northern Europe* or *the aboriginal inhabitants of the South Pacific* is generally much preferable to *the natives of northern Europe* or *the aborigines of the South Pacific*. • Despite its potentially negative connotations, *native* is enjoying increasing popularity in ethnonyms such as *native Australian* and *Alaska native*, perhaps due to the wide acceptance of *Native American* as a term of ethnic pride and respect. These compounds have the further benefit of being equally acceptable when used alone as nouns (*a native Australian*) or in an adjectival construction (*a member of a native Australian people*). Of terms formed on this model, those referring to peoples indigenous to the United States generally capitalize *native*, as in *Alaska Native* (or the less common *Native Alaskan*) and *Native Hawaiian,* while others usually style it lowercase.

(*American Heritage Dictionary of the English Language*, 4th ed.)

In the synonyms at the close of the entry, did you observe the various shades of meaning, especially the meaning of *indigenous* and *native*? A dictionary is an invaluable aid to definition, but it must be used with care if you want to express yourself clearly and precisely. No two words have exactly the same meaning, and a word may have many meanings, some that extend to very different concepts.

Avoiding Common Problems

- Do not use the expression *is where* or *is when* in beginning the main part of a definition. The verb *is* (a linking verb) should be followed by a noun, a pronoun, or an adjective.

> **Weak:**   A stadium is where they hold sports spectaculars.
>
> **Better:**   A stadium is a structure in which sports spectaculars are held.
>
> **Weak:**   Socialism is when the ownership and operation of the means of production and distribution are vested in the community as a whole.
>
> **Better:**   Socialism is a theory or system of community organization that advocates that the ownership and control of the means of production, capital, land, and so forth, be vested in the community as a whole.

- Do not use the **circular definition**, a practice of defining a term with the term itself.

> **Circular:**   An aristocracy is a form of government based on rule by the aristocrats.
>
> **Direct:**   An aristocracy is a form of government in which the power resides in the hands of the best individuals or a small privileged class.

- Do not define the subject in more complicated language than the original.

> **Murky:**   *Surreptitious* means "clandestine."
>
> **Clear:**   *Surreptitious* means "secret."

- Do not substitute the example for the definition; the example may be excellent for clarification, but it does not completely define.

> **Weak:**   Political conservatives are people like John McCain and Sarah Palin.

> **Better:**   Political conservatives are people who are dedicated to preserving existing conditions. Examples of conservatives are John McCain and Sarah Palin.

TECHNIQUES FOR WRITING EXTENDED DEFINITIONS

Essays of definition can take many forms. Among the more common techniques for writing a paragraph or short essay of definition are the patterns we have worked with in previous chapters. Consider each of those patterns when you need to write an extended definition. For a particular term, some forms will be more useful than others; use the pattern or patterns that best fulfill your purpose.

Each of the following questions takes a pattern of writing and directs it toward definition.

- *Narration*: Can I tell an anecdote or a story to define this subject (such as *jerk*, *humanitarian*, or *citizen*)? This form may overlap with description and exemplification.
- *Description*: Can I describe this subject (such as *a whale* or *the moon*)?
- *Exemplification*: Can I give examples of this subject (such as naming individuals, to provide examples of *actors*, *diplomats*, or *satirists*)?
- *Analysis by division*: Can I divide this subject into parts (for example, the parts of *a heart*, *a cell*, or *a carburetor*)?
- *Process analysis*: Can I define this subject (such as *lasagna*, *tornado*, *hurricane*, *blood pressure*, or any number of scientific processes) by describing how to make it or how it occurs? (Common to the methodology of communicating in science, this approach is sometimes called the "operational definition.")
- *Cause and effect*: Can I define this subject (such as *a flood*, *a drought*, *a riot*, or *a cancer*) by its causes and effects?
- *Classification*: Can I group this subject (such as kinds of *families*, *cultures*, *religions*, or *governments*) into classes?

Subject	**Class**	**Characteristics**
A republic	is a form of government	in which power resides in the people (the electorate).

- *Comparison and contrast*: Can I define this subject (such as *extremist* or *patriot*) by explaining what it is similar to and different from? If you are defining *orangutan* to a person who has never heard of one but is familiar with the gorilla, then you could make comparison-and-contrast statements. If you want to define *patriot*, then you might want to stress what it is not (the contrast) before you explain what it is: a patriot is not a one-dimensional flag waver, not someone who hates "foreigners" because America is always right and always best.

When you use prewriting strategies to develop ideas for a definition, you can effectively consider all the patterns you have learned by using a modified clustering form (Figure 14.1). Put a double bubble around the subject to be defined. Then put a single bubble around each pattern and add appropriate

Figure 14.1
Bubble Cluster Showing How a Term Could Be Defined Using Different Essay Patterns

words. If a pattern is not relevant to what you are defining, leave it blank. If you want to expand your range of information, you could add a bubble for a simple dictionary definition and another for an etymological definition.

Order

The organization of your extended definition is likely to be one of emphasis, but it may be space or time, depending on the subject material. You may use just one pattern of development for the overall sequence. If so, you would use the principles of organization discussed in previous chapters.

Transitional Words

Consider using the following transitional words to improve coherence by connecting ideas with ideas, sentences with sentences, and paragraphs with paragraphs.

FOR DEFINITION: originates from, means, derives from, refers to, for example, as a term, as a concept, label, similar to, different from, in a particular context, in common usage, in historical context.

FOR ALL PATTERNS OF WRITING: The <u>HOTSHOT CAT</u> words: <u>H</u>owever, <u>O</u>therwise, <u>T</u>herefore, <u>S</u>imilarly, <u>H</u>ence, <u>O</u>n the other hand, <u>T</u>hen, <u>C</u>onsequently, <u>A</u>lso, <u>T</u>hus (See pages 427–428 for additional transitional words.)

Introduction and Development

Consider these ways of introducing a definition: with a question, with a statement of what it is not, with a statement of what it originally meant, or with a discussion of why a clear definition is important. You may use a combination of these ways or all of them before you continue with your definition.

Development is likely to represent one or more of the patterns of narration, description, exposition (with its own subdivisions), and argumentation.

Whether you personalize a definition depends on your purpose and your audience. Your instructor may ask you to write about a word from a subjective or an objective viewpoint.

FINDING PATTERNS IN PHOTOS

EXERCISE 2   A Text-Based Activity for Groups or Individuals

American Indian veterans saluting during D-Day anniversary celebrations at Omaha Beach

© Owen Franken/Corbis

At the center of arguments about patriotism is, of course, a definition of the word *patriotism*. These three photos—two veterans at a ceremony, protesters at a demonstration, and two people voting (with child)—show American citizens in public life. Do all three photos demonstrate parts of a comprehensive definition of democracy or would you exclude one or more? What other components should be added? Complete the outlines (altering them as needed) to show some main characteristics of your definition of patriotism in terms of what it is and is not. Include supporting information under the Roman-numeral headings if you like.

Patriotism is not

    I. _____

    II. _____

    III. _____

Patriotism is

    I. _____

    II. _____

    III. _____

If your instructor directs, write a paragraph or an essay of definition based on the outlines. Consider explaining some of the parts of your definition by using examples from your personal experience or your studies.

Protest by surveillance camera players

Texas: Voting polling place

Practicing Patterns of Definition

Doing the following exercise will help you remember the patterns of writing used in extended definitions.

EXERCISE 3   Completing Patterns of Definition

Fill in the double bubble with a term to be defined. You might want to define *culturally diverse society, educated person, leader, role model, friend, infatuation, true love, success,* or *intelligence*. Then complete a bubble on the right for each paragraph or essay pattern. If the pattern does not apply (that is, if it would not provide useful information for your definition), mark it NA ("not applicable").

A. Using Patterns in Definitions

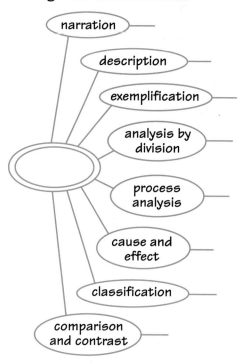

B. Using Patterns in Definitions

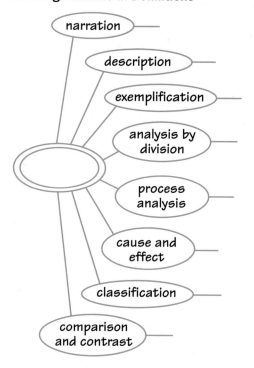

EXERCISE 4   Techniques for Introducing and Developing Definitions

Pick one of the topics you selected for Exercise 3: _____

A. Place an "X" beside each of the following techniques that might be useful in introducing the topic.

_____ A question calling for a definition.

_____ A statement about what the term does not mean.

_____ A statement about what the term meant originally (etymology).

_____ A statement about why a definition would help clarify an ongoing public debate.

B. Place an "X" beside each of the patterns that might be used in developing the topic.

_____ Exemplification

_____ Process analysis

_____ Analysis by division

_____ Cause and effect

_____ Comparison and contrast

Readings for Critical Thinking, Discussion, and Writing

READING STRATEGIES AND OBJECTIVES

Underlining and annotating these reading selections will help you answer the questions that follow the selections, discuss the material in class, and prepare for reading-based writing assignments. As you underline and annotate, pay special attention to the author's writing skills, logic, and message, and consider the relevance of the material to your own experiences and values.

Some selections begin with a Mindset suggestion that can help you create a readiness for connecting with what you are about to read.

PARAGRAPH

Burnout

GREGORY MOORHEAD AND RICKY W. GRIFFIN

Occupational sociologists Gregory Moorhead and Ricky W. Griffin provide the following definition of burnout *adapted from their book* Organizational Behavior *(2001). Their definition pertains mainly to vocational work, but burnout can occur in any organization—church, government, recreation, even marriage and family.*

Burnout, a consequence of stress, has clear implications for both people and organizations. Burnout is a general feeling of exhaustion that develops when a person simultaneously experiences too much pressure and has too few sources of satisfaction. Burnout usually develops in the following way. First, people with high aspirations and strong motivation to get things done are prime candidates for burnout under certain conditions. They are especially vulnerable when the organization suppresses or limits their initiative while constantly demanding that they serve the organization's own ends. In such a situation, the individual is likely to put too much of himself or herself into the job. In other words, the person may well keep trying to meet his or her own agenda while simultaneously trying to fulfill the organization's expectations. The most likely effects of this situation are prolonged stress, fatigue, frustration, and helplessness under the burden of overwhelming demands. The person literally exhausts his or her aspiration and motivation, much as a candle burns itself out. Loss of self-confidence and psychological withdrawal follow. Ultimately, burnout results. At this point, the individual may start dreading going to work in the morning, may put in longer hours but accomplish less than before, and may generally display mental and physical exhaustion.

EXERCISE 5   Discussion and Critical Thinking

1. Underline the sentence that best conveys the basic definition.

2. What other pattern—comparison and contrast, classification, cause and effect, or narration—provides structure for this definition?

3. If you were going to personalize this definition, what other pattern would you use?

ESSAYS

Bully, Bully

JOHN LEO

John Leo, staff writer for U.S. News and World Report, *offers his observations on the currently hot-button issue of bullying in the United States. Focusing on definitions in a national study, he argues that rumors and dirty looks and putting up with horrible classmates are all part of growing up and should not be classified as bullying.*

MINDSET

Lock It In

How do you define *bullying*? You'll probably agree that physical attacks (the "sticks and stones will break my bones" school of thought) constitute bullying. But what about repeated teasing and name-calling (the "words will never hurt me" view)? The author of the essay you are about to read believes we are being too broad with our definition. If you strongly agree or disagree, then underline and annotate passages, and jot down a few of your own examples.

1   Now we have a big national study on bullying, and the problem with it is right there in the first paragraph: Bullying behavior may be "verbal (e.g., name-calling,

threats), physical (e.g., hitting), or psychological (e.g., rumors, shunning/exclusion)." Uh-oh. The study may or may not have put bullying on the map as a major national issue. But it rather clearly used a dubious tactic: taking a lot of harmless and minor things ordinary children do and turning them into examples of bullying. Calling somebody a jerk and spreading rumors counted as bullying in the study. Repeated teasing counted too. You achieved bully status if you didn't let the class creep into your game of catch, or if you just stayed away from people you didn't like (shunning, exclusion).

2   With a definition like that, the total of children involved in either bullying or being bullied themselves ought to be around 100 percent. But no, the bullying study says only 29.9 percent of the students studied reported frequent or moderate involvement—and that total was arrived at by lumping bullies and their victims together in the statistics.

3   **Debatable Definitions.**   The low numbers and highly debatable definitions undercut the study's conclusion that bullying is "a serious problem for U.S. youth." Of the 29.9 figure, 13.0 percent were bullies, 10.6 percent were targets of bullying, and 6.3 percent were both perpetrators and victims. The study, done by the National Institute of Child Health and Human Development, is based on 15,686 questionnaires filled out by students in grades six through 10 in public and private schools around the country.

4   We have seen this statistical blending of serious and trivial incidents before. The American Association of University Women produced a 1993 report showing that 80 percent of American students have been sexually harassed, including a hard-to-believe 76 percent of all boys. The AAUW got the numbers up that high by including glances, gestures, gossip, and naughty jokes. The elastic definition encouraged schools and courts to view many previously uncontroversial kinds of expression as sexual harassment. Before long, schools were making solemn lists of harassing behaviors that included winking, and calling someone "honey."

5   Another set of broad definitions appeared when zero-tolerance policies descended on the schools. Antidrug rules were extended to cover aspirin. Antiweapons regulations covered a rubber knife used in a school play. Just two months ago, a third grader in Monroe, Louisiana, was suspended for drawing a picture of G.I. Joe. Now the antibullying movement is poised to provide a third source of dubious hyperregulation of the young. One antibullying specialist says "hard looks" and "stare downs"—everyday activities for millions of hormone-driven adolescents—should be punishable offenses under student codes.

6   This has all the makings of an antibullying crusade with many of the same wretched excesses of the zero-tolerance and antiharassment campaigns. Serious bullying can be ugly. Parents and schools should stop it and punish offenders. And schools should do whatever they can to create a culture of civility and tolerance. But rumors and dirty looks and putting up with horrible classmates are a part of growing up. So are the teenage tendencies to form cliques and snub people now and then. Adults shouldn't faint when they see this behavior, or try to turn it into quasi-criminal activity.

7   Another pitfall: In focusing on gossip, rumors, and verbal offenses, the crusade has the obvious potential to infringe on free speech at schools. Will comments like "I think Catholicism is wrong," or "I think homosexuality is a sin," be turned into antibullying offenses? The crusade could also demonize those who bully, instead of helping them change. Some of the antibully literature circulating in Europe is hateful stuff. One screed calls "the serial bully" glib, shallow, evasive, incapable of intimacy, and a practiced liar who "displays a seemingly limitless demonic energy." Yet a lot of the academic literature reports that bullies often aren't very psychologically different from their victims. And the national study says a fifth of bullying victims are bullies themselves.

8   The example of Europe's more advanced antibullying crusade should make Americans cautious. The European campaign has expanded from schools into the adult world and the workplace. Several nations are considering antibullying laws, including Britain. Definitions are expanding too. A proposed antibullying law in Portugal would make it illegal to harass workers by giving them tasks for which they are overqualified. Deliberately giving employees erroneous information would count as bullying too. Ireland's antibullying task force came up with a scarily vague definition of bullying: "repeated inappropriate behavior, direct or indirect," which could "reasonably be regarded as undermining the individual's right to dignity at work." Imagine what the American litigation industry could do with wording like that.

9   It's time to stop and ask: Where is our antibullying campaign going?

EXERCISE 7   Vocabulary Highlights

Write a short definition of each word as it is used in the essay. (Paragraph numbers are given in parentheses.) Be prepared to use these words in sentences.

dubious (1)   civility (6)

perpetrators (3)   tendencies (7)

trivial (4)   evasive (7)

uncontroversial (4)   vague (8)

hyperregulation (5)   litigation (8)

EXERCISE 8   Discussion and Critical Thinking

1. Circle the thesis sentence.

2. The definition in question defines *bullying* as "verbal," "physical," or "psychological" behavior (paragraph 1) directed against the victim. Of those three characteristics, which two does Leo find troublesome?

3. Why does Leo find those two characteristics troublesome?

4. Does he have a good point in criticizing the definition or is he unfairly ridiculing the definition? Explain your answer.

5. Does Leo believe there should be no antibullying campaign?

6. What does Leo say about bullying?

7. What part of the questioned definition does Leo say is actually part of growing up?

8. How does Leo use comparison and contrast to evaluate the definition of *bullying*, according to the national study?

9. Leo does not provide us with his definition of *bullying*. Write a definition for him or explain what kind of regulation he would use to confront bullying.

Whose Values?

JANET PEARSON

Janet Pearson is an editorial writer for Tulsa World, *a metropolitan newspaper. Notice the care with which she identifies her sources as she deals with the important and difficult question posed in the title.*

MINDSET

Lock It In

Imagine that a political candidate says to you, "I believe in family values." What question do you ask?

1 The terms are all over the newspapers and the airwaves: Family values. Moral values. Traditional values. Judeo-Christian values. Elections are decided based on values. Contentious public battles are fought over values. People are killed every day over values. But what exactly do Americans mean by these terms? How do we view the family and what do we believe about religion in schools? divorce? gay marriage? sex education?

2 If polls are to be believed, there is no one set of traditional American values anymore, if there ever was. The traditional, nuclear American family, along with its accompanying values, has become an elusive species, and taking its place is a new animal. American views about family life and values have become a sometimes-contradictory mishmash, perhaps of necessity. According to a recent poll on religion and the family conducted by Greenberg Quinlan Rosner Research Inc., most Americans still view the traditional, one-man, one-woman union-for-life as "God's plan" for us all. But at the same time, majorities of Americans don't feel divorce is a sin and about half find cohabitation acceptable.

3 Changing American values probably are a reflection of the new status quo: The latest Census data show only 24 percent of American households have a traditional family structure—mother, father and their children. The Greenberg survey reflected these changes: Sixty-nine percent of respondents were single parents and 19 percent were living with a steady partner. Sixty percent had been married but were not currently married. The survey-ors concluded: "We observe a disconnection between attitudes toward the family and lived experiences. . . . Americans in traditional and nontraditional arrangements hold fast to the traditional ideal of marriage and family, where the lucky couples get to live 'happily ever after.' This vision is the aspiration."

4   Though values were deemed a major factor in recent elections, there is not widespread agreement on what the term means. For about a third of those surveyed, the term means honesty and responsibility. About a quarter cited protecting children from sex and violence in the media. Only about 10 percent pointed to abortion or gay marriage and another 10 percent said moral values mean social justice. About 8 percent cited compassion and concern for the sick and needy. "Despite the intense focus on abortion and gay marriage during the election season, most Americans view moral values individualistically, as a set of values that motivate an individual toward acting responsibly and with integrity. They feel that family should remain in the private sphere and tend to balk at the notion that government should be involved in such things as marriage initiatives," surveyors concluded.

5   When it comes to defining the family, Americans also offered a variety of meanings. Nearly two-thirds defined family as their own immediate family unit; only a third of those surveyed defined family in the most traditional sense—married parents and their biological children. Further indication of this broadening definition of family was the affirmative response rate—from 55 to 74 percent, depending on family structure—to this statement: "Love is what makes a family and it doesn't matter if parents are gay or straight, married or single." The survey found some surprising differences among religious groups. Traditional evangelical parents were more likely than other traditional parents to believe children suffer when the mother has a full-time job, but the evangelicals also were more likely to have two-income households. Religious devoutness, the survey also found, "does not make one immune to unsuccessful marriage." Protestants and evangelicals are more likely to get married than other religious groups, but they are no more likely than others to stay married. In fact, about half or more of respondents from all faiths agreed that divorce "is usually the best solution" when a couple can't work out marital problems.

6   There were even more surprises on subjects such as sex education and religion in the classroom. Most parents said they would speak to a teacher if objectionable religious material were presented in their child's classroom. But surprising numbers said they would allow the child to be exposed to the material and then explain why it was wrong. Evangelicals were most inclined to try to have the material removed. Respondents had a "fairly pragmatic view" about sex education, with about 39 percent favoring instruction that focuses on abstinence but also offers instruction about contraception. About 38 percent preferred programs that teach teens how to make responsible decisions about sex. Only 18 percent favored abstinence-only programs.

7   If the shifting beliefs of adult Americans surprise you, wait till you hear views from the younger generation, a majority of whom have had one parent leave the household before the child graduated from high school, and 87 percent of whom had working mothers. A sampling by the same research firm of 892 Generation Y young people—Americans ages 18–24—could portend what is to come for the American family. A shocking 57 percent majority agreed that the "institution of marriage is dying in this country," and an equal number support gay marriage. A similar number also agreed that cohabitation without intent to marry is acceptable. The fact so many of this age group report having gay friends (more than 80 percent know a gay person and a third have a close gay or lesbian friend) explains their acceptance of gay marriage.

8   Of course, views can change with age, so it remains to be seen if the younger generation represents yet another shift in American family life. But history suggests that more than anything, the American family is adaptable and flexible. There's a good explanation for that: It has to be.

EXERCISE 9   Vocabulary Highlights

Write a short definition of the word as it is used in the essay. Paragraph numbers are given in parentheses. Be prepared to use these words in sentences.

contentious (1)	status quo (3)
nuclear (2)	aspiration (3)
elusive (2)	deemed (4)
cohabitation (2)	immune (5)
reflection (3)	portend (7)

EXERCISE 10   Discussion and Critical Thinking

1. Pearson begins paragraph 2 with the words "If polls are to be believed." Do you believe in polls? To what extent? What about the polls referred to in this article?

2. How do you reconcile the statement "Most Americans still view the traditional, one-man, one-woman union-for-life as 'God's plan' for us all" (paragraph 2) with the statement "But at the same time, majorities of Americans don't feel divorce is a sin and about half find cohabitation acceptable" (paragraph 2)?

3. What does Pearson mean by her statement that "Changing American values probably are a reflection of the new status quo" (paragraph 3)?

4. The author says, "Americans in traditional and nontraditional arrangements" believe in the "traditional idea of marriage and family" (paragraph 3). Why is this vision called an "aspiration"?

5. How do you rank these ideas as they relate to values: concern for the sick and needy, honesty, social justice, compassion, abortion, responsibility, protection of children from sex and violence in the media, and gay marriage?

6. How do you interpret the following statement? "Traditional evangelical parents were more likely than other traditional parents to believe children suffer when the mother has a full-time job, but the evangelicals also were more likely to have two-income households" (paragraph 5).

7. Pearson says, "A shocking 57 percent majority agreed that the 'institution of marriage is dying in this country,' and an equal number support gay marriage. A similar number also agreed that cohabitation without intent to marry is acceptable" (paragraph 7). Should she feel that these figures are shocking? Explain.

8. What possible explanations does Pearson have for the younger generation's views and values?

9. What do the last two sentences mean? "But history suggests that more than anything, the American family is adaptable and flexible. There's a good explanation for that: It has to be."

Graffiti: Taking a Closer Look

CHRISTOPHER GRANT

First published as a cover story in the FBI Law Enforcement Bulletin, *this article is included as general-interest material in* Info Trac, *a data service provider mainly for libraries. It offers a thorough analysis, but it also takes an argumentative position. See how it compares to your own views.*

MINDSET
Lock It In

Situation: A tagger has just spray-painted your block wall by your home. Then the tagger jumps into his or her car, and the engine won't start. What do you say—words only—to the tagger?

1   Not long ago, the word *graffiti* conjured images of innocent messages, such as "Tom loves Jane," or "Class of '73." Such simple and innocuous scribblings, although occasionally still seen, have become essentially messages of the past. Most of the graffiti that mars contemporary American landscape—both urban and rural—contains messages of hatred, racism, and gang warfare. Public attitudes toward graffiti tend to fluctuate between indifference and intolerance. On a national level, the criminal justice system has yet to adopt a uniform response to graffiti and the individuals who create this so-called street art. While some jurisdictions combat the problem aggressively, others do very little or nothing at all to punish offenders or to deter the spread of graffiti.

2   To a large degree, society's inability to decide on a focused response to graffiti stems from the nature of the offense. It could be argued that graffiti falls into the grey area between crime and public nuisance. If graffiti is considered in a vacuum, such an argument could appear to have some credence. However, it is unrealistic, and ultimately foolhardy, to view such a public offense in a vacuum. There is a growing consensus in communities around the country that the problem of graffiti, if left unaddressed, creates an environment where other more serious crimes flourish and can quickly degrade once low-crime areas. At a time when law enforcement agencies nationwide are adopting more community-based policing philosophies, administrators are exploring ways to address the basic factors that lead to crime and neighborhood decline. The time has come to take a closer look at graffiti.

Wall Writing

3 **Graffiti** is a general term for wall writing, perhaps humankind's earliest art form. The crude wall writings of prehistoric times and the highly stylized street art of today's inner-city youths share one common feature: Each stems from a basic human need to communicate with others. For youths who may not be able to express themselves through other media, such as prose or music, graffiti represents an easily accessible and effective way to communicate with a large audience. Anyone can obtain a can of spray paint and "make their mark" on a highway overpass or the side of a building.

4 Modern graffiti generally falls into one of three categories—junk graffiti, gang graffiti, and tagging. **Junk graffiti** messages are not gang-related but often involve obscene, racist, or threatening themes. The line separating gang graffiti and tagging has become blurred in recent years. **Tagging**, once seen as a nonviolent alternative to more threatening gang activities, is now considered an entry level offense that can lead to more serious crimes, including burglary and assault. In addition, tagging often results in direct gang affiliation. While all types of graffiti threaten the quality of life in affected areas, tagging and graffiti tied to gang activities represent the most widespread and formidable challenges to communities around the country.

Tagging

5 Tagging as a form of graffiti first appeared in the early 1980s and has grown immensely popular in many parts of the country, in both rural and urban areas. A tagger is someone who adopts a nickname, or tag, and then writes it on as many surfaces as possible, usually in highly visible locations. Although spray paint is the most common medium, taggers—sometimes referred to as "piecers," "writers," and "hip-hop artists"—also may use magic markers or etching tools to create their images.

6 The motivation behind tagging involves fame, artistic expression, power, and rebellion—all integral parts of what has been referred to as the hip-hop culture. Tagging may fill an even deeper void for youths without a strong sense of personal identity. Interviews with taggers reveal a deep desire simply to be known, to create an identity for themselves, and to communicate it to others. The thrill of risk taking also appears to be an underlying motivation for many taggers. While the images taggers create may not necessarily be gang-related, research shows that most taggers hope to join gangs and use tagging as a way to gain the attention of gang members. The more often their monikers appear in different locations, the more publicity they receive. Consequently, a small number of taggers can cause a disproportionate amount of property damage in a community. Tagging messages usually resemble handwriting, but may be difficult, if not impossible, to read. Taggers also have been known to invent their own letters or symbols, often adding to the confusion over the message and the author. . . .

Communication and Territoriality

7 In an article about the increase in area gang violence, a local California newspaper accurately described graffiti as a "crude but effective way for gang members to communicate among themselves, with the community, and with rival gangs." Communication is an important attribute of graffiti that law enforcement and community leaders should understand as they attempt to address the problem. While neighborhood residents and police might see graffiti simply as a blight, gang members and many taggers view it not so much as property damage but as a means to send messages understood within the gang community.

8   The expressive value of graffiti also forms an important component of gang territoriality. Gangs, and potential gang members, use graffiti to identify and mark their territory. Although the traditional perception of gang territoriality has been altered by increased mobility via the automobile, research of a noted gang expert indicates that gangs continue to "mark, define, claim, protect, and fight over their turf." In fact, territoriality among rival gangs continues to be a major source of gang violence. Graffiti as a primary form of communication and turf identification plays a direct part in feeding this violence.

True Impact of Graffiti

9   The threat posed by graffiti to neighborhoods and society in general goes much deeper than territorial gang violence. Community leaders need only to consider the reverberating effects of graffiti to understand how a seemingly low-grade misdemeanor can threaten or destroy the quality of life in an entire community. The monetary damages attributed to graffiti speak for themselves. In one year, the City of Los Angeles spent more than $15 million on graffiti eradication. This figure does not include the volunteer time devoted to graffiti cleanup or the estimated millions of dollars spent by private businesses taking care of the problem themselves. In addition, the Southern California Rapid Transit District spent $12 million on graffiti removal during the same year. . . .

10   James Q. Wilson, UCLA criminologist and framer of the "broken windows" theory, states that signs of disorder in society—such as graffiti, abandoned cars, broken windows, and uncollected trash—frighten law-abiding citizens into avoiding public places. Those places are then left to criminals who further deface them, creating a downward spiral in which the fear of crime leads to an increase in criminal activity. The presence of graffiti discourages citizens from shopping or living in affected areas. As established businesses relocate or close, new businesses might be reluctant to move into areas where customers would feel unsafe. As property values decline and law-abiding citizens with resources move, once-thriving neighborhoods can quickly degrade into dangerous places. Thus, the seemingly trivial offense of graffiti ultimately can have devastating consequences for a community.

Response

11   Most experts agree that allowing graffiti to remain visible in a community sends a message that this type of behavior is acceptable to residents. Further, allowing graffiti in an area encourages other offenders to degrade the community with more graffiti or other acts of vandalism. As stated in a newspaper article, ". . . removing graffiti as soon as it appears is the best way to deter further vandalism."

12   Recognizing the serious threat posed by graffiti, a number of communities across the country have developed programs to respond to the problem. The City of Anaheim, California, is considered a leader in developing innovative programs dealing with taggers and the damage they cause. The city developed "Adopt-a-Block" and "Wipeout Graffiti" programs and also established a 24-hour graffiti hotline that encourages residents to report graffiti damage, as well as information about suspects. Information leading to an arrest and conviction can net the caller up to $500. The hotline has proven to be quite successful. To date, callers have received more than $16,500 for information provided about offenders. The courts sentence convicted taggers to perform community service that includes graffiti removal. Anaheim also adopted an antigraffiti ordinance that assigns responsibility for the cost of graffiti removal to taggers, prohibits possession of implements used to create graffiti, and requires merchants to keep aerosol spray cans or other implements used to create graffiti out of direct reach of the general public. . . . To enhance graffiti-related

investigations, Orange County, California, uses a forensic scientist specializing in handwriting analysis to help identify chronic offenders. Several other localities in California have passed ordinances calling for convicted taggers to perform up to 80 hours of graffiti removal as part of their sentences.

The Future

13   Although these approaches represent a step in the right direction, they are reactive measures and do little to address the causes of the graffiti problem. The causes lie deep within the roots of social structure; it will require much more than rollers and paint to correct the problem.

14   One of the first steps is to educate the public about graffiti—its meaning and its potential impact on a community. Citizens must understand that this type of behavior cannot be tolerated because its insidious nature threatens communities from within. To deter new graffiti, young people should be taught that their actions can have far-reaching consequences. Law enforcement agencies may consider augmenting drug- and gang-prevention efforts with lessons on graffiti. Students should be advised that damaging property with graffiti is a serious crime and offenders will be punished. As part of the lesson, instructors also may suggest and encourage alternative methods of self-expression.

Conclusion

15   Like prostitution and illegal gambling, people often view graffiti as a victimless crime. But as communities around the country have learned, there is no such thing as a victimless crime. In fact, crimes that do not produce a single, identifiable victim generally have more impact on the entire community. As a highly visible offense, graffiti represents a particularly menacing threat to the quality of life in a community. The residual effects of reduced property values, lost business, increased gang territoriality, and heightened fear of crime escalate the severity of graffiti-related offenses beyond their impact as visual pollution. Communities that do not develop measures to deter and prevent graffiti now may find themselves confronting more intractable problems in the future.

EXERCISE 11   Vocabulary Highlights

Write a short definition of each word as it is used in the essay. (Paragraph numbers are given in parentheses.) Be prepared to use these words in sentences.

fluctuate (1)	enhance (12)
consensus (2)	insidious (14)
disproportionate (6)	augmenting (14)
reverberating (9)	escalate (15)
innovative (12)	intractable (15)

EXERCISE 12   Discussion and Critical Thinking

1. Underline the sentence in paragraph 2 that indicates what the author is trying to do.

2. Underline the sentence in paragraph 4 that takes a clear position on graffiti and, therefore, can be called the proposition.

3. Draw vertical lines in the left margin to indicate the sentences in paragraphs 1 and 2 that tie this essay to an audience concerned with law enforcement.

4. According to Grant, what motivates taggers?

5. Why do many gang members do graffiti?

6. What is the "broken window" theory?

7. What form of writing is used in paragraph 10?

8. What is the best way to deter further graffiti?

9. What should be done to deal with the causes of graffiti problems?

10. Does the solution of educating young people about the problems caused by graffiti suggest that the writer has faith in human beings?

11. What parts of this essay do you agree and not agree with? Explain.

12. If you could add one more strong section (or strengthen one), what would it be? Discuss.

STUDENT PARAGRAPH AND ESSAY

Linda Wong looked at a list of abstract terms for her assignment to write an extended definition and almost immediately found one that intrigued her. She had often heard people say things such as "I just can't love him [or her] enough," and "It was too much of a good thing," and she connected those ideas with one of the terms: *extremist.*

Wong's Writing Process Worksheet shows you how her writing evolved from idea to final draft. To conserve space here, the freewriting and the rough drafts marked for revision have been omitted. The balance of the worksheet has been lengthened for you to be able to see her other work in its entirety.

You will find a full-size blank worksheet on page 6, which can be photocopied, filled in, and submitted with each assignment if your instructor directs you to do so.

Writing Process Worksheet

Name Linda Wong   **Title** Going Too Far   **Due Date** Monday, December 4, 8 a.m.

Use the back of this page or separate paper if you need more space.

Assignment

In the space below, write whatever you need to know about your assignment, including information about the topic, audience, pattern of writing, length, whether to include a rough draft or revised drafts, and whether your paper must be typed.

Write a paragraph that defines an abstract word. Use at least three patterns of writing in your extended definition. Keep in mind that members of your audience may use your term in different ways, so using examples and clear explanations will be helpful for clarification. Submit your completed worksheet, one or more rough drafts marked for revision, and a typed final draft of about 300 words.

Stage One

Explore Freewrite, brainstorm (list), cluster, or take notes as directed by your instructor.

Clustering

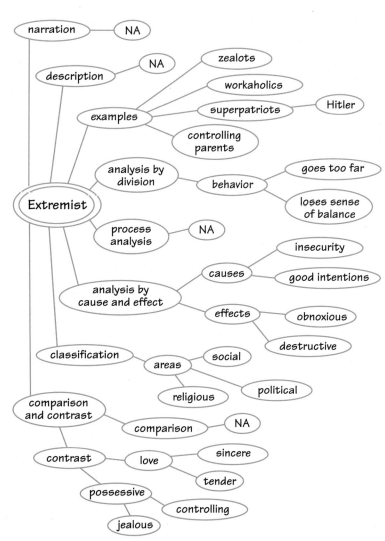

Stage Two

Organize Write a topic sentence or thesis; label the subject and the focus parts.

Extremists are involved people who lose their sense of balance and go too far
     subject   focus
in concentrating on one thing.

Write an outline or an outline alternative. For reading-based writing, include references and short quotations with page numbers as support in the outline.

I. Going too far
   A. Become preoccupied with one thing
   B. Lose sense of balance
II. Produce bad effect
   A. Are unpleasant to be around
   B. Are often destructive
III. Become incomplete
   A. Are often thought of as one kind of person
      1. Workaholics
      2. Zealots
      3. Superpatriots
   B. Diminished by loss of perspective

Stage Three

Write On separate paper, write and then revise your paragraph or essay as many times as necessary for **c**oherence, **l**anguage (usage, tone, and diction), **u**nity, **e**mphasis, **s**upport, and **s**entences (**CLUESS**). Read your work aloud to hear and correct any grammatical errors or awkward-sounding sentences.

Edit any problems in fundamentals, such as **c**apitalization, **o**missions, **p**unctuation, and **s**pelling (**COPS**).

Final Draft

GOING TOO FAR
Linda Wong

What the term does not mean

    Some people believe that it is good to be an extremist in some areas, but those people are actually changing the meaning of the word. According to the

Simple definition

Random House Dictionary of the English Language, the word *extremism* itself

Topic sentence

means "excessively biased ideas, intemperate conduct." The extremist goes too far; that means going too far in whatever the person is doing. I once heard someone say that it is good for people to be extremists in love. But that is not

Example/contrast

true. It is good to be enthusiastically and sincerely in love, but extremists in love love excessively and intemperately. People who love well may be tender and sensitive and attentive, but extremists are possessive or smothering. The

Example/contrast

same can be said of parents. We all want to be good parents, but parental extremists involve themselves too much in the lives of their children, who, in turn, may find it difficult to develop as individuals and become independent. Even in patriotism, good patriots are to be distinguished from extreme

Example/contrast

patriots. Good patriots love their country, but extreme patriots love their country so much that they think citizens from other countries are inferior and suspect. Extreme patriots may have Hitler-like tendencies. Just what

Examples

is wrong with extremists then? It is the loss of perspective. <u>The extremists are so preoccupied with one concern that they lose their sense of balance.</u> They are the <u>workaholics</u>, the <u>zealots</u>, the <u>superpatriots</u> of the world. They may begin with a good objective, but they focus on it so much that they can

Effect and concluding sentence

become destructive, obnoxious, and often pitiful. <u>The worst effect is that these extremists lose their completeness as human beings.</u>

EXERCISE 13   Discussion and Critical Thinking

1. Wong says that extremists "can become destructive, obnoxious, and often pitiful." Can you think of any good effects from people who were extremists? For example, what about a scientist who works fifteen hours a day to find a cure for a horrible disease? Is it possible that the scientist may succeed in his or her profession and fail in his or her personal life? But what if the scientist does not want a personal life? Discuss.

2. Why does Wong use contrast so much?

3. According to Wong, is it bad for a person to be an extremist in religion? Discuss.

READING-BASED WRITING

. . . .

My-graines

VINCENT SHEAHAN

The assignment was to read several essays related to health and write a reading-based, documented essay of extended definition about one health condition as it related to the student's experience. The final product would include at least two quotations and several paraphrases from the source, each to be formally identified. The source would be listed at the end, according to MLA style for an article in an anthology. (Your instructor may not ask you to formally document an essay based on a single textbook source.)

1   The aura set in like a suffocating stillness before a tropical storm. "This is going to be a bad one," I told myself as I shut off the lights, took my medication, lay down, and prepared for the inevitable—the relentless throbbing in my temple. About three hours of incapacitating agony later, I recovered, feeling strangely drained, and skimmed through my reading assignment for my college English class. What a coincidence! It included "In Bed," an essay about migraines by Joan Didion. Because I had only recently been diagnosed with migraines (although I had long suffered), I naturally had enormous curiosity about the subject, and now homework coincided with my private need for information. By closely comparing my family history, my triggers for attacks, and my personality with Joan Didion's, perhaps I could find some informed answers to my questions and be able to define *migraines* more precisely.

2   A year ago when I decided to seek medical help, the matter of family history was of immediate concern. At my first appointment, my neurologist informed me that, although no one knows why, migraines tend to run in families. I said the only person in my family who has migraines is my Uncle Joe, my father's brother. For Didion, the family connection is more apparent and pervasive: Both of her grandmothers, her father, and her mother all suffer from migraine headaches. But she does go on to explain, "One inherits, of course, only the predisposition" (59). Therefore, it is possible that everyone on my father's side has carried the gene for migraines, but only Uncle Joe has ever actually developed the headaches.

3   After the doctor asked his questions, I had one of my own: What actually causes migraine headaches? I was fearful that my job as an emergency medical technician (E.M.T.), with its debilitating stress and irregular hours, was the main reason. He explained that the exact causes are not completely understood and that my fatigue and irregular sleep patterns are not the causes of my migraines, because there are plenty of E.M.T.s who have the same sleep patterns as I do yet do not have migraines. Nevertheless, the fatigue and irregular sleep may trigger migraine headaches. For Didion, the triggers are varied. She says, "Almost anything can trigger a specific attack of migraine: stress, allergy, fatigue, an abrupt change in barometric pressure, a contretemps over a parking ticket. A flashing light. A fire drill" (60). Yet she explains that her headaches are not triggered at times when she needs to be alert and thinking clearly, such as an emergency situation, but instead, they are triggered when she is feeling overwhelmed or extremely stressed (60).

4   In addition to the exposure to these triggers, a migraine sufferer like me usually has what is called a "migraine personality." Didion offers a good definition of that term, saying that she is typical, a perfectionist who is "ambitious, inward, intolerant of error, rather rigidly organized" (60). But she points out that not all perfectionists have migraines and not all people with migraines are perfectionists. She says that she is a perfectionist about writing, not housekeeping (60). And, as for me, I try—probably harder than most—to be organized when it comes to my education, work, and personal life.

5   Like Joan Didion, I am intensely interested in migraines, and I am learning about them. We migraine sufferers have much in common, though each of us has his or her own family history of migraines, triggers, and migraine personality. Knowing that others go through what I do and having more information about my condition make it easier for me to deal with the pain of my migraines. I will continue to do the same thing Joan Didion does when she has an aura: I will not try to fight it. I will lie down and endure. When it is finally over, I will count my blessings.

Work Cited

Didion, Joan. "In Bed." *Health Views*. Ed. Marjorie Ford and Jon Ford. Boston: Houghton, 1998. 58–61. Print.

EXERCISE 14   Discussion and Critical Thinking

1. Circle the thesis and underline the topic sentences in the support paragraphs.

2. Forms of writing other than definition are often used to define. Which form provides structure for this extended definition?

3. How is Sheahan's introduction connected to his conclusion?

4. How do you explain Sheahan's change of verb tenses?

Suggested Topics and Prompts for Writing Definition

You will find a blank Writing Process Worksheet on page 6 of this book and on your Student Companion Site. It can be photocopied or printed out, filled in, and submitted with your assignment, if your instructor directs you to do so.

READING-BASED WRITING

Reading-based writing requires you to read critically, write a reply that shows you understand what you have read, and give credit for ideas you borrow and words you quote. The form can be a summary, a reaction, or a two-part response (with separated summary and reaction). Documentation, in which you give credit for borrowed ideas and words, can be either formal (MLA) or informal, as directed by your instructor. Both the forms of reading-based writing and documentation are discussed with examples in Chapter 1. Definitions of the three forms follow. Any form can be used for any reading selection in this book.

Summary

- The summary is a statement presenting only the main points of what you have read by using different wording without altering the meaning, adding information, or showing bias.
- It is the purest form of reading-based writing.

Reaction

- In the reaction, the meaning of what you have read will be central to your topic sentence of your paragraph or to the thesis of your essay.
- Although the reaction is not a personal narrative by itself, it may include personal experience to explain elements of the text. For example, if your source is about driving styles, your own experiences as a driver or an observer of drivers could be relevant in your analysis of the text.
- The reaction may incorporate a summary to convey a broad view of what you have read, but your summary should never be the main part of your reaction.

The Two-Part Response

- The two-part response separates the summary from the reaction.
- This form will give you practice in separating your objective summary in the first part from your more personal evaluation, interpretation, or application in the second part, the reaction.

READING-BASED WRITING TOPICS

"Burnout"

1. Borrow the definition from this paragraph and in a reaction develop it with an extended example of someone you know who is or was a burnout.

"Bully, Bully"

2. Write a reaction to Leo's essay, and evaluate his ideas. To what extent do you agree with him? Examine the definitions along with him and explain what you think is and is not workable. Ask your instructor if you should separate your main summary from your critical reaction and, therefore, write a two-part response.

3. In a reaction, discuss Leo's reservations about the definition of *bullying* from the national study as they apply to the examples of bullying and consequent bullying in "Disarming the Rage." Explain how the definition should be narrowed, if at all.

"Whose Values?"

4. Write a two-part response in which you first summarize Pearson's report on values and then, in a separate section, evaluate the views as they stand and seem to be changing. Explain how you feel about the reported changes, especially from generation to generation. Use references and quotations as you discuss whether current values are good or bad for society. Has reading this article made you reexamine or redefine your own definition of family values?

5. Write a paragraph or an essay of reaction with summary points incorporated. This will be much like the previous topic but will integrate rather than separate the parts.

"Graffiti: Taking a Closer Look"

6. Write a reaction to Grant's definition of *graffiti* in which you take issue with some of his views. Use quotations from and references to his essay.

7. Write a reaction that is generally in agreement with Grant's view, using your own examples to refer to neighborhoods or towns damaged by graffiti.

8. If you know people who do or have done graffiti, interview them with questions framed around Grant's argument. Then write an essay that accepts or rejects their views. Use quotations and references.

"Going Too Far"

9. Apply Wong's definition of *extremist* to a situation or situations with which you are familiar: an overprotective parent, a controlling companion, an over-controlling boss, a too-strict police officer or teacher, a too-virtuous friend or preacher, a too-clean housekeeper, a zealous patriot, a person fanatical about a diet, or a person concerned too much with good health or exercise.

You might begin your paragraph or essay with the statement: "It is good to be _____, but when _____ is carried to the extreme, the result is _____."

GENERAL TOPIC

10. The following topics are appropriate for extended development of definitions; most of them will also serve well for writing simple definitions.

   a. Cult

   b. Workaholic

   c. Clotheshorse

   d. Educated

   e. Body language

   f. Hero

   g. Psychopath

   h. School spirit

   i. Jock

   j. Cool

CROSS-CURRICULAR TOPIC

11. Define one of the following terms in a paragraph or an essay.

   a. History and government: socialism, democracy, capitalism, communism

   b. Philosophy: existentialism, free will, determinism, ethics, stoicism

   c. Education: charter schools, school choice, gifted program, ESL class, paired teaching, digital school

   d. Music: symphony, sonata, orchestra, tonic systems

   e. Health science: autism, circulatory system, respiratory system, thyroid, cancer, herbal remedies, acupuncture

   f. Marketing: depression, digitalization, discretionary income, electronic commerce, globalization, marketing channel, free trade, telemarketing, warehouse clubs

CAREER-RELATED TOPICS

12. Define one of the following terms by using other patterns of development (such as exemplification, cause and effect, narration, comparison and contrast): total quality management, quality control, business ethics, customer satisfaction, cost effectiveness, Internet, temporary worker, union, outsource, or downsize.

13. Define a good boss, good employee, good workplace, good employer, or good job. Analysis by division is a useful form.

14. Define a term from computer technology, such as Internet, World Wide Web, search engine, or chat room.

WRITER'S GUIDELINES: Definition

Simple Definition

1. No two words have exactly the same meaning.

2. Several forms of simple definitions can be blended into your discussion: basic dictionary definitions, synonyms, direct explanations, indirect explanations, and analytical definitions.

3. For a formal or an analytical definition, specify the term, class, and characteristic(s).

   <u>Capitalism</u> is <u>an economic system</u> <u>characterized by investment</u>
      term   class

   <u>of money, private ownership, and free enterprise</u>.
               characteristics

4. Avoid "is where" and "is when" definitions, circular definitions, and the use of words in the definition that are more difficult than the word being defined.

Extended Definition

1. Use clustering to consider other patterns of development that may be used to define your term.

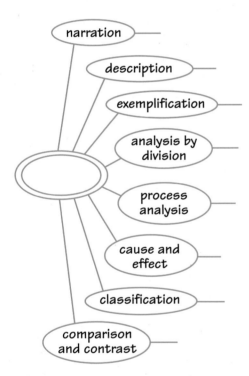

2. The organization of your extended definition is likely to be one of emphasis, but it may be space or time, depending on the subject material. You may use just one pattern of development for the overall organization.

3. Consider these ways of introducing a definition: with a question, with a statement of what it is not, with a statement of what it originally meant, or with a discussion of why a clear definition is important. You may use a combination of these ways before you continue with your definition.

4. Whether you personalize a definition depends on your purpose and your audience. Your instructor may ask you to write about a word within the context of your own experience or to write about it from a detached, clinical viewpoint.

5. Use the writing process.

- Write and then revise your paragraph or essay as many times as necessary for **c**oherence, **l**anguage (usage, tone, and diction), **u**nity, **e**mphasis, **s**upport, and **s**entences (**CLUESS**).
- Read your work aloud to hear and correct any grammatical errors or awkward-sounding sentences.
- Edit any problems in fundamentals, such as **c**apitalization, **o**missions, **p**unctuation, and **s**pelling (**COPS**).

Chapter 15

Argument
Writing to Persuade

FLOW OF WRITING

WHEN TO USE ARGUMENT

FOR COLLEGE WRITING ASSIGNMENTS

- You will use argument and persuasion in all college writing—paragraphs, essays, tests, reports, and research papers—that requires you to discuss and support your views on topics about which others may disagree or reluctantly follow. You may argue that a theory in biology is sound, that a system in philosophy is inadequate, or that a short story in literature is flawed. You may persuade in nursing that a particular diet or exercise program is desirable.

IN CAREERS AND AT THE WORKPLACE

- Business and other institutions require persuasive and argumentative writing in memos to employers or fellow employees about team standards, in proposals to clients about projects, in promotional material about selling items and services, and in application letters about getting hired.

ARGUMENT IN A CARTOON

THE QUIGMANS   by Buddy Hickerson

B. Hickerson, copyright Los Angeles Times Syndicate. Reprinted by permission.

"Looks like the work of that vampire from the Nursing Home."

Writing Argument

Persuasion is a broad term. When we persuade, we try to influence people to think in a certain way or to do something.

Argument is persuasion on a topic about which reasonable people disagree. Argument involves controversy. Whereas exercising appropriately is probably not controversial because reasonable people do not dispute the idea, an issue such as gun control is. In this chapter, we will be concerned mainly with the kind of persuasion that involves argument and uses evidence (see cartoon).

TECHNIQUES FOR DEVELOPING ARGUMENT

Statements of argument are informal or formal. An opinion column in a newspaper is likely to have little set structure, whereas an argument in college writing is likely to be tightly organized. Nevertheless, the opinion column and the college paper have much in common. Both provide a proposition, which is the main point of the argument, and both provide support, which is the evidence or the reasons that back up the proposition.

For a well-structured college paragraph or essay, an organization plan is desirable. Consider these elements when you write an argument, and ask yourself the following questions as you develop your ideas:

Background: What is the historical or social context for this controversial issue?

Proposition (the thesis of the essay): What do I want my audience to believe or to do?

Qualification of proposition: Can I limit my proposition so that those who disagree cannot easily challenge me with exceptions? If, for example, I am in favor of using animals for scientific experimentation, am I concerned only with medical experiments or with any use, including experiments for the cosmetic industry?

Refutation (taking the opposing view into account, mainly to point out its fundamental weakness): What is the view on the other side, and why is it flawed in reasoning or evidence?

Support: In addition to sound reasoning, can I use appropriate facts, examples, statistics, and opinions of authorities?

This is the most commonly used pattern for an essay, which is abbreviated for a paragraph.

Background	Discussion of the problem, reason for concern, historical development, etc.
Proposition	
Refutation (often omitted)	The other view and its fundamental inadequacy.
Support	
Support	The evidence—why your solution is valid.
Support	
Emphatic restatement of proposition	The clinching statement, often with generalization based on evidence.

There are, of course, other variants, and there are also several methods of developing the material within each pattern. You may organize your support by a pro and con arrangement, presenting one side at a time or one issue at a time (discuss an issue favoring your position, then refute your opponent's claims). You may also develop the argument (or persuasive writing, in a broader sense) by a method such as cause and effect, definition, and comparison and contrast or by a combination of methods.

YOUR AUDIENCE

Your audience may be uninformed, informed, biased, hostile, receptive, apathetic, sympathetic, empathetic—any one, several, or something else. The point is that you should be acutely concerned about who will read your composition. If your readers are likely to be uninformed about the social and historical background of the issue, then you need to set the issue in context. The discussion of the background should lead to the problem for which you have a proposition or solution. If your readers are likely to be biased or even hostile to your view, take special care to refute the opposing side in a thoughtful, incisive way that does not further antagonize them. If your readers are already receptive and perhaps even sympathetic, and you wish to move them to action, then you might appeal to their conscience and the need for their commitment.

KINDS OF EVIDENCE

In addition to sound reasoning generally, you can use these kinds of evidence: facts, examples, statistics, and authorities.

First, you can offer facts. Martin Luther King Jr. was killed in Memphis, Tennessee, on April 4, 1968. Because an event that has happened is true and can be verified, this statement about King is a fact. But that James Earl Ray acted alone in killing King is, to some, questionable. That King was the greatest of all civil rights leaders is also opinion because it cannot be verified.

Some facts are readily accepted because they are general knowledge—you and your reader know them to be true, because they can be or have been verified. Other "facts" are based on personal observation and are reported in various publications but may be false or questionable. You should always be concerned about the reliability of the source for both the information you use and the information used by those with other viewpoints. Still other so-called facts are genuinely debatable because of their complexity or the incompleteness of the knowledge available.

Second, you can cite examples. Keep in mind that you must present a sufficient number of examples and that the examples must be relevant.

Third, you can present statistics. Statistics are numerical facts and data that are classified and tabulated to present significant information about a given subject.

Avoid presenting a long list of figures; select statistics carefully and relate them to things familiar to your reader. The millions of dollars spent on a war in a single week, for example, become more comprehensible when expressed in terms of what the money would purchase in education, highways, or urban renewal.

To test the validity of statistics, either yours or your opponent's, ask: Who gathered them? Under what conditions? For what purpose? How are they used?

Fourth, you can cite evidence from, and opinions of, authorities. Most readers accept facts from recognized, reliable sources—governmental publications, standard reference works, and books and periodicals published by established firms. In addition, they will accept evidence and opinions from individuals who, because of their knowledge and experience, are recognized as experts.

In using authoritative sources as proof, keep these points in mind:

- Select authorities who are generally recognized as experts in their field.
- Use authorities who qualify in the field pertinent to your argument.
- Select authorities whose views are not biased.
- Try to use several authorities.
- Identify the authority's credentials clearly in your essay.

Transitional Words

Consider using the following transitional words to improve coherence by connecting ideas with ideas, sentences with sentences, and paragraphs with paragraphs.

FOR ARGUMENT: it follows that, as a result, causes taken collectively, as a concession, even though, of course, in the context of, in the light of, in the final analysis, following this, further, as additional support, moreover, consequently, according to, in support of, contrary to

FOR ALL PATTERNS OF WRITING: The HOTSHOT CAT words: However, Otherwise, Therefore, Similarly, Hence, On the other hand, Then, Consequently, Also, Thus (See pages 427–428 for additional transitional words.)

LOGICAL FALLACIES

Certain thought patterns are inherently flawed. Commonly called **logical fallacies**, these thought patterns are of primary concern in argument. You should be able to identify them in the arguments of those on the other side of an issue, and you should be sure to avoid them in your own writing.

Eight kinds of logical fallacies are very common.

1. ***Post hoc, ergo propter hoc*** ("after this, therefore because of this"): When one event precedes another in time, the first is assumed to cause the other. "If *A* comes before *B*, then *A* must be causing *B*."

    "I knew I'd have a day like this when I saw that black cat run across my driveway this morning."

    "What did I tell you? We elected him president, and now we have high inflation."

2. **False analogy**: False analogies ignore differences and stress similarities, often in an attempt to prove something.

    "People have to get a driver's license because unqualified drivers could have bad effects on society. Therefore, couples should also have to get a license to bear children because unqualified parents can produce delinquent children."

    "The leader of that country is a mad dog dictator, and you know what you do with a mad dog. You get a club and kill it."

3. **Hasty generalization**: This is a conclusion based on too few reliable instances.

    "Everyone I met this morning is going to vote for Johnson, so I know Johnson is going to win."
    "How many people did you meet?"
    "Three."

4. **False dilemma**: This fallacy presents the reader with only two alternatives from which to choose. The solution may lie elsewhere.

"Now, only two things can be done with the savings and loan places. You either shut them down or let them go bankrupt."

"The way I see it, you either bomb them back into the Stone Age or let them keep on pushing us around."

5. **Argumentum ad hominem** ("argument against the person"): This is the practice of abusing and discrediting your opponent rather than keeping to the main issues of the argument.

"Who cares what he has to say? After all, he's a wild-eyed liberal who has been divorced twice."

"Let's put aside the legislative issue for a moment and talk about the person who proposed it. For one thing he's a Southerner. For another he's Catholic. Enough said."

6. **Begging the question**: This fallacy assumes something is true without proof. It occurs when a thinker assumes a position is right before offering proof.

"Those savages can never be civilized."

"I have one simple question. When is he going to stop ripping off his customers? Case closed."

7. **Circular reasoning**: This thought pattern asserts proof that is no more than a repetition of the initial assertion.

"You can judge good art by reading what good critics say about it."
"But who are good critics?"
"The people who spend their time judging good art."

8. **Non sequitur**: This fallacy draws a conclusion that does not follow.

"He's my first cousin, so of course you can trust him."

"You can count on Gizmo computers; they were designed by native Californians."

EXERCISE 1   Identifying Logical Fallacies

Identify the logical fallacy (or fallacies) in the following sentences.

1. "If politicians can hire ghostwriters, why can't a little student like me be allowed to buy a research paper?"

2. "Stamp out dirty books, I say. Just look at all the crime we have since they started allowing this stuff."

3. "I was starting to have my doubts about the accuracy of newspapers until I read a newspaper editorial last week saying how reliable newspapers actually are."

4. "I can tell from listening to my family that the school bond issue will never pass."

5. "Blaming a company for making big profits is like blaming a cow for giving too much milk."

6. "Okay, so my spouse left me. Who cares? They're like buses; you miss one, and another one'll come along in a minute or two."

7. "I used to think Hemingway was a great writer until I read about his life. The guy was a self-centered, pompous jerk, and I'll never read any of his stuff again."

8. "I was really shocked until she told me it happened in New York, and then I just said, 'What's new?'"

9. "Like I say, you either fish or you cut bait. Will you marry me or won't you? Take your choice."

10. "Mark my words. If they start controllin' handguns, it's just a matter of time 'til we're back to defendin' ourselves with clubs and rocks against criminals with bazookas."

EXERCISE 2   Writing Examples of Logical Fallacies

Provide examples of the following logical fallacies. Work in a group or individually as directed by your instructor.

1. *Post hoc*: _____

_____

_____

2. False analogy: _____

_____

_____

3. Hasty generalization: _____

_____

_____

4. False dilemma: _____

_____

_____

5. *Argumentum ad hominem*: _____

_____

_____

6. Begging the question: _____

_____

_____

7. Circular reasoning: _____

_____

_____

8. Non sequitur: _____

_____

_____

PROPOSALS FOR THE WORKPLACE

In the workplace, the proposal is the purest expression of persuasion. Although it does not have a precise form, there are different kinds of proposals and different situations from which proposals arise. In this chapter, we will attempt to summarize the main forms and purposes of the proposal, but we will not try to teach how to write a long, complicated one that requires extensive research. Learning to work with the basic form will give you useful practice in this kind of writing. On the job you will experience the many ways of framing proposals.

Notice the remarkable similarities between conventional college writing assignments and workplace proposals.

Paragraph or Essay of Persuasion (or Argument)	Proposal
Background (placing the issue into a social or historical perspective)	Background (indicating the problem or the need, emphasizing the urgency)
Proposition, with possible qualification	Solution to the problem, or need, stated concisely
Possible refutation	Possible explanation of why other solutions are inadequate
Support (reasoning and evidence)	In detail, what you can do
Support (reasoning and evidence)	How you can do it
Support (reasoning and evidence)	When you can do it
Support (reasoning and evidence)	What it will cost
Conclusion (clinching statement)	Conclusion (emphasizing the problem and solution)

The body of your proposal will usually have the parts shown in the proposal list. You will be able to determine what is necessary. For example, if you are proposing a change in procedure for an internal solution to a problem such as miscommunication, the cost may not be mentioned. As for order, the sequence shown in the list is common, but you can easily change the sequence to fit your needs.

Longer and highly technical proposals often begin with an executive summary, a statement that carries the major ideas but not the explanations. Such a component would be read by executives, who would depend on others to evaluate and report on the remaining parts of the extensively detailed proposal.

FINDING PATTERNS IN PHOTOS

EXERCISE 4   A Text-Based Activity for Groups or Individuals

Business person multitasking while driving

Take a close look at the driver in the photo—listening to the Bluetooth in his ear, sipping coffee from a cup in his left hand, texting with his cell phone in his right hand, steering with his right wrist. What's your reaction? Would you wish to nominate him for the *Guinness Book of Records* for multitasking? Or would you wish him off the road, signing an unsafe driving ticket just issued by the highway patrol?

If your second wish were to be granted, you would have to select your place of residence carefully, for the cell phone laws vary greatly from state to state. According to the American Automobile Association (AAA) studies (as of the writing of this exercise), only five states prohibit all drivers from the use of hand-held cell phones while driving, twenty-one ban all cell phone use by novice drivers, seventeen ban school bus drivers from all cell phone use when passengers are present, fourteen ban text messaging for all drivers, and nine ban text messaging for novice drivers.

Imagine you are a federal congressperson and you are on a committee studying the issue of whether to have a national law banning or partially banning the use of cell phones while driving. Trying to be objective, first list the reasons for not having restrictions on the use of cell phones while driving—the no restrictions, the con side. Then list the reasons for having a law with restrictions, the pro side.

Reasons for No Restrictions	Reasons for Restrictions
_____	_____
_____	_____
_____	_____
_____	_____
_____	_____

Now write a federal law that reads like the proposition, or thesis, in an argument in this chapter: one with a subject and a focus. Your proposed law should be specific and include any intended qualifications of key words, such as "all drivers," "novice drivers," "school bus drivers," "hand-held cell phones," and "text messaging." Limit your statement to one or two (probably with semicolon) sentences.

If your instructors requires, write a paragraph or an essay on the proposition that you have proposed for a federal law. Use this basic form:

Proposition: _____

Support 1: _____

Support 2: _____

Support 3: _____

Practicing Patterns of Argument

The formal pattern of argument is not always followed in a set sequence, but the main components—the proposition and the support—are always included. You should also consider whether to qualify your proposition and whether to include a refutation.

EXERCISE 5   Completing Patterns of Argument

Fill in the blanks with supporting statements for each proposition. Each outline uses the following pattern:

Proposition

I. Support 1

II. Support 2

III. Support 3

A. Proposition: College athletes should be paid.

   I. _____

   II. They work long hours in practice and competition.

   III. They have less time than many other students for study.

B. Proposition: Zoos are beneficial institutions.

   I. _____

   II. They preserve endangered species by captive breeding.

   III. They study animal diseases and find cures.

EXERCISE 6   Writing Patterns of Argument

Complete the following outline. Use your own topic or write on the topic "There should be no curfew for teenagers" or "There should be a curfew for teenagers."

Proposition: _____

I. _____ (Support 1)

II. _____ (Support 2)

III. _____ (Support 3)

EXERCISE 7   Writing Patterns of Argument

Complete the following outline. Use your own topic or write on the topic "Known gang members should be prohibited from using public parks" or "Known gang members should not be prohibited from using public parks."

Proposition: _____

I. _____ (Support 1)

II. _____ (Support 2)

III. _____ (Support 3)

Readings for Critical Thinking, Discussion, and Writing

READING STRATEGIES AND OBJECTIVES

Underlining and annotating these reading selections will help you answer the questions that follow the selections, discuss the material in class, and prepare for reading-based writing assignments. As you underline and annotate, pay special attention to the author's writing skills, logic, and message, and consider the relevance of the material to your own experiences and values.

Most selections begin with a Mindset suggestion that can help you create a readiness for connecting with what you are about to read.

ESSAYS

Shouldn't Men Have "Choice" Too?

MEGHAN DAUM

Meghan Daum is the author of The Quality of Life Report *and the essay collection* My Misspent Youth *and writes a weekly column for the* Los Angeles Times. *Known for her humor and acute cultural observations, she has inspired controversy over a range of topics, including social politics and class warfare.*

MINDSET

Lock It In

Imagine "Pro-Life for Men" and "Pro-Choice for Men" bumper stickers.

1   For pro-choicers like myself, Supreme Court nominee Samuel A. Alito Jr.'s position regarding spousal consent for abortion seems like one more loose rock in the ongoing erosion of Roe vs. Wade. Even those of us who are too young to remember the pre-Roe era often see any threat to abortion rights as a threat to our very destinies. We are, after all, the generation that grew up under Title IX, singing along to "Free to Be You and Me" (you know, the 1972 children's record where Marlo Thomas and Alan Alda remind us that mommies can be plumbers and boys can have dolls). When it comes to self-determination, we're as determined as it gets.

2   But even though I was raised believing in the inviolability of a woman's right to choose, the older I get, the more I wonder if this idea of choice is being fairly applied. Most people now accept that women, especially teenagers, often make decisions regarding abortion based on educational and career goals and whether the father of the unborn child is someone they want to hang around with for the next few decades. The "choice" in this equation is not only a matter of whether to carry an individual fetus to term but a question of what kind of life the woman wishes to lead.

3   But what about the kind of life men want to lead? On December 1, Dalton Conley, director of the Center for Advanced Social Science Research at New York University, published an article on the Op-Ed page of the *New York Times* arguing that Alito's position on spousal consent did not go far enough. Describing his own experience with a girlfriend who terminated a pregnancy against his wishes, Conley took some brave steps down the slippery slope of this debate, suggesting that if a father is willing to assume full responsibility for a child not wanted by a mother, he should be able to obtain an injunction stopping her from having an abortion—and he should be able to do so regardless of whether or not he's married to her. Conley freely acknowledges the many obvious caveats in this position—the most salient being the fact that regardless of how "full" that male responsibility might be, the physical burden of pregnancy and childbirth will always put most of the onus on women. But as much as I shudder at the idea of a man, husband or not, obtaining an injunction telling me what I can or cannot do with my own body, I would argue that it is Conley who has not gone far enough.

4   Since we're throwing around radical ideas about abortion rights, let me raise this question: If abortion is to remain legal and relatively unrestricted—and I believe it should—why shouldn't men have the right during at least the first trimester of pregnancy to terminate their legal and financial rights and responsibilities to the child?

5   As Conley laments, the law does not currently allow for men to protect the futures of the fetuses they help create. What he doesn't mention—indeed, no one ever seems to—is the degree to which men also cannot protect their own futures. The way the law is now, a man who gets a woman pregnant is not only powerless to force her to terminate the pregnancy, he also has a complete legal obligation to support that child for at least 18 years. In other words, although women are able to take control of their futures by choosing from at least a small range of options— abortion, adoption or keeping the child—a man can be forced to be a father to a child he never wanted and cannot financially support. I even know of cases in which the woman absolves the man of responsibility, only to have the courts demand payment anyway. That takes the notion of "choice" very far from anything resembling equality.

6   I realize I've just alienated feminists (among whose ranks I generally count myself) as well as pro-lifers, neither of whom are always above platitudes such as "You should have kept your pants on." But that reasoning is by now as reductive as suggesting that a rape victim "asked for it." Yes, people often act irresponsibly and yes, abortion should be avoided whenever possible. But just

as women should not be punished for choosing to terminate a pregnancy, men should not be punished when those women choose not to.

7   One problem, of course, is that the child is likely to bear the brunt of whatever punishment remains to be doled out. A father who terminates his rights, although not technically a deadbeat dad, has still helped create a kid who is not fully supported. And (in case you were wondering) there are dozens of other holes in my theory as well: What if a husband wants to terminate his rights—should that be allowed? What if a father is underage and wants to terminate, but his parents forbid him? Should a father's decision-making time be limited to the first trimester? Should couples on first dates discuss their positions on the matter? Should Internet dating profiles let men check a box saying "will waive parental rights" next to the box indicating his astrological sign?

8   There's also the danger that my idea is not just a slippery slope but a major mudslide on the way to Conley's idea. If a man can legally dissociate himself from a pregnancy, some will argue, why couldn't he also bind himself to it and force it to term? That notion horrifies me, just as my plan probably horrifies others. But that doesn't mean these ideas aren't worth discussing. Though it may be hard to find an adult male who's sufficiently undiplomatic to admit out loud that he'd like to have the option I'm proposing, let alone potentially take it, I know more than a few parents of teenage boys who lose sleep over the prospect of their sons' landing in the kind of trouble from which they'll have no power to extricate themselves.

9   And although the notion of women "tricking" men into fatherhood now sounds arcane and sexist, we'd be blind not to recognize the extent to which some women are capable of tricking themselves into thinking men will stick around, despite all evidence to the contrary. Allowing men to legally (if not always gracefully) bow out of fatherhood would, at the very least, start a conversation for which we haven't yet found the right words.

10   Actually, there's one word we've had all along: choice. We just need to broaden its definition.

EXERCISE 8   Vocabulary Highlights

Write a short definition of each word as it is used in the essay. (Paragraph numbers are given in parentheses.) Be prepared to use these words in sentences.

erosion (1)	laments (5)
inviolability (2)	absolves (5)
injunction (3)	platitudes (6)
salient (3)	doled (7)
trimester (4)	extricate (8)

EXERCISE 9   Discussion and Critical Thinking

1. Which paragraph contains Daum's thesis?

2. How does Daum introduce her proposition?

3. What qualified support does she offer in paragraph 3?

4. Which paragraph contains the rebuttal?

5. If you were to support Daum's proposition, how would you answer the questions Daum poses in paragraph 7?

6. In paragraph 8, Daum says males might be reluctant to admit publicly that they agree with her proposition. How do you think most men would respond? most women?

7. Daum has redefined the word *choice*. Use your own words to write her proposition.

8. Do you agree with the proposition? Why or why not?

Rape and Modern Sex War

CAMILLE PAGLIA

Camille Paglia is a distinguished and controversial professor, author, and speaker. Her books include Sex, Art, and American Culture: Essays, Vamps and Tramps: New Essays, *and* Alfred Hitchcock's "The Birds." *This essay was first published in* New York Newsday.

MINDSET
Lock It In

Is date rape primarily an act of violence or sex?

1   Rape is an outrage that cannot be tolerated in civilized society. Yet feminism, which has waged a crusade for rape to be taken more seriously, has put young women in danger by hiding the truth about sex from them.

2   In dramatizing the pervasiveness of rape, feminists have told young women that before they have sex with a man, they must give consent as explicit as a legal contract's. In this way, young women have been convinced that they have been the victims of rape. On elite campuses in the Northeast and on the West Coast, they have held consciousness-raising sessions, petitioned administrations, demanded inquests. At Brown University, outraged, panicky "victims" have scrawled the names of alleged attackers on the walls of women's rest rooms. What marital rape was to the 1970s, "date rape" is to the 1990s.

3   The incidence and seriousness of rape do not require this kind of exaggeration. Real acquaintance rape is nothing new. It has been a horrible problem for women for all of recorded history. Once, fathers and brothers protected women from rape. Once, the penalty for rape was death. I come from a fierce Italian tradition where, not so long ago in the motherland, a rapist would end up knifed, castrated, and hung out to dry.

4   But the old clans and small rural communities have broken down. In our cities, on our campuses far from home, young women are vulnerable and defenseless. Feminism has not prepared them for this. Feminism keeps saying the sexes are the same. It keeps telling women they can do anything, go anywhere, say anything, wear anything. No, they can't. Women will always be in sexual danger.

5   One of my male students recently slept overnight with a friend in a passageway of the Great Pyramid in Egypt. He described the moon and sand, the ancient silence and eerie echoes. I am a woman. I will never experience that. I am not stupid enough to believe I could ever be safe there. There is a world of solitary adventure I will never have. Women have always known these somber truths. But feminism, with its pie-in-the-sky fantasies about the perfect world, keeps young women from seeing life as it is.

6   We must remedy social injustice whenever we can. But there are some things we cannot change. There are sexual differences that are based in biology. Academic feminism is lost in a fog of social constructionism. It believes we are totally the product of our environment. This idea was invented by Rousseau.[1] He was wrong. Emboldened by dumb French language theory, academic feminists repeat the same hollow slogans over and over to each other. Their view of sex is naïve and prudish. Leaving sex to the feminists is like letting your dog vacation at the taxidermist's.

7   The sexes are at war. Men must struggle for identity against the overwhelming power of their mothers. Women have menstruation to tell them they are women. Men must do or risk something to be men. Men become masculine only when other men say they are. Having sex with a woman is one way a boy becomes a man.

8   College men are at their hormonal peak. They have just left their mothers and are questing for their male identity. In groups, they are dangerous. A woman going to a fraternity party is walking into Testosterone Flats, full of prickly cacti and blazing guns. If she goes, she should be armed with resolute alertness. She should arrive with girlfriends and leave with them. A girl who lets herself get dead drunk at a fraternity party is a fool. A girl who goes upstairs alone with a brother at a fraternity party is an idiot. Feminists call this "blaming the victim." I call it common sense.

9   For a decade, feminists have drilled their disciples to say, "Rape is a crime of violence but not of sex." This sugar-coated Shirley Temple nonsense has exposed young women to disaster. Misled by feminism, they do not expect rape from the nice boys from good homes who sit next to them in class.

10   Aggression and eroticism, in fact, are deeply intertwined. Hunt, pursuit and capture are biologically programmed into male sexuality. Generation after generation, men must be educated, refined, and ethically persuaded away from their tendency toward anarchy and brutishness. Society is not the enemy, as feminism ignorantly claims. Society is woman's protection against rape. Feminism, with its solemn Carry Nation[2] repressiveness, does not see what is for men the eroticism or fun element in rape, especially the wild, infectious delirium of gang rape. Women who do not understand rape cannot defend themselves against it.

[1] A French political writer and philosopher (1712–1778) (editors' note).
[2] A nineteenth-century reformer who advocated the abolition of alcohol (editors' note).

11   The date-rape controversy shows feminism hitting the wall of its own broken promises. The women of my 1960s generation were the first respectable girls in history to swear like sailors, get drunk, stay out all night—in short, to act like men. We sought total sexual freedom and equality. But as time passed, we woke up to cold reality. The old double standard protected women. When anything goes, it's women who lose.

12   Today's young women don't know what they want. They see that feminism has not brought sexual happiness. The theatrics of public rage over date rape are their way of restoring the old sexual rules that were shattered by my generation. Yet nothing about the sexes has really changed. The comic film *Where the Boys Are* (1960), the ultimate expression of 1950s man-chasing, still speaks directly to our time. It shows smart, lively women skillfully anticipating and fending off the dozens of strategies with which horny men try to get them into bed. The agonizing date-rape subplot and climax are brilliantly done. The victim, Yvette Mimieux, makes mistake after mistake, obvious to the other girls. She allows herself to be lured away from her girlfriends and into isolation with boys whose character and intentions she misreads. *Where the Boys Are* tells the truth. It shows courtship as a dangerous game in which the signals are not verbal but subliminal.

13   Neither militant feminism, which is obsessed with politically correct language, nor academic feminism, which believes that knowledge and experience are "constituted by" language, can understand preverbal or nonverbal communication. Feminism, focusing on sexual politics, cannot see that sex exists in and through the body. Sexual desire and arousal cannot be fully translated into verbal terms. This is why men and women misunderstand each other.

14   Trying to remake the future, feminism cut itself off from sexual history. It discarded and suppressed the sexual myths of literature, art and religion. Those myths show us the turbulence, the mysteries and passions of sex. In mythology we see men's sexual anxiety, their fear of woman's dominance. Much sexual violence is rooted in men's sense of psychological weakness toward women. It takes many men to deal with one woman. Woman's voracity is a persistent motif. Clara Bow,[3] it was rumored, took on the USC[4] football team on weekends. Marilyn Monroe, singing "Diamonds Are a Girl's Best Friend," rules a conga line of men in tuxes. Half-clad Cher, in the video for "If I Could Turn Back Time," deranges a battleship of screaming sailors and straddles a pink-lit cannon. Feminism, coveting social power, is blind to woman's cosmic sexual power.

15   To understand rape, you must study the past. There never was and never will be sexual harmony. Every woman must be prudent and cautious about where she goes and with whom. When she makes a mistake, she must accept the consequences and, through self-criticism, resolve never to make that mistake again. Running to mommy and daddy on the campus grievance committee is unworthy of strong women. Posting lists of guilty men in the toilet is cowardly, infantile stuff.

16   The Italian philosophy of life espouses high-energy confrontation. A male student makes a vulgar remark about your breasts? Don't slink off to whimper with the campus shrinking violets. Deal with it. On the spot. Say, "Shut up, you jerk! And crawl back to the barnyard where you belong!" In general, women who project this take-charge attitude toward life get harassed less often. I see too many dopey, immature, self-pitying women walking around like melting sticks of butter. It's the Yvette Mimieux syndrome: make me happy. And listen to me weep when I'm not.

[3]A movie star from the Roaring Twenties era (editors' note).
[4]University of Southern California (editors' note).

17   The date-rape debate is already smothering in propaganda churned out by the expensive Northeastern colleges and universities, with their overconcentration of boring, uptight academic feminists and spoiled, affluent students. Beware of the deep manipulativeness of rich students who were neglected by their parents. They love to turn the campus into hysterical psychodramas of sexual transgression, followed by assertions of parental authority and concern. And don't look for sexual enlightenment from academe, which spews out mountains of books but never looks at life directly.

18   As a fan of football and rock music, I see in the simple, swaggering masculinity of the jock and in the noisy posturing of the heavy-metal guitarist certain fundamental, unchanging truths about sex. Masculinity is aggressive, unstable, combustible. It is also the most creative cultural force in history. Women must reorient themselves toward the elemental powers of sex, which can strengthen or destroy.

19   The only solution to date rape is female self-awareness and self-control. A woman's number-one line of defense against rape is herself. When a real rape occurs, she should report it to the police. Complaining to college committees because the courts "take too long" is ridiculous. College administrations are not a branch of the judiciary. They are not equipped or trained for legal inquiry. Colleges must alert incoming students to the problems and dangers of adulthood. Then colleges must stand back and get out of the sex game.

EXERCISE 10   Vocabulary Highlights

Write a short definition of each word as it is used in a sentence. (Paragraph numbers are given in parentheses.) Be prepared to use these words in sentences.

explicit (2)	motif (14)
intertwined (10)	coveting (14)
delirium (10)	cosmic (14)
suppressed (14)	espouses (16)
voracity (14)	syndrome (16)

EXERCISE 11   Discussion and Critical Thinking

1. Paglia begins her essay by saying that feminism "has put young women in danger by hiding the truth about sex from them" (paragraph 1). What truth is she referring to?

2. Which sentence in paragraph 6 is central to Paglia's argument?

3. What does Paglia mean when she says, "The sexes are at war" (paragraph 7) at college? Do you agree with her view? Why or why not?

4. What does Paglia say about rape as a violent act?

5. Why does she say women cannot "do anything, go anywhere, say anything, wear anything" (paragraph 4)?

6. Does she say masculinity is bad?

7. What is Paglia's solution to date rape?

8. With what parts of her argument do you agree and disagree? Explain.

Let Granny Drive If She Can

SUZANNE FIELDS

A syndicated columnist for the Washington Times, *Suzanne Fields writes opinion articles twice a week on topics that often polarize her readers. Here she addresses the idea of restricting drivers' privileges because of age.*

1   My mother at 85 was alert, with good vision and sharp reflexes for her age, but one day she smashed into three parked cars on a supermarket parking lot. We never found out exactly how it happened—she was not sure, either—but the investigators figured Mom hit the accelerator instead of the brake. When the car didn't slow down, she panicked and pushed down harder on the wrong pedal. This may be what happened to the 86-year-old man who plowed through that California farmers' market.

2   Mom was lucky, even though she spent two weeks in the hospital with two broken ribs. But we reluctantly concluded that it was time to take Mom's car keys. This was the hardest thing I have ever had to do. She pleaded, cajoled and demanded to keep her car. I was "mean" and "unfeeling," and her gentle voice grew strident. Tears trickled down her cheeks. I think she never felt old until that moment, when I took away the independence provided by the car. I felt like the wicked witch of the west, and the other points of the compass as well.

3   In the days that followed, we suggested that she take taxis to visit friends and to shop, but she wouldn't do it: "That's not my style." A driver was out of the question because she had no set places she had to go. She was not a lady for "Driving Miss Daisy." Fortunately, she lived in the city and quickly slipped into the routine of taking the bus, which she hadn't done since high school. She got to know the bus drivers and waved at them as they drove past her on her frequent strolls through the neighborhood. She began to enjoy her new life. But most old people have no convenient public transportation or shops within walking distance.

4   Hard as it was on both of us, we made the right decision in Mom's case. But is tragedy like that in Santa Monica a reason to take away the car keys of the elderly? I think not. Unless we learn how to play God, foreseeing accidents, that's the wrong lesson to learn.

5   Age doesn't necessarily prove anything. Slower reflexes or not, senior citizens are much better drivers than, for example, teenagers. They usually drive more slowly. They get honked at a lot, but their slower speed reduces the risk of death and destruction that accompanies speeding tons of metal. The worst risk-takers on the highway are young men between the ages of 18 to 25, but no one suggests taking away their keys or raising the driving age to 26.

6   The fatality rate in 2001 for motorists between 16 and 20, according to the National Highway Traffic Safety Administration, was more than double that for drivers over 70. The AARP estimates that drivers 55 and older compose a quarter of the driving population, but have only 18 percent of the accidents. The older the driver, the fewer miles he puts on his car. As the baby boomers age, the numbers of older drivers will increase. Large majorities of them live in the suburbs or in the countryside without public transportation. Rural and suburban communities must arrange for alternative kinds of transportation for those who are failing in their driving ability; demand can drive public and entrepreneurial innovation.

7   Preventive remedies for the aging driver abound. Their licenses could be renewed at shorter intervals, with tougher physical tests. At the first signs of diminished alertness, a designated adult in the family should monitor the elderly driver closely for the good of everyone else. They shouldn't drink and drive, but who should? Doctors who prescribe medications for the elderly must make them aware of their influence on driving.

8   The older citizen who tries to avoid danger is likely to take personal responsibility with considerably more seriousness than a younger person who courts danger through partying and risk. I like the example of Lord Renton, the 94-year-old "Father of the House of Lords" in London, who volunteered the other day to take his first driving test. He first drove a car in England before 1935, the year a driver's license was first required. He enjoyed a grandfather clause, you might say.

9   Deciding he owed it to himself and his fellow drivers to submit to a test, he submitted himself to the indignity of taking the test on a small and unfamiliar Ford sedan, not his usual cup of tea. He succeeded brilliantly. We could expect no less from seniors on this side of the Atlantic. So, let's let Granny drive for as long as she can. Road age is a lot less dangerous than road rage.

EXERCISE 12   Discussion and Critical Thinking

1. What two paragraphs state the author's proposition and summarize her support?

2. What two other patterns of writing (narration, exemplification, comparison and contrast, process analysis, analysis by division) does Fields use significantly to advance her argument?

3. List the several forms of evidence Fields uses.

4. She mentions that young men between the ages of 18 and 25 are the worst drivers, but no one suggests taking their licenses away because of age. Why does that view prevail?

5. What is your reaction to Fields's argument?

6. Fields personalizes her argument by discussing her mother's situation. What effect does that approach have on her overall presentation?

STUDENT PARAGRAPH, ESSAY, AND PROPOSAL

After Angela DeSarro received a list of topics from which to select, she went to the library to obtain some information about the ones that interested her. One such topic was euthanasia. Her textbook contained an essay originally published in the *Journal of the American Medical Association* about a doctor who illegally assisted a suffering, terminally ill patient. DeSarro's mind and emotions came together on the issue and she had her topic.

DeSarro's Writing Process Worksheet shows how her writing evolved from idea to final draft. Notice how she turns her listing into an outline, which becomes the structure for her paragraph. To conserve space here, the freewriting and two rough drafts marked for revision and editing have been omitted. The balance of her worksheet has been lengthened for you to be able to see her other work in its entirety.

You will find a full-size blank worksheet on page 6, which can be photocopied, filled in, and submitted with each assignment if your instructor directs you to do so.

Writing Process Worksheet

Name Angela DeSarro   **Title** My Life to Live—or Not   **Due Date** Tuesday, October 14, 10 a.m.

Use the back of this page or separate paper if you need more space.

Assignment   In the space below, write whatever you need to know about your assignment, including information about the topic, audience, pattern of writing, length, whether to include a rough draft or revised drafts, and whether your paper must be typed.

Write a paragraph of 200 to 300 words in which you argue for a particular action or restraint. Include at least three supporting points. Keep in mind that some thoughtful readers will disagree with your proposition. Submit this completed worksheet, a rough draft marked for revision and editing, and a typed final draft.

Stage One   **Explore** Freewrite, brainstorm (list), cluster, or take notes as directed by your instructor.

Listing

Debbie's struggle	*Proposal*
(from JAMA)	—physician-assisted suicide
—terminally ill with cancer	—patient terminally ill,
—nauseous, emaciated, suffering	little time left
—wants to die with a bit of	—must be suffering
dignity intact	—must want suicide
—physician helps her	—physician can assist
—an illegal act	—must be regulated
—shouldn't be illegal	—should be national law
	—similar to the one in Oregon

Stage Two

Organize Write a topic sentence or thesis; label the subject and the focus parts.

The time has come for a national law legalizing physician-assisted suicide for
               subject   focus
the terminally ill.

Write an outline or an outline alternative. For reading-based writing, include references and short quotations with page numbers as support in the outline.

  I. Person dying
     A. Pain
     B. Extreme discomfort
     C. Example: Debbie
 II. Person desiring death with dignity
     A. Not wanting to wither away
     B. Not wanting to be alive on tubes and machines
     C. Example: Debbie
III. Person demanding choice in dying
     A. Of time
     B. Of method
     C. Example: Debbie
IV. A law that works
     A. Chosen by voters in Oregon
     B. Is not abused
 V. Plea for a national law

Stage Three

Write On separate paper, write and then revise your paragraph or essay as many times as necessary for **c**oherence, **l**anguage (usage, tone, and diction), **u**nity, **e**mphasis, **s**upport, and **s**entences (**CLUESS**). Read your work aloud to hear and correct any grammatical errors or awkward-sounding sentences.

Edit any problems in fundamentals, such as **c**apitalization, **o**missions, **p**unctuation, and **s**pelling (**COPS**).

Final Draft

MY LIFE TO LIVE—OR NOT
Angela DeSarro

Proposition	Debbie, 20, was dying of ovarian cancer. Racked with pain, nauseous, emaciated, she sought the ultimate relief and found it in euthanasia. A doctor administered a drug and she died. It was a hidden, secret act. It was also illegal in Debbie's state, but this case was written up in the *Journal of the American Medical Association*. <u>Surely the time has come for a nationwide law legalizing this practice under specific provisions and regulations</u>. Debbie
Support	had reached the point of not only enduring terrible pain but of vomiting constantly and not being able to sleep. Pain-killing medication no longer worked. She wanted to die with what she regarded as a degree of dignity. She had already become a withered, suffering human being with tubes coming out of her nose, throat, and urinary tract, and she was losing all self-control.
Support	She also believed that it should be up to her, under these conditions, to decide when and how she should die. Laws in most places prohibit terminally ill patients from choosing death and physicians from assisting them. One state, Oregon, has a law favoring physician-assisted suicide, at least in the limited cases of terminally ill people expected to live less than six months. In 1998,
Concluding sentence as a restated proposition	fifteen people benefited from that law; it was not abused. <u>It, or a similar form, should be enacted nationwide</u>.

EXERCISE 13   Discussion and Critical Thinking

1. What kinds of evidence does DeSarro use to support her argument?

2. What might be the objections to her reasoned argument?

3. Do you agree or disagree with DeSarro's argument? Why?

READING-BASED WRITING
. . . .

Schools as Political Combat Zones

ERIC HORNER

Student Eric Horner was required to write a reaction or a two-part response to one of the assigned professional essays in his textbook. He was to analyze the source he selected and provide documented references and quotations to it. He chose to write a critical reaction to "Educators Declare War on Traditional Values" by Thomas Sowell.

Text thesis	1	According to Thomas Sowell in "Educators Declare War on Traditional Values," American society is involved in political combat with educators, and most citizens do not know that shots are being fired. The target, he says, is wholesome mainstream traditions and the parents who want to and should pass their values along to their children.

Topic sentence

Logical fallacy

Sowell position

Short questions

2   His argument sticks to the image of warfare he mentions in his title. Instead of dealing with issues of sex education and personal counseling in a thoughtful way, he resorts to *argumentum ad hominem*. Educators are the "anointed," and the "zealots" (351) who "carry on unrelenting guerilla warfare against the traditional values of the society and against the very role of families in making decisions about their own children." They "camouflage what they are doing" on their "battlefields" in "an undeclared war" (352).

Topic sentence
Transition
Evidence
Short quotation

Sowell position

Student reaction

3   Two examples of this warfare are his sole evidence, though he says they are typical of what is happening across this country. The first comes from a recent program in San Francisco, in which he says outside speakers "shocked and outraged" students and parents with tales of their sexual experiences. Sowell says it was just another instance of educators promising to teach biology and using that as a cover to replace traditional American values (352). He does not see that because of rampant pregnancy and sexually transmitted diseases among the young something must be done differently in schools. That is what people such as Sowell should be shocked and outraged about. Depending on parents talking to their children is obviously far too often not enough. In that respect Sowell should offer some concrete suggestions.

Topic sentence

Evidence

Short quotation
Sowell position

Student reaction

4   His second example concerns a young female student who broke up with her boyfriend and said she "might as well be dead." Her boyfriend reported her statement to her mother and the school counselor. The counseling staff contacted the mother and daughter. Sowell saw this procedure as the school "busybodies . . . driving a wedge between parent and child" (351–52). He does not mention that schools have rules requiring counselors to take action when they hear that a student has talked about wanting to be dead. The rules were adopted because of the high rate of suicide among the young. Is it not better to risk interfering with the privacy, and even values, of a family if it is possible that in some instances doing so might save lives? In this instance the mother complained. What would the mother and Sowell have said if the daughter had not been counseled and had killed herself?

Concluding student evaluation

Logical fallacy

5   Public schools are just that—public—and, of course, people should be involved in what is and what should be taught. But it will take more than the two examples Sowell gives—one vague and one, I think, not typical—to support his views that devious educators are attacking virtuous families. At best he uses hasty generalizations. If he wants to make a case for the public schools being taken over by a counterculture, his argument would be better served by dealing with statistics and specific information and by going light on the name calling.

Work Cited

Sowell, Thomas. "Educators Declare War on Traditional Values." *Paragraphs and Essays with Culturally Diverse Readings*. Ed. Lee Brandon. 7th ed. Boston: Houghton, 1998. 351–53. Print.

CAREER-RELATED WRITING: PROPOSAL

In writing career-related persuasion, you will write either an essay about some aspect of the workplace or a proposal. Each is a useful form. The essay about work will give you an opportunity to explore a topic and explain your view; a topic might be union membership, management style, or government regulation of business.

The proposal can be about a student, a neighborhood, or a family issue, which is written in the form of a business proposal, or it can be about a business issue (to purchase an item, to modify a practice, to hire a certain kind of person, to discontinue or modify a product or service, or the like). Regardless of the topic, writing a form according to a format commonly used in the marketplace will give you practice for your future or continuing career.

Mandatory Tipping at BoBo's

ROBERTO BENTANCOURT

The assignment was for students to consider a problem they are encountering or have encountered at a job and to write a proposal to the appropriate manager who would have the authority to change a policy or practice. The assignment proposal would not have to be sent to that manager, but it should be generally accurate in the use of evidence. Students were asked to write the proposal as if they still worked at the establishment and to label the parts. Some of the suggested topics were working conditions, pay, uniforms, management style, parking, fringe benefits, worker behavior, worker appearance, cell-phone use, shifts, security, and safety. Bentancourt had recently worked as a shift manager at BoBo's Diner, a little restaurant near a large, urban community college. A favorite with student customers, it should have been a great place to work. But there was one main problem that led to a rapid turnover of food servers.

Background

1   Our student customers really like to eat at this restaurant. One can hear students say, "I'll meet you at BoBo's." Business is obviously good. But it could be better. When one hears a complaint, it is usually about service. The food servers are often inexperienced in dealing with multiple orders in a brief time and in separating work from friendly conversations. There is a reason for that. As you know, we have a high turnover in food servers. Some leave for personal reasons such as dropping out of school, moving, or getting married. Others obtain a job that is more closely related to their intended careers or a job that simply pays more or offers better hours or benefits. But the main reason for leaving work here at BoBo's is the low pay. The pay should not be an issue. You pay a dollar over minimum wage, and with tip money, that should be very rewarding. But it is not—because of the tips, or should I say, lack of tips.

2   Many of our customers eat light, drink as much as they can get with refills, and leave without tipping. That creates several problems. One, it makes the food servers unhappy and ultimately cynical, so many of them become unfriendly or cranky before they quit. And they usually do quit after a short period of time. Two, not getting tips has a double effect on food servers. They do not get the money and then when it is time to pay income tax, they have to pay 8 percent on total sales, so they are, in effect, being further penalized for not getting tips.

3   Of course, some students do tip. A few even tip generously. But far too many hardly tip at all, and the trend is getting worse. As I have said, when customers do not give tips, food servers may become surly and uncaring. When that happens, the customers may feel they have a reason for not tipping. The two problems feed on each other.

Solution to the Problem

4   The solution is to include a 10 percent tip in each bill.

Explanation of Why Other Solutions Are Unworkable

5　Other solutions that come to mind are not practical. Trying to educate customers on this issue will not work because they already know that argument. Paying the food servers more would not be a good idea because you are already selling food and drinks at a low percentage of profit.

What, How, and When Something Can Be Done

6　The addition of 10 percent to each check is a highly workable solution. The food server would automatically receive that tip. Customers could leave an additional amount if they like. Customers would continue to come to BoBo's. In fact, the food servers would be less inclined to leave to go down the street to work at a restaurant with more diverse clientele for better tips. Instead they would be more likely to stay, and they would be more cheerful and efficient, behavior that would bring in more business. Everyone would win. If you feel the food servers would not work hard if they already knew they would get the tip, then make out a receipt that says the customer, upon receiving poor service, could check a box and the tip would go to a charity such as the Salvation Army.

What It Will Cost

7　The cost of this change will be slight. You would need to insert a message inside the menu and post that message near the entrance and cash register. The message should include a brief explanation, with emphasis on the point that a food server who does not get a tip must pay additional income taxes on salary. You would also need to have new receipts printed to make a line for the new item.

Conclusion

8　As one of your shift managers and as a person who knows our customers from the college well, I would talk to individuals during the "breaking-in" period. I will also help you write a letter of explanation. I could even write a letter to the editor of the campus newspaper, explaining the new rule and the reason for the rule. Actually, as a little test, I have mentioned this idea to several of our customers, and they seemed very understanding. One even said that knowing everyone would be tipping at least 10 percent could make the customers happier because with the current practice, those who tipped sometimes felt they were being regarded as fools because other students were, in effect, paying less for their food.

EXERCISE 14   Discussion and Critical Thinking

1. If you were the manager, what would be your response?

2. How do you think nontipping customers would react?

3. Which section carries the thesis in this workplace version of persuasive writing?

4. Which section carries the refutation?

5. Which section carries the most support for this proposal?

Suggested Topics and Prompts for Writing Argument

You will find a blank Writing Process Worksheet on page 6 of this book and on your Student Companion Site. It can be photocopied or printed out, filled in, and submitted with your assignment, if your instructor directs you to do so.

READING-BASED WRITING

Reading-based writing requires you to read critically, write a reply that shows you understand what you have read, and give credit for ideas you borrow and words you quote. The form can be a summary, a reaction, or a two-part response (with separated summary and reaction). Documentation, in which you give credit for borrowed ideas and words, can be either formal (MLA) or informal, as directed by your instructor. Both the forms of reading-based writing and documentation are discussed with examples in Chapter 1. Definitions of the three forms follow. Any form can be used for any reading selection in this book.

Summary

- The summary is a statement presenting only the main points of what you have read by using different wording without altering the meaning, adding information, or showing bias.
- It is the purest form of reading-based writing.

Reaction

- In the reaction, the meaning of what you have read will be central to your topic sentence of your paragraph or to the thesis of your essay.
- Although the reaction is not a personal narrative by itself, it may include personal experience to explain elements of the text. For example, if your source is about driving styles, your own experiences as a driver or an observer of drivers could be relevant in your analysis of the text.
- The reaction may incorporate a summary to convey a broad view of what you have read, but your summary should never be the main part of your reaction.

The Two-Part Response

- The two-part response separates the summary from the reaction.
- This form will give you practice in separating your objective summary in the first part from your more personal evaluation, interpretation, or application in the second part, the reaction.

READING-BASED WRITING TOPICS

"Shouldn't Men Have 'Choice' Too?"

1. Rely on what you have witnessed and experienced and what you believe to write a reaction to Daum's argument. Be sure to refer directly to her essay and use quotations. Your reaction should be an answer to the question posed in the essay title.

2. Write a two-part response in which you summarize Daum's view and then react with answers to the question in the title and the questions in paragraph 7.

"Rape and Modern Sex War"

3. Paglia says, "There are sexual differences that are based in biology" (paragraph 6). Placing herself in opposition to those who believe that the environment— not current social behavior and values—plays the more important role, she maintains that women must protect themselves against date rape by exercising self-awareness and self-control and by calling the police to report rapes. Write an argument (reaction) in which you agree or disagree with her. Are men who practice unwanted sexual aggression generally following social or culture values or are they following their biological instincts in the form of hormones? Is culture or are genes to blame? Do men mainly learn or inherit their feelings toward women? Select some key sentences (maybe four to six) to quote or refer to directly. Examine the evidence Paglia uses to support her argument. Take into account your own experience and inclinations.

"Let Granny Drive If She Can"

4. Write an argument of reaction in which you disagree with Fields's views. Make it a critique of Fields's argument, its logic and overall effectiveness. Use references to and quotations from her article.

5. Write an argument of reaction in which you agree with Fields's views. Your argument should be either personalized with your own examples or presented as a more formal argument without personal examples, but it should be tied to her article with references and quotations.

"My Life to Live—or Not"

6. Use the library or Internet sources to research the state law in Oregon that allows physicians to assist in suicides under certain conditions. In a two-part response, write a summary of that law in one paragraph and your reaction to the law in another. Print out a copy of the law you are summarizing if your instructor requires.

"Mandatory Tipping at BoBo's"

7. Write an argument from a customer's point of view in which you either agree or disagree with Bentancourt's view. Consider using your own examples from restaurants you have frequented. Discuss the effectiveness of his proposal. Use references and short quotations.

GENERAL TOPIC

8. The following are broad subject areas. You will have to limit your focus for a paragraph or an essay of argument. Modify the subject to correspond with your experiences and interests. Some of these subjects will benefit from research in the library or on the Internet. Some will overlap with subject material from classes you have taken and with studies you have made.

   a. School metal detectors
   b. Sex education
   c. Defining sexual harassment
   d. Changing the juvenile justice system
   e. Endangered species legislation
   f. Advertising tobacco
   g. Combating homelessness
   h. State-run lotteries
   i. Jury reform
   j. Legalizing prostitution
   k. Censoring rap or rock music
   l. Cost of illegal immigration
   m. Installation of local traffic signs
   n. Foot patrols by local police
   o. Change in (your) college registration procedure
   p. Local public transportation
   q. Surveillance by video (on campus, in neighborhoods, or in shopping areas)
   r. Zone changes for stores selling liquor
   s. Curfew for teenagers
   t. Laws keeping known gang members out of parks

CROSS-CURRICULAR TOPIC

9. From a class you are taking or have taken or from your major area of study, select an issue on which thoughtful people may disagree and write an essay of persuasion or argument. It could be an interpretation of an ambiguous piece of literature for an English class; a position on global warming, public land management, or the Endangered Species Act for a class in ecology; an argument about the effectiveness of a government program in a political science class; a view on a certain kind of diet in a food-science class; a preference for a particular worldview in a class on philosophy; or an assertion on the proper role of chiropractors as health-care practitioners in a health-science class.

CAREER-RELATED TOPIC

10. Write a proposal to solve a problem in your family, neighborhood, school, or workplace. The problem is likely to be the purchase or modification of something, the introduction or modification of a procedure, or the introduction of a service. For this assignment, use basically the same form regardless of the location or circumstances of the problem. You can use a basic pattern,

background, solution (as a proposition), support (how it can be done, when it can be done, what it will cost, if anything). The problem that you are proposing to alleviate or eliminate can be based on your experiences or it can be purely fictional. If you are suggesting the purchase of an item or items to solve a problem, the Internet can provide you with prices and specifications. Those data could be integrated into your proposal or photocopied and attached, with references. (See "Mandatory Tipping at BoBo's" on pages 363–364 for a student proposal.)

Following are a few specific topic suggestions:

a. *Home*: contracting with a gardener or a housekeeper, dividing the chores, respecting the privacy and space of others

b. *Neighborhood*: limiting noise; dealing with dogs—vicious, wandering, barking; parking recreational vehicles out front

c. *College*: parking, enrollment and registration, classroom procedure, safety

d. *Workplace*: doing your job (or part of it) at home rather than at the workplace, fringe benefits, evaluation procedures, staggering lunch hours and work breaks, communication between workers on different shifts

WRITER'S GUIDELINES: Argument

1. Ask yourself the following questions; then consider which parts of the persuasive statement or argument you should include in your essay.

   * *Background*: What is the historical or social context for this controversial issue?
   * *Proposition* (the topic sentence of the paragraph or the thesis of the essay): What do I want my audience to believe or to do?
   * *Qualification of proposition*: Can I limit my assertion so that those who disagree cannot easily challenge me with exceptions?
   * *Refutation* (taking the opposing view into account, mainly to point out its fundamental weakness): What is the view on the other side, and why is it flawed in reasoning or evidence?
   * *Support*: In addition to sound reasoning, can I use appropriate facts, examples, statistics, and opinions of authorities?

2. The basic pattern of a paragraph or an essay of persuasion or argument is likely to be in this form:

   Proposition (the topic sentence of the paragraph or the thesis of the essay)
   I. Support 1
   II. Support 2
   III. Support 3

3. The proposal has the following parts, which can be adjusted to a particular need:

   * Background (indicating the problem or the need, emphasizing the urgency)
   * Solution to the problem, or need, stated concisely
   * Possible explanation of why other solutions are inadequate
   * In detail what you can do

- How you can do it
- When you can do it
- What it will cost
- Conclusion (emphasizing the problem and the solution)

4. Write and revise.

- Write and then revise your paragraph or essay as many times as necessary for **c**oherence, **l**anguage (usage, tone, and diction), **u**nity, **e**mphasis, **s**upport, and **s**entences (**CLUESS**).
- Read your work aloud to hear and correct any grammatical errors or awkward-sounding sentences.
- Edit any problems in fundamentals, such as **c**apitalization, **o**missions, **p**unctuation, and **s**pelling (**COPS**).

Part IV USING SOURCES

Never before have students been able to access information so easily and swiftly. In little more than a decade, libraries have broadened searches from the shuffle of card catalogs to the click of the electronic keyboard. Cyberspace and electronic databases extend everywhere. They give us more as they require more from us as critical thinkers.

For the course you are now taking, connecting with sources, good sources, is essential. Your sources may help you understand yourself by providing you with information that will give you insights and challenge your views. Across the curriculum, your sources can connect you with a deeper understanding of the variety of subjects you study. In career-related writing, you can investigate vocational fields and workplace issues.

Some of these searches will take the form of research papers or other documented written assignments, usually moving away from personal writing. This part of the book will help you generate topics, do research in various ways, organize a paper, and write it in the appropriate form.

Chapter 16

Writing the Research Paper

The Research Paper Defined

The **research paper** is a long documented essay based on a thorough examination of your topic and supported by your explanations and by both references to and quotations from your sources. The traditional research paper in the style of the Modern Language Association, typically called MLA style (**here with 2009 MLA Update**), includes a title page and an outline (if your instructor requires them), a thesis, a documented essay (text), and a list of sources (called "Works Cited," referring to the works used specifically in the essay).

This chapter presents ten steps for writing a research paper. Don't be apprehensive; if you can write an effective essay, you can write an effective research paper. Pick a feasible topic and stay on schedule. (The two main problems for students working on research papers are [1] they select topics that are too broad or too narrow and [2] they fall behind schedule.) The form for documentation is shown in Step 3. Completing a research paper using the following ten steps will give you practice in finding sources in your school library and on the Internet, and it will give you experience in writing a longer, more complicated essay. It will help you master skills so that you can communicate better.

Although specific aims and methods may vary from one research activity to another, most nonexperimental, objective research tasks depend on ten basic steps. See the following explanation and then review the student work for illustration. A partial, annotated student final draft follows this discussion.

Ten Steps to Writing a Research Paper

STEP 1 SELECT A TOPIC

Select a topic and make a scratch outline. Then construct a thesis as you did for writing an essay by choosing what you intend to write about (subject) and by deciding how you will limit or narrow your subject (focus). Your purpose will be either to inform (explain) or to persuade (argue). For persuasive issues, see General Topics on page 367.

- Your topic should interest you and be appropriate in subject and scope for your assignment.
- Your topic should be researchable through library and other relevant sources, such as the Internet. Avoid topics that are too subjective or are so new that good source material is not available.

To write a focus for your subject, you may need to scan a general discussion of your topic area so that you can consider it in perspective and begin to see the parts or aspects on which you will want to concentrate. Relevant sections of encyclopedias and comprehensive books, such as textbooks, are often useful in establishing the initial overview. At this point, the closer you can come to a well-defined topic with a functional scratch outline of its divisions, the more likely you are to make a smooth, rapid, effective journey through the process. Try to divide your thesis into its functional parts.

Student Example:

Tentative thesis: Despite some valid criticism, <u>the zoo as an institution</u> will
subject

<u>probably survive because of its roles in entertainment, education, and conservation</u>.
focus

    I. Entertainment
      A. Money
      B. Problems
   II. Education
      A. General public
      B. Students
 III. Conservation
      A. Science
      B. Breeding
 IV. Criticism
      A. Pro
      B. Con
  V. Zoos of future
      A. Education
      B. Conservation

STEP 2 FIND SOURCES

Find sources for your investigation. With your topic and its divisions in mind, use the resources and the electronic databases available in your college library and on the Internet to identify books, articles, and other materials pertaining to your topic. The list of these items, called the **bibliography**, should be prepared on cards in the form appropriate for your assignment. (MLA style is used in this text. See this book's Instructor Companion Site for other styles.) Seek different kinds of materials, different types of source information (primary, meaning coming from direct study, participation, observation, involvement; and secondary, meaning coming from indirect means—usually reporting on what others have done, observed, or been involved in), and credible writers (authorities and relatively unbiased, reliable reporters on your topic).

The main parts of the library pertaining to most research papers are the book collection and the periodical collection. Books are arranged on shelves by subject according to the Library of Congress system or the Dewey Decimal system. Periodicals, including newspapers, are stored in a variety of ways: in unbound form (very recent editions), in bound form, on microfilm, in databases, and in online computer systems.

Books

Today most academic and municipal libraries provide information about books online, with databases accessible by author, title, subject, or other key words. Usually a printout of sources is available. As with the Internet, selecting key words and their synonyms is crucial. A combination of words will help you focus your search. In the following sample printout on the topic *animal?* and *conservation*, the user has keyed in the topic and then clicked to the title to check for location and availability:

```
BOOK - Record 1 of 20 Entries Found                    Brief View
-------------------------------------------------------------------
  Title:       The atlas of endangered species
  Published:   New York : Macmillan : Toronto : Maxwell Macmillan
               Canada, 1991.
  Subjects:    Endangered species.
               Endangered plants.
               Nature conservation.
               Rare animals.
               Rare plants.
               Wildlife conservation.
               Environmental protection.
--------------------------------------------------+ Page 1 of 2 -------
Search Request:  K-ANIMAL? AND CONSERVATION MS<ENTER>-Book catalog
BOOK - Record 1 of 20 Entries Found                    Brief View
-------------------------------------------------------------------
  Title:        The atlas of endangered species
-------------------------------------------------------------------
LOCATION:                  CALL NUMBER            STATUS:
REFERENCE SHELVES          333.9516 At65          Not checked out
(Non-Circulating)
```

Printed Material Other Than Books

For the typical college research paper, the main printed nonbook sources are periodicals, such as newspapers, magazines, and journals. Various indexes will provide you with information for finding the source material you need. Depending on the library and the publication, periodicals are listed in indexes printed on paper or in electronic form. The most common index in bound volumes is the *Readers' Guide to Periodical Literature* (now also computerized). It indexes more than 200 popular magazines such as *Time* and *Newsweek*, which means it is useful for basic research but not for more scholarly studies. The *New York Times* and numerous other metropolitan newspapers are also covered by indexes. For more academic searches, check with a reference librarian for indexes in specific fields such as anthropology or art. Indexes are usually kept in one area of the reference section. The following figure shows three sample entries from the *Readers' Guide.*

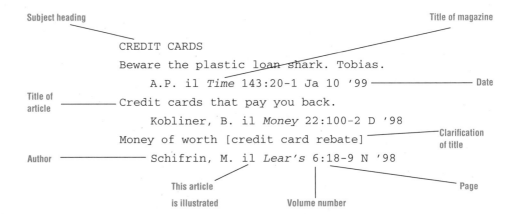

Computerized Indexes and Other Online Services

Computerized indexes, such as *InfoTrac*, *Periodical Abstracts*, and *Newspaper Abstracts Ondisc*, can be accessed in basically the same way as the online book catalogs, using key words and word combinations. They provide source information, perhaps with printouts. Some indexes include short abstracts (brief summaries) of the individual entries. Some indexes even provide the full text of material. One such index is *LexisNexis*, an online service that can help you find sources and then provide the text of the original source material, all of which can be printed out.

An online essay originally published in, say, *Time* magazine usually will be published without illustrations and in a different format. Therefore, it is important that you give full bibliographical information about your particular source (source citation instructions appear in Step 3).

Government publications, pamphlets, and other materials are cataloged in several ways. Procedures for searching all electronic indexes and sources routinely are posted alongside terminals, and librarians are available for further explanations and demonstrations. Many libraries also have pamphlets listing the periodicals they carry, their arrangements with other libraries for sharing or borrowing materials, access to the Internet, databases stored on CD-ROMs, and various online services.

Search engines, such as Google, Windows Live, and Yahoo!, will yield an abundance of material on your topic. Just key in your subject and choose among sources with discrimination. As with all sources, credibility depends on the expertise of the writer(s). You should ask the following questions: What are the qualifications of the author? What is the reputation of the publication? How reliable is the support? When was the material published?

STEP 3 LIST SOURCES

List tentative sources in a preliminary bibliography.

Bibliography and Works Cited, MLA Style (with 2009 MLA Update)

You will list source material in two phases of your research paper project: the preliminary bibliography and the Works Cited list.

The 2009 MLA Update makes only a few major style changes.

- It replaces underlining with italics.
- It uses URLs only when they are requested or needed for finding sources.
- It uses abbreviations (*N.p.* for *no publisher*, *n.d.* for *no date*, and *n. pag.* for *no page*).
- It specifies the medium of publication (e.g., Print , Web, Performance, or TV).

These changes are shown in examples in this chapter. For more obscure changes, consult the *MLA Handbook*, 7th edition, or use your search engine on your computer.

When you begin your research, make a list of works that may provide useful information on your topic. At this time, do not stop to make a careful examination and evaluation of each entry, although you should keep in mind that your material usually should come from a variety of sources and that those sources ideally should be objective, authoritative, and current. For various reasons, some sources may not find their way into your research paper at all. As you read, you may discover that some sources are superficial, poorly researched, overly technical, off the topic, or unavailable. The preliminary bibliography is nothing more than a list of sources to consider and select from.

The sources that you actually use in the paper—meaning those that you refer to by name or quote—become part of the Works Cited list at the end of the final draft. Whether you use cards, sheets of paper, or computer files, become familiar with the form you will use in writing your paper and take care in recording the detailed information you will need for documentation.

The MLA research paper form is commonly used for both the preliminary bibliography and the list of works cited. This format is unlike the formats used in catalogs and indexes. The following examples show the difference between printout forms from library files and the MLA research paper forms.

Books
Printout Form

```
Author:      DiSilvestro, Roger L.
Title:       The African elephant: twilight in Eden
Published:   New York: Wiley. ©1991.
```

MLA Research Paper Form

Titles of longer works are italicized.

DiSilvestro, Roger L. *The African Elephant: Twilight in Eden*.
New York: Wiley, 1991. Print.

Periodicals

Printout Form

Author: Ormrod, Stefan A.

Title: Boo for zoos.

Source: *New Scientist* v. 145 (Mar. 18 '95) p. 48

MLA Research Paper Form

Ormrod, Stefan A. "Boo for Zoos." *New Scientist* 18 Mar. 1995:
48. Print.

Form for Printed Sources

Books

A Book by One Author

Adeler, Thomas L. *In a New York Minute*. New York: Harper, 1990.
Print.

An Anthology or Textbook

List the name(s) of the editor(s), followed by a comma, a space, and "ed." or "eds."

Grumet, Robert S., ed. *Northeastern Indian Lives*. Amherst: U of
Massachusetts P, 1996. Print.

Two or More Books by the Same Author

Walker, Alice. *The Color Purple: A Novel*. New York: Harcourt,
1982. Print.

———. *Meridian*. New York: Harcourt, 1976. Print.

A Book by Two or Three Authors

Current, Richard Nelson, Marcia Ewing Current, and Louis Fuller.
Goddess of Light. Boston: Northeastern UP, 1997. Print.

Use et al., or you may use all names, for four or more authors.

Danziger, James N., et al. *Computers and Politics: High
Technology in American Local Governments*. New York: Columbia
UP, 1982. Print.

A Book with a Corporate Author

Detroit Commission on the Renaissance. *Toward the Future*.
Detroit: Wolverine, 1989. Print.

Articles

Article in a Journal

Butterick, George. "Charles Olson's 'The Kingfishers' and the
Poetics of Change." *American Poetry* 6.2 (1989): 28-59. Print.

Article in a Weekly or Biweekly Magazine: Author Unknown, Known

"How the Missiles Help California." *Time* 1 Apr. 1996: 45. Print.

Keizer, Garret. "How the Devil Falls in Love." *Harper's* Aug. 2002: 43–51. Print.

Article in a Newspaper: Author Unknown, Known

"A Steadfast Friend on 9/11 Is Buried." *New York Times* 6 June 2002: B8. Print.

Franklin, Deborah. "Vitamin E Fails to Deliver on Early Promise." *New York Times* 2 Aug. 2005, late ed.: F5. Print.

Article or Other Written Selection in an Anthology or Textbook

Brownmiller, Susan. "Let's Put Pornography Back in the Closet." *Take Back the Night: Women on Pornography.* Ed. Laura Lederer. New York: Morrow, 1980. 252–55. Rpt. in *Conversations: Readings for Writing.* Ed. Jack Selzer. 4th ed. New York: Allyn, 2000. 578–81. Print.

Editorial in a Newspaper or Magazine: Author Unknown, Known

Gergen, David. "A Question of Values." Editorial. *US News and World Report* 11 Feb. 2002: 72. Print.

"It's Subpoena Time." Editorial. *New York Times* 8 June 2007, late ed.: A28. Print.

A Work in an Anthology or Textbook with Readings

Booth, Wayne C. "The Scholar in Society." *Introduction to Scholarship in Modern Languages and Literatures.* Ed. Joseph Gibaldi. New York: MLA, 1981. 116–43. Print.

An Article in an Encyclopedia

Cheney, Ralph Holt. "Coffee." *Collier's Encyclopedia.* 1993 ed. Print.

Government Publications

United States. Dept. of Transportation. National Highway Traffic Safety Admin. *Driver Licensing Laws Annotated 1980.* Washington: GPO, 1980. Print.

Citations from the *Congressional Record* require only a date and page number.

Cong. Rec. 11 Sept. 2008: 12019–24. Print.

Treat particular presentations in the proceedings as you would pieces in a collection.

Wise, Mary R. "The Main Event Is Desktop Publishing." *Proceedings of the 34th Annual International Technical Communication Conference, Denver, 10–13 May 1987.* San Diego: Univet, 1987. Print.

A Lecture, a Speech, or an Address

Kern, David. "Recent Trends in Occupational Medicine." AMA Convention. Memorial Hospital, Pawtucket, RI. 2 Oct. 1997. Address.

A Personal Interview

```
Thomas, Carolyn. Personal interview. 5 Jan. 2009.
```

Films, Filmstrips, Slide Programs, and Videotapes

```
It's a Wonderful Life. Dir. Frank Capra. Perf. James Stewart, Donna
    Reed, Lionel Barrymore, and Thomas Mitchell. RKO, 1946. DVD.
```

Form for Electronic Sources

Formats vary widely in electronic media because of rapidly changing systems and terms. The information you provide in your bibliography and works cited will inform your reader about such matters as the subject of each source, who has worked on it, where it came from originally, when it was first written and last changed, when you found it, where you found it, and how you found it. Be sure that you give enough information. If you cannot find directions for citing a source, you should identify a form used for similar content as a model, improvise if necessary, and be as consistent as possible. Usually the URL is unnecessary.

Do not be intimidated by the length and seeming complexity of the citations. Every part is reasonable and every part is necessary. If you are not certain whether to include some information, you probably should. As you present an orderly sequence of parts in your entries, you must take great care in attending to detail, for a single keystroke can leave your source concealed in cyberspace with no electronic map for your reader.

The examples in this section follow MLA style from the 2009 MLA Update. More details can be found at *www.mla.org*. Because the nature of electronic sources and references to them are constantly evolving, if you must include a URL, check each website for changes and updates.

This is the basic form for Internet and World Wide Web sources for your bibliography and Works Cited entries:

- Author's [editor's, compiler's, translator's, director's, narrator's, performer's] last name, first name, middle initial
- "Title of article or other short work" or *Title of Book*
- Title of the overall website
- Version or edition used
- Publisher or sponsor of the site
- Publication date
- Medium of publication
- Date of access to the source

Online Services—Library and Personal

Library Subscription Services (database with full texts)

Online library subscription services provide databases mainly of articles in journals, magazines, and newspapers. They are accessed either at a library terminal or by the student's computer. They often include hundreds of publications and enable students to find and print out entire texts rapidly. Although most have complete printed versions, the illustrations are usually omitted, page numbers are changed or not given, and some material may be reformatted. For brief documented papers, instructors sometimes ask their students to include copies of the printouts with the final submission. Content ranges from works intended for the general reader to those written for scholarly purposes. Some are listed as "juried," which means that the selections have been evaluated for credible content by a group of experts in the field. Library online services include ProQuest Direct, LexisNexis, and EBSCOhost.

The basic form for citing sources is author, title, publication information, service company, library, medium of publication, and date of access. Include the URL of the service in angle brackets if the reader needs it to find the source.

Here are three examples. See page 382 for others.

> Meyer, Greg. "Answering Questions about the West Nile Virus." *Dayton Daily News* 11 July 2002: Z3-7. *LexisNexis*. Web. 17 Feb. 2003.
>
> Folks, Jeffrey J. "Crowd and Self: William Faulkner's Sources of Agency in *The Sound and the Fury*." *Southern Literary Journal* 34.2 (2002): 30+. *EBSCO*. Web. 6 June 2003.
>
> Taylor, Steven J. "Caught in the Continuum: A Critical Analysis of the Principle of the Least Restrictive Environment." *Research and Practice for Persons with Severe Disabilities* 29.4 (2004): 218-30. *ERIC*. Web. 3 Mar. 2009.

Personal Subscription Services (databases with full texts supplied by companies such as AOL)

Typically indicate author, title, publication information (if any), name of service, medium of publication, date of access, and the *Keyword* you used or the *Path* (sequence of topics) you followed in locating the source.

> "Cloning." *BioTech's Life and Science Dictionary*. 30 June 1998. Indiana U. *America Online*. 4 July 1998. Path: Research and Learning; Science; Biology; Biotechnology Dictionary.
>
> "Tecumseh." *Compton's Encyclopedia Online*. Vers. 3.0. 1998. *America Online*. Web. 8 Apr. 2000. Keyword: Compton's.

Professional Site

> *The Purdue OWL Family of Sites*. The Writing Lab and OWL, at Purdue and Purdue U, 2008. Web. 9 Sept. 2009.

Personal Site

> Gladwell, Malcolm. Home page. N.p., 8 Mar. 2005. Web. 2 Mar. 2009.

Web Log (blog)

> Cuthbertson, Peter. "Are Left and Right Still Alright?" *Conservative Commentary*. N.p., 7 Feb. 2005. Web. 18 Feb. 2005.

Book Online

> Douglass, Frederick. *My Bondage and My Freedom*. Boston, 1855. *Google Book Search*. Web. 8 June 2005.

Poem Online

> Hampl, Patricia. "Who We Will Love." *Woman Before an Aquarium*. Pittsburgh: U of Pittsburgh P, 1978: 27-28. *A Poem a Week*. Rice University. Web. 13 Mar. 1998.

Article in a Journal Online

DeKoven, Marianne. "Utopias Limited: Post-Sixties and Postmodern
American Fiction." *Modern Fiction Studies* 41.1 (1995): 75–97.
Web. 20 Jan. 2005.

Article in a Magazine Online

Keillor, Garrison. "Why Did They Ever Ban a Book This Bad?"
Salon.com. Salon Media Group, 13 Oct. 1997. Web. 14 Oct.
1997.

Article in a Newspaper Online

"Tornadoes Touch Down in S. Illinois." *New York Times*. New York
Times, 16 Apr. 1998. Web. 20 May 1998.

Newspaper Editorial Online

"The Proved and the Unproved." Editorial. *New York Times*. New York
Times, 13 July 1997. Web. 13 July 1997.

Review Online

Ebert, Roger. Rev. of *Star Wars: Episode I—The Phantom Menace*,
dir. George Lucas. *Chicago Sun-Times*. Digital Chicago,
8 June 2000. Web. 22 June 2000.

Government Publication Online

Cite an online government publication as you would cite a print version; end with
the information required for an electronic source.

United States. Dept. of Justice. Office of Justice Programs.
*Violence against Women: Estimates from the Redesigned National
Crime Victimization Survey*. By Ronet Bachman and Linda E.
Saltzman. Aug. 1995. *Bureau of Justice Statistics*. Web.
10 Jan. 2008.

Newspaper Article in a Library Database

Weeks, Linton. "History Repeating Itself; Instead of Describing
Our Country's Past, Two Famous Scholars Find Themselves Exam-
ing Their Own." *Washington Post* 24 Mar. 2002: N. pag. *Lexis-
Nexis*. Web. 3 Aug. 2005.

Journal or Magazine Articles in a Library Database

Fabel, Robin F. A. "The Other War of 1812: The Patriot War and
the American Invasion of Spanish East Florida." *Alabama Review*
57.4 (2004): 291–92. *ProQuest*. Web. 8 Mar. 2005.
Priest, Ann-Marie. "Between Being and Nothingness: The 'Aston-
ishing Precipice' of Virginia Woolf's *Night and Day*." *Journal
of Modern Literature* 26.2 (2002–03): 66–80. *InfoTrac*. Web. 12
Jan. 2004.
Suggs, Welch. "A Hard Year in College Sports." *Chronicle of Higher
Education* 19 Dec. 2003: 37. *LexisNexis*. Web. 17 July 2004.

An Article in an Encyclopedia

Include the article's title, the title of the database (italicized), the version number (if available), the sponsor, the date of electronic publication, the publication medium, and the date of access.

> "Hawthorne, Nathaniel." *Encyclopaedia Britannica Online.*
> Encyclopaedia Britannica, 2008. Web. 16 May 2008.

Personal E-Mail Message

> Watkins, Jack. "Collaborative Projects." Message to Gabriel
> Mendoza. 12 Apr. 2009. E-mail.

EXERCISE 1   Form for Bibliography and Works Cited

Change the following items from printouts to MLA research paper form.

1. A Book by One Author
   Printout Form
   Author: Colin Tudge
   Title: Last Animals at the Zoo: How Mass Extinction Can Be Stopped
   Publisher: Hutchinson Radius
   Place of Publication: London
   Date of Publication (or Copyright): 1991

   MLA Research Paper Form

2. A Work in an Anthology (May Be a Textbook)
   Printout Form
   Author of Work (Essay): Adam Goodheart
   Title of Essay: How to Paint a Fresco
   Title of Anthology: From Self to Sources: Essays and Documented Essays
   Editor of Anthology: Lee Brandon
   Publisher: Houghton Mifflin Company
   Place of Publication: Boston
   Date of Publication (or Copyright): 2003
   Page Numbers of Work (Essay): 262–264

   MLA Research Paper Form

3. Article in a Weekly or Biweekly Magazine
   Printout Form
   Author: Betsy Carpenter
   Title of Article: Upsetting the Ark
   Title of Magazine: U.S. News & World Report
   Date of Publication: August 24, 1992
   Page Numbers of Article: 57–61

MLA Research Paper Form

4. Newspaper Article
Printout Form
  Author of Article: Malcolm W. Browne
  Title of Article: They're Back! Komodos Avoid Extinction
  Title of Newspaper: New York Times
  Date of Publication: March 1, 1994
  Page Numbers of Article: C1 and C4

· *MLA Research Paper Form*

STEP 4   TAKE NOTES

Take notes in an organized fashion. Resist the temptation to record everything that interests you. Instead, take notes that pertain to divisions of your topic as stated in your thesis or scratch outline. Locate, read, and take notes on the sources listed in your preliminary bibliography. Some of these sources need to be printed out from electronic databases or from the Internet, some photocopied, and some checked out. Your notes will usually be on cards, or on your computer, with each notation indicating key pieces of the information:

A. Division of topic (usually the Roman-numeral part of your scratch outline or the divisions of your thesis)

B. Identification of topic (by author's last name or title of piece)

C. Location of material (usually by page number)

D. Text of statement as originally worded (with quotation marks; editorial comments in brackets), summarized or paraphrased (in student's own words, without quotation marks), and statement of relevance of material, if possible

Student Example of Organization on a Card:

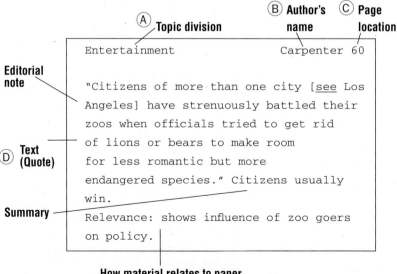

EXERCISE 2   Completing Note Cards

Transfer the following information to the incomplete note card at the end of this exercise.

1. Quotation:

   "The lucky or well-born find homes at accredited zoos, but many are put to death or sold to game ranges, roadside menageries, amusement parks or circuses."

2. Author: Betsy Carpenter

3. Title: "Upsetting the Ark" (the only selection by Carpenter in this paper)

4. Location: p. 59

5. Division of Topic (how it relates to thesis): No easy solution to problem

---

STEP 5   REFINE YOUR THESIS AND OUTLINE

Refine your thesis statement and outline to reflect more precisely what you intend to write.

Student Example:

Thesis: Throughout the world, despite determined opposition, the modern zoo with a new image and compound purpose is taking shape.

   I. Zoos as entertainment
      A. Attendance
      B. Income
      C. Customer preferences
  II. Captive breeding success
      A. National
      B. International
 III. Scientific success
      A. Embryo transfers
      B. Artificial insemination
      C. Test-tube fertilization
      D. Storage of eggs, sperm, and tissue
      E. Computer projects
         1. Lab studies
         2. Animal tracking

IV. Education
    A. Purpose—change attitude
    B. Basic idea—show animals in ecosystem
    C. School applications
V. Different models of zoos
    A. Zoo/park
    B. Safari park
    C. Regional zoo

STEP 6   WRITE YOUR FIRST DRAFT

Referring to your thesis, outline, and note cards keyed to your outline, write the first draft of your research paper. Use the following guidelines to include proper MLA research paper form in documentation.

Plagiarism

Careful attention to the rules of documentation will help you avoid **plagiarism**, the unacknowledged use of someone else's words or ideas. It occurs when a writer omits quotation marks when citing the exact language of a source, fails to revise completely a paraphrased source, or gives no documentation for a quotation or paraphrase. The best way to avoid this problem is to be attentive to the following details.

When you copy a quotation directly into your notes, check to be sure that you have put quotation marks around it. If you forget to include them when you copy, you might omit them in the paper as well.

When you paraphrase, keep in mind that it is not sufficient to change just a few words or rearrange sentence structure. You must completely rewrite the passage. One of the best ways to accomplish this is to read the material you want to paraphrase; then cover the page so that you cannot see it and write down the information as you remember it. Compare your version with the original and make any necessary changes on the note card. If you cannot successfully rewrite the passage, quote it, or part(s) of it, instead.

The difference between legitimate and unacceptable paraphrases can be seen in the following examples:

> **Source:** "What is unmistakably convincing and makes Miller's theatre writing hold is its authenticity in respect to the minutiae of American life. He is a first-rate reporter: he makes the details of his observation palpable."

> **Unacceptable Paraphrase:** What is truly convincing and makes Arthur Miller's theatrical writing effective is its authenticity. He is an excellent reporter and makes his observation palpable.

> **Legitimate Paraphrase:** The strength of Arthur Miller's dramatic art lies in its faithfulness to the details of the American scene and in its power to bring to life the reality of ordinary experience.

The differences between the two paraphrased versions are enormous. The first writer has made some token changes, substituting a few synonyms (*truly* for *unmistakably*, *excellent* for *first-rate*), deleting part of the first sentence, and combining the two parts of the second sentence into a single clause. Otherwise, this is a word-for-word copy of the original, and if the note were copied into the paper in this form, the writer would be guilty of plagiarism. The second writer has changed the vocabulary of the original passage and completely restructured the sentence so that the only similarity between the note and the source is the ideas.

Check to see that each of your research notes has the correct name and page number so that when you use information from that note in your paper, you will be able to credit it to the right source.

Documentation: Parenthetical References, MLA Style

Although you need not acknowledge a source for generally known information such as the dates of the Civil War or the names of the ships that carried Columbus and his followers to the New World, you must identify the exact source and location of each statement, fact, or original idea you borrow from another person or work.

In the text of the research paper, MLA style requires only a brief parenthetical source reference keyed to a complete bibliographical entry in the list of works cited at the end of the paper. For most parenthetical references, you will need to cite only the author's last name and the number of the page from which the statement or idea was taken, and, if you mention the author's name in the text, the page number alone is sufficient. This format also allows you to include within the parentheses additional information, such as title or volume number, if it is needed for clarity. Documentation for some of the most common types of sources is discussed in the following sections.

References to Articles and Single-Volume Books

Articles and single-volume books are the two most common types of works you will be referring to most often in your research paper. When citing them, either mention the author's name in the text and note the appropriate page number in parentheses immediately after the citation or acknowledge both name and page number in the parenthetical reference, leaving a space between the two. If punctuation is needed, insert the mark outside the final parenthesis.

> **Author's Name Cited in Text:** Marya Mannes has defined *euthanasia* as "the chosen alternative to the prolongation of a steadily waning mind and spirit by machines that will withhold death or to an existence that mocks life" (61).

> **Author's Name Cited in Parentheses:** *Euthanasia* has been defined as "the chosen alternative to the prolongation of a steadily waning mind and spirit by machines that will withhold death or to an existence that mocks life" (Mannes 61).

> **Corresponding Works Cited Entry:** Mannes, Marya. *Last Rights*. New York: Morrow, 1973. Print.

References to Works in an Anthology

When referring to a work in an anthology, either cite in the text the author's name and indicate in parentheses the page number in the anthology where the source is located, or acknowledge both name and page reference parenthetically.

> **Author's Name Cited in Text:** One of the most widely recognized facts about James Joyce, in Lionel Trilling's view, is "his ambivalence toward Ireland, of which the hatred was as relentless as the love was unfailing" (153).

Author's Name Cited in Parentheses: One of the most widely recognized facts about James Joyce is "his ambivalence toward Ireland, of which the hatred was as relentless as the love was unfailing" (Trilling 153).

Corresponding Works Cited Entry: Trilling, Lionel. "James Joyce in His Letters." *Joyce: A Collection of Critical Essays*. Ed. William M. Chace. Englewood Cliffs: Prentice-Hall, 1974. 151–59. Print.

References to Works of Unknown Authorship

If you borrow information or ideas from an article or a book for which you cannot determine the name of the author, cite the title instead, either in the text of the paper or in parentheses, and include the page reference as well.

Title Cited in Text: According to an article titled "Going Back to Booze," surveys have shown that most adult alcoholics began drinking heavily as teenagers (42).

Title Cited in Parentheses: Surveys have shown that most adult alcoholics began drinking heavily as teenagers ("Going Back to Booze" 42).

Corresponding Work Cited Entry: "Going Back to Booze." *Time* 30 Nov. 1999: 41–46. Print.

References to Internet Material

Treat Internet material as you would other material. If the author's name is not available, give the title. Consider using page and paragraph numbers if they are available; usually they are not.

References in Block Quotations

Quotations longer than four typewritten lines are indented ten spaces or one-half inch without quotation marks, and their references are placed outside end punctuation.

Reference Cited After End Punctuation: Implicit in the concept of Strange Loops is the concept of infinity, since what else is a loop but a way of representing an endless process in a finite way? And infinity plays a large role in many of Escher's drawings. Copies of one single theme often fit into each other, forming visual analogues to the canons of Bach. (Hofstadter 15)

Corresponding Works Cited Entry: Hofstadter, Douglas. *Gödel, Escher, Bach: An Eternal Golden Braid*. New York: Vintage, 1980. Print.

EXERCISE 3   Giving Credit to Sources

Complete the parenthetical references and punctuation according to MLA style.

1. Quotation, taken from page 60 of the source, is introduced with the author's name (with only one source by this author in this paper).

   Schmidt reports that the Cincinnati Zoo Center for Reproduction of Endangered Wildlife has frozen "eggs from a rare female Sumatran rhino that died, hoping one day to obtain some sperm and learn how to make test-tube rhino embryos" ___.

2. Paraphrased information by James Rainey from an Internet source with no page numbers given (with only one source by this author in this paper).

   The Los Angeles Zoo faced similar opposition in 1994 when directors proposed a multimillion-dollar expansion of the education program rather than spending that money on facilities for animals popular with zoo-goers _____.

3. Quotation, from page 52 of the source, is introduced with the author's name. One other source by the same author is used in this paper. The title of this source is "Captive Audiences for Future Conservation."

   As Tudge points out, "Captive breeding is not an alternative to habitat protection. Increasingly, however, it is a vital backup" _____ _____.

STEP 7   REVISE YOUR FIRST DRAFT

Evaluate your first draft and amend it as needed (perhaps researching an area not well covered for additional support material and adding or deleting sections of your outline to reflect the way your paper has grown).

Use the writing process guidelines as you would in writing any other essay:

- Write and then revise your paper as many times as necessary for **c**oherence, **l**anguage (usage, tone, and diction), **u**nity, **e**mphasis, **s**upport, and **s**entences (**CLUESS**).
- Correct problems in fundamentals such as **c**apitalization, **o**missions, **p**unctuation, and **s**pelling (**COPS**). Before writing the final draft, read your paper aloud to discover any errors or awkward-sounding sentence structure.

STEP 8   PREPARE YOUR WORKS CITED SECTION

Using the same form as in the preliminary bibliography, prepare a Works Cited section (a list of works you have referred to or quoted and identified parenthetically in the text).

STEP 9   WRITE YOUR FINAL DRAFT

Write the final version of your research paper with care for effective writing and accurate documentation. The final draft will probably include the following parts:

1. Title page (sometimes omitted)

2. Thesis and outline (topical or sentence, as directed)

3. Documented essay (text)

4. List of sources used (Works Cited)

STEP 10   SUBMIT REQUIRED MATERIALS

Submit your research paper with any preliminary material required by your instructor. Consider using a checklist to make sure you have fulfilled all requirements. A comprehensive checklist might look like this:

Research Paper Checklist

❏ Title page (sometimes omitted, especially if the outline is not required)
❏ Thesis and outline
❏ Documented essay (text)
_____ Approximate total number of words
_____ Approximate number of words quoted (Usually, more than 20 percent quoted words would be excessive.)
❏ List of sources used (Works Cited)
_____ Number of sources used
❏ Preliminary materials, such as preliminary bibliography, note cards, and rough draft, as required
❏ Double-spaced text, one-inch margins

Student Essay

The following material is an excerpt from a ten-page research paper by Michael Chung. Other parts of his assignment were shown in the ten-step approach in the previous pages. The material here includes a title page (which your instructor may not require), a full outline, the introduction, a sampling of body material, the conclusion, and a Works Cited section. The material is annotated to indicate form and technique in a well-written research paper.

Title page is optional; check with your instructor.

ZOOS—AN ENDANGERED SPECIES?

Michael Chung

Professor Lee Brandon

English 1A
8 January 2009

Double-space throughout (thesis and outline section is optional; check with your instructor).

Heading for all pages starting on the second page of the paper: last name, one space, page number (small Roman numerals for outline pages, Arabic for paper)

Align entries in columns

Chung ii

Thesis statement: Throughout the world, despite determined opposition, the modern zoo with a new image and compound purpose is taking shape.

I.   Zoos as entertainment
   A.   Attendance
   B.   Income
   C.   Customer preferences
      1.   Favoring certain animals
      2.   Favoring animals over education
II.   Pandas for profit
   A.   Criticism
   B.   Benefits
      1.   Money for zoo conservation projects
      2.   Money back to natural habitat
III.   Captive breeding success
   A.   National
   B.   International
IV.   Scientific success
   A.   Embryo transfers
   B.   Artificial insemination
   C.   Test-tube fertilization
   D.   Storage of eggs, sperm, and tissue
      1.   For use shortly
      2.   Awaiting future development
   E.   Computer projects
      1.   Lab studies
      2.   Animal tracking in field

Chung iii

V. Education
  A. Purpose--change attitude
  B. Basic idea--show animals in ecosystem
  C. School applications
    1. Field trips
    2. Sleepovers
    3. Entire high school education in zoo
VI. Different models of zoos
  A. Zoo/Park
  B. Safari park
  C. Regional zoo
VII. Humane treatment of animals
  A. Problems without easy solution
    1. Unruly animals
    2. Animals with diseases
    3. Surplus animals
  B. Problems and solutions
    1. Providing better living areas
    2. Engaging animals in nature activities
VIII. Response to critics
  A. Acknowledging contributions
  B. Pointing out flaws
    1. Zoos and support for wildlife linked
    2. Much habitat destruction inevitable and irreversible

Chung 1

½" from top

1" from top
Information here only
if you do not use a title page

Michael Chung
Professor Lee Brandon
English 1A
8 January 2009

[Introduction]

Title

Zoos—An Endangered Species?

Uses historical perspective for
introduction

Early zoos were usually little more than crude holding
pens where animals, often serving dually with circuses,
died off and were replaced by a seemingly unlimited supply
from the wilds. In the first seven decades of the twentieth
century, zoos became institutions that offered some education,
a little conservation of species, and mostly entertainment.
Meanwhile, many vocal critics emerged, arguing for animal
rights and questioning the effectiveness and appropriateness
of zoo programs. They brought into focus the question, Are

Basic thesis idea as question

zoos necessary?

[Excerpt from body]

In addition to the entertainment aspect of zoos is the captive
breeding program. In one spectacular captive breeding success,
the National Zoo in Washington, D.C., may have saved the
endangered Komodo dragon from extinction by successfully

Statistics

incubating thirty eggs. This ten-foot, dangerous, ugly creature

Chung 2

that resembles a dinosaur numbers only somewhere around 5,000–8,000 in the wild but soon will be represented in numerous zoos (Browne C1). Now that the incubation process is in place, the entire program offers an opportunity to restock the Komodo's habitat in Indonesia.

Not all captive breeding projects can end with a reintroduction of the species to the wild. For those species, the zoos have turned to science, which has been used in a variety of ways. In "Preserving the Genetic Legacies," Karen F. Schmidt says:

> Zoos are increasingly adapting the latest in human and agricultural reproductive technologies to aid beleaguered species by boosting their numbers, increasing gene variety in small populations and controlling inbreeding. . . . Although still in the early stages, embryo transfers, artificial insemination and even test-tube fertilization are seen by zoologists as having real or potential application in conserving endangered wildlife. (60)

These scientific activities began in the 1970s and now some of them are commonplace. Female apes are on the pill and surrogate mother tigers are receiving embryos. Schmidt reports that the Cincinnati Zoo Center for Reproduction of Endangered Wildlife has frozen "eggs from a rare female Sumatran rhino that died, hoping one day to obtain some sperm and learn how to make test-tube rhino embryos" (60). In many zoos, eggs, sperm, and skin for DNA storage have been frozen in zoo labs, awaiting scientific development by future generations.

Paraphrased material
Citation

Quotation introduced with title and author's name
Block-indented quotation, no quotation marks

Words omitted (ellipses)

Citation after period for long quotation

Reference introduced with author's name
Blended paraphrase and quotation
Citation after quotation marks for short quotation

Chung 3

[Conclusion]

The zoo of the future will almost surely be a projection of the contemporary model, one that teaches, conserves, explores, experiments, and entertains. Captive breeding cannot save thousands of creatures facing extinction but, as Tudge points out, "Captive breeding is not an alternative to habitat protection. Increasingly, however, it is a vital backup" ("Captive Audiences for Future Conservation" 51). Of course, the whole zoo operation must be monitored by those who know, appreciate, and understand animals. Nevertheless, zoos have demonstrated their value, and they have the potential to continue with their benefits.

Works Cited

Browne, Malcolm W. "They're Back! Komodos Avoid Extinction." *New York Times* 1 Mar. 1994: C1, C4. Print.

Carpenter, Betsy. "Upsetting the Ark." *U.S. News & World Report* 24 Aug. 1992: 57–61. Print.

Cohn, Jeffrey. "Decisions at the Zoo." *Bioscience* Oct. 1992: 654–60. Print.

---. "The New Breeding Ground." *National Parks* Jan./Feb. 1997: 20–26. Print.

Diamond, Jared. "Playing God at the Zoo." *Discover* Mar. 1995: 78–86. Print.

Douglas-Hamilton, Ian and Oria. *Battle for the Elephants.* New York: Viking, 2002. Print.

Citation, author with two cited sources

Ends with emphasis on thesis

Chung 4

Fravel, Laura. "Critics Question Zoo's Commitment to
    Conservation." *National Geographic News*. Web. 13 Nov.
    2003.

"Not Endangered." *The Economist* 13 Apr. 1991: 55–56. Print.

"Project Technology." *Malaysian Elephant Satellite Tracking
    Project*. Web. 27 Apr. 1997.

Rainey, James. "Dogfight at the Zoo." *Los Angeles Times* 30
    Jan. 1994: C1, C4. Web. 29 Apr. 1997.

Schmidt, Karen F. "Preserving the Genetic Legacies." *U.S.
    News & World Report* 24 Aug. 1992: 60. Print.

Tarpy, Cliff. "New Zoos." *National Geographic* July 1993:
    6–37. Print.

Tudge, Colin. "Captive Audiences for Future Conservation."
    New Scientist 28 Jan. 1995: 51. Print.

---. *Last Animals at the Zoo: How Mass Extinction Can Be
    Stopped*. London: Hutchinson Radius, 1991. Print.

WRITER'S GUIDELINES: The Research Paper

1. The research paper is a long documented essay based on a thorough examination of a topic and supported by explanations and by both references to and quotations from sources.

2. The research paper is no more difficult than other writing assignments if you select a good topic, use a systematic approach, and do not get behind with your work.

3. A systematic approach involves these ten steps:

- Select a topic.
- Find sources.
- List sources.
- Take notes.
- Refine your thesis and outline.
- Write your first draft.
- Revise your first draft.
- Prepare your Works Cited section.
- Write your final draft.
- Submit required materials.

4. Your library almost certainly mixes traditional and electronic indexes and sources; you should become familiar with them.

5. MLA style for works cited differs from that used in traditional and electronic indexes.

6. You can avoid plagiarism by giving credit when you borrow someone else's words or ideas.

7. Use the writing process.

- Write and then revise your work as many times as necessary for **c**oherence, **l**anguage (usage, tone, and diction), **u**nity, **e**mphasis, **s**upport, and **s**entences (**CLUESS**).
- Read your work aloud to hear and correct any grammatical errors or awkward-sounding sentences.
- Edit any problems in fundamentals, such as **c**apitalization, **o**missions, **p**unctuation, and **s**pelling (**COPS**).

Part V

HANDBOOK

*In your personal, reading-based cross-curricular, and career-related writing, almost all of your work will be in sentences. This part of your textbook will help you write correctly and effectively, enabling you to say what you want to say and even enhancing the flow of your message. Within the writing process, this handbook pertains especially to the "S" (**s**entences) part of **CLUESS** and all parts (**c**apitalization, **o**missions, **p**unctuation, and **s**pelling) of **COPS**.*

Chapter 17

Handbook
Writing Effective Sentences

Parts of Speech

To classify a word as a part of speech, we observe two simple principles:

- The word must be in the context of communication, usually in a sentence.
- We must be able to identify the word with others that have similar characteristics—the eight parts of speech: nouns, pronouns, adjectives, verbs, adverbs, prepositions, conjunctions, or interjections.

The first principle is important because some words can be any of several parts of speech. The word *round*, for example, can function as five:

1. I watched the potter *round* the block of clay. [verb]

2. I saw her go *round* the corner. [preposition]

3. She has a *round* head. [adjective]

4. The astronauts watched the world go *round*. [adverb]

5. The champ knocked him out in one *round*. [noun]

NOUNS

- **Nouns** are naming words. Nouns may name persons, animals, plants, places, things, substances, qualities, or ideas—for example, *Bart, armadillo, Mayberry, tree, rock, cloud, love, ghost, music, virtue*.
- Nouns are often pointed out by noun indicators. These noun indicators—*the, a, an*—signal that a noun is ahead, although there may be words between the indicator and the noun itself.

the slime	*a* werewolf	*an* aardvark
the green slime	*a* hungry werewolf	*an* angry aardvark

PRONOUNS

A **pronoun** is a word that is used in place of a noun.

- Some pronouns may represent specific persons or things:

I	she	they	you
me	her	them	yourself
myself	herself	themselves	yourselves
it	he	we	who
itself	him	us	whom
that	himself	ourselves	

- Indefinite pronouns refer to nouns (persons, places, things) in a general way:

each	everyone	nobody	somebody

- Other pronouns point out particular things:

Singular	**Plural**
this, *that*	*these*, *those*
This is my treasure.	*These* are my jewels.
That is your junk.	*Those* are your trinkets.

- Still other pronouns introduce questions.

  Which is the best CD player?

  What are the main ingredients of a Twinkie?

VERBS

Verbs show action or express being in relation to the subject of a sentence. They customarily occur in set positions in sentences.

- **Action verbs** are usually easy to identify.

  > The aardvark *ate* the crisp, tasty ants. [action verb]
  > The aardvark *washed* them down with a snoutful of water. [action verb]

- The **being** verbs are few in number and are also easy to identify. The most common *being* verbs are *is*, *was*, *were*, *are*, and *am*.

  > Gilligan *is* on an island in the South Pacific. [*being* verb]
  > I *am* his enthusiastic fan. [*being* verb]

- The form of a verb expresses its tense, that is, the time of the action or being. The time may be in the present or past.

  > Roseanne *sings* "The Star-Spangled Banner." [present]
  > Roseanne *sang* "The Star-Spangled Banner." [past]

- One or more **helping verbs** may be used with the main verb to form other tenses. The combination is called a *verb phrase*.

  > She *had sung* the song many times in the shower. [Helping verb and main verb indicate a time in the past.]
  > She *will be singing* the song no more in San Diego. [Helping verbs and main verb indicate a time in the future.]

- Some helping verbs can be used alone as main verbs: *has*, *have*, *had*, *is*, *was*, *were*, *are*, *am*. Certain other helping verbs function only as helpers: *will*, *shall*, *should*, *could*.

  The most common position for the verb is directly after the subject or after the subject and its modifiers.

  > At high noon only two men [subject] *were* on Main Street.
  > The man with the faster draw [subject and modifiers] *walked* away alone.

ADJECTIVES

Adjectives modify nouns and pronouns. Most adjectives answer the questions *What kind? Which one?* and *How many?*

- Adjectives answering the *What kind?* question are descriptive. They tell the quality, kind, or condition of the nouns or pronouns they modify.

red convertible	*dirty* fork
noisy muffler	*wild* roses
The rain is *gentle*.	Bob was *tired*.

- Adjectives answering the *Which one?* question narrow or restrict the meaning of a noun. Some of these are pronouns that become adjectives by function.

my money	*our* ideas	the *other* house
this reason	*these* apples	

- Adjectives answering the *How many?* question are, of course, numbering words.

some people	*each* pet	*few* goals
three dollars	*one* glove	

- The words *a*, *an*, and *the* are adjectives called *articles*. As "noun indicators," they point out persons, places, and things.

ADVERBS

Adverbs modify verbs, adjectives, and other adverbs. Adverbs answer the questions *How? Where? When?* and *To what degree?*

Modifying Verbs: They <u>did</u> their work <u>quickly</u>.
                                    v   adv

Modifying Adjectives: They were <u>somewhat</u> <u>happy</u>.
                                             adv   adj

- Adverbs that answer the *How?* question are concerned with manner or way.

  She ate the snails *hungrily*.
  He snored *noisily*.

- Adverbs that answer the *Where?* question show location.

  They drove *downtown*.
  He stayed *behind*.
  She climbed *upstairs*.

- Adverbs that answer the *When?* question indicate time.

  The ship sailed *yesterday*.
  I expect an answer *soon*.

- Adverbs that answer the *To what degree?* question express extent.

  She is *entirely* correct.
  He was *somewhat* annoyed.

Most words ending in *-ly* are adverbs.

  He completed the task *skillfully*. [adverb]
  She answered him *courteously*. [adverb]

However, there are a few exceptions.

  The house provided a *lovely* view of the valley. [adjective]
  Your goblin mask is *ugly*. [adjective]

PREPOSITIONS

A **preposition** is a word or group of words that functions as a connective. The preposition connects its object(s) to some other word(s) in the sentence. A preposition and its object(s)—usually a noun or pronoun—with modifiers make up a **prepositional phrase**, which will function as an adjective or adverb.

  Bart worked <u>against</u> great <u>odds</u>.
                     prep   object
                   └─────────────────────┘
                     prepositional phrase

Everyone <u>in</u> his <u>household</u> cheered his effort.
prep   object
prepositional phrase

A storm is forming <u>on</u> the <u>horizon</u>.
prep   object
prepositional phrase modifying the verb phrase *is forming*
adverb

Some of the most common prepositions are the following:

about	before	but	into	past
above	behind	by	like	to
across	below	despite	near	toward
after	beneath	down	of	under
against	beside	for	off	until
among	between	from	on	upon
around	beyond	in	over	with

Some prepositions are composed of more than one word and are made from other parts of speech:

according to	as far as	because of	in spite of
ahead of	as well as	in back of	instead of
along with	aside from	in front of	together with

Caution: Do not confuse adverbs with prepositions.

I went *across* slowly. [without an object—adverb]

I went *across* the field. [with an object—preposition]

We walked *behind* silently. [without an object—adverb]

We walked *behind* the mall. [with an object—preposition]

CONJUNCTIONS

A **conjunction** connects and shows a relationship between words, phrases, or clauses. A phrase is two or more words acting as a part of speech. A clause is a group of words with a subject and a verb. An independent clause can stand by itself: *She plays bass guitar.* A dependent clause cannot stand by itself: *when she plays bass guitar.*

There are two kinds of conjunctions: coordinating and subordinating.

Coordinating conjunctions connect words, phrases, and clauses of equal rank: noun with noun, adjective with adjective, verb with verb, phrase with phrase, main clause with main clause, and subordinate clause with subordinate clause. The seven common coordinating conjunctions are *for, and, nor, but, or, yet,* and *so.* (An easy way to remember them is to think of the acronyn FANBOYS, which is made up of the first letter of each conjunction.)

Two Nouns: Bring a <u>pencil</u> <u>and</u> some <u>paper</u>.
noun   conj   noun

Two Phrases: Did she go <u>to the store</u> <u>or</u> <u>to the game?</u>
prep phrase   conj   prep phrase

Paired conjunctions such as *either/or*, *neither/nor*, or *both/and* are usually classed as coordinating conjunctions.

<u>Neither</u> the coach <u>nor</u> the manager was at fault.
conj   conj

Subordinating conjunctions connect dependent clauses with main clauses. The most common subordinating conjunctions include the following:

after	because	provided	whenever
although	before	since	where
as	but that	so that	whereas
as if	if	till	wherever
as long as	in order that	until	
as soon as	notwithstanding	when	

Sometimes the dependent clause comes *before* the main clause, where it is set off by a comma.

<u>Although</u> <u>she</u> <u>was</u> in pain, she stayed in the game.
conj   subj   v
|_____|
dependent clause

Sometimes the dependent clause comes *after* the main clause, where it usually is *not* set off by a comma.

She stayed in the game <u>because</u> <u>she</u> <u>was needed</u>.
conj   subj   v
|_____|
dependent clause

Caution: Certain words can function as either conjunctions or prepositions. It is necessary to look ahead to see if the word introduces a clause with a subject and verb—conjunction function—or takes an object—preposition function. Some of the words with two functions are these: *after, for, since, until*.

After the concert was over, we went home. [clause follows—conjunction]
After the concert, we went home. [object follows—preposition]

INTERJECTIONS

An **interjection** conveys strong emotion or surprise. When an interjection appears alone, it is usually punctuated with an exclamation mark.

Awesome!   Curses!   Cowabunga!   Yaba dabba doo!

When it appears as part of a sentence, an interjection is usually followed by a comma.

Oh, I did not consider that problem.

The interjection may sound exciting, but it is seldom appropriate for college writing.

EXERCISE 1   Identifying Parts of Speech

Identify the part of speech of each italicized word or group of words by placing the appropriate abbreviations in the blanks.

n	noun	pro	pronoun
v	verb	adj	adjective
adv	adverb	prep	preposition
conj	conjunction		

1. I could *never* do *that* hard work at my age.   _____ _____

2. We *must leave* for the seashore at once *before* the shower.   _____ _____

3. *Until* Steve signs the checks, *we* must remain here.   _____ _____

4. *These* men are anxiously awaiting your *instructions*.   _____ _____

5. What is the *price* of those new *foreign* cars?   _____ _____

6. Your *sister* is later than *you* this time.   _____ _____

7. The coach is always *nervous before* the game begins.   _____ _____

8. The *Norwegian* people protested the visit *of* the alleged terrorist.   _____ _____

9. *I* shall have been absent a week *tomorrow*.   _____ _____

10. That *reckless* driver hurt only *himself* in the accident.   _____ _____

11. Her attitude *toward* the suspension of the students was *somewhat* cool.   _____ _____

12. We *found* the answer to those difficulties *since* he was last present.   _____ _____

13. Joan is much *wiser* now, *and* she will never forget the lesson.   _____ _____

14. We saw the ship *that* was in the *collision*.   _____ _____

15. *Behind* the store is a *winding* road that leads to the farms.   _____ _____

16. *If* you wish, I *will take* down his message for you.   _____ _____

17. A *group* of students *asked* to see those new paintings earlier.   _____ _____

18. When Kristin had finished talking, she came *over*
    to *my* side of the room.   _____   _____

19. *Certainly*, you may see *his* answers.   _____   _____

20. I will *not* agree to *your* criticism.   _____   _____

EXERCISE 2   Identifying Parts of Speech

Identify the part of speech of each italicized word or group of words by placing the appropriate abbreviations in the blanks.

n	noun	pro	pronoun
v	verb	adj	adjective
adv	adverb	prep	preposition
conj	conjunction		

1. *According to* legend, silk *was discovered* by
    Empress Hsi Ling-shi.   _____   _____

2. Empress Hsi Ling-shi *lived around* 2500 BCE.   _____   _____

3. *One* day while walking, *she* saw a mulberry tree
    covered with caterpillars.   _____   _____

4. The *caterpillars* were eating the *mulberry* leaves.   _____   _____

5. A few days *later* she saw the branches filled *with*
    the caterpillars' cocoons.   _____   _____

6. She plucked a cocoon *from* a branch and *took*
    it home.   _____   _____

7. *There* she placed *it* in a pot of water.   _____   _____

8. She *watched as* it loosened into a web.   _____   _____

9. She picked the *web apart*.   _____   _____

10. She discovered that *it* was a *long* thread of silk.   _____   _____

11. The process of making silk *became* China's
    special secret.   _____   _____

12. The *secret lasted* for the next 3,000 years.   _____   _____

13. Foreign gold poured *into* China from the *silk* trade.   _____   _____

14. To pass on the secret of silk-making *to* the
    outside world was forbidden.   _____   _____

15. Betraying the secret was punishable *by death*.   _____   _____

16. *Anyone* who has ever seen or worn a garment of
    pure silk knows why the Chinese had to guard
    their invention so jealously.   _____   _____

17. Silk is *petal* soft and lighter than the *sheerest* cotton.   _____   _____

18. It is *stronger* than *some* kinds of steel thread of equal thickness.   _____   _____

19. Silk *drapes* and flows *gracefully*.   _____   _____

20. It can be dyed to *richer* hues than any other natural *fabric*.   _____   _____

EXERCISE 3   Supplying and Identifying Words in Context

STUDENT COMPANION SITE
For additional practice visit www.cengage .com/devenglish/ brandon/PE11e.

Luke and Lisa LaRue made a handsome couple at their wedding. Everyone had said so. But now, after seven years of marriage, they are not always happy with each other. After one heated argument, Lisa left, and Luke sat down with his guitar to write a song describing their situation.

Fill in the blanks with words that you think would fit the context of the song. Then identify the part of speech of each of your choices by placing the appropriate abbreviation in the blanks at the left. The lines from the songs have been converted to sentences and may seem a bit less lyrical than Luke's inspired original creation, "You Hurt My Feelings."

_____   You always burn my (1) _____ TV dinners.

_____   You (2) _____ my brand-new station-wagon car.

_____   You said (3) _____ didn't like to do housekeeping.

_____   By accident you broke my best (4) _____.

_____ _____   You went (5) _____ and spent my hard-earned (6) _____.

_____ _____   Then you (7) _____ a dozen bouncing (8) _____.

_____ _____   And then (9) _____ had to go and hurt my (10) _____

_____   when you ran (11) _____ with my best friend named Tex.

Chorus:

_____ _____   You (12) _____ my feelings, and I'm feeling (13) _____.

_____ _____   You hurt my (14) _____ (15) _____ I'm feeling sad.

                You hurt my feelings, ran away with my friend.

_____ _____   (16) _____ hurt my feelings, and (17) _____ is the end.

_____   You went out drinking on my (18) _____.

_____ _____   Then you (19) _____ my mother is a (20) _____.

_____   You made (21) _____ of my special mustache.

_____   You (22) _____ it gives you a funny itch.

_____   You broke all my Dolly Parton (23) _____.

_____   Then you went (24) _____ dancing with your ex.

_____   And then you had to go and (25) _____ my feelings

_____   when you ran away with my best (26) _____ named Tex.

Chorus:

You hurt my feelings, and I'm feeling sad.

_____ _____   You hurt my (27) _____, and I'm feeling (28) _____.

_____   You (29) _____ my feelings, and I'm feeling sad

_____   because Tex was the best (30) _____ I ever had.

Scale for correctly labeled parts of speech (have your instructor check your answers):

  0–10 = need help with grammar
11–20 = starting to catch on to parts of speech
21–25 = becoming highly capable with parts of speech
26–30 = excellent knowledge of parts of speech

Scale for correct answers (exact matches or close enough, as determined by your instructor) of word selections.

  0–10 = need help with basic song writing
11–20 = ready for simple ditties
21–25 = becoming highly capable in dealing with sentimentality
26–30 = ready for advanced country song writing

Subjects and Verbs

The two most important parts of any sentence are the subject and the verb. The **subject** is who or what causes the action or expresses a state of being. The **verb** indicates what the subject is doing or is being. Many times the subject and verb taken together carry the meaning of the sentence. Consider this example:

The <u>woman</u> <u>left</u> for work.
     subject verb

The subject *woman* and the verb *left* indicate the basic content of the sentence while providing structure.

SUBJECTS

The simple subject of a sentence is usually a single noun or pronoun.

The judge's <u>reputation</u> for order in the courtroom is well known.
       simple subject

The complete subject is the simple subject with all its modifiers—that is, with all the words that describe or qualify it.

<u>The judge's reputation for order in the courtroom</u> is well known.
complete subject

To more easily understand and identify simple subjects of sentences, you may want to review the following information about nouns and pronouns.

Nouns

Nouns are naming words. Nouns may name persons, animals, plants, places, things, substances, qualities, or ideas—for example, *Bart, armadillo, Mayberry, tree, rock, cloud, love, ghost, music, virtue.*

Pronouns

A **pronoun** is a word that is used in place of a noun.

- Pronouns that can be used as subjects of sentences may represent specific persons or things and are called **personal pronouns**:

I	we
you	you
he, she, it	they

  Example: <u>They</u> recommended my sister for the coaching position.

     subject

- **Indefinite pronouns** refer to nouns (persons, places, things) in a general way:

  each   everyone   nobody   somebody

  Example: <u>Everyone</u> wants a copy of that paragraph.

     subject

- Other pronouns point out particular things:

  Singular: *this, that*   **Plural:** *these, those*

This is my treasure.   *These* are my jewels.

That is your junk.   *Those* are your trinkets.

- Still other pronouns introduce questions:

  Which is the best iPod?

What are the main ingredients in a Twinkie?

Who understands this computer command?

Note: To be the subject of a sentence, a pronoun must stand alone.

This is a treasure. [Subject is *this*; pronoun stands alone.]

This *treasure* is mine. [Subject is *treasure*. *This* is an adjective—a word that describes a noun; *This* describes *treasure*.]

Compound Subjects

A subject may be **compound**. That is, it may consist of two or more subjects, usually joined by *and* or *or*, that function together.

The *prosecutor* and the *attorney* for the defense made opening statements.

He and his *friends* listened carefully.

Steven, Juan, and *Alicia* attended the seminar. [Note the placement of commas for three or more subjects.]

Implied Subjects

A subject may be **implied** or understood. An **imperative sentence**—a sentence that gives a command—has *you* as the implied subject.

(You) Sit in that chair, please.
(You) Now take the oath.
(You) Please read the notes carefully.

Trouble Spot: Prepositional Phrases

A **prepositional phrase** is made up of a preposition (a word such as *at, in, of, to, with*) and one or more nouns or pronouns with their modifiers: *at the time, by the jury, in the courtroom, to the judge and the media, with controlled anger.* Be careful not to confuse the subject of a sentence with the noun or pronoun (known as the object of the preposition) in a prepositional phrase. The object of a preposition cannot be the subject of a sentence.

The <u>car</u> <u>with the dents</u> is mine.
   subject   prepositional
           phrase

The subject of the sentence is *car*. The word *dents* is the object of the preposition *with* and cannot be the subject of the sentence.

<u>Most</u> <u>of the pie</u> has been eaten.
subject prepositional
        phrase

The <u>person</u> <u>in the middle</u> <u>of the crowd</u> has disappeared.
   subject   prepositional   prepositional
            phrase   phrase

Trouble Spot: The Words *Here* and *There*

The words *here* and *there* are adverbs (used as filler words) and cannot be subjects.

There is no <u>problem</u>.
         subject

Here is the <u>issue</u>.
        subject

VERBS

Verbs show action or express being in relation to the subject of a sentence.

Types of Verbs

Action verbs indicate movement or accomplishment in idea or deed. Someone can "consider the statement" or "hit the ball." Here are other examples:

She *sees* the arena.
He *bought* the book.
They *adopted* the child.
He *understood* her main theories.

Being verbs indicate existence. Few in number, they include *is, was, were, am,* and *are.*

The movie *is* sad.
The book *was* comprehensive.
They *were* responsible.
I *am* concerned.
We *are* organized.

Verb Phrases

Verbs may occur as single words or as phrases. A **verb phrase** is made up of a main verb and one or more helping verbs such as the following:

is	was	can	have	do	may	shall
are	were	could	had	does	might	should
am		will	has	did	must	
		would				

Here are some sentences that contain verb phrases:

The judge *has presided* over many capital cases.
His rulings seldom *are overturned* on appeal.

Trouble Spot: Words Such as *Never, Not,* and *Hardly*

Never, not, hardly, seldom, and so on, are modifiers, not verbs.

The attorney could *not* win the case without key witnesses. [*Not* is an adverb. The verb phrase is *could win.*]
The jury could *hardly* hear the witness. [*Hardly* is an adverb; *could hear* is the verb phrase.]

Compound Verbs

Verbs that are joined by a word such as *and* or *or* are called **compound verbs**.

As a district attorney, Sumi *had presented* and *had won* famous cases.
She *prepared* carefully and *presented* her ideas with clarity.
We *will go* out for dinner or *skip* it entirely.

Trouble Spot: Verbals

Do not confuse verbs with verbals. **Verbals** are verblike words in certain respects, but they do not function as verbs. They function as other parts of speech. There are three kinds of verbals.

An **infinitive** is made up of the word *to* and a verb. An infinitive provides information, but, unlike the true verb, it is not tied to the subject of the sentence. It acts as a noun or describing unit.

He wanted *to get* a bachelor's degree.
To get a bachelor's degree was his main objective.

(In the first example, the word *wanted* is the verb for the subject *He*. The word *get* follows *to*; *to get* is an infinitive.)

A **gerund** is a verblike word ending in *-ing* that acts as a noun.

Retrieving her e-mail was always an exciting experience.
She thought about *retrieving* her e-mail.

Retrieving in each sentence acts as a noun.

A **participle** is a verblike word that usually has an *-ing* or an *-ed* ending.

Walking to town in the dark, he lost his way.
Wanted by the FBI, she was on the run.
The *starved* dog barked for food.

In the first example, the word *walking* answers the question *when*. In the second example, the word *wanted* answers the question *which one*. In the third example, *starved* describes the dog. *Walking, wanted,* and *starved* are describing words; they are not the true verbs in the sentences.

LOCATION OF SUBJECTS AND VERBS

Although the subject usually appears before the verb, it may follow the verb instead:

Into the court <u>stumbled</u> the <u>defendant</u>.
              verb   subject

From tiny acorns <u>grow</u> mighty <u>oaks</u>.
            verb   subject

There <u>was</u> little <u>support</u> for him in the audience.
     verb   subject

Here <u>are</u> your <u>books</u> and your <u>papers</u>.
    verb   subject   subject

Verb phrases are often broken up in a question. Do not overlook a part of the verb that is separated from another in a question such as "Where had the defendant gone on that fateful night?" If you have trouble finding the verb phrase, recast the question, making it into a statement: "The defendant *had gone* where on that fateful night." The result will not necessarily be a smooth or complete statement, but you will be able to see the basic elements more easily.

Can the defense lawyer *control* the direction of the trial?

Change the question to a statement to find the verb phrase:

The defense lawyer *can control* the direction of the trial.

EXERCISE 4 Finding Subjects and Verbs

Write the simple subject, without modifiers, in the first blank; write the verb in the second blank. Some sentences have compound subjects, compound verbs, or both; some sentences have an implied ("you") subject.

1. Every afternoon Joyce watches her favorite soap opera, *The Blameless and the Doomed*.   _____ _____

2. Never again will José order the mystery meat stew.   _____ _____

3. Jack and Jill should have been more careful on that hill.   _____ _____

4. Maybe you and I will learn to tango.   _____ _____

5. In Key West is the southernmost point of the United States.   _____ _____

6. Several of the players are already stretching and warming up.   _____ _____

7. Please knock three times on the window.   _____ _____

8. Al Franken, a former *Saturday Night Live* comedian, was elected senator in Minnesota.   _____ _____

9. Before long he will discover the sunken treasure and become famous.   _____ _____

10. Whom can we persuade to clean the skunk's cage?   _____ _____

11. There is plenty of borscht for everyone.   _____ _____

12. How will you crack the code?   _____ _____

13. The boxers, just before the fight, touched gloves and returned to their corners of the ring.   _____ _____

14. In no time at all, Snow White had cleaned the whole cottage.   _____ _____

15. Many of the ice skaters were injured during the last race.   _____ _____

16. Has he ever wished upon a star?   _____ _____

17. Please bring me flies for my Venus fly trap.   _____ _____

18. His response to her marriage proposal was to ask if he would get a diamond ring.   _____ _____

19. In the jar floats a lone pickled egg.   _____ _____

20. Write your name on the paper.   _____ _____

EXERCISE 5   Finding Subjects and Verbs

Write the simple subject, without modifiers, in the first blank; write the verb in the second blank. Some sentences have compound subjects, compound verbs, or both; some sentences have an implied ("you") subject.

1. The earliest evidence of Chinese writing comes from the Shang dynasty.   _____   _____

2. Archaeologists have found and studied hundreds of animal bones and tortoise shells with written symbols on them.   _____   _____

3. These strange objects are known as oracle bones.   _____   _____

4. Priests used them in fortune telling.   _____   _____

5. People 3,500 years ago developed part of the culture existing in China today.   _____   _____

6. Some of the characters are very much like those in a modern Chinese newspaper.   _____   _____

7. In the Chinese method of writing, each character stands for an idea, not a sound.   _____   _____

8. On the other hand, many of the Egyptian hieroglyphs stood for sounds in their spoken language.   _____   _____

9. But there were practically no links between China's spoken language and its written language.   _____   _____

10. One might read Chinese and not speak it.   _____   _____

11. The Chinese system of writing had one great advantage.   _____   _____

12. People with different dialects in all parts of China could learn the same system of writing and communicate with it.   _____   _____

13. Thus, the Chinese written language aided the unification of a large and diverse land.   _____   _____

14. The disadvantage of the Chinese system is the enormous number of written characters.   _____ _____

15. A barely literate person needs at least 1,000 characters.   _____ _____

16. A true scholar needs about 10,000 characters.   _____ _____

17. For centuries, this requirement severely limited the number of literate, educated Chinese.   _____ _____

18. A noble's children learned to write.   _____ _____

19. A peasant's children did not.   _____ _____

20. Consider these ideas as a background to modern educational systems.   _____ _____

Kinds of Sentences

The four kinds of basic sentences in English are simple, compound, complex, and compound-complex. The terms may be new to you, but if you can recognize subjects and verbs, with a little instruction and practice you should be able to identify and write any of the four kinds of sentences. The only new idea to master is the concept of the *clause*.

CLAUSES

A **clause** is a group of words with a subject and a verb that functions as a part or all of a complete sentence. The two kinds of clauses are independent (main) and dependent (subordinate).

> **Independent Clause:**   I have the money.
>
> **Dependent Clause:**   When I have the money

Independent Clauses

An **independent (main) clause** is a group of words with a subject and a verb that can stand alone and make sense. An independent clause expresses a complete thought by itself and can be written as a separate sentence.

She plays the bass guitar.
The manager is not at fault.

Dependent Clauses

A **dependent clause** is a group of words with a subject and verb that depends on a main clause to give it meaning.

> since Shannon came home [no meaning alone]
>
> <u>Since Shannon came home</u>, <u>her mother has been happy</u>. [has meaning]
>   dependent clause   independent clause
>
> because she was needed [no meaning alone]
>
> <u>She stayed in the game</u> <u>because she was needed</u>. [has meaning]
>   independent clause   dependent clause

Relative Clauses

One type of dependent clause is called a relative clause. A **relative clause** begins with a relative pronoun, a pronoun such as *that*, *which*, or *who*. Relative pronouns *relate* the clause to another word in the sentence.

> that fell last night [no meaning alone]
>
> The snow <u>that fell last night</u> is nearly gone. [has meaning]
>   dependent clause

In the sentence above, the relative pronoun *that* relates the dependent clause to the subject of the sentence, *snow*.

> who stayed in the game [no meaning alone]
>
> <u>She was the only one</u> <u>who stayed in the game</u>.
>   independent clause   dependent clause

In the sentence above, the relative pronoun *who* relates the dependent clause to the word *one*.

Trouble Spot: Phrases

A **phrase** is a group of words that go together. It differs from a clause in that a phrase does not have a subject and a verb. In the previous section, we discussed prepositional phrases (*in the house*, *beyond the horizon*) and saw some verbal phrases (infinitive phrase: *to go home*; participial phrase: *disconnected from the printer*; and gerund phrase: *running the computer*).

TYPES OF SENTENCES

This section covers sentence types according to this principle: On the basis of the number and kinds of clauses it contains, a sentence may be classified as simple, compound, complex, or compound-complex. In the examples in the following list, the dependent clauses are italicized, and the independent clauses are underlined.

Type	Definition	Example
Simple	One independent clause	<u>She did the work well</u>.
Compound	Two or more independent clauses	<u>She did the work well</u>, and <u>she was paid well</u>.
Complex	One independent clause and one or more dependent clauses	*Because she did the work well*, <u>she was paid well</u>.
Compound-complex	Two or more independent clauses and one or more dependent clauses	*Because she did the work well*, <u>she was paid well</u>, and <u>she was satisfied</u>.

Simple Sentences

A **simple sentence** consists of one independent clause and no dependent clauses. It may contain phrases and have more than one subject and/or verb.

The *lake looks* beautiful in the moonlight. [one subject and one verb]

The *Army*, *Navy*, and *Marines sent* troops to the disaster area. [three subjects and one verb]

We sang the old songs and *danced* happily at their wedding. [one subject and two verbs]

My *father*, *mother*, and *sister came* to the school play, *applauded* the performers, and *attended* the party afterward. [three subjects and three verbs]

EXERCISE 6   Writing Simple Sentences

Write six simple sentences. The first five have been started for you.

1. The mall _____

_____

2. The parking _____

_____

3. The sale _____

_____

4. After two hours _____

_____

5. Then _____

_____

6. _____

_____

Compound Sentences

A **compound sentence** consists of two or more independent clauses with no dependent clauses. Take, for example, the following two independent clauses:

He opened the drawer. He found his missing disk.

Here are two ways to join the independent clauses to form a compound sentence.

1. The two independent clauses can be connected by a connecting word called a coordinating conjunction. The coordinating conjunctions are *for*, *and*, *nor*, *but*, *or*, *yet*, *so*. (Remember the acronym FANBOYS.)

   He opened the drawer, *and* he found his missing disk.
   He opened the drawer, *so* he found his missing disk.

   Use a comma before the coordinating conjunction (FANBOYS) between two independent clauses (unless one of the clauses is extremely short).

2. Another way to join independent clauses to form a compound sentence is to put a semicolon between the clauses.

   He opened the drawer; he found his missing disk.

EXERCISE 7   Writing Compound Sentences

Write five compound sentences using coordinating conjunctions. The sentences have been started for you. Then write the same five compound sentences without the coordinating conjunctions. Use a semicolon to join the independent clauses.

1. It was the car of her dreams, _____

   _____

2. She used the Internet to find the dealer's cost, _____

   _____

3. She now was ready to bargain, _____

   _____

4. Armed with facts, she went to the dealer, _____

   _____

5. The dealer made an offer, _____

   _____

6. _____

   _____

7. _____

_____

8. _____

_____

9. _____

_____

10. _____

_____

Complex Sentences

A **complex sentence** consists of one independent clause and one or more dependent clauses. In the following sentences, the dependent clauses are italicized.

> *When lilacs are in bloom*, we love to visit friends in the country. [one dependent clause and one independent clause]
>
> *Although it rained last night*, we decided to take the path *that led through the woods*. [one independent clause and two dependent clauses]

Punctuation tip: Use a comma after a dependent clause that appears before the main clause.

> *When the bus arrived*, we quickly boarded.

A relative clause (see page 418) can be the dependent clause in a complex sentence.

> I knew the actress *who played that part in the 1980s*.

EXERCISE 8   Writing Complex Sentences

Write six complex sentences. The first four have been started for you.

1. Although the job paid well, _____

_____

2. Before she went to work each day, _____

_____

3. When she returned home each night, _____

_____

4. Because her social life was suffering, _____

_____

5. _____

_____

6. _____

_____

Compound-Complex Sentences

A **compound-complex sentence** consists of two or more independent clauses and one or more dependent clauses.

Compound-Complex Sentence:	Albert enlisted in the Army, and Jason, who was his older brother, joined him a day later.
Independent Clauses:	Albert enlisted in the Army Jason joined him a day later
Dependent Clause:	who was his older brother
Compound-Complex Sentence:	Because Mr. Sanchez was a talented teacher, he was voted teacher of the year, and his students prospered.
Independent Clauses:	he was voted teacher of the year his students prospered
Dependent Clause:	Because Mr. Sanchez was a talented teacher

EXERCISE 9 Writing Compound-Complex Sentences

Write six compound-complex sentences. The first five have been started for you.

1. When he began his research paper, he was confident, but _____

_____

2. Although his college library offered good traditional sources, he wanted

some online sources, so _____

_____

3. After he found sources for background information, he focused on one

issue, and then _____

_____

4. When he discovered that an expert in his study lived nearby, he _____

_____

5. After he wrote his final draft on his computer, he _____

_____

6. _____

_____

_____

_____

EXERCISE 10   Identifying Types of Sentences

Indicate the kind of sentence by writing the appropriate letter(s) in the blank.

S	**simple**
CP	**compound**
CX	**complex**
CC	**compound-complex**

_____ **1.** The *Titanic*, a British passenger liner, began its maiden voyage from England to New York on April 10, 1912.

_____ **2.** It was the largest and most luxurious ship ever built, and it carried 2,227 passengers and crew members.

_____ **3.** The ship was described as a floating palace, and because its hull included a complicated system of watertight compartments, it was also declared to be "practically unsinkable."

_____ **4.** After three days of calm, clear weather at sea, the captain received seven warnings of ice in the area.

_____ **5.** At 11:40 p.m. on April 14, lookouts in the ship's crow's nest saw an iceberg directly in the vessel's path, but it was too late to change course.

_____ **6.** The *Titanic* struck the iceberg in the North Atlantic Ocean.

_____ **7.** Because the ship was supposedly unsinkable, it carried only twenty lifeboats.

_____ **8.** Women and children were first to board the lifeboats, which offered room for only about half of the people aboard.

_____ **9.** Water poured into the ship, and by 1:15 a.m., its bow sank.

_____ **10.** At 2:17 a.m., as the stern rose almost vertically into the air,

the lights finally flickered and went out.

_____ **11.** At 2:18 a.m. on April 15, the sinking ship broke in two, and at

2:20 a.m., it disappeared beneath the waves.

_____ **12.** Those who did not drown froze to death in the icy water.

_____ **13.** The disaster claimed 1,522 lives; 705 people were rescued.

_____ **14.** After this tragedy occurred, new agreements revised lifeboat

standards and created the International Ice Patrol in North

Atlantic sea lanes.

_____ **15.** Immediately, people began talking about ways to find the

Titanic and raise it to the surface.

_____ **16.** Not until 1985, though, did a team of U.S. and French researchers

locate the wreck off the coast of Newfoundland at a depth of two

and a half miles.

_____ **17.** Several subsequent expeditions sent cameras, lights, and manned

submarines down to the eerie scene, where they explored and

photographed the rusted wreckage and collected artifacts from it.

_____ **18.** The photos revealed that the iceberg ripped a hole in six of the

watertight compartments; the ship might have survived if only four

of its compartments had been ruptured.

_____ **19.** In 1996, when researchers tried to salvage a section of the ship's

hull by raising it to the surface with balloons, a storm caused the

lines to break, and the piece fell back to the bottom of the sea.

_____ **20.** The ship is deteriorating rapidly in its saltwater grave, and it will

eventually melt into the floor of the sea.

EXERCISE 11   Identifying Types of Sentences

Indicate the kind of sentence by writing the appropriate letter(s) in the blank.

S   simple
CP   compound
CX   complex
CC   compound-complex

_____   1. Throughout history there have been truth tests for the innocent and the guilty.

_____   2. Many of these methods relied (unknowingly) on the basic physiological principles that also guided the creation of the polygraph.

_____   3. For example, one method of lie detection involved giving the suspect a handful of raw rice to chew.

_____   4. After the suspect chewed for some time, he or she was instructed to spit out the rice.

_____   5. An innocent person was expected to do this easily, but a guilty person was expected to have grains of rice sticking to the roof of the mouth and tongue.

_____   6. This technique relied on the increased sympathetic nervous system activity in the presumably fearful and guilty person.

_____   7. This activity would result in the drying up of saliva.

_____   8. That, in turn, would cause grains of rice to stick in the mouth.

_____   9. A similar but more frightening technique involved placing a heated knife blade briefly against the tongue.

_____   10. An innocent person would not be burned, but the guilty person would immediately feel pain, again because of the relative dryness of the mouth.

_____   11. A more primitive but functional technique for detecting liars was supposedly used by a Persian king.

_____   12. He was presumed to have a very special donkey, one that had the ability to tell an innocent person from a guilty one.

_____ **13.** When a crime was committed, the suspects would be gathered in a hall next to the room that held the donkey.

_____ **14.** According to directions, each suspect entered the room alone, found the donkey in the dark, and pulled its tail.

_____ **15.** The donkey did the rest.

_____ **16.** If an innocent person pulled the tail, the donkey was said to remain silent.

_____ **17.** If a guilty person pulled the tail, the donkey would bray loudly.

_____ **18.** In fact, the donkey's tail was dusted with graphite.

_____ **19.** The guilty person emerged with clean hands because he or she wanted to avoid detection.

_____ **20.** The king knew that the person with clean hands was guilty, and he proceeded with punishment.

Combining Sentences

The simple sentence, the most basic sentence in the English language, can be exceptionally useful and powerful. Some of the greatest statements in literature have been presented in the simple sentence. Its strength is in its singleness of purpose. However, a piece of writing made up of a long series of simple sentences is likely to be monotonous. Moreover, the form may suggest a separateness of ideas that does not serve your purpose well. If your ideas are closely related, some equal in importance and some not, you can combine sentences to show the relationships between your ideas.

COORDINATION: THE COMPOUND SENTENCE

If you intend to communicate two equally important and closely related ideas, you certainly will want to place them close together, probably in a compound sentence.

Suppose we take two simple sentences that we want to combine:

I am very tired. I worked very hard today.

We have already looked at coordinating conjunctions as a way of joining independent clauses to create compound sentences. Depending on which coordinating conjunction you use, you can show different kinds of relationships. (The following list is arranged according to the FANBOYS acronym discussed earlier. Only the first conjunction joins the original two sentences.)

For shows a reason:

> I am very tired, *for* I worked very hard today.

And shows equal ideas:

> I am very tired, *and* I want to rest for a few minutes.

Nor indicates a negative choice or alternative:

> I am not tired, *nor* am I hungry right now.

But shows contrast:

> I am very tired, *but* I have no time to rest now.

Or indicates a choice or an alternative:

> I will take a nap, *or* I will go out jogging.

Yet indicates contrast:

> I am tired, *yet* I am unable to relax.

So points to a result:

> I am tired, *so* I will take a nap.

Punctuation with Coordinating Conjunctions

When you combine two sentences by using a coordinating conjunction, drop the first period, change the capital letter that begins the second sentence to a small letter, and insert a comma before the coordinating conjunction.

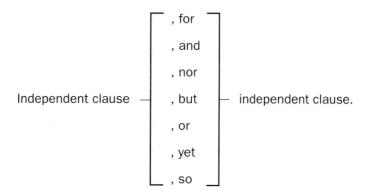

Independent clause — [, for / , and / , nor / , but / , or / , yet / , so] — independent clause.

Semicolons and Conjunctive Adverbs

In the previous section, we saw that a semicolon can join independent clauses to make a compound sentence. Here are two more simple sentences to combine:

> We were late. We missed the first act.

We can make one compound sentence out of them by joining the two clauses with a semicolon:

> We were late; we missed the first act.

We can also use words called conjunctive adverbs after semicolons to make the relationship between the two clauses clearer. Look at how the conjunctive adverb *therefore* adds the idea of "as a result."

We were late; *therefore*, we missed the first act.

Conjunctive adverbs include the following words and phrases: *also, consequently, furthermore, hence, however, in fact, moreover, nevertheless, now, on the other hand, otherwise, soon, therefore, similarly, then, thus.*

Consider the meaning you want when you use a conjunctive adverb to coordinate ideas.

As a result of: *therefore, consequently, hence, thus, then*

To the contrary or with reservation: *however, nevertheless, otherwise, on the other hand*

In addition to: *moreover, also*

To emphasize or specify: *in fact, for example*

To compare: *similarly*

Punctuation with Semicolons and Conjunctive Adverbs

When you combine two sentences by using a semicolon, replace the first period with a semicolon and change the capital letter that begins the second sentence to a small letter. If you wish to use a conjunctive adverb, insert it after the semicolon and put a comma after it. (However, usually no comma follows *then, now, thus*, and *soon*.) The first letters of ten common conjunctive adverbs make up the acronym HOTSHOT CAT.

Independent clause — [; however, / ; otherwise, / ; therefore, / ; similarly, / ; hence, / ; on the other hand, / ; then / ; consequently, / ; also, / ; thus] — independent clause.

SUBORDINATION: THE COMPLEX SENTENCE

Whereas a compound sentence contains independent clauses that are equally important and closely related, a complex sentence combines ideas of unequal value. The following two sentences can be combined as either a compound sentence or a complex sentence, depending on whether the writer thinks the ideas are of equal value.

My neighbors are considerate. They never play loud music.

Combined as a compound sentence, suggesting that the ideas are of equal value, the new sentence looks like this:

<u>My neighbors are considerate</u>, and <u>they never play loud music.</u>
  independent clause   independent clause
      (main idea)   (main idea)

Here are the same two ideas combined as a complex sentence, suggesting that the ideas are of unequal value:

<u>Because my neighbors are considerate</u>, <u>they never play loud music.</u>
     dependent clause   independent clause
   (less important idea)   (main idea)

Although both the compound and the complex forms are correct, the complex form conveys the ideas more precisely in this sentence because one idea does seem to be more important—one idea depends on the other.

Thus if you have two sentences with closely related ideas and one is clearly more important than the other, consider combining them in a complex sentence. Compare these two paragraphs:

1. This version contains six simple sentences, implying that the ideas are of equal value:

> (1) I was very upset. (2) The Fourth of July fireworks were especially loud. (3) My dog ran away. (4) The animal control officer made his morning rounds. (5) He found my dog in another part of town. (6) I was relieved.

2. This version consists of two simple sentences and two complex sentences, showing that some ideas are more important than others:

> (1) I was very upset. (2) Because the Fourth of July fireworks were especially loud, my dog ran away. (3) When the animal control officer made his morning rounds, he found my dog in another part of town. (4) I was relieved.

You will probably consider Version 2 superior to Version 1. In Version 1, sentences 2 and 3 are closely related, but 3 is more important. Sentences 4 and 5 are closely related, but 5 is more important. In Version 2, the revision made each pair into a complex sentence.

Although you could combine sentences 1 and 2, the result would be illogical because the wrong idea would be conveyed:

Illogical Combination: I was very upset because the Fourth of July fireworks were especially loud.

The person was very upset because the dog ran away, not because the fireworks were especially loud.

Subordinating Conjunctions

As you learned in the previous section, a complex sentence is composed of one independent clause and one or more dependent clauses. In combining two independent clauses to write a complex sentence, your first step is to decide on a word that will best show the relationship between the clauses. Words that show the relationship of a dependent clause to an independent one are called

subordinating conjunctions. The italicized words in the following sentences are subordinating conjunctions. Consider the meaning as well as the placement of each one.

> *Because* the storm hit, the game was canceled.

> *After* the storm passed, the dogs began to bark.

> *When* she read her poem, they were moved to fits of hysterics.

> He did not volunteer to work on the holiday, *although* the pay was good.

> No one has visited her *since* she moved into town.

> They decided to wait *until* the cows came home.

> They refused to work *unless* they were allowed to wear chef's hats.

> *Before* the session ended, all the "hep cats" blew some sweet sounds.

Other subordinating conjunctions include the following:

as	provided that	whereas
as if	rather than	wherever
even if	so that	whether
even though	than	while
if	whenever	
in order that	where	

Punctuation with Subordinating Conjunctions

If the dependent clause comes *before* the main clause, set it off with a comma.

> Before Mike wrote his final draft, he looked over his outline.

If the dependent clause comes *after* or *within* the main clause, set it off only if the clause is not necessary to the meaning of the main clause or if the dependent clause begins with the word(s) *although*, *though*, or *even though*.

> We went home *after* the concert had ended.

> He continued painting, *although* he had repainted the cabinet twice.

Punctuation with Relative Pronouns

As you learned earlier, a relative clause begins with a relative pronoun, a pronoun such as *that*, *which*, or *who*.

> The decision <u>that I made</u> is final.
>   relative clause

> A student <u>who uses a computer</u> can save time in revising.
>   relative clause

Set off the dependent (relative) clause with commas when it is not necessary to the sentence. Do not set off the clause if it is necessary for the meaning of the sentence.

> Everyone *who tries* will pass this class. [The dependent clause is necessary because one would not say, "Everyone will pass this class."]

Rachel, *who tries*, will pass this class. [The dependent clause is not necessary because one can say, "Rachel will pass this class."]

The relative pronoun *which* usually refers to things. The word *which* almost always indicates that a clause is not necessary for the meaning of the sentence. Therefore, a clause beginning with *which* is almost always set off by commas.

My car, *which* is ten years old, has a flat tire.

The relative pronoun *that* also usually refers to things. However, the word *that* almost always indicates that the clause *is* necessary for the meaning of the sentence. Therefore, a clause beginning with *that* is almost always *not* set off by commas.

The car *that* has a flat tire is ten years old.

The relative pronouns *who* and *whom*, as well as *whoever* and *whomever*, usually refer to people. Clauses that begin with those relative pronouns are not set off by commas if they are necessary for the meaning of the sentence; if they are not necessary, they are set off.

A person *who* has a way with words is often quoted. [necessary for the meaning of the sentence]

My uncle, *whom* I quote often, has a way with words. [not necessary for the meaning of the sentence]

COORDINATION AND SUBORDINATION: THE COMPOUND-COMPLEX SENTENCE

At times you may want to show the relationship of three or more ideas within one sentence. If that relationship involves two or more main ideas and one or more supporting ideas, the combination can be stated in a compound-complex sentence (two or more independent clauses and one or more dependent clauses).

Before he learned how to operate a computer,

dependent clause

he had trouble with his typewritten assignments,

independent clause

but now he produces clean, attractive pages.

independent clause

In our previous discussion of the complex sentence, we presented this group of six sentences:

I was very upset. The Fourth of July fireworks were especially loud. My dog ran away. The animal control officer made his morning rounds. He found my dog in another part of town. I was relieved.

We then converted the group of six sentences to four:

I was very upset. Because the Fourth of July fireworks were especially loud, my dog ran away. When the animal control officer made his morning rounds, he found my dog in another part of town. I was relieved.

But what if we wanted to show an even closer relationship of ideas? One solution would be to combine the two complex sentences in this way (the italicized sentence is compound-complex):

> I was very upset. *Because the Fourth of July fireworks were especially loud, my dog ran away; but when the animal control officer made his morning rounds, he found my dog in another part of town.* I was relieved.

Punctuation of Complicated Compound or Compound-Complex Sentences

If a compound or compound-complex sentence has one or more commas in the first clause, you may want to use a semicolon before the coordinating conjunction between the two clauses. Its purpose is to show the reader very clearly the division between the two independent clauses. The preceding example illustrates this use of the semicolon.

OTHER WAYS TO COMBINE IDEAS

1. Use an **appositive**, a noun or a noun phrase that immediately follows a noun or pronoun and renames it.

   Garth Brooks claims Yukon, Oklahoma, as his hometown. He is a famous singer.

   Garth Brooks, *a famous singer*, claims Yukon, Oklahoma, as his hometown.

2. Use a **prepositional phrase**, a preposition followed by a noun or pronoun object.

   John Elway led the Denver Broncos to two Super Bowl victories. Both triumphs occurred in the 1990s.

   John Elway led the Denver Broncos to two Super Bowl victories *in the 1990s*.

3. Drop the subject in the sentence that follows and combine the sentences.

   Emily Dickinson's poetry went mostly unpublished during her lifetime. It was finally discovered and celebrated more than a half century later.

   Emily Dickinson's poetry went mostly unpublished during her lifetime but was finally discovered and celebrated more than a half century later.

4. Use a **participial phrase**, a group of words that includes a participle, which is a verbal that usually ends in *-ing* or *-ed*.

   Michael rowed smoothly. He reached the shore.

   Rowing smoothly, Michael reached the shore.

EXERCISE 12   Combining Sentences

Combine each group of sentences into a single sentence. Use coordination, subordination, or one of the other ways of combining ideas.

1. Cobras are among the most feared of all snakes.
   They are not the deadliest of all snakes.

2. Cobras do not coil before they strike.
   They cannot strike for a long distance.

3. Cobras do not have a hood.
   They flatten their neck by moving their ribs when they are nervous or frightened.

4. Cobras use their poison in two ways.
   One way is by injecting venom with their fangs.
   Another way is by spitting venom at their victims.

5. Human beings will not die from the venom that has been spit.
   It can cause blindness if it is not washed from the eyes.

6. A person can die from a cobra bite.
   Death may come in only a few hours.

7. Snake charmers have long worked with cobras.
   They use only a snake, a basket, and a flute.

8. The snakes cannot hear the music.
   They respond to the rhythmic movements of the charmers.

9. The snake charmers are hardly ever in danger of being bitten.
   They defang the cobras or sew their mouths shut.

10. Most cobras flee from people.
    They attack if they are cornered or if they are guarding their eggs.

EXERCISE 13 Combining Sentences

Combine each group of sentences into a single sentence. Use coordination, subordination, or one of the other ways of combining ideas.

1. Henry David Thoreau grew tired of living in society.
   He wanted to face his essential self.

2. He built a cabin in the woods.
   He lived there for more than a year.

3. Gilligan had a plan.
   He would float in a shipping crate to Hawaii.

4. It would be a surprise.
   He would send help to his friends on the island.

5. A storm came up.
   Gilligan's craft sank in three feet of water in the lagoon.
   The skipper cried bitter tears over the loss of his little buddy.

6. The professor made a submarine out of coconut shells, Mrs. Howell's corset,
   Ginger's jewelry, and fish bones.
   Gilligan was rescued.

7. Captain Ahab set sail for the South Seas.
   Captain Ahab had an obsession.

8. He wanted to kill the great white whale.
   The name of the great white whale was Moby Dick.

9. The captain and the whale had their encounter. Moby Dick was easily
   the victor.

10. Hamlet was sad.
    His father was dead.
    His mother had married his uncle.

11. Hamlet believed that his uncle had killed his father.
    Hamlet plotted to kill his uncle.

12. Romeo and Juliet were young.
    They fell in love.

13. Their families were feuding.
    Romeo and Juliet decided to run away.

14. They tried to trick their families.
    Their plans turned sour.
    They both died.

15. The contestant spun the wheel one more time.
    Vanna White clapped her hands with glee.

16. Pat Sajak made a wry joke about greed.
    Only one letter remained.

17. The wheel stopped.
    The contestant lost his turn.

18. The audience groaned.
    Vanna White slumped, and Pat Sajak comforted her sad heart.

19. Several tabloids have reported that Elvis has not left us.
    He has been sighted in several parts of this country and even on other planets.

20. The tabloids report that the King is just tired and wants privacy.
    They give credit to unnamed reliable sources.

Omissions

Do not omit words that are needed to make your sentences clear and logical. Of the many types of undesirable constructions in which necessary words are omitted, the following are the most common.

1. **Subjects.** Do not omit a necessary subject in a sentence with two verbs.

   Illogical: The cost of the car was $12,000 but would easily last me through college. (subject of *last*)

   Logical: The cost of the car was $12,000, but the car would easily last me through college.

2. **Verbs.** Do not omit verbs that are needed because of a change in the number of the subject or a change of tense.

Illogical:	The bushes were trimmed and the grass mowed.
Logical:	The bushes were trimmed, and the grass was mowed.
Illogical:	True honesty always has and always will be admired by most people. (tense)
Logical:	True honesty always has been and always will be admired by most people.

3. *That* **as a conjunction.** The conjunction *that* should not be omitted from a dependent clause if there is danger of misreading the sentence.

Misleading:	We believed Eric, if not stopped, would hurt himself.
Clear:	We believed that Eric, if not stopped, would hurt himself.

4. **Prepositions.** Do not omit prepositions in idiomatic phrases, in expressions of time, and in parallel phrases.

Illogical:	Weekends the campus is deserted. (time)
Logical:	During weekends the campus is deserted.
Illogical:	I have neither love nor patience with untrained dogs. (parallel phrases)
Logical:	I have neither love for nor patience with untrained dogs.
Illogical:	Glenda's illness was something we heard only after her recovery.
Logical:	Glenda's illness was something we heard about only after her recovery.

EXERCISE 14   Repairing Omissions

STUDENT COMPANION SITE

For additional practice visit www.cengage .com/devenglish/ brandon/PE11e.

Identify the kinds of omissions by writing one of the following words in the blanks to the right: *preposition, verb, subject, that*. Insert the necessary words in the sentences.

1. Courage always has and always will be admired.   _____

2. In the trees or the ground the squirrel is a fascinating animal.   _____

3. Mornings they went to the coffee house to think.   _____

4. I never have and never will like her.   _____

5. He has neither love nor patience with children.   _____

6. The price of the leather jacket was $763, but was something

   I'd always wanted.   _____

7. The parking problem is getting worse, and already is unable

   to handle all the cars.   _____

8. Doretta's victory was announced in the local newspaper

   and the community television channel.   _____

9. The puck was stopped by the goalie, and went down to defeat. _____

10. He discovered his feet were wet.   _____

Variety in Sentence Types, Order, Length, Beginnings

Do not bother to look for formulas in this section. Variety may be desirable for its own sake, to avoid dullness. However, it is more likely you will revise your compositions for reasons that make good sense in the context of what you are writing. The sentence variations available to you are types, order, length, and beginnings.

Types

You have learned that all four types of sentences are sound. Your task as a writer is to decide which one to use for a particular thought. That decision may not be made until you revise your composition. Then you can choose on the basis of the relationship of ideas:

Simple: a single idea

Compound: two closely related ideas

Complex: one idea more important than the other

Compound-Complex: a combination of compound and complex

These types were all covered earlier in this Handbook (pages 418–422). This section provides further practice, as you combine sentences.

Order

You will choose the order of parts and information according to what you want to emphasize. Typically the most emphatic location is at the end of any unit.

Length

Uncluttered and direct, short sentences commonly draw attention. But that focus occurs only when they stand out from longer sentences. Therefore, you would usually avoid a series of short sentences.

Beginnings

A long series of sentences with each beginning with a subject followed by a verb may become monotonous. Consider beginning sentences in different ways:

With a prepositional phrase: *In the distance* a dog barked.

With a transitional connective (conjunctive adverb) such as *then*, *however*, **or** *therefore*: *Then* the game was over.

With a coordinating conjunction such as *and* **or** *but*: *But* no one moved for three minutes.

With a dependent clause: *Although he wanted a new Corvette*, he settled for a used Ford Taurus.

With an adverb: *Carefully* he removed the thorn from the lion's paw.

EXERCISE 15   Providing Sentence Variety

STUDENT COMPANION SITE
For additional practice visit www.cengage .com/devenglish/ brandon/PE11e.

Revise the following passage to achieve better sentence variety by changing the types of sentences, order of information, length of sentences, and beginnings of sentences. Use the skills you have learned about combining sentences. Compare your revisions with those of others in your class. There is no single correct way of making these changes.

MY SCHOOL NIGHTMARE
Anna Kuang

My first day of school in America was also my worst nightmare. I woke up early in the morning. My uncle took me to school. I sat in the classroom during the first period and listened. I could not understand what the teacher was talking about. Fifty minutes passed. I saw others walk out of the classroom. I did not know what they were doing. I walked out with them. I still did not realize that the school system in America was different from that in China. Students in China do not change classrooms every period. The teachers do. Students in America rather than teachers change classrooms. So I went back to the same classroom again. I stayed in that room until noon. Lunch hour was coming. In China, everybody goes home for lunch. I thought people did the same thing here. I left for home. A school security man stopped me outside the school. He talked to me. I did not know what he was saying. I was frustrated and scared. I wanted to cry. Some of my schoolmates looked at me as if I were an alien. My face turned red. My heart was crying. I hid my tears. A Chinese girl came up and talked to me in Chinese. She told me we had to stay in school until the last period. I did not know she would become my best friend. I did know my worst nightmare had ended.

Correcting Fragments, Comma Splices, and Run-Ons

You have learned about subjects and verbs, and you have identified and written different kinds of sentences. With the information you now have, you will be able to spot and correct three problems that sometimes creep into what is otherwise good writing. Those problems are sentence fragments, comma splices, and run-on sentences.

FRAGMENTS

A correct sentence signals completeness. The structure and punctuation provide those signals. For example, if I say to you, "She left in a hurry," you do not necessarily expect me to say anything else, but if I say, "In a hurry," you do. If I say, "Tomorrow I will give you a quiz on the reading assignment," and I leave the room, you will merely take note of my words. But if I say, "Tomorrow when I give you a quiz on the reading assignment," and leave the room, you will probably be annoyed, and you may even chase after me and ask me to finish my sentence. Those examples illustrate the difference between completeness and incompleteness.

A **fragment** is a word or group of words without a subject ("Is going to town.") or without a verb ("He going to town.") or without both ("Going to town."). A fragment can also be a group of words with a subject and verb that cannot stand alone ("When he goes to town."). Although the punctuation signals a sentence (a capital letter at the beginning and a period at the end), the structure of a fragment signals incompleteness. If you said it or wrote it to someone, that person would expect you to go on and finish the idea.

Other specific examples of common unacceptable fragments are these:

* *Dependent clause only*: When she came.
* *Phrase(s) only*: Waiting there for some help.
* *No subject in main clause*: Went to the library.
* *No verb in main clause*: She being the only person there.

Acceptable Fragments

Sometimes fragments are used intentionally. When we speak, we often use the following fragments:

* *Interjections*: Great! Hooray! Whoa!
* *Exclamations*: What a day! How terrible! What a bother!
* *Greetings*: Hello. Good morning. Good night. Good evening.
* *Questions*: What for? Why not? Where to?
* *Informal conversation*: Eight o'clock. Really.

In novels, plays, and short stories, fragments are often used in conversation among characters. However, in your typical college assignments, you need to be able to identify fragments and turn them into complete sentences.

Dependent Clauses as Fragments: Clauses with Subordinating Conjunctions

You have learned that words such as *because, after, although, since, before* (see page 430 for a more complete list) are subordinating conjunctions, words that show the relationship of a dependent clause to an independent one. A dependent clause punctuated like a sentence (capital letter at the beginning; period at the end) is a sentence fragment.

While the ship was sinking.

You can choose one of many ways to fix that kind of fragment.

Incorrect: They continued to dance. *While the ship was sinking.*

Correct: They continued to dance *while the ship was sinking.*

Correct: *While the ship was sinking,* they continued to dance.

Correct: The ship was sinking. They continued to dance.

Correct: The ship was sinking; they continued to dance.

In the first two correct sentences above, the dependent clause *while the ship was sinking* has been attached to an independent clause. Note that a comma is used when the dependent clause appears at the beginning of the sentence. In the next two sentences, the subordinating conjunction *while* has been omitted. The two independent clauses can then stand alone as sentences or as parts of a sentence joined by a semicolon.

Dependent Clauses as Fragments: Clauses with Relative Pronouns

You have also learned that words such as *that, which,* and *who* can function as relative pronouns, words that relate a clause back to a noun or pronoun in the sentence. Relative clauses are dependent. If they are punctuated as sentences (begin with a capital letter; end with a period), they are incorrect. They are really sentence fragments.

Which is lying on the floor.

The best way to fix such a fragment is to attach it as closely as possible to the noun to which it refers.

Incorrect: That new red sweater is mine. *Which is lying on the floor.*

Correct: The new red sweater, *which is lying on the floor,* is mine.

Reminder: Some relative clauses are restrictive (necessary to the meaning of the sentence) and should not be set off with commas. Some are nonrestrictive (not necessary to the meaning of the sentence), as in the example above, and are set off by commas.

Phrases as Fragments

Although a phrase may carry an idea, a phrase is a fragment because it is incomplete in structure. It lacks both a subject and a verb. (See pages 413–414 for verbal phrases, pages 404–405 and 412 for prepositional phrases, and page 432 for appositive phrases.)

Verbal Phrase

Incorrect: *Having studied hard all evening.* John decided to retire.

Correct: *Having studied hard all evening,* John decided to retire.

The italicized part of the incorrect example is a verbal phrase. As you have learned, a verbal is verblike without being a verb in sentence structure. Verbals include verb parts of speech ending in *-ed* and *-ing.* To correct a verbal phrase fragment, attach it to a complete sentence (independent clause). When the phrase begins the sentence, it is usually set off by a comma.

Prepositional Phrase

Incorrect: *For the past ten hours.* I have been designing my home page.

Correct: *For the past ten hours,* I have been designing my home page.

In this example, the fragment is a prepositional phrase—a group of words beginning with a preposition, such as *in, on, of, at,* and *with,* that connects a noun or pronoun object to the rest of the sentence. To correct a prepositional phrase fragment, attach it to a complete sentence (independent clause). If the prepositional phrase is long and begins the sentence, it is usually set off by a comma.

Appositive Phrase

Incorrect: He lived in the small town of Whitman. *A busy industrial center near Boston.*

Correct: He lived in the small town of Whitman, *a busy industrial center near Boston.*

Incorrect: Many readers admire the work of the nineteenth-century American poet. *Emily Dickinson.*

Correct: Many readers admire the work of the nineteenth-century American poet *Emily Dickinson.*

In these examples, the fragment is an appositive phrase—a group of words following a noun or pronoun and renaming it. To correct an appositive phrase fragment, connect it to a complete sentence (an independent clause). An appositive phrase fragment is set off by a comma or by commas only if it is not essential to the meaning of the sentence.

Fragments as Word Groups Without Subjects or Without Verbs

Incorrect: Kristianna studied many long hours. And received the highest grade in the class. [without subject]

Correct:	Kristianna studied many long hours and received the highest grade in the class.
Incorrect:	Fcw children living in that section of the country. [without verb]
Correct:	Few children live in that section of the country.

Each sentence must have an independent clause, a group of words that contains a subject and a verb and that can stand alone. As you may recall from the discussion of subjects, a command or direction sentence, such as "Think," has an understood subject of *you.*

COMMA SPLICES AND RUN-ONS

The comma splice and the run-on are two other kinds of faulty "sentences" that give false signals to the reader. In each instance the punctuation suggests that there is only one sentence, but, in fact, there is material for two.

The **comma splice** consists of two independent clauses with only a comma between them:

> The weather was disappointing, we canceled the picnic. [A comma by itself cannot join two independent clauses.]

The **run-on** differs from the comma splice in only one respect: It has no comma between the independent clauses. Therefore, the run-on is two independent clauses with *nothing* between them:

> The weather was disappointing we canceled the picnic. [Independent clauses must be properly connected.]

Because an independent clause can stand by itself as a sentence and because two independent clauses must be properly linked, you can use a simple technique to identify the comma splice and the run-on. If you see a sentence that you think may contain one of these two errors, ask yourself this question: "Can I insert a period at some place in the word group and still have a sentence on either side?" If the answer is yes and there is no word such as *and* or *but* following the inserted period, then you have a comma splice or a run-on to correct. In our previous examples of the comma splice and the run-on, we could insert a period after the word *disappointing* in each case, and we would still have an independent clause—therefore, a sentence—on either side.

Four Ways to Correct Comma Splices and Run-Ons

Once you identify a comma splice or a run-on in your writing, you need to correct it. There are four different ways to fix these common sentence problems.

1. Use a comma and a coordinating conjunction.

Incorrect:	We canceled the picnic the weather was disappointing. [run-on]

> Correct: We canceled the picnic, *for* the weather was disappointing. [Here we inserted a comma and the coordinating conjunction *for*.]

Knowing the seven coordinating conjunctions will help you in writing sentences and correcting sentence problems. Remember the acronym FANBOYS: *for, and, nor, but, or, yet, so.*

2. Use a subordinating conjunction.

> Incorrect: The weather was disappointing, we canceled the picnic. [comma splice]

> Correct: *Because* the weather was disappointing, we canceled the picnic.

By inserting the subordinating conjunction *because*, you can transform the first independent clause into a dependent clause and correct the comma splice. Knowing the most common subordinating conjunctions will help you in writing sentences and correcting sentence problems. Here again is a list of frequently used subordinating conjunctions.

after	if	until
although	in order that	when
as	provided that	whenever
as if	rather than	where
because	since	whereas
before	so that	wherever
even if	than	whether
even though	unless	while

3. Use a semicolon.

> Incorrect: The weather was disappointing, we canceled the picnic.

> Correct: The weather was disappointing; we canceled the picnic.

> Correct: The weather was disappointing; *therefore*, we canceled the picnic.

This comma splice was corrected by a semicolon. The first correct example shows the semicolon alone. The second correct example shows a semicolon followed by the conjunctive adverb *therefore*. The conjunctive adverb is optional, but, as we have already seen, conjunctive adverbs can make the relationship between independent clauses stronger. Here is a list of conjunctive adverbs you saw on page 428.

however	on the other hand
otherwise	then
therefore	consequently
similarly	also
hence	thus

Consider using the acronym HOTSHOT CAT, made up of the first letter of each of these common conjunctive adverbs. The acronym will help you remember them. Other conjunctive adverbs include *in fact*, *for example*, *moreover*, *nevertheless*, *furthermore*, *now*, and *soon*.

4. **Make each clause a separate sentence.**

Incorrect: The weather was disappointing, we canceled the picnic.

Correct: The weather was disappointing. We canceled the picnic.

To correct the comma splice, replace the comma with a period and begin the second sentence (the second independent clause) with a capital letter. This method is at once the simplest and most common method of correcting comma splices and run-ons. For a run-on, insert a period between the two independent clauses and begin the second sentence with a capital letter.

TECHNIQUES FOR SPOTTING PROBLEM SENTENCES

1. For the fragment, ask yourself: "If someone were to say or write this to me, would I expect the person to add to the statement or rephrase it?"

2. In checking for the comma splice or run-on, ask yourself: "Is there a point in this word group at which I can insert a period and create a sentence on either side?" (The question is not necessary if there is a coordinating conjunction—FANBOYS—at that point.)

3. If you have trouble with comma splices and run-ons, check these constructions as you revise:

   a. A comma preceded by a noun or pronoun followed by a noun or pronoun

   b. A sentence beginning with a subordinating conjunction

3. If you have trouble with fragments, look for these clues:

   a. A word group with a single verb ending in -ing

   b. A word group without both a subject and a verb

5. Use the grammar checker on your computer to alert you to possible problem sentences. Then use instructions from this book to make necessary corrections.

EXERCISE 16   Correcting Fragments, Comma Splices, and Run-Ons

Write the appropriate identification in each blank. Correct the faulty sentences.

OK   correct
CS   comma splice
RO   run-on
FRAG   fragment

_____   1. King Henry VIII, who ruled England from 1509 to 1547,

accomplished a number of important things.

_____   2. He separated the Church of England from Roman Catholicism, this

act significantly altered his country's history.

_____ 3. Credited with changing the king's role to include head of church.

_____ 4. However, Henry VIII's accomplishments are often overshadowed by the fact that he had six wives.

_____ 5. Many people believe that he executed all six, but that is not true.

_____ 6. He beheaded only two of them he divorced two of the others.

_____ 7. Of the other two, one died in childbirth, and one outlived him.

_____ 8. Wanting to divorce his first wife, Catherine of Aragon, who had not been able to give him an heir, and marry Anne Boleyn.

_____ 9. Unfortunately, the pope refusing to annul his marriage to Catherine.

_____ 10. Anne, already pregnant with Henry's daughter Elizabeth, who would eventually rule England as Queen Elizabeth I for forty-five years.

_____ 11. Henry was forced to take drastic measures he declared that he was head of the Church of England and would decide whether he was still married to Catherine.

_____ 12. But then Anne, Henry's second wife, failed to produce a male heir, she was unpopular and made many enemies, Henry became interested in Jane Seymour, one of Anne's attendants.

_____ 13. Henry had Anne arrested and charged with treason and infidelity she was beheaded in 1536.

_____ 14. Within 24 hours of Anne's execution, Henry was engaged to Jane Seymour, they wed two weeks later.

_____ 15. Jane gave birth to a son, but she died two weeks later.

_____ 16. For political reasons, Henry married Anne of Cleves next she was unattractive, and Henry was already smitten with young Kathryn Howard, cousin of Anne Boleyn.

_____ 17. Right after he annulled his marriage to Anne of Cleves, he married Kathryn.

_____ 18. She was nineteen, young, and vivacious, he was forty-nine, fat, and suffering from a painful leg ulcer.

_____ **19.** Kathryn sought the company of handsome young men in 1542,

she, too, was beheaded for infidelity.

_____ **20.** Henry's last wife, Katherine Parr, who became his widow when he

died in 1547.

EXERCISE 17   Correcting Fragments, Comma Splices, and Run-Ons

Write the appropriate identification in each blank. Correct the faulty sentences.

OK	**correct**
CS	**comma splice**
RO	**run-on**
FRAG	**fragment**

_____ **1.** During the eighteenth and nineteenth centuries, many people

developed an intense fear of being buried alive.

_____ **2.** Doctors couldn't measure brainwaves and other vital signs,

diagnosing death was an inexact science.

_____ **3.** A person who was only in a coma could appear dead, lead

poisoning, for example, led to a long state of unconciousness that

mimicked death.

_____ **4.** Premature burial was a real possibility people passed around

hundreds of stories about re-opened caskets revealing lids with

claw marks and corpses with bloodied fingers.

_____ **5.** The horror stories of writer Edgar Allan Poe often included

premature burials, in "The Fall of the House of Usher," a young

woman breaks out of her tomb.

_____ **6.** Poe's stories "The Premature Burial," "The Cask of Amontillado,"

and "The Black Cat."

_____ **7.** Such stories contributed to the phobia, people developed customs

designed to confirm that someone was actually dead.

_____ **8.** The ceremony known as a "wake" allowed family and friends to sit

with the deceased and give him or her time to wake up.

_____ 9. "Waiting mortuaries" were started in 1791 they were places where the deceased was kept for two weeks.

_____ 10. A system of cords and pulleys attached to the dead person's fingers, toes, and head that caused bells to ring if he or she made the slightest movement.

_____ 11. Although some people left instructions for their doctors to prod, poke, and pierce them in a variety of ways to confirm death.

_____ 12. In addition, numerous patents were issued for coffin escape devices.

_____ 13. One particular design gave the English language several phrases still in use today.

_____ 14. The deceased person's wrist was tied with a string attached to a bell above the ground, in the event of premature burial, he or she could ring the bell and be dug up by a person hired to keep watch.

_____ 15. Thus, the "dead ringer" "saved by the bell" by someone working the "graveyard shift."

_____ 16. An inventor named Herr Gusmuth, who invented a "security coffin" with a speaking tube.

_____ 17. Allowed the prematurely buried to yell for help.

_____ 18. The tube also permitted food and drink to be served to the awakened corpse while he or she was awaiting exhumation.

_____ 19. Some designs included flags or lights as signaling devices others were outfitted with heaters and stocked with food and beverages.

_____ 20. Today, of course, medical science is more advanced, we have more confidence in our doctors' abilities to recognize death.

EXERCISE 18   Correcting Fragments, Comma Splices, and Run-Ons

Write the appropriate identification in each blank. Correct the faulty sentences.

OK	**correct**
CS	**comma splice**
RO	**run-on**
FRAG	**fragment**

_____   1. Piranhas live in freshwater streams and rivers of South America, they travel through the water in groups.

_____   2. These ferocious-looking fish have a protruding lower jaw revealing a mouthful of sharp teeth.

_____   3. Piranhas are meat-eaters they will eat just about any live or dead creature.

_____   4. A school of piranhas consuming an animal the size of a pig in just minutes.

_____   5. Like sharks, they are drawn toward the scent of blood in the water, movements such as splashing attract them, too.

_____   6. When a school of piranhas is in a feeding frenzy.

_____   7. The water appears to boil and become red with blood.

_____   8. The piranha owes its savage reputation, in part, to adventurer Theodore Roosevelt.

_____   9. Who wrote in a 1914 book that these ruthless predators would "devour alive any man or beast."

_____   10. Roosevelt had heard of a man who went out alone on a mule, the mule returned to camp without its rider.

_____   11. The man's skeleton was found in the water every bit of flesh had been stripped from his bones.

_____ **12.** Still, Americans intrigued by stories bought piranhas for aquarium pets.

_____ **13.** Fascinated by the fish's grisly reputation.

_____ **14.** Perhaps admiring the silver body and bright red belly of this handsome creature.

_____ **15.** As aquarium owners realized that their pets could be quite aggressive and dangerous.

_____ **16.** Piranhas dumped into ponds, lakes, and reservoirs across the United States.

_____ **17.** Fortunately, most of the waters were too cold for the piranhas to survive.

_____ **18.** Truthfully, though, piranhas rarely attack humans, South Americans even bathe in piranha-infested waters.

_____ **19.** South Americans also think piranhas are tasty and like to net, cook, and eat them.

_____ **20.** However, U.S. officials are taking no chances, piranhas are illegal in many states.

Verbs

This section covers the use of standard verbs. To some, the word *standard* implies "correct." A more precise meaning is "that which is conventional among educated people." Therefore, a standard verb is the right choice in most school assignments, most published writing, and most important public-speaking situations. We all change our language when we move from these formal occasions to informal ones: We don't talk to our families in the same way we would speak at a large gathering in public; we don't write letters to friends the same way we write a history report. But even with informal language we would seldom change from standard to nonstandard usage.

REGULAR AND IRREGULAR VERBS

Verbs can be divided into two categories, called *regular* and *irregular*. Regular verbs are predictable, but irregular verbs—as the term suggests—follow no definite pattern.

Verbs always show time. **Present-tense verbs** show an action or a state of being that is occurring at the present time: I *like* your hat. He *is* at a hockey game right now. Present-tense verbs can also imply a continuation from the past into the future: She *drives* to work every day.

Past-tense verbs show an action or a state of being that occurred in the past: We *walked* to town yesterday. Tim *was* president of the club last year.

Regular Verbs

Present Tense

For *he*, *she*, and *it*, regular verbs in the present tense add an *-s* or an *-es* to the base word. The following chart shows the present tense of the base word *ask*, which is a regular verb.

	Singular	**Plural**
First Person:	I ask	we ask
Second Person:	you ask	you ask
Third Person:	he, she, it asks	they ask

If the verb ends in *-y*, you might have to drop the *-y* and add *-ies* for *he*, *she*, and *it*.

	Singular	**Plural**
First Person:	I try	we try
Second Person:	you try	you try
Third Person:	he, she, it tries	they try

Past Tense

For regular verbs in the past tense, add *-ed* to the base form:

Base Form (Present)	**Past**
walk	walked
answer	answered

If the base form already ends in *-e*, add just *-d*:

Base Form (Present)	**Past**
smile	smiled
decide	decided

If the base form ends in a consonant followed by *-y*, drop the *-y* and add *-ied*.

Base Form (Present)	**Past**
fry	fried
amplify	amplified

Regardless of how you form the past tense, regular verbs in the past tense do not change forms. The following chart shows the past tense of the base word *like*, which is a regular verb.

	Singular	**Plural**
First Person:	I liked	we liked
Second Person:	you liked	you liked
Third Person:	he, she, it liked	they liked

Past Participles

The past participle uses the helping verbs *has*, *have*, or *had* along with the past tense of the verb. For regular verbs, the past-participle form of the verb is the same as the past tense.

Base Form	Past	Past Participle
happen	happened	happened
hope	hoped	hoped
cry	cried	cried

Following is a list of some common regular verbs, showing the base form, the past tense, and the past participle. The base form can also be used with such helping verbs as *can*, *could*, *do*, *does*, *did*, *may*, *might*, *must*, *shall*, *should*, *will*, and *would*.

Regular Verbs

Base Form (Present)	Past	Past Participle
answer	answered	answered
ask	asked	asked
cry	cried	cried
decide	decided	decided
dive	dived (dove)	dived
finish	finished	finished
happen	happened	happened
learn	learned	learned
like	liked	liked
love	loved	loved
need	needed	needed
open	opened	opened
start	started	started
suppose	supposed	supposed
walk	walked	walked
want	wanted	wanted

Irregular Verbs

Irregular verbs do not follow any definite pattern.

Base Form (Present)	Past	Past Participle
shake	shook	shaken
make	made	made
begin	began	begun

Some irregular verbs that sound similar in the present tense don't follow the same pattern.

Base Form (Present)	Past	Past Participle
ring	rang	rung
swing	swung	swung
bring	brought	brought

Present Tense

For *he*, *she*, and *it*, irregular verbs in the present tense add an *-s* or an *-es* to the base word. The following chart shows the present tense of the base word *break*, which is an irregular verb.

	Singular	**Plural**
First Person:	I break	we break
Second Person:	you break	you break
Third Person:	he, she, it breaks	they break

If the irregular verb ends in *-y*, you might have to drop the *-y* and add *-ies* for *he*, *she*, and *it*.

	Singular	**Plural**
First Person:	I cry	we cry
Second Person:	you cry	you cry
Third Person:	he, she, it cries	they cry

Past Tense

Like past-tense regular verbs, past-tense irregular verbs do not change their forms. This chart shows the past tense of the irregular verb *do*.

	Singular	**Plural**
First Person:	I did	we did
Second Person:	you did	you did
Third Person:	he, she, it did	they did

The following list includes the past tense of many irregular verbs.

Past Participles

Use the past-tense form with the helping verbs *has*, *have*, or *had*.

Here is a list of some common irregular verbs, showing the base form (present), the past tense, and the past participle. Like regular verbs, the base forms can be used with such helping verbs as *can*, *could*, *do*, *does*, *did*, *may*, *might*, *must*, *shall*, *should*, *will*, and *would*.

Irregular Verbs

Base Form (Present)	Past	Past Participle
arise	arose	arisen
awake	awoke (awaked)	awoken (awaked)
be	was, were	been
become	became	become
begin	began	begun
bend	bent	bent
blow	blew	blown
break	broke	broken
burst	burst	burst
buy	bought	bought
catch	caught	caught
choose	chose	chosen

Base Form (Present)	Past	Past Participle
cling	clung	clung
come	came	come
cost	cost	cost
creep	crept	crept
deal	dealt	dealt
do	did	done
drink	drank	drunk
drive	drove	driven
eat	ate	eaten
feel	felt	felt
fight	fought	fought
fling	flung	flung
fly	flew	flown
forget	forgot	forgotten
freeze	froze	frozen
get	got	got (gotten)
go	went	gone
grow	grew	grown
hang	hung	hung
have	had	had
hit	hit	hit
know	knew	known
lead	led	led
leave	left	left
lose	lost	lost
make	made	made
mean	meant	meant
put	put	put
read	read	read
ride	rode	ridden
ring	rang	rung
see	saw	seen
shine	shone	shone
shoot	shot	shot
sing	sang	sung
sink	sank	sunk
sleep	slept	slept
slink	slunk	slunk
speak	spoke	spoken
spend	spent	spent
spread	spread	spread
steal	stole	stolen
stink	stank (stunk)	stunk
sweep	swept	swept
swim	swam	swum
swing	swung	swung
take	took	taken
teach	taught	taught

Base Form (Present)	Past	Past Participle
tear	tore	torn
think	thought	thought
throw	threw	thrown
thrust	thrust	thrust
wake	woke (waked)	woken (waked)
weep	wept	wept
write	wrote	written

EXERCISE 19   Selecting Verbs

Cross out the incorrect verb form.

1. Mark (knew/knowed) he could not finish the term paper that semester.
2. They (dragged, drug, drugged) the cart into the back yard.
3. I was sure that I hadn't (ate, eaten) the lobster.
4. When we arrived, the windows were (broke, broked, broken).
5. Vanessa (dive, dived) from the high board and swam over to us.
6. Imelda had (spread, spreaded) the maps out on the table before the meeting.
7. Have they (began, begun) to gather that material this early?
8. Shawna (swimmed, swam, swum) that distance twice last week.
9. The water pipes have (burst, busted, bursted) again.
10. I (ran, runned) over to Colleen's house for help.

"Problem" Verbs

The following pairs of verbs are especially troublesome and confusing: *lie* and *lay*, *sit* and *set*, and *rise* and *raise*. One way to tell them apart is to remember which word in each pair takes a direct object. A direct object answers the question *whom* or *what* in connection with a verb. The words *lay*, *raise*, and *set* take a direct object.

He *raised* the window. (He *raised* what?)

Lie, *rise*, and *sit*, however, cannot take a direct object. We cannot say, for example, "He rose the window." In the following examples, the italicized words are direct objects.

Present Tense	Meaning	Past Tense	Past Participle	Example
lie	to rest	lay	lain	I lay down to rest.
lay	to place something	laid	laid	We laid the *books* on the table.
rise	to go up	rose	risen	The smoke rose quickly.
raise	to lift, bring forth	raised	raised	She raised the *question*.
sit	to rest	sat	sat	He sat in the chair.
set	to place something	set	set	They set the *basket* on the floor.

EXERCISE 20   Selecting Verbs

Cross out the incorrect verb form.

1. The book is (lying, laying) on top of the bureau.

2. Will we (receive, received) your package soon?

3. His recent decision will certainly (change, changed) our policy.

4. When he heard Lenore call, he (rose, raised) and left the room.

5. That dog can (sit, set) in the yard for hours and bark constantly.

6. Marcia (done, did) many chores before she left for school.

7. Why are you (sitting, setting) those plants in the hot sun?

8. My mother (don't, doesn't) understand why Victor takes so long to come

    home from kindergarten.

9. A stray cat (drowned, drownded) in the river yesterday.

10. The spy (fool, fooled) his captor by disguising himself as a workman.

11. My cousins will (left, leave) Europe soon.

12. We (learn, learned) from his conversation that he did not wish to go again.

13. Kim hasn't been able to (taught, teach) those boys anything.

14. Have you (tryed, tried) to relax for a few minutes this evening?

15. The police officers could not (see, saw) us cross the bridge during the heavy

    rainstorm.

16. You (lie, lay) down here and rest for a few minutes before class.

17. The cost of those articles has (raised, risen) considerably since the first of

    the year.

18. Pam (rose, raised) the window and waved to me as I passed.

19. My brother (lay, laid) the money on the table and looked hopefully at Mother.

20. Please (sit, set) the shoes down on the rack and come over here.

EXERCISE 21   Writing Sentences with Troublesome Verbs

Use each of these words in a sentence of ten words or more.

1. *lie, lay* (rest), *lain, laid* _____

_____

_____

_____

_____

_____

2. *sit, sat, set* _____

_____

_____

_____

_____

_____

_____

3. *is, was, were* _____

_____

_____

_____

_____

_____

4. *do, does* (or *don't, doesn't*) _____

_____

_____

_____

_____

_____

THE TWELVE VERB TENSES

Some languages, such as Chinese and Navajo, have no verb tenses to indicate time. English has a fairly complicated system of tenses, but most verbs pattern in what are known as the simple tenses: present, past, and future. Altogether there are twelve tenses in English. The four sections that follow illustrate those tenses in sentences. The charts place each verb on a time line; they also explain what the different tenses mean and how to form them.

Simple Tenses

Present: I, we, you, they *drive*.
He, she, it *drives*.

Past: I, we, you, he, she, it, they *drove*.
Future: I, we, you, he, she, it, they *will drive*.

Perfect Tenses

Present Perfect: I, we, you, they *have driven*.
He, she, it *has driven*.

Past Perfect: I, we, you, he, she, it, they *had driven*.
Future Perfect: I, we, you, he, she, it, they *will have driven*.

Progressive Tenses

Present Progressive: I *am driving*.
He, she, it *is driving*.
We, you, they *are driving*.

Past Progressive: I, he, she, it *was driving*.
We, you, they *were driving*.

Future Progressive: I, we, you, he, she, it, they *will be driving*.

Perfect Progressive Tenses

Present Perfect Progressive: I, we, you, they *have been driving*.
He, she, it *has been driving*.

Past Perfect Progressive: I, we, you, he, she, it, they *had been driving*.

Future Perfect Progressive: I, we, you, he, she, it, they *will have been driving*.

Simple Tenses

Tenses	Time Line	Time	Verb Form
Present I *drive* to work. She *drives* to work.	past —— XXX —— future **Now**	Present; may imply a continuation from past to future	Present: *drive* *drives*
Past I *drove* to work.	X —— **Now**	Past	Past: *drove*
Future I *will drive* to work.	—— X **Now**	Future	Present preceded by *will*: *will drive*

Perfect Tenses

Tenses	Time Line	Time	Verb Form
Present Perfect I *have driven* to work.	past —— XXX —— future **Now**	Completed recently in the past; may continue into the present	Past participle preceded by *have* or *has*: *have driven*
Past Perfect I *had driven* to work before I moved to the city [event].	Event XO —— **Now**	Prior to a specific time in the past	Past participle preceded by *had*: *had driven*
Future Perfect I *will have driven* to work thousands of times by December [event].	Event X O **Now**	At a time prior to a specific time in the future	Past participle preceded by *will have*: *will have driven*

Progressive Tenses

Tenses	Time Line	Time	Verb Form
Present Progressive I *am driving* to work.	past ——XXX—— future Now	In progress now	Progressive (-*ing* ending) preceded by *is*, *am*, or *are*: *am driving*
Past Progressive I *was driving* to work.	XXX Now	In progress in the past	Progressive (-*ing* ending) preceded by *was* or *were*: *was driving*
Future Progressive I *will be driving* to work.	XXX Now	In progress in the future	Progressive (-*ing* ending) preceded by *will be*: *will be driving*

Perfect Progressive Tenses

Tenses	Time Line	Time	Verb Form
Present Perfect Progressive I *have been driving* to work.	past ——XXX—— future Now	In progress before now or up to now	Progressive (-*ing* ending) preceded by *have been* or *has been*: *have been driving*
Past Perfect Progressive I *had been driving* when I began ride-sharing [event].	Event XXX O Now	In progress before another event in the past	Progressive (-*ing* ending) preceded by *had been*: I *had been driving*
Future Perfect Progressive By May 1 [event], I *will have been driving* to work for six years.	Event XXX O Now	In progress before another event in the future	Progressive (-*ing* ending) preceded by *will have been*: *will have been driving*

EXERCISE 22   Selecting Verbs

Underline the correct verb form.

1. I wished I (stayed, had stayed) home.

2. I remembered that I (paid, had paid) him twice.

3. After parking their car, they (walk, walked) to the beach.

4. I (have, had) never encountered a genius until I met her.

5. I hoped that we (could have gone, went) to the big game.

6. They know that they (will complete, will have completed) the job before the first snow.

7. We (are considering, consider) the proposal.

8. He told us of the interesting life he (had led, led).

9. We went to the desert to see the cabin they (built, had built).

10. Tomorrow I (drive, will drive) to the supermarket for party items.

EXERCISE 23   Selecting Verbs

Underline the correct verb form.

1. The scholars (worked, had worked) many hours before they solved the problem.

2. The shipping clerks wished they (had sent, sent) the package.

3. We (study, are studying) the issue now.

4. We (decide, will decide) on the winner tomorrow.

5. They reminded us that we (made, had made) the same promise before.

6. Before she went to Mexico, Jill (had never been, never was) out of the country.

7. Jake (had been napping, napped) when the alarm sounded.

8. By the time he finished talking, he realized that he (said, had said) too much.

9. At the end of the semester, the course grade (depends, will depend) on your ability to write well.

10. After he retired, I realized how much I (had learned, learned) from working with him.

SUBJECT-VERB AGREEMENT

This section is concerned with number agreement between subjects and verbs. The basic principle of **subject-verb agreement** is that if the subject is singular, the verb should be singular, and if the subject is plural, the verb should be plural. There are ten major guidelines. In the examples under the following guidelines, the simple subjects and verbs are italicized.

1. Do not let words that come between the subject and verb affect agreement.

   - Modifying phrases and clauses frequently come between the subject and verb:

     The various *types* of drama *were* not *discussed*.

     Angela, who is hitting third, *is* the best player.

     The *price* of those shoes *is* too high.

   - Certain prepositions can cause trouble. The following words are prepositions, not conjunctions: *along with, as well as, besides, in addition to, including, together with*. The words that function as objects of prepositions cannot also be subjects of the sentence.

     The *coach*, along with the players, *protests* the decision.

   - When a negative phrase follows a positive subject, the verb agrees with the positive subject.

     Philip, not the other boys, *was* the culprit.

2. Do not let inversions (verb before subject, not the normal order) affect the agreement of subject and verb.

   - Verbs and other words may come before the subject. Do not let them affect the agreement. To understand subject-verb relationships, recast the sentence in normal word order.

     Are Juan and his *sister* at home? [question form]

     Juan and his *sister are* at home. [normal order]

   - A sentence filler is a word that is grammatically independent of other words in the sentence. The most common fillers are *there* and *here*. Even though a sentence filler precedes the verb, it should not be treated as the subject.

     There *are* many *reasons* for his poor work. [The verb *are* agrees with the subject *reasons*.]

3. A singular verb agrees with a singular indefinite pronoun.

   - Most indefinite pronouns are singular.

     Each of the women *is* ready at this time.

     Neither of the women *is* ready at this time.

     One of the children *is* not paying attention.

- Certain indefinite pronouns do not clearly express either a singular or plural number. Agreement, therefore, depends on the meaning of the sentence. These pronouns are *all*, *any*, *none*, and *some*.

  All of the melon *was* good.

  All of the melons *were* good.

  None of the pie *is* acceptable.

  None of the pies *are* acceptable.

4. Two or more subjects joined by *and* usually take a plural verb.

   The *captain* and the *sailors were* happy to be ashore.

   The *trees* and *shrubs need* more care.

   - If the parts of a compound subject mean one and the same person or thing, the verb is singular; if the parts mean more than one, the verb is plural.

     The *secretary* and *treasurer is* not present. [one]

     The *secretary* and the *treasurer are* not present. [more than one]

   - When *each* or *every* precedes singular subjects joined by *and*, the verb is singular.

     Each *boy* and each *girl brings* a donation.

     Each *woman* and *man has asked* the same questions.

5. Alternative subjects—that is, subjects joined by *or, nor, either/or, neither/ nor, not only/but also*—should be handled in the following manner:

   - If the subjects are both singular, the verb is singular.

     Rosa or *Alicia* is responsible.

   - If the subjects are plural, the verb is plural.

     Neither the *students* nor the *teachers were* impressed by his comments.

   - If one of the subjects is singular and the other subject is plural, the verb agrees with the nearer subject.

     Either the Garcia *boys* or their *father goes* to the hospital each day.

     Either their *father* or the Garcia *boys go* to the hospital each day.

6. Collective nouns—*team, family, group, crew, gang, class, faculty*, and the like—take a singular verb if the verb is considered a unit, but they take a plural verb if the group is considered as a number of individuals.

   The *team is playing* well tonight.

   The *team are getting* dressed.

(In the second sentence the individuals are acting not as a unit but separately. If you don't like the way the sentence sounds, substitute "The members of the team are getting dressed.")

7. Titles of books, essays, short stories, and plays, a word spoken of as a word, and the names of businesses take a singular verb.

The Canterbury Tales was written by Geoffrey Chaucer.

Ives is my favorite name for a pet.

Markel Brothers has a sale this week.

8. Sums of money, distances, and measurements are followed by a singular verb when a unit is meant. They are followed by a plural verb when the individual elements are considered separately.

Three dollars was the price. [unit]

Three dollars were lying there. [individual]

Five years is a long time. [unit]

The *first five years were* difficult ones. [individual]

9. Be careful of agreement with nouns ending in -*s*. Several nouns ending in -*s* take a singular verb—for example, *aeronautics, civics, economics, ethics, measles, mumps.*

Mumps is an unpleasant disease.

Economics is my major field of study.

10. Some nouns have only a plural form and so take only a plural verb—for example, *clothes, fireworks, scissors, pants.*

His *pants are* badly wrinkled.

Marv's *clothes were* stylish and expensive.

EXERCISE 24   Making Subjects and Verbs Agree

Underline the correct verb form.

1. There (is, are) very little remote wilderness left in the world.

2. Neither the jungles, nor the oceans, nor the desert (has, have) gone unexplored.

3. Mount Everest, the world's highest mountain, (is, are) no exception.

4. Before 1953, though, many a thrill-seeker (was, were) hoping to be the first to stand on its summit.

5. Everyone (know, knows) that George Mallory died trying in 1924.

6. Although we can never be sure, some of us (believe, believes) Mallory was the first to make it to the top.

7. According to the record books, Sir Edmund Hillary, along with his partner Tenzing Norgay, (was, were) the first to reach the highest place on Earth on May 29, 1953.

8. There (is, are) many reasons why someone would want to climb Mount Everest.

9. (Is, Are) personal satisfaction or prestige more important to today's climbers?

10. (Is, Are) mountaineers driven by passion or by sport?

11. Now, $65,000 (is, are) the price anyone can pay for a guided hike to the summit.

12. Trips to the top of Mount Everest (is, are) now routine.

13. A 64-year-old man, a legally blind person, and an amputee (has, have) successfully climbed the mountain.

14. A solo climber or a group (take, takes) about eleven hours to ascend.

15. Everest has been climbed more than 1,300 times; however, not all of the attempts (was, were) successful.

16. Either falls or an avalanche (has, have) caused numerous deaths.

17. *Into Thin Air* (is, are) a riveting tale of one catastrophic expedition during which eight people died.

18. The majority of the 175 people who have died (is, are) still on the mountain.

19. The news (is, are) always bad when people make mistakes and lose their lives.

20. But adventurers like Sir Edmund Hillary (is, are) always willing to take the risk.

EXERCISE 25   Making Subjects and Verbs Agree

Underline the correct verb form.

1. Three varieties of poison ivy (grow, grows) in her garden.

2. Enrique, an executive with Sony Records, (is, are) looking for new talent.

3. Someone with psychic abilities (is, are) what you need.

4. My face, as well as my legs, (is, are) sunburned.

5. One B, not just A's, (was, were) on her report card.

6. (Is, Are) Bert and Ernie still roommates?

7. There (is, are) several skeletons in his particular closet.

8. Each of the bongo songs (sound, sounds) the same.

9. Neither of the girls (is, are) good at bagging groceries.

10. One of the Indians (shoot, shoots) better than the cowboys.

11. Some of the jelly (has, have) been stolen.

12. Some of the jelly beans (was, were) stuck together.

13. (Do, Does) your family or your friends know that you've joined the circus?

14. Neither the baton twirlers nor the band (like, likes) to march behind the horse-drawn carriages.

15. Every person, place, or thing (is, are) a noun.

16. My mentor and friend (advise, advises) me to read the *Wall Street Journal*.

17. *The Shell Seekers* (is, are) one of my favorite books.

18. McDonald's (stays, stay) open late.

19. My glasses (is, are) at the bottom of the pool.

20. Your thanks (is, are) much appreciated.

CONSISTENCY IN TENSE

Consider this paragraph:

> We (1) went downtown, and then we (2) watch a movie. Later we (3) met some friends from school, and we all (4) go to the mall. For most of the evening, we (5) play video games in arcades. It (6) was a typical but rather uneventful summer day.

Does the shifting verb tense bother you (to say nothing about the lack of development of ideas)? It should! The writer makes several unnecessary changes. Verbs 1, 3, and 6 are in the past tense, and verbs 2, 4, and 5 are in the present tense. Changing all verbs to past tense makes the paragraph much smoother.

> We went downtown, and then we watched a movie. Later we met some friends from school, and we all went to the mall. For most of the evening, we played video games in arcades. It was a typical but rather uneventful summer day.

In other instances you might want to maintain a consistent present tense. There are no inflexible rules about selecting a tense for certain kinds of writing, but you should be consistent, changing tense only for a good reason.

The present tense is ordinarily used in writing about literature, even if the literature was composed long in the past:

> *Moby Dick* is a novel about Captain Ahab's obsession with a great white whale. Ahab *sets* sail with a full crew of sailors who *think* they *are going* on merely another whaling voyage. Most of the crew *are* experienced seamen.

The past tense is likely to serve you best in writing about your personal experiences and about historical events (although the present tense can often be used effectively to establish the feeling of intimacy and immediacy):

In the summer of 1991, Hurricane Bob *hit* the Atlantic coast region. It *came* ashore near Cape Hatteras and *moved* north. The winds *reached* a speed of more than ninety miles per hour on Cape Cod but then *slackened* by the time Bob *reached* Maine.

EXERCISE 26   Making Verbs Consistent in Tense

In each sentence, the last verb is in the wrong tense. Cross it out and write the correct form above it.

1. Ralph Waldo Emerson said that a success was defined as leaving the world a better place.

2. After Lou graduated from college, he joins the Peace Corps.

3. She lost the game because she wasn't sure where the Galapagos Islands were.

4. Joe was determined to shed twenty pounds before he goes to his high school reunion.

5. I'd like to fight you in the Tough Man contest, but I had a pedicure appointment.

6. After having dated only losers for fifteen years, Roxanne decides to remain single.

7. Not everyone who tries out got to play on the team next year.

8. She hopes ₒₒ be a star some day, but she was not going to give up her day job.

9. The guest did not realize that caviar was fish eggs.

10. Albert Einstein said that imagination was more important than knowledge.

11. The lawyer answered all of her questions; then he sends her a bill for $200.

12. She always claims to be on a diet, but she ordered dessert every time we go out to eat.

13. As Taloola cuts your hair, she gossiped about everyone in town.

14. Tanya takes her lunch to school because she disliked the smell of the cafeteria food.

15. When Rhonda pulled the gun from her purse, everyone in the room runs for cover.

16. Trixie wondered aloud if the 1930s were called the Great Depression because everyone is so depressed.

17. He did fifty sit-ups every morning before he takes a shower.

18. She regretted not telling him that she will always love him.

19. George thinks that he's in trouble when the police car pulled up behind him.

20. Tex and his bride chose a home site where the buffalo were roaming and the antelopes are playing.

EXERCISE 27   Making Verbs Consistent in Tense

Change the verbs in the following paragraph as necessary to maintain a mostly consistent past tense.

(1) Tarzan spoke to Jane in simple language. (2) His most famous words were "Me Tarzan, you Jane." (3) Before the arrival of Jane, there are only jungle friends for Tarzan. (4) Those animals seldom used the full eight parts of speech. (5) For example, lions seldom utter verbs. (6) Elephants had no patience with prepositions. (7) Chimps condemn conjunctions. (8) Their punctuation was replaced largely by snarls, growls, and breast-beating. (9) Their language is well suited to Tarzan. (10) To him, jungle language was like swinging on a vine. (11) A one-syllable yell is a full oration. (12) Jane never ridiculed his grammar or even his yelling. (13) She holds back criticism of the king of the apes. (14) Despite their difference in language skills, they establish hutkeeping. (15) They were very poor and wore simple garments made of skins. (16) Their main transportation is well-placed hanging vines. (17) Tarzan and Jane had a child. (18) They name him "Boy." (19) Fortunately, they did not have another male child. (20) Such an occurrence could have caused a language gridlock.

EXERCISE 28   Making Verbs Consistent in Tense

Change the verbs in the following paragraph as necessary to maintain a mostly consistent past tense.

(1) Once upon a time, a Professor Glen was very popular with his students. (2) He kept long office hours and always speaks nicely to his students on campus. (3) He even brought popcorn for them to munch on during tests. (4) Respecting their sensitivity, he marks with a soothing green ink instead of red. (5) He often told jokes and listened attentively to their complaints about assignments. (6) The leaders of student government elect him teacher of the century. (7) Who would not admire such a person? (8) Then late one semester, a strange and shocking thing happens. (9) Everywhere there were students in despair. (10) Professor Glen no longer speaks openly to students. (11) During his office hours, he locked his door and posted a pit bull. (12) He corrects student papers in flaming scarlet. (13) Instead of popcorn, he gave them hot scorn. (14) He told no more jokes and sneered at their complaints about assignments. (15) He sticks out his tongue at students on campus. (16) He offered good grades for cash. (17) Professor Glen even accepts Visa cards and validated parking. (18) One day the students heard a thumping sound in a classroom closet. (19) Looking inside, they find the true Professor Glen. (20) The other one was an evil twin professor.

ACTIVE AND PASSIVE VOICE

Which of these sentences sounds better?

> Ken Griffey Jr. slammed a home run.

> A home run was slammed by Ken Griffey Jr.

Both sentences carry the same message, but the first expresses it more effectively. The subject (*Ken Griffey Jr.*) is the actor. The verb (*slammed*) is the action. The direct object (*home run*) is the receiver of the action. The second sentence lacks the vitality of the first because the receiver of the action is the subject; the one who performs the action is embedded in the prepositional phrase at the end of the sentence.

The first sentence demonstrates the active voice. It has an active verb (one that leads to the direct object), and the action moves from the beginning to the end of the sentence. The second exhibits the passive voice (with the action reflecting back on the subject). When given a choice, you should usually select the active voice. It promotes energy and directness.

The passive voice, though not usually the preferred form, does have its uses.

- When the doer of the action is unknown or unimportant:

    My car was stolen. [The doer, a thief, is unknown.]

- When the receiver of the action is more important than the doer:

    My neighbor was permanently disabled by an irresponsible drunk driver. [The neighbor's suffering, not the drunk driver, is the focus.]

As you can see, the passive construction places the doer at the end of a prepositional phrase (as in the second example) or does not include the doer in the statement at all (as in the first example). In the first example the receiver of the action (the car) is in the subject position. The verb is preceded by the *to be* helper *was*. Here is another example:

> **Passive:**   The book was read by her.

> **Active:**   She read the book.

Weak sentences often involve the unnecessary and ineffective use of the passive form; Exercise 29 gives you practice in identifying the passive voice and changing it to active.

EXERCISE 29   Using Active and Passive Voice

Rewrite these sentences to convert the verbs from passive to active voice.

1. A letter has been written by me to you.

2. An honest dollar was never made by his ancestors, and now he is following in their fingerprints.

3. The assignment was approved by the instructor.

4. The instructor was given a much-deserved medal of valor by the president of the student body.

5. Few people noticed that most of the work was done by the quiet students.

6. The ballgame was interrupted by bats catching flies in the outfield.

7. The commotion at the apathy convention was caused by a person who attended.

8. The air was filled with speeches by him.

9. He doesn't have an enemy, but he is hated by all his friends.

10. His lips are never passed by a lie—he talks through his nose.

STRONG VERBS

Because the verb is an extremely important part of any sentence, it should be chosen with care. Some of the most widely used verbs are the *being* verbs: *is, was, were, are, am.* We couldn't get along in English without them, but writers often use them when more forceful and effective verbs are available. Consider these examples:

Weak Verb:	He *is* the leader of the people.
Strong Verb:	He *leads* the people.
Weak Verb:	She *was* the first to finish.
Strong Verb:	She *finished* first.

EXERCISE 30   Using Strong Verbs

Rewrite the following sentences to strengthen the weak verbs.

1. He is the writer of that essay.

2. She was the driver of the speeding car.

3. He was the player of the guitar.

4. They were the leaders of the entire region in sales.

5. The medicine was a cure for the cold.

6. The last entertainer was the winner of the award.

7. The yowling cat was the cause of my waking up last night.

8. The mechanic is the fixer of my car.

9. He was in attendance at the computer seminar.

10. She is a shoe salesperson.

SUBJUNCTIVE MOOD

Mood refers to the intention of the verb. Three moods are relevant to our study: indicative, imperative, and subjunctive.

The **indicative mood** expresses a statement of fact.

I considered the issue.

I was tired.

The **imperative mood** expresses a command (and has a *you* understood subject).

Go to the store.

The **subjunctive mood** expresses a statement as contrary to fact, conditional, desirable, possible, necessary, or doubtful. In current English the subjunctive form is distinguishable only in two forms: The verb *to be* uses *be* throughout the present tense and *were* throughout the past tense.

He requires that we *be* [instead of *are*] on time.

If she *were* [instead of *was*] the candidate, she would win.

In other verbs, the final -*s* is dropped in the third person singular [*he*, *she*, *it*] of the present tense to make all forms the same in any one tense.

I request that he *report* [instead of *reports*] today.

Here are examples of the common forms:

If I *were* [instead of *was*] you, I wouldn't do that. [contrary to fact]

She behaves as if she *were* [instead of *was*] not certain. [doubt]

I wish I *were* [instead of *was*] in Texas. [wish]

EXERCISE 31 Selecting Subjunctive Verbs

STUDENT COMPANION SITE
For additional practice visit www.cengage .com/devenglish/ brandon/PE11e.

Underline the subjunctive verbs.

1. If I (was, were) going to work, I would give you a ride.

2. I wish I (were, was) on the beach.

3. I demand that you (will return, return) the deposit.

4. They act as if they (are, were) rich.

5. I require that my workers (are, be) on time.

6. You may wish you (are, were) an adult, but you must show your ID.

7. You talk as if winning (was, were) possible.

8. My manager insists that I (be, am) tactful with clients.

9. Suppose, for sake of argument, your statement (was, were) true.

10. Sometimes I wish I (were, was) of the younger generation.

Pronouns

Should you say, "Between you and *I*" or "Between you and *me*"? What about "Let's you and *I* do this" or "Let's you and *me* do this"? Are you confused about when to use *who* and *whom*? Is it "Everyone should wear *their* coat [or *his* coat or *his or her* coat]"? Is there anything wrong with saying, "When *you* walk down the streets of Laredo"?

The examples in the first paragraph represent the most common problems people have with pronouns. This section will help you identify the standard forms and understand why they are correct. The result should be expertise and confidence.

PRONOUN CASE

Case is the form a pronoun takes as it fills a position in a sentence. Words such as *you* and *it* do not change, but others do, and they change in predictable ways. For example, *I* is a subject word and *me* is an object word. As you refer to yourself, you will select a pronoun that fits a certain part of sentence structure. You say, "*I* will write the paper," not "*Me* will write the paper," because *I* is in the subject position. But you say, "She will give the apple to *me*," not "She will give the apple to *I*," because *me* is in the object position. These are the pronouns that change:

Subject	Object
I	me
he	him
she	her
we	us
they	them
who, whoever	whom, whomever

Subjective Case

	Singular	Plural
First Person:	I	we
Second Person:	you	you
Third Person:	he she it	they
	who	

Subjective-case pronouns can fill two positions in a sentence.

1. Pronouns in the subjective case fill subject positions.

   a. Some will be easy to identify because they are at the beginning of the sentence.

I dance in the park.

He dances in the park.

She dances in the park.

We dance in the park.

They dance in the park.

Who is dancing in the park?

b. Others will be more difficult to identify because they are not at the beginning of a sentence and may not appear to be part of a clause. The words *than* and *as* are signals for these special arrangements, which can be called incompletely stated clauses.

He is taller than *I* (am).

She is younger than *we* (are).

We work as hard as *they* (do).

The words *am*, *are*, and *do*, which complete the clauses, have been omitted. We are actually saying, "He is taller than *I am*," "She is younger than *we are*," and "We work as hard as *they do*." The italicized pronouns are subjects of "understood" verbs.

2. Pronouns in the subjective case refer back to the subject.

a. They follow a form of the verb *to be*, such as *was*, *were*, *am*, *is*, and *are*.

I believe it is *he*.

It was *she* who spoke.

The victims were *they*.

b. Some nouns and pronouns refer back to an earlier noun without referring back through the verb.

The leading candidates—Juan, Darnelle, Steve, Kimlieu, and *I*—made speeches.

Objective Case

	Singular	**Plural**
First Person:	me	we
Second Person:	you	you
Third Person:	him her it	them
	whom	

Objective-case pronouns can also fill two positions in sentences.

1. Pronouns in the objective case fill object positions.

   a. They may be objects after the verb.

   - A direct object answers the question *what* or *whom* in connection with the verb.

     We brought *it* to your house. [*What* did we bring? *it*]

     We saw *her* in the library. [*Whom* did we see? *her*]

   - An indirect object answers the question *to whom* in connection with the verb.

     I gave *him* the message. [*To whom* did I give the message? *to him*]

     The doctor told *us* the test results. [*To whom* did the doctor tell the results? *to us*]

   b. Objective-case pronouns are objects after prepositions.

     The problem was clear to *us*.

     I went with Steve and *him*.

2. Objective-case pronouns may also refer back to object words.

   They had the costumes for us—Judy and *me*.

   The judge addressed the defendants—John and *her*.

Techniques for Determining Case

Here are three techniques that will help you decide which pronoun to use when the choice seems difficult.

1. If you have a compound element (such as a subject or an object of a preposition), consider only the pronoun part. The sound alone will probably tell you the answer.

   She gave the answer to Marie and (I, me).

   Marie and the pronoun make up a compound object of the preposition *to*. Disregard the noun, *Marie*, and ask yourself, "Would I say, 'She gave the answer *to me* or *to I*'?" The way the words sound would tell you the answer is *to me*. Of course, if you immediately notice that the pronoun is in an object position, you need not bother with sound.

2. If you are choosing between *who* (subject word) and *whom* (object word), look to the right to see if the next verb has a subject. If it does not, the pronoun probably *is* the subject, but if it does have a subject, the pronoun probably is an object.

   The person (*who*, whom) works hardest will win. [*Who* is the correct answer because it is the subject of the verb *works*.]

The person (who, *whom*) we admire most is José. [*Whom* is the correct answer because the next verb, *admire*, already has a subject, *we*. *Whom* is an object.]

A related technique works the same way. If the next important word after *who* or *whom* in a statement is a noun or pronoun, the correct word will almost always be *whom*. However, if the next important word is not a noun or pronoun, the correct word will be *who*.

To apply this technique, you must disregard qualifier clauses such as "I think," "it seems," and "we hope."

Tyrone is a natural leader (*who*, whom) has charisma. [*Who* is the correct answer; it is followed by something other than a noun or pronoun.]

Tyrone is a natural leader (*who*, whom), we think, has charisma. [*Who* is the correct answer; it is followed by the qualifier clause *we think*, which is then followed by something other than a noun or pronoun.]

Tyrone is a natural leader (who, *whom*) we supported. [*Whom* is the correct answer; it is followed by a pronoun.]

3. *Let's* is made up of the words *let* and *us* and means "you *let us*"; therefore, when you select a pronoun to follow it, consider the two original words and select another object word—*me*.

Let's you and (I, *me*) take a trip to Westwood. [Think of "You let us, you and me, take a trip to Westwood." *Us* and *me* are object words.]

EXERCISE 32   Selecting Pronouns: Case

Underline the correct pronoun form.

Compounds

1. Sacagawea and (he, him) helped Lewis and Clark as they explored the West.

2. Did you and (she, her) practice throwing curve balls?

3. She insisted on setting up Roxanne and (them, they) with blind dates.

4. The fortune cookie revealed to (they, them) and me the truth.

Appositives

5. Let's you and (I, me) order the crawfish platter.

6. Two of the dancers—Cheyenne and (she, her)—couldn't high-kick very well.

7. She has narrowed her suitors down to three—you, Bob, and (he, him).

8. (We, Us) know-it-alls consider it our duty to correct those who are wrong.

9. They frowned upon (we, us) women showing off our tattoos.

Comparisons

10. My friend Raj is a better rapper than (I, me).

11. Lucy has more freckles than (she, her).

12. He makes a lot more money than (they, them).

13. The chimpanzee knew as many words as (he, him).

Who/Whom

14. (Who, Whom) did you invite to the luau?

15. She is a person (who, whom) we can trust.

16. (Who, Whom) leaked the information to the press?

17. She is now dating the fellow (who, whom) she accidently ran over last month.

18. (Who, Whom) do you predict will be our first female president?

Refer Back to Subject

19. Was it (I, me) you hoped to find?

20. It is (she, her) for whom he sold his soul.

EXERCISE 33   Selecting Pronouns: Case

Underline the correct pronoun form.

1. She did not realize that you and (I, me) would be asked to testify.

2. Give the award to (whoever, whomever) is voted most valuable player.

3. We need one person (who, whom) we can rely on.

4. Would you support (her, she) in the election?

5. Let's you and (I, me) take that trip next year.

6. Everybody but (he, him) was ready for the test.

7. Only two were chosen, Kathy and (he, him).

8. She thinks more clearly than (I, me).

9. Distribute the cards among John, Joe, and (he, him).

10. Gilligan knows the answer better than (we, us).

11. The person (whom, who) came will call on you again.

12. You know that much better than (I, me).

13. The police believed (they, them) to be us.

14. The court found (us, we) to be responsible.

15. (Whoever, Whomever) they choose will receive the promotion.

16. I would have taken (she, her) to the meeting.

17. Is it (I, me) you are looking for?

18. Just between you and (I, me), I think we should go.

19. It could have been (he, him) whom you saw.

20. The soldiers (who, whom) they trained were sent to the front.

PRONOUN-ANTECEDENT AGREEMENT

Every pronoun refers to an earlier noun, which is called the **antecedent** of the pronoun. The antecedent is the noun that the pronoun replaces. The pronoun brings the reader back to the earlier thought. Here are some examples:

I tried to buy *tickets* for the concert, but *they* were all sold.

Roger painted a *picture* of a pickup truck. *It* was so good that *he* entered *it* in an art show.

A **pronoun** agrees with its antecedent in person, number, and gender. **Person**—first, second, or third—indicates perspective, or point of view. **Number** indicates singular or plural. **Gender** indicates masculine, feminine, or neuter.

| | **Subject Words** | | | **Object Words** | |
	Singular	Plural		Singular	Plural
First Person:	I	we	**First Person:**	me	we
Second Person:	you	you	**Second Person:**	you	you
Third Person:	he, she, it	they	**Third Person:**	him, her, it	them
	who			whom	

Agreement in Person

Avoid needless shifting of person, which means shifting of point of view, such as from *I* to *you*. First person, second person, and third person indicate perspectives from which you can write. Select one point of view and maintain it, promoting continuity and consistency. Needless shifting of person, meaning changing perspectives without reasons important for your content and purpose, is distracting and awkward. Each point of view has its appropriate purposes.

First Person

Using the word *I* and its companion forms *we*, *me*, and *us*, the first-person point of view emphasizes the writer, who is an important part of the subject of the composition. Choose first person for friendly letters, accounts of personal experience, and, occasionally, business correspondence, such as a letter of application for a job, which requires self-analysis.

Observe the presence of the writer and the use of *I* in this example.

I could tell that the wedding would not go well when the caterers started serving drinks before the ceremony and the bride began arguing with her future mother-in-law. After the sound system crashed, the band canceled and *I* wished *I* hadn't come.

Second Person

Using or implying the word *you*, the second-person point of view is fine for informal conversation, advice, and directions. Although it is occasionally found in academic writing, most instructors prefer that you use it only in process analysis, directions in how to do something.

In this example, note that the word *you* is sometimes understood and not stated.

> To juggle three balls, first *you* place two balls (A and B) in one hand and one ball (C) in the other. Then toss one of the two balls (A), and before *you* catch it with your other hand, toss the single ball (C) from that hand. Before that ball (C) lands in the other hand, toss the remaining inactive ball (B). Then pick up the balls and repeat the process until balls no longer fall to the ground.

Third Person

Referring to subject material, individuals, things, or ideas, the third-person point of view works best for most formal writing, be it academic or professional. Third-person pronouns include *he, she, it, they, him, her,* and *them*. Most of your college writing—essay exams, reports, compositions that explain and argue, critiques, and research papers—will be from this detached perspective with no references to yourself.

In this example, written in the third person, the name *Bartleby* is replaced by forms of *he*.

> *Bartleby*, one of Herman Melville's most memorable characters, has befuddled critics for more than a century. At a point in *his* life chosen for no obvious reason, *he* decides not to work, not to cooperate with others, and not to leave the premises of *his* employer because *he* "prefers not to." Most readers do not know what to make of *him*.

Correcting Problems of Agreement in Person

Most problems with pronoun agreement in person occur with the use of *you* in a passage that should have been written in the first or third person. If your composition is not one of advice or directions, the word *you* is probably not appropriate and should be replaced with a first- or third-person pronoun.

If you are giving advice or directions, use *you* throughout the passage, but, if you are not, replace each *you* with a first- or third-person pronoun that is consistent with the perspective, purpose, and content of the passage.

Inconsistent: *I* love to travel, especially when *you* go to foreign countries.

Consistent: *I* love to travel, especially when *I* go to foreign countries.

Inconsistent: When *you* are about to merge with moving traffic on the freeway, *one* should not stop *his or her* car.

Consistent: When *you* are about to merge with moving traffic on the freeway, *you* should not stop *your* car.

Consistent: When *one* is about to merge with moving traffic on the freeway, *one* should not stop *his or her* car. [using third-person pronouns, including the indefinite pronoun *one*]

Consistent: When *drivers* are about to merge with moving traffic on the freeway, *they* should not stop *their* car. [using third-person plural pronouns to match plural noun]

Agreement in Number

Most problems with pronoun-antecedent agreement involve **number**. The principles are simple: If the antecedent (the word the pronoun refers back to) is singular, use a singular pronoun. If the antecedent is plural, use a plural pronoun.

1. A singular antecedent requires a singular pronoun.

   Vincent forgot *his* notebook.

2. A plural antecedent requires a plural pronoun.

   Many *students* cast *their* votes today.

3. A singular indefinite pronoun as an antecedent takes a singular pronoun. Most indefinite pronouns are singular. The following are common indefinite singular pronouns: *anybody, anyone, each, either, everybody, everyone, no one, nobody, one, somebody, someone.*

   Each of the girls brought *her* book.

   When *one* makes a promise, *one* [or *he or she*] should keep it.

4. A plural indefinite pronoun as an antecedent takes a plural pronoun.

   Few knew *their* assignments.

5. Certain indefinite pronouns do not clearly express either a singular or plural number. Agreement, therefore, depends on the meaning of the sentence. These pronouns are *all, any, none,* and *some.*

   All of the apple *was* wormy.

   All of the apples *were* wormy.

   None of the cake *is* acceptable.

   None of the cakes *are* acceptable.

6. Two or more antecedents, singular or plural, take a plural pronoun. Such antecedents are usually joined by *and* or by commas and *and.*

   Howard and his *parents* bought *their* presents early.

Students, instructors, and the *administration* pooled *their* ideas at the forum.

7. Alternative antecedents—that is, antecedents joined by *or, nor, whether/or, either/or, neither/nor, not only/but also*—require a pronoun that agrees with the nearer antecedent.

   Neither Alex nor his *friends* lost *their* way.

   Neither his friends nor *Alex* lost *his* way.

8. In a sentence with an expression such as *one of those _____ who,* the antecedent is usually the plural noun that follows the preposition *of.*

   He is one of those *people who* want *their* money now.

9. In a sentence with the expression *the only one of those _____ who,* the antecedent is usually the singular word *one.*

   She is the *only one* of the members *who* wants *her* money now.

10. When collective nouns such as *team, jury, committee,* and *band* are used as antecedents, they take a singular pronoun if they are considered as units.

    The *jury* is doing *its* best.

    When individual behavior is suggested, antecedents take a plural form.

    The *jury* are putting on *their* coats.

11. The words *each, every,* and *many a(n)* before a noun make the noun singular.

    Each child and *adult* was *his* or *her* own authority.

    Each and *every person* doubted *himself* or *herself.*

    Many a person is capable of knowing *himself* or *herself.*

Agreement in Gender

The pronoun should agree with its antecedent in gender, if the gender of the antecedent is specific. Masculine and feminine pronouns are gender-specific: *he, him, she, her.* Others are neuter: *I, we, me, us, it, they, them, who, whom, that, which.* The words *who* and *whom* refer to people. *That* can refer to ideas, things, and people, but usually does not refer to individuals. *Which* refers to ideas and things, but never to people.

   My *girlfriend* gave me *her* best advice. [feminine]

   Mighty *Casey* tried *his* best. [masculine]

   The *people* with *whom* I work are loud. [neuter]

Indefinite singular pronouns used as antecedents require, of course, singular pronouns. Handling the gender of these singular pronouns is not as obvious; opinion is divided.

1. Traditionally, writers have used the masculine form of pronouns to refer to the indefinite singular pronouns when the gender is unknown.

   Everyone should work until *he* drops.

2. To avoid a perceived sex bias, use *he or she* or *his or her* instead of just *he* or *his*.

   Everyone should work until *he or she* drops.

3. Although option 1 is more direct, it is illogical to many listeners and readers, and option 2 used several times in a short passage can be awkward. To avoid those possible problems, writers often use plural forms.

   All people should work until *they* drop.

In any case, avoid using a plural pronoun with a singular indefinite pronoun; such usage violates the basic principle of number agreement.

   Incorrect: *Everyone* should do *their* best.

   Correct: *Everyone* should do *his or her* best.

   Correct: *People* should do *their* best.

EXERCISE 34   Making Pronouns Agree

Underline the correct pronoun form.

1. When someone does a favor for you, (he or she, they) must be thanked.

2. The audience clapped and cheered to communicate (their, its) approval.

3. No one in the maze could find (his or her, their) way out.

4. The corporation has decided to move (its, their) headquarters to Hawaii.

5. Everyone wearing high heels knew that (she, they) had made a bad shoe choice.

6. Ricardo is one of those people who like to do everything (himself, themselves).

7. Lynn's name was on the list of people (that, who) still owed money.

8. The drill sergeant required perfection from everyone and everything (who, that, which) was part of his platoon.

9. Ellen is the only one in the whole class who can laugh at (himself or herself, themselves, herself) after making a mistake.

10. Both of my parents are conscientious about taking care of (his or her, their) health.

11. The team faces (its, their) toughest challenge this Friday.

12. Neither of the men wanted to carry (his, their) wife's purse while she shopped.

13. Either John or Ralph will win the contest and see (his, their) hard work pay off.

14. A parent should read to (you, his or her, their) child every day.

15. Either of the mothers will be willing to tell you (her, their) story.

16. The writer and the artist have joined forces to produce (his or her, their) next book.

17. Neither George nor his brothers have been able to locate (his, their) grandmother's jewelry box.

18. Students must keep up with the reading if (he or she, they) want to pass the exam.

19. A babysitter should learn CPR in case (you, he or she, they) faces an emergency.

20. We assumed that everyone would take (his or her, their) time.

EXERCISE 35   Making Pronouns Agree

Underline the correct pronoun form.

1. I like to ride roller coasters, especially when (I, you) flip upside down.

2. He was the only one of the three judges who gave (his, their) honest opinion.

3. The music was lively and upbeat; (you, one) couldn't help tapping a foot in time with the rhythm.

4. Each of the men sucked in (his, their) stomach as the beautiful woman approached.

5. Neither Eric nor his brothers would take responsibility for (his, their) actions.

6. Todd is one of those people who like to get (his, their) own way all of the time.

7. She is the only one of the cast who did not flub (their, her) lines.

8. The members of the audience clapped (its, their) hands together.

9. Everybody should be treated as though (they, he or she) is a valued customer.

10. Only a few had brought (their, his or her) books to class.

11. Everyone likes to get discounts on (their, his or her) purchases.

12. To get ahead in life, (you need, one needs) a good education.

13. Too late, I realized that (you, one) should not eat a sloppy joe sandwich and drive at the same time.

14. Each of the rabbits had dug (its, his or her) way out of the pen.

15. She is the only one in her group of friends who is sure about (her, their) career path.

16. A fortune-teller should keep (his or her, their) crystal ball smudge-free and shiny.

17. Either of the tour guides will enlighten you with (his or her, their) vast knowledge.

18. The poet and the peasant declared (their, his) boundless love for her.

19. The committee submitted (their, its) recommendation to the president.

20. Every American must vote in order to do (his or her, their) civic duty.

PRONOUN REFERENCE

A pronoun must refer clearly to its antecedent. Because a pronoun is a substitute word, it can express meaning clearly and definitely only if its antecedent is easily identified.

In some sentence constructions, gender and number make the reference clear.

> Kevin and Latisha discussed *his* absences and *her* good attendance. [gender]

> If the three older boys in the *club* carry out those plans, *it* will break up. [number]

Avoid ambiguous reference. The following sentences illustrate the kind of confusion that results from structuring sentences with more than one possible antecedent for the pronoun.

> **Unclear:** Tyler gave Walt *his* money and clothes.

> **Clear:** Tyler gave his own money and clothes to Walt.

> **Unclear:** Lynette told her sister that *her* car had a flat tire.

> **Clear:** Lynette said to her sister, "Your car has a flat tire."

When using a pronoun to refer to a general idea, make sure that the reference is clear. The pronouns used frequently in this way are *this, that, which,* and *it.* The best solution may be to recast the sentence to omit the pronoun in question.

> **Unclear:** She whistled the same tune over and over, which irritated me.

> **Clear:** She whistled the same tune over and over, a *habit* that irritated me.

> **Recast:** Her whistling the same tune over and over irritated me.

EXERCISE 36   Correcting Problems in Pronoun Reference

Some of the following sentences contain pronouns that are examples of faulty reference; cross out these pronouns and correct them. If the sentence is correct, write OK in the blank.

_____   1. Tyrone said he would not be going on the trip, which worried his friends.

_____   2. Yolanda criticized Monique because she was closed-minded and intolerant.

_____   3. If that child doesn't get his own way, he has a temper tantrum.

_____   4. During a recession, you find it harder to get a good job.

_____   5. Fred told Barney that he may be laid off from his job at the quarry.

_____   6. To cook sufficiently well, one must know how to read a cookbook.

_____   7. That is Rachel's husband you met yesterday.

_____   8. She loved to visit the Bahamas, but she did not want to live there.

_____   9. In that state, they don't require motorists to wear seatbelts.

_____   10. Dottie asked her mother if she could wear her high heels to the dance.

_____   11. Jolene gave her daughter her dinner.

_____   12. Rita told her boss that she was sorry.

_____   13. It was one of those days that we'd like to forget.

_____   14. Robert hinted that he would love a new watch.

_____   15. Julio was able to get a discount, which pleased him.

_____   16. Most Americans admit to speeding, eating while driving, and running yellow or even red lights. This is what causes accidents.

_____   17. My father made a fortune by dealing in real estate. I want that, too.

_____   18. If a victim catches on fire, you should stop, drop, and roll.

_____   19. In this brochure, it says that the hotel's pool has a waterslide.

_____   20. Paul listens to his mother and follows her advice.

EXERCISE 37   Correcting Problems in Pronoun Reference

The following sentences contain pronouns that are examples of faulty reference. Correct the sentences.

1. They treated him like a child and that angered him.

2. Noel talked while he was eating, which annoyed his companions.

3. You could disagree with the idea, but it would not be easy.

4. Marcus handed Jim his keys.

5. Jannis told Jannel that her hair was too long.

6. We installed mud flaps, but some of it still got on the fenders.

7. The instructor told the student that his deadline was tomorrow.

8. This is my sister's house, whom you met yesterday.

9. They say unemployment is causing social problems.

10. Timothy never looked at me when he talked, which made me distrust him.

11. He often interrupted other people, which I found annoying.

12. They regarded him as incompetent, which embarrassed him.

13. You could come to her aid, but would it be appreciated?

14. Franklin told Jeff that his car needed to be repaired.

15. They say that the big bands are coming back.

16. In prison, you have little freedom.

17. This is my uncle's dog, who has a hundred-acre farm.

18. You could build a baseball field, but would it be worth the bother?

19. They say on television that anyone can buy a new car.

20. Hans put his finger into a hole in the dike at the edge of the ocean, but some of it still came in.

Adjectives and Adverbs

Adjectives modify (describe) nouns and pronouns and answer the questions *Which one? What kind?* and *How many?*

Which one? The <u>new</u> <u>car</u> is mine.
adjn

What kind? <u>Mexican</u> <u>food</u> is my favorite.
adjn

How many? A <u>few</u> <u>friends</u> are all one needs.
        adj   n

Adverbs modify verbs, adjectives, or other adverbs and answer the questions *How? Where? When?* and *To what degree?* Most words ending in *-ly* are adverbs.

Where? The cuckoo <u>flew</u> <u>south</u>.
        v   adv

When? The cuckoo <u>flew</u> <u>yesterday</u>.
        v   adv

Why? The cuckoo <u>flew</u> <u>because of the cold weather</u>.
        v   adv phrase

How? The cuckoo <u>flew</u> <u>swiftly</u>.
        v   adv

<u>Without adjectives and adverbs</u>, <u>even</u> John Steinbeck, the <u>famous</u>
    adv phrase   adv   adj

<u>Nobel Prize–winning</u> author, <u>surely</u> could <u>not</u> have described the
    adj   adv   adv

<u>crafty</u> octopus <u>very</u> <u>well</u>.
 adj   adv adv

We have two concerns regarding the use of adjectives and adverbs (modifiers) in writing. One is a matter of diction, or word choice—in this case, selecting adjectives and adverbs that will strengthen the writing. The other is how to identify and correct problems with modifiers.

SELECTING ADJECTIVES AND ADVERBS

If you want to finish the sentence "She was a(n) _____ speaker," you have many adjectives to select from, including these:

distinguished	dependable	effective	sly
influential	impressive	polished	astute
adequate	boring	abrasive	humorous

If you want to finish the sentence "She danced _____," you have another large selection, this time of adverbs such as the following:

bewitchingly	angelically	quaintly	zestfully
gracefully	grotesquely	carnally	smoothly
divinely	picturesquely	serenely	unevenly

Adjectives and adverbs can be used to enhance communication. If you have a thought, you know what it is, but when you deliver that thought to someone else, you may not say or write what you mean. Your thought may be eloquent and your word choice weak. Keep in mind that no two words mean exactly the same thing. Further, some words are vague and general. If you settle for a common word such as *good* or a slang word such as *neat* to characterize something that you like, you will be limiting your communication. Of course, those who know you best may understand fairly well; after all, certain people who are really close may be able to convey ideas using only grunts and gestures.

But what if you want to write to someone you hardly know to explain how you feel about an important issue? Then the more precise the word, the better the communication. By using modifiers, you may be able to add significant information. Keep in mind, however, that anything can be overdone; therefore, use adjectives and adverbs wisely and economically.

Your first resource in searching for more effective adjectives should be your own vocabulary storehouse. Another resource is a good thesaurus (book of synonyms), either in print form or on a computer.

Supply the appropriate modifiers in the following exercises, using a dictionary, a thesaurus, or the resources designated by your instructor.

EXERCISE 38   Supplying Adjectives

Provide adjectives to modify these nouns. Use only single words, not adjective phrases.

1. A(n) _____ cat

2. A(n) _____ politician

3. A(n) _____ echo

4. A(n) _____ friend

5. A(n) _____ waiter

6. A(n) _____ conference

7. A(n) _____ comedian

8. A(n) _____ street

9. A(n) _____ school

10. A(n) _____ vacation

EXERCISE 39   Supplying Adverbs

Provide adverbs to modify these verbs. Use only single words, not adverb phrases.

1. stare   _____

2. flee   _____

3. yell   _____

4. approach _____

5. taste   _____

6. smile _____

7. look _____

8. leave _____

9. cry _____

10. eat _____

COMPARATIVE AND SUPERLATIVE FORMS

For making comparisons, most adjectives and adverbs have three different forms: the positive (one), the comparative (comparing two), and the superlative (comparing three or more).

Adjectives

1. Some adjectives follow a regular pattern:

Positive (one)	Comparative (two)	Superlative (three or more)
nice	nicer	nicest
rich	richer	richest
big	bigger	biggest
tall	taller	tallest
lonely	lonelier	loneliest
terrible	more terrible	most terrible
beautiful	more beautiful	most beautiful

These are the general rules:

a. Add *-er* (or *-r*) to short adjectives (one or two syllables) to rank units of two.

Julian is *nicer* than Sam.

b. Add *-est* (or *-st*) to short adjectives (one or two syllables) to rank units of three or more.

Of the fifty people I know, Julian is the *kindest*.

c. Add the word *more* to long adjectives (three or more syllables) to rank units of two.

My hometown is *more beautiful* than yours.

d. Add the word *most* to long adjectives (three or more syllables) to rank units of three or more.

My hometown is the *most beautiful* in all America.

2. Some adjectives are irregular in the way they change to show comparison:

Positive (one)	Comparative (two)	Superlative (three or more)
good	better	best
bad	worse	worst

Adverbs

1. Some adverbs follow a regular pattern.

Positive (one)	Comparative (two)	Superlative (three or more)
clearly	more clearly	most clearly
quickly	more quickly	most quickly
carefully	more carefully	most carefully
thoughtfully	more thoughtfully	most thoughtfully

a. Add -er to some one-syllable adverbs for the comparative form and add -est for the superlative form.

My piglet runs *fast*. [positive]

My piglet runs *faster* than your piglet. [comparative]

My piglet runs *fastest* of all known piglets. [superlative]

b. Add the word *more* to longer adverbs for the comparison form and *most* to longer adverbs for the superlative form.

Judy reacted *happily* to the marriage proposal. [positive]

Judy reacted *more happily* to the marriage proposal than Nancy. [comparison]

Of all the women Clem proposed to, Judy reacted *most happily*. [superlative]

c. In some cases, the word *less* may be substituted for *more*, and *least* for *most*.

Mort's views were presented *less effectively* than Craig's. [comparative]

Of all the opinions that were shared, Mort's views were presented *least effectively*. [superlative]

2. Some adverbs are irregular in the way they change to show comparisons.

Positive (one)	Comparative (two)	Superlative (three or more)
well	better	best
far	farther (distance)	farthest (distance)
	further	furthest
badly	worse	worst

USING ADJECTIVES AND ADVERBS CORRECTLY

1. Avoid double negatives. Words such as *no, not, none, nothing, never, hardly, barely,* and *scarcely* should not be combined.

Double Negative:	I do *not* have *no* time for recreation. [incorrect]
Single Negative:	I have *no* time for recreation. [correct]
Double Negative:	I have *hardly never* lied. [incorrect]
Single Negative:	I have *hardly* ever lied. [correct]

2. Do not confuse adjectives with adverbs. Among the most commonly confused adjectives and adverbs are *good/well*, *bad/badly*, and *real/really*. The words *good*, *bad*, and *real* are always adjectives. *Well* is sometimes an adjective. The words *badly* and *really* are always adverbs. *Well* is usually an adverb.

To distinguish these words, consider what is being modified. Remember that adjectives modify nouns and pronouns and that adverbs modify verbs, adjectives, and other adverbs.

Incorrect:	I feel *badly* today. [We're concerned with the condition of *I*.]
Correct:	I feel *bad* today. [The adjective *bad* modifies the pronoun *I*.]
Incorrect:	She feels *well* about that choice. [We're concerned with the condition of *she*.]
Correct:	She feels *good* about that choice. [The adjective *good* modifies the pronoun *she*.]
Incorrect:	Lazarro plays the piano *good*. [The adjective *good* modifies the verb *plays*, but adjectives should not modify verbs.]
Correct:	Lazarro plays the piano *well*. [The adverb *well* modifies the verb *plays*.]
Incorrect:	He did *real* well. [Here the adjective *real* modifies the adverb *well*, but adjectives should not modify adverbs.]
Correct:	He did *really* well. [The adverb *really* modifies the adverb *well*.]

3. Do not use an adverb such as *very*, *more*, or *most* before adjectives such as *perfect*, *round*, *unique*, *square*, and *straight*.

Incorrect:	It is *more* round.
Correct:	It is round.
Correct:	It is *more nearly* round.

4. Do not double forms, such as *more lonelier* or *most loneliest*.

| Incorrect: | Julie was *more nicer* than Jake. |
| Correct: | Julie was *nicer* than Jake. |

5. Do not confuse standard and nonstandard forms of adjectives and adverbs.

- **Accidently.** This is a substandard form of *accidentally*.
- **All ready, already.** *All ready* means "completely prepared." *Already* means "previously."

We are *all ready* to give the signal to move out. [prepared]

When he arrived at the station, we had *already* left. [previously]

- **All right, alright.** *All right* (two words) means "correct," "yes," "fine," "certainly." *Alright* is a substandard spelling of "all right.

  Yes, I am *all right* now.

- **All together, altogether.** *All together* means "in a group." *Altogether* means "completely," "wholly," "entirely."

  The boys were *all together* at the end of the field.

  The manuscript is *altogether* too confusing.

Be careful to place such words as *also*, *almost*, *even*, *just*, *hardly*, *merely*, *only*, and *today* in the right position to convey the intended meaning. As these words change position in the sentence, they may also change the meaning of the sentence.

I *only* advised him to act cautiously.
I advised *only* him to act cautiously.
Only I advised him to act cautiously.
I advised him *only* to act cautiously.

EXERCISE 40   Selecting Adjectives and Adverbs

Cross out the mistake in each sentence and write in the correction above it.

1. Ping-Sim thought his teacher had a most unique method of lecturing.

2. Some jobs are done easier by blind people than by those with sight.

3. It was up to the parents to decide if this kind of movie is real bad for children.

4. The adventure of life is too impossible to discuss.

5. Oscar felt badly about rejection slips but worse about his bank account.

6. Victor was not the stronger of the pair, but he was the best boxer.

7. The whole class thought Kyoka's sunglasses the most perfect they had seen.

8. The suspect became violenter as the police drew nearer.

9. Of all the potential winners, the judges agreed that Miss Idaho was more beautiful.

10. The United States has no central educational authority, but overall it does good.

11. An unambiguous word only can mean one thing.

12. It is real easy to forget that "liquor" used to mean "liquid."

13. Hurtful experiences in childhood don't fade out easy.

14. She said he had all ready ruined his reputation by making her buy her own flowers.

15. A trembling voice may indicate that the speaker does not feel alright.

16. Julian had two ways of starting a speech: One way was with a definition, but

    the easiest way was with a joke.

17. Sherman choked as if the very words tasted badly to him.

18. Natasha made a real good decision.

19. Erika didn't say the food was terrible; only she said it was bad.

20. On controversial topics, he was all together too easily offended.

EXERCISE 41   Selecting Adjectives and Adverbs

Cross out the mistake in each sentence and write in the correction above it.

1. I remember one real good experience.

2. It left me feeling alright.

3. Of the two cars I have owned, the '69 Camaro was best.

4. It was also the beautifulest car I have ever seen.

5. When I drove it, I felt like the most rich person in town.

6. For a year I didn't have no time for anything except polishing my car.

7. I had it painted green so that it was real handsome.

8. My name for it was the "Hornet," and when people gave me glances as I

    drove it, I felt well.

9. I hardly never abused that vehicle.

10. When I finally traded it in, I didn't never look back for fear I would cry.

11. All I can say is that it was most perfect.

12. Later I went back to the dealer, but I was all ready too late.

13. The Hornet had been bought by a young man who thought it was the better of

    all the cars on the lot.

14. He said he couldn't find no better car anywhere.

15. I could see he felt real good.

16. He and his family were standing altogether.

17. It was no time for me to feel badly.

18. In fact, as I said, I felt alright about the transaction.

19. I didn't shed no tears.

20. That experience is a real happy memory for me.

DANGLING AND MISPLACED MODIFIERS

Modifiers should clearly relate to the word or words they modify.

1. A modifier that fails to modify a word or group of words already in the sentence is called a **dangling modifier**.

Dangling:	*Walking down the street*, a snake startled him. [Who was walking down the street? The person isn't mentioned in the sentence.]
Correct:	*Walking down the street*, *Don* was startled by a snake.
Correct:	*As Don walked down the street*, *he* was startled by a snake.
Dangling:	*At the age of six*, my uncle died. [Who was six years old? The person isn't mentioned in the sentence.]
Correct:	*When I was six*, my uncle died.

2. A modifier that is placed so that it modifies the wrong word or words is called a **misplaced modifier**. The term also applies to words that are positioned to unnecessarily divide closely related parts of sentences such as infinitives (*to* plus verb) or subjects and verbs.

Misplaced:	The sick man went to a doctor *with a high fever*.
Correct:	The sick man *with a high fever* went to the doctor.
Misplaced:	I saw a great movie *sitting in my pickup*.
Correct:	*Sitting in my pickup*, I saw a great movie.
Misplaced:	Kim found many new graves *walking through the cemetery*.
Correct:	*Walking through the cemetery*, Kim found many new graves.
Misplaced:	I forgot all about my sick dog *kissing my girlfriend*.
Correct:	*Kissing my girlfriend*, I forgot all about my sick dog.
Misplaced:	They tried to *earnestly and sincerely* complete the task. [splitting of the infinitive *to complete*]
Correct:	They tried *earnestly and sincerely* to complete the task.
Misplaced:	My neighbor, *while walking to the store*, was mugged. [unnecessarily dividing the subject and verb]
Correct:	*While walking to the store*, my neighbor was mugged.

Try the following procedure in working through Exercises 42 and 43.

1. Circle the modifier.

2. Draw an arrow from the modifier to the word or words it modifies.

3. If the modifier does not relate directly to anything in the sentence, it is dangling, and you must recast the sentence.

4. If the modifier does not modify the nearest word or words, or if it interrupts related sentence parts, it is misplaced and you need to reposition it.

EXERCISE 42   Correcting Dangling and Misplaced Modifiers

In the blank, write D for dangling modifier, M for misplaced modifier, and OK for correct sentences. Correct the sentences with modifier problems.

_____ 1. Late again, there was no time for breakfast.

_____ 2. Racking up points, the video-game player was close to setting a new record.

_____ 3. Bathed, clipped, and perfumed, she allowed the dog to enter the house again.

_____ 4. We guessed approximately that the jar contained 3,000 jelly beans.

_____ 5. Filling out the form, my pen ran out of ink.

_____ 6. With grim determination, the mountain had been conquered.

_____ 7. Rudely, the interrupting child burst into the room without knocking.

_____ 8. The student made an appointment to see the teacher with a complaint.

_____ 9. By brushing and flossing every day, cavities can be avoided.

_____ 10. Sitting in the back row, the speaker was hard to hear.

_____ 11. He asked her to marry him yesterday.

_____ 12. Right after buying it, the popcorn was spilled all over the floor.

_____ 13. Strolling through the garden, the hot sun beat down.

_____ 14. I only have one objection to your devious plan.

_____ 15. To be healthy, smoking must be given up.

_____ 16. To find the gold, the map was followed by the treasure hunters.

_____ 17. When I was two years old, my mother enrolled me in swimming lessons.

_____ 18. I only signed up for one class.

_____ 19. Bill tried to slowly and persistently worm his way into her heart.

_____ 20. As the mother of six children, her grocery bill is always high.

EXERCISE 43   Correcting Dangling and Misplaced Modifiers

In the blank, write D for dangling modifier, M for misplaced modifier, and OK for correct sentences. Correct the sentences with modifier problems.

_____ 1. When I was in the third grade, my family moved to Texas.

_____ 2. When ten years old, my father won the lottery.

_____ 3. During the summer, I worked at the mall.

_____ 4. Raynelle went after the game was over, to the banquet.

_____ 5. Traveling over the mountain road, the inn was reached.

_____ 6. To be a successful runner, one needs strength and stamina.

_____ 7. Driving through the forest, many deer were seen from our car.

_____ 8. After studying it for many weeks, the plan was discontinued.

_____ 9. Searching the computer screen, we found the answer.

_____ 10. After driving the car for ten years, it was sold.

_____ 11. After three hours of walking, they rested.

_____ 12. The ring sparkled on her hand, which she had bought in Italy.

_____ 13. Climbing the mountain, we stopped to admire the view.

_____ 14. Ms. Prank wanted to buy a car for her husband with a large trunk.

_____ 15. He found a wallet in the park that didn't belong to him.

_____ 16. Standing on top of the hill, we could see Catalina Island.

_____ 17. Ginny took, to miss the construction, a detour.

_____ 18. To play basketball well, good coordination is needed.

_____ 19. After playing all the game, the coach knew that Jean was tired.

_____ 20. It is desirable to usually avoid splitting an infinitive.

Balancing Sentence Parts

We are surrounded by balance. Watch a colorful cross-frame, or diamond, kite as it soars in the sky. If you draw an imaginary line from the top to the bottom of the kite, you will see corresponding parts on either side. If you were to replace one of the sides with a loose-fitting fabric, the kite would never fly. A similar lack of balance can also cause a sentence to crash.

Consider these statements:

"To be or not to be—that is the question." [dash added]

This line from *Hamlet*, by William Shakespeare, is one of the most famous lines in literature. Compare it to the well-balanced kite in a strong wind. Its parts are parallel and it "flies" well.

"To be or not being—that is the question."

It still vaguely resembles the sleek kite, but now the second phrase causes it to dip like an unbalanced kite. Lurching, the line begins to lose altitude.

"To be or death is the other alternative—that is the question."

The line slams to the floor. Words scatter across the carpet. We return to the revision board.

The first sentence is forceful and easy to read. The second is more difficult to follow. The third is almost impossible to understand. We understand it only because we know what it should look like from having read the original. The point is that perceptive readers are as critical of sentences as kite-watchers are of kites.

BASIC PRINCIPLES OF PARALLELISM

Parallelism as it relates to sentence structure is usually achieved by joining words with similar words: nouns with nouns, adjectives (words that describe nouns and pronouns) with adjectives, adverbs (words that describe verbs, adjectives, and other adverbs) with adverbs, and so forth.

Men, women, and *children* enjoy the show. [nouns]

The players are *excited*, *eager*, and *enthusiastic*. [adjectives]

The author wrote *skillfully* and *quickly*. [adverbs]

You can create parallel structure by joining groups of words with similar groups of words: prepositional phrase with prepositional phrase, clause with clause, sentence with sentence.

She fell *in love* and *out of love* in a few minutes. [prepositional phrases]

Who he was and *where he came from* did not matter. [clauses]

He came in a hurry. He left in a hurry. [sentences]

Parallelism means balancing one structure with another of the same kind. Faulty parallel structure is awkward and draws unfavorable attention to what is being said.

Nonparallel: Gary Payton's reputation is based on his ability in *passing, shooting*, and *he is good at rebounds*.

Parallel: Gary Payton's reputation is based on his ability in *passing, shooting*, and *rebounding*.

In the nonparallel sentence, the words *passing* and *shooting* are of the same kind (verblike words used as nouns), but the rest of the sentence is different. You do not have to know terms to realize that there is a problem in smoothness and emphasis. Just read the material aloud. Then compare it with the parallel statement; *he is good at rebounds* is changed to *rebounding* to make a sentence that's easy on the eye and ear.

SIGNAL WORDS

Some words signal parallel structure. If you use *and*, the items joined by *and* should almost always be parallel. If they are not, then *and* is probably inappropriate.

The weather is hot *and* humid. [*and* joins adjectives]

The car *and* the trailer are parked in front of the house. [*and* joins nouns]

The same principle is true for *but*, although it implies a direct contrast. Where contrasts are being drawn, parallel structure is essential to clarify those contrasts.

He *purchased a Dodger Dog, but* I *chose the Stadium Peanuts*. [*but* joins contrasting clauses]

She *earned* an A in math *but failed* her art class. [*but* joins contrasting verbs]

You should regard all the coordinating conjunctions (FANBOYS: *for, and, nor, but, or, yet, so*) as signals for parallel structure.

COMBINATION SIGNAL WORDS

The words *and* and *but* are the most common individual signal words used with parallel constructions. Sometimes, however, **combination words** signal the need for parallelism or balance. The most common ones are *either/or, neither/nor, not only/but also, both/and*, and *whether/or*. Now consider this faulty sentence and two possible corrections:

Nonparallel: *Either we will* win this game, *or let's* go out fighting.

Parallel: *Either we will* win this game, *or we will* go out fighting.

The correction is made by changing *let's* to *we will* to parallel the *we will* in the first part of the sentence. The same construction should follow the *either* and the *or*.

Nonparallel: Flour is used *not only* to bake cakes *but also* in paste.

Parallel: Flour is used *not only to bake* cakes *but also to make* paste.

The correction is made by changing *in* (a preposition) to *to make* (an infinitive). Now an infinitive follows both *not only* and *but also*.

EXERCISE 44 Correcting Faulty Parallelism

Mark each sentence as P for parallel or NP for nonparallel. Correct the sentences with nonparallel structure.

_____ 1. Jacques Cousteau was an adventurer, explorer, and educated people.

_____ 2. He will be remembered not only as a pioneer but also he was an environmentalist of great influence.

_____ 3. His love for the sea led him to devote his life to research, protecting, photographing, and writing about it.

_____ 4. His passion for the world's oceans made him an environmentalist, inventive, and a romantic.

_____ 5. He is credited with co-inventing scuba gear, developing a bathyscaphe, and helped start the first human undersea colonies.

_____ 6. Cousteau also helped invent skin-diving gear that freed divers from air hoses and to allow them to float at will.

_____ 7. His famous boat, the _Calypso_, was not only his transportation but also giving him a marine laboratory for experiments.

_____ 8. He not only was a filmmaker who created many documentaries but also the author of countless books.

_____ 9. His famous adventures included unearthing an ancient Greek shipwreck and photography of Antarctica's underwater ice sculptures.

_____ 10. Millions recognized Cousteau, who was thin, bespectacled, and he wore a red cap.

_____ 11. Cousteau was born in 1910, and his death occurred in 1997.

_____ 12. Although he was a sickly child, he liked going to the beach, swimming, and to dive.

_____ 13. He started out aiming for the skies in naval aviation school but ending up in the water.

_____ 14. He was honored both with France's Legion of Honor for his military service and forty Emmy nominations for his documentaries.

_____ 15. In his eighties he gave up diving, but he did not give up his mission to protect the sea for future generations.

_____ 16. To preserve the oceans for future generations was as important to him as teaching people.

_____ 17. Not long before he died at age 87, Cousteau said that he was proudest of helping to save the environment and with informing people everywhere.

_____ 18. He was not only beloved in France but also the subject of American songs such as John Denver's "Calypso."

_____ 19. Cousteau's films and what he believed influenced people of all ages.

_____ 20. He brought the mystery and beauty of the sea into the lives of even those who were landlocked.

EXERCISE 45   Correcting Faulty Parallelism

STUDENT COMPANION SITE

For additional practice visit www.cengage .com/devenglish/ brandon/PE11e.

Mark each sentence as P for parallel or NP for nonparallel. Correct the sentences with nonparallel structure.

_____ 1. Both children and people who are adults enjoy fairy tales.

_____ 2. You may be interested to know who wrote them and their origins.

_____ 3. When asked to name authors of fairy tales, most people either say the Grimm brothers or Hans Christian Andersen.

_____ 4. But these men didn't write the stories; they merely collected or retold them.

_____ 5. Many originated hundreds of years ago as oral folk stories told by women who wanted to pass on their knowledge and what they had experienced.

_____ 6. These women, who had no rights in their male-dominated society, had two other purposes: rebelling against their many restrictions and to make their opinions known.

_____ 7. Their stories, which were imaginative, gruesome, and with frightening parts, were not meant for children.

_____ 8. They included cannibalistic witches, murderous parents, and animals that eat men.

_____ 9. Their tales were filled not only with scary characters but also gory violence.

_____ 10. In the original "Cinderella," one of Cinderella's greedy stepsisters cuts off her toe so that her foot would fit into the slipper, and the other cutting off her heel.

_____ 11. As blood oozes from their shoes, pigeons peck out their eyes to punish them for their wickedness and being liars.

_____ 12. In Charles Perrault's seventeenth-century version of "Little Red Riding Hood," the heroine not only fails to outsmart the wolf but also to escape being devoured.

_____ 13. In the Grimm brothers' version, a woodcutter is Red Riding Hood's rescuer and who slices open the wolf's belly to let her out.

_____ 14. The original "Snow White" contained neither dwarves nor a magic mirror.

_____ 15. In that version, it is Snow White's natural mother and father who drive her cruelly and with malice out of the house and into the woods.

_____ 16. The Grimm brothers changed the story so that she is abandoned by a male servant, protected by male dwarves, and a male prince rescues her.

_____ 17. It is their version that adds the wicked stepmother, the poisoned apple, and putting the girl in the glass coffin.

_____ **18.** The story "Sleeping Beauty" had to be stripped of cannibalism, sex crimes, and people being unfaithful to their spouses.

_____ **19.** The old versions taught people what were punishable sins and those deserving rewards.

_____ **20.** In today's versions, the good still win. The bad still are losers.

Punctuation and Capitalization

Understanding punctuation will help you to write better. If you are not sure how to punctuate a compound or compound-complex sentence, then you probably will not write one. If you do not know how to show that some of your words come from other sources, you may mislead your reader. If you misuse punctuation, you will force your readers to struggle to get your message. So take the time to review and master the mechanics. Your efforts will be rewarded.

END PUNCTUATION

Periods

1. Place a period after a statement.

The weather is beautiful today.

2. Place a period after common abbreviations.

Dr.   Mr.   Mrs.   Dec.   a.m.

Exceptions: FBI   UN   NAACP   FHA

3. Use an ellipsis—three periods within a sentence and four periods at the end of a sentence—to indicate that words have been omitted from quoted material.

He stopped walking and the buildings . . . rose up out of the misty courtroom. . . .

(James Thurber, "The Secret Life of Walter Mitty")

Question Marks

1. Place a question mark at the end of a direct question.

Will you go to the country tomorrow?

2. Do *not* use a question mark after an indirect (reported) question.

She asked me what caused that slide.

Exclamation Points

1. Place an exclamation point after a word or a group of words that expresses strong feeling.

Oh!   What a night!   Help!   Gadzooks!

2. Do not overwork the exclamation point. Do not use double exclamation points. Use the period or comma for mild exclamatory words, phrases, or sentences.

> Oh, we can leave now.

COMMAS

Commas to Separate

1. Use a comma to separate main clauses joined by one of the coordinating conjunctions—*for, and, nor, but, or, yet, so*. The comma may be omitted if the clauses are brief and parallel.

> We traveled many miles to see the game, *but* it was canceled.

> Mary left and I remained. [brief and parallel clauses]

2. Use a comma after introductory dependent clauses and long introductory phrases (generally, four or more words is considered long).

> *Before the arrival of the shipment*, the boss had written a letter protesting the delay. [two prepositional phrases]

> *If you do not hear from me*, assume that I am lost. [introductory dependent clause, an adverbial modifier]

> *In winter* we skate on the river. [short prepositional phrase, no comma]

3. Use a comma to separate words, phrases, and clauses in a series.

> *Red, white,* and *blue* were her favorite colors. [words]

> He ran *down the street, across the park,* and *into the arms of his father.* [prepositional phrases]

> *When John was asleep, when Mary was at work,* and *when Bob was studying,* Mother had time to relax. [dependent clauses]

4. However, when coordinating conjunctions connect all the elements in a series, the commas are omitted.

> He bought *apples* and *pears* and *grapes.*

5. Use a comma to separate coordinate adjectives not joined by *and* that modify the same noun.

> I need a *sturdy, reliable* truck.

6. Do not use a comma to separate adjectives that are not coordinate. Try the following technique to determine whether the adjectives are coordinate: Put *and* between the adjectives. If it fits naturally, the adjectives are coordinate; if it does not, they are not, and you do not need a comma.

> She is a kind, beautiful person.

> kind *and* beautiful [natural, hence the comma]

> I built a red brick wall.

> red *and* brick wall [not natural, no comma]

7. Use a comma to separate sentence elements that might be misread.

> Inside the dog scratched his fleas.

> *Inside*, the dog scratched his fleas.

Without benefit of the comma, the reader might initially misunderstand the relationship among the first three words.

Commas to Set Off

1. Use commas to set off (enclose) adjectives in pairs that follow a noun.

> The scouts, *tired and hungry*, marched back to camp.

2. Use commas to set off nonessential (unnecessary for meaning of the sentence) words, phrases, and clauses.

> My brother, *a student at Ohio State University*, is visiting me. [If you drop the phrase, the basic meaning of the sentence remains intact.]

> Marla, *who studied hard*, will pass. [The clause is not essential to the basic meaning of the sentence.]

> All students *who studied hard* will pass. [Here the clause *is* essential. If you remove it, you would have *All students will pass*, which is not necessarily true.]

> I shall not stop searching *until I find the treasure*. [A dependent clause at the end of a sentence is usually not set off with a comma. However, a clause beginning with the word *though* or *although* will be set off regardless of where it is located.]

> I felt unsatisfied, *though we had won the game*.

3. Use commas to set off parenthetical elements such as mild interjections (*oh, well, yes, no,* and others), most conjunctive adverbs (*however, otherwise, therefore, similarly, hence, on the other hand,* and *consequently* but not *then, thus, soon, now,* and *also*), quotation indicators, and special abbreviations (*etc., i.e., e.g.,* and others).

> *Oh*, what a silly question! [mild interjection]

> It is necessary, *of course*, to leave now. [sentence modifier]

> We left early; *however*, we missed the train anyway. [conjunctive adverb]

> "When I was in school," *he said*, "I read widely." [quotation indicators]

> Books, papers, pens, *etc.*, were scattered on the floor. [The abbreviation *etc.* should be used sparingly, however.]

4. Use commas to set off nouns used as direct address.

> Play it again, *Sam*.

> Please tell us the answer, *Jane*, so we can discuss it.

5. Use commas to separate the numbers in a date.

> June 4, *1965*, is a day I will remember.

6. Do not use commas if the day of the month is not specified, or if the day is given before the month.

> June 1965 was my favorite time.

> One day I will never forget is 4 June 1965.

7. Use commas to separate the city from the state. No comma is used between the state and the zip code.

> Walnut, CA 91789

8. Use a comma after both the city and the state when they are used together in a sentence.

> Our family visited Anchorage, *Alaska*, last summer.

9. Use a comma following the salutation of a friendly letter and the complimentary closing in any letter.

> Dear John,

> Sincerely,

10. Use a comma in numbers to set off groups of three digits. However, omit the comma in dates, serial numbers, page numbers, years, and street numbers.

> The total assets were *$2,000,000*.

> I look forward to the year *2050*.

EXERCISE 46   Using Commas

Insert all necessary commas in the following sentences.

1. Commas are used to separate words phrases and clauses in a series.

2. A strong assertive comma separates coordinate adjectives.

3. After long introductory modifiers a comma is used.

4. A comma is used between independent clauses and a period is usually found at the end of a sentence.

5. After all the meaning of the sentence is often clarified by a comma.

6. Inside the car smelled new and clean.

7. In the beginning of the game there was nothing but noise and chaos.

8. The crazy-looking car was painted pink black green and lavender.

9. Cherise worked at her desk all night but the job was not finished in time.

10. The sharp burning rays of the sun would soon be hidden by the trees.

11. Having finished the banquet the diners moved to the living room.

12. Bach and Handel both born in 1685 were the two greatest baroque composers.

13. Motor racing not horse racing is the more popular sport.

14. "When I was a boy" Arturo said "one dollar a week was enough!"

15. Dwight Jones the salesperson will take your order now.

16. Well that's the way it's going to be!

17. The new car all sleek and shiny was nowhere to be found.

18. He arrived in Tribbey Oklahoma on February 21 1934.

19. The old boxer was only down not out.

20. The Eiffel Tower which is located in Paris is no longer the highest tower in the world.

EXERCISE 47   Using Commas

Insert all necessary commas in the following sentences.

1. Before most people were superstitious.

2. People now know that superstitions are silly but many of these beliefs are still alive and well.

3. I know you believe dear friend that blowing out all the candles on your birthday cake will make your wish come true.

4. Do you knock on wood say "bless you" when someone sneezes and avoid opening your umbrella indoors?

5. When you knock on wood you're calling upon the good spirits that live in trees to protect you.

6. Pope Gregory passed a law requiring people of the sixth century to bless a sneezer who had probably contracted the deadly plague.

7. If you break a mirror you face seven years of bad luck.

8. The bird which had flown into the house was an omen of death.

9. Brides must wear something old something new something borrowed and something blue.

10. It is however bad luck for the groom to see his bride before the wedding.

11. "Don't step on a crack or you'll break your mother's back."

12. You've heard I'm sure that pulling out a gray hair causes ten more to grow back.

13. The young guy well schooled in superstition waited beneath the mistletoe for the object of his affection to happen by.

14. If you take a test with the same pencil you used when you studied the pencil will remember the answers.

15. He carried at all times a rabbit's foot a four-leaf clover and a horseshoe.

16. Throw a coin into the fountain and make a wish.

17. Edmund Burke said "Superstition is the religion of feeble minds."

18. But Johann Wolfgang von Goethe a German novelist said that "superstition is the poetry of life."

19. The wishbone clean and dry was ready to be pulled in two.

20. Don't harm a cricket or a ladybug for they both bring good luck.

SEMICOLONS

The **semicolon** indicates a stronger division than the comma. It is used principally to separate independent clauses within a sentence.

1. Use a semicolon to separate independent clauses not joined by a coordinating conjunction.

   You must buy that car today; tomorrow will be too late.

2. Use a semicolon between two independent clauses joined by a conjunctive adverb such as one of the HOTSHOT CAT words (*however, otherwise, therefore, similarly, hence, on the other hand, then, consequently, accordingly, thus*).

   It was very late; therefore, I remained at the hotel.

3. Use a semicolon to separate main clauses joined by a coordinating conjunction if one or both of the clauses contain distracting commas.

   Byron, the famous English poet, was buried in Greece; and Shelley, who was his friend and fellow poet, was buried in Italy.

4. Use a semicolon in a series between items that themselves contain commas.

> He has lived in Covina, California; Reno, Nevada; Prague, Oklahoma; and Bangor, Maine.

EXERCISE 48   Using Commas and Semicolons

Each sentence needs one or more semicolons or commas. Insert the appropriate marks.

1. Each year many species of birds fly south for the winter for example ducks and geese migrate to warmer areas to find more abundant food.

2. Most insects cannot fly the distances that these birds can fly instead they time their development so that they are in eggs or cocoons during the winter.

3. There is one exception however the Monarch butterfly is different from other insects.

4. Birds avoid lethal cold by getting away from it the Monarch butterfly does the same thing.

5. The long, hot days begin to grow shorter the temperatures grow colder and the beautiful, black and orange Monarch butterflies know that it's time to make their amazing journey.

6. These butterflies have tiny insect brains however, those brains somehow guide them over thousands of miles they've never seen before.

7. On their way to central Mexico, eastern Monarch butterflies stop in places like San Angelo, Texas Bracketville, Texas and Eagle Pass, Texas.

8. Thousands of them travel together in the same "flyways" to see all of them flying together at once is truly awesome.

9. They don't mind crowds as a matter of fact a 10-acre colony can contain five to six million butterflies per acre.

10. Biologists estimate that 15,000 to 20,000 butterflies perch on a single tree bough as a result the trees appear to be covered with bright autumn leaves.

11. They arrive in their winter home in November and they remain until March of the next year.

12. The Monarch butterfly breeds four or five times per year in a cycle each generation migrates either north or south.

13. The generation of butterflies that migrates to Mexico returns to the Gulf Coast states of the South and this generation lays eggs on milkweed plants.

14. The next generation lives only four to six weeks its mission is to get to the northern states and southern Canada.

15. Milkweed is plentiful at north latitudes so the butterflies spend their summer there eating and increasing their numbers.

16. Milkweed is the only thing these butterflies eat and this plant has one additional benefit.

17. Milkweed contains toxins therefore the butterflies become poisonous to predators when they ingest these toxins.

18. These butterflies need no camouflage for their bright colors signal poison to animals looking for a snack.

19. The generation that makes the journey to Mexico is rewarded for its hard work with a longer life those butterflies live eight months instead of two.

20. The Monarch butterfly is a fascinating creature and its travels are one of the world's biological wonders.

EXERCISE 49   Using Commas and Semicolons

Each sentence needs one or more semicolons or commas. Insert the appropriate marks.

1. The oldest science is the study of the stars and planets even ancient peoples looked up at the night sky with wonder and awe.

2. Early scientists plotted the positions and changing brightness of the stars and people worshipped the Sun and the Moon as gods.

3. Modern scientific discoveries have led to new knowledge about our solar system but astronomers continue to gather more information every day.

4. We've learned that our Sun is a star it radiates heat and light because of nuclear reactions inside its core.

5. The mass of the universe, including our bodies, is made up of elements from stars that exploded billions of years ago therefore humans are the stuff of stars.

6. A galaxy is a huge collection of stars bound together by gravity our Sun and its satellites are part of the spiral-shaped Milky Way Galaxy.

7. The universe is unbelievably vast astronomers estimate that there are at least one *billion* different galaxies close enough to photograph.

8. Our own solar system is so big that it could take up to twelve years to journey from Earth to the outermost planet yet it occupies only a tiny area of this vast universe.

9. There are two types of planets Earth and the three planets like it (Mercury, Venus, and Mars) are known as the terrestrial planets.

10. The other group consists of the planets that resemble Jupiter these Jovian planets include Jupiter, Saturn, Uranus, and Neptune.

11. Pluto does not resemble either Earth or Jupiter so some astronomers suggest that it be classified as an asteroid rather than a planet.

12. The farthest planet from the Sun is Pluto it orbits the Sun only once every 248 years.

13. Pluto is the only planet that has not been visited by a probe from Earth but scientists hope to launch one in the near future.

14. Venus is the closest planet to Earth as a result it is the brightest object in our nighttime sky.

15. Jupiter is the largest planet of our solar system also it has sixteen moons, more than any other planet.

16. One of Jupiter's moons, Europa, may have an ocean of liquid water if it does, it could contain life.

17. Saturn is distinctive because of its rings they are believed to be composed of ice and rocks.

18. Many scientists believe that Mars may have once supported life for a Martian asteroid contains what looks like fossils of tiny organisms.

19. Neptune and Uranus are twins both have rings like Saturn and a similar composition.

20. Mercury is closest to the Sun thus its average surface temperature is 350 degrees Fahrenheit during the day.

QUOTATION MARKS

Quotation marks are used principally to set off direct quotations. A direct quotation consists of material taken from the written work or the direct speech of others; it is set off by double quotation marks. Single quotation marks are used to set off a quotation within a quotation.

Double Quotation Marks: He said, "I don't remember."

Single Quotation Marks: He said, "I don't remember if she said, 'Wait for me.'"

1. Use double quotation marks to set off direct quotations.

   Erin said, "Give me the book."

   As Edward McNeil writes of the Greek achievement: "To an extent never before realized, mind was supreme over faith."

2. Use double quotation marks to set off titles of shorter pieces of writing such as magazine articles, essays, short stories, short poems, one-act plays, chapters in books, songs, and separate pieces of writing published as part of a larger work.

   The book *Literature: Structure, Sound, and Sense* contains a deeply moving poem titled "On Wenlock Edge."

   Have you read "The Use of Force," a short story by William Carlos Williams?

   My favorite Elvis song is "Don't Be Cruel."

3. Use double quotation marks to set off slang, technical terms, and special words.

   There are many aristocrats, but Elvis is the only true "King." [special word]

   The "platoon system" changed the game of football. [technical term]

4. Use double quotation marks in writing dialogue (conversation). Write each speech unit as a separate paragraph and set it off with double quotation marks.

   "Will you go with me?" he asked.

   "Yes," she replied. "Are you ready now?"

5. Use single quotation marks to set off a quotation within a quotation.

> Professor Baxter said, "You should remember Shakespeare's words, 'Nothing will come of nothing.'"

6. Do *not* use quotation marks for indirect quotations.

> **Incorrect:**   He said that "he would bring the supplies."
>
> **Correct:**   He said that he would bring the supplies.

7. Do *not* use quotation marks for the title on your own written work. If you refer to that title in another piece of writing, however, you need the quotation marks.

PUNCTUATION WITH QUOTATION MARKS

1. A period or comma is always placed *inside* the quotation marks.

> Our assignment for Monday was to read Poe's poem "The Raven."
>
> "I will read you the story," he said. "It is a good one."

2. A semicolon or colon is always placed *outside* the quotation marks.

> He read Robert Frost's poem "Design"; then he gave the examination.
>
> He quoted Frost's "Stopping by Woods on a Snowy Evening": "But I have promises to keep."

3. A question mark, an exclamation point, or a dash (see page 512) is placed *outside* the quotation marks when it applies to the entire sentence and *inside* the quotation marks when it applies to the material in quotation marks.

> He asked, "Am I responsible for everything?" [quoted question within a statement]
>
> Did you hear him say, "I have the answer"? [statement within a question]
>
> Did she say, "Are you ready?" [question within a question]
>
> She shouted, "Impossible!" [exclamation]
>
> Roy screamed, "I'll flunk if I don't read Poe's short story 'The Black Cat'!" [exclamation belongs to the material inside the quotation marks]
>
> "I hope—that is, I—" he began. [dash]
>
> "Accept responsibility"—those were his words. [dash that does not belong to the material inside the quotation marks]

4. A single question mark is used in sentence constructions that contain a double question—that is, a quoted question following a question.

> Mr. Martin said, "Did he say, 'Are you going?'"

ITALICS

Italics (slanting type) is used to call special attention to certain words or groups of words. In handwriting, such words are underlined; however, computers provide italics.

1. Italicize (underline) foreign words and phrases that are still listed in the dictionary as foreign.

   c'est la vie

   Weltschmerz

2. Italicize (underline) titles of books (except the Bible); long poems; plays; magazines; motion pictures; musical compositions; newspapers; works of art; names of aircraft and ships; and letters, figures, and words.

   I think Hemingway's best novel is *A Farewell to Arms*.

   His source material was taken from *Time*, *Newsweek*, and the Los Angeles *Times*. [Sometimes the name of the city in titles of newspapers is italicized—for example, the *New York Times*.]

   The *Mona Lisa* is my favorite painting.

3. Italicize (underline) the names of ships, airplanes, spacecraft, and trains.

   Ships: *Queen Mary*   *Lurline*   *Stockholm*

   Spacecraft: *Challenger*   *Voyager 2*

4. Italicize (underline) to distinguish letters, figures, and words when they refer to themselves rather than to the ideas or things they usually represent.

   Do not leave the *o* out of *sophomore*.

   Your *3*'s look like *5*'s.

DASHES

The dash is used when a stronger break than the comma is needed. The dash may be typed as two hyphens with no space before or after them (--).

1. Use a dash to indicate a sudden change in sentence construction or an abrupt break in thought.

   Here is the true reason—but maybe you don't care.

2. Use a dash after an introductory list. The words *these*, *those*, *all*, and occasionally *such* introduce the summarizing statement.

   English, French, history—these are the subjects I like.

COLONS

The colon is a formal mark of punctuation used chiefly to introduce something that is to follow, such as a list, a quotation, or an explanation.

1. Use a colon after a main clause to introduce a formal list, an emphatic or long restatement (appositive), an explanation, an emphatic statement, or a summary.

> The following cars were in the General Motors show: Cadillac, Chevrolet, Buick, Oldsmobile, and Pontiac. [list]

> He worked toward one objective: a degree. [restatement or appositive]

> Let me emphasize one point: I do not accept late papers. [emphatic statement]

2. Use a colon to introduce a formal quotation or a formal question.

> Shakespeare's Polonius said: "Neither a borrower nor a lender be." [formal quotation]

> The question is this: Shall we surrender? [formal question]

3. Use a colon in the following conventional ways: to separate a title and subtitle, a chapter and verse in the Bible, and hours and minutes; after the salutation in a formal business letter; and between the act and the scene of a play.

Title and subtitle:	*Korea: A Country Divided*
Chapter and verse:	Genesis 4:12
Hour and minutes:	8:25 p.m.
Salutation:	Dear Ms. Johnson:
Act and scene:	*Hamlet* III:ii

PARENTHESES

Parentheses are used to set off material that is of relatively little importance to the main thought of the sentence. Such material—numbers, supplementary material, and sometimes explanatory details—merely amplifies the main thought.

1. Use parentheses to set off material that is not part of the main sentence but is too relevant to omit altogether. This category includes numbers that designate items in a series, amplifying references, explanations, directions, and qualifications.

> Jay offered two reasons for his losing: (1) he was tired, and (2) he was out of condition. [numbers]

> Review the chapters on the Civil War (6, 7, and 8) for the next class meeting. [references]

> Her husband (she had been married about a year) died last week. [explanation]

2. Use a comma, semicolon, and colon after the parentheses when the sentence punctuation requires their use.

> Although I have not lived here long (I arrived in 2006), this place feels like my only true home.

3. Use the period, question mark, and exclamation point in appropriate positions depending on whether they go with the material within the parentheses or with the entire sentence.

The greatest English poet of the seventeenth century was John Milton (1608–1674).

The greatest English poet of the seventeenth century was John Milton. (Some might not agree; I myself favor Andrew Marvell.)

BRACKETS

Brackets are used within a quotation to set off editorial additions or corrections made by the person who is quoting.

Churchill said: "It [the Yalta Agreement] contained many mistakes."

APOSTROPHES

The **apostrophe** is used with nouns and indefinite pronouns to show possession; to show the omission of letters and figures in contractions; and to form the plurals of letters, figures, and words referred to as words.

1. A possessive shows that something is owned by someone. Use an apostrophe and *s* to form the possessive of a noun, singular or plural, that does not end in *s*.

   man's coat   women's suits

2. Use an apostrophe alone to form the possessive of a plural noun ending in *s*.

   girls' clothes the Browns' house

3. Use an apostrophe and *s* or the apostrophe alone to form the possessive of singular nouns ending in *s*. Use the apostrophe and *s* only when you would pronounce the *s*.

   James' hat *or* (if you would pronounce the *s*) James's hat

4. Use an apostrophe and *s* to form the possessive of certain indefinite pronouns.

   everybody's idea   one's meat   another's poison

5. Use an apostrophe to indicate that letters or figures have been omitted.

   o'clock (short for *of the clock*) in the '90s (short for *1990s*)

6. Use an apostrophe with pronouns only when you are making a contraction. A contraction is a combination of two words. The apostrophe in a contraction indicates where a letter has been omitted.

it is	=	it's
she has	=	she's
you are	=	you're

   If no letters have been left out, do not use an apostrophe.

   Incorrect: The dog bit it's tail.

   Correct: The dog bit its tail. [not a contraction]

Incorrect:	Whose the leader now?
Correct:	Who's the leader now? [a contraction of *who is*]
Incorrect:	Its a big problem.
Correct:	It's a big problem. [a contraction of *it is*]

7. Use an apostrophe to indicate the plural of letters, figures, and words used as words.

Dot your *i*'s.   five *8*'s   *and*'s

Note that the letters, figures, and words are italicized, but the apostrophe and *s* are not.

HYPHENS

The **hyphen** brings two or more words together into a single compound word. Correct hyphenation, therefore, is essentially a spelling problem rather than one of punctuation. Because the hyphen is not used with any degree of consistency, consult your dictionary for current usage. Study the following as a beginning guide.

1. Use a hyphen to separate the parts of many compound words.

brother-in-law   go-between

2. Use a hyphen between prefixes and proper names.

all-American   mid-Atlantic

3. Use a hyphen to join two or more words used as a single adjective modifier before a noun.

bluish-gray eyes   first-class service

4. Use a hyphen with spelled-out compound numbers up to ninety-nine and with fractions.

twenty-six   two-thirds

Note: Dates, street addresses, numbers requiring more than two words, chapter and page numbers, time followed directly by a.m. or p.m., and figures after a dollar sign or before measurement abbreviations are usually written as figures, not words.

CAPITALIZATION

Following are some of the many conventions concerning the use of capital letters in English.

1. Capitalize the first word of a sentence.

2. Capitalize proper nouns and adjectives derived from proper nouns.

Names of persons
Edward Jones

Adjectives derived from proper nouns

a Shakespearean sonnet   a Miltonic sonnet

Countries, nationalities, races, languages

Germany   English   Spanish   Chinese

States, regions, localities, other geographical divisions

California   the Far East   the South

Oceans, lakes, mountains, deserts, streets, parks

Lake Superior   Sahara Desert   Fifth Avenue

Educational institutions, schools, courses

Santa Ana College   Joe Hill School   Rowland High School   Spanish 3

Organizations and their members

Boston Red Sox   Audubon Society   Boy Scouts

Corporations, governmental agencies or departments, trade names

U.S. Steel Corporation   Treasury Department
Coca-Cola   White Memorial Library

Calendar references such as holidays, days of the week, months

Easter   Tuesday   January

Historic eras, periods, documents, laws

Romantic Age   First Crusade
Declaration of Independence   Geneva Convention

3. Capitalize words denoting family relationships when they are used before a name or substituted for a name.

He walked with his nephew and Aunt Grace.

but

He walked with his nephew and his aunt.

Grandmother and Mother are away on vacation.

but

My grandmother and my mother are away on vacation.

4. Capitalize abbreviations after names.

Henry White Jr.   Juan Gomez, M.D.

5. Capitalize titles of essays, books, plays, movies, poems, magazines, newspapers, musical compositions, songs, and works of art. Do not capitalize short conjunctions and prepositions unless they come at the beginning or the end of the title.

Desire Under the Elms   *Terminator*
Last of the Mohicans   *Of Mice and Men*
"Blueberry Hill"

6. Capitalize any title preceding a name or used as a substitute for a name. Do not capitalize a title following a name.

Judge Wong	Alfred Wong, a judge
General Clark	Raymond Clark, a general
Professor Fuentes	Harry Fuentes, the biology professor

EXERCISE 50   Using Punctuation and Capitalization

One punctuation mark, a capital letter, or italic type is omitted in each of the following sentences. Insert them as needed. Pairs of quotation marks, parentheses, or dashes are considered one unit.

1. Odyssey is a famous epic poem of Greek mythology.

2. The professor said, The poem tells of the wanderings and sufferings of Odysseus, who is also known as Ulysses.

3. This poem is a great classic of literature; its famous for its beautiful poetry as well as its exciting tales of adventure.

4. The author was Homer, who wrote this poem and the equally well-known Iliad in the ninth century BCE.

5. The story begins at the end of the Trojan war as Odysseus and his band of Greeks prepare to sail back to their home in Ithaca.

6. It would take Odysseus if you can believe it ten years to get back.

7. He and his companions encounter many obstacles people, creatures, and gods who seek to kill them.

8. A one-eyed giant called the Cyclops eats several of Odysseus men and imprisons the rest in his cave.

9. Odysseus blinds the giant, and his men must sneak out of the cave by tying themselves under the bellies of the Cyclops sheep.

10. The sea-god Neptune the Cyclops' father tries to sink the Greek ships in a storm.

11. Many of Odysseus' sailors are eaten by cannibals called lestrigonians.

12. For a year, Odysseus and his men remain captives of the beautiful sorceress circe on her enchanted island.

13. Circe turns Odysseus' twenty two companions into pigs but finally lets them go.

14. The Sirens half women and half birds enticed sailors to their doom with their sweet songs.

15. Odysseus evades their charms by putting wax in his mens ears and lashing himself to the mast of the ship, where he can enjoy the songs but resist temptation.

16. Next, he manages to get past two more monsters Scylla and Charybdis.

17. Scylla is a six headed female monster, with six mouths containing three rows of sharp teeth.

18. Did you know that Charybdis is a dangerous whirlpool.

19. This is a great story! exclaimed the students.

20. It's amazing that a poem so old can be so action packed.

EXERCISE 51   Using Punctuation and Capitalization

STUDENT COMPANION SITE

For additional practice visit www.cengage .com/devenglish/ brandon/PE11e.

Twenty punctuation marks are needed in the following paragraph; the locations are indicated by the numbers. Pairs such as quotation marks and parentheses are considered one unit. Insert the marks as needed.

    1   2   3   4

Shakespeares age was like ours it was full of change and turmoil" the old
                5   6

gentleman said. New ideas were not confined exclusively to one social class
            7

one religion or one political party. Outer space stirred the imaginations of most
            8   9   10

of the people not just the astronomers. They went to see Hamlet for fun and

they bought all the books available on the strange customs of other cultures.
     11   12   13 14   15   (14)

And whos to say that when Hamlets father says I am thy fathers spirit he is any
                                     16   17

less visible than the ghosts some people say they see today. There wasnt much
          18   19

Shakespeare didnt know about us. Thats why we still quarrel about the meaning
      20   (5)

of his plays we are still discovering the truth about ourselves in them.

Spelling

SPELLING TIPS

The following tips will help you become a better speller.

1. Do not omit letters.

Many errors occur because certain letters are omitted when the word is pronounced or spelled. Observe the omissions in the following words. Then concentrate on learning the correct spellings.

Incorrect	Correct	Incorrect	Correct
aquaintance	acquaintance	irigation	irrigation
ajourned	adjourned	libary	library
agravate	aggravate	paralell	parallel
aproved	approved	parlament	parliament
artic	arctic	paticulaly	particularly
comodity	commodity	readly	readily
efficent	efficient	sophmore	sophomore
envirnment	environment	stricly	strictly
familar	familiar	unconsious	unconscious

2. Do not add letters.

Incorrect	Correct	Incorrect	Correct
athelete	athlete	ommission	omission
comming	coming	pasttime	pastime
drownded	drowned	priviledge	privilege
folkes	folks	similiar	similar
occassionally	occasionally	tradgedy	tragedy

3. Do not substitute incorrect letters for correct letters.

Incorrect	Correct	Incorrect	Correct
benefisial	beneficial	offence	offense
bullitins	bulletins	peculier	peculiar
sensus	census	resitation	recitation
discription	description	screach	screech
desease	disease	substansial	substantial
dissention	dissension	surprize	surprise
itims	items	technacal	technical

4. Do not transpose letters.

Incorrect	Correct	Incorrect	Correct
alunmi	alumni	prehaps	perhaps
childem	children	perfer	prefer
dupilcate	duplicate	perscription	prescription
irrevelant	irrelevant	principels	principles
kindel	kindle	yeild	yield

Note: Whenever you notice other words that fall into any one of these categories, add them to the list.

5. **Apply the spelling rules for spelling *ei* and *ie* words correctly.**
Remember this poem?

> Use *i* before *e*
> Except after *c*
> Or when sounded like *a*
> As in *neighbor* and *weigh*.

i* before *e

achieve	chief	niece	relieve
belief	field	piece	shield
believe	grief	pierce	siege
brief	hygiene	relief	variety

*Except after **c***

ceiling	conceive	deceive	receipt
conceit	deceit	perceive	receive

Exceptions: either, financier, height, leisure, neither, seize, species, weird
*When sounded like **a***

deign	freight	neighbor	sleigh
eight	heinous	rein	veil
feign	heir	reign	vein
feint	neigh	skein	weigh

6. **Apply the rules for dropping the final *e* or retaining the final *e* when a suffix is added.**

Words ending in a silent *e* usually drop the *e* before a suffix beginning with a vowel; for example, *accuse + -ing = accusing*. Here are some common suffixes beginning with a vowel: *-able, -age, -al, -ary, -ation, -ence, -ing, -ion, -ous, -ure*.

admire + *-able* = admirable	imagine + *-ary* = imaginary
arrive + *-al* = arrival	locate + *-ion* = location
come + *-ing* = coming	please + *-ure* = pleasure
explore + *-ation* = exploration	plume + *-age* = plumage
fame + *-ous* = famous	precede + *-ence* = precedence

Exceptions: *dye + -ing = dyeing* (to distinguish it from *dying*), *acreage, mileage*.

Words ending in a silent *e* usually retain the *e* before a suffix beginning with a consonant; for example: *arrange + -ment = arrangement*. Here are some common suffixes beginning with a consonant: *-craft, -ful, -less, -ly, -mate, -ment, -ness, -ty*.

entire + *-ty* = entirety	manage + *-ment* = management
hate + *-ful* = hateful	safe + *-ly* = safely
hope + *-less* = hopeless	stale + *-mate* = stalemate
like + *-ness* = likeness	state + *-craft* = statecraft

Exceptions: Some words taking the *-ful* or *-ly* suffixes drop the final *e*:

awe + *-ful* = awful   true + *-ly* = truly

due + *-ly* = duly   whole + *-ly* = wholly

Some words taking the suffix *-ment* drop the final *e*; for example:

acknowledgment   argument   judgment

Words ending in silent *e* after *c* or *g* retain the *e* when the suffix begins with the vowel *a* or *o*. The final *e* is retained to keep the *c* or *g* soft before the suffixes.

advantageous   noticeable

courageous   peaceable

7. **Apply the rules for doubling a final consonant before a suffix beginning with a vowel.**

Words of one syllable:

blot	blotted	get	getting	rob	robbed
brag	bragging	hop	hopped	run	running
cut	cutting	hot	hottest	sit	sitting
drag	dragged	man	mannish	stop	stopped
drop	dropped	plan	planned	swim	swimming

Words accented on the last syllable:

acquit	acquitted	equip	equipped
admit	admittance	occur	occurrence
allot	allotted	omit	omitting
begin	beginning	prefer	preferred
commit	committee	refer	referred
concur	concurring	submit	submitted
confer	conferring	transfer	transferred
defer	deferring		

Words that are not accented on the last syllable and words that do not end in a single consonant preceded by a vowel do not double the final consonant (regardless of whether the suffix begins with a vowel).

FREQUENTLY MISSPELLED WORDS

a lot	athletics	committee	discipline
absence	awkward	competition	discussed
across	becoming	complete	disease
actually	beginning	consider	divide
all right	belief	criticism	dying
among	benefit	definitely	eighth
analyze	buried	dependent	eligible
appearance	business	develop	eliminate
appreciate	certain	development	embarrassed
argument	college	difference	environment
athlete	coming	disastrous	especially

etc.	knowledge	prejudice	similar
exaggerate	laboratory	privilege	sincerely
excellent	leisure	probably	sophomore
exercise	length	professor	speech
existence	library	prove	straight
experience	likely	psychology	studying
explanation	lying	pursue	succeed
extremely	marriage	receipt	success
familiar	mathematics	receive	suggest
February	meant	recommend	surprise
finally	medicine	reference	thoroughly
foreign	neither	relieve	though
government	ninety	religious	tragedy
grammar	ninth	repetition	tried
grateful	nuclear	rhythm	tries
guarantee	occasionally	ridiculous	truly
guard	opinion	sacrifice	unfortunately
guidance	opportunity	safety	unnecessary
height	parallel	scene	until
hoping	particular	schedule	unusual
humorous	persuade	secretary	using
immediately	physically	senior	usually
independent	planned	sense	Wednesday
intelligence	pleasant	separate	writing
interest	possible	severely	written
interfere	practical	shining	
involved	preferred	significant	

CONFUSED SPELLING AND CONFUSING WORDS

The following are more words that are commonly misspelled or confused with one another. Some have similar sounds, some are often mispronounced, and some are only misunderstood.

a	An adjective (called an article) used before a word beginning with a consonant or a consonant sound, as in "I ate *a* donut."
an	An adjective (called an article) used before a word beginning with a vowel (*a, e, i, o, u*) or with a silent *h*, as in "I ate an artichoke."
and	A coordinating conjunction, as in "Sara *and* I like Alison Krauss."
accept	A verb meaning "to receive," as in "I *accept* your explanation."
except	A preposition meaning "to exclude," as in "I paid everyone *except* you."
advice	A noun meaning "guidance," as in "Thanks for the *advice*."
advise	A verb meaning "to give guidance," as in "Will you please *advise* me of my rights?"
all right	An adjective meaning "correct" or "acceptable," as in "It's *all right* to cry."
alright	Not used in formal writing.
all ready	An adjective that can be used interchangeably with *ready*, as in "I am *all ready* to go to town."

already	An adverb meaning "before," which cannot be used in place of *ready*, as in "I have *already* finished."
a lot	An adverb meaning "much," as in "She liked him *a lot*," or a noun meaning "several," as in "I had *a lot* of suggestions."
alot	Misspelling.
altogether	An adverb meaning "completely," as in "He is *altogether* happy."
all together	An adverb meaning "as one," which can be used interchangeably with *together*, as in "The group left *all together*."
choose	A present-tense verb meaning "to select," as in "Do whatever you *choose*."
chose	The past-tense form of the verb *choose*, as in "They *chose* to take action yesterday."
could of	A misspelled phrase caused by confusing *could've*, meaning *could have*, with *could of*.
could have	Correctly spelled phrase, as in "I *could have* left."
could've	Correctly spelled contraction of *could have*, as in "He *could've* succeeded."
affect	Usually a verb meaning "change," as in "Ideas *affect* me."
effect	Usually a noun meaning "result," as in "That *effect* was unexpected."
hear	A verb indicating the receiving of sound, as in "I *hear* thunder."
here	An adverb meaning "present location," as in "I live *here*."
it's	A contraction of *it is*, as in "*It's* time to dance."
its	Possessive pronoun, as in "Each dog has *its* day."
know	A verb usually meaning "to comprehend" or "to recognize," as in "I *know* the answer."
no	An adjective meaning "negative," as in "I have *no* potatoes."
lead	A present-tense verb, as in "I *lead* a stable life now," or a noun referring to a substance, such as "I sharpened the *lead* in my pencil."
led	The past-tense form of the verb *lead*, as in "I *led* a wild life in my youth."
loose	An adjective meaning "without restraint," as in "He is a *loose* cannon."
lose	A present-tense verb from the pattern *lose, lost, lost*, as in "I thought I would *lose* my senses."
paid	The past tense form of *pay*, as in "He *paid* his dues."
payed	Misspelling.
passed	The past-tense form of the verb *pass*, meaning "went by," as in "He *passed* me on the curve."
past	An adjective meaning "former," as in "That's *past* history," or a noun, meaning "a time gone by," as in "He lived in the *past*."
patience	A noun meaning "willingness to wait," as in "Job was a man of much *patience*."
patients	A noun meaning "people under care," as in "The doctor had fifty *patients*."
peace	A noun meaning "a quality of calmness" or "absence of strife," as in "The guru was at *peace* with the world."

piece	A noun meaning "part," as in "I gave him a *piece* of my mind."
quiet	An adjective meaning "silent," as in "She was a *quiet* child."
quit	A verb meaning "to cease" or "to withdraw," as in "I *quit* my job."
quite	An adverb meaning "very," as in "The clam is *quite* happy."
receive	A verb meaning "to accept," as in "I will *receive* visitors now."
recieve	Misspelling.
stationary	An adjective meaning "not moving," as in "Try to avoid running into *stationary* objects."
stationery	A noun meaning "paper material to write on," as in "I bought a box of *stationery* for Sue's birthday present."
than	A conjunction, as in "He is taller *than* I am."
then	An adverb, as in "She *then* left town."
their	An adjective (possessive pronoun), as in "They read *their* books."
there	An adverb, as in "He left it *there*," or a filler word, as in "*There* is no time left."
they're	A contraction of *they are*, as in "*They're* happy."
thorough	An adjective, as in "He did a *thorough* job."
through	A preposition, as in "She went *through* the yard."
to	A preposition, as in "I went *to* town."
too	An adverb meaning "exceeding or going beyond what is acceptable," as in "You are *too* late to qualify for the discount," or "also," as in "I have feelings, *too*."
two	An adjective of number, as in "I have *two* jobs."
truely	Misspelling.
truly	An adverb meaning "sincerely" or "completely," as in "He was *truly* happy."
weather	A noun meaning "condition of the atmosphere," as in "The *weather* is pleasant today."
whether	A conjunction, as in "*Whether* he would go was of no consequence."
write	A present-tense verb, as in "Watch me as I *write* this letter."
writen	Misspelling.
written	A past participle verb, as in "I have *written* the letter."
you're	A contraction of *you are*, as in "*You're* my friend."
your	A possessive pronoun, as in "I like *your* looks."

YOUR SPELL CHECKER

Your computer spell checker is an important tool with many benefits and some limitations. With about 100,000 words in a typical database, the spell checker alerts you to problem words in your text that should be verified. If you agree that the spelling of a word should be checked, you can then select from a list of words with similar spellings. A likely substitute word will be highlighted. With a keystroke, you can correct a problem, add your own word to the database, or ignore the alert. With a few more keystrokes, you can type in your own correction, and you can add an unusual spelling or word to the database. You will be amazed at how many times your computer will catch misspellings that your eye did not see.

However, the spell checker has limitations. If you intended to type *he* and instead typed *me*, the spell checker will not alert you to a possible problem because the word you typed is spelled correctly. If you use the wrong word, such as *herd* instead of *heard*, the spell checker will not detect a problem. Thus you should always proofread your writing after you have spell checked it.

Avoiding Wordy Phrases

Certain phrases clutter sentences, consuming our time in writing and our readers' time in reading. Watch for wordy phrases as you revise and edit.

Wordy: *Due to the fact that* he was unemployed, he had to use public transportation.

Concise: *Because* he was unemployed, he had to use public transportation.

Wordy: *Deep down inside* he believed that the Red Sox would win.

Concise: He believed that the Red Sox would win.

Wordy	Concise
at the present time	now
basic essentials	essentials
blend together	blend
it is clear that	(delete)
due to the fact that	because
for the reason that	because
I felt inside	I felt
in most cases	usually
as a matter of fact	in fact
in the event that	if
until such time as	until
I personally feel	I feel
in this modern world	today
in order to	to
most of the people	most people
along the lines of	like
past experience	experience
at that point in time	then
in the final analysis	finally
in the near future	soon
have a need for	need
in this day and age	now

EXERCISE 52   Wordy Phrasing

Circle the wordy phrases and revise them to form concise phrases.

1. Past experience tells me I should read the fine print.

2. In the final analysis, I feel inside that the college courses will blend together.

3. It is clear that most of the people can be fooled.

4. For the reason that I am too young, I must say no to your marriage proposal.

5. In most cases I would agree with you.

6. I am learning the basic essentials in this class.

7. In the near future I will have some investment money.

8. I personally feel that success is within my grasp.

9. I have no other comment at the present time.

10. I don't have a need for a pocket tool kit.

Brief Guide for ESL Students

If you came to this country knowing little English, you probably acquired vocabulary first. Then you began using that vocabulary within the basic patterns of your own language. If your native language had no articles, you probably used no articles; if your language had no verb tenses, you probably used no verb tenses, and so on. Using the grammar of your own language with your new vocabulary may initially have enabled you to make longer and more complex statements in English, but eventually you learned that your native grammar and your adopted grammar were different. You may even have learned that no two grammars are the same, and that English has a bewildering set of rules and an even longer set of exceptions to those rules. This Handbook presents grammar (the way we put words together) and rhetoric (the way we use language effectively) that can be applied to your writing. The following are some definitions, rules, and references that are of special help to writers who are learning English as a second language (ESL).

USING ARTICLES IN RELATION TO NOUNS

Articles

Articles are either indefinite (*an, a*) or definite (*the*). Because they point out nouns, they are often called *noun determiners*.

Nouns

Nouns can be either singular (*book*) or plural (*books*) and are either count nouns (things that can be counted, such as "book") or noncount nouns (things that cannot be counted, such as "homework"). If you are not certain whether a noun is a count noun or a noncount noun, try placing the word *much* before the word. You can say, "much homework," so *homework* is a noncount noun.

Rules

- **Use an indefinite article (*a* or *an*) before singular count nouns and not before noncount nouns.** The indefinite article means "one," so you would not use it before plural count nouns.

Correct:	I saw a book. [count noun]
Correct:	I ate an apple. [count noun]
Incorrect:	I fell in a love. [noncount noun]
Correct:	I fell in love. [noncount noun]
Incorrect:	I was in a good health. [noncount noun]
Correct:	I was in good health. [noncount noun]

- **Use the definite article (*the*) before both singular and plural count nouns that have specific reference.**

Correct:	I read the book. [a specific one]
Correct:	I read the books. [specific ones]
Correct:	I like to read a good book. [nonspecific, therefore the indefinite article]
Correct:	A student who works hard will pass. [any student, therefore nonspecific]
Correct:	The student on my left is falling asleep. [a specific student]

- **Use the definite article with noncount nouns only when they are specifically identified.**

Correct:	Honesty (as an idea) is a rare commodity.
Correct:	The honesty of my friend has inspired me. [specifically identified]
Incorrect:	I was in trouble and needed the assistance. [not specifically identified]
Correct:	The assistance offered by the paramedics was appreciated. [specifically identified]

- **Place the definite article before proper nouns (names) of the following:**

  oceans, rivers, and deserts (for example, *the* Pacific Ocean and *the* Red River)
  countries, if the first part of the name indicates a division (*the* United States of America)
  regions (*the* South)
  plural islands (*the* Hawaiian Islands)
  museums and libraries (*the* Los Angeles County Museum)
  colleges and universities when the word *college* or *university* comes before the name (*the* University of Oklahoma)

These are the main rules. For a more detailed account of rules for articles, see a comprehensive ESL book in your library.

SENTENCE PATTERNS

The Kinds of Sentences section in this Handbook defines and illustrates the patterns of English sentences. Some languages include patterns not used in standard English. The following principles are well worth remembering:

- **The conventional English sentence is based on one or more clauses, each of which must have a subject (sometimes the implied "you") and a verb.**

  Incorrect: Saw the book. [subject needed even if it is obvious]

  Correct: I saw the book.

- **English does not repeat a subject, even for emphasis.**

  Incorrect: The book that I read it was interesting.

  Correct: The book that I read was interesting.

VERB ENDINGS

- **English indicates time through verbs.** Learn the different forms of verb tenses and the combinations of main verbs and helping verbs.

  Incorrect: He watching the game. [A verblike word ending in *-ing* cannot be a verb all by itself.]

  Correct: He is watching the game. [Note that a helping verb such as *is*, *has*, *has been*, *will*, or *will be* always occurs before a main verb ending in *-ing*.]

- **Take special care in maintaining consistency in tense.**

  Incorrect: I went to the mall. I watch a movie there. [verb tenses inconsistent]

  Correct: I went to the mall. I watched a movie there.

All twelve verb tenses are covered with explanations, examples, and exercises in the Verbs section of the Handbook, pages 449–460.

IDIOMS

Some of your initial problems with writing English are likely to arise from trying to adjust to a different and difficult grammar. If the English language used an entirely systematic grammar, your learning would be easier, but English has patterns that are both complex and irregular. Among them are idioms, word groups that often defy grammatical rules and mean something other than what they appear to mean on the surface.

The expression "He kicked the bucket" does not mean that someone struck a cylindrical container with his foot; instead, it means that someone died. That example is one kind of idiom. Because the expression suggests a certain irreverence, it would not be the choice of most people who want to make a statement about death; but if it is used, it must be used with its own precise wording, not "He struck the long cylindrical container with his foot," or "He did some bucket-kicking." Like other languages, the English language has thousands of these idioms. Expressions such as "the more the merrier" and "on the outs" are ungrammatical. They are also very informal expressions and therefore seldom used in college writing, although they are an indispensable part of a flexible, effective, all-purpose vocabulary. Because of their twisted meanings and illogic, idioms are likely to be among the last parts of language that a new speaker learns well. A speaker must know the culture thoroughly to understand when, where, and how to use slang and other idiomatic expressions.

If you listen carefully and read extensively, you will learn English idioms. Your library will have dictionaries that explain them.

MORE SUGGESTIONS FOR ESL WRITERS

1. Read your material aloud and try to detect inconsistencies and awkward phrasing.

2. Have others read your material aloud for the same purposes.

3. If you have severe problems with grammatical awkwardness, try composing shorter, more direct sentences until you become more proficient in phrasing.

4. On your Self-Evaluation Chart, list the problems you have (such as articles, verb endings, clause patterns), review relevant parts of the Handbook, and concentrate on your own problem areas as you draft, revise, and edit.

EXERCISE 53   Correcting ESL Problems

STUDENT COMPANION SITE

For additional practice visit www.cengage .com/devenglish/ brandon/PE11e.

Make corrections in the use of articles, verbs, and phrasing.

GEORGE WASHINGTON AT TRENTON

One of most famous battles during the War of Independence occur at Trenton, New Jersey, on Christmas Eve of the 1776. The colonists outmatched in supplies and finances and were outnumbered in troop strength. Most observers in other countries think rebellion would be put down soon. British overconfident and believe there would be no more battles until spring. But George Washington decide to fight one more time. That Christmas, while large army of Britishers having party and thinking about the holiday season, Americans set out for surprise raid. They loaded onto boats used for carrying ore and rowed across Delaware River. George Washington stood tall in lead boat. According to legend, drummer boy floated across river on his drum, pulled by rope tied to boat. Because British did not feel threatened by the ragtag colonist forces, they unprepared to do battle. The colonists stormed living quarters and the general assembly hall and achieved victory. It was good for the colonists' morale, something they needed, for they would endure long, hard winter before fighting again.

Text Credits

Maya Angelou, "Liked for Myself" (editor's title), from *I Know Why the Caged Bird Sings* by Maya Angelou, copyright © 1969 and renewed 1997 by Maya Angelou. Used by permission of Random House, Inc. and Virago, an imprint of Little, Brown Book Group as publisher.

John Batchelor, "Food, Service Hit and Miss at Gianno's," *Greensboro News & Record*, January 12, 2006. Reprinted by permission.

Geraldine Baum, "Flirting Fundamentals: A Glance, A Smile—So Sexy, So Subtle . . . So Scientific," *Los Angeles Times*, October 3, 1994. Copyright © 1994 by the Los Angeles Times. Reprinted by permission.

Suzanne Britt, "Neat People vs. Sloppy People," from *Show and Tell*. Reprinted by permission of the author.

José Antonio Burciaga, "Tortillas." Copyright José Antonio Burciaga. Reprinted with permission of Cecilia P. Burciaga.

Judith Ortiz Cofer, "More," reprinted with permission from the publisher of *Silent Dancing: A Partial Remembrance of a Puerto Rican Childhood* (Houston: Arte Público Press—Univ. of Houston, 1990).

Meghan Daum, "Shouldn't Men Have 'Choice' Too?" *Los Angeles Times*, December 10, 2005. Reprinted by permission of the author.

Definitions of "indigenous" and "native." Copyright © 2000 by Houghton Mifflin Company. Reproduced by permission from *The American Heritage Dictionary of the English Language, Fourth Edition*.

Effective E-mail Practices, adapted from *Contemporary Business Communication*. Reprinted by permission of Houghton Mifflin Company.

S. Feshbach and B. Weiner, "Pity, Anger, and Achievement Performance" and "Primitive Methods of Lie Detection," from *Personality*, 1991, pp. 505 and 359. Reprinted with permission of Houghton Mifflin Company.

S. Feshbach and B. Weiner, "Total Institutions." from *Personality*, D.C. Heath, 1991. Reprinted with permission of Houghton Mifflin Company.

Suzanne Fields, "Let Granny Drive If She Can," from *The Washington Times*, Op-Ed, July 24, 2003. Reprinted by permission of the author.

Francis Flaherty, "The Ghetto Made Me Do It," *In These Times*, April 5, 1993. Article is reprinted with the permission of *In These Times*, www.inthesetimes.com.

Avi Friedman, "Living Environments" originally appeared in *The Montreal Gazette* and is reprinted by permission of the author.

Eric Gall, "Little Brother Is Watching," is reprinted by permission of the author.

Excerpts from C. Edward Good and William Fitzpatrick, "A Successful Interview," Prima Publishing, 1993. Reprinted by permission of C. Edward Good, author of *A Grammar Book for You and I . . . Oops, Me!* and developer of GrammaRight at Grammar.com.

Christopher Grant, "Graffiti: Taking a Closer Look," *The FBI Law Enforcement Bulletin*, August 1, 1996.

John Gray, excerpt from "Mr. Fix-It and the Home-Improvement Committee" pp. 15–23, from *Men Are from Mars, Women Are from Venus*. Copyright © by John Gray. Reprinted by permission of HarperCollins Publishers.

Gina Greenlee, "No Tears for Frankie," from *The New York Times Magazine*, June 10, 2001. Reprinted by permission of the author.

Rose Del Castillo Guilbault, "Americanization Is Tough on 'Macho,'" from *This World*, a weekly magazine of the *San Francisco Chronicle*, 1989. Reprinted by permission of the author.

Mary Ann Hogan, "Why We Carp and Harp," *Los Angeles Times*, March 10, 1992. Reprinted by permission of the author.

Garrison Keillor, "Attitude," reprinted with the permission of Scribner, a Division of Simon & Schuster, Inc., from *Happy to Be Here* by Garrison Keillor. Copyright © 1979 by Garrison Keillor. All rights reserved.

Adair Lara, "Who's Cheap?" from *San Francisco Chronicle*. Reprinted by permission of the author.

John Leo, "Bully, Bully," *U.S. News & World Report*, May 21, 2001, vol. 130, issue 20, p. 15. Copyright 2001 U.S. News & World Report, L.P. Reprinted with permission.

N. Scott Momaday, "The Story of a Well-Made Shield," from *In the Presence of the Sun: Stories and Poems, 1961–1991* (New York: St. Martin's Press, 1992), pp. 73–75, 80–81. Copyright © by N. Scott Momaday. Permission to reprint granted by N. Scott Momaday.

Bharati Mukherjee, "Two Ways to Belong in America," *New York Times*, September 27, 2996. © 1996, The New York Times. Reprinted by permission.

Camille Paglia, "Rape and Modern Sex War," from *Sex, Art and American Culture* by Camille Paglia, copyright © 1992 by Camille Paglia. Used by permission of Vintage Books, a division of Random House, Inc., and Penguin Books Ltd., and the author.

Janet Pearson, "Whose Values?" from *Tulsa World*, October 30, 2005. Reprinted by permission of the author, an editorial writer for *Tulsa World* Newspaper.

Kathy Shaskan, "Chick Flicks vs. Macho Movies: Can You Tell the Difference?" Copyright © 1999–2000 by Kathy Shaskan. Reprinted by permission of the author.

Irwin Shaw, "The Girls in Their Summer Dresses," from *Five Decades* by Irwin Shaw. Reprinted With Permission. © Irwin Shaw. All rights reserved.

Judy Sheindlin and Josh Getlin, "Enough Is Enough." Excerpt from *Don't Pee on My Leg and Tell Me It's Raining* by Judy Sheindlin and Josh Getlin. Copyright © 1996 by Judy Sheindlin and Josh Getlin. Reprinted by permission of HarperCollins Publishers.

Robert J. Trotter, "How Do I Love Thee?" from *The Three Faces of Love*, September 1986, p. 47. Reprinted with permission from *Psychology Today* magazine. Copyright © 1986, Sussex Publishers, LLC.

Elizabeth Wong, "The Struggle to Be an All-American Girl" is reprinted by permission of the author, www.elizabethwong.net.

Author/Title Index

Subject Index